Will to Murder

THE TRUE STORY BEHIND THE CRIMES & TRIALS
SURROUNDING THE *Glensheen* KILLINGS

Fourth Edition

GAIL FEICHTINGER

WITH

JOHN DeSANTO & GARY WALLER

X-comm

X-communication
Duluth, Minnesota
www.x-communication.org

Will to Murder: the true story behind the crimes and trials surrounding the Glensheen killings

Text by Gail Feichtinger with John DeSanto and Gary Waller.
Copy editing and additional research by Scott Pearson.
Proofreading by Kate Elliott, Chris Godsey, Catherine Winter, and Jennifer Derrick.
Cover and interior layout and design and additional editing by Tony Dierckins.

A complete list of photo and image credits appears in the Appendix.

FOURTH EDITION
(FIRST PRINTING MAY 2009)

09 10 11 12 13 ♦ 5 4 3 2 1

Library of Congress Control Number: 2009925750

ISBNs: 1-887317-35-X ♦ 978-1-887317-35-1

Printed in Brainerd, Minnesota, USA, by Bang Printing

For Velma Pietila,
Glensheen's forgotten victim and unsung hero.

The authors and publisher would like to thank...

Gabrielle Allen, David Arnold, Mike Arra, Dr. Elizabeth Bagley,
Christina Baldwin, Charles Barnes, Chris Bialke, David Bouschor, Susan Budig,
Howard Caldwell Jr., Pauline Chandra, Thomas Congdon, Gabrielle David,
Betty Dawson, Donald J. Dierckins, Ray DiPrima, Lana DeSanto, Bill Dickinson,
Vera Dunbar, Gary Esler, Dr. Jessica Gaynor, Bob Geiger, Ann Glumac,
Dr. Volker Goldschmidt, Ernie Grams, Paula Granquist, Jack Greene, Tom & Julie Hagen,
Bob Harmon, Bob Harvey, Sandra Immerman, Deborah Johnson, Jennifer & Chuck Johnson,
Nancy Hagen Kaufmann, Barb Kucera, Chuck Laszewski, Dick LeRoy,
Jack Litman, Dennis Loberg, Mary Logue, Dan Mabley, Kenneth Maine,
Michael McNabb, Diana Meerovich, Ronald Meshbesher, Bob Metz, Ellen Quinn,
Mannette Allen Rauth, Jason Rice, Mark Rubin, Sylvia Savalas, Pat Shannon,
Millie Smrz, Bill Talty, Tom Taylor, Doug Thomson, Karl Vick, Mary Waller,
Bob Wyness, Richard Yagoda, Cynthia Thompson Zuk,
and the many individuals who have asked to remain anonymous...

Glensheen and its staff,
the Minnesota Historical Society,
the ever-helpful staff of the Duluth Public Library,
Dr. Maureen O'Brien of the UMD School of Economics,
Pat Maus and the Northeast Minnesota Historical Center,
the St. Louis County Court Administrator and Probate Offices,
Dan Brenan of the Minnesota Department of Transportation,
Bob King and Tom Borich of the *Duluth News-Tribune*,
WDIO-TV, KARE-11 TV, Genetic Technologies,
the Ajo Historical Society,
the Arizona Historical Society,
the Ajo Chamber of Commerce,
the Pima County Attorney's Office,
the Pima County Sheriff's Department,
the Pinal County Sheriff's Department,
the Arizona Department of Corrections,
Tobies Restaurant of Hinckley, Minnesota,
TeaSource of St. Paul,
and as always the good folks at Adventure Publications.

For Bob, Alexandra, and Elena

— G.F.

Contents

Foreword

THE NEWS THAT ELISABETH CONGDON AND VELMA PIETILA were found dead inside Glensheen shook the city of Duluth. The story received national press coverage, and Minnesotans daily scoured newspapers and tuned to TV news to learn of the latest developments in the investigation and prosecutions. Detective Gary Waller (the case's chief investigator) and Prosecutor John DeSanto felt the media coverage of the investigation and trials hadn't been entirely accurate, and that the complete story had never been told. One day, they told each other, we will have our chance to explain everything the way it really happened. It was a personal goal: outside of those close to the victims, the case affected no one as much as it did Waller and DeSanto. They felt compelled to tell their story, and felt the people affected by the crimes—as well as the citizens of Duluth and St. Louis County, whose tax dollars paid for the investigation and prosecutions—deserved to have the entire story told.

When that day came, Waller and DeSanto also knew they wouldn't be able to do it themselves. They had the firsthand experience and volumes of information and evidence the press had never seen, but they had never written a book. They would also need a writer who could approach the subject free of bias and go beyond what they knew in order to make the book as accurate as possible. In the mid-1980s, the two turned to former *Duluth News-Tribune* journalist Gail Feichtinger, who knew both men from her work as the paper's crime reporter. After she had left Duluth for another job and, eventually, attended law school (she now practices law with the Minnesota Attorney General's Office), Waller and DeSanto asked her to help them put all they knew and had experienced into words and also to research aspects of the story never before presented.

Together the three gathered information. Waller and DeSanto provided their own diaries and reports from the investigation and trials. They also sat down with Feichtinger many times to tell the stories that couldn't be found in newspapers—behind-the-scenes discussions and events that never reached the courtroom. Feichtinger sifted through countless stacks of books, newspaper and magazine articles, letters, police reports, court records and transcripts, and other documents. She also interviewed those associated with the case—investigators, attorneys, judges, and jurors as well as friends, acquaintances, former

Glensheen staff, and family members of the accused and the victims (including members of the Congdon family).

In addition to the three authors, many other individuals and organizations contributed to the content and shape of this book. A list of most of them appears on the acknowledgments page. But not everyone who helped has been mentioned on that list. Some asked that their names not be included for privacy concerns. Others asked to be left out of the acknowledgments because they feared reprisal from Marjorie Caldwell Hagen. The authors and publisher again thank them and anyone who may have been accidentally overlooked. Without their help and the help of those listed, the authors could not have assembled such a unique and comprehensive volume.

But the project took longer than they expected. Years longer. Because of their busy lives, none of the three could absolutely dedicate themselves to the manuscript. In fact, they even shelved the project at one time. In all, more than fifteen years of intermittent work went into the book.

The wait turned out to be a blessing. Along the way the authors discovered some exciting new information that wouldn't have been available to them until recently. David Arnold, Roger's friend and legal advisor, came forward with three boxes and a suitcase filled with documents Caldwell wrote and collected while in prison. Their contents provided valuable insight. And, for a case over twenty-five years old, the authors were fortunate enough to have access to a great deal of physical evidence. Once the case was officially closed, evidence belonging to the Congdon family was returned to the Congdon Office; the rest was scheduled to be destroyed. Instead, John DeSanto got permission to save some of the evidence, took it home, and stored it in his basement. In 2003 the authors dug through the boxes of evidence. They found a garment bag and an envelope that played key roles in the case, clothing and other bits of physical evidence recovered from the crime scene as well as fingerprints, hair samples, and known saliva samples from Roger Caldwell. Some of the evidence was subjected to DNA testing, unavailable to investigators in 1977. The results of those tests—which indeed shed new light on the case, and could well have changed the outcome of the trials had they been available at the time—can be found in the book's epilogue.

Since the book's 2003 release, Marjorie Hagen herself was released from prison. She started calling herself "Maggie Wallis" and soon returned to her old ways. In 2007—thirty years after the killings at Glensheen—she was arrested for check fraud and evidence indicates she may have gotten away with another murder. She plead guilty to attempted forgery in February 2009 was sentenced again. Gail Feichtinger has kept up with Hagen's activities, and you can read all of her exploits since her 2003 release from prison in this updated third edition of the book.

— TONY DIERCKINS, PUBLISHER

CHAPTER I

The Scene of the Crime

THE WEATHER-BEATEN CITY OF DULUTH, MINNESOTA, sits roughly 150 miles north of the Twin Cities of Minneapolis-St. Paul on a rocky hillside above the westernmost point of Lake Superior, the largest expanse of fresh water in the world. The lumber and mining industries in Minnesota's Arrowhead region helped Duluth boom in the late nineteenth and early twentieth centuries—by 1905, Duluth boasted more millionaires than any other city in the U.S. Touted early on as "The Zenith City of the Unsalted Seas," Duluth enjoyed many prosperous years as a major U.S. port. But by the 1970s, the economy had slowed down. A shortage of trees reduced the lumber industry, and mine after mine shut down due in part to an influx of foreign steel. While Duluth hosted many visitors, drawn to the lake and such sights as the Aerial Bridge, its great tourism boom wouldn't begin until the late 1980s. In 1977, Duluth was perhaps best known as the home of millionaire entrepreneur Jeno Paulucci of Jeno's, Inc., the man credited with inventing the pizza roll. None of its 100,000 residents could have imagined their small city would soon be the scene of the most notorious double murders in Minnesota history.

On the Sunday afternoon of June 26, 1977, Elisabeth Congdon—daughter of Clara Congdon and her husband Chester, an attorney who created a fortune investing in the mining industry—returned to her family's estate after a weekend at Swiftwater Farm, her summer lodge located along the cold, racing waters of northwestern Wisconsin's Brule River. Every Friday after lunch, Elisabeth, her chauffeur Richard Kartes, and a nurse left for "the Brule," returning each Sunday before dinner. At eighty-three years old, Elisabeth had lived in the same house for seventy-two years: "Glensheen," a thirty-nine room Jacobean mansion her parents had built on a sprawling estate with Lake Superior as its backdrop. Filled with stands of cedar, birch, and cottonwood, the woods that bordered Glensheen played host to foraging deer, raccoons, and even bears. In winter months, storms on the big lake brought ice floes crashing against the estate's rocky beach.

Elisabeth had outlasted all her brothers and sisters, as the family portraits on the walls constantly reminded her. "Miss Elisabeth" to the household staff, she was a heavyset woman with a strong, expressive face, kind eyes, and upturned eyebrows that rose above her metal-frame glasses. Her fine gray hair curled softly away from her face. A stroke twelve years earlier had left her comatose for ten days, destroying massive amounts of brain tissue and crippling her right side. Partial paralysis confined her to a wheelchair and made her dependent on around-the-clock nursing care and live-in servants. She was nearly deaf and also suffered from diabetes, which required daily insulin shots.

Since the stroke, Elisabeth suffered from aphasia, a loss of the ability to speak and express ideas. Although she could say yes and no, she had difficulty with full sentences and her words were distorted and halting, particularly when she was tired. Early on after her stroke, flashcards helped her communicate. Later, when she forgot a word, her family, friends, nurses, and servants would recite the alphabet until she stopped them at a certain letter. They would then list off words beginning with that letter until she nodded and said, "Yes, that is the one."

Despite her handicaps, Elisabeth refused to be pitied or coddled. There were times when Elisabeth longed for the independence and physical activity of her youth, but when she had to accept the help of her nurses and staff, she was gracious and uncommonly dignified.

She tried to lead as active a life as she could. Each morning after breakfast she did her physical therapy exercises on Glensheen's third floor. Walking was extremely difficult, but with the help of a nurse she could manage a few steps along the parallel bars on good days. Since the stroke, she had learned to write, brush her teeth, and feed herself with her left hand.

Following her exercises, her daily routine included reading, receiving visits from friends, or conferring with household staff in the library. Lunch was usually served in the breakfast room on the main floor during the winter; in warmer months, Elisabeth enjoyed her noon meal sitting on the porch overlooking the stone bridge that crossed Tischer Creek, which flowed through the estate on its way to empty into Lake Superior. She was particularly fond of the outdoors; when she was younger she had loved to play tennis, picnic, and take walks on the estate. In her later years, on afternoons when the weather was pleasant, Elisabeth was wheeled outside onto the broad, sunny brick terrace so she could enjoy Glensheen's formal gardens. She regularly provided fresh flowers to the Methodist church she attended on Sundays as often as her health permitted—like her parents before her, Elisabeth donated generously to a number of charities and nonprofit organizations. When housebound, she enjoyed a game of cards, a visit with friends, listening to classical music, or having one of her nurses read to her. She enjoyed a good murder mystery.

Elisabeth led a quiet life, as a rule, which had made it all the more surprising back in 1972 when she had allowed Universal Studios to use Glensheen as the setting for its suspense film *You'll Like My Mother*. Elisabeth and other family members attended the premiere showing at the NorShor Theatre in downtown Duluth. Elisabeth had been so taken aback by the film's dramatic and violent moments that she kept repeating "oh my word" throughout the showing.

On that last Sunday of June 1977, Elisabeth was tired when they arrived at Glensheen around 4:30 P.M. after the almost two-hour trip from Swiftwater Farm. Nurse Mildred Klosowsky, nicknamed "Miss Kay," brought Elisabeth's things in from the car. She took two suitcase-like wicker baskets upstairs and put them along with Elisabeth's purse and several dresses on the bed in the heiress's bedroom. She then went downstairs and helped Elisabeth to the large green sofa in the living room facing the windows so Elisabeth could rest.

Klosowsky went back upstairs to unpack the wicker baskets and hang up Elisabeth's clothes. The smaller wicker basket had been used to carry two small white pillows that were usually placed under Elisabeth's arms while she slept. The larger basket contained medication, visitation charts, underwear, a pair of shoes, and several pillow cases. After unpacking the baskets, Klosowsky placed them one inside the other on a stool in the closet.

At about 5 P.M., Elisabeth awoke from her nap and asked Klosowsky to play gin rummy with her. Cards were a favorite pastime, and Elisabeth could beat any of the nurses at gin rummy or hearts. Unable to hold the cards, she used a special board with a groove down the center. Slowly, with great effort, she was able to shuffle the cards.

Klosowsky and Elisabeth stopped playing at about 6:30 P.M. to eat a light supper of tuna salad and egg salad sandwiches, fresh fruit, and skim milk served by the maid, Hazel Conger, in the library. More gin rummy and television followed. Elisabeth was very happy and looked forward to celebrating the Fourth of July at the Brule the next weekend. At about 9 P.M., Elisabeth's personal secretary, Vera Dunbar, called to give nurse Klosowsky an important message: a call was expected from one of Elisabeth's adopted daughters, Marjorie Caldwell. The previous Friday night Conger had intercepted a call from a woman who refused to identify herself. Conger had told the caller, whom she believed was Marjorie, that Miss Elisabeth would be back Sunday afternoon. Since Marjorie often wanted something from her mother—usually money—Dunbar told Klosowsky not to put the call through. Klosowsky had been told the same thing by Dunbar in the past. The servants knew Elisabeth couldn't refuse to bail her daughter out of another financial mess.

Despite Dunbar's warning, the phone never rang. At 10 P.M., Klosowsky wheeled Elisabeth into the elevator, which they exited on the second floor. Klosowsky pushed Elisabeth around a corner, down the hall, and turned left into a simply-decorated bedroom. Through the door, she turned left again and maneuvered the chair beside Elisabeth's metal hospital bed, with its matching nightstands and lamps on both sides. Along the wall across from the other side of the bed was a door to the closet, a dresser, the bathroom door, and a vanity. The far corner of the room jutted out, forming a nook with windows facing the lake; a chair, small desk, and memorabilia case of family heirlooms filled the nook. In front of the nook, a sofa faced the bed, covered with needlepoint throw pillows. A television stood just to the right of the sofa, opposite the bedroom door. A stone mosaic fireplace dominated the wall to the right of the entrance.

Klosowsky lifted her patient into bed. She opened a window to let in fresh air, as Elisabeth preferred. As part of the bedtime routine, Klosowsky removed Elisabeth's hearing aid and disconnected her phone. As usual, Elisabeth wore to bed her gold watch and her favorite ring—a platinum strawberry dome ring containing twelve diamonds and fifteen round sapphires.

Elisabeth was so tired that she didn't need the medication she sometimes took in order to sleep. She also didn't watch any television, as she did most nights. Her favorite programs included The Waltons, Ironsides, and Streets of San Francisco. She had enjoyed a pleasant weekend at the Brule, including an unexpected visit from her grandson Stephen LeRoy, Marjorie's oldest son. Settled in bed by 10:45 P.M., Elisabeth appeared "tired but content," after a "quiet, peaceful P.M.," nurse Klosowsky wrote in the daily medical log.

"I need a good night's rest," Elisabeth told the nurse before closing her eyes. Then she gently touched Klosowsky's cheek and said, "I'll see you tomorrow, dear." Klosowsky left one of the nightstands' small lamps on and the bedroom door open. Elisabeth went to sleep lying on her right side, facing the fireplace.

Velma Pietila, the night nurse for Sunday, arrived at the mansion shortly before 11 P.M. Nurse Klosowsky, standing at the window in the nurse's room, watched as Pietila parked her car near Glensheen's front door and walked toward the mansion. Pietila prided herself on her well-kept appearance. Her nurse's uniform revealed a slender figure and tanned, muscular legs. A petite woman, she was surprisingly strong from years of playing golf, swimming, and lifting Elisabeth in and out of her wheelchair. Her blond-tinted gray hair was swept up in a chignon, and she wore stylish, dark-framed glasses.

A registered nurse since 1933, Pietila, 66, had spent the previous seven years working at Glensheen. She had just retired the month before, eager to travel and spend more time with her husband. However, head nurse Mildred Garvue, who'd taken over Pietila's daily 7 A.M. to 3 P.M. shift, had called Friday sounding desperate. The regular night nurse was on vacation and the substitute nurse had company. Could Pietila fill in Sunday night? Pietila hated working nights and her husband strongly objected, but she had loved working for Elisabeth. Her sense of duty and affection won out. "I miss Miss Elisabeth so I'll do it this one night," she told Garvue. "But only this once."

After Klosowsky let Pietila in, the two women chatted upstairs for several minutes as Klosowsky described Elisabeth's condition and handed Pietila the key to the medicine cabinet. Then Pietila looked at her watch as Klosowsky glanced at hers. It was five past eleven.

"My goodness it's getting late," Pietila said. "I'd better let you go home."

Pietila spent the night in the nurse's room across the hall from Elisabeth's bedroom. She sipped fruit juice, saving a sandwich, apple, and piece of cake for later. After propping open a window with her thermos of juice, Pietila read the book she had brought from home, Peg Bracken's *I Didn't Come Here to Argue*. Soon she would be involved in much more than an argument—soon she would be fighting for her life.

As part of her morning routine as Glensheen's maid, Hazel Conger unlocked Glensheen's front door for head nurse Mildred Garvue so the doorbell wouldn't disturb Elisabeth. But when she went to unlock the door Monday morning, Conger was surprised to find the chain off and bolt lock undone. The nurses were supposed to follow a specific lockup routine. The nurse working the 3 P.M. to 11 P.M. shift would check the windows in the library to make sure they were locked. She would also test the front door's push button lock, put on the chain, and engage the deadbolt lock. The night nurse, on the 11 P.M. to 7 A.M. shift, would never knock on the door or ring the doorbell when she arrived. Instead, the nurse on duty would watch for the night nurse to arrive and unlock the door. The night nurse would then relock the doors after her colleague left. But Pietila must have forgotten to finish locking up this time, the maid guessed as she popped open the push button lock.

Garvue arrived shortly before 7 A.M. Her first task was to get Elisabeth's insulin from the refrigerator in the pantry, where cook Prudence Rennquist was organizing the breakfast tray.

"How is Miss Elisabeth this morning?" Rennquist asked.

"I don't know. I haven't been upstairs yet," Garvue answered. Insulin, coat, and purse in hand, she headed upstairs to confer with the night nurse about Elisabeth's condition.

As Garvue started up the stairs, she was startled to see bare legs dangling on the landing between the first and second floors. Pietila lay motionless, awkwardly sprawled on a red velour window seat beneath a picturesque view of Lake Superior. Her position was deceiving. At first glance, Garvue thought the night nurse was resting or had perhaps fallen down the stairs. Pietila's legs hung over the side of the window seat, but her upper body was twisted around on the seat cushion. Her arms half hid her face, and her hands were nearly clasped, as if in prayer.

Climbing farther up the stairs, Garvue spotted blood crusted on the carpet. She stopped as she began to realize something terrible had happened. Garvue slowly looked up to where the night nurse lay and saw a pool of blood beneath Pietila's head. She approached the window seat and bent down, but could not bring herself to look at Pietila's body. She did manage to lift the night nurse's stiff arm to check for signs of life. Pietila's cold arm felt like cement in Garvue's hand. There was no pulse.

Shaking with fear, Garvue gathered the courage to look closely at Pietila's body. Her face was a rust-colored mask of dried blood, her jaw appeared broken. Blood spattered her uniform and pooled on the polished hardwood floor beneath the window seat, staining the Oriental carpeting. A blood-covered brass candlestick stood on the carpet several feet from the body.

Horrified, Garvue ran upstairs in a panic, concerned for Elisabeth. She flung her purse and coat into the nurse's room as she rushed into the heiress's bedroom. Often in the mornings, Elisabeth, already waking up, would smile and say "How are you?" before Garvue had a chance to ask Elisabeth the same question. This morning the room was in disarray. Dresser drawers had been pulled out and jewelry boxes lay open and empty on the floor near the vanity. Elisabeth lay face up in her bed, her legs bare and the sheets pulled back. Her left arm was bruised. Her gold watch and diamond-and-sapphire ring were missing from her wrist and hand. A pink, blood-flecked satin pillow covered her face. Garvue nervously lifted a corner. Miss Elisabeth's face was purple. Garvue didn't need to take a pulse.

Instead she rushed downstairs to the kitchen where Conger waited to bring up the breakfast tray.

"Velma's dead—Miss Elisabeth's been murdered," Garvue said, her face and voice numb with shock. Conger, suddenly weak, clung to Garvue for support. They knew they had to call the police, but fearing they would upset Rennquist, who had a heart condition, they avoided using the kitchen phone. Arm in arm, the two women guided each other slowly toward the front hall phone. They phoned the police at 6:58 A.M. The Duluth Police Department recorded the emergency call from Glensheen:

"Severe emergency. Thirty-three hundred London Road. Homicide," Garvue urgently told the dispatcher.

The dispatcher repeated the address, "Thirty-three hundred London Road," and waited for her to continue.

"Yes, sir. The Congdon estate."

"What's the problem?"

"Homicide."

"O.K. Just a minute, we'll get an ambulance. Thirty-three hundred London Road."

"Yes, please."

"Okay. Possible ten-eighty-nine. Homicide," the dispatcher told police and paramedics.

Conger and Garvue then tried to call Dunbar and Miss Elisabeth's physician, Dr. Elizabeth Bagley. But when the head nurse picked up the phone, there was no dial tone. The two women looked at each other in horror. The phone had just worked, and now it was dead. Conger went to fetch Glensheen's maintenance man, leaving Garvue alone in the mansion. Fearing that the line had been cut and that the killer was still inside Glensheen, Garvue anxiously waited for police to arrive, praying that the killer—or killers—wouldn't get to her first.

CHAPTER 2

Family Ties

CHESTER ADGATE CONGDON, ELISABETH'S FATHER, was the richest man in Minnesota when he died in 1916, according to news accounts at the time. Local legend has it that the conservative Republican died of a broken heart after Democrat Woodrow Wilson won the presidency.

As attorney, land owner, and state legislator, Chester Congdon would have been remembered in Minnesota even if his daughter had died peacefully. The Congdon name is sprinkled throughout Duluth—Congdon Park, Congdon Boulevard, and Congdon Park Elementary School, to name just a few tributes. At one time, Chester even had a ship named after him, but on November 7, 1918, the Great Lakes iron ore carrier *Chester A. Congdon* ran aground on a reef. It remained there, in a rocky area called Canoe Rocks near Isle Royale, until a storm sank it. The wreck site is now called Congdon Shoal.

Chester was born in 1853 in Rochester, New York, the son of a Methodist minister. As a young boy, he moved with his family to Syracuse, where his father led a new, larger church. His childhood was uneventful until he reached age fourteen. During one tragic month in 1868, Chester's father died of pneumonia and three of Chester's siblings died of scarlet fever. Suddenly the patriarch of the Congdon family, Chester took his new responsibilities very seriously. When the time came, he decided to attend college at Syracuse University, which allowed him to be near his mother, brother Bertie, and sister Laura. He also sent money when he could to help his mother with payments for the family farm.

"It is a close shave for us all now," he wrote his mother from school. "But we're going to pull through, don't worry over the note—I can take care of that if needs be—I had hoped to send some $10 bills as Christmas presents, all around, but I don't see how I can do it and raise the $200 [tuition] in January. But we will all revel in luxury some day. If we don't get any harder up than we are now. We will be infinitely better off than the large majority—but that's a weak sort of consolation—I want to be better off than everybody else."

During his freshman year in 1871, Chester met Clara Hesperia Bannister of San Francisco, and they soon discovered they had something in common—Methodist minister fathers. They made a striking couple. Chester stood tall and stately with dark hair, a straight patrician nose, and deep-set blue eyes. He wore a neatly trimmed mustache that hid his upper lip, a feature he hated. Clara Bannister was petite, with cascading brown hair she liked to put up in a French twist. She usually wore a black grosgrain ribbon choker.

Both excellent students, Chester and Clara graduated Phi Beta Kappa in Syracuse University's first class of 1875. Clara further distinguished herself as one of the university's first women graduates. During college, the couple had become engaged, but they postponed marriage until Chester established himself professionally.

Clara found a job as a schoolteacher at a small women's college in Belleville, Ontario, on the north shore of Lake Ontario, where she taught art and modern languages. Chester remained in Syracuse, studying law at a local firm, and was admitted to the New York bar in 1877. But wanderlust hit, and the next year Chester traveled west to Chippewa Falls, Wisconsin. Apparently, he hoped a teaching career would bring prosperity, but he lasted just one year. Tired of teaching and being poor, Chester inquired about legal opportunities in the Midwest and back East, where his family remained. His cousin C.H. Green in Fairport, New York, wrote back:

> "...If you hear of a place where there are not lawyers keep away for if there had been any good picking there would have been someone on the ground. Pitch in where there is a crowd. When you see a lot of crows hovering around you may know that there is a rich feast of carrion near....
>
> "I would be happy to show you the place and give you the reasons pro and con if you would come here...we have a flourishing village of 2000, 10 mile s from Rochester. Three lawyers. One gutter drunkard, one thief. And another man who does all of the business would I think take someone into his office."

Chester decided, however, to remain in the Midwest and moved to St. Paul, Minnesota, in 1879. The next year he was admitted to the Minnesota bar and hired by a St. Paul law firm. But his early days were marked by a scarcity of money and a wealth of doubts. Chester worried about his worth as a lawyer and prospective husband. Dr. Charles Bennett, one of Chester's closest friends, tried to snap Chester out of his depression in this letter postmarked January 1880:

> "How is Minneapolis? I am glad you are there rather then in Dacotah [North Dakota]. It is the place for you to plant yourself now. Mom told me of your financial condition. I think, in view of even the extreme case which you made that you are in the right plan. You may find your funds wasting away, but why leave? It is certainly as expensive to be on the move as to stay in one place. Has not this been one mistake which you have made—to be moving too soon?"

Despite his friend's good intentions, Chester continued to suffer bouts of depression. He felt he had failed himself and Clara—five years after graduation he was still struggling. Chester wrote Clara that his net worth consisted of $9.67 in cash, $5 receivable from his firm, $8 in prepaid rent, a $5.75 meal ticket, two pounds of crackers, two pounds of canned meat, and a half pound of coffee. In a letter dated January 30, 1880, a discouraged Chester confides in his fiancée:

> "I am afraid I can't have any good coffee until you come & make it for me. You ask me if I have ever thought of going into the wilderness—I certainly have. When I think that perhaps the greatest wrong I could do would be to marry you, then I think of getting away. Do you remember, dear, about a year ago you had some fears that it might be a mistake for you to marry me? I was very much surprised & since that time I have watched your letters very closely to see if you still had that idea.
>
> "No one realizes better than I that there is no reason why anyone should wish to share my life; & so when I think of how poor my own prospects are; & that there may be some doubts in your own mind, I very naturally think of the wilderness. For I should never have come here had it not been for you—& I would not stay here a week were it not for you. Not that I would go & kill myself; as that would occasion unpleasant notoriety—nor deliberately throw myself away. But I have become something of a gambler in feeling. I would risk everything on a small chance—go into the territories after money and in all human probability fail. Here is a slower & safer course.... I have seen a good many poor lawyers make money, so I may make some some day."

In another letter to his fiancée, Chester berated himself as "nothing more than a second rate lawyer." He told Clara, "certainly I should have the good sense to be a cowboy on the plains."

Chester's poor prospects suddenly improved months later when he was asked to serve as assistant to the U.S. Attorney for Minnesota, William W. Billson. His career finally launched, Chester told Clara to make wedding plans. They were married in a small ceremony in Syracuse on September 29, 1881, and honeymooned at Niagara Falls.

Theirs was a traditional marriage, based on a strong religious faith. Although the Methodist church didn't prohibit them, Clara would not allow drinking, smoking, or card playing in her home. Chester and Clara's first of seven children, Walter Bannister Congdon, was born in St. Paul in November 1882. The family lived in St. Paul for eleven years and had four more children, but little is known of their activities during this time.

In 1892, Chester, Clara, and their growing family of five children moved 150 miles north to Duluth. There Chester set up a law partnership with his old boss, William Billson. The law firm of Billson & Congdon quickly earned a statewide reputation for its expertise in civil litigation. But perhaps more significantly, on October 19, 1892, not long after the move, Clara noted in her diary that she "saw first car of ore from the Mesabi range."

The Mesabi, together with the Vermilion Iron Range, is an ore-rich region in northern Minnesota stretching over a hundred miles in a northeasterly direction from Grand Rapids to Ely. The Mesabi Iron Range became known for its soft ore, which lay close to the surface; extracting the ore didn't require the deep mining that the Vermilion Range did, nor the special processing necessary at the smaller Cuyuna Range west of Duluth, which had a high manganese content. The Mesabi generated a string of towns along its range from Grand Rapids to Babbitt, some with mining-inspired names like Taconite (a low-grade iron ore) and Mountain Iron.

Pittsburgh mining magnate Henry Oliver came to Duluth to research the Mesabi Range for himself, and visited the firm without advance notice. Oliver wanted to talk to Billson, who was out of the office, but was persuaded to speak with the younger partner. He was so impressed he hired Chester that day as chief counsel for the Oliver Iron Mining Company, which became one of the largest copper and iron ore producers on Minnesota's Iron Range—the result of a lucky break and Chester's legal talents.

Chester became a self-taught expert on iron ore properties as an investor, consultant, and landowner. His biggest coup and moneymaker came at age forty-eight, when he purchased land containing lower grade ore initially ignored by the mining companies, who eventually leased the land from him. Soon, Chester Congdon was turning iron ore into gold.

The late nineteenth century was a time of significant iron ore exploration and discovery in northern Minnesota—the major players included the Rockefellers, the Carnegies, and J.P. Morgan. Chester became increasingly active as a business consultant for the mining companies, serving on numerous boards but always protecting Oliver Mining interests. He continued as counsel for the company during its sale to J.P. Morgan's United States Steel Corporation in 1901. The sale left its mark on the region by creating two towns along the St. Louis River just south of Duluth—Oliver, Wisconsin, and Morgan Park, a company town built for workers at the U.S. Steel plant.

After the sale, Congdon and Oliver started their own business leasing iron ore properties. Chester's investments went beyond mining properties, however. He bought large tracts of land in the South, including some in Louisiana, for their farming value, raising muskrats, or the development of a hunting resort, depending on which family members remember correctly. This property increased significantly in value after his death, when oil was discovered.

During a trip to the West Coast in the late 1800s, Chester had fallen in love with Washington state's Yakima Valley and recognized its agricultural potential. He began purchasing land, which he eventually developed into a 375-acre orchard and cattle ranch. He helped build Congdon Ditch, one of the largest irrigation systems in Yakima Valley, for his apple, cherry, pear, and peach orchards. As for his cattle, Chester's herd of Aberdeen Angus was one of the largest in the country, and nationally known. On his ranch he built a family home out of native basalt stone on the side of a hill overlooking the orchards. Named "Westhome," the mansion was known to locals as "Congdon Castle" for its castle-like design, including turrets. Westhome was also distinctive for its indoor swimming pool, the first in the region.

Besides his vast wealth and land holdings, Chester Congdon earned a reputation for his civic contributions. One example is the large sum of money Chester donated to the city of Duluth to purchase land along Lake Superior. This property later became part of panoramic Highway 61 north of the city, now called the Scenic North Shore Drive.

Chester had little patience for political deals and favors, but became increasingly active in the Republican Party. He was a member of the Republican National Committee and served two terms in the Minnesota House of Representatives from 1909–1913. During his tenure, he denounced legislation to tax St. Louis County at the state's highest property tax rate as a backhanded way to raise taxes on the iron and steel industries. The measure was defeated. Reapportionment of political districts, an issue still prickly today, kept Chester so busy during his last House term that Clara noted it in her diary.

Despite his work as an attorney, investor, and legislator, Chester's family came first. After living in several houses in Duluth—including "The Redstone," architect Oliver Traphagen's sandstone-and-red-brick duplex masterpiece located at 1511 East Superior Street—Chester and Clara decided to build their own house. At the turn of the century, they purchased a fourteen-acre tract along Lake Superior beyond Duluth's fashionable East End. The July 23, 1903, entry in Clara's diary reads, "Chester and I went to Tischer's Creek to measure the place for house." Construction didn't begin until May 1905.

The site the Congdons chose for their new home was flanked by stands of pine and birch trees growing along Tischer Creek. Chester named the estate Glensheen, in part for his family's village of origin, Sheen, in Surrey, England, and, as the family story goes, for the way the sun shone on the waters of Tischer Creek. Glen derived from the deep ravines or glens carved out by the creek on the west end of the property.

From the selection of the building site to the mansion's architectural and interior design, Glensheen was Chester's special project. During the four years of construction, he spared no expense. He commissioned Clarence H. Johnston, Sr., a prominent architect for the State of Minnesota, to build the family home. A few years earlier, Johnston had been appointed architect to the Board of Regents of the University of Minnesota, and is credited with designing many of the university's buildings on all its campuses. Chester hired one of the Midwest's top interior designers, William A. French Company of St. Paul, to decorate Glensheen with furnishings from around the globe—Italy, Ireland, Algeria, Germany, the Orient, and the Middle East.

Glensheen's Jacobean design reflects the architect's classical training and Chester's fondness for English architecture. The thirty-nine-room mansion's external features include large, rectangular windows with divided panes, three curbed gables rising above the roof, and a series of tall brick chimneys. The décor also features Jacobean-style touches such as handcrafted pilasters in the main hall, an intricate central staircase carved to resemble leather strapwork, ornamental plaster ceiling accents, and stained glass windows in a Tudor rose pattern. Red brick terraces with marble pillar railings overlook manicured lawns, formal gardens, and a fountain.

Each of Glensheen's rooms featured international furnishings personally selected or crafted for the mansion. The main hall's rich, dark wood paneling greeted visitors entering the house. The architect had the oak woodwork specially stained or "fumed" by exposing the wood to ammonia fumes in sealed rooms. Former workers of the Tiffany Glass Company designed the leaded light fixtures, wall sconces, and stained glass windows. The living room's stately fireplace was made of Algerian marble, its chairs and sofa upholstered in tapestry woven in Germany. Mosque lamps bought in the Middle East flanked the library mantle, and silk damask wallpaper framed the golden-hued reception room, crowned by a ceiling accented with gold leaf. Marble imported from Sienna, Italy, faced the dining room fireplace.

In June 1906, Clara and Chester traveled back east to Burlington, Vermont, "to see granite," according to Clara's diary, which they purchased for Glensheen. By the following summer, the mansion's third floor was plastered, Clara wrote, and Glensheen was more than halfway complete. On November 24, 1908, three months before Glensheen was completed, Clara noted in her diary that the Congdon family "moved in and all spent the night there." While typical lakefront houses in 1909 cost between $11,000 and $16,000, Glensheen's price tag at completion was $864,000—given modern construction techniques and the limited availability of the raw materials, experts estimate a current price tag as high as $30 million.

While Chester took an opulent approach to Glensheen's magnificent design and interior decoration, he also equipped the mansion with practical features, such as buttons under the breakfast and dining room tables to summon staff. Glensheen had state-of-the-art appliances for the time, including a vacuum system that extended throughout the mansion. Hot water ran through pipes installed under the sink in the butler's pantry to warm plates and keep food hot for second helpings. The house originally had gas light fixtures, but the Congdons had the foresight to have wiring installed for the eventuality of electricity. Chester also irrigated Glensheen's grounds with water from a holding pond on Tischer Creek.

Over time, the estate grew to include a cottage for the gardener, a clay tennis court, a bowling green, a carriage house with an apartment, horse stables, and room for several Jersey cows, which provided the family with fresh milk and butter. Glensheen also boasted a large vegetable garden with a wealth of crops such as corn, broccoli, asparagus, Brussels sprouts, cabbage, cauliflower, peppers, tomatoes, and squash. In back of the main house on the lakefront, the Congdons constructed a boathouse with an attached L-shaped pier. The estate also included four greenhouses: the palm, rose, carnation, and general plant house, named for the plants grown in each. Several years after the Congdons moved into Glensheen, they ate ripe bananas and oranges from their own trees that grew in the palm house—the property's largest greenhouse—along with orchids, palm trees, and other exotic plants. Other greenhouses supplied fresh flowers for the family to enjoy each day.

Following Glensheen's completion, the estate became a gathering place for Congdon family members and friends from around the country, and the house was often filled with guests. Chester and Clara frequently hosted parties at the mansion or, in warmer weather, dances on the roof of the boathouse and boat rides on Lake Superior. To the children growing up within its brick walls, Glensheen could be stuffy and formal. Elisabeth and her siblings dressed formally for dinner every night. The boys wore black tuxedos and the girls long dresses.

But the mansion also made a wonderful playground. Glensheen had secret compartments and numerous hiding places for games like "sardines in the dark," a combination of hide-and-seek and tag. One person hid and as each seeker found the hider, they too squeezed into the hiding place.

Winters meant skating and hockey on the grounds at Tischer Creek or the Congdon Park rink just up the hill from Glensheen. The children also enjoyed sledding down the steep slope a couple blocks east of the mansion.

The Congdons celebrated Christmastime in grand fashion and elaborately decorated Glensheen. Three Norfolk Island pine trees, grown in Glensheen's own greenhouses, were brought into the mansion and put up in the main hall, the living room, and the recreation room. The family decorated the living room tree with traditional Christmas ornaments and silver tinsel. The rose greenhouse supplied red poinsettias to decorate the mansion. The gardener fashioned evergreen boughs gathered on Glensheen's grounds into eighty-foot-long garlands that adorned the mansion's staircase and fireplaces, as well as the Congdons' church, First Methodist Episcopal of Duluth.

Clara personally selected gifts for each child and grandchild. Chester distributed $20 gold pieces to the household staff. The Congdon clan would gather at Glensheen on Christmas Day, a tradition that held through the years.

Elisabeth's nephew, Tom Congdon, lived at Glensheen for eighteen months with his parents, sister, and brother while their house was being remodeled. He remembered the traditional Christmas breakfast of flummery, a "gritty, grainy hot cereal" of Scottish origin.

Like her cousin, Elisabeth's daughter, Jennifer Johnson, recalled hearty Christmas breakfasts in Glensheen's dining room with sister Marjorie, their mother, and grandmother Clara. After breakfast, the four sang Christmas carols as they walked downstairs one at a time, oldest to youngest, to the recreation room. They would find a fire blazing in the fireplace and gaily wrapped presents stacked beneath the Christmas tree. Then, before the Congdon relatives arrived for the big meal at noon, the family opened their gifts.

The Christmas noon meal consisted of a turkey and trimmings—mashed potatoes, sweet potatoes, cranberries, and mincemeat and pumpkin pie—served in the dining room. As a young child, Jennifer enjoyed visiting with her cousins as the children ate their Christmas meal in the less formal breakfast room.

Tom's sister, Mary Congdon Van Evera, said Christmas night was celebrated with friends and neighbors. "We invited people around town that didn't have family. Family friends who didn't have any connection like bachelors and former boyfriends of Aunt Elisabeth's. Dinner was held in the basement with all the food on the billiard table.

We ate and then we teased everybody to play games," Van Evera said. Charades were a popular Christmas night pastime.

In early spring, while the woods were still blanketed with snow, Chester and Clara's grown children and their children would have a cookout and make maple syrup candy. "We would boil maple syrup and make our initials in the snow," Mary Van Evera recalled.

As the weather became warmer, family activities often revolved around the lake and lakefront. The Congdons held parties on the beach and, on the Fourth of July, they picnicked and set off Roman candles. Chester bought a pleasure boat and named it the Hesperia, after Clara's middle name. The boat was docked at the pier behind Glensheen. During the summer, Chester and Clara entertained friends on the boat, taking it out on the lake while a live orchestra played on the boathouse roof. Unfortunately, a mishap with the boat's fuel destroyed the Hesperia in a July 1916 fire that also damaged the boathouse.

Chester and Clara were seasoned travelers who visited many European countries, the Orient, and the Middle East. They displayed special mementos they brought home in the "little museum," a room at the west end of the mansion's basement. The mementos included miniature tea sets, souvenir teaspoons, wooden carvings, and ceramic tiles. Additionally, Clara collected seashells and coral from their travels to tropical destinations such as the Caribbean, South Seas, and Roratonga.

Some items, like a Persian rug, became part of the mansion's décor. As their children grew, Clara became more of a homebody, preferring to remain behind at Glensheen while Chester traveled on business. Family vacations, however, remained important to Clara and Chester. The Congdon family visited Clara's relatives in California and New York, toured historic sites, and attended World's Fairs and Expositions, including those in Seattle, Chicago, San Francisco, and Portland.

As a father, Chester was caring and supportive. Although he expected his children to excel academically, and was a stricter disciplinarian than Clara, Chester also enjoyed a close relationship with each of his six children. While he and Clara had a large family, they tried hard to spend time with each child individually. Chester had a special way of getting to know his children better—each year, Chester took one child on a trip. One year, Elisabeth and her father sailed Lake Superior on an iron ore carrier. Another time, Chester took Elisabeth's brother Walter on a trip down the Nile.

Clara was a loving mother, but, as was the practice in those days, not an overly demonstrative parent. Her children were encouraged to be self-reliant. As Clara explained to one of her grandchildren years later, "In the old days, we didn't believe it was proper to fill our children with love and affection. We had to be stoic and teach them to be good sports and overcome all obstacles." But Clara took an active interest in her children's activities. She screened her children's books to make sure they were suitable. Gifted at sewing, needlepoint, appliqué, and other handicrafts (including making lace, which she collected from around the world), Clara taught her daughters those skills.

Clara's children also received lessons in thriftiness. When the seamstress came to Glensheen to sew clothes for the children, Clara had her make over any reusable clothes belonging to her older children as hand-me-downs. Torn bed sheets that couldn't be mended became pillowcases. Frayed towels found a new home in the maid's bathroom.

Chester and Clara instilled in their children a sense of noblesse oblige. For the Congdon children this meant that because they had more money than most, they had a duty to give to others. Community service would become a priority in their daughter Elisabeth's life.

Clara, a devoutly religious woman, made sure her children regularly attended services at First Methodist, where she was an active volunteer. She insisted that grace be said before each meal. She forbade card playing on Sundays, when the minister often joined the family for dinner at noon. Instead, she encouraged reading books, including the Bible. Jennifer recalled that she and Marjorie had to go into their grandmother Clara's bedroom each Sunday, where she would assign the girls a Bible verse to memorize that week. The following Sunday, Clara would ask the girls to recite the verse.

As she had done in their previous homes, Clara did not allow alcohol to be served at Glensheen. But when Chester hosted his business associates for dinner, he liked to serve brandy after the meal. He had a secret liquor cabinet in the basement in a closet off the playroom, which was not accessed until after Clara and the other wives retired to the living room. Jennifer Johnson remembered a family story about the night Chester had to repeatedly ask the butler to bring up brandy for his guests. "I'm sorry, Mr. Congdon, there isn't any brandy," the butler said each time. Chester asked him to look more thoroughly. Finally, the fourth time the butler was unsuccessful, Chester could see and smell the real reason why: there was indeed brandy, but unfortunately it was inside the butler. Clara discovered the liquor after Chester's death and promptly donated it to St. Luke's Hospital to use for medicinal purposes.

When Clara was in her late twenties, she lost most of her hearing to an unspecified illness, and sometimes wore an ear trumpet as a hearing aid. She found the device cumbersome and unhelpful, and instead began carrying a pad and pencil around to better communicate with family and friends. Although she never learned sign language, Clara became skilled at reading letters traced with a finger on her children's and Chester's hands, and at reading lips. Even from across the room, Clara could make out an unkind word or harsh retort, as her children and grandchildren learned the hard way.

Chester and Clara wanted their children to receive a good education, so they sent them off to prestigious East Coast preparatory schools and colleges. Elisabeth's older brothers attended prep schools in Massachusetts and Pennsylvania before attending Yale. Elisabeth and her sisters Helen and Marjorie attended Dana Hall, a private boarding school for girls in Wellesley, Massachusetts. Elisabeth was a good student who excelled at history and English, and her parents encouraged her to continue her education. After graduating from Dana Hall in 1915, she enrolled at Vassar College in Poughkeepsie, New York, where her sister Helen had also gone.

Chester Congdon died of pleurisy on November 21, 1916, in his apartment at the Saint Paul Hotel, where he stayed during the legislative session. He was sixty-three years old. He had become ill shortly after returning from Duluth, where he had gone to vote in the presidential election. The *Duluth Herald* published a special editorial:

> Mr. Congdon was a close student of government and state policies, a foe of waste and inefficiency, a friend of political progress as he saw it, a champion of clean public life and sound government.... Not because he was a rich man but because he was a good man with sound instincts and large capacities for service and with an ever increasing will to give his energy and means to wholesome public enterprises the loss of Chester A. Congdon is a great blow to the community, to the state and to the nation.

Her father's death brought Elisabeth home to Duluth after her freshman year of college. She did not go back to Vassar, feeling it was her duty to remain at Glensheen and look after her mother. In 1913 Chester had established two trusts "to provide and maintain for my wife and children a home so long as any of them shall live.... [m]aking it easy for any of my children, who so may wish, to occupy Glensheen." Elisabeth became her mother's closest companion, a special relationship the two women shared for thirty-four years, until Clara's death at age ninety-six in 1950. Elisabeth stayed until her own death, the last of Chester and Clara's children and the only one to live in Glensheen her entire adult life.

Soon after her return to Duluth, Elisabeth devoted herself to volunteer work. Although Elisabeth avoided publicity, her generous donations of money and time to charitable and civic organizations put her in the public eye. She filled her calendar with fundraisers and meetings for causes that included the symphony orchestra, the public library, the Lighthouse for the Blind, the St. Louis County Heritage and Arts Center, and the Duluth Rehabilitation Center. Like her mother, Elisabeth became an active volunteer at her family's church, which would eventually relocate to Skyline Parkway in 1966 and become First United Methodist, known to Duluthians as the "Coppertop Church" for its distinctive roof. In later years, Elisabeth attended church as often as her health allowed and continued to regularly donate fresh flowers from Glensheen's gardens, as her mother had done.

Educational institutions, long important to both sides of Elisabeth's family, became one of her priorities. She served as a member of the Chancellor's Group at Syracuse University, her parents' alma mater. She was a trustee of Dana Hall, the preparatory school she'd attended, and nearby Pine Manor Junior College. Years later, Elisabeth received an honorary doctorate from the University of the Pacific in Stockton, California, where her maternal grandfather had been the first president and founder.

Elisabeth shared her father's interest in civic affairs. She served as president of the King's Daughters Society of Duluth and, when it became the local Junior League in 1920, members selected Elisabeth as its first president. She held a seat on the board of the St. Luke's Hospital Guild and, as a board member, took charge of a major decorating project. She helped redecorate an entire wing, selecting wallpaper and traveling to Mexico to buy decorative art pieces.

During World War II, Elisabeth organized and headed the American Red Cross Nurse's Aid Committee in Duluth. The women volunteers rolled bandages, prepared care packages, knit mittens and scarves, and helped however they could to support the war effort and the local hospitals. Although Elisabeth didn't knit, she rolled hundreds of bandages and coordinated volunteers.

Those who knew Elisabeth well said she didn't give the impression of belonging to one of the richest families in town. She shunned fancy clothes, preferring instead to wear simply styled, fine cotton dresses and sensible pumps. She wore her hair neatly coifed, but in a simple, unfussy style. Elisabeth adorned herself with little jewelry, typically a simple strand of cultured pearls and matching earrings.

According to a friend, Elisabeth "liked to do things for people, but she was very natural with people—they never thought of her as hoity-toity."

Elisabeth did sometimes indulge a more flamboyant side. Her pride and joy for many years was a Stutz Bearcat sports car, followed by a Cadillac, in the family's favorite color—a pine green they called "Congdon green."

Although Elisabeth remained single, it wasn't for lack of attention. In her late twenties she seriously considered marrying Fred Wolvin, a handsome Duluth beau and longtime acquaintance, considered "a good catch" by Elisabeth's friends and family. [Wolvin's father, Captain August B. Wolvin, was a business acquaintence of Chester's and in 1902 built the Wolvin Building in Duluth at 227 West First Street; the building has since been renamed the Missabe Building.] Elisabeth accepted a diamond engagement ring from Wolvin, although their engagement was never officially announced. Elisabeth later told Wolvin she didn't love him enough to spend the rest of her life with him. The story goes that after she returned the large diamond engagement ring, her distraught suitor threw it into Lake Superior. Wolvin never married and, when he died, he left Elisabeth money in his will to buy a ring to commemorate their friendship. She purchased a diamond-and-sapphire dome ring she wore faithfully on her little finger until she died. For reasons she kept to herself, Elisabeth never married.

Nevertheless, Elisabeth loved children and didn't let convention stand in her way when, in her late thirties, she decided she wanted children of her own. Although adoption by single women was virtually unheard of in the 1930s, Elisabeth had family and financial resources that many adoptive couples did not, which likely assisted the adoption process. In 1932, at the age of thirty-eight, she contacted an adoption agency in Greensboro, North Carolina, and brought home a three-month-old baby girl named Jacqueline Barnes. "I want to help her. I can give her a good home and schooling," Elisabeth told family members and friends. She renamed her new daughter Marjorie, after her sister, and Mannering, after her mother's father. Marjorie Mannering Congdon slept in a bassinet in her mother's bedroom.

"There was a kind of feeling that Marjorie was to be the answer to Aunt Elisabeth's lonesomeness and her feeling of being unfulfilled as a single person," Mary Van Evera recalled. "But that also made Marjorie sort of a toy. I remember reading in [Clara's] diary 'Elisabeth was away again today,' and I think that Elisabeth left the baby-sitting job to her mother a whole lot."

Three years later, Elisabeth Congdon adopted her second daughter, this time through a Chicago adoption agency. As part of the adoption proceedings, she obtained a letter of recommendation from attorney Harold Stassen, Minnesota's future governor. Elisabeth adopted a baby girl whose parents, unmarried college students, could not afford to raise a child. She called her new daughter Jennifer Susan because she "liked the name."

The two girls couldn't have been more different.

CHAPTER 3

The Investigation Begins

DESPITE THE WARMTH AND SUNSHINE that greeted Duluthians Monday morning, June 27, 1977, Duluth Police Sergeant Gary Waller knew it was going to rain. The air was heavy and humid, a perfume of steaming wet leaves and grass, unusual for a city used to Lake Superior's brisk breezes. Dressed in athletic shorts and a sweatshirt with the sleeves pushed high, the thirty-two-year-old detective was sweating after only a couple blocks of his daily three-mile run through Lakeside, the neighborhood just east of Glensheen. One more drop of moisture in the air, Waller thought, and rain would spill out.

Waller took the time to stay in shape, dress stylishly, and carefully groom his dark blond hair. This, together with his blue eyes and wide smile, caused him to suffer a good deal of ribbing from his fellow police officers, some of whom tagged him the department's "golden boy." He shrugged off the good-natured teasing—the "golden boy" had become a heavy smoker and let himself go a bit around the middle, about fifteen pounds' worth by his estimation. Jogging, one of the things he hated most in life, was a necessary evil. Besides, it gave him time to review the burglary case he and his partner in the Detective Bureau, Dave Cismoski, had recently solved. More than one hundred residential burglaries had taken place in the city in just half a year. They now had two suspects in custody—a couple of local teenagers—and planned to take one of them out of jail for the day to identify homes he and his associates had burglarized. Within days, however, Waller would realize that the challenges of that case paled when compared with the Congdon case, and not just because the latter involved two murders.

Some police officers thought of law enforcement as just a job, but to Waller it was his career and his life. Law enforcement ran in his family. His father was a twenty-five-year Duluth police veteran. His brother, an uncle, and a cousin were police officers. After working his way up from a street cop, Waller found himself where he wanted to be, the detective bureau. But police work hadn't always been part of his plans.

Waller had grown up in Piedmont Heights, largely a blue collar, middle class neighborhood. As a teenager, he'd worked at the business his father ran in addition to his patrol job, a dental lab that made dentures. When Waller first attended the University of Minnesota Duluth, he intended to become a dentist. But he soon found the prerequisite math classes, especially calculus, too much. Waller changed his major from dentistry to sociology with a criminology focus. He liked to joke about his decision, saying he'd gone from working with one end of the anatomy to the other.

Like many young men in the 1960s, Waller had his education interrupted by the military. He signed up with the Minnesota National Guard in 1964 and completed basic training the following winter at Fort Knox, Kentucky. He then returned to college, waiting to be called up to Vietnam. But his unit never saw active duty. In the years since, Waller felt fortunate compared to many of his friends who were injured or killed in the war. He also felt guilt pangs for not having fought.

The Duluth Police Department hired Waller in 1966. After only three years on patrol, he took an assignment with the identification bureau, along the way gaining expertise in fingerprint analysis. By the time of the murders at Glensheen, he had risen to detective sergeant specializing in criminal investigation.

By 7:30 a.m., Waller had finished his run and was about to shower when the phone rang. Sergeant Richard Yagoda, one of the department's most experienced detectives, was calling from headquarters with a message from their boss, Duluth Police Inspector Ernie Grams.

A large man, Yagoda stood over six feet tall and weighed in at about 230 pounds. He had dark, wavy hair and a prominent nose even he kidded about. Waller considered Yagoda one of his mentors. He particularly admired the veteran detective's interview skills. Yagoda had a certain folksy charm that, when combined with persistent questioning, persuaded subjects to open up. Grams usually asked him to take charge of the department's tough cases.

"Gary. What are you doing?"

"I just got back from jogging. What do you think? I'm getting ready for work."

"There's been a double homicide at the Congdon estate."

"Go screw yourself, Dick."

Waller wasn't in the mood for another of Yagoda's practical jokes. Duluth didn't have a high crime rate. In the late seventies the city recorded an average of two or three homicides per year, far fewer than other communities its size.

"No, I'm serious, Gary. Elisabeth Congdon and her nurse were murdered last night. Ernie wants you at the estate right away."

"Who else is down there?"

"Chris Kucera. Jack Greene. ID's been called. Ernie's asking you to handle the crime scene."

"I can't come dressed like this. I'll be down there as fast as I can."

Waller showered, dressed hurriedly, and drove his 1974 Oldsmobile toward the Congdon estate. He snubbed out a half-smoked cigarette and lit another. He was up to a couple packs of Winston filters a day, a chain smoker when stressed. He had been thinking about quitting. Bad timing.

This case would mean a lot of pressure from the media and the victims' families, particularly the Congdons. He'd grown up with the Congdon name. To Waller and others outside the family it meant one thing—wealth. The Congdons were among Duluth's richest, oldest, and best-known families. Conscious of their position in the community, the Congdons prided themselves on their civic contributions made with little or no fanfare. But no citizen could miss the Congdon name. It appeared on everything in the city. Schools. Streets. Parks. Recreational halls. Boardrooms. The name also signified Glensheen, the mansion Waller drove by daily on the way to work. He'd never been inside, but he had investigated a killing involving the Congdon family before.

Seven years earlier Waller had been a crime scene technician in the Identification Bureau of the Duluth Police Department and had investigated the death of a teenage boy at the Robert and Dorothy Congdon mansion located at 3700 London Road, a few blocks east of Glensheen. The late Robert Congdon was Elisabeth's brother. His widow, Dorothy, had retired for the night to her second floor bedroom when she heard the sound of breaking glass outside and below her bedroom. An intruder was kicking out the glass panes in a terrace door on the first level, using the door as a ladder to climb to a second floor balcony on the Lake Superior side of the mansion.

The feisty seventy-year-old later told Waller that she was an experienced hunter and marksman. As the young man had attempted to climb onto the balcony she pointed a shotgun at him and ordered him to leave; he didn't take advantage of the opportunity. She had then aimed at his leg, hoping to only injure him, and fired. Unfortunately, one bb from the shotgun blast severed the femoral artery of his leg and he bled to death before medical assistance arrived. The intent of the young man, who had been under the influence of drugs, would never be known. Later that day Waller and his partner were pictured on the front page of the evening paper. It had been Waller's first press coverage, and he knew there would be much more this time.

Duluth police officer Chris Kucera was the first to reach Glensheen, at 7:03 A.M. He had driven in through the estate's east gate and circled the gardener's residence when he saw a man working outside the garage. Kucera pulled the marked blue squad alongside and got out of the car.

"Did you call for help?" Kucera asked gardener Robert Wyness.

"No, it must be from the main house," the gardener replied matter-of-factly, obviously unaware of the reported homicides.

Kucera got back in the car and sped around the driveway to the mansion's front entrance. Two women, one dressed in a white nurse's uniform and the other in a conservative suit, paced outside the door.

As the nurse came toward him, he noticed the dazed expression on her face. Conger and Garvue had been afraid the killer was still in Glensheen and had cut the phone line. But the line wasn't dead—there was no dial tone because the police operator had kept the line open between dispatch and the house until the first unit arrived, a common safety measure before the 911 emergency system could automatically identify a caller's location.

"What happened?" he asked.

"Both of them are dead," Conger said, pointing inside the house.

"Where?"

"Up there," she said, motioning toward the stairs.

Officer Kucera rushed past the women to the central staircase and climbed to the landing. He stopped in front of the first body and instinctively touched one leg to check for vital signs. The body was cool; no pulse. Kucera ran upstairs to Elisabeth Congdon's bedroom and saw the second body on the bed. He touched her lifeless right leg. Nothing to do but call for backup.

As Kucera headed downstairs, he saw his partner, Steve Rolland, and paramedics coming up. "No need for an ambulance," Kucera told them.

Rolland pulled out his radio. "We have a homicide. Send more help," he instructed headquarters.

At police headquarters, Sergeant Jack Greene had planned to continue working on a missing person case with local FBI agents. But as he parked his car on the ramp, a uniformed officer shouted at him.

"Hey, Jack. You've got a homicide on London Road."

From the police garage another male voice broke in: "Now you've got a double homicide."

Greene immediately called Ernie Grams at home, interrupting the inspector's breakfast. Grams assigned Greene and Yagoda to interview Glensheen servants and household staff.

At Glensheen, Lieutenant Nick Radulovich arrived next on the scene and ordered the mansion searched. He and Officer Kucera checked the second and third floors while Rolland took the first. They found no one hiding.

Within minutes, Grams and Greene arrived. As ranking officer at the crime scene, Grams confirmed the homicides and radioed the dispatcher to send tracking dogs and additional investigators. He also verified that identification experts were on the way.

A thirty-year police veteran, Grams, fifty-three, was a short, stocky balding man with deep-set eyes and a heavy, furrowed brow. He had started his career in Duluth on the other side of First Street, as the police reporter for the *Duluth News-Tribune*. He joined the Duluth Police Department in 1948, moving across the street from the newspaper's offices to the granite building that served in part as the city's police station. Fellow officers liked to describe Grams as TV detective Kojak with a little hair left. Grams had a dry sense of humor, often self-effacing. He wisecracked to reporters that he was just a hick cop from Duluth. He enjoyed a good cigar even in the office, and kept a stockpile in his desk drawer. Beneath the friendly banter and easygoing manner was an old pro with a track record for wrapping up difficult cases.

Detective Waller looked for Inspector Grams as he pulled up to the estate shortly after 8 A.M. He parked illegally on the grass outside Glensheen's wrought iron fence—one perk of being a cop. He spotted the uniformed officers posted around the grounds. The officer stationed at the main gate motioned for the crowd, which had gathered within minutes of news bulletins, to let Waller pass. The media, using police scanners, had found out about the murders just moments after the dispatcher had, so television and radio news bulletins had gone out within fifteen minutes of Garvue's call. Forecasts of a storm hadn't dissuaded reporters or spectators. Forcing his way through the crush of people on the sidewalk, Waller refused to answer questions.

As Waller entered the mansion, he saw before him a polished wooden stairway with Persian runners. To the left of the staircase, sun streamed in through a heavy cut-glass door leading to the patio. The house was dim except for the prism-like door and the patterns it cast on the dark, paneled walls.

Waller felt like he was walking into a museum, as though time had suddenly stopped. The air smelled musty, like someone had just opened an old manuscript or a sealed room after many years. The others present—police officers, paramedics, and household staff—spoke in hushed, grave voices. "Even though people lived in the house, there was absolutely no feeling of warmth," Waller recalled later. "It was ornate and dark and somber."

For a moment, Waller was overwhelmed by the enormous task that he and the other officers faced—ensuring that the three-story, thirty-nine-room mansion and seven-and-a-half-acre estate were not disturbed. But any security police now provided for the crime scene would be more than had previously existed at Glensheen. Waller was surprised to learn that despite the estate's vast size, there was no electronic security system at the mansion and other security measures were few. They included triple locks on Glensheen's massive front doors, a live-in staff, and a local security company under contract for emergency calls. Violent crime in Duluth was so rare in the mid-'70s that the Congdon family trustees felt confident they needed no further safety measures. Obviously, that confidence had been shattered.

The scene reminded Waller of "a Chinese fire drill: lots of people running around, much activity, but little control. We had a shift commander, inspector of detectives, three detective sergeants, and two patrol sergeants all wanting to take charge." FBI Special Agent Robert Harvey was also there, having tagged along with Greene, but the FBI wasn't officially on the case yet. "Harvey wasn't a Hoover-type agent," Waller recalled. "He was a team player."

Inspector Grams met Waller in the hallway. The two men stood talking at the foot of the main staircase.

"What have we got?" Waller asked.

"We found the nurse's body on the landing. She's been badly beaten. Miss Congdon appears to have been smothered with a pillow."

"What can I do?"

"I want you to handle the crime scene," said Grams, assigning Waller to supervise the processing and collection of evidence. But first, Grams wanted Waller to view the bodies with him, to try and reconstruct what had happened.

Inspector Grams and Waller climbed the stairs. Sunlight filled the window above the body on the window seat. The familiar sweet, coppery smell of blood concentrated on the landing made Waller wince. Even before he got close, he could sense the lifelessness. "There is a definite absence of life, you can feel the vacuum when you enter a room with a dead body," Waller said later. "It's instinctual, and it has nothing to do with being a policeman or an investigator."

Waller had investigated dozens of violent deaths, but the brutality of this attack sickened him. Velma Pietila was beaten beyond recognition. Her chiseled Nordic features—she was Finnish—were crushed, her blond-gray hair matted with blood. Her white nurse's uniform was spattered with blood, bunched to her waist, and unzipped halfway, exposing her slip. This suggested a sexual assault, though lab tests later ruled that out.

Pietila's body had apparently been arranged on the seat, her torso awkwardly angled in a different direction than her arms and legs. Her arms were badly bruised, and a dark nylon stocking was wound tightly around her left wrist. Perhaps the killer had first tried to just tie her up, Waller thought. Whoever had killed her and rested her body there might have felt a certain degree of remorse.

The two men moved upstairs, careful to step around other pieces of evidence scattered on the landing and up the stairs. They then entered Elisabeth Congdon's bedroom. The lamp next to her bed remained lit. The heiress's pillow, bedspread, and nightgown were bloodstained. Judging from the light-colored flecks of blood, many of them smeared, Waller guessed Pietila had been killed first. The murderer had then transferred traces of the nurse's blood to Congdon's bedroom. If the police were lucky, the killer had also been injured during the struggle on the stairs and left traces of his or her own blood behind.

Waller removed the pink satin pillow from Congdon's face. One crumpled corner had obviously been clenched in the killer's fist. Waller noticed a raw patch of skin on her nose. He could also see dark bruises on her left arm where the killer had held her down.

Waller looked around, surprised by the muted colors and rather plain furnishings in the bedroom. Except for a few knickknacks and decorative pieces acquired during her globe-trotting days, it showed few outward signs of Congdon's vast wealth. A dull pinkish gray dominated the room: as in all the other bedrooms, the wallpaper, draperies, carpeting, and woodwork matched. Aside from a hospital bed with its overhead ring and railings, only a pale green couch and a large wooden dresser stood out.

The tall dresser caught the investigators' eyes. All eight drawers were pulled out exactly the same distance, about six inches. Hardly wide enough for a burglar to search inside. Yet empty jewelry boxes and plastic trays were scattered on the floor by the vanity. The burglar had taken time to neatly arrange the dresser, Waller noted, perhaps to stage the appearance of a break-in.

Directly across the hall, in the nurse's room, Pietila's purse lay open on the bed, obviously rifled through by the killer, who, it would later be determined, had taken her car keys. In the adjoining bathroom, faint bloodstains showed on the door jamb, and several nearly invisible spots dotted on the white sink and white-tiled floor. The stains suggested the murderer had stopped to hurriedly wash before escaping.

In the meantime, canine units went through Glensheen from top to bottom before the crime scene was sealed. One of the German shepherds picked up a scent in Congdon's bedroom that led to the basement and a possible entry point, a broken window at the rear of the mansion, inside an enclosed porch. The other dog followed a track to the porch that continued outside beyond the well-manicured lawn and gardens toward the lake. Officers found a single set of fresh tracks and a lollipop stick on the pier at the lake's edge. Did the lollipop stick belong to the killer, or just some trespassing kid? There was no way to know.

Once the dogs moved outside, Waller and three officers from the Duluth Police Department's identification bureau began the tedious task of processing the crime scene, documenting and collecting each item of evidence. They started by photographing the bodies and all visible physical evidence. The officers worked their way up the central staircase to Pietila's body, then into Elisabeth Congdon's bedroom, before finishing with the nurse's bedroom and bathroom.

Dr. Volker Goldschmidt, the St. Louis County medical examiner, arrived about 8:45 A.M. He knelt on the landing and closely examined Pietila's body. The dark nylon stocking was wound around her left wrist so tightly it would have to be cut free at the autopsy. Goldschmidt was puzzled by a pattern of tattoo-like puncture wounds on her face, forearm, and finger, unsure of what had caused them. He noted the strange markings in his pre-autopsy observations. Based on the condition of the blood on the landing, Dr. Goldschmidt believed that Pietila died sometime after midnight. Next, he and Mildred Garvue went up to the nurse's bedroom to look at the medical log maintained by the nurses during each shift. Pietila's uneaten dinner and thermos were on the sill of the window overlooking the driveway.

The log was usually kept on the larger of two desks in the nurse's room. The lone entry for the evening of June 26 was Velma's sign-in at the beginning of her shift: "V. Pietila, R.N., eleven to seven." Between 11 P.M. and 2:30 A.M., Elisabeth was often repositioned in bed and typically received sedatives or pain medication and sometimes a glass of warm milk to aid her sleep. There was no notation in the log of any medication in the early morning hours of June 27. An inventory of Elisabeth's medications the day of the murders also indicated that none had been dispensed during Pietila's shift. The lack of any additional entries by Pietila therefore suggested a time frame for the killings between 11 P.M. and 2:30 A.M.

Goldschmidt next examined Elisabeth's body. Rigor mortis had set in.

He also observed the abrasion on the tip of her nose, small hemorrhages in the pupils of her eyes, and a severe bruise on her left forearm. She appeared to have suffocated while fighting off her killer: as she had twisted from side to side, the satin pillow had rubbed the tip of her nose raw.

While Waller and others processed physical evidence, Greene had begun his first interview with sixty-two-year-old Vera Dunbar. Scottish, strong-willed, and square-jawed, Dunbar was a prim, petite woman. She wore a conservative suit, her gray hair styled in a pageboy. She had managed Elisabeth Congdon's daily schedule for nine years and ran the household, giving orders to the servants and nurses. Three years earlier, she'd been appointed one of Miss Congdon's personal conservators. Her new duties included screening her employer's calls and visitors to ensure no one tried to take advantage of the heiress and that Miss Elisabeth didn't overexert herself.

Dunbar escorted Sergeant Greene to a small room used as the servants' dining area. Seated at the formica table, Greene started the conversation: "Tell me something. Tell me about this family, this house. Get me going."

Dunbar said Elisabeth owned two of the four Congdon homes; a winter home in Tucson, Arizona, and Swiftwater Farm. Glensheen and Westhome in Yakima, Washington, belonged to the Congdon estate. Elisabeth divided her time between Duluth, the Brule, and Tucson. The last time Dunbar saw her employer was after lunch on Friday, June 24, when Miss Elisabeth left for a weekend at Swiftwater Farm.

Greene was particularly interested to learn that whenever Elisabeth visited the winter home, the family hired a security guard because Tucson was over 300 miles closer to Golden, Colorado—where her adopted daughter Marjorie lived—than Duluth was. Duluth. Dunbar retrieved a family photo album and showed Greene a smiling photograph of Marjorie and her first husband, Richard LeRoy. Dunbar told Greene that Marjorie's second husband, Roger Caldwell, had visited Glensheen in May—without Marjorie—to meet Elisabeth and ask the Congdon trustees for a large sum of money. Dunbar said the meeting took place in the library and lasted a half hour. Dunbar then drove Caldwell back to his Duluth hotel.

When Greene asked about any family problems, Dunbar mentioned a rift between Marjorie and other family members over her mishandling of money. Marjorie was constantly in debt. Greene would hear this repeatedly from most of the family and staff he interviewed. Dunbar had more to confide. Marjorie manipulated her mother, she told Greene, and as conservator Dunbar had tried to protect Miss Elisabeth from her daughter's advances, particularly after an incident three years earlier, on November 3, 1974.

Marjorie had visited her mother at Glensheen and brought along a loaf of homemade bread and jar of sugar-free marmalade, Dunbar recalled. There had been trouble before with Marjorie concerning Elisabeth's diet. (Marjorie's daughter Suzanne would later state that during holiday meals at Glensheen her mother would place sweets on Elisabeth's plate and tell her she should have some, even though Elisabeth, a diabetic, was not medically permitted to do so.) Dunbar continued to explain that within hours after Elisabeth had eaten the sandwich her daughter had prepared, she became very ill. Her blood pressure dropped drastically, she couldn't be roused the next morning, and she was sleepy for two days. Blood tests performed by her doctor revealed traces of meprobamate, a powerful sedative not on Elisabeth's prescription list. But tests could not pinpoint how and when Elisabeth was drugged or by whom.

Determined to avoid adverse publicity, the Congdon family did not notify Duluth police. The family also decided against confronting Marjorie. They had no proof, just circumstantial evidence and suspicions, particularly because Marjorie abruptly left the morning her mother's condition was discovered. After the scare, however, household staff and nurses were told never to leave Elisabeth alone with Marjorie. Trustees of the Congdon Office Corporation, established in Duluth to manage and oversee the Congdon family's finances, also ordered the household and nursing staff to monitor all phone calls between the two women.

Next, Greene interviewed sixty-four-year-old Prudence Rennquist, who'd joined the household as cook two months earlier. Rennquist told Greene she went to her bedroom around 8:30 P.M., took a bath, watched television, and let Muffin, her black miniature poodle, outside before going to bed shortly before eleven. She awoke around 3 A.M. to find Muffin scratching at her arm and barking excitedly.

Rennquist later said, "I'm very time conscious, especially if I get woke up in the middle of the night. And I looked at my watch and it was ten minutes to three, and I said, 'What's your story, Muffin?' And she just ran to the door and wanted me to come with her. I took her in my arms and held her mouth shut and went to the bathroom. But when I was coming out of the bathroom, she got away from me and ran to the door that leads from the servants' quarters to Miss Congdon's room." A thick wooden door separated the servants' quarters from the rest of Glensheen's second floor. "And she scratched on the door and I remember the thought went through my mind, well, tomorrow morning I'll just have to see if there's any scratches on that door."

Even after being spanked with a newspaper, Muffin continued to bark and whine and refused to stay in bed. Rennquist said, "I had my Bible laying by the bed and I had some favorite letters that my four daughters sent and I read through all the letters first, and hushed Muffin in between reading. And in one of my girl's letters she said 'read the psalms,' so I was reading the psalms." The dog remained agitated and kept Rennquist awake until about 4:50 A.M. Muffin had behaved the same way only once before, when Rennquist's previous employer's garage was burglarized.

Glensheen maid Hazel Conger had worked at the mansion for nine years. She occupied the front bedroom in the servants' quarters. A heavy sleeper, Conger told officers she hadn't heard any strange noises after going to bed around 11:15 P.M. Sunday. She'd slept so soundly she didn't wake up until her alarm went off at 6:30 A.M.

Once dressed, Conger's morning routine was to turn off the front hall and outside lights and unlock the front door for the day nurse. She then set up Miss Elisabeth's breakfast tray in the pantry; Miss Elisabeth always ate breakfast in bed. This morning, as Conger finished setting out the food, she heard someone at the pantry door calling her.

Conger thought it was Velma Pietila. But when she turned, she saw Mildred Garvue instead. Garvue's wide eyes and pained expression said something wasn't right. "What's wrong?" Conger had nervously asked. It was then she learned Miss Elisabeth was dead.

Glensheen gardener Robert Wyness had lived all but six of his sixty-two years on the estate, where his father had served as gardener before him. Wyness told police he'd had relatives visiting from Springfield, Illinois. They'd had a fish fry on the beach behind Wyness's small house on the grounds from 7 to 9 p.m. Sunday. Wyness then drove the relatives to their motel about 10 p.m., when it was getting dark. After he returned, he and his wife went to bed. They heard nothing unusual at the estate that night.

The death of Elisabeth, whom he thought of as a sister, traumatized Wyness so much that he refused to enter the main house for nearly two years.

Velma Pietila's husband, Loren, arrived at Glensheen at 8:50 a.m. Inspector Grams had the unpleasant responsibility of informing him that his wife

had been murdered, but Grams was too late. Pietila, a retired forester, already knew he was a widower. He'd heard a radio news report shortly after 7:15 a.m. in his home, just two miles east of Glensheen on London Road. It was about the time his wife should have been getting home.

Shaken by the news, Loren Pietila eventually called a close friend to drive him to the mansion. As he walked up the driveway, he noticed his car, a Ford Granada, was missing. He told Inspector Grams that Velma had driven the car to work. Duluth police immediately issued a statewide alert.

He told Grams that when his wife was asked to work Sunday night, he "pleaded with her not to go." Velma had never worked a night shift before during the seven years she'd cared for Elisabeth Congdon. He said goodbye to his wife about 10:45 p.m. Sunday. That was the last time they spoke.

The Pietilas had been married nearly forty-five years. Childhood sweethearts from northern Minnesota's Iron Range, the Pietilas were still deeply in love. They spent as much time together as possible. The parents of three grown children, the couple eagerly looked forward to Velma's retirement when they could travel more and play golf. As Loren Pietila explained simply, "We had things planned."

Grams asked Pietila if he knew anyone who'd want to harm his wife or Elisabeth Congdon. Velma had confided to her husband that she'd had problems with Marjorie, Pietila said. During one of Marjorie's visits, she and Velma argued over Miss Congdon. Marjorie grabbed Velma's wrists hard and wouldn't let go. Velma told her husband she "shook off Marjorie's hands."

This incident was recounted in a letter from Vera Dunbar to one of the Congdon trustees on August 7, 1975. Dunbar, who had been out shopping, returned to Glensheen to find a car belonging to Fran Bouche, one of Marjorie's friends from the Twin Cities, parked in front. As Dunbar walked toward the front door, Hazel Conger came hurriedly toward her and told her to go right upstairs because Marjorie was with her mother and she had heard shouting. Dunbar immediately went up to the second floor and found Marjorie and Bouche seated in Elisabeth's bedroom. "[Elisabeth] was in her wheelchair," Dunbar wrote, "and the nurse, Velma Pietila, met me at the door at the room saying 'you don't know what I've been through.' She told me that Marjorie grabbed her wrists while she was attempting to back out of the room with [Elisabeth], explaining that [Elisabeth] had a one o'clock at the hairdresser. Marjorie said that her mother was going to stay right where she was." Eventually, Congdon cousins Tom Congdon—a trustee—and Dr. Terry d'Autremont were summoned to the mansion, and Marjorie informed them that she expected her mother to take her and Bouche to lunch at the Kitchi Gammi Club, the exclusive private club founded in part by Chester Congdon and his friend, Guilford Hartley.

Loren Pietila believed Miss Congdon had been "set up" by Marjorie. "Bad blood" existed between the mother and daughter, he told Grams. Loren Pietila had heard Marjorie owed her mother more than $1 million.

While Loren Pietila talked with detectives, news of the murders reached Elisabeth Congdon's family. Jennifer and her husband, Chuck, were in the middle of having the upstairs of their Racine, Wisconsin, home painted. When the phone rang, Chuck had taken their dog for a walk on the beach and Jennifer was getting dressed. "Bill Van Evera called, and I picked up the phone," Jennifer remembered. Van Evera was her cousin Mary's husband and a Congdon trustee. "He said, which I thought was pretty blunt, 'Your mother's been murdered.' The first thing I said was 'Marjorie did it. I've got to find Chuck.' Never thinking about the painters, I went out the door in my nightgown, down the stairs. I was screaming at Chuck down at the beach to get up here. That afternoon we left to go to Duluth."

North of St. Paul, Marjorie Caldwell's oldest daughter, Suzanne LeRoy, received word of her grandmother's death from her sister, who had called the stable where Suzanne worked. LeRoy's first thought was that her mother was probably involved. She told stable owner Hans Ecklund she suspected her mother because of her desperate need for money. Her mother might even have hired a Mafia hit man, LeRoy said, referring to the number of suspected organized crime figures who owned horses near Marjorie's home and prospective horse ranch in Colorado. Ecklund quickly pointed out that if Marjorie's finances were so bad, the Caldwells couldn't cover the advance hit men usually require. (Subsequent police investigation failed to turn up any organized crime connection to Marjorie Caldwell or the murders.) Suzanne's father, Dick LeRoy—Marjorie's first husband—also found out soon, contacted at work by his second wife, Sherry. Dick told his colleagues that he thought Marjorie was involved.

In Denver, Elisabeth's nephew Tom Congdon took matters into his own hands after learning of the murders. He considered his cousin Marjorie and her husband, Roger Caldwell, who lived less than an hour away in Golden, Colorado, suspects. Assuming Roger had committed the murders and would be fleeing back to Colorado, he telephoned airport police only to discover the likely flight from Minneapolis to Denver had already landed. He then contacted the Denver Police and asked for the name of a private investigator. He was given the name of private detective William Furman of Denver. Congdon called Furman and arranged for immediate protection of his family. He also hired Furman to tail Marjorie and Roger. To help collect information on the Caldwells and the murders, Furman told Congdon he would use "a kind of device that enables you to hear conversations from a distance." Furman also said he would "put some money on the streets" to see what he could dig up on the Caldwells. The choice would eventually prove regrettable—Furman had a questionable reputation with certain police officers.

As one of three trustees for the funds established by Chester Congdon, Tom Congdon was aware of every family member's financial status. The Caldwells had serious money problems. He'd recently paid $400 so they wouldn't be thrown out of the Holland House Hotel in Golden, where they and Marjorie's youngest son, Rick, had lived since March.

Bob Harmon, an agent with the Colorado Bureau of Investigation, also had suspicions regarding the Caldwells. He'd spent months investigating an alleged burglary at the couple's former home. Harmon suspected the crime had been staged. The Caldwells faced possible charges of insurance fraud.

Waller authorized the removal and dispatch of the bodies, Pietila's at 9:50 A.M. and Elisabeth's at 10:50 A.M., to St. Luke's Hospital for the autopsy. Once the paramedics removed the bodies, Waller and officers Bob Cox and Bob Gracek of the department's identification bureau began their painstaking examination of the landing and stairs where Pietila had struggled. The apparent murder weapon sat upright on the landing next to her body—a heavy, ten-inch brass candlestick bent above its base. Across from the window seat, on the hardwood floor, they found a bloody footprint. Unfortunately the print, made by what looked like a shoe heel, was blurred, and of little help to police. Over the next several hours, the trio carefully examined the bizarre array of items strewn on the landing and stairway—a dented flashlight, batteries, a bloody shoe with its heel broken off, hairpins, earrings, broken eyeglasses, pills, and teeth fragments. They recovered thirty-seven pieces of evidence from the staircase alone, proof of the horrible struggle between Pietila and her killer.

While the officers continued to process the central staircase, Vera Dunbar took a preliminary inventory of her employer's bedroom. Police soon learned many pieces of Elisabeth's jewelry were missing. A diamond-and-sapphire ring, a gold watch, a double string of pearls, a cameo pin, a choker necklace, several bracelets, a gold Tiffany pin, and eighteen pairs of earrings could not be located. The stolen jewelry, most of it custom-made, included Elisabeth's favorite charm bracelet with thirteen gold charm silhouette heads, each representing one of her grandchildren.

Detectives received a call from Loren Pietila around 10 A.M., shortly after he'd returned home. The keys to Pietila's stolen car had been found at the Minneapolis-St. Paul International Airport at about 8:30 that morning. Mark Fuelling, an airport maintenance worker, told Pietila he'd discovered the keys after removing a plastic trash bag from a can outside the terminal's main entrance. Fuelling noticed an identification tag on the key ring listing Pietila's name, address, and phone number.

Since the killer—or killers—had apparently abandoned the car at the airport, Duluth police phoned airport security with a description of the car

and license plate number. About 11 A.M., two airport police officers found

the Ford Granada in the short-term parking lot. The Minnesota Bureau of Criminal Apprehension, headquartered in St. Paul, was called in to process the car. The organization specializes in the collection and laboratory examination of physical evidence, which in this case meant hair, fiber, blood, and fingerprints. Meanwhile, airport police asked Fuelling to point out the trash can where he found the car keys. Inside the trash container, they discovered a short-term parking lot ticket for the airport lot stamped 6:35 A.M. June 27.

Back at headquarters, Duluth police began checking commercial airline schedules for early morning flights out of the Twin Cities. Because Congdon family members suspected Marjorie and her husband (privately, Duluth police did too), investigators focused on direct and connecting flights to Colorado.

Eventually, a fingerprint on the driver's window would be identified as belonging to Loren Pietila. A blood stain on the floor near the gas pedal came from someone with blood type O. Velma Pietila and Elisabeth Congdon both had type-O blood. So did Roger Caldwell.

After talking with the Glensheen staff, detectives Greene and Yagoda began interviewing the Congdon family. The detectives were interested in the absence of a formal security system at the mansion. The family had hired off-duty Duluth police officers to direct traffic and provide security for a family reunion two years before. It was at the reunion that Pietila had had her argument with Marjorie Caldwell; Bill Van Evera told detectives that Marjorie had ejected the nurse from her mother's room. Afterward, the family decided to pay the Midwest Patrol security firm $25 a month to be on call for emergencies. But more recently, the family had relied on around-the-clock nurses, live-in servants, and the two families living on the grounds: the male chauffeur and groundskeeper, who lived in separate homes, and the telephone hookups from their quarters to the mansion, comprised Glensheen's internal security system. The interviews with Congdon relatives would last into the evening. Detectives Greene and Yagoda continued to hear the same story over and over. Family members suspected that Elisabeth's daughter Marjorie and her husband, Roger, were involved in the murders. The motive? The couple's heavy and mounting debt. Marjorie stood to inherit millions upon Elisabeth's death.

Waller and police identification technicians Cox and Gracek continued their evidence gathering on the central staircase throughout the morning. Gracek sketched the crime scene and items of evidence while Waller measured each object and its location on the stairs. Cox photographed, recorded, labeled, and collected the evidence in new paper bags. Police prefer paper bags because they are sterile, untouched by human hands until opened. And unlike plastic, paper breathes. In this case, officers could collect the victims' bloody clothing and bedding without worrying that the material would decompose before trial. Each bag was sealed and initialed by Waller. The evidence was then sent either to the state crime lab or FBI for analysis or to the police evidence room for storage.

The investigators left the apparent murder weapon, the dented, bloodied brass candlestick, upright on the landing. Police would dust it for fingerprints later. The blood-soaked carpeting on the landing would be pulled up several days later and sent to the state crime lab along with the stained cushion from the window seat.

While the officers worked their way up the staircase, a massive thunderstorm moved in over Lake Superior. Through the window they saw ominous black clouds rolling across the vast horizon and lightning dancing upon the lake, its flashes lighting up the staircase. The officers fell silent, momentarily overcome by the scene in front of them. The storm forced police to slightly alter the crime scene; someone removed Pietila's thermos from the nurse's room window so the window could be shut. Continuing his way up the stairs, Waller noticed a deep, crescent-shaped dent in the wall paneling near the head of the stairs. The killer had either missed a swing at Velma Pietila with the heavy candlestick or dropped the weapon against the wall.

Blood splatters marked the walls going up the stairs and above the window seat. Investigators found spattered blood as far as six feet from the window—including blood casting on the molded ceiling at the top of the stairs—made by the killer while swinging the bloody candlestick. They recorded numerous bloodstains in the nurse's room and bathroom. The state crime lab technicians, experts in blood splatter analysis, would be on the scene two days later. Waller counted on the blood splatter analysis to confirm the sequence of the murders and provide details on Pietila's struggle with her killer. Next, the officers examined a low, wooden bureau in the hallway at the top of the stairs. To its right sat a chair, to the left stood a small statue of the Roman poet Virgil perched on a stone obelisk (nearby, the statue's counterpart, a matching statue of Italian poet Danté, flanked the left side of a guest room door). On top of the bureau, on the left side, a single brass candlestick remained. The candle and drip ring from the bloody candlestick on the landing lay on the right side, where they had fallen when the murderer grabbed his or her weapon. From there, Waller, Cox, and Gracek moved into Elisabeth's bedroom.

Once the written narrative, photographs, measurements, and sketches had been completed, officers collected latent prints at the crime scene. Investigators lifted a partial print from the brass candlestick, and Waller hoped for good news from the crime lab. No usable prints were found in Elisabeth's bedroom. The nurse's room and bathroom would not be processed for prints until after the state crime experts examined the faint bloodstains.

Since neither the live-in staff nor the families living on the grounds had seen or heard anything suspicious, Waller hoped to find physical evidence as the first day of the investigation progressed. Detectives couldn't afford to overlook anything at this stage of the investigation. Every conceivable relevant item was painstakingly photographed, measured, and documented in a written log.

"We were documenting the original condition of the crime scene, recording exactly what we saw," Waller recalled. "When we walked up the stairs and saw that amount of blood on the floor and the blood splattering on the walls and the battered body of Velma Pietila...it's hard not to let your emotions get in the way. But the first thing we had to do was control our emotions before we could begin."

It would take police three days to search and collect evidence at the mansion and 7.6-acre estate, even with outside help from the state crime lab experts. This was the most challenging crime scene of Waller's experience—and the most frustrating.

"First and foremost, the crime scene has to be protected from contamination until all the evidence is gathered," Waller said. "The worst offenders are usually the law enforcement officers assigned to investigate the case.

"We did secure the house and the grounds, but we failed to protect them. We had cigarette butts in the toilet of the nurse's bathroom. Who threw their cigarettes in the toilet? The police officer protecting the scene. I didn't see it at the time. I looked at pictures of the crime scene a million times and missed seeing the cigarettes. It gave the appearance of being careless and sloppy and worst of all, of a contaminated crime scene. How can you defend that in court?

"Good crime scene investigations involve complete control of everyone entering the area. Now anyone who comes to a crime scene has to be there for a legitimate reason," Waller said. This murder resulted in a policy change for the police department, requiring officers to sign in and state their purpose for being at the crime scene.

Waller was mad as hell about the initial lack of security to protect the evidence— and he had good reason to be. Every time people enter a crime scene they risk taking away a bit of evidence. They might also deposit fibers, fingerprints, hairs, and other matter not there before. Contamination of the crime scene is the fastest way to destroy a solid, physical evidence case. A small army of police officers and representatives of the county attorney's office had tramped through the crime scene, especially around Velma Pietila's body. The large number of visitors raised a nagging question for Waller.

Could hair strands found near the nurse's body, assumed to be the murderer's, have been tracked there from somewhere else in the mansion? The possibility was mathematically remote, but not impossible.

Pietila's clothing and Congdon's nightgown and bedding were among the dozens of items Duluth police forwarded to the FBI. The FBI lab had the technology to lift prints off porous surfaces like cloth by using special chemicals. All other evidence, hundreds of items, was sent to the Minnesota Bureau of Criminal Apprehension.

The volume of physical evidence was impressive. Waller had already earned a reputation for submitting large quantities of evidence to the state crime lab. His fellow officers teased that only his uncle, Floyd Bowman, a twenty-one-year veteran with the Duluth Police Department and at that time a BCA agent, could top him. They said that if it were possible, Waller would have put Glensheen on wheels and rolled it down Interstate 35 to the BCA in St. Paul.

Monday afternoon, Grams held a press conference in his ground-floor office at city hall. The grisly news had spread throughout Duluth, down to the Twin Cities, and hit the wire services. The news media demanded to know what had gone on inside Glensheen. Reporters nationwide wondered if the police had any suspects or a motive for the killings. The story made banner headlines:

"ELISABETH CONGDON, NIGHT NURSE MURDERED" — *The Duluth Herald*

"DULUTH SOCIALITE, NURSE MURDERED" — *The Minneapolis Star*

"2 WOMEN SLAIN IN DULUTH" — *The St. Paul Dispatch*

"HEIRESS, NURSE FOUND SLAIN" —*T he Milwaukee Journal*

"DULUTH HEIRESS AND NURSE SLAIN" — *Chicago Sun-Times*

"TUCSON BENEFACTRESS AND NURSE SLAIN IN MANSION NEAR DULUTH"
— *Arizona Daily Star*

Grams told reporters burglary was the presumed motive for the murders. The killer had apparently entered Glensheen through a window at the rear of the house. The murders had occurred sometime between midnight and 7 A.M.

Grams dispelled rumors that Elisabeth Congdon had slept with a gun under her pillow. He also informed reporters that Glensheen's main gates were open during the night. They were only locked during the smelting season to discourage trespassing in the creek on their property. (Smelting was a popular spring ritual along Lake Superior's North Shore. Mouths of creeks and rivers filled with smelt, a small, silvery fish, swimming upstream to spawn. Thousands gathered to catch the smelt with bare hands, buckets, and nets. Since the late 1980s, the smelt population—and, therefore, smelting—has dramatically declined.)

Pietila apparently had been killed after encountering the intruder just before or after Elisabeth Congdon's murder. Judging by the force of the blows to Pietila, "We know the murderer was a man," said Grams. "I can't imagine a woman being that vicious." But they had no official suspects. "The suspect could be four-foot-nine or six-foot-ten. We just don't know. Anybody could be a suspect."

What the reporters in Grams' office didn't know until much later was that police almost immediately discarded the burglary theory. The disarray in Elisabeth Congdon's room was too well organized. They were looking at premeditated murder. There was one killer for sure, possibly two.

Back at Glensheen, Duluth police processed the suspected entry point. The broken window led into the basement from an enclosed porch which ran much of the length of the lake side of the mansion. It was called the "subway" by the Congdon family, a space where the children had once played and ridden their bicycles. A door at the far end of the subway had been left unlocked, and a number of the exterior windows had been removed by the gardener for repair, resulting in easy access to the basement windows.

Police collected fibers and glass shards from the subway and the recreation room inside the basement. A partial heel print was visible on a couch beneath the open entry window. Investigators were puzzled by the absence of any object that could have been used to break the glass, and wondered if the entry had been staged. Could someone break the window, reach an arm through, unlatch the lock, and then reach further in to release the window stop? The hole in the glass was narrow and jagged, and the window stop was not easily reached. The stop made it possible to leave the window unlocked and partially open while ensuring the window could not be opened far enough to permit entry; the stop was not reachable through the partial opening.

Officer Barry Brooks, assigned to process the suspected entry point, decided to conduct his own experiment to see if it were possible to reach the window stop through the hole in the glass without being severely cut. He enlisted four officers, but of the group, only Brooks could get his right arm far enough through to disengage the sash lock, allowing him to open the window all the way.

Later, this unauthorized experiment would prove to be another costly mistake for Duluth police. When the case reached the courts, arm length comparisons, biceps measurements, and even a life-sized cardboard cutout of the window would be used to distract from the physical evidence.

Another problem with the window evidence would surface at trial. Police had not prevented contamination of the crime scene. When the canine unit had made its sweep before processing, one of the dogs had jumped through the open window and the canine handler had followed right behind the dog. Worse yet, Waller learned that Lieutenant Radulovich, the third officer at Glensheen, had gone through the open window before the dogs arrived. The scent the dogs tracked from Elisabeth's bedroom, through the window, and onto the grounds—as well as the heel print on the couch—could have been his.

Police investigated for any possible connection to the earlier killing involving Dorothy Congdon, but found no leads in that regard. Equally fruitless was the seizure of clothing discarded at a Duluth gas station and the forty bags of garbage removed from all the trash containers at roadside rest areas between Duluth and Minneapolis. As officers sorted through the garbage, they retrieved a pair of surgical gloves and a piece of costume jewelry. But, like the clothes from the gas station, they amounted to nothing.

Duluth police also received help from other law enforcement agencies. The FBI had officially joined the case when reports of the stolen jewelry's estimated worth topped $50,000. The Minnesota State Patrol conducted a twenty-mile helicopter search of the shoreline behind Glensheen, north to the town of Two Harbors.

Calls continued to pour into police headquarters from people reporting suspicious people and vehicles. One man reported seeing a motorcycle turn into the estate grounds at 4 A.M. June 27. Another caller told police he heard gunshots in the neighborhood Sunday night. The calls even included several from off-duty police officers. Nothing came of any of these, ultimately, but Duluth police tried to follow up on every lead.

Because of the money at stake, many family members were possible suspects. Twenty-three people were mentioned in Elisabeth's will. In addition to the Elisabeth Congdon Living Trust, valued at $4,078,101, Elisabeth had been an heir to various trusts set up by her father that totaled $45,106,453. Some people who had been getting up to $40,000 a year might now receive $1 million. But only one family member had a history of desperate financial problems and a sometimes volatile relationship with Elisabeth.

Police even received a postcard with just such a tip. "Sad indeed to read about Miss Congdon's murder. One daughter, Marjorie Caldwell of Golden, Colorado, has always been a Big Spender. Would she know anything? Attempt anything? She would seem worth questioning." Signed, "Merchant she dealt with when living in Minneapolis."

They dropped the ball, however, on one lead in particular. Later, there would be controversy over their lack of follow-up on the sighting of a white male in his twenties with shoulder-length hair and a slender build wearing a sleeveless jean jacket. A caller had spotted the man in front of the Congdon estate about 2:30 A.M. Monday, June 27. Police made no effort to track down persons matching this description. The information was sketchy, and it wasn't uncommon for young people to be out late in the summer walking along the lakeshore on London Road, a major thoroughfare through the east end of town. A defense attorney would later exploit the failure to follow through on the lead.

This wasn't the only oversight Duluth law enforcement made during the initial investigation. Hundreds of pictures were taken of the crime scene and physical evidence the day of the murder. But police failed to keep a photo inventory with a description of where and when each picture was taken and in what order. This omission eventually caused serious problems for the prosecution. Police would have a difficult time refuting defense allegations that evidence could have been moved or removed by officers at the crime scene.

As the officer in charge, Waller hated these screw ups. Later he would insist the police department had done its best. The department only had 130 officers; fewer than a dozen were trained to investigate homicides. With a case of this magnitude, the department's resources were stretched thin, and the investigation was just beginning.

CHAPTER 4

The Black Sheep

No one could have mistaken Elisabeth Congdon's adopted daughters Marjorie and Jennifer for biological sisters. Petite with short, pixie-like brownish-black hair and olive-hued skin, Marjorie wore thick glasses—tied on when she was a small child—that hid her nearsighted, dark brown eyes. Jennifer stood tall and fair, with long, wavy blond hair, blue eyes, and a pale complexion.

The differences between Marjorie and Jennifer went far beyond physical appearance. Jennifer had an outgoing, bubbly personality that allowed her to make friends easily. She got along well with people, including her Congdon relatives, and didn't share Marjorie's sensitivity or insecurity about being adopted. Like her mother, Jennifer loved the outdoors, and played outside whenever she could. Family members and Glensheen staff remember Jennifer as a well-mannered, thoughtful girl who liked to help her mother. She seldom disobeyed Elisabeth.

Marjorie was a more complex child to raise. An introvert, Marjorie would play with toys by herself or spend hours lost in a book, reading. As she later said, "I was alone but not lonesome." She was also a spirited child who said she enjoyed sliding down Glensheen's main staircase banister, or down the laundry chute to the baskets below. When Marjorie didn't want to eat her vegetables, she claimed she hid them in the Oriental vases in the dining room—until the stench exposed her secret. On rainy days, she played house in Glensheen's attic. She loved to look for secret compartments behind the wall panels throughout the mansion. When Elisabeth hosted dinner parties, Marjorie would spy on her mother's guests until the creaky boards of the main staircase gave her away.

But the spirited child could turn willful, even volatile, if she didn't get what she wanted. "Marjorie liked attention and she was bossy," said her cousin Mary Van Evera. When playing with her friends and cousins, she insisted on being in charge of the games or toys. Marjorie also needed to have more toys or doll clothes than the children she played with, a childhood friend recalled.

From an early age, Marjorie learned to get her way with her mother by throwing temper tantrums. She would fling herself on the floor, kicking her feet and screaming. When Marjorie got older, if her mother denied her something she wanted, she might flail at Elisabeth with her fists, sometimes striking her, according to Jennifer. Elisabeth gave in to her elder daughter's demands in order to keep the peace. "I don't remember Aunt Elisabeth having any disciplinary issues with her when there was a crowd," said Van Evera. "But I know there were plenty, and not all Marjorie's fault. Aunt Elisabeth did have a difficult time being a single mother."

Yet as suddenly as Marjorie could turn prickly, she could ooze charm. She could be unexpectedly demonstrative, showering friends and family with affection and presents. Even as a girl, Marjorie had the gift of gab; she could talk her way into or out of just about anything.

While Jennifer was open about her adoption, Marjorie was shy and defensive. She disliked having to explain to others why her mother was a Miss. Jennifer recalled that, as a child, Marjorie would tell strangers she was related to royalty. Not just any royalty; she said she was a direct descendant of King Charlemagne of France.

As she grew older, Marjorie complained that her cousins in Duluth teased her about being illegitimate. She also claimed that because she was not a blood relative, her mother's family did not accept her and did not allow her to sit at the dining room table for family dinners. As Marjorie said later, "I never felt a part of the family. The animosity goes back to Day One." She began calling herself the black sheep of the Congdon family.

But some family members say Marjorie manufactured her bitter memories. Her claims were nonsense, according to Van Evera. "Marjorie used to say she was rejected because she had to sit at the other table. Well, there were so many of us that the younger kids had a table in the window," Van Evera said.

While Elisabeth's daughters may have lacked a father, two of her brothers, Robert and Edward "Ned" Congdon, provided them with a male presence. Elisabeth relied particularly on her older brother, Ned, for help. She had always been close to Ned, the family practical joker. One Christmas morning when the children were young, he gave Elisabeth and Robert chewing tobacco. Elisabeth and Robert each chewed a wad and their Christmas was ruined—they were sick to their stomachs the entire day.

Ned lived nearby and frequently looked in on his mother, sister, and nieces. He was godfather to Marjorie and Jennifer and a loving uncle to both girls. Jennifer recalled that Uncle Ned could tell wonderful stories, and she and Marjorie would take turns sitting on his lap and listening to his tales.

Elisabeth's youngest brother, Robert, was also one of her closest confidantes, especially after Ned's sudden death from a heart attack in 1940. Jennifer enjoyed a good relationship with her Uncle Bob and, when she married, Uncle Bob gave her away. Marjorie, however, did not get along with her uncle from a young age, most likely because he had advised his sister to practice tough love when Marjorie first began acting out. When Marjorie threw tantrums, he insisted that his sister not give in to the child's demands. After Marjorie repeatedly ran up her mother's charge cards and spent money she didn't have, he told his sister to stop bailing Marjorie out. Marjorie became furious when she learned of her uncle's recommendations, but it didn't matter. Elisabeth continued to rescue her daughter financially and give her what she wanted because, as she told her brother, she wanted to uphold the Congdon name. Of her mother's relatives, Marjorie preferred the company of her Uncle Harry Dudley and his wife Marjorie, her namesake and godmother. Perhaps, her sister Jennifer speculated, this was because the Dudleys felt sorry for Marjorie and, when it came to family matters, they listened to her side of the story.

While Glensheen was home to Clara, Elisabeth, Marjorie, and Jennifer, the family divided their time between Duluth, Tucson, Yakima, and the Brule. Throughout their grammar school years, the girls spent the fall semester until Christmas at Glensheen. Marjorie and Jennifer attended the Duluth Normal School, where both girls were good students. Jennifer was a serious student who loved school but had to work hard at it. Good grades came easily for Marjorie, who, although she was a gifted, straight-A student, didn't care for school. However, while Marjorie excelled at most subjects such as English and history, she had no aptitude for math.

After the Christmas holidays, Elisabeth, her mother Clara, and her daughters traveled by train from Duluth to Chicago. After an overnight in Chicago, the four then took the Golden State Limited from Chicago to the family's winter home in Tucson, where they stayed through Easter. In those glory days of train travel, tuxedoed waiters served four-course meals on bone china, with silver utensils, crystal glasses, and white linen tablecloths. Elisabeth and the girls occupied one room in a sleeper car with a private bath while Clara had a room to herself.

Elisabeth had built her Tucson adobe ranch-style home in the late 1920s, at a time when desert surrounded the property. Tucson's main street, Broadway, was a packed dirt road during the time Jennifer and Marjorie grew up. Elisabeth's only neighbors for years were the El Conquistador Hotel and Julia and Caroline Marshall, close friends from Duluth, who built a house on a small parcel of land Elisabeth sold them. Marjorie and Jennifer boarded horses at the hotel's stables and took frequent rides up into the foothills. They attended the private Arizona Sunshine School for the winter semester, and Elisabeth took watercolor painting lessons.

Winters in Tucson included Sunday afternoon picnics. Clara, Elisabeth, and the girls loaded the car's trunk with lunch prepared by cooks—fried chicken, mashed potatoes, vegetables, salad, and dessert—and then drove up into the foothills. "My grandmother would go off into the desert with her cane and poke around for wildflowers," Jennifer recalled. "Marjorie and I would hike and explore. Sometimes we'd go up to Sabino Canyon where there was a stream coming through and we'd go wading."

Tucson gave Elisabeth, her aging mother, and the girls a respite from Duluth's harsh winters. But having to repeatedly change schools was not always easy for Jennifer and Marjorie. Jennifer said, "The last year I transferred from Duluth to Tucson was when I was a freshman in high school, and that was very difficult. I was taking both

Spanish and Latin and math, and the Tucson schools were so far ahead of the Duluth schools. Of course, when I transferred back it was great."

In April, after Easter, Clara, Elisabeth, Marjorie, and Jennifer took the train from Tucson to Westhome, Chester's other dream home, in Yakima. Westhome was a welcome destination for Jennifer. She loved the house's castle-like appearance with its lava stone walls and turret. Elisabeth and other family members also cherished Westhome for its scenic view overlooking the Congdon fruit orchards. Jennifer remembered the orchards as one of her favorite things. "We'd go out in the orchards and get up on the hood of this old Chrysler that was kept in the barn, and we'd pick cherries," she recalled. One time, however, the day before Jennifer, Marjorie, Elisabeth, and Clara were leaving for Duluth, Jennifer ate as many cherries as she could. "I ate so many cherries that I was terribly ill on the train ride back," Jennifer said. After visiting Westhome, they all returned to Duluth for the girls' spring semester.

Once the final school semester was completed, Elisabeth and her daughters spent summers in Duluth and at Swiftwater Farm, named for the rushing river and rapids near the house. Elisabeth had bought the old six-bedroom farmhouse in 1947, remodeled it, and built a guest house and caretaker cottage. The girls went swimming, canoeing, tubing, and exploring and ran around in swimsuits, shorts, and bare feet. Goats provided further entertainment, and Elisabeth's brother Edward had a summer home nearby, so the girls had more Congdon relatives to visit and play with.

Elisabeth relaxed at her summer house; she particularly enjoyed painting watercolors, canoeing, picnicking, and playing tennis on the courts at her brother Ned's house. For the girls, the casual lifestyle at the Brule was a welcome contrast to Glensheen's formality. "At Glensheen, we always had to dress for dinner. You had to have a dress and shoes on. You couldn't come barefoot to the table. The only place we didn't have to dress up was at the Brule," Jennifer said. She recalled that Fourth of July celebrations at the Brule included strawberry shortcake for dessert and sparklers and firecrackers before bedtime.

In addition to traveling between the family homes, Elisabeth took her children to Europe and Mexico. As her parents had for her, Elisabeth wanted her children to see the world and experience other cultures. Marjorie first visited Europe as a toddler with Clara and Elisabeth. Jennifer recalled a trip with her mother during high school when they visited twelve countries in three months. Elisabeth wanted Jennifer to get an overview of Europe so that Jennifer could decide which countries she wanted to explore further.

Life at Glensheen served to remind Marjorie and Jennifer that they weren't ordinary little girls. Like many children, the two girls took piano lessons. But unlike most, Jennifer and Marjorie practiced on a Steinway grand piano in Glensheen's living room. When Marjorie or Jennifer needed new clothes, they didn't shop with their mother in the department stores. Instead, the stores ferried boxes and boxes of clothes to Glensheen for the girls to try on. The girls wore classic, expensive clothing with timeless styling. As a child, Marjorie had a brown woolen winter coat trimmed with beaver pelts that was later worn by other family members' children. In the wintertime, when it was too cold to play outside, Elisabeth allowed the girls to roller-skate and ride their bikes on the subway's marble floors.

Mansion life even affected how they got around town. Whenever the girls visited friends the chauffeur drove them. Jennifer particularly hated the fuss. She would lie on the back seat of the Cadillac so no one could see her. A half block away from a friend's house she made the driver let her out so she could walk to the door unescorted. The first time Marjorie was allowed to walk home from school, the chauffeur followed her in the family car.

At school, Jennifer had many friends and loved to take part in activities such as glee club. Marjorie spent a lot of time by herself, often reading. According to one childhood friend who attended Duluth Normal School (and, later, Dana Hall) at the same time as Marjorie, the older Congdon sister didn't have many friends. "Marjorie was quiet and serious…, a little, dark-eyed kid with glasses," while her sister Jennifer "was bouncy, cheerful, and outgoing," the friend recalled. "Marjorie was not a happy camper." When it came to boys, Jennifer dated regularly throughout school, while Marjorie didn't have her first real boyfriend until she was eighteen.

It didn't matter that only three years separated Marjorie and Jennifer, or that they shared a bedroom in Tucson each winter and spring, or that they had both been adopted. The sisters were not close, and they spent little spare time together as children, usually choosing to play apart and make separate friends.

Marjorie talked about being a veterinarian when she grew up, seeming to prefer the company of animals to that of most humans. She particularly loved horses; she thought they were beautiful creatures, and she loved the feeling of power she had when riding. Marjorie took riding lessons for a number of years during the winter in Tucson and in the summers at Duluth's Skyline Stables.

Marjorie demonstrated her rebellious streak at an early age. When she was about seven years old, she would take her mother's special diamond-and-sapphire ring and wear it outside to play in the sandbox. Another childhood friend recalled that Marjorie had a "thing" about that piece of jewelry. The maid would have to come and retrieve the ring and return it to Elisabeth's jewelry box. Marjorie's fixation on the ring would continue into adulthood. Her daughter Suzanne later recalled that when she was a young girl Elisabeth told Suzanne she would receive the ring someday. Marjorie immediately corrected her mother, saying that she would get the ring, not Suzanne.

Marjorie would sometimes sneak away from the estate without her mother's permission. Jennifer recalled a number of occasions when Marjorie dragged her along on a "misadventure." One afternoon the two girls left home without telling anyone and hopped the bus downtown to the movie theater. Chauffeur James Roper, however, saw the sisters get off the bus returning home. Although the movie was

Marjorie's idea, Jennifer remembers they were punished equally. Elisabeth did not tolerate dishonesty.

Jennifer recalled that her sister began having money troubles as a young child. "She always had a spending problem. Even when she was little, she'd steal money from my mother's purse in her bedroom. I've seen her steal from mother's purse. We got a quarter a week, and fifteen cents of that had to go to Sunday School. She always had to have money," Jennifer recalled. For many years, Elisabeth was unaware that her daughter was stealing money from her. If Elisabeth's wallet had less cash than she remembered, it was money she must have forgotten she'd spent at the grocery or drugstore.

Elizabeth Oakerland, a childhood friend, recalled that Marjorie learned early on she could get away with overspending, even when caught.

As a teen, Oakerland clerked at Wahl's Department Store in Duluth, where Marjorie was a frequent customer. "Marjorie would come in and charge three or four cashmere sweaters and then Elisabeth Congdon would make a telephone call to the store telling them not to let Marjorie charge things," Oakerland remembers. Eventually, Marjorie's continued charging without consent led to a special arrangement with the store. Elisabeth would give Marjorie a signed note when she had permission to use Elisabeth's charge account. But Oakerland said the arrangement did nothing to reign in Marjorie's spending. Marjorie simply forged her mother's signature as needed.

One winter in Tucson, when Marjorie was a teenager, she entreated Elisabeth to buy her a thoroughbred stallion. Jennifer recalled that Marjorie, without their mother's knowledge or permission, signed papers and put money down on the stallion. Marjorie could not come up with the remaining money and, when the owners threatened to sue Elisabeth, she bailed her daughter out and bought the stallion.

Maybe because her scheme had worked so well, Marjorie tried it again with a palomino mare, "Fara." Elisabeth bought the second horse, but told Marjorie the palomino would be Jennifer's to ride as Marjorie already had the stallion. But Marjorie wasn't finished. She insisted she should have the stallion to ride in Duluth. Elisabeth was allergic to horses, but Marjorie's power of persuasion was strong. Marjorie arranged to have it transported by trailer to Duluth and Elisabeth got stuck with the bill. The Congdons kept the stallion in Glensheen's stables while Fara remained in Tucson for Jennifer, who rode the palomino for many years.

Marjorie's theatrical flair reminded one family friend of actress Tallulah Bankhead. "She can make herself do anything she wants," the friend said. One longtime Glensheen employee described Marjorie as "smart and scheming...Marjorie could talk her mother into almost anything."

In the fall of 1947, Elisabeth decided to send Marjorie to Dana Hall, the exclusive girls' boarding school she had attended outside Boston. Elisabeth hoped her daughter would outgrow her emotional problems at a school known for academic excellence and strict supervision.

In her first letter home on September 28, 1947, Marjorie wrote "Well I suppose you are pretty disgusted that I haven't written to you before but I've been so doggone busy and all since classes have started that I don't know where the time goes." She was most excited about her first riding experience at the school's stables, because she was put into the second-class advanced riders. The instructor "said I didn't have much form (he is a stickler on form) but I...would someday be an excellent horse woman." After mentioning how well she was doing in her classes, Marjorie continued, "By the way sprained my ankle slightly. It's very slight and no there is nothing to worry about but I thought you might like to know." She signed off "Love, Me."

Marjorie was a loner, a school friend remembered, who spent as much time as possible around horses and rode every day at Dana Hall. Marjorie had one friend who was very tall, and together they made a real Mutt and Jeff combination. "They were two lonely girls and their horses," the friend said.

Marjorie earned good grades at Dana Hall and reportedly possessed one of the highest IQs in the school's history. But even in her first year she had money trouble and run-ins with the headmistress, as her letters home revealed:

January 27, 1948

Dear Mom,

I have enclosed the reports you asked for plus a note from Peg. She wrote it herself with no priming from me because things were in a mess here and she figured this would calm you down. Boy, you really fixed things with Mrs. Johnson. She was so mad at me she was about to have little kittens but I told her I had talked everything over with you and that it was all O.K. Finally I got her calmed down and she said she would disregard your letter and you won't have to write her anymore. For heaven's sake don't do that again. Everything was horribly messed for awhile and I got so wrought up about it all I just about flunked a Spanish test. I got a C- on it. After this discuss things with me first and leave the school out of it. It is none of Mrs. Johnson's business anyhow. Now she has poked her nose in everything....

I AM COMING BACK ON ONE CONDITION ONLY. We can talk about it later I've got to go to bed now, but I'll write just as soon as I get back from Peg's.

Love, Marj

The enclosed note from Marjorie's friend and classmate Peg read: "I don't think that Marjorie wastes money or that she gets too much." Marjorie also included a list of her recent expenditures in an attempt to persuade her mother she was conscientious and charitable:

September 2	$20.00	Subscription to the *Western Horseman,* the *Quarter Horse* and having two pictures framed and buying one for me
October 9	$3.16	to buy the book *Equestrianare* and rental due on rental books
October 15	$21.50	to Congregational Church for aid to France and Belgium
November 8	$21.50	to Congregational Church for aid to Germany

November 8	$3.50	to the Horsemans book club for *Great Horse Stories* for me
December 24	$80.00	for white french poodle, nightgown and Grandma presents
December 27	$10.00	to me for cash for miscelanious [sic] things
January 14	$41.00	to Thurmans for photographs and frames
January 16	$1.85	to The Craftloom for yarn to finish my green sweater
January 17	$24.00	to Sue Page for pictures (antique) and frames. One was given away for a present (birthday) and three were kept

Marjorie returned to Dana Hall for her junior year. Her letter to her mother dated Valentine's Day, 1949, described her continued problems at school and her overspending. It also reflected Marjorie's sensitivity about her adoption:

Dear Mom,

It was swell to talk to you on the phone yesterday. You don't know how much I miss you and want to get home. As you know I have from the 23rd until the 6th, that is 15 days of freedom. I really will stay home more this time and only go riding once a day for half a day at a time instead of all day.

My bill for rides at Colonel Beasley's was my biggest expense this vacation. Jean is going to let me ride for considerably less. I was paying about $20 a week at the Colonel's, but I certainly got my money's worth with the amount of riding I did. Ye gads, I hate to think what it would have been by the hour. Anyway that and paying for a few of the girls' rides when they went as my guests mounted the amount. They just cashed my check apparently and I got a letter from Mr. Berg [of the Congdon Office in Duluth] saying I had overdrawn my account. He put in my March allowance to cover it though and I assure you it won't happen again. I am now going to try and see how big a bank balance I can pile up.

I have a suggestion to make. What do you think about lowering my allowance considerably during the summer months? I really won't need as much money there as during the winter....

Mrs. J says that she's going to answer your letter. She says that she feels it her duty to help you bring me up as I don't have two parents. I just about slapped her face I was so furious. As if you couldn't bring me up as well or better than most girls.... If there is anything you want to discuss with me do it spring vacation, but leave that woman out of it. She says since I am an adopted child I should feel much more grateful to you and realize what a privilege I have been given. She won't even say "your mother." She says "your guardian" or "your aunt" when she says anything to me about you. Then she says I have an adoption complex. I have never hated anyone so damn much in all my life and if you will have any more correspondence with her about me I'll clear out of here and never come back to this place again. I mean it. She says I get too much money, when I know four girls that get $125 a month. Anyway, it's none of her damn business....

So long and write me any questions you want answered before her.

Love, Marj

Jennifer recalled that her mother was extremely frustrated by Marjorie's irresponsibility with money—either Marjorie hadn't registered all the checks she'd written or she'd lost track of her bank balance. But the spending didn't stop with an overdraft notice. That summer Marjorie attended camp in Maine. In her postcards, Marjorie asked her mother to send more clothes and money.

Following Marjorie's junior year at Dana Hall, Elisabeth took her for evaluation at the Menninger Clinic, a well-known psychiatric treatment center in Topeka, Kansas. Marjorie's compulsive lying, her stealing, irresponsibility with money, and her acting out at home added up to a bigger problem than adolescence, Congdon family members remembered. Menninger doctors diagnosed Marjorie as a sociopath: a person who ignores social and moral norms.

After a short stay at the clinic, Marjorie went to a group home in St. Louis and completed her senior year at a special school, Jennifer said. Elisabeth hoped this change would help Marjorie, who did successfully graduate and made plans to attend St. Louis University. Soon after she met her first real boyfriend, Richard "Dick" LeRoy, a handsome man with dark hair and a long, thin face distinguished by deep-set, serious eyes. Nearly a foot taller than Marjorie and five years her senior, he would become her first husband.

Dick LeRoy was born in February 1927, the last of Harris and Beth LeRoy's eight children. Raised in Winchester, Massachusetts, as a child he learned the virtues of hard work and fiscal responsibility from his father, who was director of the Boston area chapter of the Boys Club of America. "His biggest job was fundraising," Dick recalled. "When he came in 1910, they had $3,000 and a couple of rooms. When my father retired, the club had five buildings and an annual income of $350,000."

His fiscal lessons continued after his father's stroke and death in 1938. When he was eleven, financial problems forced his family to move from their seventeen-room house to one less than half its size. But his mother always made sure there was food on the table and scraped together money for her children's needs. Years later, Dick still remembered the day she sold rickrack to the neighbors for bus fare, so his brother and sister could look for work.

After high school, Dick enlisted in the Navy, where he specialized in radio communications and combat gunnery. After two years of service, during which World War II ended, Dick returned home to enroll at the University of Massachusetts. He majored in political science, originally hoping to go on to law school after graduation. But money was tight, so he accepted his brother Robert's invitation to come live and job hunt in St. Louis.

Dick started working as an underwriter for General Insurance Company of America and spent his first six weeks in St. Louis living with Robert. From there he moved into a rooming house that didn't provide meals. Most evenings, he walked down the street to take his supper at Mom and Pop Lippert's boarding house, where Marjorie Congdon happened to live.

On an October night in 1950, Dick was introduced to a talkative young woman seated across the table. Her thick glasses did little to hide her dark, inquisitive eyes. Marjorie told him she was taking a nursing course at Washington University. For months he would learn little of her family background—or her family's wealth.

Soon after they met, Dick asked Marjorie out. That winter they dated steadily, often meeting at the rooming house or at a favorite local restaurant, Parentes, for pizza and Coke. Dick and Marjorie regularly attended Centenary Methodist Church, where they participated in the young adults' club. The couple played volleyball with other club members, attended church potluck suppers, and went to concerts and plays. When the weather was warm, they enjoyed the municipal opera, which performed outdoors, and took excursions on the river boat *Admiral*.

"She was exuberant, so full of fun," said Dick, recalling what had first attracted him. "She was very intelligent, from an upper-middle class family whose values were similar to my own."

Marjorie confided to Dick that she had been in some trouble during her early teens and been taken to the Menninger Clinic. She explained that her overprotective, eccentric mother had insisted on the visit—he shouldn't take it seriously.

She didn't need to make excuses for her visit to the clinic: Dick had fallen in love with the spunky woman who seemed to him a whirlwind of activity. One night in January or February 1951, while the couple was alone helping paint the church, Dick asked Marjorie to marry him. She said yes, but would have to wait a year for her diamond engagement ring, which Dick couldn't yet afford.

Elisabeth learned of the wedding plans in a phone call from Marjorie just as she and Jennifer were returning to the U.S. after a trip to Europe. She and Jennifer traveled straight to St. Louis to see the newly engaged couple, concerned that Marjorie, at age nineteen, was too young. Elisabeth talked to her about the importance of getting an education, of perhaps seeing more of the world before committing to marriage—Elisabeth hoped she and Marjorie could go to Europe together—but it did no good. Marjorie had made up her mind to get married. If opposites attract, spendthrift Marjorie couldn't have chosen a more suitable partner than Dick. Beyond his austere upbringing, his last name—from the French le roi, "the king"—made him a fitting companion for a young woman who liked to believe she descended from royalty.

Marjorie Mannering Congdon and Richard Webster LeRoy were married on June 30, 1951, in a large, formal Methodist ceremony held in Glensheen's living room before approximately 150 guests. Dick's mother, Beth, had flown in for the wedding, and to meet her new daughter-in-law.

The wedding announcement in Dick's hometown newspaper described the wedding as taking place "[b]efore a fireplace banked with caladium, ivy and maidenhair fern." Marjorie wore a long-sleeved, traditional white Italian silk satin dress trimmed in heirloom rosepoint lace with a Juliet cap. Marjorie's floor-length veil of silk illusion had belonged to her namesake, her aunt Marjorie Congdon Dudley, and she was given away by her uncle Harry Dudley, both of whom were among the few relatives with whom she enjoyed a close relationship. Jennifer was her maid of honor, and her bridesmaids were childhood friends: Betsy Congdon, Ann Paine, Helen Moore, and Caroline Lewis. Dick's best man was unable to make it to Duluth from St. Louis, so Marjorie's cousin Chester d'Autremont took his place; other Congdon cousins and friends served as his groomsmen. The simple, elegant reception consisted of a beautiful wedding cake and buffet served in Glensheen's dining room. Marjorie tossed her bouquet from the main staircase landing.

The newlyweds honeymooned for two weeks at Swiftwater Farm before returning to St. Louis. Dick recalled years later how happy they were to simply be together for that brief time, enjoying the outdoors as they went swimming, took canoe rides, and picnicked. They never once discussed money.

CHAPTER 5

Suspect News

AS POLICE LEARNED OF THE KILLINGS AT GLENSHEEN, Marjorie Caldwell took her usual seat in the coffee shop of the Holland House Hotel in Golden, Colorado, a thousand miles southwest of Duluth. Across from Golden State Bank in the central business district, the fifty-year-old hotel catered to travelers looking for a bargain. A few, like Marjorie, called the worn two-story white stucco building home. Since March, Marjorie, her sixteen-year-old son, Rick, and her second husband, Roger Caldwell, had occupied two adjacent rooms at the back of the second floor. She and Roger had met in 1975. They had decided to live together after they'd known each other one weekend; they were married within three months of meeting. As waitress Mildred Smith poured coffee that Monday morning, Marjorie told her, "I'm going to surprise you and have breakfast." Normally Marjorie preferred barbecued-beef sandwiches, even for breakfast, but today she ordered French toast and a side of bacon. It was 6 A.M. on a Monday morning, 7 A.M. in Duluth.

Golden, an unpretentious small town on the edge of the Rocky Mountains just west of Denver, is home to several sites of interest, including the Buffalo Bill Museum, the Adolph Coors Company headquarters, and the Colorado School of Mines, whose signature letter M lights up Lookout Mountain, illuminating the campus at night. Once a boomtown known as "the gateway to the golden fields," Golden was Colorado's first territorial capital. Signs of the town's frontier past are abundant. The main street's storefronts and a historic district recall the Old West of the 1800s.

Marjorie had moved to Colorado two years earlier, in May 1975. Soon after arriving in Denver she had been arrested and jailed—her AMC Pacer had not been paid for. This inauspicious arrival had its origins back in Minnesota.

When Marjorie had decided to move she called E. Thomas Welch. Since 1973, Welch, senior vice president in charge of the trust office of the Marquette National Bank in Minneapolis, had administered the two trusts that Elisabeth had set up for Marjorie in 1968. The trust office, due to past problems with Marjorie, had instituted a policy of sending money directly to her creditors instead of to her.

During the phone call Marjorie told Welch she was moving her family out to Colorado for a new start. The climate would be better for her son Rick's asthma, and he would be closer to his asthma specialist in Denver. At the time, the trust office already had an outstanding $30,000 bill from Dayton's department store in Minneapolis for clothing Marjorie had bought. Nevertheless, a short time after Marjorie's move Welch got a call from Dayton's. On the day Marjorie left Minnesota she had charged hundreds of dollars more at the downtown store for items including designer clothes, hair styling, and electrolysis.

Next, Welch discovered through a call from a car dealer that on the day she left Minnesota, Marjorie had driven to a Bloomington dealership and traded in her GMC for two Pacers for her and her children to drive to Colorado. But the dealer had subsequently learned that the trade-in car had a lien against it, and Marjorie's check for the difference on the cars had bounced. The dealer assumed the trust would pay up. When Welch contacted Marjorie about this her only response was that she needed transportation.

The car dealer took the situation into his own hands and went out to Colorado to repossess the cars. He had Marjorie jailed and, since Welch was out of town, she spent the weekend incarcerated. Welch came back the following Monday, bailed Marjorie out, paid for one car so Marjorie had transportation, and let the dealership repossess the other.

After recovering from this shaky start, Marjorie eventually decided her Colorado dream was to breed and train horses and own a ranch. Her friends were used to seeing her dressed casually in worn Levi's and cowboy boots. She was most comfortable, she told them, hanging out in the barn with her horses. She didn't even mind the menial chores; she was a real "stall mucker." With shovel and pitchfork she cleaned out horse manure and laid down fresh hay.

Marjorie would be working toward her dream later the morning of her mother's murder. She had a meeting with Crown Realty agent Fran Beyer. Marjorie had first met Beyer in May when she was intrigued by an igloo-shaped house listed with Beyer's office. Though Marjorie decided against buying the house, she'd asked Beyer to help her find a ranch. They had made plans the previous night over dinner at a Mr. Steak restaurant. Marjorie wanted to look at some new properties and revisit others. She also needed to finalize the purchase of two properties, including one the Caldwells were already calling "Roger's Retreat." The previous night after the restaurant closed, Beyer had drawn up the purchase agreements in the front seat of Beyer's car, parked next to a light post.

After breakfast, Marjorie planned to do laundry down the street at the Landmark Laundromat. "Do you know what time it opens?" Marjorie asked the waitress. She didn't know.

Marjorie reached down and grabbed her plastic garbage pail of dirty clothes, mostly horse blankets and riding apparel, and walked briskly toward the laundromat three blocks away. Even to the casual observer, Marjorie was a kinetic woman, with dark, cropped hair and emotive brown eyes hidden behind thick glasses. Her hands constantly moved, and her strong chin hinted at a woman used to getting her own way.

She arrived at the coin-operated laundromat shortly before it opened at 7:30 A.M. Owner Fred Golnar leaned against the counter as she waited impatiently at the door. Minutes later, he watched her load clothes as a man Golnar didn't recognize came in and approached her. The man stood by the side door, and he and Marjorie laughed and talked animatedly for fifteen minutes before he left. Golnar later learned that man was Frank Wilbur "Bill" Kay, Jr.

Kay looked like a genuine cowboy, with a deep tan, long wavy brown hair, and western clothes and boots. He flaunted a laid-back approach to life and called himself an artist. Local law enforcement wasn't so sure. They had investigated his possible connection to a suspected burglary insurance fraud involving the Caldwells' former Bailey, Colorado, ranch, Pine Valley Farms. Though no charges were ever filed, authorities continued to track his activities.

Kay had first met the Caldwells in November 1976, when they bought Pine Valley Farms. After the purchase, he sometimes watched the property for the Caldwells. The Caldwells had recently disclosed to Kay they were desperate for cash. Only five days earlier, Kay had gotten an urgent call from Roger.

"Can you help me? Do you know some place where Marge and I could hock or sell some of our jewelry?"

"Why, what's going on?" Kay asked.

Roger explained they owed hundreds of dollars in horse boarding and feed bills at Table Mountain Ranch in Golden. "We're not going to sell the horses," Roger insisted. Especially not his horse, Puppy, that he wouldn't let anyone else ride.

"I'll take you two out tomorrow morning," Kay offered.

This was not the first time Roger had confided in Kay about his troubles. On a boozy night two or three months earlier, Kay had listened to Roger loudly complain about his wife, and certain comments had stuck in Kay's mind.

"I'm thinking of leaving Marjorie," Roger had said to him, "because she is capable of anything." Roger angrily told Kay, "It's hard to believe anything she says." Roger also talked about how his lawyers had suggested he file bankruptcy and divorce Marjorie.

But Kay doubted Roger would ever make good on his threat. Kay knew Roger was unemployed and virtually penniless, living off his wife's trust income. Besides, Roger struck Kay as too passive. "Roger was a hardworking man before he met Marjorie," Kay recalled. "She turned him into a gentleman farmer."

On Thursday morning, June 23, about 9:30 A.M., Kay had arrived at the Holland House Hotel to pick up the Caldwells. Kay noticed that Roger was so groggy he could hardly keep his eyes open. Kay then drove the couple to L&L Coin, a Denver pawn shop where he was a regular. The owner gave the Caldwells a $3,000 check in exchange for $8,000 worth of gold, silver, and turquoise jewelry. Marjorie made sure the owner knew she planned to buy the jewelry back. Store policy gave the Caldwells thirty days to repurchase the jewelry, but it would cost them an extra $1,000. "I'm expecting to come into a sizable amount of money soon," Marjorie announced during the transaction. Kay again observed that Roger could barely stay awake. Aware he was being watched, Roger wondered aloud about what type of medication Marjorie had given him that morning.

After the pawn shop, Marjorie insisted that Kay drive her to a nearby bank so she could immediately cash the check for $3,000 worth of ten- and twenty-dollar bills. Next Marjorie asked Kay to drive them to the Hertz office in Denver so they could rent a car for the weekend. Kay and Roger waited in Kay's car while Marjorie went inside and returned a short time later, stating that her rental car was at the airport. Again Kay chauffeured the couple, dropping Roger and Marjorie off at the airport's upper level at about 1:30 P.M.

On Monday morning Kay wanted to talk with Roger to see how bill-paying had turned out. But when he arrived at the Holland House, the front desk clerk said that Roger was out and Marjorie was at the laundromat. She also told Kay there was a wake-up call and note for Rick, which Kay volunteered to take to the boy. He went upstairs and knocked loudly until he awakened Rick, handed him the note, and left the hotel.

When he found Marjorie at the laundromat he asked about Roger's whereabouts. "Roger had to go downtown to meet with the lawyer," Marjorie explained. She told Kay that she had driven him to John Moorhead's office in downtown Denver. Kay talked about the Caldwells' horses with Marjorie for a short time before leaving. While fun to talk to, Marjorie's outward charm soon wore thin, as her need to impress became overbearing even to casual acquaintances like Kay. As Kay said later, Marjorie boasted of her riches and tried to surround herself with people she could easily impress. But Kay knew she had nearly depleted her family trust funds.

Minutes after Kay had left, as Marjorie folded her laundry, the phone rang. Golnar answered, then called out "Marjorie, phone call!" The Caldwells' personal attorney, David Arnold, was on the line from Minnesota. His secretary had tracked her down after calling the hotel.

"Are you alone?" Arnold asked.

"Yes. Roger's gone out to get a six-pack of Coke." She told Arnold that Roger was at the 7-Eleven store, located three blocks from the laundromat. This was the second excuse for her husband's absence that morning.

"I have some bad news—" Arnold began.

Marjorie broke in, "Oh my God. Is it the children?"

"No, your mother." Arnold's voice softened. "Your mother and her nurse were murdered last night." The news had already reached her sister, Jennifer. The first reports said that the women had been killed during a break-in. Rumors were rampant, Arnold continued. According to an unofficial report, a young man in bloodstained clothing had been seen running away from Glensheen around the time of the murders. But there were few details Arnold could share.

Upon hearing the news, Marjorie sounded distraught. She sobbed loudly and fired question after question at Arnold. However, by conversation's end, Arnold realized

Marjorie had changed her tone. She had become businesslike, unnaturally composed and organized as she ticked off funeral details and travel plans. Arnold would arrange to wire money ahead for the Caldwells' plane tickets. "At the time it didn't seem at all strange," Arnold later recalled. "But shortly after I thought, how can one, after being advised of murder, and having the response that she did, suddenly have the clarity of mind to go through a checklist?"

After Marjorie hung up the phone, she turned to Golnar.

"I'm going to look for my children," she announced, before repeating the grim news of her mother's murder. "The burglar took $7,000 worth of jewelry," she added. Not even police had an estimation of the jewelry's worth at the time.

"Are you going to tell your husband?" Golnar asked.

"I don't know where he is. He's someplace downtown," said Marjorie, shrugging off the question with her third version of Roger's whereabouts. She folded two wet shirts before asking Golnar, "Would you mind folding the rest of the laundry for me?" Marjorie then left the laundromat, and Golnar assumed she went home.

Instead, Marjorie drove to the National Asthma Center in Denver. She asked to see Dr. Hyman Chai, the specialist who had regularly treated Rick since they had moved to the Denver area. Dr. Chai was busy in a meeting, and she spoke instead with Shirley Herman, his administrative assistant. "A terrible thing has happened in my family," Marjorie said, her voice nearly hysterical. "My mother's been murdered." Marjorie then asked dramatically, "What should I do with Rick if he breaks down when he hears about his grandmother's death? We'll be going to Duluth tomorrow because we can't get into Duluth today." Before she left, Marjorie insisted that the center should be ready in case her son's asthma flared up and he required hospitalization. Later that day, Dr. Chai confirmed with his assistant that, if necessary, Rick could be brought to the center for treatment.

From the Asthma Center, Marjorie drove to the ranch home of her horse trainer, Dion Dana. The two women had met at the National Western Stock Show at the Denver Colosseum back in January, when Marjorie wanted to find a horse to buy. Dana helped Marjorie buy a horse, "Jinx." Dana had insisted on cash payment, having learned of Marjorie's history of bounced checks from another horse trainer. Since then, she'd given Marjorie and Rick riding lessons.

Around 9 A.M. on June 27, Marjorie ran into Dana's house, talking rapidly and not making much sense. She was visibly upset as she told Dana, "My mother was murdered last night." Marjorie said her mother kept little "real money" at Glensheen, but noted that the mansion did have some valuable paintings, implying a plausible motive for murder.

While at Dana's ranch, Marjorie called her cousin Tom in Denver shortly before 9:30 A.M. Senior trustee for the family trust funds, Tom Congdon was regarded as the patriarch of the Congdon clan. A mild-mannered man with dark hair and tortoise-shell glasses, he had a youthful face that belied his fifty-one years. Congdon was usually nattily attired in rumpled yet obviously expensive tailored suits, seersucker in summer. He worked as president of St. Mary Parish Land Company, a Denver oil and gas exploration firm.

Stuttering, crying, and seemingly in shock, Marjorie told Congdon she had gotten a phone call from her attorney at the laundromat. "Mother's been killed," Marjorie said. She asked Congdon if he "knew who did it," and then launched into an unprompted rundown of her and Roger's activities the evening before and that morning. She told Congdon that she and Roger had both been at the laundromat that morning. But Roger was "out on an errand" when she got the bad news, she explained. This, her fourth story of Roger's whereabouts the morning of the killings, was closer to the version she had told Arnold.

"Oh, I thought my mother would also be at the Brule through the Fourth of July. I was just going to call her on Sunday and Roger and I went out to dinner and when we got back to the hotel it was ten o'clock and he advised me that it was then eleven o'clock in Duluth and much too late to call mother. And now I can never call her again," Marjorie tearfully told her cousin. But if she really thought Elisabeth would be at the Brule through the Fourth, she would have known Elisabeth wouldn't be home that Sunday.

Congdon was "skeptical as hell" of what Marjorie told him. As he said later, "I took all of this with a lot of salt." Since Glensheen staff and Elisabeth's nurses monitored her incoming calls, Congdon knew that Marjorie didn't call her mother frequently. He didn't think she'd been truthful about Roger's presence at the laundromat and her immediate and unrequested itinerary of their whereabouts struck Congdon as odd.

Congdon and Marjorie discussed travel arrangements for the funeral. Elisabeth would be buried in Duluth, the city she had called home all her life. Marjorie and Roger would fly from Denver to Minneapolis-St. Paul the next morning. They would be joined by Arnold, who would fly with them to Duluth the same day.

"Tom, you're the only one in the family that gives me the straight facts," Marjorie told her cousin. "I want my mother buried in the family plot," Marjorie said emphatically, and asked Congdon to relay her instructions to family members and Glensheen staff.

After the phone call, Marjorie and Dana talked further about the murders, and Dana asked where Roger was. Once more Marjorie brushed off her husband's absence. She went back to the story that she had dropped Roger off that morning at John Moorhead's law office in downtown Denver. She told Dana that she planned to go downtown and look for him after she took care of Rick.

Rick had gone to Hillcroft Acres, a neighboring stable, to feed the family's horses. Marjorie asked Dana to look after Rick for the day and not tell him about his grandmother's death. "I'm going to find Roger and call Rick's doctor," Marjorie explained. At Marjorie's request, Dana called Hillcroft Acres and asked Louise McConnell, the owner, to send Rick over. McConnell called down to the barn and Rick answered the phone. He told McConnell he had just gotten there and he stayed about fifteen minutes after McConnell told him to go to Dana's house. Marjorie left Dana's house about 10:15 A.M., just as Rick arrived. Mother and son chatted briefly, but Marjorie said nothing to Rick about the murders; she planned to tell him of his grandmother's death that night.

Next, Marjorie kept her scheduled appointment with realtor Fran Beyer. They had arranged to meet at their usual spot, a Heritage Drug in the suburbs of Denver. Marjorie had picked the drugstore meeting place because it was close to the stables where Marjorie kept her favorite horse, Jeffrey.

When Fran Beyer pulled up to the drug store, she spotted Marjorie coming from the delicatessen next door, carrying a large cup of iced tea. Marjorie seemed strangely calm as she told Beyer that her attorney had called with the terrible news that her mother and her mother's nurse had been murdered. Police had sealed off her mother's house and even family members weren't being allowed inside. She apologized for her spaciness, saying she'd gotten a shot of Valium and some pills from her doctor.

Beyer suggested they cancel their appointments. No, Marjorie insisted. "Roger and my doctor feel I should stay busy during the day," she told Beyer. Roger had taken her son Rick to the mountains surrounding Boulder, she said, so Rick wouldn't hear any news reports. This fifth version of Roger's activities departed radically from her earlier stories. She said Rick's doctor was on standby with emergency equipment in case Rick had a bad asthma attack after learning of his grandmother's death.

The two women spent the afternoon touring ranch properties near Denver even though Marjorie had yet to make the down payment on a $97,500 ranch the Caldwells had agreed to purchase two weeks before. (Today the ranch would list for more than $290,000.) The owners had accepted the Caldwells' offer, including a $5,000 payment due Friday the 24th.

The previous week, when Beyer had telephoned about the late payment, Marjorie apologized and explained she'd just been released from the hospital after being kicked by a horse. She'd been sedated and in traction, and hadn't had time to contact her attorney or banker to redeem the $5,000 note. She promised to have the down payment on Monday.

But at this Monday-morning meeting, neither Beyer nor Marjorie mentioned the $5,000. Marjorie signed purchase agreements for the two properties she'd admired over the weekend—a ranch next door to the ranch they were already buying and the separate property they called "Roger's Retreat." Both required a $5,000 down payment within ten days. At Marjorie's insistence, the women also toured a $1.3 million, 450-acre ranch near Colorado Springs.

While Marjorie was with Beyer, Roger called the Holland House Hotel at about 1:45 P.M. and asked for his wife. When front desk clerk Bertha Huskins told him no one answered the phone in their room, Roger left a message.

"Tell her to pick me up. I'm ready."

"Where?"

"It doesn't matter. She'll know where." Roger abruptly hung up.

Beyer last saw Marjorie at 4 p.m., when she dropped her off outside the drugstore. Before she left, Marjorie told Beyer she was glad they'd been together so late Sunday. Her family was not very fond of her, she said. They might think she had something to do with the murders.

Living just an hour's drive from Roger and Marjorie, Tom Congdon was the family member in closest touch with his cousin and her husband—and their financial troubles. Roger had first begun calling Congdon in late May and June, desperate for money and financial advice.

Congdon hadn't seen his cousin since her move to Colorado two years earlier. The two had never socialized and had never been close, despite the months that Congdon had lived at Glensheen as a child while his parents remodeled their home. He was one of the three Congdon Office trustees whose duties included overseeing trust payments to Marjorie. He knew she chafed at other family members' tight control over the trust funds, but her behavior over the years had left them no choice.

In May, Roger had met with Congdon to ask about the Congdon family annual financial report that Roger and Marjorie had not received. Roger wanted to know how much Marjorie stood to inherit upon the death of Elisabeth Congdon. Tom Congdon told Roger that Marjorie's share of the inheritance came to around $8 million.

On May 31, Roger had contacted Congdon at home, despondent because the bank had started foreclosure proceedings on Caldwells' ranch, Pine Valley Farms. The couple had failed to come up with a $45,000 installment due on the $290,000 ranch. They faced more than just eviction. The sheriff's department planned to auction $26,000 worth of furnishings to pay off outstanding bills from their former townhouse in Denver. Other creditors had lined up as well. Roger asked if the Congdon estate's legal staff could represent the Caldwells.

On Wednesday, June 1, Roger called Congdon at Congdon's office. Roger stated that he and Marjorie had been served with foreclosure papers on their Bailey, Colorado, ranch. Their furniture had been hauled away, and if it was recovered from one creditor, another lined up to take it away again.

Later that day Roger stopped by Congdon's office and described the couple's recent activities, some of them illegal. Besides owing creditors thousands of dollars, Roger said the couple had written a series of bad checks.

In December of 1976, they had opened an account at the First Bank of Evergreen by depositing a $35,000 bad check drawn on the First National Bank of Duluth. They managed to keep this account open until March 1977, writing approximately 130 overdrafts totaling nearly $7,500. Among many other things, they had written bad checks for horses, horse tack, and stable bills.

"Roger, I cannot help you myself," said Congdon, giving Roger the name of a criminal attorney.

Though she had driven with her husband to Tom's office, Marjorie refused to accompany Roger inside. Supposedly she'd eaten something that made her queasy. When Congdon walked Roger to the car, he saw Marjorie lying on the back seat. It was the first time he'd seen his cousin since her move to Colorado. He almost felt sorry for Marjorie as she tried to look ill in a pitiful attempt to save face. Congdon strongly urged the couple to live within their means. Don't expect the family to pay off your debts, he warned.

On June 15 and 16 Roger called Congdon, saying he and Marjorie had decided to hire F. Lee Bailey's law firm and needed money. On June 18, Roger met with Congdon at his office. Roger, neatly dressed in a denim jacket and blue jeans, paced back and forth, extremely agitated. Roger repeated that he and Marjorie wanted to retain the Bailey law firm to sue Marquette Bank and asked for $250,000. Tom refused. During the conversation, Roger confided that he and Marjorie were doing what they could to stay alive, which meant besides bad checks, they were using expired credit cards, and putting slugs in soda machines. That very day Marjorie would write two more bad checks to the Lapins of Wildwood Farms in Englewood, Colorado—one for another horse for $6,000 and a second for $881.44 worth of equipment, boarding, and training for the horse.

Roger told Congdon that the couple was again behind in payments to the Holland House Hotel. Each morning, Roger had to put a twenty dollar bill on the counter to avoid being kicked out. He also repeated his and Marjorie's grand plan to purchase a horse ranch and train and breed horses. The problem was that Roger was living on his $97-per-week unemployment checks, and Marjorie supposedly was down to a $150-per-month annuity. The couple needed at least $106,000, Roger told Tom Congdon; $81,000 to pay off debts to keep them out of jail and $25,000 for down payment on a nearby ranch that included a large horse barn that would hold the Caldwells' remaining five horses. Roger never mentioned selling the horses as an option to raise cash.

"Why don't you go to work?" Tom asked in exasperation. "Every other person works."

"I only earned $12,000 a year in my last job."

Tom, unsympathetic, reminded him that $12,000 plus Marjorie's annual income of $22,000 from her trust fund added up to more than many other couples made. Roger said that Marjorie's mounting debt made it difficult to look for work or hold a job.

Congdon would say later, "I said 'If you could just get employment with the compensation you had before.' I suggested that Marjorie—she likes horses so much—go to work in a stable."

The day of his mother-in-law's murder, Roger sought out Congdon once more. About 9 P.M. Monday, June 27, he phoned Congdon at home.

"Is there any word about what happened?" Roger asked, his voice sounding shaky and strained.

"Well, police think it's a burglary, you know."

"Well, Marjorie is terribly upset."

Congdon could hear his cousin in the background screaming at her husband. She yelled that Bill Van Evera and Vera Dunbar had arranged to kill her mother.

"I got Marjorie some sedatives. I'm trying to get her to take them."

"Roger, why don't you wait until Wednesday to come up? The family will be so upset." Since relations between Marjorie and the rest of the family had been strained over the years, he added, "I think you should follow your idea to bring David Arnold with you."

"What about the funeral arrangements?"

"Well, it's going to be 1:30 P.M. Thursday."

Congdon could hear Marjorie's screaming protests. "I'm the oldest daughter. I'll make the funeral arrangements," she yelled.

Congdon quickly said, "That's the only time we could get the minister." Repeated by Roger, the lie seemed to pacify Marjorie, for the moment. Marjorie loudly insisted that she and Roger would be staying at Glensheen.

"Nobody is even getting into the place," Tom told Roger, which he knew wasn't true. When Tom hung up, he had a creepy feeling that Roger had called simply to check in—to let Congdon know he was in Colorado.

CHAPTER 6

Marriage & Money

DICK AND MARJORIE LEROY'S FIRST HOME CONSISTED OF a one-bedroom apartment in Audubon Park, a new complex in Brentwood, Missouri, a St. Louis suburb. Small and plainly furnished, the apartment stood in stark contrast to Glensheen's vast opulence, and that seemed to be all right with Marjorie, at least at first. But within several months of the marriage, Dick began to receive threatening phone calls from creditors demanding payment of bills run up by Marjorie. He was particularly upset by a call from a local grocery store demanding $400. Even after the $25 raise he got when they married, Dick was making just $260 a month. For someone whose mother had been so good at handling money, he had trouble understanding his new wife's spending habits. "That $400 was like the national debt to me at that time," he said later.

Dick recalled another time just after his mother-in-law had visited the couple in St. Louis. He received calls from several department stores regarding payment for several thousand dollars' worth of merchandise charged to his account. When he confronted Marjorie, she insisted her mother had charged the items on the account because it was more convenient. But a phone call to Elisabeth soon disproved Marjorie's story. His mother-in-law did, however, send money to help clear up this round of debts, and talked with her son-in-law about Marjorie's problems.

Finally, Dick began to see the other side of the story: his wife's weakness with money and her propensity for lying and exaggerating the truth. He had never seen her studying for any nursing classes or met her on campus; he later suspected that she was riding a stallion she owned, Bomber, instead. When Elisabeth asked Dick if Marjorie had told him about being admitted to the Menninger Clinic, he replied, "Not in the way that you told me." It was the beginning of a picture that would grow bleaker and bleaker as time went on.

By the end of 1951, Marjorie was behind on payments for a horse she'd bought from a breeder in Tremont, Illinois. A letter dated December 26, 1951, to Marjorie from the breeder read:

Dear Marjorie:
    I received your telegram and I must admit I am a little confused. As I understand it, you are offering to send the colt back here until you get the Duluth office straightened out concerning this final payment and then take him back again.

I cannot understand why there is so much difficulty in getting my address in order to mail this last payment. We received your Xmas card only a day or so after you mailed it and that address was correct.

It would fall to Dick to make good on this debt. Soon afterward he received a promotion, which moved the LeRoy family to Minneapolis in 1952. But Marjorie's spending outpaced the extra income that came with Dick's new job—and the spending multiplied with the birth of every child in their growing family. Their first, Stephen, had been born in St. Louis in May of 1952; Peter followed in September, 1953.

A May 18, 1954, letter from Marjorie to Elisabeth provided a glimpse into Marjorie's reliance on her mother's money and how she continued to manipulate her mother into buying her what she wanted. While pregnant with her third child, Suzanne (who would be born in November), and only days after a visit from Elisabeth, Marjorie wrote:

> Dayton's [department store] has had some more maternity clothes come in since Saturday morning.... I found a darling 2 piece dress of pale pink.... It is very becoming and they will hold it for me for one week while I write you. It costs $35 and with the cotton seersucker slip [for $4] and $6 pants you said you would treat me to also, the bill comes to $45 even. If this is too expensive let me know and I'll cancel it, but it is very sweet and such a heavenly shade of pink.

While Marjorie forged a new life for herself as a wife and mother, Jennifer graduated from Dana Hall and attended Garland College, a small women's school in Boston. During college, she met Charles (Chuck) Johnson, a graduate student at the Massachusetts Institute of Technology. When they were first introduced, Jennifer refused to believe Chuck was a student. "You're too old to be a student," she told him. Only after he produced a driver's license was she satisfied, and extremely embarrassed.

The couple became engaged during Jennifer's senior year. In September 1955, after her graduation, they wed in Glensheen's formal gardens, overlooking Lake Superior. Duluth's unpredictable weather, however, nearly spoiled the outdoor ceremony before it ever began. A nor'easter blew through Duluth several days before the wedding, ruining the flower gardens. Glensheen's gardener made the rounds of Duluth's flower shops, buying up flowers, which he placed in the gardens.

Jennifer knew how much family and tradition meant to Elisabeth, so she reluctantly asked Marjorie to be her matron of honor, while Dick was one of the groomsmen. After the wedding, Jennifer said, "We went into the army." Chuck was stationed in Washington, D.C., for two years, after which the couple moved to Racine, Wisconsin, Johnson's hometown. Chuck spent a year working for his father then took a job with IBM, where he worked for many years before he and Jennifer started Visual Numerics, Inc., a computer software company, in 1970. The couple had six children, five girls and one boy, and they named their oldest daughter Elisabeth.

"Marjorie had no conception of money whatsoever. She always had to have the best and most expensive of everything," said Jennifer. "But Mother always said we had to uphold the Congdon name.... Mother would talk about Marge and the spending and she really didn't know how to stop it. I said, 'Well, Mom, don't let her charge on your charge accounts. Put a stop to it.' She finally did that. The spending still went on and the stores still kept letting Marge charge."

Over the years, other family members noted Marjorie's pattern of deficit spending. "Marjorie always spent more and Aunt Elisabeth would have to bail her out at some point," recalled Bill Van Evera. "Not big amounts considering the family, but it was always that way, almost every year."

"She'd adopted this girl and she was trying to raise her the best that she could," Jennifer said. "Maybe she felt she had done something wrong in raising her the way she turned out."

Throughout their marriage, Dick assumed the role of Marjorie's financial front man. He not only warded off creditors, but at Marjorie's request repeatedly called her mother to ask for money. Dick also contacted the Congdon Office trustees on Marjorie's behalf to inquire about accelerating his wife's trust fund interest payments. Dick insisted he should be completely in charge of the family finances, given Marjorie's track record. He reminded her to stay within their budget and to clear expenditures with him. Sometimes Marjorie reacted angrily to her husband's directives and berated Dick for thinking she was incapable of exercising restraint or showing concern for their family. Other times, she was more demure, and told him she appreciated how hard he worked to keep their finances in order, promising almost sheepishly to be more budget conscious.

In November 1956, in a move he hoped would help curb Marjorie's spending, Dick wrote the Credit Bureau of Minneapolis and asked that a restriction be placed on his family's credit accounts. The restriction, noted in Dick's credit reporting file, stated "I will not be responsible for any purchases made in my name without my signature."

After that, whenever Marjorie contacted her mother for money, she pretended to seek help for her husband or children. Their fourth child, Andrew (Andy), had been born in March of 1956. Rebecca, their fifth, would be born in November 1957. In a June 26, 1957, letter, Marjorie asked her mother for money regarding insurance policies Elisabeth had purchased from Dick:

> Mr. Berg [at the Congdon Office] will not pay Dick for the present bill he sent him. This happened last year too and if you remember you had to get after him then, too. Dick would like to clear up all this. When it is as large an amount as yours it makes it extremely hard when Dick has to pay his company and doesn't receive the money he is owed.
>
> Dick thinks maybe this winter we will need to get some kind of household help for either cleaning or ironing with 5 children. I keep on having high blood pressure and headaches, but I hope they will disappear with the baby's arrival. I've never had such trouble before during pregnancies on such a scale.

At the time of this letter, the LeRoys were living in St. Louis Park, a Minneapolis suburb, and Marjorie had decided they needed a bigger house—despite the fact they couldn't afford one and her husband liked their current six-room home. When Marjorie's relentless campaigning failed to change Dick's mind, she took action without him. One day, she brought home an earnest money contract in Dick's and Marjorie's names for a large $32,000 house on Fremont Avenue in an upscale neighborhood near Lake Harriet in Minneapolis. After Dick refused to sign the purchase agreement, Marjorie scratched off his name and gave the real estate agent a $1,000 check from an account that didn't exist. Marjorie also lied to the realtor, saying she had thousands of dollars coming from one of her Duluth trust funds when, in reality, no trust fund monies were available to cover a purchase that large at that time.

Dick was furious when he found out what she had done, but it was too late. Once more, Elisabeth came to her daughter's rescue, providing the $32,000 to purchase the house on Fremont. Over the years the couple would repay Elisabeth on a contract for deed. But every payment reminded Dick how indebted he was to his mother-in-law, and how his wife had deceived him.

Just weeks after buying the house, Marjorie implored Dick to redecorate. He firmly told her no, there was no money for luxuries like that, especially after the stunt she had pulled.

One Sunday morning a few weeks later, the family returned home from church to a nasty surprise. They found the family dog and the neighbors' dog loose inside the house and all the living room furniture ripped apart.

Marjorie insisted the dogs were responsible for the destruction. Dick suspected Marjorie had cut up the furniture with a knife. Regardless, the claim was submitted and the LeRoys' insurance company paid for new living room furnishings, selected by Marjorie. "Marjorie was the last one out of the house," Dick said years later. "I confronted her. I knew she'd done it. But she swore up and down she didn't do it. I was never convinced."

Dick recalled that they had two fires at the Fremont house. One broke out in the basement incinerator after their son Peter and his friend stuffed it too full of cardboard. The origin of the other fire, in 1966, was never definitely established. Dick came home to find the garage in flames, its windows blown out. He ran to the garage, backed the car out, then quickly summoned the fire department. Marjorie had been home the whole time, but had done nothing about the growing blaze; the garage was a total loss, and Marjorie submitted an insurance claim to Dick's company. The claim was paid, the fire was attributed to kids smoking in the garage, and a new garage was built.

After the family's move to the Fremont house, Marjorie began to collect eighteenth century antiques, which quickly became an expensive obsession, Dick recalled. Since Dick wasn't interested in antiques and knew little about them, Marjorie would bring home an item and tell Dick she'd paid $50, when it actually cost her $500. Sometimes when Dick tried to discourage Marjorie from buying more, he would come home from the office to find another antique piece in the house.

A family friend visited the Fremont house during this time and later wondered about Marjorie's views on parenting. The decor throughout the house included regal touches like flocked wallcoverings, velvet drapes, and eighteenth century furnishings. She decorated the children's bedrooms with antique furniture and handmade quilts. Each child had an antique cradle with his or her name carved into the headboard. But there were no toys out or clothes strewn around—no sign that children lived in the household.

Not every piece Marjorie "acquired" found its way into her collection, however. During a LeRoy family visit to Glensheen in 1958, Marjorie secretly removed a small oil painting by Henri Harpignies (1819-1916) from the library. The next time the couple visited, Elisabeth asked if they had seen the painting on their last trip. Dick didn't think much about it at the time, but after they returned home, Marjorie had given him a slip of paper to file, which he had assumed was a bill. When he examined the paper more closely, he saw it was a sales receipt for the painting from the Beard Art Gallery of Minneapolis. The Congdon Office and Dick then traced the painting to Newhouse Galleries in New York City. In January 1959, Dick wrote the gallery explaining that Marjorie had "mistakenly" sold the painting, which belonged to the Congdon estate and couldn't be sold without the trustees' permission. The dealer sold the painting back to Elisabeth for his purchase price, $225, plus $50 for expenses he had incurred through shipping charges, cleaning the painting, and varnishing and toning the frame. The Congdon Office paid the bill, and the dealer returned the painting to Glensheen; the painting hangs in the library to this day.

Jennifer Johnson recalled that besides the painting, other family treasures disappeared from Glensheen and were traced back to Marjorie. "She took my grandmother's imperial jade ring and hocked it," Jennifer said. "A friend of my aunt's spotted Marjorie in a beauty shop in Minneapolis wearing the ring."

Everything almost changed during an incident at Swiftwater Farm in 1960, while Marjorie was six months pregnant with her last child. Jennifer remembered family members, including Elisabeth, discussing Marjorie's mental health. Some suggested that Marjorie needed psychiatric counseling, even hospitalization, to address her spending, stealing, lying, and manipulation. But no matter how serious Marjorie's problems, Elisabeth hated to think about involuntary commitment. "I can't let that happen. I will not have a grandchild of mine born in an institution," she told Jennifer. The issue was never raised again in front of Elisabeth.

The LeRoys' financial picture worsened throughout the 1960s as they struggled to raise seven children—their sixth, Heather, had been born in July, 1959, and their last, Richard (Rick), Jr., in September, 1960. In 1957, at age 25, Marjorie had begun receiving income from a trust Elisabeth had established in the 1930s, amounting to $25,000 annually. She also received interest income from a trust her grandmother Clara had established that brought in another $6,000 a year, increasing over time to $8,000 by the late 1960s. But Marjorie's obsessive spending quickly wiped out the money. They even had to mortgage the house, which they owned in the clear thanks to Elisabeth. While her difficult behavior had played a constant role in their marriage, Dick noticed that when she was pregnant, her lying and spending sprees escalated.

Then one night in the early 1960s, as Marjorie sat on the bedroom floor next to Dick, she admitted her inability to accept her adoption. She had always felt like an outsider, at least in her mind, not only because she'd been adopted, but because she'd been adopted by a well-to-do family. During grade school, she and her mother had driven down to the Twin Cities and back in one day, an uncommon trip in a time when long-distance car travel was relatively rare. When she told her classmates about the trip even her teacher accused Marjorie of lying. Only at a parent-teacher conference did Elisabeth set the teacher straight.

It was the first time Dick could recall his wife really opening up, but when he pressed her, she suddenly turned the tables. "You have a shell and you won't let me in,'" she complained.

Dick believed that if his wife was more comfortable with her past she might be happier and less compulsive in the present. Marjorie had little information about her adoption, and Dick thought he knew the reason why. Elisabeth had confided to Dick's mother that, on the advice of her attorney, she destroyed Marjorie's adoption records just prior to Marjorie and Dick's wedding. In the late 1990s, however, when the Duluth Congdon Office closed, Jennifer learned that both of their adoption files had been kept there over the years. Jennifer took her file and it was her understanding that Marjorie's file was then discarded. After all those years Dick finally learned that Marjorie's file had been locked in the Congdon Office, apparently kept secret out of concern about how Marjorie might respond to its contents.

During their marriage, however, knowing only that Marjorie had been adopted from the Children's Home Society in Greensboro, North Carolina, Dick had begun a private investigation. He obtained a court order for Marjorie's birth records and received a copy of her birth certificate from the North Carolina Department of Human Services. The birth certificate identified her as Jacqueline Barnes, born in Tarboro, North Carolina, a small town in the northeastern part of the state. Florence Barnes, age nineteen, and Randolph Lee, Marjorie's father, a twenty-one-year-old farmer from a neighboring county, were not married.

Dick recalled that after receiving a notarized statement from Marjorie, the adoption agency had sent them a letter outlining what was known about her natural parents. Although not wealthy, Marjorie's birthmother's family made a comfortable living. And while the letter did not disclose the whereabouts of Marjorie's birthmother, it did mention that she had moved away and lived in a state far from both North Carolina and Minnesota.

The letter also mentioned Florence Barnes' troubled behavior, which piqued Dick's interest. The report indicated that while Marjorie's mother did not behave responsibly, her family did. Marjorie's mother had been accused of embezzlement at the store where she worked, and her family had made restitution for her. It sounded a bit like life around him.

In the mid-1960s the LeRoys took an emergency vacation at Lutsen ski resort, about eighty-five miles north of Glensheen along Lake Superior's North Shore. The trip marked the start of marital counseling for the couple. Dick said years later that Marjorie's psychiatrist at the University of Minnesota diagnosed her problem as "promiscuity with money caused by a personality defect." Another psychiatrist pronounced her borderline manic-depressive. Dick's therapist, who had previously treated Marjorie until she refused to go, warned Dick, "Protect yourself. Make sure you have a special fund—Marjorie could wipe you out."

Dick described his wife in simple terms: she was a spendthrift who constantly bought things they didn't need. From the time she was a child, Marjorie had equated having money and receiving possessions with love and affection. "Marjorie is kind of like an alcoholic. She had to have certain things. But once she got them, they didn't mean anything to her anymore," Dick said years later.

Besides antiques, figure skating had become another of Marjorie's obsessions. In 1962, she had decided that she wanted all her children to be figure skaters, and when Marjorie decided to do something, she did it full bore. Dick explained this obsession simply: "she wanted to be the mother of a figure skating champion."

Marjorie approached Mannette Allen, a twenty-eight-year-old skating instructor and coach at the Ice Center in Minneapolis, about family skating lessons for the seven children and herself. While Allen recommended individual lessons for the LeRoy children because of their varying ages and skating levels, Marjorie insisted on family lessons. The LeRoy children took lessons twice a week in compulsory school figures and freestyle skating, then the two components of competitive figure skating.

At first, Marjorie took skating lessons alongside her children, but she soon gave up, preferring to play the role of a "skating mom." She sat in the bleachers with the other parents, a loosely-knit group comprised mostly of women, each with a fierce desire to see her child win. Being a skating mother demanded an enormous time commitment. Sometimes Marjorie got up at four o'clock in the morning, sat in a cold tub to stay awake, and read the U.S. Figure Skating Association rule book. She wanted to make sure she knew all the fine points of judging. She also drove her children to the Ice Center before and after school and watched their practices, lessons, and competitions. As another skating mother recalled, "I don't know who raised the children who weren't on the ice, because Marjorie was always at the rink."

While Marjorie watched her children practice and compete, she gossiped with the other parents and kept busy with some sort of handiwork, usually knitting. Marjorie could knit a sweater faster than anyone. Marjorie also constantly studied her children's competitors. When she learned that one of Stephen's figure skating competitors took ice dancing lessons and that the boy's coach thought it was a good idea, she immediately signed up Stephen for daily lessons.

Figure skating is an expensive sport. In addition to paying for lessons and ice time, Marjorie outfitted each child with dozens of skating costumes and multiple pairs of skates, which she had custom-made by the best skate manufacturer in Minnesota. Although Dick tried to talk to Marjorie about reducing the number of lessons and amount of equipment, Marjorie wanted her children to have the best skates and skating attire that money could buy, even just for practices. Most children practiced in the afternoons in the same clothes they had worn to school. Stephen, on the other hand, wore spotless white jeans topped off with cashmere sweaters in an assortment of colors, one skating mother remembered. Another mother recalled seeing Suzanne practice in different skating dresses each day of the week. One day she asked how many skating dresses Suzanne owned and Suzanne said "about forty."

Allen said that for a while, she considered Marjorie her best friend. They both lived in southwest Minneapolis and had eleven children between them. The children ate and played together and had sleepovers; the moms took turns ferrying one another's children. Although Marjorie didn't have many close friends, Allen remembers her as fiercely loyal to those she had, and generous to a fault. Once Allen picked up some of the LeRoy children when Marjorie couldn't and fed them and her own kids hot dogs for dinner. The next day Marjorie presented her with a gold pin, saying "thank you for feeding my kids." Other gifts Allen received included extravagant floral arrangements, silk scarves, pieces of jewelry including gold earrings and gold charms, and an expensive pair of ice skates. Marjorie gave Allen's daughter Stephanie a pedigreed Siamese kitten, "just because Stephanie and I had helped her out."

Allen described Marjorie as a woman with a great sense of humor—she loved sharing funny stories about her children—who enjoyed entertaining friends on a grand scale. She invited the Allens out for Thanksgiving dinner at the Minneapolis Women's Club, a private club, for a "sumptuous feast," recalled Allen. "All we knew was that Marjorie had all the money in the world, but spent it accordingly without being obnoxious," Allen said.

Allen said she and the other skating mothers "thought Marjorie had married a sugar daddy who had a ton of money. I had maybe known her a year and a half when we went up to Brule River and got a look at [Swiftwater Farm] and the guest house, and I went 'whoa,' I haven't had this right at all."

But Marjorie's use of her money was erratic and often selfish. According to one of the coaches' wives, when Marjorie wanted to create skating dresses for her daughters, she went to the fabric store and bought an entire bolt of fabric so that no other skater in town could wear the same outfit. Marjorie then had a dressmaker sew the costumes, but she would ask the dressmaker to leave the dresses unhemmed. Marjorie would then bring the dresses to the rink and sit and hem them, giving the impression she had sewn the dresses. She and her son Stephen once flew to Detroit so he could have his competition jumpsuits and jackets made by a tailor Marjorie considered superior to any in the Twin Cities. (Dick LeRoy remembered this incident differently. Marjorie and Stephen flew to Detroit without his knowledge. He only discovered the trip a week later when Stephen told him about it. Stephen said they went to Detroit to be fitted for custom skates.)

Stephen, to Marjorie's delight, won figure skating competitions almost from the start. Marjorie spent an average of $15,000 a year on his lessons, rink rental, and entry fees for competitions throughout the United States. She even paid her son's way and accompanied him to an international skating competition in France. During the same trip she also indulged Stephen's interest in golf by taking him to play at the exclusive Saint Andrews Royal and Ancient Golf Club in Scotland.

While Stephen possessed natural talent and a strong drive, his mother's competitiveness on his behalf was excessive. One of the skating mothers recalled that Marjorie had Stephen taking so many skating lessons that the mothers referred to them as "baby-sitting on ice." She also recalled how Marjorie bought up extra ice time and practice spaces, called "patches," at the Ice Center. Unclaimed patches were advantageous for adjacent skaters because certain school figures were too large to be executed in a single patch. Skaters would have to overlap one another's patches to practice these figures but an empty patch meant a skater could execute them on clean ice. One skating mother recalled that Marjorie would also instruct her children to occupy the empty patches facing their competitors so those skaters would not have clean ice to practice on.

Another skater's mother said that Marjorie downplayed Stephen's skating experience at his first competition to give him an edge with the judges. "She told the judges that he'd only been skating a year, which sounded very good—until it turned out that he had been playing hockey for years before that," the woman remembered.

She also said that Marjorie had Stephen take advantage of a rule allowing ill skaters to be exempted from a competition. On a number of occasions, when Stephen performed poorly in a particular competition, Marjorie had him feign illness in order to get an exemption. In this way, Stephen advanced to the next round without really facing all of his competitors.

The same woman also observed Stephen advance to nationals as a result of "very interesting circumstances" that occurred at a regional figure skating competition in Green Bay, Wisconsin. Stephen was in fourth place after the compulsory or school figures competition. Shortly after the skaters took the ice to warm up, the boy in third place slipped, lost his edge, and slammed into the boards hard, knocking him unconscious. When the woman looked up, "Marjorie was standing at the edge of the boards right on top of him, beet red, and crying. No child was ever injured going around the curve of the rink. The skates had to have been tampered with. It had to have been that someone got hold of his blades, ran them over the concrete, and made it so the edge would be gone." Marjorie's tears following the accident could have been tears of relief, the woman thought, because the injured boy had to withdraw from the competition. Stephen, now in third place by default, went to nationals.

This skating mom witnessed another incident involving the LeRoy children. Just before the competition began, a girl in competition against Suzanne could not find her skates. Marjorie offered to lend the girl a pair of Rebecca's or Suzanne's skates, the woman recalled. However, because the fit is so important, competitive skaters use custom-made skates—no matter whose skates the girl borrowed, she could not skate. Marjorie's generous offer was disingenuous. Suzanne won the competition.

Allen said that Marjorie became friends with one of the other skating mothers, Helen Hagen, possibly because their children did not compete against each other. The LeRoy children skated as individuals, while Tom and Nancy Hagen, Helen's children, competed as a pair. Although Helen was "just as ambitious for her kids as Marjorie" and just as strong minded, the two women got along well, Allen recalled. Marjorie and Helen both went to the Ice Center every day, would often sit together during practices, and sometimes even socialized outside the rink.

The time demands of skating further strained a marriage burdened by Marjorie's lying and overspending. Dick and Marjorie spent increasingly fewer hours together as husband and wife. Marjorie woke at 5:15 A.M. to take the children involved in figure skating to the Ice Center for two hours of practice before she drove them to school. Dick took responsibility for waking the remaining children at 6:45 A.M., fixing them breakfast, and seeing them off to school, which included driving Suzanne and Andy to their separate schools. Only then was Dick free to go to work at his insurance agency.

After school, Marjorie picked up the children who participated in skating and drove them back to the Ice Center. On days when Marjorie took Suzanne for riding lessons, Dick had to leave the office at 4 P.M. to pick up the children after skating practice. At home before dinner, Dick helped his children with their homework and ate dinner with them. He also took charge of baths for the younger children. Marjorie often didn't get home from the ice rink before 8:30 P.M. or later. She usually fell into bed exhausted, only to get up the next morning before Dick awoke.

Marjorie's excessive focus on winning figure skating competitions didn't displace her compulsive spending outside of the rink. One winter, Marjorie bought Dick an expensive cashmere coat. He couldn't take the coat back to the store because it had been special-ordered. Spending money on their kids, Dick recalled, was like a "recreational sport" for her. At Marjorie's insistence, all of the LeRoy children except Peter—who went to a vocational high school in Minneapolis—attended private schools. Allen recalled a shopping trip to a furniture store to buy the LeRoy children study desks. Marjorie asked a sales clerk about purchasing an expensive hardwood desk she liked. The sales clerk assumed she wanted to buy a single desk until Marjorie corrected him, telling him to order one for each of her children. If one of her daughters needed a new dress, Marjorie would buy six. When her sons needed new shirts, she'd buy a dozen of the same style, one in every available color and all monogrammed, so they couldn't be returned. Marjorie not only wanted the most, but it also had to be the best—her daughters wore Florence Eiseman designer dresses, her boys Brooks Brothers shirts. But Marjorie didn't believe in her children sharing hand-me-down clothes. Word spread in the neighborhood that she discarded designer children's clothes in mint condition. According to Robert "Red" Kairies, manager of the Ice Center, people went so far as to sift through the LeRoys' garbage on trash day to see Marjorie's rejects.

In 1967, on her thirty-fifth birthday, Marjorie received capital from the Clara Congdon Trust, set up by her grandmother. Dick recalled that Marjorie received nearly $290,000. The extra money wouldn't last long.

Christmas best displayed Marjorie and Dick's different approaches to money. She filled the Fremont house's enclosed side porch knee-deep with gifts—thousands of dollars worth. Dick had suggested a number of times that he and Marjorie give each of their children one nice present and donate the rest of the Christmas money to charity. "She thought I was nuts," said Dick.

Marjorie liked to make statements with her Christmas gifts. She had always loved horses, so for Christmas in 1968 each LeRoy child received a horse from their mother. Dick recalled that Marjorie, despite having promised to discuss major purchases in advance, had secretly raided one of her trust accounts to buy the seven horses. To make financial matters worse, the present turned into a gift that kept on giving—besides the cost of the horses, Marjorie paid for competition fees, weekly riding lessons at a local stable, and room-and-board costs totaling more than $500 a month. During the time two of her daughters competed in equestrian events she purchased dozens of boots—custom-made for $133 a pair—and close to 300 riding outfits for the girls. By the early 1970s, Marjorie owned at least nineteen horses in the Twin Cities; her passion for horseback riding became another obsession.

Suzanne soon acquired her mother's passion for riding. As a teenager, she and Marjorie regularly drove out to Jonathan Stables, just southwest of the Twin Cities, for riding lessons. Parents gathered under a large apple tree beside the lesson ring, recalled Willie Wakefield, whose daughter took lessons at the stable with Suzanne. Just as she had done at the Ice Center, Marjorie sat with the other parents, talking and doing needlepoint. Wakefield also recalled that Marjorie gave needlepoint lessons at The Needle Nest, a needlepoint store in Wayzata, an upscale Minneapolis suburb, and regularly bought furniture at an antique store in the same neighborhood "that gave Marjorie lots of items she never ended up paying for."

Wakefield said that Marjorie, like Suzanne, also dressed in expensive riding clothes and had hundreds of riding outfits. Marjorie shopped at an exclusive New York City store that specialized in English riding clothes. An acquaintance of Marjorie heard that, much as she had done with fabric for skating costumes, she made sure no one else had the same clothes by buying the entire stock of riding outfits. While she may have dressed the part, Wakefield said that Marjorie was not an accomplished rider. "Marjorie seldom rode," Wakefield remembers. "She rode in a couple of horse shows and did so-so."

While Suzanne took lessons and competed in horse shows, Marjorie bought up "every horse that hit the barn," Wakefield said. "If the manager at the stables got a new horse, Marjorie would want dibs on that horse for Suzie to ride in competition."

Suzanne soon learned that riding was a mixed blessing. When she had first told Marjorie she was quitting skating, Marjorie had pulled Suzanne off her bed by the hair. Riding had eased tensions, but Marjorie expected Suzanne to be a tough competitor. Suzanne recalled that Marjorie told her that if she fell off a horse she had better not cry or Marjorie would bloody her up.

One of Wakefield's most vivid memories of Marjorie involved a bridle that belonged to Wakefield's husband, Lyman. "She stole one of Lyman's best bridles," Wakefield recalled. "Then she used it in front of God and everybody." When Lyman confronted Marjorie about the bridle, she told him that she guessed she had made a mistake. The excuse sounded to Wakefield just like the explanation she had received when a needlepoint project she had been working on at the stables disappeared and wound up in the LeRoys' garage.

While there were no Rolls-Royces or trips around the world, Dick recalled how his wife liked to treat herself to extravagant gifts. Marjorie favored expensive jewelry, particularly with horse designs. Much of her jewelry and clothing was special order or custom-made. He remembers his wife returning from forays to Dayton's Oval Room—a clothing department within the upscale department store—with pricey designer clothes. Marjorie was depleting her trust funds, going through hundreds of thousands of dollars, but despite her excessive purchases, no one could quite figure out where it all went.

Regardless of the turmoil between Dick and Marjorie over her spending and lies, they tried to maintain a semblance of stable family life. The family usually spent Sundays together, when all the LeRoys dressed up in their best clothes, attended the local Methodist church, and went out for brunch. They also enjoyed occasional family activities such as roasting marshmallows at a neighborhood park or visiting a museum, the Como Park Zoo in St. Paul, or the state fair. Getting the whole family together was difficult, however, given Marjorie's obsession with figure skating.

Dick soon became grateful for his wife's absences. When home, Marjorie would bring up some controversial subject that they ended up fighting about. As Dick described it, there was "never any quietness or smoothness about the life in the house," with Marjorie at home. "I appreciated the fact that she was not there because it was more of an ordeal when she was around." Dick was concerned, however, about the impact of Marjorie's schedule on those children not as involved in skating or horseback riding. Heather, Peter, Andy, and Ricky tried figure skating but did not have the interest necessary for full-time commitment. The family paid for Marjorie's focus on Stephen's skating.

It also led to a falling out with her best friend Mannette Allen over two incidents in the 1960s. At a major skating competition, Allen missed Stephen's short program. Not a morning person, Allen didn't hear the alarm clock and slept on as Stephen completed his compulsory figures. She felt terrible for letting her student down, but Marjorie knew Allen always slept late in the morning. "All Marjorie had to do was pick up the phone and I would have been there," Allen said. Angered about the missed appearance, Marjorie decided Allen would no longer coach her son.

The second incident had a more lasting effect on the friendship. Allen's daughter Stephanie was scheduled to take an ice dancing test in July, 1966, and needed a male partner. Due to the shortage of male skaters, she had recruited Stephen to be her partner. The two made an attractive couple, an important consideration in ice dancing competition. At the last minute, with no satisfactory explanation, Marjorie would not permit Stephen to partner with Stephanie, and Allen could not find a substitute. Stephanie was going to have to skate with her coach who, aside from being considerably older, was also quite a bit taller. Allen spoke with the judges about the situation, knowing that the judges would not respond favorably to the odd pairing. When Marjorie found out that Allen had talked to the judges, she sued Allen for defamation of character.

Allen consulted with the father of one of the skaters she knew from the Minneapolis figure skating club, an attorney. He advised suing Marjorie for breach of contract, so Allen sued. The case settled out of court on August 23, 1967. Marjorie had to pay Allen $500. Allen later said it wasn't about the money, but rather getting Marjorie to back down and admit she was wrong. The women did not speak for months afterward.

Marjorie entered into another legal battle in 1968 after the Figure Skating Club of Minneapolis refused to renew the LeRoy family's membership. As Dick later explained, the refusal resulted from derogatory remarks Marjorie had made about a number of members of the club. Marjorie and Dick sued, and the case went up to the Minnesota Supreme Court. Marjorie lost the case.

Marjorie's lying and reckless spending, already a huge issue for Dick in their marriage, continued to increase. Dick recalled the time that Marjorie borrowed $3,000 from Northwestern National Bank in Minneapolis for ninety days. At the end of the ninety days, she went back to the bank, renewed the loan, and got an additional $2,000, for a total of $5,000. Three months later, when she couldn't repay the money, Marjorie admitted she'd forged her mother's name as cosigner. When Dick contacted his mother-in-law about Marjorie's transgression, Elisabeth discreetly repaid the bank, ensuring that bank officials had no idea about the forgery.

"I spent a lot of time cleaning up her messes," Dick recalled. He loved Marjorie, but he couldn't take the constant strain of being hounded by creditors. "I became her enabler because she realized I would take care of all these things. She never seemed able to accept the consequences of her actions."

Dick knew that as soon as he shut off one line of credit, Marjorie would lie, saying "I have my own money," and she'd open up a new line or apply for a new card. They were playing a financial version of hide-and-seek. Elisabeth and the Congdon trustees were well aware of Marjorie's inability to control her spending. So in 1968, Elisabeth set up two trust funds for her daughter at the First American National Bank in Duluth with the intent of restricting Marjorie's access to her inheritance, while putting Dick in charge of paying off Marjorie's debts and paying bills with the trust money. The MCL (Marjorie Congdon LeRoy) Trust was established with $500,000, while the Marjorie LeRoy Family Trust contained $1,000,000. Marjorie could not touch the principal on the larger trust, but Dick was allowed, with the bank's permission, to use capital from the MCL trust to pay Marjorie's debts.

After finding that joint checking invited overdrafts by Marjorie, Dick opened separate accounts for himself, Marjorie, and the children. He opened a checking account for Marjorie called the Marjorie C. LeRoy Trust Account. Only he had legal authority to write checks on these accounts. But that didn't stop Marjorie from attempting to bypass him and cash checks with just her signature. She continued to spend money without telling her husband.

In January 1969, Dick came home from work and found an Oriental rug being laid down in his living room. He was upset to see the new rug in place of one from his childhood home that had great sentimental value. When Dick learned the Oriental rug cost $4,000, he told the man who was laying the rug "that he better roll up his rug and take it back" because there was no money to pay for it. Unfortunately, the rug was actually two rugs sewn together, a special order by Marjorie. Dick was stuck with another unnecessary expense.

Dick was fast becoming fed up—no matter how hard he tried, or how many times they talked, Marjorie refused to cut back on the number of horses they owned, the antiques she purchased, or the skating expenditures. As Dick learned early in the marriage, Marjorie's promises were meaningless because she would turn around and do exactly as she pleased. If Dick persisted too much, Marjorie could become extremely unpleasant to live with, and he didn't want the children to suffer. Dick explained later, "as long as you would go along with what she wanted to do, she was happy and everything was all right. But if you disagreed, then there was immediately stress in the household and things would get very uncomfortable."

The next year, Marjorie lost a battle of wills with her son Stephen after he decided to quit competitive figure skating. Stephen had won a number of championships, and was the Upper Great Lakes Juvenile Men's Champion. He based his decision to quit partly on an ankle injury he suffered while competing for the nationals and his plans to attend college out of state at Stanford University in California. According to Dick, once Stephen made his decision, "he absolutely put his foot down and would not go into the rink." Marjorie, however, would not accept her son's decision, perhaps reluctant to relinquish her role as the mother of a skating champion.

She lied to Stephen's coach and told him that her son had mononucleosis and would return, Dick recalled. As insurance agent for the coach and his wife, Dick learned that the couple was unaware that Stephen had stopped skating. The couple was counting on income from Stephen's lessons. The unfortunate task of informing the couple that there would be no more lessons fell to Dick.

Marjorie was angry at Stephen for stopping skating, and Dick noticed his wife's caustic tone and unpleasant behavior toward their son. The same behavior extended to her daughter Suzanne when, not long after Stephen quit skating, Suzanne decided to discontinue competitive horseback riding. "She acts like a martinet as far as her children are concerned," Dick said later.

That same year, while attending a national figure skating competition, Marjorie took rooms at the Broadmoor Hotel in Colorado Springs, Colorado. She brought her son Peter and daughter Suzanne on the two-week trip. Marjorie ran up a $2,000 hotel bill and purchased jewelry totaling $8,000, including custom-made items. Dick discovered the expenditures when the hotel's jewelry store called to talk with Marjorie about the custom designs.

"All the ingredients were there for a beautiful life and a good marriage," Dick said, "but she blew it. The overspending, the lying. She liked to play the grand lady." As he said years later, despite his business and the couple's seven children—he had scant time for either, since the majority of his waking hours were spent contacting creditors and Congdon trustees—he felt as if he'd lost his identity. He also worried about his sons Andy, Peter, and Rick, who he felt had been neglected by Marjorie because of her absences.

So Dick decided to take the three boys for a two-week vacation to Alaska in 1970. The tour of Alaska, which included taking a boat cruise down the Chena River, riding the Alaskan Railroad, hiking in McKinley Park, and riding a ferry down the coast, was a father-and-sons bonding experience, Dick recalled. Unfortunately, the closeness would not last long.

By 1970, even Marjorie's mother had run out of patience with her daughter's spending habits and repeated requests for money. In a September 16, 1970, letter from the Congdon Office to Dick, trustee C.A. Hoekstra described Elisabeth's reaction to Marjorie's request for $449.50 to cover entry fees for a horse show. The letter read, in part, "Although Miss Congdon's check has gone forward as she promised Marjorie over the telephone, I feel constrained to advise you that she was not very happy about this request being made of her, particularly in view of the largesse just recently bestowed by her upon Marjorie and her family directly and in trust."

The last straw, Dick said, was when Marjorie obtained a $20,000 unsecured loan from Northwestern National Bank of Minneapolis to start a horse breeding business.

Marjorie told the loan officer that she had money from her trust to serve as collateral, when the trust funds actually would not be available for several years. To make matters worse, the bank that approved the loan was the same one that Dick had asked not to lend his wife money without his approval. Dick wrote the bank informing them that "the $20,000 note was signed by Mrs. LeRoy only and I do not know by what means she plans to repay it." He went on to advise the bank "I assume no responsibility for repayment."

So, after nearly twenty years of marriage, Dick decided his only alternative was to leave. On October 31, 1970, when Marjorie came home from her children's skating lessons, she found her husband waiting by the front door with his suitcase. That night he moved into the Curtis Hotel in downtown Minneapolis.

Several days later, Marjorie came to Dick's office. "She got down on her knees and begged me to come back," he recalled. Dick told Marjorie he would think it over. But even as he agreed to consider Marjorie's request, he knew reconciliation was not possible. "We had talked about our problems for years. Marjorie never kept her promises," he said.

After Dick moved out, Marjorie turned vindictive. She demanded her children's allegiance and told them that the pending divorce was their father's fault. Marjorie tried to turn the children against their father, fabricating hateful stories about how he was a callous womanizer who didn't really care about

them. She restricted Dick's access to the children, would not allow him inside the Fremont house, and interfered with scheduled visitations. According to Stephen, Marjorie had always used loyalty as a lever for her children's privileges—and as a measure of their affection. With the exception of Stephen, Dick saw little of his children for several years after his split with Marjorie. He felt the alienation so keenly that in November 1970 he started a diary he kept during the divorce proceedings titled "Estrangement of Children."

In the midst of his parents' separation, Stephen came home from Stanford University, spending winter quarter at the University of Minnesota in order to be closer to the family. Although he moved back in with his mother, Stephen tried to remain impartial, and stayed in touch with his father.

On November 23, 1970, Dick wrote in his diary, "There was a hearing on restraining order. Marjorie said she did not want a divorce then in the next breath she said she was afraid I was going to hit her." That night, Dick noted in his diary, he got a call at his hotel room from his daughter Rebecca. She wanted to know why her father was telling lies about her mother, why he was cutting off Marjorie's credit, and why he was running around with other women.

Dick had scheduled visitation time on Wednesday evenings. He learned from Stephen that Marjorie made sure Rebecca and Heather were in bed by 6:30 P.M. those days, making it impossible for them to visit with their father. The other children—Peter, Suzanne, Andy, and Rick—were not on speaking terms with their father.

While Dick was not welcome to see his children at Thanksgiving that year, he accepted an invitation from Elisabeth to have Thanksgiving dinner in Duluth. After he arrived at Glensheen, Dick received a long distance call from Stephen who reported that Marjorie had thrown him out of the house. Marjorie had become furious at Stephen after his siblings refused to talk to the guardian ad litem, appointed by the court to represent the children's interests during the divorce. At Dick's suggestion, Stephen took the train up from Minneapolis to join his grandmother and father on Thanksgiving Day. Marjorie was further enraged to learn that Stephen had spent the holiday with his father. She had Rebecca call Glensheen on Thanksgiving with a message for Stephen. Marjorie wanted him to come back home and she loved him.

Stephen returned home and Marjorie confronted him, informing him that he could not see his father except on visitation days. He was upset by her comments and the two got into an argument that became physical—Marjorie ended up on the floor. She screamed that he should leave and not come back. Stephen immediately moved in with a friend. Later that day, Dick began receiving hang-up calls in his hotel room. He suspected Marjorie of making the calls, which continued for a number of months.

The next day, November 29, 1970, Stephen met with his father and talked about the altercation with Marjorie. "He related to me that his mother had physically provoked him and that he had tried to defend himself," Dick noted in his diary. The LeRoys' housekeeper, Hester Norwood, told Dick that Marjorie had kicked Stephen when he told her he would see his father whenever he wanted. Stephen had turned around and shoved her and she fell down. Norwood insisted that Stephen had not slapped his mother. However, soon after the incident Marjorie began claiming Stephen had slapped her, and later claimed that she needed surgery for injuries allegedly suffered as a result of his pushing her.

On December 4, 1970, Dick received a call from Rebecca and asked her why she refused to see him. "She said she didn't like the things I was doing to her mother," Dick wrote in his diary. "She said she had gone down to Arjohn's, a picture framing shop, and been refused credit. She wanted to know why I wouldn't let the bank in Duluth give her mother money. I told her I had nothing to do with it anymore and to have her mother talk to the bank. She angrily hung up."

Dick soon learned that Marjorie was not only trying to alienate him from his children but that she was also spreading lies about him to their friends and acquaintances. On December 6, 1970, he met with the associate pastor of the family's church. Dick noted in his diary that the pastor "told me that a Mrs. Schnoor of the church had called the house and asked that Marjorie make some cookies for the church. She told this woman, who to the best of my knowledge she does not know, that her husband was divorcing her and had left her with no food in the house and no money and that she was in poverty circumstances. This was reported to the church."

Even during the separation, creditors sought Dick for help with debts that Marjorie had incurred. Marjorie had selected a large color television set at Dayton's as a

Christmas present from her mother. Elisabeth had no idea she was giving her daughter this present. Dick got a call from an official at Marjorie's bank, which had been contacted by Dayton's for credit authorization. Marjorie had told Dayton's to send the bill to Elisabeth. Meanwhile, Dick had learned from Stephen that the television had already been delivered to the Fremont house.

Dick contacted the Congdon Office. Hoekstra immediately wrote back asking that Dick make clear to Marjorie that she should not expect her mother to cover her credit card purchases: "Miss Congdon was very emphatic in her denial that she ever made such an offer to Marjorie and seemed to be quite astounded and very disturbed that Marjorie would make such a statement."

The letter concluded, "I would hope that Marjorie would refrain from creating any further involvements of this nature for her mother, because they are very upsetting emotionally to her in her present physical condition. On Miss Congdon's behalf I want to thank you, Dick, for calling this incident to her attention and hope that this reply will serve to forestall any further similar incidents in the future."

But Marjorie didn't stop spending. The December 29, 1970, entry in Dick's diary noted that a Wayzata dress shop owner stopped by Dick's office to ask whether he was going to be paid soon. The following day a bank called about one of Marjorie's accounts being overdrawn. Dick told the bank representative to call Marjorie.

Dick finally filed for divorce, citing cruel and inhuman treatment. In a 1970 deposition, taken as part of the divorce proceedings, Dick detailed Marjorie's reckless spending and habitual lying, and how her lack of grace ruined their social life.

"Marjorie does not seem to have the ability of being able to get along with people and seems to constantly put them in a position of being uncomfortable by either a display of wealth on her part or just extolling the fact that she came from a very fine background," Dick said.

He provided examples of how Marjorie had alienated their friends and acquaintances: "Several months ago Marjorie and I attended a Sunday School Class at Hobart Methodist Church and in this church there are a number of minority group couples. There was a woman, her husband is half Indian and half African-American and she is half white and half African-American. Somehow or other the topic of conversation came around to dissenters and protesters and Marjorie got very emotional about it and blasted away at people and apparently got to the point where she was making very derogatory statements about minority groups to the point where this woman got up and left the room very upset."

In his deposition, Dick said that he had kept financial records since 1958. Based on his conservative calculations, Marjorie had spent more than $1 million in twelve years time. He told the attorneys that Elisabeth Congdon had bailed her daughter out of approximately $365,000 of debt.

During the time of the depositions, Dick briefly visited with Rebecca several times at the Ice Center. After months of no contact during the separation, Dick was thrilled to be able to reconnect with his daughter. Within days, however, Rebecca told her father she could no longer talk to him. Marjorie had learned about their visits and threatened to stop Rebecca's skating lessons.

Marjorie counter-sued for divorce citing Dick on the same grounds he had used—cruel and inhuman treatment—and she was the party granted the divorce. Dick said, "It was on record that I filed for divorce. So whether she got it or I got it didn't make any difference to me." What mattered was that he was free. In a bitter divorce battle, Dick and Marjorie both sought custody of the children. Dick, however, had limited financial resources. Marjorie hadn't asked for alimony or child support because of her trust funds. The judge awarded her full custody of the children and Dick gave Marjorie her adoption records.

After the divorce was final in April, 1971, Dick wrote each child a letter attempting to explain what had happened and that he loved them. Suzanne, Andy, Rebecca, Heather, and Rick still lived with their mother. Stephen was in college and Peter was married. Dick arranged for a housekeeper to personally deliver each one. The estrangement from his children was very painful for Dick; after all, they were the only reason he had stayed with Marjorie for so long. In the years immediately following the divorce, he tried to initiate contact by phone and in person, but his overtures were largely rebuffed, with the exception of Stephen. Dick hoped that over time his children would see how their mother had manipulated the facts surrounding the divorce and unfairly cast him as the bad guy. But Marjorie not only demanded her children's allegiance, she made threats of serious consequences for having contact with their father.

Nonetheless, Dick sent his children birthday cards, having friends address and mail them in an attempt to evade Marjorie's scrutiny. But inevitably the cards would be returned to Dick in a different envelope, apparently sent back by Marjorie.

In July 1971, Myrtle Humphrey, mother of the LeRoys' housekeeper, told Dick that Marjorie was having trouble accepting the divorce. Dick wrote in his diary that Humphrey reported that, "Marjorie has been going out on dates and has begun drinking.... She said that Marjorie has been going to Duluth almost weekly for financial reasons. She also indicated that Marjorie has been telling Suzanne that I have been trying to take her horses away from her."

That same month, Dick spoke with Marjorie's old friend Elizabeth Oakerland, who reported that Marjorie had recently shared "several untruths" about him. Oakerland told Dick that she had talked with Marjorie several months earlier and, as Dick wrote in his diary, Oakerland related that "Marjorie really sounded sick, mentally." Oakerland was so upset after the conversation with Marjorie that she couldn't sleep that night.

Those closest to Marjorie were aware of her tremendous imagination and knack for believing things she wanted to be true. Months after her divorce, she told Jennifer and Chuck Johnson that she had met a Trans World Airlines pilot. Marjorie claimed that she flew with him back and forth between Minneapolis and New York. The Johnsons had one problem with her story—TWA didn't fly into Minneapolis at that time. But Marjorie insisted the couple was living it up in New York City. "We flew out to New York and saw all these plays," she said confidently, as if she believed her own lies.

Dick's troubles continued, and so did his children's. In September of 1971 someone egged the dashboard and floors of his car. The knobs to the radio and lights had been stolen. Dick had parked the car at a Minneapolis restaurant where he was having dinner with a date. The parking attendant told Dick that it was the first time he'd seen a car in the lot vandalized. Dick learned from Stephen that Marjorie had seen him at the same restaurant several days earlier.

In 1973, at the age of seventeen, Andy stopped attending high school and got a job. Marjorie complained to her attorney that she could not control Andy and never knew his whereabouts. She went to court to have her son declared incorrigible and placed in a juvenile correctional facility. Dick noted in his diary on May 5, 1973, that his second wife, Sherry, had called about Marjorie's efforts against Andy. He sent his son a message that "the door was open" and Andy could get in touch if he wanted.

Andy soon needed his father's help. Dick received a phone call one Friday from Marjorie's lawyer that Andy had been picked up at work for truancy and was being held at the juvenile detention center in Minneapolis. A hearing was set for the following Monday.

On Monday, Dick was in court with his attorney to fight the action, while Marjorie was conspicuously absent, supposedly at a doctor's appointment. When the court asked Andy who he wanted to live with, Andy said his father. The court dismissed the charges and permitted Andy to move in with Dick.

During the summer of 1973, Rebecca moved in with Dick after a confrontation with Marjorie, but only for several months. According to Dick, Rebecca had to move back to her mother's house if she wanted to continue figure skating and have Marjorie pay for it, as he could not afford it.

The divorce didn't improve Marjorie's ability to manage money. In November 1973, she went to Duluth and convinced her mother to cosign a $125,000 bank loan, which she later defaulted on. Marjorie bought an old farmhouse she dubbed the "Homestead" in Marine On St. Croix, an affluent community east of the Twin Cities near the St. Croix River, bordering Wisconsin. She hired contractor Michael Billingsley and spent approximately $500,000 to remodel the house, build a guesthouse, and landscape the grounds. A room in the garage was built for Rick, fitted with a hospital bed and an oxygen supply for his asthma. She adorned the house with imported woods, antique furniture, and decorative details including gold faucets and animal-shaped sprinkler heads made in Italy and speakers in the garden disguised as bird houses. Rick lived with Marjorie most of the time, while Heather and Rebecca were in and out; Suzanne would live in the guesthouse for awhile.

Meanwhile, Billingsley told Marjorie he was separated from his wife, and by the summer of 1974 the two were engaged. Marjorie received an engagement ring and Billingsley moved in with her in September. Jennifer recalled the time late that summer when Marjorie brought Billingsley to Glensheen. Marjorie took him to Duluth's Northland Country Club, bought him outfits, golf shoes, and a set of clubs, and charged them to her mother.

Skilled at spending well beyond her means, Marjorie knew how to find money— even if it meant taking it from her children. At the time of her divorce from Dick, he turned over six savings account passbooks which he had been keeping for their children. Because he had already turned eighteen, Stephen received his passbook. The other children later told Dick they never received any of the money.

Because the children were benefactors of Congdon trust income, Dick had filed individual income tax returns for each. For the year 1971 several of the LeRoy children were entitled to tax refunds. When the checks arrived, Marjorie told her kids that the money belonged to her, not them. She then forced them to sign the checks over to her. The children never received any money from the tax returns.

In 1958, Elisabeth Congdon had purchased payment life policies through the Connecticut Mutual Life Insurance Company for Marjorie and each of her children. The policies had a face value of $50,000 and, when paid in full, a cash value of approximately $40,000. All of the policies had been paid up by the time of the divorce. Peter and Andy managed to secure their policies, but the other children discovered that Marjorie had withdrawn all of the cash value from the rest. Suzanne told police she remembered when her mother had probably had her and her sisters sign over theirs. She and her sisters opened up the mail one day and found checks made out to them in excess of $40,000 each. When Marjorie came home she was very upset the girls had opened up the letters and she insisted that they sign the checks. Suzanne and her sisters never saw the money. No one knows how Marjorie spent it all.

Elisabeth's problems with Marjorie continued as well. In 1972, on her fortieth birthday, Marjorie had received $1.5 million from two of the family trust funds. By 1974, Elisabeth Congdon was so upset by her daughter's behavior that she amended special instructions in her Living Trust Agreement to read: "...in the exercise of their discretion, the trustees are warned that Marjorie C. LeRoy has shown a strong inclination to spend more than her means will properly warrant." That September, Marjorie was sued for nonpayment of a bank note for $126,000 that had been co-signed by her mother.

Although trustee Bill Van Evera supervised Elisabeth's major expenditures, she continued to make smaller gifts of money to her daughter. Whether out of a sense of duty, a need to protect her child, or doubts about how she raised her daughter, Elisabeth just couldn't abandon Marjorie financially.

But Marjorie went too far when she coerced her mother to co-sign yet another loan on May 28, 1974, this time for $345,000 from Marquette National Bank of Minneapolis to pay for the renovation of the Marine On St. Croix property. The nurse on duty that day later said that Marjorie instructed the nurse to leave her alone with Elisabeth. Congdon trustees believed that Marjorie obtained her mother's signature during this time—and wondered about the means Marjorie might have used to persuade Elisabeth to sign. "With Mom, when it came to Marjorie, I don't think she could say 'no,'" Jennifer said. "She was vulnerable. And Marjorie was a con artist." Marjorie defaulted on the loan and the bank sued Elisabeth, forcing the trustees to settle the debt. During a civil lawsuit over the loan, on August 6, 1975, Marjorie admitted to obtaining her mother's signature by duress and under false pretenses.

After this incident, Congdon trustees ordered household staff and nurses to monitor Marjorie's visits to Glensheen as well as restrict Marjorie's phone contact with her mother. Jeannette Wisherd, a caretaker at Swiftwater Farm with her husband, Scott, later recalled that security at the Brule became an issue after the loan incident. Scott had to sleep on a mattress in a small screen porch off the kitchen whenever Elisabeth was at her summer home, due to family concern that Marjorie might come or send someone to request that Elisabeth sign additional loan documents.

In the fall of 1974, Wisherd made several large Christmas wreaths for Marjorie at a cost of about $40. She called Marjorie about getting paid and sent her a bill. Marjorie never paid it. Finally, after repeated excuses, Marjorie said that she didn't have the money to pay for the wreaths because of her youngest son Rick's "terminal" medical condition. Marjorie's story proved to be another fabrication.

Marjorie's behavior began to alienate the children whose allegiance she had struggled to keep. Fed up with her mother's efforts to control her life, Suzanne would move out of the guesthouse in Marine On St. Croix in April 1975. According to Suzanne, Marjorie used Suzanne's name to spread lies, opened and read her mail, and listened in on her phone calls. Peter disliked how his mother kept reminding him that she had helped buy things for him and his wife after they were first married. The summer after her parents' divorce, Rebecca, between her sophomore and junior years in high school, had moved in with Stephen, who had already moved out.

Billingsley's wife eventually sued Marjorie for alienation of affections. David Arnold represented Marjorie at a couple of motions, but her liability insurer handled most of the case. Lorraine Billingsley received $50,000 in the settlement, which was paid by Marjorie's insurance company. It was one of the last alienation suits in Minnesota. Marjorie and Billingsley split up in March 1975. When Marjorie moved to a suburb of Denver that May, only Rebecca, Heather, and Rick went with her. Heather and Rebecca lived in a separate apartment in the same complex as her mother and brother. Rebecca had relocated to Colorado not to be with her mother, but to pursue her figure skating.

Problems soon arose between the girls and their mother. Suzanne heard from her sisters that Marjorie had taken out the telephone at the girls' apartment as part of her efforts to control them, which began to escalate. That summer Heather fell off her bike and cut her leg. Rebecca was going to take her sister to the hospital, but discovered her car keys and purse were missing. At the time, she noted that Rick started laughing about the missing items. Rebecca had to borrow a friend's van.

When she returned from the hospital, Rebecca went to her mother's apartment. She learned that Marjorie, for reasons unknown, had sent Rick to Heather's apartment to take Heather's purse and Rebecca's purse and car keys. Rebecca later told police that she and her mother started arguing, and the argument ended "with Marjorie sitting on top" of her on the floor, "shaking and choking" her. Rebecca knocked her mother off and called the police. But when they arrived, the officers only told Rebecca to behave. She immediately decided to return to Minnesota, and to bring Heather with her. Marjorie tried to convince the girls to stay. According to Rebecca, Rick, acting on orders from Marjorie, slashed the tires of her Firebird. The two girls left anyway, flying back to Minnesota. The Firebird, which was in both Rebecca and her mother's name, remained behind.

That fall, Rebecca moved into a Macalester College dormitory and Heather moved in with her brother Stephen. Even after Heather returned to Minnesota, she said her mother caused trouble in her life. In October 1975, Heather was picked up by the police in Stillwater, Minnesota, and placed in juvenile detention because Marjorie had reported her as a runaway—even though Heather was living with her brother in the Twin Cities. Dick recalled that Marjorie wanted Heather returned to Colorado, but not out of concern for her daughter's well-being. Marjorie was trying to buy a ranch and part of her argument to the trustees for funding was that she needed more space for her two children. Dick went to court and instead of Heather being sent back to Colorado, she returned to live with Stephen, who eventually became her legal guardian.

By the time he was a teenager, Stephen and a friend had come up with a succinct nickname for Marjorie: "The Major."

CHAPTER 7

Attorneys & Autopsies

A S DULUTH POLICE CORDONED OFF THE CRIME SCENE at Glensheen with yards of yellow tape, Assistant St. Louis County Attorney John DeSanto arrived early at his office. That Monday morning he began his routine weekly review of the manila case files stacked on his well-organized desk. At thirty-one, DeSanto was the chief criminal prosecutor, responsible for tracking trial and hearing assignments in the criminal division. DeSanto worked out of St. Louis County's main office in Duluth, though he occasionally traveled to the two branch offices in northeastern Minnesota's Mesabi Iron Range, known simply as "The Range" to locals. He was preparing to go to court on two cases. Nothing big—the justice process traditionally slowed in the summer months when judges and court personnel scheduled vacations. DeSanto's shock of brown hair—parted on the side and styled long over the ears—his neatly trimmed mustache, wide oval tortoise-framed glasses, and clean-shaven cheeks gave him a boyish appearance. To counter it in the courtroom, he wore conservatively cut dark suits with matching vests.

DeSanto's office was tucked away on the fifth floor of the county courthouse, a granite rectangle flanked by the federal courthouse and city hall. Prominent Chicago architect Daniel Burnham designed Duluth's civic center complex in the neoclassical tradition, a style popular in the early Twentieth century. The county courthouse, completed in 1909 at a cost of $1 million, incorporates such neoclassical features as stone lions, a series of high, arched windows on the ground floor, and Ionic stone columns with detailed scrollwork extending several floors high.

DeSanto's windows at the rear of the courthouse overlooked Second Street and the county jail. Appropriate enough, he thought, for a prosecutor. From his desk, he could almost make out half of the carved inscription in the granite above the jail's steel front entrance: "The great privilege is given to all to develop strength of character, to lead clean and honest lives, to render diligent and worthy service, to help others, and to be loyal citizens of the Republic and obedient to its laws."

As DeSanto intently read the case files, the telephone rang, startling him. His desk clock read 8:25 A.M. Although the courthouse doors opened at 8 A.M., arraignments, trials, or other official proceedings were not scheduled until 9 or 9:30. He didn't expect early calls. On the phone was a Duluth Police Department detective. DeSanto leaned forward, elbows braced on his desk, and waited. Detectives seldom made social calls. Two bodies had been found at Glensheen, the detective said. Heiress Elisabeth Congdon and her nurse had been murdered, one apparently suffocated and the other obviously bludgeoned. Police had no suspects in custody. DeSanto had never been to Glensheen before; that was about to change.

"June 27, 1977, is a date I'll always remember, like my birth date, my wedding anniversary, and the birth dates of my children and other loved ones," DeSanto said years later. That morning, as he hung up, he believed the murders were nothing more than a burglary gone bad. Probably a couple of Duluth's local crooks who'd been surprised and panicked.

DeSanto had prosecuted five homicides and boasted a one-hundred percent conviction rate. But those cases paled beside a double murder. And he knew this case wouldn't be tried in a vacuum. The Congdon name would attract statewide, even national media attention. Prosecuting a high-profile case could help make or break a legal career and, as head prosecutor, DeSanto counted on trying this one.

DeSanto had begun chasing his dream of becoming a lawyer during his high school years at Duluth Cathedral, a parochial school. A Duluth native, born twenty-one minutes behind his fraternal twin Will, DeSanto grew up in a conservative, religious household. His father, an Italian-Catholic, worked as an accountant for Chun King, the Chinese food manufacturer based in Duluth and owned until 1964 by the city's most famous businessman, Jeno Paulucci. DeSanto's Finnish-Lutheran mother, an insurance agent, stayed home to raise the boys.

In 1948, when the twins turned two, the DeSantos moved to a picture perfect white Colonial house in Lakeside, a middle class Duluth neighborhood on the city's east end, bordered to the west by Tischer Creek and Congdon Park and dotted with family-owned businesses. Life for the DeSanto twins centered around the neighborhood. They lived in its heart, just three blocks from St. Michael's Catholic Church where they attended Mass each Sunday and the boys went to grade school, a block from their barbershop, and a block from the movie theater. John and Will could be found at the Lakeside Theatre almost every Saturday, entranced by Francis the Talking Mule and the adventures of the crime-fighting Green Hornet. As young John lay in his bed at night, listening to the rumble of the trains from the Duluth, Missabe and Iron Range Railroad, he dreamed that one day he too would fight crime.

DeSanto's parents stressed the importance of a good education and even offered their son career advice. "My parents always suggested law, because I talk so much," said DeSanto. "And I liked what I saw on television." At first DeSanto wanted to be a criminal defense attorney. "Everything you read in books and see in the movies about criminal trials focuses on the flamboyant defense lawyer who's making lots of money and getting wrongly charged people off. I grew up watching Perry Mason."

After distinguishing himself as junior and senior class president at Cathedral, De-Santo attended the University of Minnesota Duluth and studied psychology and political science. He heeded his parents' career advice, anxiously determined to attend law school. But the draft delayed his plans two years. The Army assigned him to Frankfurt, Germany, as a clerk for the Third Armored Division—the same unit that Elvis Presley had served in. DeSanto received an early discharge in 1970 to attend summer school, and finally entered law school at the University of Minnesota that fall.

In the summer of 1972, before his final year of law school, DeSanto earnestly pursued his goal of becoming a defense attorney by applying to work in the St. Louis County public defender's office. At the last minute, the office turned him down, a decision that ultimately affected not only his life, but the lives of hundreds of criminals. Instead, he spent the summer clerking for the county attorney's office, going in with only the faintest idea of what being a prosecuting attorney entailed. By the end of the summer, he was hooked. After graduation, he applied only to county attorney offices and accepted a job in his hometown that fall. Soon he was prosecuting major felony cases—and winning.

When DeSanto joined the county attorney's office, relations between his office and Duluth police were strained and communication terse. DeSanto's boss, Keith Brownell—well-known for plea bargaining cases—frustrated investigating officers with his willingness to settle. During one of his first cases, a residential burglary, De-Santo met Duluth police officer Gary Waller, then assigned to the identification bureau, responsible for crime scene processing including fingerprints. Despite the tensions, Waller went out of his way to assist DeSanto with the prosecution. Investigators had found a fingerprint on the entry window, the only physical evidence found. As a new prosecutor, DeSanto knew little about fingerprint evidence or fingerprint expert testimony. So during trial preparation, when DeSanto told Waller the questions that he planned to ask Waller to establish him as a print expert, Waller told DeSanto he had a better idea. "John, with all due respect, I've been a latent print examiner for three years, and I've testified as an expert in several cases. Why don't I tell you the questions that you need to ask me?" Waller asked. Waller also graciously gave DeSanto a quick lesson in print development and analysis. DeSanto got his conviction and the two men became professional allies.

In October 1974, DeSanto and Waller teamed up again on John's first murder prosecution, the Ed Reilly case, a breakthrough for its use of bite mark evidence. A developmentally disabled woman in her fifties had been raped and strangled in her apartment. The victim, Mary Mahalich, had worked at Woodland Hills, a home for troubled youth in Duluth. Police discovered extensive bite marks the killer had made on her shoulders and breasts. Waller, one of the crime scene investigators, had the bite marks photographed to scale. He explained to DeSanto, the case prosecutor, that if someone was arrested, the photos could be used to try and match the suspect's teeth with the bite marks on the body. Bite marks, like fingerprints, are unique to individuals, a fact Waller had learned working in his father's dental lab, where his father made dentures from bite impressions dentists sent him. Waller and DeSanto used the bite mark evidence to match the suspected killer. The case marked the first time in Minnesota a prosecutor employed bite-mark evidence to help obtain a murder conviction. Waller's one-time passion for dentistry paid off in his detective work.

DeSanto and Waller became fast friends. They frequently enjoyed beers together after work and were racquetball partners at the YMCA. They also complemented one another's personalities. While Waller was a driven perfectionist, DeSanto was an easygoing procrastinator. Waller took a cynical approach to gauging others; DeSanto assumed the best about people. Ambitious professionals who put their jobs first, both made steady progress in their careers.

The county attorney's office appointed DeSanto chief prosecutor in April 1976, making him responsible for supervising six other attorneys. Now, one year later, at age thirty-one, he might have a chance to prosecute the biggest case of his career. He pushed aside the stack of case files and grabbed his car keys. Since office protocol called for the criminal prosecutors to attend all autopsies in the homicide cases, DeSanto assigned himself. He tried to attend murder autopsies whenever possible; as lead prosecutor, he wanted to see the brutality for himself. If he wanted to learn more about these murders, the autopsies made a good place to start.

That afternoon, while police continued to collect evidence at Glensheen, Waller and detective Bob Gracek drove to nearby St. Luke's Hospital to observe the autopsies. Inked fingerprints would need to be taken to compare with prints recovered at the scene, eliminating those that belonged from those that did not. In addition, Waller would usually assist the medical examiner with the collection of blood and hair samples for similar elimination purposes. If investigators were lucky, any unknown samples left after eliminating the known samples would eventually be matched to a suspect.

Police officers routinely attend autopsies in case any unusual evidence is discovered and in order to preserve the chain of custody for evidence obtained during the procedure. Maintaining a clear line of possession helps authenticate any evidence at trial, and officers who regularly attend autopsies learn to view the body as a major item of evidence. Their first autopsy often leaves officers sickened or numbed, and Waller was no exception. He had since learned to live with it. Seven years earlier he had observed the autopsy of a middle-aged man who'd blown his head off with a shotgun. The man had been drinking, and Waller would never forget the smell of blood and alcohol in the room. "You have to build up some insulation when you're dealing with death," says Waller. "The body isn't that person anymore; it's just the empty house in which the person once lived."

St. Luke's housed the county morgue in a discreetly marked room on the second floor. It had stark white walls, a walk-in cooler along one wall, and, in the center, a white porcelain table with a large, stainless steel sink built into its side. The chalkboard on the wall closest to the table listed autopsy protocol. As the officers walked into the cramped room, Waller noted that assistant St. Louis County attorneys Alan Mitchell, Rick Hansen, and John DeSanto all came to observe. Waller nodded to DeSanto, neither knowing they soon would team up again on the Congdon-Pietila case.

Velma Pietila's autopsy, conducted by assistant medical examiner Dr. Stanley Irving, began about 2:30 P.M. After cleaning away the blood and shaving her hair, he found a series of twenty-three wounds to the front and back of Pietila's head. The gashes were deep enough to have penetrated her skull, some of them down to the brain tissue.

The wounds to Pietila's face had been caused by downward blows from a heavy object—the brass candlestick, Dr. Irving determined. One of the blows had nearly cut her left ear in half. During the attack the killer and Pietila had apparently changed positions; the lacerations to the back of her head, caused by the edge of the base of the candlestick, had been inflicted with sideways and upwards blows. The attacker severely fractured Pietila's skull, particularly on the left side of her face, where it crushed her cheekbones. The force of the blows had split her skull into four quadrants and broke her jaw on both sides—the fracture started behind her left ear and extended across to the outside of her right ear. Dr. Irving told the officers that the broken jaw could have resulted from a blow from a hand or fist. Two of Pietila's teeth had broken off and Dr. Irving confirmed that teeth fragments police had recovered from the staircase matched the breaks. Dr. Irving determined that small puncture marks on her face, arms, and finger had been inflicted by exposed nails on the bottom of one of her shoes. His official cause of death: Velma Pietila died from a fractured skull and massive bleeding.

"Of all the pictures from the Congdon-Pietila homicide," DeSanto recalled, "the one that remains most firmly planted in my mind's eye is that of Velma Pietila's head, showing the deep lacerations, her hair cut away and head cleaned up. I could see the repeated blows and the kind of force used to kill her."

Despite the detailed examination of Pietila's body, everyone failed to note that the bloodied silver watch on her left wrist had stopped at 2:50. If noticed at the autopsy this could have been a clue to the time of the fatal struggle between Pietila and her killer. It would have been easy to assume the watch had stopped at 2:50 A.M. as it wound down after Pietila's death, or that it had been broken and stopped during the struggle. If it did stop early that morning, then the killer had enough time to get to the airport parking lot by 6:35 A.M., even if he didn't leave until 2:50 A.M. (or up to an hour after that—the killer still had to go to Elisabeth's room). But it wasn't until years later that a defense attorney preparing for trial noticed both that the watch was stopped at 2:50 and that a picture taken at the autopsy also showed the watch at 2:50. It seemed more likely that the watch had already stopped by the time the picture was taken than that the picture had been taken of a running watch at the very time at which the watch would eventually stop. However, since the autopsy began around 2:30 P.M. and there was no clear record of when the picture was taken, it was also possible that the watch could have stopped at 2:50 that afternoon and the picture was taken after that. Once entered into evidence, the watch could not be tampered with; this included simply winding it to see if it still worked. If it did work, how long it would have continued to run without winding was still unknown. The afternoon stop time remains a distinct possibility, a reasonable doubt about the significance of the time on the watch.

Chief Medical Examiner Dr. Volker Goldschmidt performed Elisabeth Congdon's autopsy. He had conducted more than three thousand such procedures during his lengthy career. He attended medical school in Germany, graduating from the University of Munich. When St. Louis County ended its 120-year-old coroner system in 1975, it appointed Goldschmidt its first medical examiner. Unlike coroners, who are not required to have medical training, medical examiners must be doctors trained in pathology and are responsible only for determining the cause of death. In his distinctive German accent, Goldschmidt tape-recorded every observation into the microphone hanging above the autopsy table.

With Dr. Goldschmidt, Waller, DeSanto, a police photographer, and a lab assistant present, the autopsy began at 4:25 P.M. Despite her partial paralysis, Elisabeth had obviously given her killer a fight. Bruises covering her upper body and her left arm (the arm she could still use after her stroke) indicated that she had struck out and, most significantly, the abrasion on her nose showed she had struggled beneath the satin pillow.

Goldschmidt studied the piece of skin that loosely clung to the tip of her nose. If she had been found without the pillow over her head or without her nose rubbed raw, the autopsy report might have listed the cause of death as congestive heart failure. Instead, the killer had left evidence of a struggle and clues that the heiress had suffocated.

There were small hemorrhages in Elisabeth Congdon's eyes and a bluish discoloration of her upper shoulders, neck, and face. Goldschmidt noted a streak of blood had escaped from her mouth and dried on her right cheek. Constriction marks on her left little finger and left wrist indicated her diamond-and-sapphire ring and gold watch had been removed after her death. He determined that the large bruise on her left forearm was fairly fresh, made within six hours of her death.

Although his examination revealed arteriosclerosis and other changes due to aging, Goldschmidt concluded that Elisabeth Congdon had died of heart failure resulting from "homicidal suffocation by a pillow." He estimated the time of death around 2 A.M., plus or minus an hour or two. When someone is suffocating, an interruption of the brain's oxygen supply causes unconsciousness after several minutes. Once unconscious, the person can live for four or five minutes. If the victim can catch a breath of air, she may live as long as eight minutes. Goldschmidt could not be certain how long Elisabeth fought to stay alive, but he could see how hard she had struggled. She had probably tried to grab onto the side bed railing or the support bar hanging overhead.

Elisabeth's personal physician, seventy-three-year-old Dr. Elizabeth Bagley, also attended the procedure. Personal physicians rarely attend their patients' autopsies, but Bagley, a longtime family friend, was more than Elisabeth's doctor. Bagley had cared for Elisabeth's mother Clara until her death, and Elisabeth had been her special patient since 1948. She had seen Elisabeth through a gall bladder operation, breast and stomach surgery, and a severe stroke. Now Bagley had to know what had happened to her friend. She also wondered how much damage the stroke had done. The autopsy revealed extensive brain damage, but as she later said "it is amazing the amount of the brain that can be destroyed and still function."

Dr. Bagley and Vera Dunbar had been appointed Elisabeth's co-conservators in 1974. The Congdon trustees and family wanted Elisabeth looked after more closely. Her memory lapses and partial paralysis left her vulnerable to manipulation. The appointment closely followed the marmalade incident and Elisabeth's cosigning several large bank loans that Marjorie defaulted on. As co-conservator, Bagley helped Dunbar manage Elisabeth's schedule and business affairs and screened her visitors and phone calls.

"She could be easily involved with groups that would be almost overwhelming at times," Bagley said. "She was always very kind to people and did not recognize her own [physical] limitations."

After the autopsies, Waller joined Inspector Grams and Detectives Greene and Yagoda at the Chinese Lantern restaurant in the historic Duluth Athletic Club building across the street from police headquarters. A wooden bridge at the entrance, painted gold dragons, and deep red-and-black decor marked one of law enforcement's regular watering holes.

Waller ordered a stinger—white créme de menthe and brandy—and tried to unwind. But he and the others were still pumped up after the first day of the investigation. They all looked forward to a shower and change of clothes, particularly Waller. He wanted to wash away the smell of death—the scent of blood had penetrated his clothes, skin, and hair.

He thought back to the uniform disarray in Elisabeth Congdon's bedroom. If the burglary had been staged, Waller wondered what the killer or killers had really been after. But the most significant piece of information he had learned on the first day of the investigation was Roger Caldwell's absence from Golden, Colorado, in the days leading up to and including the day of the murders.

Late that afternoon, DeSanto drove to Glensheen. He wanted to view the crime scene and try to picture what had happened. His presence and that of several other attorneys from his office was a strategic mistake—more feet contaminating the crime scene before police and state crime lab technicians could fully process it.

A lifelong Duluth resident, DeSanto had long been aware of Glensheen, but just as part of the scenery, one of a string of fine old homes he passed each day driving to and from the courthouse. Now as he pulled in front, Glensheen stood out, distinguished by yellow plastic police tape warning the press and curious bystanders to stay out.

As DeSanto entered Glensheen's main hall, he was struck by the mansion's enormity and extravagance. But the ornate woodwork and fancy furnishings—or even the Congdon name—didn't impress him as much as did the number of officers at work throughout the mansion and the sheer volume of physical evidence they photographed, processed, and collected. If assigned the case, DeSanto would have to explain this massive amount of evidence to a jury.

Uniformed officers guarded the crime scene and detectives cordoned off the area where the bodies were found with more yellow police tape. DeSanto walked up to the landing of the central staircase for a close-up look at where Pietila had been killed. Then he turned away from the police tape and went back down to the main hallway to take the back stairs all the way up to the second floor to Elisabeth's bedroom and the nurse's bathroom. The bedroom furnishings seemed plain and drab, which surprised DeSanto—he had imagined a woman of Elisabeth's means to live in high style. The modesty impressed him.

Out of curiosity, DeSanto wandered up to the third floor and poked around the attic. He perused a stack of yellowed newspapers dating back to when the Congdons built Glensheen in the early 1900s. DeSanto also noted that the large cedar-lined closets had lost none of their distinctive aroma through the years. Late that afternoon, after he finished inspecting the crime scene, DeSanto headed downtown to his favorite bar, Mr. Pete's, to meet up with other attorneys from his office.

"Prosecution of this homicide won't be easy," he thought as he downed his beer. The crime scene and victims' bodies produced more physical evidence than in any past case he'd handled—and already a lot more publicity. The victims were older women with no known enemies, one an invalid known for her philanthropy—a motive would be hard to determine.

As the table of attorneys sat debating the killer's or killers' motives, a muscular African-American man stopped by their table. "You'll never catch the person who did this," Bobby Daniels teased DeSanto. Daniels, an ex-boxer, maintained his fighting shape. One of the best athletes ever to come out of Duluth, he had recently had some legal trouble. But this was a good-natured jab.

"I bet you we'll have somebody behind bars in ten days," DeSanto replied, his tone serious and determined.

"How much you want to bet?" Daniels asked. They sealed the $10 bet with a firm handshake.

CHAPTER 8

Colorado Cowboys

MARJORIE CONGDON LEROY MET ROGER SIPE CALDWELL the winter after her move to Colorado. Her daughters had left and she and Rick had moved into a new townhouse development in a Denver suburb. After the move, Marjorie made an effort to get out and make new friends.

One night she attended a Parents Without Partners meeting and struck up a conversation with Roger. Blue-eyed with sandy brown hair and a pronounced widow's peak, Roger stood just a couple inches under six feet tall. When he offered to take her out for coffee after the meeting, she agreed. After coffee, they stopped by his place. Marjorie didn't go home that night—or for the next couple of nights. The couple was inseparable. When three days had passed, Marjorie decided to move in with her new boyfriend.

Roger knew that Marjorie had relatives in Minnesota, but had no idea the Congdons were one of the state's wealthiest families. That much he would eventually learn. But he would never really know the extent of his girlfriend's debt.

Strangers usually found the soft-spoken Roger friendly and easy to approach, according to his ex-wife Martha. However, his former employers soon came to know him as a "passive dreamer" and a man with "delusions of grandeur." He also drank heavily at times, one reason behind his separation and divorce from Martha.

Roger grew up in Latrobe, Pennsylvania, a small town about forty miles east of Pittsburgh. Latrobe sits at the base of the Allegheny Mountains, one thousand feet above sea level, surrounded by fertile, sloping farmlands and wooded hills. Home to Rolling Rock beer, golf pro Arnold Palmer, and public television's Fred "Mr. Rogers" Rogers, Latrobe also bills itself as the birthplace of professional football and the banana split—and a good place to raise a family.

Roger's father, Howard, worked in the local steel mill while his mother, Cecile, stayed home to raise their four boys. Cecile named her third son Rogers, after the hero in one of the romance novels she read during her pregnancy. Rogers hated the name, and eventually dropped the "s."

In high school, Roger belonged to the chemistry club and excelled at athletics. He ran track and played halfback for the Latrobe Wildcats football team. After graduation,

Roger attended college in his hometown for a year and worked for Kenna Metal. That winter, Roger and Martha—his high school sweetheart—eloped, marrying on January 9, 1954, in Cumberland, Maryland.

From Latrobe they moved to Springfield, Ohio, where Roger enrolled in Wittenberg, a Lutheran college. He studied to become a Lutheran minister and worked part-time as a campus custodian. He and his wife also started their family. They had three children, Christi, Caren, and Scott, during their twenty-year marriage.

Roger abandoned his religious studies after a year and began to work a variety of jobs for a succession of companies in Ohio, California, and Colorado. From 1957 to 1972, Roger was employed by no less than eleven companies in jobs which included bread deliveryman, machine repairman, grocery store clerk, construction company buyer, production controller for an instrument company, and purchasing agent for an orthodontics firm.

While living in California in 1961, the couple separated over Roger's drinking, which had surfaced several years into the marriage. During the separation he responded to a newspaper advertisement for Alcoholics Anonymous and joined the program. According to his ex-wife, they attended a number of meetings together. After Roger stopped drinking, Martha felt they'd been given a second chance. When he landed a sales job in Denver, the reunited family moved to Colorado in July 1967. Sometime during those next few years, however, his drinking resumed.

When Roger got drunk, he could also get mean. He became verbally abusive; the couple had ugly arguments that upset Martha. In July 1974, while Roger worked as a buyer for Gallagher Steel in Denver, they divorced. Martha Caldwell later said simply, they "were not getting along."

Roger and Martha both remained in the Denver area. Martha talked to her ex-husband, however, only when he came to visit their children. The divorce settlement made Roger responsible for child support, but his support payments soon ended. He had lost his job.

Though short on cash, forty-two-year-old Roger had other attributes, including a wry smile that matched his sense of humor. He confided in Marjorie that he'd had a drinking problem, but now attended Alcoholics Anonymous meetings. Marjorie felt she'd found a kindred soul in Roger. They were both black sheep estranged from their families.

After dating for two months, the couple was engaged on St. Patrick's Day, 1976. They married in a private religious ceremony on March 20 at United Methodist Church in Littleton, Colorado. Marjorie's closest friends, Barb Lyons and Ruth McDermott, acted as her personal attendants and witnesses. Marjorie and Ruth had met through Ruth's son Patrick, who had a paper route in the apartment complex where Marjorie and Rick lived after moving to Colorado. Lyons had gotten to know Marjorie through McDermott. A small wedding reception was held at the Brown Palace, a popular Denver hotel, where Marjorie, Roger, and their friends ran up an $800 tab. Elisabeth did not attend her oldest daughter's second marriage.

After their marriage, friends said that Roger adopted Marjorie's ambitions and passions and tried to overlook her excesses. But like Dick LeRoy, Roger quickly became the buffer between her, the Congdon trustees, and her family. Within the first month after the marriage, McDermott recalled, Roger phoned and said they'd had a big fight over $7,000 in bad checks Marjorie had written. He told friends that he was making an effort to hold Marjorie's spending "in check." On another occasion, he called and told McDermott, "You girls go out to lunch a lot," insinuating Marjorie always picked up the tab for her friends. McDermott explained she and Lyons paid for their own meals, but Marjorie charged her lunches on a Bank Americard. During their conversation, Roger discovered his credit cards missing from his wallet and hung up in a rage. Despite these problems, Marjorie's friends believed Roger genuinely cared about her. Once he called McDermott from his office and confided that Marjorie had threatened to commit suicide and would not answer his calls at home. At Roger's request, McDermott went to visit Marjorie, who said Roger was the one with the problem, not her.

Less independent than Dick, Roger was not the type of man to shape his own future. Although Roger, a friend recalled, "couldn't ride to save his life" and failed to show up for riding lessons he signed up for at a local ranch, he decided to live the part of the Western rancher. Back in Pennsylvania, he wore conservative, bland clothing. Now in Colorado, he exchanged his sports coats and trousers for western garb: cowboy boots, string ties, Western shirts, denim jackets, and blue jeans. He became known as a flashy dresser and started collecting silver and turquoise jewelry and accessories. The bigger and gaudier the pieces, the better. The owner of one ranch where the Caldwells boarded their horses recalled, "Roger had on enough turquoise to choke a horse." At the National Western Horse Show at the Denver Coliseum in January 1977, Roger bought nearly $4,000 worth of silver and turquoise jewelry.

The drinking problems that plagued Roger's first marriage would resurface in his second. When Lyons had first met Roger, he seemed quiet and reserved, but pleasant. Marjorie had announced that Roger didn't drink because he had a problem and was a member of Alcoholics Anonymous. However, the first time McDermott met Roger over dinner at her home, she offered him a drink at Marjorie's insistence. "I want to test his willpower," Marjorie explained. He refused that night. When he did drink, McDermott recalled he sometimes lost his temper and became verbally abusive. The last time she saw Roger, in the summer of 1976, he showed up at her home drunk and upset.

He told McDermott and her husband that Marjorie had invited his boss, the owner of a local manufacturing company, to dinner. During dinner, Marjorie planned to offer his boss a $150,000 check to make Roger an equal partner in the business. But Roger knew Marjorie didn't have the money, and he wouldn't be able to cover the amount himself.

The more he talked with the couple, the more agitated and belligerent Roger became. "Fuck you. Come here you cocksucker and listen to me," he yelled at McDermott, who called Marjorie to warn her of her husband's condition. Marjorie sent Rick over to pick Roger up, but Roger shouted at the boy to go away. The McDermotts then offered Roger a ride, but he refused and drove his own car. Later, McDermott learned Marjorie had left the house shortly before Roger arrived home.

Marjorie told McDermott a story she found hard to believe. She said Roger, intensely angry when he got home, beat their cat against the side of the house until it died. She claimed to have found the dead cat in the trash compactor the next day.

But her closest friends heard Marjorie lie so convincingly they'd swear she almost believed it herself. Lyons recalled an incident involving the Caldwells' insurance company. Marjorie claimed a nonexistent motorcycle belonging to Rick had been stolen. She tried to get Lyons to back up her report to the insurance company. "Remember the motorcycle Ricky had a couple weeks ago?" Marjorie prompted. No, Lyons replied. She had never seen a motorcycle.

Financial problems aside, the Caldwells bought their dream ranch. In September 1976, they signed a contract for a 227-acre ranch valued at $290,000 near Denver in Bailey, Colorado. They named their ranch Pine Valley Farms, and moved into their new home just before Thanksgiving.

Almost immediately after moving in, the Caldwells reported a burglary at their ranch. Marjorie claimed a loss of $80,000. The Colorado Bureau of Investigation assigned Agent Bob Harmon to look into the burglary. According to Harmon's investigation, Marjorie first reported that $700 in ski boots and a television set had been stolen. She then told authorities the stolen items included jewelry, a priceless collection of bone porcelain, and heirloom silver handed down from her grandparents. Harmon's suspicions were further aroused when he learned Roger was seen ten days after the break-in wearing Navajo jewelry reported stolen.

The insurance company agreed to settle for $74,529.60 because Marjorie came from "a fine family in Minnesota"—an old refrain—and Park County authorities, who first investigated the case, never filed charges. Park County officials later explained to Harmon and Duluth police that they had lacked funds to prosecute the case.

When notified of the settlement, the Caldwells made plans to spend the money, despite a long list of creditors. Marjorie took the settlement notification to the First Bank of Evergreen and negotiated a $35,000 loan. She also obtained a $15,000 loan from Citicorp Person to Person and made a down payment on a $300,000 tract of land adjacent to Pine Valley Farms.

Marjorie, always skilled at shifting money, then managed to talk an employee at Aetna into quickly issuing the settlement checks in spite of the CBI investigations of the bad checks and the alleged burglary, but the insurance company still hedged its bets. It issued two checks, both requiring bank endorsements in addition to Marjorie's signature, one naming the First Bank of Evergreen as co-payee, the other Citicorp. Marjorie got a Citicorp clerk's endorsement, but Evergreen would not endorse the other check because of the investigations. So Roger forged the endorsement of a nonexistent Evergreen employee and the Caldwells deposited the Evergreen check into a new account at the Colorado National Bank. The bank gave the Caldwells twenty counter checks, which they immediately used—and bounced. Colorado National had never actually opened the account, but instead had returned the check to Aetna as improperly endorsed.

Judy McCoy and her husband, who raised Arabian stallions used for jumping and hunting, had wanted to befriend the Caldwells, as did a number of horse people in the Denver area, for two simple reasons. First, the Caldwells presented themselves as a wealthy couple intent on buying purebred horses. Second, the Caldwells seemed interested in the training and breeding of hunter jumper horses. The McCoys believed the friendship, at least at the start, was a perfect fit.

Marjorie told McCoy that Elisabeth Congdon, heir to the Bethlehem Steel fortune, had adopted her. But Elisabeth's father Chester had nothing to do with the Pennsylvania steel giant. Marjorie also said she had an adopted sister in Arizona who was married to a Johnson Wax heir, who did not need or deserve any of the Congdon money. She claimed that her family did not allow her "to see or talk" to Elisabeth; they considered her the "black sheep of the Congdon family" and wanted nothing to do with her.

McCoy began to see some of the real reasons the Congdon family had to distance themselves from Marjorie. In December 1976, while the two women vacationed together, Marjorie surprised McCoy by asking her if she knew any syndicate people in the Denver area. She told McCoy that she wanted to put a murder contract out on her trust officer in Minneapolis. As Marjorie explained the situation to McCoy, Thomas Welch had control of her finances and he held the reins tightly—too tightly. Marjorie said she had organized crime connections in Chicago, but she wanted a contact further away from Minnesota. If she could wipe Welch out of her life, Marjorie said, then she "would no longer have any financial problems." As McCoy listened to her, she thought about how much Marjorie liked to talk tough and impress people with the supposed magnitude of her wealth and power. McCoy then realized that Marjorie could just as likely be dead serious—and that scared her.

Roger had his scary moments as well. In January 1977, Roger and Marjorie left a party at which Roger had gotten drunk. Although Marjorie didn't want him to drive, he insisted and wrested away the car keys. On the drive home the two argued loudly and the car began to weave down the road. Rick, driving behind them, saw the fight in progress and sped ahead to block his stepfather's car and force it to stop. The two quarreled frequently, particularly over the way Roger treated Marjorie when drunk. When Roger stopped, Marjorie grabbed the car keys and jumped out. "I'm going to get you," Roger yelled at Rick. Roger pulled a twelve-inch tire chain from the back seat and began hitting his stepson. Rick punched Roger, then ran with his mother to his own car while Roger got in his car and fled. A passing patrol officer arrested Roger for assault and driving while intoxicated. After Roger agreed to go through chemical dependency treatment, Marjorie had the charges dismissed.

While Roger was in a local hospital drying out, Marjorie told her friends that he had been admitted for stomach surgery. During this time period Marjorie confided to her friend Judy McCoy that if Roger "didn't straighten out his drinking problem," she was going to "dump him."

In February 1977, Roger and Marjorie spent ten days at the exclusive Broadmoor Hotel in Colorado Springs. Their bill, which included many purchases from the complex's shops, came to $5,275.39. They paid with a $6,000 Colorado National Bank check from the account the bank had never opened. They received $300 cash back and used the $424.61 difference as a down payment for a reservation in March. They had planned to celebrate their first wedding anniversary, March 20, 1977, in a penthouse suite that cost from $350 to $400 a day.

The couple repeatedly fell behind on car payments. On February 15, the Caldwells defaulted on their $21,620 bank loan for three Jeep vehicles. Ten days later they paid their February/March installments with a bad check. In early March, Roger presented Golden State Bank vice president John Hannigan $1,944 in cash toward the loan. "You're my first stop today before I pay off all the other bad checks," he told Hannigan.

The Caldwells also fell thousands of dollars behind in their horse boarding and training bills. They boarded most of their show horses at Table Mountain Ranch, a local country club. At one time, they paid general manager Larry Souza $3,000 a month to feed and board their horses—not including training expenses.

Roger had paid off the overdue bills for the horses in February. He gave Souza $3,000 cash. "From now on, I'm going to handle all finances," Caldwell told Souza. But Souza knew that Marjorie would continue to do as she pleased, and the Caldwells were soon delinquent again. Souza sent a letter that threatened to sell their horses to recoup the debt. On March 10, 1977, Roger came in and again paid off the balance. But the late payments continued, Souza recalled, through that spring and summer.

That March, other creditors closed in. The local sheriff's department ordered the Caldwells' furniture and vehicles seized. The telephone company disconnected their phone service after it reported to the sheriff that the Caldwells had sizable unpaid long distance bills. The Colorado Bureau of Investigation had targeted Roger and Marjorie in a fraud investigation for the dozens of bad checks they had written in December 1976 and January 1977 and found that the Caldwells had used checkbooks from five different closed bank accounts. The couple was months late on the $45,000 first payment for their Bailey, Colorado, ranch. Foreclosure was only a matter of time and paperwork.

With the few possessions they owned outright, the couple and Rick moved into the Holland House Hotel in Golden. The Caldwells' money troubles continued.

Though management and other residents depicted the couple as friendly, one tenant added, "They had a hard time paying their bills." Desk clerk Bertha Huskins recalled, "They told me so many cock-and-bull stories for so many months, it was hard to believe anything they said."

Marjorie's reckless spending, her indiscriminate use of the Congdon name to extend credit limits, and the couple's large debt attracted more than her family's attention.

In a series of confidential memos on the status of the Caldwells' finances, Marjorie's cousin Tom Congdon voiced his concern to the other trustees. One three-page memo, dated March 8, 1977, contained the following excerpts:

> The pace of Marj's activities has quickened. I have been contacted by the Colorado National Bank, the Colorado Bureau of Investigation, and the Park County Sheriff's Department. Marjorie will very soon face the consequences for her behavior. We must make sure we agree as to any action...or non-action...we might take. We also must look fairly far into the future. The Colorado National Bank called me one week ago today. I had recently repeated my warning of eighteen months ago to the major bank holding companies of this area, with the added news of Marj's remarriage and new name....
>
> Late yesterday the Colorado Bureau of Investigation asked to call on me as quickly as possible. ...I met this morning with Mr. Bob Harmon of the CBI and Mr. Dave Olmstead of the Park County Sheriff's Department.... At the outset of our meeting their general attitude was: couldn't I and other members of the Congdon Family take action to pay off Marj's growing Colorado debts and then persuade her to behave herself. My general response was: this is an old story and little truth lies behind Marj's representations; furthermore, little purpose seems to be served by paying off Marj's problems, and allowing her to proceed to the next chapter....

In March 1977, the Park County Sheriff's Department interviewed McCoy as part of an investigation of the Caldwells for possible insurance fraud in connection with several home burglaries. McCoy told investigators that after the first Caldwell burglary in November 1976, she had seen items the Caldwells had listed as missing. McCoy also said that several weeks after the February 1977 burglary she saw Roger wearing two silver-and-turquoise bracelets and two matching rings that had been reported as stolen.

Barb Lyons told investigators about an incident involving trust officer Thomas Welch. After Marjorie came to Colorado she had repeatedly contacted him for funds. Within months of the move Marjorie called Welch and asked for $150,000 to buy a house she claimed had been specially built for a asthmatics like Rick. Welch denied his client's latest request. She told McDermott that she was going to tell Rick that they couldn't get the house because of Welch. In front of her two friends Marjorie said, "That bastard Welch won't pay for the house. I'm going to take care of him." Then she used the phone to supposedly instruct someone in Chicago, "Hi, this is Marjorie LeRoy. I need someone taken care of," as if she were hiring a hit man. Lyons and McDermott said nothing, but chalked it up as another Marjorie stunt, dismissing it much like Roger's occasional drunken outbursts—he could be quite nice while sober and Marjorie could be a good friend when not concocting one of her stories.

Another incident involving Welch occurred after Rick had been admitted to the National Asthma Center for treatment. McDermott recalled that Marjorie "blamed Welch for Rick LeRoy being in the hospital" and when Marjorie spoke of Welch "her voice became louder and squeakier." McDermott also remembered that Marjorie would "continually feed her son" accusations about Welch being responsible for not providing them trust money or for not having Rick's dogs sent from Minnesota. "Marjorie Caldwell was capable of working people up emotionally and knew what she was doing while doing so," McDermott told Duluth police.

Welch recalled receiving a phone call from Marjorie. She screamed at him and delivered a warning: "My son is very upset with you! We don't know where he is. And we think he might be on his way out there to try and hurt you." Welch didn't know whether Marjorie was lying, but he didn't want to risk his family's safety. He immediately contacted the local police.

That evening, Marjorie appeared at McDermott's house and told her that Rick had disappeared from the center. Marjorie said that her son had last been seen fleeing into traffic with "tears streaming down his cheeks," and that he had left behind a note. McDermott said the note was addressed "To Whoever Gives A Damn," and was written in a childish scribble with misspelled words. The note that Rick had supposedly written made reference to how no one cared about him and that he was going to get Tom Welch. Curiously, Marjorie told McDermott she was too upset to stay at home and planned instead to go to the Marriott Inn, then gave McDermott the room number. When McDermott called she reached Marjorie only after asking for Elisabeth Congdon's room.

Three or four days later, Marjorie called McDermott from the Marriott to report that Rick was with her. Eventually, McDermott learned from Marjorie that Rick had been out at all-night movies and, although Marjorie claimed to be broke, she had given her son money before he disappeared.

Even as their ever-present money troubles continued, Marjorie and Roger talked about buying a large ranch and starting a horse training and breeding business. They had already purchased expensive show horses for thousands of dollars. But to make their dreams a reality, the Caldwells needed more money— lots of it. Roger collected just $97 a week in unemployment. Marjorie also received $150 per month from an insurance company annuity her mother had bought years before. But Marjorie had dipped into her family trust funds for years and the well had nearly run dry. Most of the trust fund distributions went to creditors.

However, Marjorie would inherit a considerable fortune upon her mother's death. Her share of the various Congdon family trust funds would more than erase her debts, with money left over for her dream ranch. She and her sister, Jennifer, would inherit the second largest single shares of a family fortune worth at least $50 million.

The trust under the will of her grandfather, Chester A. Congdon, entitled Marjorie to a one-twelfth share of $31.4 million—about $2.5 million. Marjorie's share of the Congdon trust, with a $14 million principal, amounted to $60,000 annually for twenty-one years and approximately $1.2 million after twenty-one years. From the Elisabeth Mannering Congdon living trust, worth about $3.7 million, Marjorie's share was forty percent or approximately $1.5 million. (This amount would have to be adjusted for the many advance payments trustees had made to her.) Finally, from the conservatorship account of her mother, with $250,000 assets, she would be awarded around $100,000. All totaled, she stood to gain roughly $8.2 million upon her mother's death.

On April 1, 1977, Roger went to Duluth on Marjorie's behalf, along with David Arnold, to attend the annual accounting of the Congdon family trusts. The trustees and some of the Congdon relatives met Roger for the first time. The amount of turquoise jewelry he wore led one family member to describe him as a "rhinestone cowboy." Nevertheless, Arnold liked the soft-spoken Roger, and the two men were friends from that day on. That same day in Colorado, Marjorie went into Golden State Bank and told banker John Hannigan her purse had been stolen. "Roger is out of town and Rick and I have no money. Could you give me a $200 cash advance?" she pleaded.

He gave Marjorie the money. But several weeks later, when Hannigan saw Roger, he reminded him about repaying the $200. "What $200?" Roger asked. After hearing about the loan, Roger told Harmon, "That bitch. I run around trying to put out all her fires."

On May 24, at Marjorie's insistence, Roger flew to Minnesota and met his mother-in-law Elisabeth for the first time the following day at Glensheen. He had flown to Duluth to ask Congdon trustees for a $750,000 loan to fund the Caldwell's horse breeding business. He'd brought along a letter, supposedly from Rick's doctor at the National Asthma Center. The letter said the boy suffered from severe asthma and cystic fibrosis. His critical condition required him to live in a ranch-type environment, with lots of open space and clean air. The trustees turned Roger down. They soon learned the Caldwells had forged the letter on old stationery taken from the National Asthma Center. Rick did not have cystic fibrosis, and the Center had diagnosed his asthma as moderate, not life threatening. Roger had typed while Marjorie dictated every word.

The Caldwell's fraudulent activity and escalating debts weren't lost on Congdon trustees and family members. In a confidential memo marked "Marjorie Congdon Le-Roy Caldwell Chapter VI," Tom Congdon informed trustees in early June of Roger's confession that he and Marjorie had cashed bad checks and falsified the Aetna insurance check endorsement. The letter continued:

> It seems when the two of them thought they had successfully deposited the account at the Colorado National Bank, they decided to celebrate instead of paying creditors, so they dashed off to this luxury hotel where Caldwell acknowledges they spent $6,000 in ten days. I imagine he drank his share and she bought out most of the gift shops. My mind ran immediately to the grinning image of Robert Redford in The Sting.... Seemingly, he and

Marge enjoyed spreading a little confusion and try[ing] to mitigate the severity of their criminal acts....

This story gets crazier by the moment, but I believe it is reaching a climax. I am in agreement with all of you that no useful purpose is served by permitting Marjorie to take further advantage of her mother and charge these new debts. Such an action by us would simply lead to more of the same. Further, in my position as trustee of Aunt Elisabeth's assets held in the custody account, I am not about to invest in a horse breeding farm as suggested by Jordan Hockstadt [an attorney who represented the Caldwells for a time] and Roger Caldwell. In fact, I told the latter I doubt that any trustee under the sun, including those in Lexington, Kentucky, would do such a thing. However, I do feel it is appropriate that Aunt Elisabeth would wish us to provide [Marjorie] with appropriate legal counsel as she stands at the bar of justice.

In mid-June, Golden State Bank had repossessed the Caldwells' three Jeeps. By special arrangement, Rick could drive one Jeep to and from his summer job, but the Jeep had to be returned to the bank parking lot each evening. The couple still owed $20,305.

Money was so tight that Marjorie turned one final time to cousin Tom Congdon for help. Unable to pay the $20-a-day per room hotel tabs and behind $400, the Caldwells faced eviction. Marjorie pleaded with her cousin; they had nowhere to go. On June 20, 1977, Tom forked out ten days' rent for their two adjoining rooms.

On June 22, 1977, five days before Elisabeth Congdon and Velma Pietila were murdered, the Caldwells' checking account ran dry. On the same day the owner of the Shamrock gas station in Golden confiscated a Carte Blanche credit card from Rick LeRoy—a phony. An unsolicited application for a Carte Blanche card had been sent to "M. Congdon" at a Littleton, Colorado, address back in 1976. When the application was returned to Carte Blanche in July 1976, the name had been changed to E.M. Congdon. The company canceled the card on March 31, 1977, for nonpayment of charges. Roger, present with Rick at the gas station, told the owner, "This is going to cause me some trouble."

In eight years, Marjorie had spent $3 million—and she had little to show for it.

CHAPTER 9

Façades & Farewells

WHEN WALLER AND OTHER INVESTIGATORS returned to Glensheen at 7 A.M. Tuesday, June 28, only the bodies and scattered items on the staircase had been removed. Large, brown leather briefcases containing crime scene kits were spread wide open as investigators readied measuring tape, sketch pads, fingerprint brushes, dusting powder, and lift tape for another day of collecting evidence.

The blood spatters had darkened on the landing and central staircase, and the blood-soaked carpeting had hardened. The pungent, metallic odor of blood permeated the air. The murder weapon—the brass candlestick—still stood upright on the landing in the same spot the killer had left it.

Investigators stretched a rope from the bannister to the wall on the landing to protect the area where Pietila's body was found and used heavy masking tape to barricade entryways to rooms in which they still had to collect evidence. Two uniformed officers continued an around-the-clock watch to keep the crime scene secure. Outside the mansion another officer stood guard at the front gate to warn passersby to stay on the sidewalk.

On this second day of the murder investigation, Waller and officers Cox and Gracek faced more tedious evidence gathering. But they began by reshooting a number of photographs of Elisabeth's room, the nurse's room, and the hallway. For the first and only time in Waller's experience, a new technician at the sheriff's department photo lab had burned holes in the negatives taken the previous day. Waller thought the burn marks resembled a cloud of bats flying around, a bad Rorschach test. Officers wouldn't reshoot some photos until several months after the murders had occurred, creating easy openings for defense lawyers.

By midmorning, the officers had resumed documenting and collecting evidence on Glensheen's second floor. They started by dusting Elisabeth's bedroom for fingerprints. The bed had been stripped bare the previous day, but the empty jewelry cases remained strewn on the floor.

On Monday, officers had collected several strands of hair from Velma's hands. Hair evidence was being sent to the state crime lab for microscopic comparisons with the victims' hair samples. The lab had found additional hairs: one from the stretcher sheet used to wrap Velma's body and two from the Oriental runner on the landing below her body. Investigators also searched for additional hair samples, although technology in the 1970s did not allow authorities to match hairs with the same certainty as fingerprints and blood evidence.

That morning at headquarters, Detective Sergeant Jack Greene had telephoned Tom Congdon in Denver to ask about his conversation with the Caldwells on Monday night. Greene wanted to get any details he could before Congdon left town for his aunt's funeral. Greene taped the call.

"Now I've hired, I think you're aware, some local people," Congdon told Greene, "because, frankly, I was concerned that there was just two of you in Duluth on it and I felt that there is a lot of, in a sense, dirt in the streets here in Denver. Because I've been finding out so much about these people [Marjorie and Roger] all this winter, you know, and I'm of the view that, frankly, sometimes information can be bought, so I gave some money to a group called Colorado Private Investigators and a guy named William Furman, and I told him to go out in the street and use the funds in a sense to see what he could find out…I wanted some family security out here, because my suspicion has been whether it is a murder for hire, that [the killer] was probably hired here."

"O.K. Will this Furman communicate with you if you're up here when he gets the information?" Green asked.

"Oh, yes, yes."

"Very good. Great."

"He has a detective, I believe off-duty…who thought he could get into the Radisson last night but you have a Baptist convention there and he had to sleep in his car."

"There's a Denver detective up there now?" Green asked.

"Yes," said Congdon.

"Is he surveilling these people?"

"Yes."

"O.K. Great. We were talking about this with Mr. Van Evera yesterday, we wanted to know—"

"—Now listen. I was trying to reach [Colorado Bureau of Investigation Agent Robert] Harmon this morning, and I will a little later, but my concern has been there's an awful lot of circumstantial evidence pointing toward these people and I can keep my mouth shut if people want me to and I think I am now in a position that I've seen enough evidence pointing to them, I think I had better not talk to my family about them or they are going to lynch them."

"That's right."

"But I mean, you know, they are madder than hell always at Marjorie and they think [Roger] had a direct hand in it…. And if you want, I can give you how this Furman can be reached if you want…. And I say he is doing some things that I don't think sometimes you guys are allowed to do," referring to electronic eavesdropping and purchasing information.

To keep the conversation moving, Greene said something that defense attorneys would later use in an attempt to discredit Duluth police. "I'm sure and we won't even talk about those," Greene said, seeming to condone illegal tactics. In fact, Greene, aware Congdon had to catch his flight to Minnesota soon, didn't want to waste more time talking about Furman.

Around 5:15 that afternoon, attorney David Arnold and accountant Robert Vathing met the Caldwells at the Minneapolis-St. Paul International Airport and immediately noticed Roger's face had been injured. Arnold hadn't seen Roger since their trip to Duluth in May when the Congdon trustees denied Roger's request for $750,000. Arnold and Vathing stared at Roger's cut lip and the dried blood on his forehead. Marjorie grabbed her husband's right hand and held it out so the two men could see the swelling. "Did you see this?" she asked loudly. "He was kicked by a horse." She explained he'd been cleaning a stall and the horse had become agitated. Roger said nothing.

Four years earlier, Marjorie had selected Arnold as her personal lawyer and co-conservator of her financial fortune. A tall, solidly built man with a rounded face and pleasant smile, he put Marjorie at ease, and she trusted his advice. But Arnold quickly realized his new client was surprisingly cavalier about her wealth.

Marjorie had visited Arnold's office one night after the conservatorship had been established and asked if Arnold wasn't supposed to take possession of her valuables. When Arnold told her yes, she said, "I brought in my jewelry," and dumped it on the desk. She then proceeded to play a lengthy game Arnold described as "which one do you think is the most expensive?" After Marjorie left, he realized he had no safe place in his office in which to keep the jewelry. He hastily wrapped the jewelry in a handkerchief, stuffed the bundle into his pocket, and took it home. There he pinned $300,000 worth of jewelry onto one of his wife's sweatshirts—the most unlikely place Arnold thought a thief would look—so he could closely guard it throughout the night.

Marjorie baffled Arnold most by the vast amount of money she could spend on absolutely unnecessary items. The situation was made worse by vendors who, familiar with her spending habits, increased their prices when Marjorie was buying. According to Arnold, they had three prices—wholesale, retail, and Marjorie.

Marjorie's impulse buying and unexpected generosity never failed to surprise her family and friends, including her lawyers. Arnold recalled taking a walk with Marjorie in downtown Minneapolis. They had just passed a Lincoln Town Car when Marjorie asked, "Would you like to own one of those?"

"I prefer a sports car," Arnold replied.

"Okay, well, let's go buy you one," Marjorie said. Arnold described his client as "very personable, very generous with her time and energy." The problem was "she'd go off on a tangent and want to buy this horse or that jewelry and yet, if you were able to get her through one day to the next day, she'd say, 'You know, I really don't have time to ride another horse or I really don't need that jewelry.'"

Arnold and Marjorie got along well, perhaps in part because both were adopted. Marjorie confided how she had been teased as a child; Arnold reciprocated by sharing with Marjorie his retort to childhood taunts: "At least I know my parents wanted me." Marjorie considered Arnold not only her attorney, but also a friend and, in that capacity, he saw a softer side. Marjorie was unpretentious, extremely chatty yet capable of being a good listener, and possessed a good sense of humor, he recalled. Marjorie arrived early for her appointments with Arnold and liked to chat with other waiting clients.

"In all of the time I was with Marge," Arnold recalled, "I remember only a couple of occasions when she...led someone to believe that she had or came from money.... She preferred to talk to and talk about, for example, the people who ran the knitting shop where she worked or somebody who she just met at the grocery store or my office."

Marjorie loved to tell stories, often embellishing them for dramatic effect. "Marjorie would say to me, 'You know it's a lie and I know it's a lie, so what does it matter?'" Arnold recalled. "I also saw a Marjorie who could twist things and tell a story so many times that even she believed it." He further described Marjorie as someone who needed to feel in control, "much like a chess player. You never know what her next move is, and you never know if she is directing your moves and leading you on."

In a strange coincidence, he also had something in common with his client's husband. Arnold's birth name was Harley Eugene Caldwell. When Roger eventually learned about this he joked about Arnold being his long lost brother.

Marjorie, Roger, and Rick had arrived at the Minneapolis-St. Paul International Airport shortly before 5 P.M. Their plane had been ahead of schedule, and after explaining to airport officials that they wanted privacy to avoid the press and make some phone calls, they were allowed to wait in the airport police security room for Arnold and Vathing. Arnold scheduled an evening flight to Duluth instead of the original plan of driving up from the Twin Cities. Marjorie demanded Vathing also accompany them for an impromptu audit of the Congdon trust funds. But Arnold and Vathing advised Marjorie that an audit so soon after her mother's death was in bad taste. Finally Marjorie backed down, allowing Vathing to remain in Minneapolis, but insisted that Vathing review the books as soon as possible. The trustees were conspiring to cheat her on her inheritance, she told him.

Meanwhile, up in Duluth, local reaction the day after the murders included an announcement by the NorShor Theatre. Starting July 8, the theater would begin a return engagement of *You'll Like My Mother*, the 1973 murder mystery Elisabeth had uncharacteristically allowed to be filmed at Glensheen. The *Duluth News-Tribune* said the theater deserved an award for bad taste, and four people wrote or phoned the NorShor to say that they felt the rerelease exploited the victims.

Clara Spencer waited with her husband, Stephen, on the mezzanine of the Duluth airport to greet her cousin Marjorie, scheduled to arrive on the 7:15 P.M. flight. Nearly all the passengers had deplaned when Spencer finally spotted Marjorie, Roger, Rick, and Arnold.

"Clara, what are you doing here?" Marjorie asked, looking surprised.

"I couldn't bear to have you come here on such an occasion and not have someone here to meet you," Spencer replied. She felt sorry for Marjorie and her money problems.

But what most concerned Spencer was the thought of ugly scenes and family bickering at Elisabeth's funeral. Many family members wanted to avoid another confrontation like the one at the Congdon reunion two years before between Marjorie and Velma Pietila. There had also been Marjorie's blowup at Tom Congdon over the trustees' refusal to let her spend $200,000 to renovate her house.

"How awful it was that no one was with her," Marjorie said. "Did Mother suffer?"

Spencer told Marjorie she didn't think so. According to Spencer, Marjorie told them that Roger had heard the news first, then called her at the laundromat from the Holland House. "We couldn't believe it," Marjorie said. This was her sixth version of Roger's whereabouts the morning of the murders. However, Arnold would have known this was false; he had given Marjorie the bad news himself. To the best of Arnold's recollection, Marjorie actually told Clara the truth, that he had called the laundromat.

This was the first time the Spencers had met Marjorie's new husband, rumored among the relatives to be rather handsome. But the man who stood silently beside Marjorie looked less than attractive. Roger was dressed in worn blue jeans, old cowboy boots, and a gray-and-white checked jacket. His vacant, bloodshot eyes barely registered on his face, unshaven and marked with a scab. Clara thought he looked like "the wrath of God." Marjorie explained her husband's appearance, saying, "He always looks like this, but he doesn't drink."

As the group walked toward baggage claim, Marjorie announced, "The whole thing is Bill Van Evera's fault, leaving two women alone in the house all night long without any guards." Marjorie became indignant; Vera Dunbar had refused to allow her to speak with her mother when she called the Friday before the murders. "What Mother really needed was a daughter," Marjorie said. Actually, Elisabeth had already arrived at Swiftwater Farm when Marjorie called Glensheen. Maid Hazel Conger had taken the call, and Marjorie had refused to identify herself.

Next, Marjorie asked about funeral arrangements. She said she wanted to go to Glensheen to pick out a dress for her mother to wear. When Spencer told her that a blue dress, one of Elisabeth's favorites, had already been chosen, Marjorie exploded, her eyes flashing. "Who chose it?" she asked.

"Vera consulted with your sister by phone and we all approved it."

"She had no business doing that! Her conservatorship is over." Visibly agitated, Marjorie told Spencer the FBI was investigating her movements in Colorado, and she took it personally. Clara's reminder that police had the whole family under investigation did little to calm her.

Marjorie informed the Spencers that she and Roger had spent the weekend of her mother's murder with a realtor in Colorado looking at houses. "We were with a real estate agent at the time and I can prove it," Marjorie said. Neither Clara nor Stephen Spencer attached any significance to Marjorie's explanation, given the discussion of the murder investigation. As Stephen Spencer told police, "It seemed to come out as a matter of course."

The Spencers said their good-byes as Arnold drove up in the Delta 88 he had rented for the Caldwells' use while they were in Duluth for the funeral. They would next see the Caldwells at Elisabeth's funeral, seated beside them for the service. Clean-shaven and dressed in a suit, Roger looked so different that at first the Spencers failed to recognize him.

On Wednesday, day three of the murder investigation, analysts from the Minnesota Bureau of Criminal Apprehension joined Duluth police at the murder scene. The analysts concentrated on the blood evidence. With the exception of the Persian rug, which would be rolled up and transported whole, many bloodstains were so minute that they had to be collected with cotton swabs and syringes.

One agent concentrated on analyzing the blood spattering in the central staircase area. Blood had spattered on the second floor during the struggle at the top of the staircase. A series of blood marks dotted the wood paneling leading up to the second floor. Technicians found the heaviest concentration of blood on the landing below the window seat. They concluded that Pietila had first been struck with the candlestick on the second floor, then battered down the stairs near the window seat before falling. The killer stood above Pietila on the stairs when the attack began, and swung the murder weapon with his or her right hand.

While the first technician studied the stairway blood spatters, another examined the bloodstains in the nurses' bathroom. Water had diluted the drops around the washbasin and faucet—and on the floor between the sink and toilet—and they had dried into pink rings. The murderer had obviously washed just before fleeing the mansion. The stains had been left intact for the state crime lab experts; Waller hoped they would be able to get a blood type despite the dilution.

The second technician called to Waller to come look at the bathroom. Several towels were hanging on a rack to the right of the sink. But when the towels were moved aside, a spot of blood was visible on the wall behind. Waller bent down for a closer look, resting his left hand on the sink as he leaned forward. He unknowingly made a crisp palm print, one that would take months to identify and would later prove a public embarrassment for Waller.

That afternoon, police took advantage of the warm, cloudless summer day and resumed their search for evidence outdoors. Inspector Grams had ordered a complete search of the grounds, dubbing the detail "Operation Clean Sweep." The department canceled its in-school training and, without shorting street patrols, every available officer assisted in the search.

Shoulder-to-shoulder, officers slowly walked the estate's seven-and-a-half acres, including the bed of Tischer Creek and the Lake Superior beach, looking for any possible clues. They recovered five brown paper bags containing insignificant items—wood chips, a candy wrapper, some empty cigarette packages, a plastic cigarette wrapper, and a matchbook from a Nevada casino. Not much to go on for the investigators; defense lawyers would eventually exploit the matchbook.

"Sometimes doing a good job creates unanswered questions or problems like the garbage found on Operation Clean Sweep," Waller later said. A thorough gathering of potential evidence at any crime scene inevitably yields many items that can never be identified with a suspect or eliminated by matching with someone who belonged at the scene. For example, the gathering of hair alone can produce more samples than an investigator could ever hope to match. People without "crime scene experience don't realize just how many fibers there are in any building, let alone one with not only family but also staff, both nursing and domestic. Not to mention visitors. Any unidentified hair fibers could be literally scores of folks," Waller explained. After investigators develop a suspect or suspects, they have to focus on matching unknown samples to known samples from those suspects—and the detectives were already focusing on the Caldwells.

That morning, Duluth police had reached the Caldwells at their room in the Duluth Radisson and asked them to come in for questioning. Marjorie, Roger, and David Arnold met with Inspector Grams and Waller and Greene in the inspector's office adjacent to the detective bureau around 11:30 A.M. Grams would conduct the interview; Waller would fill out the report afterward.

The detective bureau occupied a long room dimly lit by flickering fluorescent lights. Six work stations were outfitted with olive green metal desks reminiscent of military-issue furniture, butted together so tightly that Waller could reach over and answer the next detective's phone. The FBI's ten most wanted list, mug shots, department memos, offbeat letters, and travel postcards decorated the walls. When the office filled with people, little opportunity for privacy remained.

Waller's desk in the left corner faced the front of the room. He could scope out everyone who entered the bureau, but the view of the newspaper building or side glimpse of the civic center courtyard out the high windows in back hardly made for pleasant scenery. At least the inspector's office had a door and a private desk; Waller had to share his with another investigator who worked the opposite shift.

Before walking into police headquarters, Arnold advised Marjorie to "watch me, and keep your answers brief." His client ignored the advice as soon as the interview began. Throughout the interview, Grams, Waller, and Greene each noted that Marjorie did all the talking and answered questions matter-of-factly. She said she'd called Glensheen the previous Friday to talk to her mother. She claimed, contradicting Conger's story, that Conger told her Elisabeth would be at Swiftwater Farm through the Fourth of July—apparently to make it appear that the Caldwells wouldn't have known Elisabeth was home the night of the murders.

When asked about her whereabouts the morning of the murders, Marjorie said she and her husband were at the laundromat near their hotel in Golden, Colorado, the morning of June 27. "Roger had gone for a six-pack of Coca-Cola when I received the call at the laundromat," she said, going back to what she had told Arnold when he had called.

Marjorie asked whether officers had checked Glensheen's two secret compartments—disguised by wooden panels in the wall on either side of the main staircase's window seat—for the missing jewelry. She also told them of a hidden compartment in the back of Elisabeth's bedroom desk; a button underneath the desk opened it. The detectives found no hidden compartment in the desk; behind the concealed panels on the landing they found only cleaning supplies.

Then she asked, "Have you questioned Vera Dunbar about the absence of guards and security?"

During the forty-five minute interview, Waller noted Roger's eyes often closed or drooped. He looked to Waller "like a man that was ill or drugged." His left upper lip was puffed out around a small cut. More importantly, Waller and Greene noticed that Roger's right hand, which he rested on his knee, looked swollen. Pietila's jaw had been broken by a blow, possibly from a fist.

Inspector Grams said that police might ask household staff and family members to undergo lie detector tests. He then asked the Caldwells if they would be willing to take a polygraph exam. Arnold said they'd talk it over and the detectives would get their answer the next day. He seemed anxious to leave and ushered his clients out as quickly as possible.

As the interview ended, Waller stood up and blocked the doorway. He grabbed hold of Roger's hand and shook it as hard as he could. Waller felt the swelling. "I wanted to see if Roger would blink," Waller recalled. "He did."

Wednesday afternoon, while investigators continued to process evidence at Glensheen, detectives at Duluth police headquarters continued their interviews of Congdon family members, including Elisabeth's daughter Jennifer and her husband, Chuck. The Johnsons had attended an anniversary party at the Racine country club the evening of the murders, then stopped off briefly at a friend's home about 9:15 P.M. before returning home. Jennifer learned of her mother's death Monday morning when her cousin's husband, Bill Van Evera, called from Duluth.

Asked for background on her sister Marjorie, Jennifer confirmed Marjorie's psychiatric treatment as a teenager at the Menninger Clinic. Her sister also went through individual and joint counseling during her marriage to Richard LeRoy, Jennifer said.

When Yagoda and Greene pressed for additional information, the Johnsons described a Christmas 1966 gift—a beautifully wrapped voodoo doll—sent to one of Jennifer and Marjorie's uncles, Robert Congdon. The doll had a large straight pin stuck through its heart. They didn't recall a card being enclosed, but said Robert believed the doll had been sent by Marjorie. As police learned, Robert—a Congdon family trustee—managed Marjorie's trust accounts at the time he received the doll. Coincidentally, he died in June, 1967—within six months of receiving the doll.

Because of Tom Congdon's position as one of the three trustees for the Congdon Trusts, detectives Yagoda and Greene also interviewed him at police headquarters that afternoon.

"Is there anyone in your family who might benefit from the death of Elisabeth Congdon or who is in financial trouble at the present time?" Greene asked. Besides his cousin Marjorie, Congdon said, one family member in Spokane, Washington, had recently gone through a divorce. But in comparison to Marjorie's debts, the Washington relative's cash problems were minor.

Several weeks earlier, Roger Caldwell had called desperate for cash, Congdon told detectives. On June 19, Congdon went down to the Holland House to temporarily bail out his cousin and her husband. "I gave the motel a personal check from my account for $400. I informed the motel that the $400 was for the next ten days rent…not for past debts."

The detectives asked Congdon if he had any further comments concerning the death of Elisabeth Congdon or about Roger or Marjorie.

Congdon described his run-in with Marjorie at the 1975 Congdon family reunion at Glensheen. Marjorie told Congdon and cousin Terry d'Autremont she needed $200,000 to refurbish her house in Colorado because of her son's asthma. Congdon refused. "You have no right to expect housing on such a grand scale," he had told her firmly. "If my son dies as a result of this, you will be responsible for his death," she yelled, and stalked off.

He also related the story of the confrontation between Marjorie and Velma Pietila. Pietila had called the Congdon Office for help. Trustee Bill Van Evera spent the rest of the day with Elisabeth.

Later that afternoon, Marjorie drove to Glensheen and demanded to see the gardener and chauffeur, hoping to convince them to accompany her to the funeral home. They refused. The officers in charge of mansion security repeated their instructions. Marjorie was not allowed inside, only on the estate grounds. But even this arrangement enraged Vera Dunbar, long suspicious of her employer's daughter. She could do nothing, however, to eject Marjorie from the property.

Meanwhile, Sergeant Greene searched the secret compartments Marjorie had mentioned in her interview. They found none of the missing jewelry. By day's end,

Duluth police found themselves quietly but firmly on the trail of two murder suspects—Roger and Marjorie.

On Tuesday before leaving Denver, Roger had called horse breeder Richard Lapin. "Hold on to the checks I gave you to buy a horse," Roger said. "They were bad." But he had assured Lapin he was coming into about $10 million because of his mother-in-law's death. "Start looking for a $20,000 to $30,000 medal horse," Roger had instructed.

Wednesday night, the night before his mother-in-law's funeral, Roger called horse trainer Dion Dana in Colorado with much the same story. "Dion, start looking for a medal horse for Rick," Caldwell told her. She knew a horse of that caliber would cost between $40,000 and $50,000. Caldwell assured her, "We've hit it big."

Velma Pietila's funeral service had been held at 2 P.M. Wednesday at Pilgrim Congregational Church in Duluth. The private service had been given a small mention in the local papers and newscasts.

That night, Roger and Marjorie visited Loren Pietila to offer their condolences. The Pietilas' daughter-in-law, Barbara, answered the door. As soon as she recognized Marjorie, she summoned Loren to greet the visitors. The Caldwells had sent flowers, but only Marjorie had signed the card.

During the brief conversation that followed, Marjorie came into the doorway of the dining room. Roger, however, hung back, looking extremely uncomfortable. Loren noticed Roger had a cut on his lip about "three-eighths of an inch, as though a blow struck." He acted "very nervous" and tugged at Marjorie's coat sleeve to go, Loren later testified. His son, James, told police he heard Roger whisper to Marjorie, "Let's go, let's not stay."

But before they left Marjorie lied to Loren about their absence from the funeral. "We certainly would have been to the funeral, but we just got to town," she said. The Pietila family was relieved when the Caldwells finally left.

On the morning of Thursday, June 30, the Congdon family and the Glensheen staff prepared for Elisabeth's funeral. Even in death, those closest to Elisabeth looked after her and surrounded her. Family, friends, and trusted servants attended a private memorial service at Glensheen. It would be a last reunion of sorts for the Congdon clan.

That morning, driving from Swiftwater Farm to his grandmother's funeral, Andy LeRoy recalled his brother, Stephen, saying, "Do you know, they don't know where [Roger] was on the morning of the murder?" Andy later told police he didn't want to hear that his mother could be involved in the killings, but he believed it was possible.

The closed casket rested in Glensheen's main floor library. Marjorie had placed garish displays of flowers on top of the casket and at the four corners, upsetting Jennifer. The flowers obscured an elegant single spray of ferns made by Glensheen's gardener, Bob Wyness. "It covered up the ferns," Jennifer recalled. "Of course Marjorie didn't pay for any of this. But the ferns went on top of the casket before it was lowered into the ground."

About one hundred people attended the private 1 P.M. service officiated by the Reverend H. Thomas Walker of First United Methodist Church. During the funeral service, eight plainclothes police officers staked out stairways and the second floor to prevent anyone from entering the murder scene. Waller and Greene stationed themselves in the sitting room across the hall from the library. Both had a good view of Roger, cleaned up and dressed in an aqua, western-style suit. Marjorie was at his side, wearing tight white slacks and a brightly colored flowered blouse, much to her sister's embarrassment.

"My mother never liked women to wear pants. She thought women should wear dresses and they should look like ladies, not like men," said Jennifer. "Marjorie and Roger came up and they didn't have any clothes, so they went to Allenfall's and charged...so Mother paid for their funeral clothes." The trustees later received a bill from the store for $1,199.

Roger knew he was under surveillance, yet first pretended not to notice the detectives. When he finally turned to catch their gaze, Waller and Greene marveled at his cool, unwavering eyes, and let him win the stare down. Sergeant Yagoda noticed that Roger's hand appeared slightly swollen and a cut ran from Roger's upper to his lower lip.

Waller and Greene followed the funeral procession on the 3.5-mile drive to Forest Hill Cemetery and the Congdon family plot, marked by a tall white monolith topped with a Celtic cross. "Congdon" is carved on its face in large letters, and the four sides of its base display the phrase "I Sing Eternal Hope And Strong Endeavor." The grave is surrounded with those of other Congdon family members, including Dudleys, Claypools, d'Autremonts, and Spencers. The tombstones and mausoleums on the knoll where they laid Elisabeth to rest read like a one-time Who's Who of Duluth society: Hartley, Snively, Alworth, Sellwood, Bradley, Fryberger, Welles—families whose prominence continued after death by burial on higher ground than those less wealthy or well-known.

Reporters and photographers lined up along London Road as the funeral procession rolled off the estate. The limousines and cars had to pass through the media gauntlet, much to Marjorie's disdain. She turned to her children in the limousine and instructed, "Turn your heads! Don't let them take your picture." Six Duluth police officers patrolled the cemetery grounds to keep the news media and curious passersby away.

That afternoon, the *Duluth Herald* published a photograph from the funeral. Investigators had ruled out burglary as the motive: they were hunting a killer. Police theory holds that a murderer sometimes returns to pay final respects to the victim. John DeSanto and his girlfriend, Lana Eckenberg, were driving to Duluth's major shopping center, Miller Hill Mall, when he noticed the picture on the front of the paper she was reading. "The murderer must be in there somewhere," DeSanto said as he scanned the mourners.

The funeral party returned to the mansion for coffee. Marjorie approached Waller, offering to get him a plate of cookies. He declined, explaining he was on duty. But Waller also distrusted Elisabeth's older daughter. "I didn't want to eat anything that woman had touched," he said later.

Marjorie approached Dr. Elizabeth Bagley and thanked her for "being so nice, and keeping my mother alive so long." She also thanked head nurse Mildred Garvue. Marjorie's distrust of law enforcement was readily apparent to anyone watching as Marjorie picked up her handbag, announcing "there are so many cops around."

Thursday afternoon around 4 P.M., Waller and Greene interviewed Marjorie's oldest son, Stephen, at police headquarters. He told the detectives he and his girlfriend had spent June 25 and 26 at Swiftwater Farm. They had canoed the Brule River, picnicked, walked in the woods, and played cards and watched television with his grandmother. Elisabeth was in a very good mood.

He last saw Elisabeth alive about 3 P.M. Sunday, June 26, when she left with her chauffeur and nurse to return to Duluth. Stephen said the news of his grandmother's death shocked him. He had tried unsuccessfully to reach his mother after hearing the news from his sister-in-law.

Stephen was reluctant to speculate about possible suspects. He told Waller and Greene only that his suspicions were probably the same as they'd heard from other family members. "Pressure can drive people to do many things," he said.

At 6:30 P.M. Thursday, Inspector Grams called the Duluth Radisson Hotel, where the Caldwells had taken rooms while in town for Elisabeth's funeral. Police had more questions for them, including whether they had decided to consent to polygraph exams. Waller and the other detectives had their doubts about Roger's whereabouts at the time of the murders. Waller had asked the medical examiner to be ready to examine Roger's swollen hand. Could the injury have been caused by a blow to Velma Pietila, or by Pietila as she struggled with her killer? But Grams learned that Roger, Marjorie, and Rick had already checked out.

David Arnold needed to get some distance between his clients and the investigation. Not wanting to take the time to make flight arrangements, they left Duluth in the rental car. Marjorie's nervous chatter and descriptions of everyone she had met that afternoon at the funeral provided the only break to the silence of their long drive back to Minneapolis. Arnold drove; his associate James Wieland, who had flown up to Duluth on Wednesday to assist him, sat in the passenger seat, and the Caldwells rode in back. Roger, Arnold noticed, remained unusually quiet during the three-hour ride. Usually conversations with Roger, a good talker, included few lulls. But he sat silent and unresponsive as his wife loudly insisted her family and Duluth police were attempting to frame them. Earlier that day at Glensheen, Chuck Johnson and Tom Congdon had informed Arnold that everyone in the family was consenting to a polygraph, and they suggested Marjorie do so as well. Arnold had advised the Caldwells not to take the polygraph. He'd have to break the news to Duluth police.

Meanwhile in Duluth, Detectives Waller, Greene, and Yagoda accompanied Inspector Grams to the Radisson, a block-and-a-half from headquarters, just down the street from City Hall and the county and federal courthouses. They arrived just as maids were about to begin cleaning the Caldwells' room. They ordered the maids to leave the rooms alone.

While Waller and the inspector searched rooms 801 and 803, Yagoda and Greene reviewed hotel registration forms and telephone numbers called by the Caldwells. Waller and Grams collected cigarette packages, magazines, cigarette butts, scraps of paper with phone numbers, an old brown suitcase, a metal belt buckle with turquoise inset, clothing boxes, and tissue paper. Their finds also included a cash register receipt and North Central Airlines baggage claim tickets. The baggage tickets were from the flight the Caldwells had taken to Duluth for the funeral. The sales slip was marked "Host Minneapolis" and totaled $56.16 for a single item bought on June 27,1977— placing the buyer in Minneapolis the day of the murders. It had been found in a discarded box from Allenfall's, the store where the Caldwells had purchased clothes for the funeral.

Back at police headquarters, Inspector Grams asked Waller to head the murder investigation. Grams' role would then be largely administrative and include dealing with the press. "When Ernie asked me if I'd take over, I didn't hesitate," Waller recalled years later. Waller admired and trusted the inspector. Grams was more than Waller's mentor; he had worked with Waller's father and uncle. Waller's father had joined the police department just three years after Grams, and they'd worked together on the force for more than twenty years. At the same time the department promoted Waller to sergeant in the detective bureau, it also named Grams inspector. Also, Waller had a healthy ego, and took great pride in his new responsibility. He wanted the prestige of supervising the big case. Forget routine burglary investigations—he had been given command of a double homicide investigation, an opportunity to prove his credentials as a detective and establish his career. "At that time, I was the kind of person eager to take on more responsibility," Waller remembers. "I knew Jack Greene and Dick Yagoda had been asked and refused. Obviously, they had better sense than I. I really didn't know what was going to happen. It's like buying something and not knowing all the things wrong with it. I'd never had an investigation like this before. I probably never will again."

Within minutes after he accepted the inspector's offer, Grams instructed Waller to fly to Colorado and scope out the hotel and town where the Caldwells lived. The murder investigation had moved to a new front. Waller left Duluth the next day.

Waller later regretted leaving for Colorado just after taking charge of the case. The trip separated him from the officers and the investigation he was supposed to oversee. "A responsibility as great as this should be assumed from the minute the investigation begins, not several days later," said Waller. "The person in charge needs to supervise, not actively investigate the case himself."

Waller's trip also put strain on his family. He would miss his wife's thirty-third birthday and a planned trip to Michigan to visit friends over the Fourth of July weekend. Law enforcement as a profession often exacts a toll on families, and Waller's family was no exception. He had a three-year-old daughter, Bridget, and a nine-year-old son, Sean. His wife, Pat, complained that she sometimes felt like a single parent.

He had first met Pat, an attractive, blue-eyed brunette, at a party, but both were dating other people at the time. Waller, attending college at the time, worked full-time as assistant manager of a Duluth grocery store. Pat taught at the Arrowhead School of Cosmetology in downtown Duluth. They were eventually introduced in 1966, when Waller saw Pat at The Cove Cabaret, a popular bar across the St. Louis River in Superior, Wisconsin, and asked her to dance.

Waller was known as a good dancer, and he enjoyed it. Growing up as a chubby kid, he initially struck out at dating, but quickly learned how much girls appreciated a competent partner at school dances. Pat and Waller hit it off, and they began dating steadily in the summer of 1966. They married in a small private ceremony in Duluth in January 1967. That September, Waller joined the Duluth Police Department as a patrol officer.

"My family was pretty much accustomed that the number one priority in my life was my job. I'd always been a type-A personality—workaholic, often letting personal responsibilities come second to career aspirations. My family relationships did suffer," Waller recalled. "My children were quite young, and I have real guilt about how little time I spent with them, particularly when my son was growing up. I can still recall hearing the Harry Chapin song 'The Cat's in the Cradle' and feeling guilty because I could identify with the father. He never had time for his son. And in later years, when the father wants to spend time with his son, the son is too busy and tells him we will sometime, but it never happens."

The night before Waller left he had heard news that put him and the detective bureau in a celebratory mood. Detectives Greene and Yagoda had traced the $56.16 purchase. The sales slip had come from one of the Host International gift shops at the Minneapolis-St. Paul International Airport. The purchase had been made early the morning of the murders, tying in with the time stamp on the parking stub found in the trash can with the Pietila car keys. Investigators had collected vital physical evidence. Not only did this place at least one of the Caldwells in Minnesota the day of the murders, it also appeared to put that person at the airport, making a getaway.

CHAPTER 10

The Colorado Front

THE SIGHT OF THE ROCKY MOUNTAINS JUTTING OUT of the eastern Colorado plains impressed Detective Gary Waller as his plane made its final descent into Denver's Stapleton International Airport on July 1, 1977. He had flown to Denver to find proof that Roger Caldwell was not in Colorado at the time of the murders. And since police had lost track of the Caldwells, he was also on the outlook for the couple. Coincidentally, Tom Congdon had been on the plane as well, but he and Waller never spoke with one another. Tom recognized Waller from Elisabeth's funeral, but thought Waller was working for the Colorado investigator he'd hired to tail the Caldwells. As Waller exited the plane, dressed in his light blue leisure suit and dress shoes, he instantly felt out of place in what he called "cowboy country." Bob Harmon, special agent for the Colorado Bureau of Investigation (CBI), met Waller at the airport terminal.

Harmon, a slightly built man in his early fifties, worked as a sergeant for the Denver police department before joining the CBI. His wavy red hair and freckled face reminded Waller of Howdy Doody, and his friendly, relaxed manner and heavy Western drawl immediately put the Duluth detective at ease. He wore a brown, western-style suit, open-collar shirt, and cowboy boots. In the months ahead, Waller would work closely with Harmon on the Congdon-Pietila case, which would require nearly as much investigation and legwork in Colorado as it did in Minnesota.

"I was out here on Monday," Harmon told Waller, "and I must have just missed Roger." Tom Congdon had called Harmon the afternoon of June 27. Congdon told the CBI to keep a lookout for Roger, a likely suspect whom he believed would return from Minneapolis to Denver. Harmon had spent a number of hours at the Denver airport in an unsuccessful attempt to intercept him. Harmon had met Marjorie while investigating an insurance fraud case involving the Caldwells just the previous year.

Despite his unimposing appearance, Harmon, a tough, experienced cop, liked to describe himself as a "wire stringer." He had spent years installing wiretaps as part of the intelligence unit of the Denver police department and later for the CBI's organized crime strike force. Eventually, federal legislation restricted wiretaps and effectively put Harmon out of business.

While they drove to Golden police headquarters, Harmon and Waller talked about serial murderer Ted Bundy's escape from jail and capture in Aspen, Colorado, the previous month. "I was out looking for that guy. Everyone I knew was out looking for him," Harmon told Waller. He was now assisting in the search for a suspected killer.

Golden police shared a cramped, one-story building with the Fire Department in downtown Golden. Harmon introduced Waller to Sergeant Randy Gordanier, the other member of his Colorado team. A tall, handsome man in his twenties with sandy brown hair and a mustache, Gordanier was the department's only full-time detective. Like Harmon, he spoke with a Western drawl, and he too favored Western-style clothing and cowboy boots. Gordanier agreed to help interview the Caldwells' neighbors and friends.

Waller told Gordanier and Harmon he first wanted to see where the couple had been living for the past three months: the Holland House Hotel, an unassuming white three-story building with a plain and well-worn, yet tidy, interior. Waller tried to picture the daughter of an heiress living in such meager accommodations. Instead of Glensheen's opulent wall coverings, hardwood floors, and Oriental rugs, Marjorie's current home had wood veneer paneling and lime green carpeting. The officers instructed hotel staff to notify police if Marjorie or Roger called or returned home.

From the Holland House, Harmon and Waller drove out to interview Marjorie's horse trainer and friend, Judy McCoy, at her ranch in Evergreen, on the outskirts of Denver. Harmon had learned from McCoy that Marjorie had said that her mother's death would solve her financial problems. A slender woman in her mid-thirties, she had a deep, leathery tan acquired from working outside most of the time. Although she invited the officers inside, Waller noted McCoy appeared uncomfortable with their surprise visit. It took several minutes before McCoy explained the reason for her reluctance to answer questions. She was afraid to talk, she said, because of rumors that Marjorie knew some organized crime figures.

After agreeing to cooperate, McCoy described how she and Marjorie first met at a Denver horse show. A mutual love of horses brought the women together and a friendship quickly evolved. McCoy had trained some of Marjorie and Roger's horses, and they had consulted her on their plans to start a horse training and breeding business.

She told the investigators of the time Marjorie said she wanted to kill Thomas Welch. "Do you know anyone in Colorado I could hire to bump him off?" Marjorie had asked. "I can't get anyone from Chicago—that's too close."

McCoy also told the officers that on another occasion, Marjorie had stated, "I wish Mother would hurry up and kick the bucket, then my problems would be over." Then in January 1977, Marjorie appeared so depressed that McCoy asked her what was wrong. "The only way I'm going to get out of this financial mess is if my mother drops dead," Marjorie told McCoy. "You don't mean that," McCoy said. "Yes, I do," Marjorie insisted.

Before the two men left, McCoy offered her opinion of the Caldwells. She believed they were capable of murder.

With their first solid lead—the cash register receipt—in hand, Duluth detectives Yagoda and Greene drove to the Minneapolis-St. Paul International Airport on Friday, July 1. Airport security confirmed that the receipt found in the Caldwells' hotel room had come from one of the Host International gift shops, The Blue Gift Shop. The shop, naturally, was located in the airport's blue concourse—the same concourse from which the first flight to Denver left every morning at 8:20. Based on their time estimates, the detectives knew Roger could have been in the gift shop prior to catching the 8:20 A.M. flight to Denver. But the detectives still needed evidence placing him inside the gift shop.

Yagoda and Greene next stopped at the Host International offices, where they had arranged to question the two employees who had worked in the Blue Gift Shop the morning of the murders. Yagoda and Greene ushered Sandra Schwartzbauer, the cashier on duty that day, and Joanne Kelly, the supervisor, into a small conference room where Yagoda showed them a photocopy of the sales receipt. Schwartzbauer and Kelly identified the $56.16 receipt from the second sale in the Blue Gift Shop on the morning of June 27.

The first customer, a young woman, had bought four greeting cards and a book. Schwartzbauer's second sale, about 6:40 A.M.—just minutes after the time on the parking stub recovered from the same trash can as the Pietilas' car keys—had been somewhat unusual. The customer bought a suede valet-style garment bag—only the second suede garment bag she'd sold in months. Her supervisor, Kelly, had observed the sale. Kelly paid special attention because the suede bag, a newer item, was one of the more expensive articles they stocked.

Schwartzbauer and Kelly told the detectives that the man who bought the bag had carried a wicker case in his left hand. They described him as having a bit of a beer belly and recalled that he wore wrinkled clothing that looked lived in. The man paid for the bag with three $20 bills. Then Schwartzbauer unsuccessfully tried to help him cram the wicker basket into the top pouch of the garment bag.

Next the detectives showed them a photo lineup. Following standard police procedure, the lineup included a picture of Roger and five other pictures of people similar in age, build, and hair. The photos were usually black-and-white police mug shots or Polaroid pictures; in this case, the only photo they had of Roger had been taken by Agent Harmon during his investigation of the Caldwells.

Kelly pointed to photo number one, Roger's, saying the man's "complexion was right." She told detectives, "The sideburns were light. The general look was good. The size looks right." But she couldn't positively pick Roger out of the six photographs. Schwartzbauer recognized the person in photo number one as someone she "had seen before." But she couldn't remember where.

The result buoyed the detectives, but hardly left them feeling overconfident. They would have to return with a second photo lineup with a more current photograph of Roger. Maybe then the women would have stronger recall of the man in the gift shop and be able to make positive identifications.

Out in Colorado, Waller took a break from interviewing to check in with Duluth headquarters. "What's new on your end?" Waller asked Inspector Grams. Grams told him about the positive identification of the Host receipt and possible sighting of Roger the morning of the murders. Grams also reported the department's failure to locate the Caldwells in Minnesota. According to David Arnold, he had spoken with Grams earlier that day to report that the Caldwells would not be taking the polygraph, but Grams had not asked him where they were. Apparently certain that they were on their way to Colorado, and with Waller already there, Grams seemed to have his bases covered. But more time had passed and the Caldwells had still not surfaced in Minnesota nor returned to the Holland House.

Grams and Waller decided to set up surveillance at Denver's Stapleton Airport. So far police only had circumstantial evidence to link the Caldwells to the murders. Duluth police could only hope that the Caldwells would return home with the suede bag in their possession.

Not surprisingly, the Denver police department and the CBI were hardly enthusiastic about staffing an airport surveillance over the Fourth of July weekend. But both organizations assigned Waller officers to stake out the baggage claim area. The Denver Police Department also already had a two-man undercover unit at the airport to keep tabs on organized crime figures who regularly passed through Stapleton on their way to and from Las Vegas. Waller asked those detectives to check with airport police in case anyone recalled seeing a man fitting Roger's description pass through security.

That same day, Detective Gordanier interviewed Candace Byers, a waitress at the Holland House restaurant. She usually saw the Caldwells during her weekend shift. Waller added Byers' name to a growing list of people who hadn't seen Roger the weekend of the murders.

Waller told Harmon they should get a search warrant for the Caldwells' phone records. No, said Harmon, we can use an organized crime strike force grand jury subpoena instead. "I was uncomfortable with not using a search warrant, but this wasn't my jurisdiction—and Harmon suggested the subpoena," Waller recalled. Using the subpoena, police got Holland House Hotel phone records for the Caldwells from June 13 to June 28 and phone records for Pine Valley Farms for the same time period. Seizing the evidence without a search warrant would later cause Waller and DeSanto problems at trial. "I got my nuts fried later on," Waller recalled. "The defense claimed I had seized the evidence illegally. On cross-examination, defense attorney Doug Thomson asked, 'You knew, Sergeant, that that evidence was never going to be presented to a Colorado grand jury at the time you did it?' And I had to say 'Yes.'"

The next morning, Saturday, July 2, as Waller again staffed airport surveillance in Denver with Agent Steven Sedlacek, Duluth detective Jack Greene accompanied Vera Dunbar to Glensheen for a detailed inventory of items missing from Elisabeth's bedroom. The smaller of two matching wicker suitcases that the heiress frequently took with her to the Brule was missing from the bedroom closet—this could link whoever bought the garment bag with Glensheen. Greene confiscated the larger case and returned to headquarters, failing to photograph the closet beforehand to officially document that only the one case remained.

After lunch Saturday, clerk Bertha Huskins gathered up all the mail that had accumulated for the Caldwells during their absence. As she put the mail in their cubbyhole behind the front desk, she noticed an envelope addressed to Mr. Roger S. Caldwell and postmarked June 27 in Duluth. The letter had arrived three days earlier, but had escaped her attention until now. Familiar with Roger's writing from the meal receipts he signed for daily, Huskins was convinced Roger had addressed the envelope. The envelope had a Radisson Hotel Duluth logo in the upper left-hand corner and the postmark read "27 JUN, 1977, P.M., DULUTH, MN 558." Believing the letter might be important, Huskins called Golden police.

As soon as he saw the letter, Sergeant Gordanier knew he had the first possible proof that Roger was in Duluth the day of the murders. Shortly before 2 P.M., Gordanier called Waller and informed him of the find. Waller told Gordanier to immediately get a search warrant. They also needed an expert opinion. So, after talking with Waller, Gordanier arranged for Patricia Rutz, an investigator and handwriting analyst with the local District Attorney's office, to meet him at the hotel. She, too, knew Roger's handwriting. Rutz had examined samples during a check fraud investigation only months earlier. Rutz now compared the envelope's handwritten address with Roger's signature on the backs of two Holland House coffee shop meal tickets. In her opinion, the handwriting on the envelope and receipts appeared to match—both used identical flourishes, including a sweeping upwards stroke from left to right, which was not necessary to make the letter "R." Roger used a large lower case "G" to write "Golden," and had made a spelling error; he then corrected a lower "a" to an "o" in "Golden."

At this point, Gordanier left to get the warrant. Later in the afternoon, when he returned to the Holland House Hotel with the warrant, he called Waller at the airport so Waller could listen in as he opened the letter.

Inside the outer envelope Gordanier found a second, folded envelope which contained a nickel-sized gold coin, imperfectly round and crudely made. Although the coin had foreign markings and lettering, the officers could not themselves determine the country of origin.

Waller called Greene in Duluth. "We found a nickel-sized gold coin inside an envelope addressed and mailed to Roger Caldwell in Colorado," said Waller. "Ask Dunbar if she remembers any coin collection or single coin matching the description." Waller also arranged to meet Gordanier later that afternoon at the Colorado Bureau of Investigation offices where technicians would photograph and analyze the envelope for fingerprints.

Next, Gordanier contacted a reserve police officer who also collected coins. The coin's front side was imprinted with the bust of a man with a cross next to his right shoulder. The back displayed a larger cross atop what looked like a small hill or set of steps. According to Gordanier's friend, the coin was Byzantine from around A.D. 300, handmade, and worth approximately $1,200.

Before Waller left the airport Saturday evening, he picked up photographs and a tan, suede garment bag sent air express by Duluth police. The photos showed a large wicker case similar to the smaller case missing from Elisabeth's bedroom. The garment bag matched the one sold at the Host International gift shop in the Twin Cities airport. Detectives Yagoda and Greene sent the bag so that Waller would know what to look for and, since he didn't have a decent garment bag, he also used it for his trips between Duluth and Denver.

Waller then forwarded to Duluth a copy of Roger's mug shot taken at the time of his DWI arrest seven months earlier in Colorado. Duluth police hoped the recent photograph would make it easier for the Host International gift shop clerks to identify Roger as the man they'd seen the morning of the murders.

At about 9 P.M., Waller, accompanied by Agent Harmon, arrived at the Colorado Bureau of Investigation crime lab where they met Gordanier and Agent Sedlacek. Sedlacek, a fingerprint analyst, would process the envelope addressed to Roger and the envelope containing the gold coin for latent prints.

While waiting for the results, Waller phoned Duluth for an update on Greene's conversation with Dunbar. He couldn't have hoped for better news. According to Dunbar, Elisabeth kept a "Greek-like coin that might possibly have been gold" in the memorabilia case in her bedroom. Dunbar recalled the gold coin had a triangle figure on one side. The stairs on the back of the coin recovered in Colorado were wide on the bottom and narrow on top, resembling a triangle. The apparent match elated Duluth police. Waller promised to report back whatever evidence Sedlacek's analysis produced.

Sedlacek processed the envelopes using ninhydrin, a chemical that turns purple when it reacts with amino acids found in human sweat. He could find no identifiable prints on the inner folded envelope. But the test revealed a fingerprint on the hand-addressed envelope near the flap. Under a magnifying glass, Sedlacek compared the print with the DWI arrest prints of Roger on file at the state crime lab. A half hour passed before Sedlacek announced the results. "We've got a match," he told Waller, Harmon, and Gordanier. In his opinion, the latent print on the back of the envelope had been made by Roger's right thumb.

"I've got to call Ernie," Waller responded to the good news. Although it was Saturday night, Inspector Grams was still at work when Waller called.

"It was just like Christmas," said Waller. "We had Roger Caldwell's thumb print on an envelope mailed from Duluth, Minnesota, on June 27, 1977. It was pretty damning evidence." In addition, Duluth police had contacted the post office and learned the envelope must have been mailed between 5 P.M. Sunday and 11:59 P.M. Monday. Besides the garment bag receipt, and gold coin, they now had a fingerprint placing Roger in Duluth within hours of the murders.

Waller had not attempted to recover saliva from the stamps or the envelope's seal for secretor blood grouping analysis. Between eighty and ninety percent of people are secretors: they secrete their blood type into other bodily fluids, including saliva. If police could have identified a blood type in the saliva sample and matched it to Roger, it would have linked their suspect to the envelope. Secretor blood grouping analysis was important evidence for eliminating and confirming suspects in the days before DNA testing. Many people share the same blood type, however, unlike fingerprints. Waller went for the more specific match. Years later, a twist in the case would make Waller wish he had tried the secretor test, but the stamps and seal had been contaminated by the ninhydrin, and any potential secretor evidence was lost.

That night, Waller sat alone in the bar of the Writers Manor Hotel. He enjoyed a stinger and reveled in the case's progress. The gold coin and envelope confirmed what he already knew but hadn't been able to establish—Roger had been in Duluth around the time of the murders. Hundreds of miles away in Duluth, prosecutor John DeSanto learned of the recent developments and called his girlfriend, Lana. "This is it," DeSanto said. "We're going to get him."

Early Sunday morning, July 3, Waller and two CBI agents regrouped at the airport to continue their check of incoming flights. That afternoon at the Holland House Hotel, Bertha Huskins answered a phone call for the Caldwells. The caller, named "Steve," last name unknown, asked for Roger and Marjorie. She told the caller they were out. "Do you want the son's room?" Huskins asked. "No," the caller answered. "He's here with me. I'll call back at 9 P.M." Then he hung up.

Huskins notified Sergeant Gordanier, who passed the information on to the Duluth police. He believed the caller was Stephen LeRoy, Marjorie's oldest son, who lived in Fridley, a Minneapolis suburb. Rick, who lived with the Caldwells in Golden, could be staying at his brother's place; perhaps he could tell them where to find Roger and Marjorie. The Minneapolis homicide squad dispatched officers to Stephen's apartment. But when they arrived, Stephen said Rick had driven to Duluth with Stephen's girlfriend.

Back at the Denver airport, Waller called off the stakeout. After spending the afternoon and evening checking incoming flights from Aspen and other parts of the country, one thing was clear—the Caldwells weren't coming home during normal working hours.

As the local officers assigned to assist Waller went home to their families to celebrate the holiday weekend, Waller continued his surveillance alone at the Holland

House Hotel. That night he slept fitfully. He had taken a second-floor room next to the Caldwells' two rooms—Roger and Marjorie in 209 and Rick in 211—so he could hear them should they return.

The next day, the Fourth of July, Waller's surveillance ended abruptly with a call from Inspector Grams. Police had located Rick in Duluth and Grams had called him in for questioning at police headquarters.

Rick's appearance stunned investigators. How odd, they thought, that the boy whose mother described as frail and severely asthmatic looked so husky and athletic. Also curiously, Rick's description of his daily activities— including up to two hours of horseback riding, "barn work," and chores such as painting—hardly fit the lifestyle of a chronic asthmatic.

Rick said he planned to return to the Twin Cities the next day to meet his mother and stepfather. He then told police that Marjorie and Roger had rooms at a Holiday Inn near the Minneapolis-St. Paul International Airport and had booked a flight to Denver departing on July 5.

When Grams asked Rick about his parents' whereabouts the weekend his grandmother was killed, Rick said he hadn't seen them. Pressed for details, he added that Roger had left him $50 and a note at the Holland House. His stepfather rarely gave him money and never signed a note as he had, "love, Dad;" he usually signed "Roger" or "Rog." Roger and Rick frequently fought, and Rick never let Roger forget he wasn't Rick's real father. While Rick's turbulent relationship with his stepfather interested them, the detectives wanted to hear more about the contents of the note. In it, Roger instructed Rick to get the laundry ready so he and Marjorie could go to the laundromat over the weekend—in Grams' view, a weak attempt to establish an alibi.

Rick said that when he went to bed after midnight both Friday and Saturday nights, Marjorie and Roger's rental car was in the hotel parking lot. More importantly, he hadn't seen his stepfather the Saturday or Sunday before the murders. Rick finally saw Roger at the Holland House around 7:30 or 8 P.M. Monday, when his mother told him about his grandmother's death.

"Mom and Roger were there and told me what happened to Grandma. I was kind of shook-up and went off by myself for a while," Rick said. After driving around for several hours, he returned to the hotel about 1 A.M. Tuesday.

Later that day, he flew to Duluth with his mother and stepfather for Elisabeth's funeral. Rick noticed that Roger had a scab on his lip from a cut Roger claimed was caused when a frisky colt knocked him against a wall.

The boy's attitude in the interview gave detectives a sign of how he had been spoiled by his mother. He sulked when police refused to allow him to drive one of the Congdon Cadillacs from Duluth back to Denver, as Marjorie had promised. He either didn't realize or didn't care that his mother was prematurely dividing up family property before the will had gone through probate.

As soon as he learned of Roger's note, Waller arranged for a warrant to search the Caldwells' rooms at the Holland House. If Roger's note to Rick was still there, he'd find it. He spent the rest of the day with Sergeant Gordanier, continuing to make the rounds of the Caldwells' friends in the horse breeding and training business around Denver.

They first stopped at Hillcroft Acres, where the Caldwells kept four horses, to speak with owner Louise McConnell. McConnell told the officers that the Caldwells typically fell behind on boarding payments—about $600 a month—and described them as "slow to pay."

Next, detectives interviewed horse trainer Dion Dana at her home in Denver. She told police that she saw Marjorie around 9:25 A.M. on June 27, when Marjorie "burst into her house" looking upset, and announced her mother had been murdered. She then asked Dana to watch her son Rick for the day. "I have to go and find Roger and Rick's doctor," Marjorie said. Rick LeRoy had arrived as his mother drove off, and spent the day with Dana. About 8:00 that evening, Roger phoned and asked Dana to send Rick home.

Roger's behavior two days later took Dana by surprise. The night before his mother-in-law's funeral, Roger called long distance to tell her that he had found the perfect property for the Caldwells' hunter-jumper training school. He asked Dana to drive by and see if she thought it was suitable. Roger also asked her to help find a horse for his stepson Rick, and said that she and Rick could go look for a horse out East. Both McConnell and Dana had attended a horse show in Monument, Colorado, the weekend of the murders. The Caldwells, who rarely missed such events, did not attend.

The night of July 4, Roger phoned his stepson Stephen at home. Roger and Marjorie were in Minneapolis visiting their close friends, the O'Tooles, and he had been drinking vodka for several hours.

"Where the fuck is Ricky?" Roger loudly demanded as soon as Stephen answered the phone.

"Pardon?"

"Where the hell is Ricky?"

"In Duluth."

"What the hell is he doing there? Who gave you permission to let him go to Duluth?"

Stephen did not want to listen to any more of Roger's tirade, so he hung up. But when the phone rang a minute later, he answered it, only to hear Roger say, "Don't you ever do that to me again or I'll beat the shit out of you."

Roger was desperate to talk to Rick. If Rick was in Duluth, he was accessible for questioning by the Duluth police. Roger ordered Stephen to locate his brother and make him available by phone within ten minutes.

"It was beyond being mad," Stephen later said of the conversation. "I had never heard such language in my life. If you can be violent on the phone, he was violent on the phone."

Shortly before 9 A.M. the next day, Waller, Gordanier, and other local law enforcement agents began searching rooms 209 and 211 at the Holland House. Their
search warrant included the wicker case and jewelry—items reported stolen from
Glensheen. Waller figured either the Caldwells still had the items or they'd left them
behind.

Room 209, Roger and Marjorie's room, showed signs of the couple's recent activities and travels. On the top of the dresser, officers found a North Central Airlines
baggage ticket labeled "WA Flight 417." Airport police told Waller the claim ticket was
from a Western Airlines flight to Denver, leaving the Twin Cities at 3:45 P.M. CST and
arriving in Denver at 4:32 P.M. MT. But to his disappointment, the tag turned out to
be from Roger's trip to Duluth in May.

The large number of items left behind made investigators hopeful the Caldwells
would soon return. They seized a Sears Western-style brown jacket, a size 46 Haggar
sport coat, a blue knit shirt, and a pair of Levi's jeans—all with suspicious-looking
stains. Other clothing items confiscated included two pairs of leather gloves, two Western-style blue denim shirts, and a Sears Western-wear down vest.

Officers also recovered a Crown Realty Company envelope dated June 26, 1977.
It contained a purchase agreement drafted by realtor Fran Beyer and signed by Marjorie.

In a desk drawer, Waller found sheets of white stationery with the letterhead
"NAC." He dismissed the stationery as insignificant, but later regretted his decision
not to seize the paper. It was identical to the stationery Marjorie had stolen from the
National Asthma Center and used to forge the letter from her son's doctor—the letter
her husband presented to Congdon trustees a month before the murders. But Waller
did not know of the forged letter at the time.

Inside Rick's room, investigators found two gasoline charge slips from a local gas
station, signed by Roger using the alias "Roger Congdon." From the bathroom they
seized two bottles of sedatives, one for Roger and the other prescribed for Marjorie the
day her mother was murdered.

The officers also recovered the note Roger left Rick crumpled in the wastebasket.
It read:

Rick—
Mom and I will be with real estate people nearly all day Saturday & Sunday. I'm trying
to keep Mom busy with other things since the Dr. says that she can't ride until next week
at least.
Here's fifty bucks for gasoline and dates through Monday.
Mom and I both agree that you may stay till 12:30 both Saturday and Sunday nights
providing that you pick up your room and put all your dirty laundry into our wash basket
since we would like to get to the laundromat sometime this weekend, too.
Please bring all dirty horse laundry from the barn no later than Saturday so we can get
it washed and put away Sunday before noon.
Love, Mom & Dad.

Later that afternoon, after the search ended, Waller called real estate agent Fran Beyer about the contract found in the Caldwells' room. Beyer was home ill, so he had to settle for a phone interview. Had she seen Marjorie or Roger June 25 or 26? Yes, she said she'd shown Marjorie a number of properties that weekend. What about Roger? No, Beyer said, she had not seen Roger the weekend of the murders. When she met Marjorie that Monday morning, Marjorie told Beyer that Roger had taken Rick to the mountains.

From Rick's room, Waller and Gordanier also collected two pink message slips dated June 27, 1977. One reported a call at 3:20 P.M. from John Hannigan, most likely regarding the money that had been wired to the Caldwells for attending the funeral; on its back had been written "let him know I have money." The other reported a call at 8:10 A.M. On the back side of the slip Roger had jotted down the phone number of the Hyatt Regency Hotel in Indianapolis. Waller called the number and had hotel officials check the registration cards for the weekend of the murders, but no link to Roger was found. Years later, Waller regretted not flying to Indiana to personally examine the hotel records. "I told Inspector Grams we should go down there, but he had concerns about an investigation already too broad, too expensive. And I didn't press the issue. John didn't press the issue. We didn't get down there to actually go through the registration slips where we might have have recognized Caldwell's handwriting or come up with a name that would be significant later on." In hindsight, Waller said police should have obtained copies of the signed registration slips and checked for outgoing calls to Colorado the week before and after the murders. Whatever the full significance of the note—Holland House records indicated two calls to the number, on June 20 and 27—it was lost to investigators.

CHAPTER 11

Marjorie's Misinformation

WHILE POLICE IN COLORADO WATCHED FOR THEIR RETURN, Roger and Marjorie celebrated Fourth of July weekend in the Twin Cities. They had taken rooms at the Holiday Inn Airport South in Bloomington, a suburb of Minneapolis, and spent part of Saturday and Sunday with Joy O'Toole. Marjorie's children and the O'Toole children had skated and competed together, and the parents had often seen one another at early morning practices.

On Saturday, July 2, Roger and Marjorie arrived at O'Toole's house in St. Paul after lunch. The couple told her that Rick was out of town with his brother Stephen.

O'Toole had never met Marjorie's second husband before, and she asked Roger about his job and hobbies.

"I'm unemployed right now," Caldwell told her. "But I was a purchaser before I was unemployed. I'm interested in turquoise jewelry and horses." For the remainder of the visit, he kept quiet. To O'Toole, Roger seemed like someone Marjorie could easily overpower. Or perhaps he was simply an opportunist, marrying Marjorie for her family's wealth. Since she hadn't seen her friend in six years, O'Toole suggested the couple have dinner with her the next night.

The following evening, the Caldwells returned to O'Toole's house, this time joined by O'Toole's ex-husband, Richard. Roger gave Richard the impression of someone who liked to impress people. Roger bragged that he swam in the 1948 Olympics, supposedly competing in events that didn't exist at the time. Roger also bragged about owning many pairs of western boots, including a pair worth $280.

Marjorie informed the O'Tooles that Roger had a perforated ulcer and had recently had surgery, so he couldn't drink any alcohol. Marjorie said his doctor had prescribed Antabuse, an alcohol aversion drug, to help him abstain. She told the O'Tooles that she could not cook with wine because of Roger's condition and had to boil any food that contained traces of alcohol. When Roger excused himself several times while watching television with Richard, no one gave it a second thought.

Roger spoke much more on the second visit. At one point he asked his hosts if there was "anything in the paper about Grandma." The O'Tooles assumed he meant

Marjorie's mother. Roger mentioned the gruesomeness of the killings and wondered aloud if the newspaper had any new information. It didn't, she told him.

During the visit, Marjorie also talked with Joy O'Toole about Elisabeth's death. "I'm surprised Mother was home Sunday night. She was usually gone for the weekend from Glensheen," Marjorie said. She also told O'Toole that she and Roger planned to go house hunting the weekend preceding the murders. Marjorie had been at the laundromat when she heard the bad news, and Roger had gone out for a bottle of pop.

The Caldwells told the O'Tooles they had a ranch property they were going to build on in Castle Rock, Colorado. Roger had big plans for their new home: the Broadmoor Hotel had giraffes for sale, and he thought it would be nice to have a few on the ranch.

Afterward, Roger and Richard remained upstairs talking while Marjorie and Joy went downstairs to the rec room to chat. Later that evening, the two women heard pacing overhead and, when they went upstairs to investigate, they were greeted by silence. When Marjorie and Joy found Roger, Joy asked where her ex had gone. "We had an argument and he left," Roger said.

Later that night, Marjorie called Joy into the kitchen and showed her a partially empty bottle of vodka. The bottle had been full at the start of the evening. That explained Roger's frequent trips away from the television.

Susan LeRoy, Peter's wife, took her children to see their grandmother at the Holiday Inn that weekend, but she had another reason for seeing Marjorie. Peter had had to change their phone number because of the frequent calls from bill collectors. Susan spoke with Marjorie about her financial problems and the effects on the rest of the family. The conversation grew heated.

Marjorie claimed that the Congdon trustees had denied funds for Rick's medical expenses, and that Rick had almost died in Colorado from his asthma. Susan didn't buy her mother-in-law's dramatic assertions. Looking directly into Marjorie's eyes, Susan angrily told her she had talked to Rick days earlier about his asthma, and he had told her he had never felt better. Susan then confronted Marjorie about taking money from the other LeRoy children's insurance policies. Marjorie admitted she had taken the money, but said that she had used all of it to pay for Rick's doctor bills.

Finally, Susan told Marjorie the arguing could go on all day and walked out of the hotel room, slamming the door behind her. She phoned her husband and told him to come get her and the children.

After Peter arrived at the Holiday Inn, Roger encouraged him to meet with Marjorie. Peter finally agreed but when Roger went up to the room to talk with Marjorie, she refused to come down and see her son. Half an hour later, he returned without her. Roger explained that she had fallen asleep—severely upset from her argument with Susan, Marjorie had taken "twenty or twenty-five" Valium.

"How can you help Marjorie get out of her debt and money problems?" Peter asked Roger.

"I'm going to handle the money," Roger said. "I don't give a god damn about any of the Congdon money, but if she does get any money, I want control of it or I'm walking."

After that meeting, Peter considered his mother's second husband "a bum." Roger had talked about not having a job and receiving a $90 unemployment check. As for his mother, Peter later said he didn't get along with her because her chronic lying ruined the LeRoy name—that, and she had also stiffed her own son for $800 when she moved to Colorado. The day before she left, she had gone to his house looking for cash for the trip. Although leery of giving his mother money, Peter went to the bank, and got a $400 certified check and $400 in cash. He gave Marjorie the $800 in exchange for a personal check. The next week Peter learned that the check was worthless.

On Monday, July 4, Duluth police had determined where the Caldwells were staying. Greene and Yagoda returned to the Twin Cities on Tuesday, July 5, to pay the Caldwells a visit at the Holiday Inn. The Caldwells were scheduled to depart for Denver on Western Airlines Flight 417 that afternoon. But first the detectives went to the airport with another photo lineup. The new set included Roger's mug shot from his DWI arrest in January 1977, when he had assaulted Rick. The detectives hoped the more recent photo would help the airport gift shop employees make a more positive identification.

First, Sergeant Yagoda spread the five photographs out on a table in front of Schwartzbauer. She immediately reached for Roger's mug shot and confidently identified him as "the man that was in the gift shop." Yagoda and Greene asked her to sit down and tell them if she was absolutely positive. When pressed, she backed off a bit, but said, "It sure looks like him."

After several more minutes of questions, Schwartzbauer's recall became less certain. She now said she wasn't sure about the man in the photo. The man in the gift shop had worn glasses. But the detectives believed Schwartzbauer had simply become overwhelmed by all the photos and questions and, in their experience, an eyewitness's initial impression was often the most accurate.

Next, Greene and Yagoda showed the lineup to Kelly. Her recall was less certain than Schwartzbauer's. The detectives noted in their report that Schwartzbauer initially recognized Caldwell's photo. The two men blamed themselves for her wavering identification. By trying to nail down a positive identification, they'd planted doubts in the mind of their best eyewitness.

Karen Mueller served a lot of business types on her 6:30 A.M. to 2 P.M. shift at the Holiday Inn Airport South restaurant. On Tuesday, July 5, she had been working about an hour and a half when Roger, whom she recognized from serving the day before, came in. Mueller poured him a cup of coffee and he ordered an omelet with cheese, onion, and green pepper. Roger read the newspaper until Mueller returned with his omelet.

Marjorie soon joined him and ordered a breakfast steak. Minutes later, when Mueller brought the steak to their table, she noticed Roger sat with head slumped and eyes closed, though neither he nor Marjorie said anything. By the time she dropped off the check, Roger's face had turned white, his breathing was labored, and he looked in pain.

"My husband suddenly became violently ill," Marjorie told Mueller. "I think it was the eggs."

"Do you want me to call the hospital?" Mueller volunteered.

"He'll be all right. It was just something about the eggs that didn't agree with him." Marjorie then turned to Roger and said, "You'd better get to the men's room." But he couldn't get up on his own.

Mueller flagged down a hotel desk clerk for help. The clerk helped Roger to his feet and guided him to the men's room, where he leaned on the counter, his shirt soaked with sweat. Roger asked to go someplace cooler, so the clerk sat him down in a chair in the main lobby and brought him several cold, damp towels and a glass of iced tea.

Marjorie continued to eat her breakfast while the hotel staff attended to Roger. She again commented to Mueller and the other waitresses it was probably the eggs, and that her husband had blacked out earlier, while sitting at the table. More likely it was brought on by drinking while on Antabuse, which Marjorie would admit later that day. While Roger's reaction continued, Marjorie got up and left the restaurant. Mueller last saw her when she returned briefly to sign the receipt.

Shortly before noon on Tuesday, Sergeants Yagoda and Greene pulled up to the Holiday Inn Airport South. Their plans to interview the Caldwells quickly fell apart when the desk clerk told them Roger had been rushed to the hospital by ambulance that morning. He had collapsed in the hotel elevator and was in intensive care at nearby Methodist Hospital.

The detectives decided to search the Caldwells' hotel room. They hoped to find Elisabeth's stolen jewelry, the suede garment bag, and any airline receipts. Just past 7 P.M., Bloomington police officers Bob Feyereizen, Doug McComb, Duluth sergeants Greene and Yagoda, and two deputies from the Hennepin County crime lab returned to the Holiday Inn, warrants in hand.

As the officers entered room 307, they noticed clothes covered the near bed, as though someone had started packing. A wicker case stacked on top of two suitcases by the wall nearest the door caught their attention. It looked like a smaller version of the case police had recovered just days before from Elisabeth's bedroom closet. A suede garment bag lay on the left side of the bed with the clothes. It looked identical to the one they had purchased on their first visit to the Host shop, which they had air-expressed to Waller in Colorado to aid in his search. The bag's handwritten identification tag named Roger S. Caldwell of Golden, Colorado, as its owner. Everything dovetailed. On the suitcases, officers noticed luggage tags marked North Central Airlines, number

997. Police soon confirmed this was the flight the Caldwells had taken to Duluth for the funeral. The garment bag had one of the tags; it was numbered consecutively with the tag on the suitcase that had been left at the Radisson.

Hennepin County crime lab technicians Merrill Hughes and Roger Smedberg went to work. For more than an hour they slowly moved clockwise around the room, photographing the evidence.

One picture showed a number of prescription medications lined up by the bathroom sink, including one in Roger's name for Antabuse, confirming what Marjorie had told the O'Tooles. On May 3, Dr. Hyman Zuckerman prescribed Antabuse for Roger after his latest attempt at rehab at Raleigh Hills had failed. The drug marked the next step in trying to control Roger's drinking. If Roger consumed alcohol while on the medication, he would experience uncomfortable physical side effects—he could even die. Marjorie had confided in Dr. Zuckerman that a drunken Roger had beaten her up on several occasions. The doctor considered Roger a "bad lush," but during Roger's May visit, the doctor also noted that Roger appeared depressed. Roger didn't say anything about his problems.

After Hughes and Smedberg finished the pictures they moved to the next step, donning plastic gloves to process the room for fingerprints.

Tuesday afternoon in Colorado, Waller and Agent Harmon drove east of Golden toward Stapleton International Airport. Waller noticed that a line of thunderstorms had enveloped the Rockies. The indigo sky came alive with a strobe-like show of summer lightning and the sound of thunder booming as the storm passed overhead. Waller told Harmon he hadn't flown much and worried about the weather conditions. "If airplanes get hit by lightning, their engines shut down and they drop like a rock from the sky," Harmon said in mock assurance. For Waller, it was a white knuckle takeoff.

A few hours later, safely back on the ground in the Twin Cities, a relieved Detective Waller stepped off the plane. Sweltering heat and high humidity more typical of the tropics knocked him back. The early evening air felt like a Sumo wrestler sitting on his chest.

As Waller entered the terminal carrying his briefcase and overnight bag, an airport security officer, who had been given Waller's description by Duluth police, flagged him down. "Sergeant Waller? There's an urgent message for you at the central office," the officer told him. The message told Waller to call detectives Yagoda and Greene at the Holiday Inn right away. When he did, Yagoda got on the phone.

They had hit pay dirt, Yagoda reported jubilantly. The suede suit bag and the smaller wicker basket had been found in the Caldwell's room. "We got 'em, Dick," Waller said excitedly.

Yagoda then left to obtain another search warrant; the first hadn't listed the wicker basket. The law said if the basket was in full view of police officers who were legally in the room, they could seize it. But as police closed in on the Caldwells, they weren't taking chances.

At about 10:15 P.M., while the search was in progress, officers heard someone fumbling with the doorknob. Waller looked through the peephole and saw Marjorie. He quickly slid out the door, reintroduced himself, and ushered her down the hall to the command post, Room 302, for questioning. She was cordial and chatty.

Waller sat next to Marjorie on the couch. Officer McComb and Detective Greene stood across the room listening. Waller explained to Marjorie that police were searching her room for stolen jewelry and physical evidence of the murders, including blood, hair, and fibers. He read aloud the search warrant and handed her a copy. To Waller's surprise, she didn't ask why the police search targeted her and her husband.

Waller inquired about Marjorie's activities in the days leading up to her mother's death. She told the officers she and her husband had visited a Denver pawn shop on June 23 and pawned jewelry for $3,000. She had spent most of the weekend of the murders inspecting ranch properties around Denver with real estate agent Fran Beyer.

Though Marjorie had agreed to the interview, Waller and the other officers knew her cooperation was strictly voluntary at this point, and she soon became uncomfortable with the line of questioning. Waller advised her of her Miranda rights.

On July 5, David Arnold sat in his pajamas watching the evening news when the phone rang. Since Marjorie had retained Arnold four years earlier, he had become used to frequent phone calls and office visits. He later estimated he spent "from fifty to sixty percent of each and every day that I worked with Marge or on her behalf. A great deal of time was spent negotiating with creditors and claimants, prioritizing claims, and trying to get everybody covered."

Early in their relationship, she'd called him late one night at home, upset because some checks she'd written were going to bounce. "She had received a check for the sale of a horse and it had bounced and in contemplation of that money being there she had written all these checks," Arnold recalled. "I told her 'Oh, Marge, that happens to everybody. Don't worry about it.' She said, 'Well, I want you to call all these people tomorrow. Explain to them and get them covered as soon as possible.' I asked her 'How much are you overdrawn?' She said, '$120,000.' So, you know, that was kind of an indication that we had more than the traditional kind of individual here."

Arnold asked Marjorie why she had called him so late this time.

"Well, I just thought you might like to have some fun," she said. "Why don't you come on out here? We've got about fifty police officers around here."

"What do you mean 'here?' Where are you?" Perplexed, Arnold tried to picture Marjorie somewhere in Colorado surrounded by police.

Marjorie sounded cavalier. "I'm at the Holiday Inn."

"What do you mean? What are you doing there?" The news that Roger and Marjorie hadn't left town startled the attorney. Arnold recalled years later, "I started chastising her for being there. For talking. She told me, 'We really didn't have any choice, you know. We were going to go the next day and then Roger got sick and had to go to the hospital.'" Marjorie said Roger was at Methodist Hospital in St. Louis Park, a Minneapolis suburb.

Arnold recalled how Marjorie blamed the Congdon family for her mother's death and the police presence in her hotel room. Marjorie explained: The Congdons were trying to frame her and Roger for Elisabeth's murder, and the Duluth police, under the family's control, played a part in the frame-up.

Arnold cut short Marjorie's complaints. "What the hell were you doing around here? Why didn't you go back out there to Colorado? At least it wouldn't have been as easy for this entourage to have shown up. What's going on?"

"Well, they're asking me a lot of questions. They're tearing apart the room. They won't let me go to the room," Marjorie said indignantly.

"Fine. I'll be out there," Arnold assured her. Then, trying to remember what Perry Mason would advise, he ordered, "Don't say anything."

But Marjorie resumed talking to police after she hung up. She had spent the entire weekend of the killings looking at real estate from early in the day until 10 or 11 P.M. Waller interrupted her. "Before you say anything else, has your attorney advised you about making statements to the police?" he asked.

No, he hadn't, she replied. Waller assumed Arnold was en route to hotel. Waller changed his strategy and began to pump Marjorie for as much information as possible until her attorney arrived.

Waller knew he had no legal power to make Marjorie talk. She had no good reason to answer questions. But instead of the pushy woman he'd encountered in the inspector's office the week before, she now sat before him calm and controlled, like a woman with nothing to hide—a woman who wanted to cooperate. Only her flushed cheeks gave her away. Waller had noticed in an earlier interview that when something upset Marjorie, her cheeks flushed from deep red to purple.

Greene knocked on the door and asked to see Waller. Waller was annoyed by the interruption of his interrogation, but Greene insisted. Waller stepped into the hall. Hughes showed Waller what he had found—a blue plastic cylinder, a pantyhose container, brimming with jewelry. Items found inside included Elisabeth Congdon's Sutton wristwatch and diamond-and-sapphire ring—both pulled from her body, investigators surmised, by her killer. The officers were elated by their find and curious about whatever explanation Marjorie would have for the items. Waller wondered why Marjorie and Roger would bring the jewelry back to Minnesota once it had been successfully transported to Colorado. He told Hughes to give him a few minutes, then come in and dump the jewelry on the couch. Then Waller would ask if she recognized any of the pieces.

Waller reentered the room. Not prepared just yet to confront her, he let Marjorie's lies compound. Marjorie repeated her whereabouts on the morning Mildred Garvue found Elisabeth Congdon and Velma Pietila dead. Waller then asked her if Roger had been with her the morning of June 27. Yes, she said, Roger had helped her carry their dirty clothes to the laundromat. The hotel front desk clerk had spoken to them on their way out.

Marjorie said she then drove Roger to downtown Denver and dropped him off. Roger planned to meet with attorney John Moorhead and also go to the library. She went directly to the laundromat. Waller looked over in surprise at the lie: police had already verified that Moorhead had spent the entire day at the annual picnic of the Denver Bar Association.

Hughes abruptly entered the room with the blue plastic container. "Do you recognize this?" Hughes asked.

"Yes, it's mine," Marjorie answered. Hughes emptied the container's contents on the couch between Waller and Caldwell. She immediately picked up the gold Sutton watch. "This is my watch. My mother had a watch identical to it." Reaching for the diamond-and-sapphire ring, she once again said her mother had an identical one. They repeated this process with most of the jewelry.

Marjorie admitted that a silver antique-looking photograph frame with engraved initials EMC had been "ripped off" from the mansion the day of her mother's funeral. A cameo pendant and a double strand of pearls were "presents" from her mother, she said.

The container also held an incriminating mix of clip and pierced earrings. Marjorie wore pierced earrings; her mother wore clip. Much of the jewelry matched the pieces Vera Dunbar had described as missing. The day after the murders, Dunbar had gone through the mansion with Waller and compiled a handwritten inventory of items she knew to be missing, expanding on her preliminary inventory the day before.

Waller glanced across the room and saw the incredulous look on McComb's face as Marjorie explained away each item of jewelry. The interview elated Waller. They'd recovered the jewelry and, to top it off, Marjorie sat there blatantly lying to them. It seemed illogical—she had to know the police now suspected more strongly than before that she knew something about her mother's murder.

Waller continued questioning Marjorie about her husband's whereabouts. Roger had no consistent alibi. His wife had given friends and acquaintances six different versions of his whereabouts the morning of the murders. When Waller asked whether Roger had also been with realtor Fran Beyer on Sunday, June 26, Marjorie initially said yes. But she then retracted and said she'd spoken with him by phone, a story similar to the one she had told Fran Beyer over dinner Sunday night—that she had spoken to Roger that morning on the phone about ranch property.

Marjorie began to fidget, and abruptly switched the conversation back to jewelry. She told the officers they could compare the items with photographs taken of her jewelry in Colorado before her home was burglarized.

"I don't know why she lied at a time when she obviously could have shut up rather than make false statements that she rationally had to know would be disproved," Waller recalled.

About 11 P.M., when Arnold and Lou Reidenberg, Marjorie's former divorce lawyer and close friend, arrived at the motel, they found Marjorie chatting with Waller in the command post room. Waller ignored them.

"Sergeant Waller, what are you talking to Mrs. Caldwell about?" Arnold asked, spotting the pile of jewelry between Marjorie and Waller.

"We're just talking about the homicides."

"Do you think we could talk to our client?"

"Sure," Waller replied agreeably, but without leaving the room.

"Alone," Arnold demanded, ending the challenge. But the six-foot-two, two-hundred-plus pound attorney said years later that the situation left him feeling overwhelmed. Arnold knew little about criminal defense. He specialized in civil law. Police officers seemed to be everywhere, surrounding his client. "It's the feeling you get when a state trooper stops you and you didn't think you were speeding, but he's still a state trooper and he stopped you," said Arnold. "It's respect for the position, yet concern as to what the hell this asshole is doing."

Arnold also recalled how indignant Marjorie sounded during their subsequent conversation, fuming as soon as police left her alone with Arnold and Reidenberg. "You ought to see the room," Marjorie told the two men. "They won't let anybody in there."

"What've you been talking about? What's going on here?" Arnold asked.

"They're looking for stuff. They obviously think that Roger—I told them Roger and I had nothing to do with it."

"What are you talking about?" Arnold asked, confused.

"Well they've taken everything we've got. They won't let us in the room. They've taken everything we've got. They're putting it in bags. And I was just explaining to them that this is my jewelry." Marjorie was becoming exasperated.

Only half kidding, Arnold told Reidenberg to keep his hand over Marjorie's mouth—gagging her was the only sure way to prevent his client from talking. He went down the hall to the Caldwells' room where police continued processing for fingerprints.

"I'd never seen anything like it," Arnold recalled. The fingerprint powder had turned the room "absolutely black from floor to ceiling" and even covered the pipes in the bathroom. Officers had disconnected the bathroom faucets and pipes to search for hidden evidence. "It looked like it had quite literally been under construction for years."

Arnold returned to room 302. He walked in to see Marjorie yacking away with officers. While Arnold lacked any experience in criminal law, he said later of the scene before him, "It just seemed like common sense to me that you don't do that." So once again he told her to shut up.

Sergeant Yagoda, who had returned with the new warrant by 10:30, turned toward Arnold and informed him that Waller and Greene had left for Methodist Hospital to arrest Roger for murder. Looking back, Arnold said, "What do you say after that?" He again ordered Marjorie to stop talking. "We have to find you a criminal defense attorney," Arnold insisted.

The phone rang around 12:45 A.M. and an officer answered it; Roger was on the line for Arnold. He was being arrested. He asked Arnold to come over to the hospital as soon as possible. Arnold told Roger not to say anything more to police, and that he would leave as soon as officers finished with Marjorie.

Arnold then waited as police searched Marjorie and her clothes, purse, and rental car. While a female police officer strip searched her, Marjorie seemed almost giddy, joking with the officer, "I suppose you go through this all the time." The strip search produced no physical evidence, but inside Marjorie's purse officers found a purchase agreement from a Colorado realty company, dated the previous month, for a $65,000 ranch. Detectives also found a set of car keys and a rental agreement signed by Arnold. He'd rented the car for the Caldwells the day after the murders.

Even after officers completed the searches, Arnold knew better than to leave Marjorie unattended. Reidenberg would stay with her while Arnold went to the hospital to visit Roger.

The searches failed to produce Elisabeth's gold grandmother's charm bracelet, which disappointed Waller. The bracelet was the one item that no one would have any reason to duplicate, and the sole piece of stolen jewelry police never recovered. But overall, police had put in a good night's work.

Sergeant Greene went downstairs and called Inspector Grams from a pay phone in the hotel lobby. "We found a pile of jewelry and the ring is in it. We've got the wicker case and the clothing bag. We've got them," Greene told his boss. It was an exciting call for any investigator to make.

Police transported most of the evidence collected from the Caldwells' room to the Hennepin County crime lab to be photographed. They took the jewelry to the BCA lab for examination for blood and hair fibers. Efforts to identify the thirty-seven pieces of jewelry would be extensive. "It really was overkill," Waller recalled. "Because the jewelry was so critical, we asked virtually everyone if they could identify the pieces."

The jewelry and Marjorie's statements were the only tangible evidence to support police and family suspicions that Marjorie was somehow involved in her mother's murder.

CHAPTER 12

Roger's Arrest

JUST AFTER MIDNIGHT ON WEDNESDAY, JULY 6, 1977, while armed detectives paced the hospital hallways, Roger Caldwell dozed in his room. Doctors had found high levels of Valium in Roger's blood, perhaps the reason for or a factor in his collapse.

Several hours earlier, Prosecutor DeSanto and Inspector Grams had reached their decision. DeSanto remembered getting the late night call from Inspector Grams. "Well, that's it. We've got enough evidence to charge him now," Grams told him. DeSanto agreed—the physical evidence and eyewitness statements were sufficient probable cause to charge Roger with two counts of first degree murder. Thursday morning, DeSanto would draft and sign a criminal complaint which would be sworn out before a judge, who would then issue the arrest warrant. DeSanto recalled, "There's a lot of pressure from outside interests—from the public and news media—to act when you have probable cause. Should we go with Roger and Marjorie Caldwell or just Roger? I was reluctant to go with Marjorie because I knew she was in Colorado at the time of the murders. It would be a much more difficult case."

By 11:30 P.M. Tuesday, the inspector had ordered officers Waller and Greene to arrest Roger on probable cause. Accompanied by Hennepin County Sheriff's Deputy Merrill Hughes, they arrived at Methodist Hospital at 12:20 A.M.

Roger looked up without surprise as the three officers entered the room. He seemed to be in some kind of sedated trance. Roger, dressed in a hospital gown, sat up slightly, the bed cranked at a fifteen-degree angle. He had pushed his gray hair back from his high brow and folded his arms against his chest. He studied the officers for several seconds before closing his eyes.

Waller stood at the side of the bed. "Roger, we'd like to talk with you about your activities the weekend of June 25 and 26," he said.

"I'm not that clear on dates."

"Roger, that was the weekend your mother-in-law was murdered," Waller said. "But before we talk about this, I need to inform you of your rights."

After being advised of his Miranda rights, Roger said smugly, his eyes still shut, "I understand my rights. I have nothing to say to you. My lawyer told me not to talk to the cops."

Waller wasted no time responding. "You're under arrest for two counts of murder in the deaths of Elisabeth Congdon and Velma Pietila."

Roger slowly opened his eyes, shrugged his shoulders, and said, "Oh." He then gave Waller a bored look and added, "I want to call Marjorie." Roger's response struck Waller as odd. Roger should have demanded to speak to his lawyer, not call his wife.

"The call has to be to your attorney," Hughes told him. But attorney David Arnold hadn't arrived home yet. Waller phoned the Holiday Inn where Arnold was still handling Marjorie. Arnold told Roger he would be over as soon as possible and not to answer any questions.

The officers escorted Roger to the hospital's X-ray room so a doctor could examine his injured right hand. The results were disappointing for Duluth detectives: the X-rays revealed no broken bones. But when the doctor lifted Roger's hand for a closer look, he discovered an abrasion and bruise at the cuticle and first joint of Roger's left middle finger. Waller silently cheered. In his professional opinion, the injury had likely been caused by the nails in Velma Pietila's broken shoe.

Back in Roger's hospital room, Waller, Greene, and Hughes searched his belongings. They found a pair of two-toned brown cowboy boots stamped with the word "Mexico" and covered with dark stains. Police confiscated the boots in order to analyze them for possible traces of blood, but they weren't holding out much hope. The killer had probably disposed of any bloody clothing within hours of the murders. From the hospital, the men returned to the Holiday Inn, where they learned that the search of Marjorie had failed to produce additional evidence. She had already left the hotel to stay at her son Stephen's apartment. Investigators also missed Arnold, who had finally been able to go to the hospital to visit Roger.

Arnold didn't arrive until after 1:30 A.M. The sheriff's deputies standing guard outside asked to see Arnold's identification and informed him that they had placed Roger under house arrest.

As Arnold walked into Roger's room, he was struck by how vulnerable Roger looked lying in his hospital bed. "In retrospect he seemed alternatively frightened like a child and relieved…like these suspicions or the likelihood of allegations or a frame-up or whatever had been talked about, now had come to fruition," Arnold recalled.

Arnold remembers starting the conversation by asking Roger where he was at the time of the murders. "He indicated he didn't know," Arnold recalled. The comment struck Arnold as kind of odd, "but I guess I didn't think anything more of it from the standpoint of—my mind might have been going very rapidly accepting and rejecting various alternatives. One of them might be, gee, he doesn't know exactly when the murders occurred, so he doesn't know where he was at that time. Or he was off somewhere." Before leaving, Arnold reminded Roger not to say anything else unless he had an attorney with him.

Several miles away from the hospital, at a Perkins restaurant, detectives Waller, Yagoda, and Greene—along with officers McComb and Feyereizen—toasted their early morning success with coffee and cheese omelets. Waller had called his boss at home to advise him of Roger's arrest. He knew Inspector Grams had already begun work preparing a press release and arranging for Roger's transfer to Duluth.

On Wednesday morning, newspaper headlines played up the arrest. The photo circulated in the news media was the photo taken by Agent Harmon that had first been shown to the airport clerks at the Host Gift Shop. Although Inspector Grams' decision to release the photo to reporters was well intentioned, it gave the prosecution a legal headache. Any identification of Roger at a later date would arguably be tainted. Chances were too great someone would have seen the picture in the newspapers or on television.

The *Minneapolis Tribune's* headline read, "Caldwell in hospital awaiting Congdon murder charges," while across the Mississippi River the St. Paul Pioneer Press splashed its front page with "Two murder counts await son-in-law."

Back at Duluth police headquarters, Waller, Yagoda, and Greene received a celebratory welcome from fellow officers and Inspector Grams. "We had a lot of pride in our hearts that we had arrested someone in connection with this highly visible homicide," said Waller.

Two days later, on Friday, July 8, the news media looked on as sheriff's deputies wheeled Roger to a waiting squad car, his head covered by a towel. He spent the night at the Hennepin County Jail in Minneapolis. The next day, Greene and Yagoda transferred him to the St. Louis County Jail in Duluth.

Unlike reporters in New York City or Miami—where the sheer volume of murders prevents all but a few from receiving front-page coverage—Duluth reporters escorted the detectives and suspect like paparazzi pursuing celebrities. Hennepin County Sheriff Don Omodt personally led a procession of squad cars to the county line where state patrol squads then took the lead. The caravan continued until Roger, Greene, and Yagoda reached the Duluth city limits.

Saturday, upon his arrival at the St. Louis County Jail in Duluth, detectives confiscated Roger's personal possessions, including a black leather, single-fold wallet. At the time, officers neglected to carefully search the wallet and eventually the wallet and its contents would be at the center of a trial controversy.

Back at Glensheen, Waller and the identification unit officers returned to their crime scene investigation. Fingerprinting was completed in Elisabeth's bedroom and additional crime scene photos were taken, including one of the bedroom closet with and without the remaining wicker case. Although police later marked the photos with the date, time, and location, they never maintained a photo inventory. This slip-up opened up the prosecution to defense charges that the photos were inaccurately marked and out of order—and that the wicker case found in the Caldwell's hotel room had been planted.

Mannette Allen heard about Roger's arrest after returning from an out-of-town skating competition. She wanted to lend her old friend Marjorie her moral support and sympathy. Allen called Stephen, hoping to learn Marjorie's whereabouts and invite her over. Marjorie herself answered the phone. When Marjorie arrived at her house, Allen could barely recognize the woman she had called her best friend years earlier. Mannette described the old Marjorie as "prissy," with her hair in a tight little bun, wearing no makeup except lipstick occasionally, and typically dressed in full skirts, shirtwaist dresses, and ballet slippers. She had been "the most demure woman I knew" and shy around men other than her husband. She recalled one time when Stephen had forgot his practice music tape. Allen knew one of the other coaches had the same music, so she asked Marjorie to go to his apartment to pick up the cassette. "She turned bright red and said, 'I can't do that.' I said, 'Why not?' And she said, 'Dick would kill me if I ever went to a bachelor's apartment by myself.'" When Allen had persisted, reminding Marjorie she was a married mother of seven, she still refused to go, and Allen had to make other arrangements. Unlike that prim and proper Marjorie of the past, the Marjorie who stood in Allen's living room was a tough-talking, cowgirl wannabe. Her black hair, cropped and spiky, looked almost boyish, and she wore blue jeans, cowboy boots, and chunky turquoise jewelry.

"It's horrible," Marjorie said, referring to Roger's arrest. "How could anyone think Roger had anything to do with my mother's death?" She hated the media frenzy and the way the police wouldn't leave her and Roger alone. Marjorie launched into a angry verbal assault on the Duluth Police Department, ending her tirade with, "Those goddamn cops."

Allen had never before heard Marjorie swear. She didn't know if her friend had changed radically or if she had simply failed to see another side to Marjorie's personality. "It was like I was meeting a completely new person," she recalled.

On Saturday, July 9, Marjorie and her friend Joy O'Toole had lunch together at Como Park in St. Paul. The two women sat on the lawn and ate White Castle hamburgers. Joy kept asking questions about the weekend of the murders. "Would Rick be able to say Roger was in Colorado during the critical time?" O'Toole asked. Rick didn't see Roger because he wasn't there, Marjorie replied, mixing up her stories.

"You said Roger went out for pop while you were at the laundromat June 27," Joy reminded her friend.

"I must be wrong on that. I think Roger was in Denver on business." Then Marjorie told Joy that Roger had also gone to the library that day, yet another version of what Roger had been doing. "I don't live in my husband's pocket," she added. "Suppose he was drinking—he wouldn't remember where he was."

Joy asked Marjorie about the jewelry police recovered in her hotel room in Bloomington. The jewelry had been "planted" in the room, Marjorie said. Wasn't it strange, she asked Joy, that police recovered the same jewelry items "earmarked" for her to inherit upon her mother's death?

The two women talked about the viciousness of Velma Pietila's beating. Joy later told authorities that Marjorie said, "That doesn't sound like Roger. Roger would have only hit her once because he's a drinker."

Even before charges had been filed, the Caldwells and Arnold, believing it was just a matter of time, had started shopping for defense attorneys. Arnold, working with Reidenberg, had compiled a list of high-profile attorneys who might be interested in representing the Caldwells. Among those approached was renowned criminal defense lawyer F. Lee Bailey. But Bailey, like most attorneys contacted, demanded cash up front. The Caldwells had none.

Arnold and Reidenberg then decided to approach two well-known Twin Cities attorneys, Ron Meshbesher and Doug Thomson. Arnold remembers the first time he met Meshbesher and Thomson: "They both said they were very interested in representation. Then it came to a discussion of who was going to represent whom, and the attorneys talked about a coin toss."

Meshbesher, however, took the initiative and said he'd take Marjorie as his client. "I like Marjorie," Meshbesher said. "She's got the same kind of temperament that I have." Thomson said he didn't care if he represented Roger. But Thomson later confided to Arnold that he thought he'd gotten the better deal. Compared to his wife, Roger wasn't much of a talker and hadn't attempted to control how Thomson tried his case.

As one of Thomson's first actions as Roger's attorney, he bought his client a pair of shoes. Caldwell had left most of his clothes behind in Colorado, including any attire appropriate for court appearances, such as his arraignment on the murder charges.

On the afternoon of Saturday, July 9, a subdued-looking Roger Caldwell, dressed in striped gray overalls and green slippers, appeared in St. Louis County Court for a bail hearing. Thomson had driven up from St. Paul for the hearing. DeSanto requested bail in the amount of $500,000. Thomson asked that bail be set at $20,000. He argued that Roger was a fine man who had even held a job with the Atomic Energy Commission and had "secret clearance." This was news to DeSanto, but he let the claim go unchallenged. Bail was set at $200,000, Roger was returned to his cell, and there seemed little chance of freedom before his arraignment. Marjorie proclaimed his innocence but was conspicuously absent from the jail on visiting days. Marjorie turned to the news media to complain that she was destitute and looked to his family to bail him out. Roger's brother Howard said years later that he hated to hear the phone ring after several calls from Marjorie. "She was on the phone to us every night after Roger's arrest," he recalled. "She needed $50,000 to bail him out. Could I send it to him. 'Don't you own your home?' she asked me. 'Can't you take out a second mortgage?' She tried to make me feel guilty." Marjorie also told Howard that she was barely scraping by trying to help Roger. She claimed to have been reduced to menial labor like scrubbing floors because money was scarce.

After the arrest, Duluth police continued to identify the jewelry recovered from the Caldwells' hotel room. Vera Dunbar told police the diamond-and-sapphire ring and gold watch looked identical to those worn by Elisabeth.

Officers talked with Richard Heimbach, the owner of Bagley & Company Jewelers in Duluth, one of Elisabeth's favorite jewelry stores. He confirmed that the ring was the same one he had cleaned and serviced many times. She had worn the ring for twenty-five years. He recognized the pattern of wear on the stones and the setting. "I know it as I would an individual," Heimbach told them. This additional evidence confirmed that at least some jewelry

items found in the Caldwells' hotel room were among those missing from Glensheen. But Waller knew they needed more proof; it's a long jump from stolen jewels to murder. The Caldwells could argue that they received the jewelry after the murders without being directly involved.

On July 12, medical examiner Volker Goldschmidt drew blood, pulled body and head hair samples, and collected saliva samples from Roger Caldwell, standard procedure when processing someone charged in a violent crime. Police would compare these known specimens with unknown specimens collected earlier at Glensheen. The defense couldn't say the jewelry only connected the Caldwells indirectly to the crime if, as Waller hoped, the samples placed Roger in Glensheen at the time of the murders.

CHAPTER 13

Will to Murder

FIVE DAYS AFTER ROGER CALDWELL'S ARREST, Gary Waller returned to Colorado. Bob Harmon greeted Waller with a smile at the Stapleton airport the afternoon of July 11. "We haven't been able to pin down Roger's whereabouts the weekend of the homicides," the CBI agent said. So far their primary suspect had no alibi, so no news was good news.

"What else have you found out?" Waller asked, anxious for an update on what they had uncovered in the two weeks since his last visit.

Gordanier and CBI Agent Harmon had lined up an interview with realtor Fran Beyer, whose statements about Roger's absence were critical to the investigation. She'd been sick during Waller's earlier trip. Beyer had spent more time with Marjorie than anyone else in the days leading up to the murders. Waller wanted Marjorie's explanations to Beyer on the record. He also needed to question Bill Kay, the Caldwells' friend who'd helped them pawn jewelry three days before the murders.

Waller and Harmon met Gordanier at the Holland House Hotel. Inside the coffee shop, an intense looking, dark-haired man sat talking to Bill Kay. Waller and Gordanier walked up to the table and introduced themselves. The man pulled a business card from his wallet and introduced himself as Vincent Carraher, a private investigator for Ron Meshbesher.

Waller was angry. Carraher's presence came as a complete surprise. What in the hell had Kay already spilled to Carraher? Where did Carraher get off meddling in an ongoing murder investigation? Waller wanted first crack at questioning Kay and he didn't like Carraher's brazen attitude. But he knew he didn't have the authority to take Kay into custody. Gordanier did, though, and together they hauled Kay down to police headquarters.

There, Kay confirmed that he and the Caldwells had visited the L & L Coin pawn shop the morning of June 23. He told Waller the couple pawned jewelry to pay for "back horse board and feed bills." The Caldwells had struck a pretty poor bargain: The pawn broker gave them $3,000 for $8,000 worth of jewelry, with an option to buy the jewelry back for $4,000.

After the Caldwells cashed the $3,000 check, Kay drove them to a car rental agency. The Caldwells had been without a car since the local bank repossessed their three Jeeps for nonpayment of loans. He then dropped the Caldwells at the airport to pick up their car.

The morning of the murders, Kay stopped at the Holland House at about nine o'clock looking for Roger. The desk clerk said the Caldwells were out, but Marjorie was at the laundromat. She also told Kay there was a wake-up call and a note for Rick, which Kay delivered before walking to the laundromat.

Kay told Waller that he and Marjorie talked for about a half hour. "She said that Roger was in Denver with a lawyer. That she had dropped him there that morning. I left Marge at approximately 10:15 and went to Denver on business. That afternoon I stopped at the Holland House to see if Roger was back. The lady at the desk asked if I knew where they were because there had been a death in the family. I asked if it was [Marjorie's] mother because I knew she was ill. The lady said it was an aunt. I took a ride to Hillcroft Acres…but did not find them." He denied being involved with the murders in any way.

After Kay left, Waller, Harmon, and Gordanier talked about what new information he'd provided. The list of of people who hadn't seen Roger in Colorado the weekend of the murders now included Bill Kay.

Waller was troubled, however, by the claim John Hannigan, vice president for Golden State Bank, had made during his first interview. He had told investigators he saw Roger around 9:30 A.M., Monday, June 27. Roger came into the bank to notify Hannigan that Rick had taken the Caldwells' repossessed Jeep Wagoneer to drive to work. Hannigan hadn't noticed anything unusual about Roger's appearance. "Rick had to be at work at 8:30 so I told him to take it because the bank wasn't open yet," Roger had explained.

When Waller suggested Hannigan might have mixed up the day he saw Roger, the bank official said he was positive. But Hannigan's secretary told investigators Roger would have had to walk directly in front of her desk in order to speak with Hannigan, and she did not see Roger Monday morning. Roger also did not pick up $300 that had been wired to him and Marjorie for travel to the funeral until June 28.

The afternoon of June 28, Hannigan spoke with Roger when he came to pick up the money. Hannigan noticed Roger seemed nervous and in a hurry, and that he had a scratch on his lip and a swollen hand. Roger said that he had cut himself shaving and a horse had stepped on his hand. Waller remained convinced that the message Bertha Huskins had taken at the Holland House Monday afternoon signaled Roger's arrival back to Denver.

The next day, Waller continued his interviews in the Golden and Denver area. He and Agent Harmon took a statement from Fran Beyer in Waller's room at the Writers Manor Hotel.

In her six-page statement, Beyer described the ranch properties the Caldwells had looked at beginning June 2. Beyer also related Roger's behavior when he accompanied his wife on Monday, June 13. Beyer picked up Roger at the Holland House Hotel shortly after 9 A.M. and then drove to Heritage Drug to pick up Marjorie. On the way to the drugstore, Roger told Beyer that if he seemed lightheaded it was because he had just taken three Valium, upset over the insurance claim he and Marjorie had filed on Pine Valley Farms. Beyer said Roger also talked about "Marge's family and the Congdons' wealth and his and Marge's recent marriage. He also said that Marge was expected to lose her hearing within four years…. While riding along, Roger in front with me and Marjorie sitting in back, they would discuss properties and uses of the facilities and usually end up hollering and Marge would 'turn him off,' so she said, and ride quietly looking out the window. Roger liked to talk about anything. And kept up a constant conversation." Marjorie and Roger had "quick short tempers," Beyer said later, and they "were not comfortable to be around all of the time."

Two ranch prospects on South Lake Gulch Road attracted the Caldwells' attention, particularly Marjorie's. The first was a twelve-acre spread complete with a house and barn. The owners, Julius and Charlotte DeLuca, showed the Caldwells and Beyer around. Marjorie was very enthusiastic, Beyer recalled, but Roger seemed to grow quieter as the day progressed. While Roger toured the house, Marjorie made up one of her stories for Beyer, saying that she "had been married to an alcoholic before," and it was so terrible that her priest "urged her to divorce him." Marjorie claimed that since that time, her family no longer held her in their good graces.

Later that day, when Beyer called her clients at the Holland House Hotel, Marjorie told her to write up a purchase agreement for the DeLuca property. She also told Beyer that she wanted to look at the second property, located next door to the DeLuca home. Marjorie claimed that her cousin James Dudley, from Long Island, had entered semiretirement and wanted to find a large property somewhere between Colorado Springs and Denver to raise thoroughbred horses. Marjorie wanted to preview properties for him. The two women then arranged to meet the next morning.

On Tuesday, June 14, Marjorie signed a purchase agreement for the $97,500 DeLuca property, with a $5,000 note due within ten days. She and Beyer then went to look at the second property on South Lake Gulch Road. Marjorie, apparently forgetting the James Dudley story, told Beyer she wanted to purchase the property for "additional acreage" and she could "use the house for stable help." The following day, Marjorie applied for a bank loan to finance the properties and told the loan officer she had written her trust officer for authorization of trust funds to buy the two properties.

On Thursday, June 23, Beyer called to remind Marjorie and Roger that their $5,000 note on the DeLuca property would come due the following day. Beyer recalled that "When Marge heard my voice, she exclaimed how sorry she was, but that she had just gotten out of the hospital. She had been kicked by a horse and had been in traction and under sedation and hadn't had time to contact her attorney or her banker and needed until Monday [June 27] to redeem the note." Marjorie and Beyer agreed to meet again on Saturday morning, June 25, so that Marjorie could sign an extension clause and look at properties for her cousin. "I picked her up and she was telling me all about how Roger was under such a strain with all of his attorneys and their claim, and how he was going down to Colorado Springs the next day, the reason I don't remember, but that he really needed the trip. He also said we should keep our eyes open for a place with fifty to two hundred acres with an old log cabin on it to be a retreat to fix up and for their retirement."

After several appointments, the women drove past a $106,000 property for sale on Perry Park Road that was not among Beyer's listings. Marjorie insisted on stopping and while Beyer parked the car, she got out and rushed up to the owners and started asking questions. It was ideal for Roger, Marjorie told Beyer.

After viewing the ranch and several other properties, they capped the day with dinner at the Magic Pan, one of Marjorie's favorite restaurants. Marjorie paid for the two dinners with cash. When Beyer called Marjorie later that night, Marjorie said she wanted to go back on Sunday to the Perry Park Road house because Roger wanted her to measure the rooms. She was also interested in looking at more properties. They agreed to meet the following day at 10 A.M.

On Sunday morning, Marjorie informed Beyer that Roger had taken the back road to Colorado Springs that morning around 5:30. He had driven by the Perry Park Road property they'd visited the previous afternoon and phoned her to say "it was just what he wanted." The women revisited the ranch and talked with the owners before checking on a twenty-acre parcel of land for sale adjacent to the South Lake Gulch Road properties.

That night, over dinner at Mr. Steak, Marjorie told Beyer she wanted purchase agreements drawn up for the Perry Park Road property and the property at 977 South Lake Gulch Road. Since they hadn't completed the paperwork by the time the restaurant closed, Beyer finished writing up the contracts in the parking lot. They planned to meet at Heritage Drug Monday morning at 11:00. Marjorie would redeem the $5,000 note for the DeLuca property.

Beyer arrived at Heritage Drug around 11:30 A.M. Monday and spotted Marjorie coming out of the delicatessen. After Marjorie told her about the murders she apologized for her condition—she had gotten Valium from her doctor—but refused to cancel their appointments, much to Beyer's surprise.

Once again, Marjorie had an explanation for Roger's absence. "Roger had taken Ricky to the mountains surrounding Boulder so [Rick] would be away from the media and not hear about [the murders] until they knew more details and his doctor was alerted to the situation with standby equipment," Beyer told the officers. "She made the statement that she was glad she had been with me so late and since they were not particularly fond of her, they might think she was involved with the murders. I was a bit taken aback by the remark but figured the sedative probably had influenced her reasoning." The two women went to the realty office to complete details of the previous night's purchase agreements, then toured additional properties; the DeLuca note remained unredeemed.

While the Caldwells were in Duluth for Elisabeth's funeral, Beyer called the De-Lucas to update them on the unredeemed note. She learned that Marjorie, Roger, and Rick had paid a surprise visit to the DeLucas on June 23. The DeLucas had been charmed by Marjorie at the first meeting and she had apparently persuaded the couple to go along with her desire to move in within a matter of weeks. The couple had moved out all their furniture with the exception of a few items the Caldwells had wanted to purchase, but hadn't yet paid for. The DeLucas slept on the floor in sleeping bags.

Marjorie had failed to call Beyer as promised before leaving town. Beyer was re-lieved to hear from Marjorie on Friday, July 1, when she called to say she and Roger would return the following Tuesday. She told Beyer that her cousin Tom Congdon would be in town then, and that the note would be redeemed. She instructed Beyer to call the Federal Land Bank to assure Marjorie's loan officer that her trust funds remained available and would not go to probate. Marjorie ended the conversation by saying that she planned to wire Beyer authorization to complete the purchase of the land adjacent to the South Lake Gulch Road properties.

Beyer last spoke with Marjorie on July 5, when Marjorie called long distance to say Roger had collapsed that morning and was in the hospital with a heart attack or potas-sium imbalance. They wouldn't be back until Friday, Marjorie said, when they planned to move into their new ranch.

"Are the DeLucas out?" Marjorie asked.

"They haven't left because the note wasn't redeemed," Beyer reminded Marjorie. Marjorie instructed Beyer to call her attorney or Tom Congdon and arrange pay-ment.

That afternoon a close friend called Beyer after hearing a radio report of Roger's arrest. Beyer tried unsuccessfully to call Marjorie at the Holiday Inn in Minneapolis. Beyer then called Tom Congdon at his office, and he "confirmed my thoughts the De-Luca property should be returned to the market." She got the same advice from David Arnold. "We should consider the sale dead," Arnold said, until Marjorie is in a position to buy something. Beyer considered every sale she'd negotiated with Marjorie as void. The only consolation was Marjorie's tardiness meeting down payment deadlines meant she didn't have any earnest money to return. At the end of her statement, she told the investigators she had not spoken to the Caldwells since Roger's arrest.

The next day, Waller and Gordanier visited the Golden State Bank to search the safety deposit box Roger rented on June 28. Bank employees recalled that Roger ap-peared nervous and agitated as he filled out the required paperwork. He seemed in a hurry to get the box, a bank secretary told Waller. After placing his papers inside, he apologized for being abrupt and left.

Search warrant in hand, Waller and Gordanier asked the bank security guard to open the box. When no spare key could be found, they called a locksmith. But the wait paid off. Inside the small gray box, the men found several documents. One, typewrit-ten and signed by Marjorie, gave Roger power of attorney. Another was sealed inside an Arapahoe County clerk of court's office envelope. Opening the envelope, Waller removed a single, yellow legal-sized sheet covered with Marjorie's handwriting: a will giving Roger her share of her grandfather's estate upon Elisabeth's death—regardless of divorce or her children. It was dated June 24, three days before the murders.

The document read:

> I, Marjorie Caldwell do on this day of June twenty fourth, nineteen hundred and seventy seven give and bequeath to my husband Roger Sipe Caldwell all the cash benefits due to and or accruing to me from the Chester A. Congdon trust that must disperse all principal to the children of his heirs within three calendar years from the date of death of the last surviving child of his, namely, Elisabeth Mannering Congdon. This bequest is made as a deed of gift with no restrictions as to use, or any restrictions accruing from a state of divorce, separation, my death or any other conditions or restrictions. I do this with the full knowledge that this document is irrevocable under any circumstances or for any reasons whatsoever and that said document shall be binding also upon my executors, heirs or beneficiaries.

Thanks to the handwritten will, Roger could look forward to about a $2.5 million cut of his wife's $8.2 million inheritance. At trial, DeSanto would refer to the will as a "murder contract."

By mid-July the case was several weeks old. Like any criminal investigation, the longer a murder case goes, the more problems law enforcement has maintaining the energy and enthusiasm of the first days. Waller, Yagoda, and Greene were now the only officers still assigned to the case full-time.

"Initially, every officer wants to get in on the action," Waller said. "Then the more routine and uneventful the investigation becomes, the harder it is to generate interest. This is when the real detective work goes on. You make an arrest, the jail door slams, and you have to continue to build a case, while other people take on new responsibilities."

On July 15, Waller, still in Colorado, focused on disproving Marjorie's various explanations for Roger's whereabouts the weekend of the murders and tried to pin down Roger's activities during the critical time period.

Waller interviewed several people Marjorie saw the morning of the murders. The secretary to Rick's doctor at the National Asthma Center in Denver said Marjorie appeared visibly distraught on June 27. She'd demanded instructions on what to do in case her son had a bad asthma attack after learning of his grandmother's murder.

Harmon and Waller visited the Organized Crime Strike Force and met with Colorado's assistant attorney general, who drafted another subpoena so that police could examine Avis rental records for the Cordoba the Caldwells had rented from the Stapleton airport from June 23 to June 27. Mileage statements for the Cordoba indicated the Caldwells could easily have driven two round trips to the Stapleton airport the weekend of the murders.

Waller talked to Joyce Smith, a waitress at the Holland House, who frequently served the Caldwells at the hotel coffee shop. Smith told Waller she saw the Caldwells about 6:15 A.M. Saturday, June 25, in the hotel parking lot. "I spoke to them. They said they were going out of town for the day. Seemed in a hurry. Roger was putting a small suitcase in the car in the back seat," she said. Smith worked the dinner shift on Sunday and she usually saw the Caldwells for dinner. She didn't remember seeing the couple Sunday night.

Smith couldn't forget Roger's appearance, however, when the Caldwells had dinner at the coffee shop the Thursday prior to the murders. Roger had acted and sounded like he had been "drinking heavily," Smith told Waller. Roger asked her to leave the twenty-ounce T-bone steaks the couple ordered off the bill. "I'll give you a big tip," Roger insisted. The Caldwells usually tipped big. Smith assumed Roger was kidding, and responded she couldn't do that. Marjorie told Roger to shut up. "Don't get the girl in trouble," she scolded.

Waller next interviewed Smith's teenage daughter, Jacqueline, who also worked as a waitress at the Holland House coffee shop. Jacqueline Smith worked from 9 A.M. to 5 P.M. on Sundays. She told Waller that on Sunday, June 26, she saw Marjorie alone in the coffee shop doing paperwork. Marjorie was writing on what appeared to be maps, Smith said. Smith had not seen Roger that Sunday.

But investigators believed that Holland House waitresses Wilma Farley and Joyce Mynheir had provided more accurate statements. They told investigators they had seen Marjorie and Roger leaving the Holland House Sunday morning, June 26. Marjorie had said they were on their way to the airport.

Farley's and Mynheir's later sighting of the Caldwells fit the investigators' theory: Marjorie had driven Roger to the Denver airport early Sunday, where he either caught a direct flight to the Twin Cities or flew to another Midwestern city and changed planes. He flew back to the Denver airport Monday, where Marjorie eventually picked him up after he had left the short message with Bertha Huskins at the Holland House front desk.

Police had another piece of circumstantial evidence to go with this theory. During interviews with airline personnel, a North Central Airlines stewardess had told Duluth detectives a male passenger on the Denver to Minneapolis flight June 26 or 27 "was noticeable for wearing a large quantity of turquoise jewelry"—a description that fit Roger's cowboy attire.

As a result, Waller and Colorado law enforcement disregarded the new information from the Smiths. Police didn't consider the possibility that the killer could have left from the Colorado Springs airport for the trip to Duluth, so flight manifests from Colorado Springs were not investigated. In hindsight, Waller thinks this was how they missed Roger—and there was enough mileage on the rented Cordoba to allow for two round trips from Golden to Colorado Springs that weekend, with mileage left over.

By early August, Duluth police had substantial circumstantial evidence, but still had no concrete leads on how Roger got to and from the murder scene. Between 6:35

A.M., the time on the Twin Cities airport parking ticket, and Roger's call to the Holland House Hotel for a ride at 1:45 P.M. (Mountain Time), sixty-nine flights left the Minneapolis-St. Paul International Airport. Police traced all but eight of the 5,900 people who flew from the Twin Cities to Denver on June 27, including one passenger assigned to a Navy submarine in the Pacific. They found no listing for Roger Caldwell among hotel or plane reservations—or any unusual last minute bookings. But the possibility remained that any of the 5,900 names might have been a pseudonym.

The police department checked flight manifests and passenger coupons for fifteen airlines with routes between Colorado and Minnesota, some directly to Duluth and some via Chicago, Milwaukee, Sioux Falls, or the Twin Cities. From August 5 through 9, police sent out the first round of letters to passengers and crew on those flights. The letter from the police chief requested "if you are aware of any existing photographs or slides taken the morning of June 27, 1977, at the Minneapolis-St. Paul and/or Denver airports, please call collect." No passengers reported seeing the suspect. In the end, police devoted more than three hundred hours of investigation to the airlines with little to show for it.

In most criminal cases, the district judge decides whether investigators have gathered sufficient evidence for a trial. But Minnesota law says first-degree murder charges must go to a grand jury for an indictment before the prosecution can try the case. When Roger had been arraigned on July 21 in St. Louis County District Court, his bail had been raised to $400,000; on August 5, a Duluth grand jury indicted Roger Caldwell on first-degree murder charges in the deaths of his mother-in-law Elisabeth Congdon and her nurse Velma Pietila. The news surprised few people. The indictment spelled out the inheritance Marjorie expected to receive. As a legal heir, Roger could inherit from his wife on her death without a will.

Elisabeth's will, dated December 29, 1967, mentioned twenty-three individuals. As expected, Elisabeth named her two adoptive daughters, Marjorie and Jennifer, as principal heirs of her estate. She also named her daughters as benefactors of her $4.2 million living trust.

But what startled investigators was a "notice of demand" by Marjorie that had been filed with St. Louis County Probate Court the day of her mother's funeral—and was dated June 16, nearly two weeks before Elisabeth was killed. It requested that she or her attorney be notified when any action concerning her mother's will was taken. Inspector Grams told reporters that the date the document was prepared could be significant in the murder investigation, but otherwise remained vague. "I'll let you draw your own conclusions," he said. However, police soon learned from David Arnold that the notice of demand had actually been drafted the same day it was filed—the day of the funeral. The day before the funeral Arnold had called his associate James Wieland, asking him to fly up to Duluth to be a "gofer" and help with Marjorie. On the day of the funeral, Marjorie insisted she needed something to protect herself from her family regarding the will. Arnold thought it was unnecessary and in bad taste, but Marjorie insisted, so he had Wieland prepare the form at the Radisson and file it that afternoon. Wieland realized later that he had glanced at the desk pad calendar, which was not on the right month, and inserted the wrong date. Filing it on the day of the funeral may have been in poor taste, but the date on the notice of demand wasn't quite the smoking gun they once thought. It was merely a clerical error.

Four days after the indictment, Waller and Sergeant Yagoda conducted a driving experiment simulating the murderer's route. Driving an unmarked squad car from Glensheen to the Twin Cities airport, they recorded the time and mileage. They drove seventy miles per hour—the speed limit at the time was fifty-five—figuring that Roger would have been anxious to get out of Duluth and to the Twin Cities to catch an early flight.

The detectives stopped midway for coffee, then got back on the freeway with one unscheduled break. A state patrol officer stopped Yagoda for speeding. Roger wouldn't have faced this problem; at the time the Minnesota State Patrol didn't cover outstate freeways for speeding between 2 and 7 A.M. After talking their way out of a ticket, Waller and Yagoda continued, arriving at the airport security lot across from short-term parking in two hours and twenty-eight minutes—more than enough time for Roger to have killed the women between midnight and 4 A.M. and made it to the airport by 6:35 A.M., the time stamped on the parking ticket recovered from the trash can.

Waller and Yagoda next walked at a moderate pace from the spot where the Pietila car was found to the garbage can where the keys and parking ticket were discovered. From there, they continued to walk at a moderate pace into the main terminal, took the escalator up to the second floor, and finally arrived at the Host Gift Shop. The total time for the walk from the parking spot to the gift shop was under two and one-half minutes.

The case then took a bizarre turn. On the same day of the driving experiment, Marjorie reported being attacked by a man with a razor in her son Stephen's apartment. Marjorie told police she was taking a bath when she heard someone knocking loudly at the door. She opened the door leaving the chain lock intact. A man dressed in a police officer's uniform claimed he had papers for her to sign, so she let him in the house.

Once inside, the attacker allegedly pulled out a straight razor and said, "This is just a warning. Stay away from Duluth—and don't try to help your husband." Marjorie claimed he then said he wouldn't seriously hurt her this time, but would get her and her son if she didn't cooperate.

Marjorie reported the man then repeatedly slashed the left side of her body, including her shoulder, upper arm, and the upper part of her back and chest. She tried without luck to break away and run for cover to the bathroom. The man hit her several times on the left side of her head with his hand before leaving.

But Marjorie did not immediately call the police or an ambulance. Instead she called Lou Reidenberg and her old friend Mannette Allen. She told Allen that somebody had broken in, attacked her, and cut her. Marjorie asked if Allen could please come and pick her up. Allen immediately drove to Stephen's house. When she arrived she saw for herself the cuts on Marjorie's face and arms, blood on her clothes, and random blood smears throughout the apartment. Marjorie was very distraught and repeated that some unknown person had attacked her. Allen wanted to take her to an emergency room, but Marjorie insisted Allen take her to Ron Meshbesher's office. At the time, Allen believed her and was much too upset to drive anywhere. It wasn't until Allen got home and her husband asked what happened that she wondered why there wasn't more blood. As she reconstructed the scene for him it seemed to her there should have been more blood on the floor, in the bathroom, and around the apartment. Most of the blood was on Marjorie.

When police were finally called, they arrived to find Marjorie sitting on the couch next to Lou Reidenberg. The responding officers noted dried blood on the left side of her face, a cut near her scalp line, and another on her left cheek between her eye and ear. Marjorie then showed the officers numerous shallow cuts covering her upper left back, shoulder, arm, and chest. She had none of the defensive wounds—cuts to the hands or forearms—that usually result from instinctive attempts to block such an attack.

She claimed to have seen her attacker before, during the search of her hotel room at the Holiday Inn the previous month. She described him as about six feet, average build, brown hair, with a mustache above thin lips. He was dressed in a blue uniform with a police gun belt and star-shaped badge. When Waller read the police complaint, he could hardly believe it—the description of Marjorie's attacker was a thinly disguised composite of himself.

The next day, University of Minnesota security officer Bud Miller pulled out of a bank drive-through in downtown Duluth. As he exited, a woman suddenly pulled her car in front of his squad car. The woman frantically waved her arms at him as though she needed help. She then got out and walked up to his car. He couldn't miss the large, white bandage on the left side of her face and her huge, dark sunglasses. Marjorie, clearly agitated, asked Miller for directions to the offices of the *Duluth News-Tribune*.

Minutes later, Marjorie walked into the *News-Tribune* newsroom unannounced and insisted on talking to a reporter. She told reporter Jim Allen that her attacker threatened to return and scar her for life if she helped her husband. The man also promised to break her arm and go after her youngest son.

In spite of this claim, Marjorie maintained her husband's innocence. "If there was any doubt about my husband's innocence, I would turn on him," she said. Marjorie also spoke lovingly about her mother, saying, "This is the woman who took me from an orphanage."

The next day, Marjorie's ghoulish photo appeared in the paper. It showed a heavily bandaged woman with dried blood, dark glasses, and matted hair.

Two days later the Anoka County Sheriff's Department called Marjorie's claims "unfounded." Investigators said because of inconsistencies, they no longer believed the assault had occurred as reported. But Lou Reidenberg told reporters he'd asked the sheriff's department to call off the investigation based on concern for Marjorie's safety.

After the alleged assault, Marjorie called Thomas Welch because she wanted the trust to buy her a guard dog. "I'm worried about getting attacked again. Somebody's after me," she told him.

Welch said that the trust would consider paying for a dog if he could verify the attack. He decided to call the emergency room physician who had treated Marjorie. Dr. James Sipe told Welch that in his opinion, Marjorie's wounds were self-inflicted.

Welch then called Marjorie back and told her the trust would not buy her a dog. Two weeks later, as Welch sat in his office that faced a glass skyway, he saw Marjorie coming across the skyway with a Doberman pinscher on a leash.

"She comes whipping into my office," Welch recalled. Marjorie asked if he had time to see her. "I said yes, and she sits down. The dog is nervous, getting up and pacing around."

"In spite of the fact you wouldn't give me any money, I got this attack dog. And now I feel safe," Marjorie told Welch.

At the end of the conversation, Welch got up and shook hands with Marjorie.

"What do you think of the dog?" Marjorie asked.

Welch stood a few feet away from Marjorie and the dog. "It's a nice dog."

"Do you know how they train these dogs to attack?" Marjorie asked.

"They train them to go for your arm?"

"No, for your crotch," she said.

Welch quickly ushered his client and her dog out the door—his vision of Marjorie letting the dog loose on him seemed a little too real.

Marjorie's so-called assault also led to the firing of Colorado private investigator William Furman. Waller suspected the PI was a fraud, and the day after Marjorie's attack, Waller called Furman at a special number Furman had given Duluth detectives.

"Furman, this is Sergeant Waller. I was just calling to find out what's new with Marge."

"Nothing new here," Furman breezily replied.

"Do you have people watching her?"

"Oh, yeah. I've got two detectives watching her as we speak."

"Well, I was just wondering if anything happened yesterday?"

"Nothing unusual. She stayed close to her son's house. Why do you ask?"

Waller, his tone suddenly brusque, told Furman about Marjorie's attack. "She was taken to the hospital."

Furman hesitated a few seconds before answering. "Oh, I'll check on it. Let me call you back." A few minutes later Furman called with an explanation. "One of my [surveillance men] got sick and had to leave her unattended for awhile. He must have missed it."

Waller immediately called Inspector Grams at Duluth headquarters. "You better tell Barney Johnson they're getting screwed," Waller said.

Grams did call Johnson, a Congdon family attorney and trustee, who fired Furman the next day. Furman had bilked Tom Congdon out of at least $15,000. Police wanted to charge him but, embarrassed by the deception, the Congdon trustees dropped the matter.

Other members of the family were not so reluctant to take public action. Five of Marjorie's children, Peter, Andy, Suzanne, Heather, and Rebecca, filed a civil lawsuit against her in September in St. Louis County probate court in Duluth. In their petition, the children objected to the distribution of any funds to Marjorie from Elisabeth's estate, her living trust, and the two trusts established by Chester Congdon. The children challenged their mother's right to her inheritance under a state law that prohibited anyone from inheriting money from the deceased if shown to be involved in that person's murder. The petition alleged a continuing murder investigation into Marjorie's possible involvement with her mother's murder. Stephen and Rick sided with their mother, proclaiming her innocence and questioning their siblings' motives.

The dispute would not be resolved until June 29, 1983, when St. Louis County probate court approved a settlement between Marjorie and her children over the approximately $8 million Congdon estate inheritance. Under the terms of the settlement, Marjorie would receive about $1.5 million from the larger of the two trusts set up by her grandfather. Marjorie would also receive the interest from one-third of her children's share of that trust, which amounted to about $4.5 million. The remainder of the inheritance monies would go to Marjorie's seven children, including a second trust amounting to approximately $2 million.

Since Roger's arrest, DeSanto had continued to ask for a physical lineup. The typical lineup is done within days of an arrest. Yet, whenever police contacted Doug Thomson, he said his case load made that impossible and he insisted on being there. Waller insisted that the county attorney's office proceed. "It's our show," he told DeSanto. They had a suspect in custody and a witness who could identify him. They, not the defense, should say when. But two months had passed before Waller could arrange for Duluth cab driver Larry Williams to come down to police headquarters.

Williams, a part-time driver for Allied Cab, had told police that he had dropped off a man near Glensheen the night of the murders. He had been driving cab #4 on Sunday, June 26, starting at 5 P.M. At about 11:30 P.M. he had been dispatched to the Melrose Building at Fourth Avenue West and First Street, a block away from police headquarters and near the Greyhound bus depot. He picked up an older man dressed in a suit and carrying a long coat, suitcase, and small carry bag. The man asked to be taken out by the blinking light on London Road. He asked "Why aren't the cabs behind the Greyhound?" Williams assumed the man had just arrived by bus. As the cab approached the blinking light at 38th Avenue East on London Road, the man motioned for Williams to turn in the driveway of an apartment complex. Before the man got out, he and Williams haggled briefly over the $3 cab fare. The man gave Williams three $1 bills and no tip before walking to a large car.

Police hoped Williams would be a good witness, but unfortunately in the months between the arrest and the lineup, Roger's appearance had changed. His hair had grown longer, he had grown a beard, and, since he'd stopped drinking, he had dropped twenty pounds and lost his paunch. Though DeSanto had never gone to court over a lineup before, he now went to Judge C. Luther Eckman and asked that Roger be ordered to shave his beard.

Judge Eckman ruled for the prosecution. In an order dated September 7, 1977, Roger would shave his beard, give additional handwriting samples, and have his arms and biceps measured. But nothing could restore the weight he had lost.

Back on July 5, Williams had picked Roger out of a photo lineup, pointing at Harmon's picture of Roger without hesitation. But the detective sergeant who showed Williams the photo would be charged and eventually convicted on unrelated felony charges; he would have been an easy mark for a defense attorney. Waller and DeSanto needed the physical line up.

At the lineup, Williams told investigators he believed Roger was the man he'd driven in his cab. But he admitted he'd seen Roger's photo in the newspaper, which tainted his identification. Defense delay tactics and the publication of Roger's photo had cost police a valuable opportunity to place Roger in Duluth the night of the murders.

"As the prosecutor, I dropped the ball. I didn't push hard enough for the lineup in July," DeSanto said later. "Gary Waller and I were jacked around by the defense, and our inexperience cost us."

The day after Thanksgiving, Waller and DeSanto flew out to Colorado so DeSanto would have an opportunity to meet the witnesses who would testify for the prosecution.

Waller introduced DeSanto to waitresses Jan Mynheir and Wilma Farley, whose stories fit the theory that Roger didn't leave Colorado until Sunday, June 26. Accordingly, efforts to trace Roger's plane reservations also concentrated on Sunday. Years later, Waller recalled that decision as one that he would make differently today.

"We focused on Stapleton International because it was the most available," Waller said. "But when people lie, they always use part of the truth. Marge told Fran Beyer on Saturday that Roger had gone down to Colorado Springs to get away from the lawyers. If you look at the mileage on the rented car, there's enough for two trips to Colorado Springs plus other driving. It wasn't until two years later that we really looked at what was being said back then by Joyce Smith and her daughter. Then it was too late."

Waller and DeSanto also met with private investigator William Furman to corroborate his earlier statements. He said he trailed the Caldwells after they flew to

Minnesota for Elisabeth Congdon's funeral. He maintained he overheard Marjorie or Roger talking about the murders during their stay at the Radisson Hotel in Duluth. Furman insisted he'd heard them say they hoped they'd get away with it. "This was total bullshit," Waller recalled. "Both John and I knew it was, and we had the integrity not to call a man like this to the witness stand." As far as Waller could determine, Furman had never traveled to Minnesota for his supposed surveillance of the Caldwells. More likely, he was defrauding Tom Congdon.

On February 27, 1978, Roger entered a plea of not guilty. He'd been in jail since July 8, 1977, and his circumstances were an understandable source of stress for his family back in Pennsylvania. Marjorie didn't make it any easier on them. In a letter dated March 5, 1978, Roger's mother responded to accusations Marjorie had made against them:

> Dear Roger,
>   I have really been nervous and disturbed, since Marge talked to Betty, on the phone, she said, that we never write to you or send you any money. What does she mean? We all think about you and love you and want everything to turn out alright. She has never answered my letters or cards. Roger couldn't you write us something and set our minds at ease, that you do hear from us and do get the money sent you.
>   Love always, Mother and Dad

DeSanto wanted to hold the trial in Duluth, but Doug Thomson had filed a motion for a change of venue. He wanted the case heard in the Twin Cities, claiming the Duluth news media had saturated residents with news of the murders. A hearing on the motion was set for March 23.

Thomson had hired a statistics professor from the University of Minnesota to randomly survey Duluth residents on their attitudes and familiarity with the case. The results indicated that it would be nearly impossible to find any potential jurors in St. Louis County who had not been exposed to some information regarding the case. In his motion, Thomson argued that Twin Cities residents were regularly exposed to violent crime and therefore wouldn't overreact to a double murder. He told the judge he could get a less biased jury in a "heterogeneous" metropolitan area rather than a smaller city like Duluth.

DeSanto also enlisted his own University of Minnesota statistics professor to review the defense's survey. In this professor's expert opinion, the poll had no credibility because of the high margin of error in random surveys and the small number of people surveyed.

District Court Judge Jack Litman was presiding over his first murder trial. The fifty-four-year-old judge had been appointed to the bench just nine months earlier. He was no stranger to Glensheen or the Congdon family. As a teenager, he had worked several weeks every summer at a dry cleaner the Congdon family patronized. The young Litman had been allowed to enter Glensheen through the kitchen to deliver the dry cleaning. During World War II, Litman had served as a bomber pilot and flown numerous combat missions over Germany. His legal career had been launched in Duluth's legal aid office. The balding and bespectacled judge wore his black robes proudly.

Judge Litman, concerned about the case's high visibility, called DeSanto at his office to say the case would be moved to either International Falls or Brainerd. The judge favored Brainerd, a resort community in the lakes area of north-central Minnesota. But if the prosecution and defense preferred, they could hold the trial in International Falls, a lumber town on the Canadian border. DeSanto opted for Brainerd. On March 29, Judge Litman announced his decision—Roger would be tried in Brainerd.

Before jury selection began on April 10, DeSanto made a plea offer to Thomson. If Roger pleaded guilty to two counts of first-degree murder, the prosecution would agree to concurrent rather than consecutive sentences. Roger would be eligible for parole in seventeen-and-a-half years instead of thirty-five. Thomson wasted little time rejecting the offer. Roger had nothing to gain, particularly in a circumstantial evidence case with fairly even odds. He and his client would take their chances in a jury trial.

Late in May, less than a month into his trial, Roger would tell St. Louis County Deputy Sheriff Tom Rooney, "Well, Tom, in another month or less, why, this will all be over and I will be out and free."

CHAPTER 14

Trial Preparations

NINE WORDS HANG ON THE OFFICE WALL NEXT TO John DeSanto's desk: "By failing to prepare, you are preparing to fail." This simple phrase, copied from a restaurant sugar packet, comprised the prosecutor's trial strategy. DeSanto's girlfriend, Lana Eckenberg, had set the words in needlepoint and placed them in a modest wooden frame.

Influenced by television, most people believe that the most difficult part of a criminal case is spent in court. DeSanto had learned soon after law school that preparation done outside the courtroom determines how well an attorney performs inside the courtroom—months spent in law libraries, interviewing witnesses and experts, reviewing evidence. Preparation for the Caldwell case became DeSanto's full-time job, and took over his office. Even today, three drawers in one of his large metal file cabinets remain crammed with Congdon/ Pietila research and legal memoranda, which serve as a reference for county prosecutors.

At age forty-eight, Doug Thomson found himself among the top of Minnesota's criminal defense attorneys. At five-foot-nine with a receding gray hairline, wire-rimmed glasses, and wry grin, his appearance wasn't nearly as imposing as his track record. In seventeen years of practice, he'd only lost one murder case.

Born in St. Paul, Thomson moved with his family frequently as his father was promoted and transferred by Northern Pacific Railroad. The series of towns in Minnesota, North Dakota, and Montana—Bemidji, Fargo, Missoula, Billings, Glendive—read like the itinerary of a train trip. His father, also a railroad man, had worked as a dining-car conductor before going on to become superintendent of the dining-car department. During Prohibition, Thomson's father maintained a lively after-hours side business selling liquor in the dining cars.

But Thomson had no interest in continuing the family railroad tradition. Upon graduating from high school in Billings, he enrolled in the pre-law program at the University of Montana. When his father transferred to Minneapolis the following year, Thomson switched schools, to the University of Minnesota, and majors, to business administration. Drafted by the Army during the Korean War, he put his law school plans on hold. After he returned to Minnesota in 1957, Thomson entered William Mitchell College of Law in St. Paul.

"I think I always wanted to be a lawyer," Thomson said. "When I was in high school I read Gene Fowler's The Great Mouthpiece about [New York lawyer] Bill Fellon, and I think that kind of instilled in me a desire to be a criminal lawyer."

Even during high school, Thomson had known he wanted to work the defense side of the criminal justice equation. Criminal defense cases he read about seemed to have more pizzazz and drama, and courtroom personalities like defense attorney Louis Nizer fascinated him. To Thomson, being a defense attorney is "kind of a one man-against-the-world type of thing."

But after passing the Minnesota bar, Thomson first put both his Juris Doctorate and business degree to use as an auditor for the state of Minnesota. After several years, Thomson tired of tax law and opened a private law office in downtown St. Paul with a law school classmate. To pay the bills, Thomson recalled, "We took anything that came in the door. But usually it was somebody with the sheriff on their ass."

Eventually, Thomson and his partner merged with another small practice, headed by an attorney whose specialties included criminal defense. Within months, Thomson sat second chair on one of Minnesota's most sensational murder cases. He helped defend Norman Mastrian, a former professional boxer charged with first-degree murder in the March 1963 slaying of Carol Thompson. Wife of St. Paul criminal attorney T. Eugene Thompson, Carol Thompson died hours after she was attacked in her home, bludgeoned with a Luger pistol and stabbed in the neck with a paring knife.

The state accused Mastrian of acting as T. Eugene Thompson's middleman in hiring a hitman for $3,000. Prosecutors alleged the husband's motives included insurance policies worth more than $1 million and a mistress. Mastrian's defense attorneys claimed that Mrs. Thompson's murder took place as part of a botched robbery.

Jurors didn't buy the robbery story and convicted Mastrian and Eugene Thompson of first-degree murder in separate trials. Each received sentences of life in prison. But even though he'd lost the case, Doug Thomson had made an important career decision. The time had arrived for him to begin building his criminal defense practice. What he saw in the courtroom only strengthened his resolve.

"I didn't realize the imbalance between the prosecution and the defense," Thomson said. "The prosecution goes into the courtroom and you've got all the facilities of organized government, all the time, all the money that any citizen could possibly muster, and it's all directed towards one end. And that's to convict the accused. And the only thing the defendant has is a lawyer that can cross-examine witnesses."

As Thomson went to work building a career as a criminal defense attorney, he kept in mind an analogy he'd picked up during basic training in the Army. "We'd spent a Friday night, called a GI party, cleaning our rifles up for an inspection in the morning and it was about midnight when we finished," Thomson recalled. "And so the drill sergeant says now everybody's got to shine their boots. So some college graduate among us asks,

'Look, I can understand perfectly why we have to clean our rifles, but why the hell do we have to shine our boots? What's that got to do with fighting a war?' And he says, 'Look, the United States of America has never lost a war. And we don't know whether it's because we clean our rifles or because we shine our boots. And until we find out you're going to do both.'"

Thomson won most of his cases because he cleaned his rifle and shined his boots. He took no shortcuts, considering every aspect of a case important. Other lawyers admired Thomson for his tenacious and tough cross-examination, the stock in trade of a good defense attorney. Just a few of Thomson's rules of law: When you see any weakness in the prosecution's case, go for the jugular. Never cross-examine unless you have to. And if you do, better make sure you extract something helpful to the defense.

Thomson enjoyed playing the sophisticated lawyer and he dressed the part from head to toe. His trademark attire included three-piece Brooks Brothers suits, pricey silk ties, shoes custom-made in London, solid-gold belt buckles, a gold pocket watch, and cufflinks. Thomson drove a black Lincoln Continental Mark IV equipped with a radar detector and two telephones—long before everyone had a cell phone. Colleagues said that beneath Thomson's smooth exterior, he took his mission—but not himself—seriously. Thomson liked to relax with a stiff drink and often shared raunchy jokes.

After his divorce, the law became Thomson's life, and even his home reflected the profession he'd chosen. His upscale apartment in a downtown St. Paul complex came with a direct view of the federal courthouse.

Thomson's latest opponent, DeSanto, had only five years experience. But the thirty-one-year-old chief prosecutor had acquired a reputation as a determined, hardworking attorney, intimate with minute details of his cases. He had a string of five successful murder prosecutions (he only counted four, since one had ended in a manslaughter conviction) and along the way earned the nickname "Kitchen Sink DeSanto" in reference to his tendency at trial to throw in every bit of evidence available, including the kitchen sink.

Brainerd, Minnesota, the county seat of Crow Wing County, sits about 135 miles north of the Twin Cities. The county, which includes the western end of the Cuyuna Iron Range, has its share of abandoned iron-ore mines and skeletal towns, but is better known for resorts, cabins, and clear, cold lakes stocked with walleye, northern pike, and bass. Located in west-central Minnesota, the region draws vacationers and summer home dwellers from as far away as Chicago, Milwaukee, and Des Moines. From May to September, the county's population triples, yielding the largest nonresident population in Minnesota. Each May, thousands of anglers descend on the Brainerd-area lakes for the state's fishing opener weekend. In winter, tiny ice fishing shacks dot the lakes. The city of eleven thousand also claims to be the home of legendary giant lumberjack Paul Bunyan and Babe the Blue Ox.

During the trial, John DeSanto made his temporary home at the Brainerd Holiday Inn at the edge of town, as did detective Waller, Judge Litman, and Don Macheledt, the judge's court reporter. The hotel's Spanish-style budget decor featured chrome helmets and crossed swords mounted on the wall in the lobby and large, mass-produced oil paintings and orange shag carpeting in the rooms—a sharp contrast to the traditional architecture and furnishings in the courthouse where the men typically spent most of their waking hours.

The 1920 courthouse, a three-story gray stone building furnished with marble staircases and dark wood paneling, was located near the center of Brainerd's business district at Fourth and Laurel streets. A first-floor passageway connected the court-house to the adjacent county jail and sheriff's department.

Roger Caldwell's trial would be held at the rear of the third-floor, in a courtroom that featured thickly varnished wood furniture and a high ceiling. The only air conditioning was the old-fashioned kind: open windows and ceiling fans—and it was a hot summer. Spectators would sit on wooden benches resembling church pews, separated by only several feet from the attorneys. The small, L-shaped counsel table pointed like the hands of a clock toward the judge at twelve and the jury, on the spectators' left, at nine. This arrangement meant that attorneys and their clients had to choose between seats facing the judge or the jury.

In Brainerd, Waller and DeSanto worked in cramped, makeshift settings. They used the couch and a long table in DeSanto's motel room for witness interviews and paperwork early in the day and at night. During the day, Waller set up a temporary of-fice in an abandoned evidence vault in the courthouse basement, courtesy of the Crow Wing County Sheriff's Department. Waller called the tiny space his sweatbox.

DeSanto also worked at the offices of Crow Wing County Attorney Steven Rathke. Over the lunch hour and during the day when Rathke was in court, DeSanto preferred Rathke's office to the file-laden motel room.

In contrast, defense attorney Doug Thomson spent his time outside of court in more picturesque surroundings. He stayed at his lake retreat, a log cabin outside Mc-Gregor, Minnesota, sixty miles from the Crow Wing County courthouse.

Inside the courtroom, however, both sides were entitled to equal quarters. But Thomson moved quickly to gain the advantage. Arriving before DeSanto, he claimed the twelve o'clock hand of the L-shaped table, sitting with the judge to his right and facing the jury box. That left DeSanto with the jury box to his left and facing the judge, a strategic disadvantage for maintaining eye contact with jurors.

On April 10, 1978, jury selection began in Roger Caldwell's murder trial. Judge Litman's style was serious and businesslike. He expected jurors to rise when he en-tered the courtroom and demanded that attorneys stand when addressing him. This formality was not a sign of ego, but the judge's way of maintaining courtroom deco-rum.

Concerned that news stories might prejudice the eighty-nine prospective jurors, Judge Litman immediately imposed a gag order on the defense and prosecution. He also barred the news media and public from the courtroom during jury selection. Eight Minnesota newspaper and broadcast organizations asked the Minnesota Supreme Court to overrule Judge Litman's decision. A hearing before the Supreme Court was scheduled for the next morning.

For the first day of the trial, DeSanto wore a navy blazer and gray pants, while his opponent wore a three-piece designer suit. Thomson took note of DeSanto's attire, and said, "that's a nice misdemeanor suit." DeSanto would never again go to court without a suit.

On Wednesday, April 12, the Minnesota Supreme Court overturned Judge Litman's closed jury selection and the next morning he opened the courtroom as jury selection continued. The judge still continued his gag order prohibiting the attorneys from talking publicly about the case. Although the courtroom had been opened up, few attended the first days of jury selection, an often slow and plodding process. Only a half-dozen reporters and a handful of spectators looked on. News media and spectators entered the Brainerd courtroom to see Roger, seated to Thomson's right, looking nothing like the swollen-faced, scruffy man who'd pleaded not guilty only two months earlier.

Here sat a clean-shaven Roger Caldwell, his hair neatly parted and combed, in a solid dark suit, polished shoes, white shirt, and striped tie. Thomson had made sure his client had several new suits, which Roger wore in rotation throughout the trial to give the impression of a more extensive wardrobe. Once police removed his handcuffs during the elevator ride up to the third floor, Roger could easily have passed for a business executive. "The defendant is obviously the focus of everybody's attention," Thomson said. "Especially the jury. They always look to the defendant for his reaction, so the more innocuously dressed he can be, the better." This strategy annoyed DeSanto—he realized that the defendant had more suits than he did.

As jury selection began, the two sides clashed immediately. DeSanto started his questioning with the statement "I represent the people of the state of Minnesota." Thomson leapt up in protest. He objected to DeSanto's characterization of the state's residents as his clients. Judge Litman overruled the objection, and the trial continued.

Jury selection is also called voir dire, which means "to speak the truth." DeSanto wanted prospective jurors to feel comfortable enough to reveal any biases. DeSanto sought jurors willing to serve for a trial projected to go six weeks or more. He did not want jurors dropping out midway or becoming angry with the prosecution. "Do you think that you might hold it against me as a prosecutor or against the prosecution in general for taking up so much of your time?" DeSanto asked each juror.

He also needed jurors who believed that circumstantial evidence was as valid as eyewitness testimony. This was the ultimate circumstantial evidence case, DeSanto told the prospective jurors. In his opinion, circumstantial physical evidence, like hair, blood, and fingerprints, was often preferable to direct eyewitness evidence. Eyewitnesses may not have had a good view of the crime or their recall may be poor or impaired by alcohol or drugs.

In court DeSanto often used an example. If someone sees footprints on a sandy beach, he knows someone has walked there, even if no one is in sight. Based on the circumstantial evidence, without an eyewitness, one can reasonably conclude that a person made those prints.

DeSanto asked each juror, "Have you heard anybody say that they could not convict on circumstantial evidence? Are you of that mind?" If they even hinted they were, DeSanto rejected them.

DeSanto also asked, "Could you disregard the consequences of your verdict?" First-degree murder meant a life sentence. Jurors had to be able to separate the penalty from the decision of guilt or innocence.

"If you find Roger Caldwell guilty, will you be able to come into the courtroom and face the defendant and his attorney and whoever else happens to be here, and say guilty?'" DeSanto asked finally.

DeSanto had the edge on his opponent during jury selection. He had background information on each prospective juror provided by the Crow Wing county attorney, Rathke, local law enforcement, and the courtroom bailiff. The bailiff also worked for the post office and was familiar with many panelists from his route. Because he knew trials could be lost or won during jury selection, Rathke wrote descriptions of potential jurors on three-by-five index cards. At the bottom of each card he noted whether the person would make a good or bad juror for the prosecution.

According to Thomson, when selecting jurors, defense attorneys avoid conservative people, leaders, and those with precise technical jobs as they tend to be less open-minded about the presumption of innocence—and more willing to vote for conviction. Thomson, whose in-depth questioning often lasted as long as an hour, asked panelists about whether they agreed that law enforcement officials, like everyone else, made mistakes and sometimes lied. He also screened prospective jurors for signs that they would react emotionally to the brutality of the murders. "You're not selecting a jury, you're eliminating," Thomson said. Frequently, during voir dire, Thomson gestured dramatically toward Roger, seated beside him. The hand of fate had placed his client there, he reminded panelists.

DeSanto and Thomson selected only one juror during day one, fifty-three-year-old rural Brainerd housewife Fern Swartout. Her selection surprised DeSanto. Swartout, a crime victim, had testified against a twenty-one-year-

old man who was convicted in the rape of her daughter and firebombing of her daughter's house. Swartout's eight-year-old grandson, Darrin, had been severely burned in the bombing. At the bottom of Swartout's card, Rathke had written "OK." DeSanto wanted Swartout on the jury, but he had expected Thomson would quickly strike the crime victim from consideration. Yet, when Thomson finished questioning Swartout, DeSanto was elated to hear the defense attorney tell Judge Litman he would accept her.

On April 17, Marjorie wrote to Roger in the Brainerd jail. Even though he had been imprisoned for nine months, Marjorie's letter focused on her own troubles, told with her usual dramatic embellishments:

Dear Rog,

I feel you should know what has been happening down here.

1. We have no phone—our total bill for 3 months, including collect calls from the Duluth jail and your family came to $140. Welch didn't pay so we have had no phone for several months and the attorneys do nothing!

2. We have no car, several months ago the attorneys knew Welch wasn't paying but they did not go to a judge in Minneapolis to get a court order ordering him to get us transportation. Rick and I took five separate lease contracts into Lou [Reidenberg] that would have come to about $200–223 per month, but Welch turned them down and of course the attorneys did not go to court.

3. Rick took a very large overdose of his medication on Thursday and almost died. Since we had no car and no phone, I walked a mile on my bad leg to a public phone and called a taxi. The only money we have had from the bank in April is $100 and I had just go [sic] my insurance insurance check of $100. When we got to the hospital he was in emergency from 11 P.M. until 3 A.M. when they put him in the coronary care unit, still with heart monitors, vital signs every 15 minutes and intravenous. I called Ron [Meshbesher] Thursday night and again on Sunday when he said he would do something to get us transportation and he would talk to the Duluth judge. On Friday when I called back at the time he set of course he was out and didn't return my call even though I left a message. I called Lou twice on Friday but of course Rick wasn't important enough for him to return a call about even if the doctors were worried about whether he would die for quite awhile.

4. Monday I called Ron again but he had done nothing and said call back at 1:30—I did and he still had done nothing—not even talked to the judge or Welch. All our money is gone on cabs as Rick came home Sunday but had to go to the clinic today and is supposed to go on Tuesday and Wednesday also for more blood work. The attorneys feel Rick's health is totally minor and if he dies, all it means to them is a bitter lawsuit.

[Doug Thomson] as usual didn't even protest when DeSanto said he didn't want anyone going into mother's house and of course Litman backed him up! If you want me at your trial or Rick alive you better start not being so meek and mild to your idiot lawyer.

We have nothing in the refrigerator but 1/2 gallon of milk and some dry cereal. As usual there is no money when Welch says there will be and the attorneys all say the other one is supposed to see to it. As a result, we have no money, no food, no way to go to the clinic, or the store if we did have money, no phone and frankly I don't think either of us can take this much longer. I get all my information on the trial from T.V. or the papers because your attorney, like the others [doesn't] do anything but what Duluth wants.

Since Welch doesn't think it necessary for me to be at the trial he won't get me a motel room or money and of course we have no car and Rick won't be able to go to school as well as not go to the clinic. I told you the attorneys were paid off but you wouldn't listen.

Marge

In the second week of jury selection, DeSanto came close to losing his job—and the trial. On Tuesday, April 18, DeSanto's boss, St. Louis County Attorney Keith Brownell, told reporters that the evidence pointed to the involvement of other persons besides Roger Caldwell in the murders of Elisabeth Congdon and Velma Pietila. Several newspapers reported that Brownell specifically mentioned that a grand jury would be investigating whether Marjorie Caldwell was involved in her mother's death. The murderer, he said, knew something about Glensheen's layout.

Brownell's statement was problematic and improper; he had violated Judge Litman's gag order and the confidentiality of a grand jury investigation. Driving to the courthouse from his cabin, Thomson learned of Brownell's comments from a radio news report. Upon arriving in Brainerd, Thomson requested a mistrial, based on publicity about the planned grand jury investigation. Thomson was obviously upset at news during his client's murder trial that his client's wife would be investigated for the same murder.

In response to Thomson's motion, Brownell suddenly reversed himself. He insisted to reporters that he had "never mentioned Marjorie's name in the context of any further investigation." He downplayed Thomson's motion for a mistrial, calling it a common defense tactic. The *Duluth News-Tribune* stuck by its reporter's story and the reporter's notes. In an editorial critical of Brownell, the paper stated "[h]e shoots from the hip one day and throws the gun away the next," and suggested Brownell should simply admit he goofed.

The next day, Judge Litman denied Thomson's motion but ordered the attorneys to question the nine jurors about whether they'd heard news of the grand jury investigation. Juror number nine was knocked off the panel after admitting he had heard a radio news report that police had Marjorie under investigation. The judge excused two other jurors who said they'd heard friends talking about the investigation. Judge Litman also denied defense motions to dismiss the indictment, release Roger without bail, and postpone the trial for six months on grounds of adverse publicity.

Furious that his gag order had been violated, Judge Litman bellowed at DeSanto in chambers. "If this happens again we will have a mistrial," the judge warned. "I didn't know [Brownell] was going to do something like this. I'll talk to him," DeSanto assured the judge.

After leaving the judge's chambers, DeSanto talked with reporters at the courthouse, giving them the standard "no comment." Humiliated and furious, he then called Brownell from the privacy of his hotel room. Not only had his boss jeopardized the trial, but he knew full well that grand jury proceedings were supposed to remain secret. He asked Brownell what good reason, if any, he could have had for going public.

Brownell refused to talk about it. Instead, he attacked DeSanto, saying he was doing a lousy job, taking too long for jury selection. I'm going to drive out and replace you, Brownell told DeSanto. DeSanto believed that Brownell's concerns were less about DeSanto's performance and more about his upcoming fall reelection campaign—and the media exposure he'd gain prosecuting Roger Caldwell. But except to oppose moving the trial, Brownell had done little pretrial preparation for the case.

Brownell's day-to-day role as county attorney was largely administrative. An actor with the Duluth Playhouse, Brownell had a loud, dramatic voice well suited for the stage. He had thinning, wavy brown hair and a round face that flushed red when he was angered. Brownell also didn't have the best relationship with Duluth police. He had a reputation within the department for plea-bargaining and dismissing cases. The detective bureau called its blackboard the "washboard" because so many cases had been wiped off without making it to trial. As for Brownell's popularity within his own office, rumors circulated that a number of the attorneys would support his challenger that fall.

For DeSanto, Brownell's announcement couldn't have come at a worse time, in the middle of jury selection. "I'm the county prosecutor, I should be trying this case," DeSanto protested. "No, my mind is made up," his boss persisted. DeSanto couldn't bear the politics. After hanging up on Brownell, he cradled his forehead and nearly lost it. "I can't believe it. Keith's coming here to replace me," DeSanto told Waller. The news made Waller so angry he stormed out of the hotel room. He immediately called his boss at home. "I'm not staying if Brownell gets involved," he told Grams. The inspector gave Waller permission to pull out if that happened. But the next morning Brownell called DeSanto to say he'd changed his mind. This unexpected turn of events baffled DeSanto, but now he could focus on trying the case.

Throughout jury selection, DeSanto also spent time preparing and evaluating the state's evidence. Items DeSanto considered crucial included the gold coin stolen from Elisabeth's bedroom and mailed to Roger in Colorado. He wondered why Roger would mail the coin to himself instead of simply keeping it with the jewelry stolen from Glensheen.

DeSanto theorized that perhaps Roger simply wanted the coin for himself. Several weeks into jury selection, DeSanto received copies of Roger's divorce decree and property settlement from his first wife, Martha. The documents contained a stipulation that Roger receive a coin collection as part of his divorce settlement. DeSanto and Waller were ecstatic: they could use Roger's fascination with coins to establish a motive for him to take the coin and keep it for himself.

The next morning in the judge's chambers—with DeSanto, Waller, and Roger present—Thomson made his usual mistrial motion based on his claim of adverse trial publicity. He asked Judge Litman to include the most recent newspaper articles, which Thomson clipped every day, as part of the court's record.

DeSanto quickly ended Thomson's tedious ritual. He handed Thomson a copy of Roger's divorce decree and settlement.

"By the way, Doug, here's something new for you," DeSanto said.

Thomson briefly glanced at the papers and said, "Big deal." The prosecution had furnished hundreds of documents as required by rules of discovery.

"Look at item number seven in the property settlement," DeSanto urged.

Thomson read further down the page. His face turned ashen and his mood sullen. "Your honor, may I have a few moments with my client?"

Thomson ordered Roger to follow him into a small room off the judge's chambers used to lock up evidence at the end of the day—the only private space available and little more than a closet.

Waller and DeSanto could hear Thomson through the closed door as he began to chew out his unresponsive client. Thomson realized the prosecution now had a motive for Roger to pocket the Byzantine coin. He demanded to know what else his client had failed to mention.

"Roger, why the hell didn't you tell me about the coin collection?" Thomson yelled at his client. "You don't tell me anything. What the hell do you think this is—a goddamn game? This is no game! Tell me about the coin collection!"

The pair emerged minutes later—Thomson red-faced and angry, Roger sheepish.

Later in the trial, during final arguments, DeSanto would suggest another reason for Roger to mail the coin: It may have served as a signal to Marjorie that Elisabeth's murder—or the burglary—had been successful.

During jury selection, Waller interviewed Roger's cellmate, Larry Roloff. The eighteen-year-old said he had some information for authorities. Roloff told Waller that Roger had been quiet when first brought in. But after a week in jail, he began talking openly about his case.

"Did he say why the police arrested him?" asked Waller.

"Just because of the evidence that he would get so much money, that his wife would get so much money if her mother died. They didn't show any more evidence than that," said Roloff.

"Did he say anything about the evidence the police had against him?" Waller pressed.

"The only thing he said he figured was the money that he would get, and he said the only witness he figured they had was some guy at a gas station. That was the only witness he figures you guys had. When he stopped for gas some place. He didn't say where it was."

This was new, perhaps significant information a year after the murders—someone may have seen Roger as he escaped after the killings. Roger might even have discarded his bloody clothing at that particular gas station. The trail had grown awfully cold. Tracking down leads on an unknown gas station and customer a year later proved frustrating to police. Although police investigated every station along the 145-mile stretch of Interstate 35 between Duluth and the Twin Cities, they turned up no clues.

Roger kept quiet and subdued during jury selection. But during breaks, he would walk up to the press table, next to the elevator on the third floor, and ask reporters for a newspaper. He didn't care whether the papers included stories about him, he said, he just enjoyed reading.

Despite his proximity to the jury box, Roger never looked directly at the jurors. Early on he developed a technique that he used throughout the trial. He stared straight ahead at a point slightly above the head of the person he was looking at. He used the technique during testimony so it appeared that he was staring down and trying to psych out the witness while he avoided actual eye contact.

Even Roger's attorney had difficulty communicating with him. Roger spoke little with Thomson and when he did he used a low mumble. But the defendant did have a few words for Detective Waller.

When they almost bumped heads one day in the courtroom doorway, Waller said, "Excuse me."

Roger looked Waller squarely in the face and responded bitterly, "I will never excuse you."

Jubilation over the completion of jury selection on May 3 was short-lived. Judge Litman mysteriously excused Fern Swartout, the first juror selected, from the panel. He gave the press no reason for Swartout's departure.

"All I can say is we'll have jury selection again in the morning," Litman said. He also told reporters details would not be released until after the trial.

This prompted one enterprising reporter to design bright yellow T-shirts with blue lettering that said "Brainerd Press Corps" on the front and "What Ever Happened to Fern Swartout?" on the back.

Reporters later learned that on May 2, Swartout came to Judge Litman and said she'd received an anonymous letter postmarked Duluth. The typewritten note offered her a bribe to find Roger guilty. The unsigned note read:

> Due to the tragic situation of your grandchild last fall, and the fact that the person at fault was allowed to be sentenced for a lesser crime, we feel that you should be willing to cooperate with us to secure a guilty verdict in the case you are at present involved in as a juror. The Duluth Police have cooperated with us to the fullest extent in seeing that the correct evidence has been located, as you will be able to note yourself. On a verdict of guilty being rendered we shall see that you receive by immediate mail the sum of ten thousand dollars in new bills.

Under oath, Swartout swore she could remain fair and impartial. But Judge Litman decided the risk of an appeal was too great. Swartout was near tears when Litman dismissed her from the jury panel.

Jury tampering is a felony offense. The bribe was turned over to the U.S. Postal Inspector and the state crime lab. Authorities tested the typewriters in the county jail and reviewed the mandatory lists of all the visitors to Crow Wing County Jail. Marjorie, Ron Meshbesher, and Thomson had visited Roger the prior weekend.

The letter implied that someone sympathetic to the prosecution had written it. Whoever sent Swartout the letter knew what would happen—and knew she was probably the state's most sympathetic juror. But investigators were never able to nail the culprit.

On Wednesday, DeSanto and Thomson selected a thirty-nine-year-old woman who ran a grocery store and post office with her husband in a nearby small town as the jury's second alternate. Finally, eighteen working days after it began, jury selection wrapped up on May 4.

The jury's makeup pleased DeSanto. The panel, whose average age was forty-four, consisted of seven women, five men, and two women alternates. The jury included a former nurse's aide, a behavior analyst, a lumberyard foreman, a retired resort owner, a farmer, a secretary, a rehabilitation counselor, a homemaker, a part-time house cleaner, a licensed practical nurse, a garment factory supervisor, and a vocational school supervisor. DeSanto felt certain this last juror would become the jury foreman.

The weekend before opening statements, Mike McNabb, DeSanto's assistant for the trial, arrived in Brainerd. On loan from the Ramsey County Attorney's Office in St. Paul, he would sit second chair for the prosecution, assisting with legal research, courtroom analysis, and moral support. McNabb, twenty-seven, was a tall, lanky man who sported tailored suits and a perpetual five o'clock shadow. He had spent two years working alongside DeSanto in Duluth before recently moving to his current job as an assistant prosecutor with Ramsey County.

Although he'd tried felonies, including aggravated assault and rape, McNabb had never before tried a murder case. During his tenure in Duluth he had acquired a reputation as a serious, intellectual lawyer with a dry sense of humor. DeSanto joked that if he were first meeting McNabb, "I'd have pegged him as the corporate attorney type." But McNabb's low-key, levelheaded style would provide a healthy balance for DeSanto in the months ahead. The trial came as a welcome respite for McNabb, who hadn't yet become comfortable with his new, less-than-ideal job trying paternity and child support cases. He started working on the Caldwell trial by checking into the Holiday Inn—his new home and office Monday through Friday was a room adjoining DeSanto's.

Judge Litman scheduled testimony to begin Monday, May 9. The prosecution's prospective witness list named more than 160 people, including law enforcement officers from Minnesota and Colorado, the Minnesota Bureau of Criminal Apprehension, and the FBI. Velma Pietila's husband Loren and six of Marjorie Caldwell's children, all but Rebecca, were also scheduled to testify.

On the day jury selection ended, DeSanto found a handwritten note from Crow Wing County Attorney Steve Rathke taped to the door of his temporary office. DeSanto had assured Rathke at the beginning of jury selection he'd only need office space for about six weeks—but jury selection had used up four weeks by itself. The note read: "You have two weeks left. I hope you can call 160 witnesses in that time."

CHAPTER 15

People of the State

O
PENING STATEMENTS IN ROGER CALDWELL'S MURDER TRIAL began on a muggy May 9, 1978, just days before the Minnesota fishing opening weekend would loose a frenzy of anglers on the Brainerd-area lakes. Close to one hundred spectators packed the third-floor courtroom, forcing some to stand at the back or spill out into the hallways. In anticipation of the crowds, officials assigned the trial to one of the courthouse's largest courtrooms. Courthouse officials had extra telephones installed for reporters, who gathered in a makeshift press area off the main third-floor hallway elevator.

The trial attracted a number of daily spectators. Many were older, retired couples recently returned from wintering in warmer climes who wanted to see justice played out up close. The case had also drawn a number of groupies—middle-aged housewives who rooted openly for DeSanto and a younger woman who drove from Duluth and knocked on DeSanto's door late at night. She just wanted to say hi, and to give him her room number at the Holiday Inn.

Throughout the trial, Elisabeth's younger daughter, Jennifer, sat in the back row with her husband, Chuck. Jennifer had little in common with the sister whose husband was now on trial, except needlepoint, which helped Jennifer pass the time during lulls in the trial. Although much of the testimony would be painful, nothing could be as traumatic as her mother's murder. Occasional attendees included Duluth millionaire Jeno Paulucci and his wife, Lois. DeSanto's father had worked for Paulucci for many years, during which time the DeSantos and Pauluccis had become close friends.

The DeSantos liked to watch their son at work and attended the trial as often as possible. Given her son's schedule, Hazel DeSanto helped out with his wash, except for John's trial uniform—his dark suits and white button-down shirts went to the dry cleaners for a light starch. Hazel also started a scrapbook of news clippings as she had for each of her son's trials since he attended law school.

As conspicuous as the regulars were, Marjorie made herself equally conspicuous by not attending. While privately professing her husband's innocence to friends and family, she never set foot in the courtroom during the trial. Marjorie also passed on opportunities to visit Roger in jail. She remained in the Twin Cities with her son Stephen, awaiting her turn.

Before testimony began, the attorneys spent the first hour of each morning in chambers battling over defense motions. Thomson's tactic was to consistently challenge the proceedings in hopes of establishing grounds for an appeal, if necessary. Every morning, Thomson presented his most recent batch of newspaper clips to support his motion for dismissal. "Your Honor, my client cannot receive a fair trial," he argued. Judge Litman reminded Thomson that jurors had been instructed not to talk about the case and not to read or watch any news reports of the trial. After defense motions were denied, the trial would continue.

Shortly before 10 A.M. on May 9, the prosecution made its opening statement. Fighting nervousness, DeSanto rose quickly and turned toward the jury box to begin a two-hour overview of the massive amount of evidence and testimony to be presented. He would call hundreds of witnesses from Minnesota, Colorado, California, and New York, and enter more than five-hundred items into evidence.

"State's evidence will show…that on March 20, 1976, Roger Sipe Caldwell married once-divorced Marjorie Congdon LeRoy Caldwell, one of two adopted daughters of heiress-millionairess Elisabeth Congdon," DeSanto said.

"The state's evidence will show you, ladies and gentlemen, that the defendant, Roger Caldwell, was unemployed from December 1976 until the time of the murders. And the state's evidence will show you, ladies and gentlemen, an almost unimaginable buildup of financial pressures on the defendant and his wife, Marjorie Caldwell."

The motive for murder was the oldest one known to mankind, DeSanto told the jury—greed, plain and simple. "Roger Caldwell murdered his semi-invalid mother-in-law, Elisabeth Congdon, in her bed," he said. "Why? Because he and his wife were in desperate financial trouble that could only be resolved through his wife's inheritance. Roger Caldwell also was responsible for the tragic, premature death of nurse Velma Pietila, beaten senseless for being in the wrong place." DeSanto described Roger Caldwell to jurors as an "unemployed fortune seeker" who lived an "extravagant, spendthrift, dream world type lifestyle."

This last remark drew a sharp protest from Thomson. "Your honor. This is an opening statement. He's arguing and name calling during opening statement. I think it's highly improper." Judge Litman sustained the objection. "The court would suggest that references to the defendant be confined to his name or his status in this action," Judge Litman instructed.

Continuing, DeSanto detailed the Caldwells' outrageous spending sprees and the tens of thousands of dollars the couple still owed creditors. He told jurors that the Caldwells' indebtedness, capped by a series of bad checks, led to Roger Caldwell's trip to Duluth in May 1977, to ask Congdon trustees for $750,000 or "at least $500,000 to stay out of jail." The trustees sent Roger back to Colorado empty-handed.

Despite hundreds of hours work, it would emerge later that Duluth police had been unable to place Roger on a plane or bus to or from Minnesota the day of the murders. But a good prosecutor clues jurors in on his or her case's weaknesses before the defense gets a chance. DeSanto admitted that investigators could not prove Roger's mode of transportation. None of Roger's fingerprints had been found at the murder scene or on the weapons used to kill Velma Pietila and Elisabeth Congdon, though some were too faint or smudged to be identified. But DeSanto told jurors there was physical evidence placing Roger at Glensheen. Hair fibers recovered from the mansion closely matched Roger's, and some bloodstains were of his blood type.

Next, the prosecutor offered jurors a motive for the murders. The evidence included the will, handwritten and signed by Marjorie just three days before the killings, which gave her husband a $2.5 million share of her inheritance from the family trusts. "That will was a carrot not too hard to swallow," DeSanto told jurors.

Once again, Thomson broke in. "I object, your Honor," he shouted. Court quickly recessed while the judge and two attorneys met in chambers. Judge Litman asked DeSanto if he planned to offer any vegetables into evidence. "Call it what it is—a murder contract," Judge Litman wryly instructed. "Carrot is an argumentative term, and you are restricted to just the facts." Once again, he denied Thomson's motion for a mistrial.

After the short recess, DeSanto was back before the jury, asking each member for "patience and justice." DeSanto had found those two words inscribed on the gavel of the judge who normally occupied this courtroom. He first noticed the gavel during pretrial preparations and made a mental note to call the words to the jury's attention.

He finished his opening statement saying, "as Mr. Thomson himself has told each of you during jury selecting, the state has accused Roger Caldwell. We are now going to prove it."

Despite the defense's occasional interruptions, DeSanto was off to a good start. He was satisfied he had been enthusiastic and aggressive enough for jurors to see the state had the right man on trial and the evidence to prove it.

The jury would have to wait for Thomson's opening statement. The State of Minnesota allows the defense to defer its opening statement until after the prosecution has presented its case, and Thomson decided he would wait until after the state rested.

Following DeSanto's opening statement, chief investigator Waller had the unwelcome distinction of being the state's first witness. "I couldn't sleep. I kept going over and over the reports, reviewing my notes, cramming," he recalled. "Being the first one out of the chute really takes its toll." He couldn't stomach breakfast that morning, but forced down a cup of coffee for stamina.

Nervous and exhausted, his mind raced with all the evidence he had gathered in the past year just for this moment. Waller felt anything but confident, despite his new navy-blue suit. He was convinced everyone in the courtroom could see him fidgeting in the witness chair.

One by one, Waller methodically identified the photographs Duluth police had taken of the crime scene and autopsies. The photos were also passed to the jury during breaks in Waller's testimony. DeSanto wanted to establish the brutality of the murders and hoped the often grisly pictures would have an emotional impact.

After the photos, DeSanto used Waller's testimony to introduce the physical evidence collected at the murder scene. The growing pile of evidence presented a macabre reminder of the savagery unleashed at Glensheen. On one day alone, thirty-seven separate items were marked as state's evidence, ranging from Velma Pietila's hairpin, earrings, and tooth fragments to the Oriental rug and window seat cushion where her body was found.

DeSanto began questioning Waller about his contact with Roger. Waller described Roger's appearance several days after the murders, when Waller and his boss, Inspector Grams, had interviewed Roger and his wife at Duluth police headquarters. Waller had noticed a cut near Roger's lip and an abrasion below the nail on his left middle finger. In Waller's opinion, Caldwell's injuries had been sustained during a struggle with nurse Velma Pietila.

Some of Waller's most significant testimony focused on the time imprinted on the airport gift shop receipt recovered from the Caldwells' Duluth hotel room, the discovery of the handwritten will in Colorado, and Elisabeth's stolen jewelry recovered from the Caldwells' Bloomington hotel room. But Waller was prevented from disclosing to the jury his conversation with Marjorie the night police found the stolen jewels in her hotel room. Judge Litman ruled that her statements to Waller were hearsay and could not be used as evidence. The ruling upset DeSanto. He'd lost an important opportunity to point out inconsistencies in the stories Marjorie told police, family, and friends about her husband's whereabouts during the murders. (Several months after the trial, Judge Litman told DeSanto he realized his hearsay rulings were incorrect. The state had wanted to disclose Marjorie's comments as proof she was lying, the opposite of hearsay evidence, which is offered to show the truth of what someone has said.)

After Waller spent two days on the witness stand for the prosecution, Thomson began an aggressive cross-examination. Thomson started theatrically, slamming down his legal-sized briefcase on the counsel table. Over the next three days, he would blow every hole he could in the prosecution's case. As DeSanto suspected he would, Thomson accused Waller of bias against Roger and sloppy investigative work. It would become a common defense theme throughout the trial.

"There is no inventory then maintained by the Duluth Police Depart-ment of the fingerprints that were sent to the Minnesota Bureau of Criminal Apprehension?" asked Thomson.

"Not any document that's specific inventory."

"Pardon?"

"Not a document that is a specific inventory, no, sir."

"So you would have no way of knowing how many fingerprints you sent to the Minnesota Bureau of Criminal Apprehension."

"I didn't send them myself."

"Let's just go back a minute, Sergeant. I understand you testified here that you were in charge of this investigation, is that correct?"

"Yes, sir."

"And you worked full time on this investigation since June 27th, 1977, have you?"

"Most of the time, yes, sir."

"Up through, including today, is that correct?"

"Yes, sir."

"Now do you, the Duluth Police Department, have any record of how many fingerprints from this case that you sent to the Minnesota Bureau of Criminal Apprehension?"

"Not to my knowledge, no, sir."

Thomson's efforts at embarrassing and discrediting Waller succeeded. By the end of his first day of cross-examination, Waller began to doubt his abilities and job performance as chief investigator for the case. "I truly believe that no matter how old I live to be, I will have lost five years of my life because I have never ever experienced any amount of anxiety equal to that cross-examination," he said later.

Thomson's cross-examination raised Waller's stress level so high he refused to read newspapers or watch television accounts of his testimony. Each night back at the Holiday Inn, Waller tried to fight the feeling of futility by running, but it brought no relief. And when he needed sleep most, it eluded him. The next morning, Waller had to psych himself up to go back into the courtroom.

During his direct examination of Waller, DeSanto had avoided mentioning the lack of any physical evidence tying Roger to the murder scene. But Thomson seized the opportunity. In a terse exchange, Thomson forced Waller to admit that none of Roger's prints had been found in Glensheen. DeSanto had failed to explain that in most cases the killer doesn't leave prints behind.

Thomson continued his effort to make the police investigation look unorganized and incomplete by emphasizing that police had still not identified two prints, a palm print in the nurse's bathroom and a fingerprint on the bathroom door.

"Now on the sink there was a palm print that was developed and was identifiable, is that correct?" asked Thomson.

"That's correct," replied Waller.

"And where was that palm print, where on the sink was it developed?"

"It was towards the front edge of the sink."

"And whose palm print was it?"

"I don't know sir."

"Wasn't Caldwell's, was it?"

"Not to my knowledge, sir."

"As a matter of fact, it was examined against his and was excluded as being his?"

"That's correct."

"So there was an identifiable print found on the sink that of this moment has not been identified with anyone, is that correct?"

"As far as I know, sir."

Back at the motel, Waller and DeSanto agreed the unidentified prints could seriously damage their case. They needed the identifications before the prosecution rested its case, five or six weeks away at most. They contacted John Douthit, a latent print expert with the Minnesota Bureau of Criminal Apprehension, for help.

The next morning, news reporters wanted the order of witnesses, but DeSanto kept the list secret in hopes of throwing Thomson off balance. Successful trial strategy depends a great deal on the order of witnesses, and DeSanto didn't want to make the defense's job any easier. DeSanto planned to put his high-impact witnesses on first to graphically describe the crime scene and the brutality of the murders.

Next, he'd take his chances with the two airport gift shop employees he hoped would identify Roger in court. He would then continue with the witnesses interviewed during the Minnesota and Colorado investigations. DeSanto planned to end by returning to the physical evidence—ensuring jurors remembered exactly what tied Roger to the murders.

The day Velma Pietila's family took the stand, a large cold sore suddenly appeared on Roger's lip. Family members testified that when the Caldwells stopped at their home the day of Velma's funeral, Roger had a sore on his upper lip. The prosecution claimed he'd received the cut while struggling with Velma on Glensheen's staircase. But Thomson now pointed to his client's cold sore and insisted that's what the Pietilas had seen.

During the morning break, Waller told DeSanto he'd read that a person could induce a cold sore by applying ice directly to his lip. The two men became convinced Roger's cold sore was self-inflicted. Upon DeSanto's redirect of Velma's son James, he asked if the Pietilas could have mistaken a cold sore for a swollen cut lip.

"After [Roger] left the home, I said to my father it looked like Roger Caldwell had a cold sore on his lip," James Pietila testified. "My father gets cold sores all the time and I've never had one in my life and it was swollen. My father said that was no cold sore." DeSanto had succeeded in rebutting the defense's claim.

Once testimony ended for the day, Waller and DeSanto began worrying that someone had bugged their motel rooms or tapped their phones—they had no other explanation for Roger's timely cold sore. They wondered if their discussions of the witness schedule had somehow been overheard. That night DeSanto and Waller called the FBI to sweep their rooms. They found nothing.

"It was just paranoia on Gary's and my part," DeSanto recalled. "In retrospect, Doug Thomson was just an experienced, well-prepared attorney who had done his homework."

On May 22, officer Barry Brooks of the Duluth Police Department's identification unit testified that he was ordered by detective Waller to process the suspected entry point. The day after the murders he had organized an unofficial experiment involving the double-locked window in which he and four other officers had participated.

Brooks described his experiment for jurors: "We tried to determine if a person could, because of the size of the opening, insert his arm through the opening, open the center lock between the sashes, and then insert his arm even further through that opening and reach over to the west side of the window to unlock the window-stop to raise the window."

Of the five officers who participated in the experiment, only Brooks could unlatch the scissors lock and reach further through the hole and disengage the window-stop. Despite the jagged slivers of broken glass, Brooks had avoided being cut. At the time of the experiment, the circumference of Brooks' right forearm measured eleven and three-eighths inches and his biceps measured twelve inches. He had measured Roger's arm shortly after Roger's arrest. The defendant's right forearm measured eleven and three-quarters and his biceps thirteen and a quarter inches, slightly larger than Brooks' arm.

The prosecution and police believed that the difference in size was negligible and that the window experiment supported their theory that Roger had broken into Glensheen from the rear, unlocking the window without injury. But when it was time for his cross-examination of Brooks, Thomson was ready with his own window experiment. He produced a cardboard cutout created using a police tracing of the hole, which duplicated the exact dimensions of the original. Unfortunately, further experiments with the original were impossible; the broken pane at Glensheen had been repaired two weeks after the murders.

"Why don't you take your coat off and try to show the jury how this is done?" Thomson said.

Brooks peeled off his sports coat and moved toward the defense exhibit at the front of the courtroom. He slowly began reaching his arm through the hole in the cardboard, feeling the jury's rapt attention.

"Wait a minute," Thomson interrupted as the ragged edges of the cardboard brushed against Brooks' arm. "You're moving it."

"Yes, the bottom piece of the glass moved," Brooks said.

"Did it break out?"

"No."

"Did you cut yourself?" Thomson persisted.

"No."

"So your arm doesn't fit in there, does it?" Thomson concluded triumph-antly.

"It went through it," Brooks said stubbornly, as he pushed his arm completely through the hole. But Brooks had moved the simulated glass edges about three-quarters of an inch. Looking on, Waller cursed the original unauthorized experiment and hoped the jurors wouldn't attach too much significance to this failed reenactment.

On May 17, a week into the trial, DeSanto put St. Louis County medical examiner Volker Goldschmidt on the stand to describe to jurors the details of Elisabeth's death. Before he began his explicit testimony, Jennifer Johnson left the courtroom. She did not want to relive her mother's suffering.

Goldschmidt testified that the extensive hemorrhaging above Elisabeth's shoulders and raw skin on her nose were telltale signs of murder. In his thick German accent, Goldschmidt motioned toward the pink satin pillow flecked with blood on the counsel table. "Miss Congdon was killed as a result of suffocation with this pillow that we found over her face," he said. The struggle with her killer had brought on congestive heart failure, he told jurors.

Jurors were visibly shaken when Goldschmidt testified that Elisabeth could have fought for her life for more than five minutes. "The interruption of blood supply to the brain only takes about a minute in order to make a person unconscious and unable to react," he explained. "And then, until a person dies, it takes a minimum of four minutes. If there was any struggle involved or any opportunity for the deceased to catch a breath in between by moving the head and gaining some air, she could take a breath, this would have taken longer."

But Goldschmidt's testimony could not eliminate the defense's claim that the murders could have been committed as late as 5 A.M., when the cook's dog finally stopped barking. By his best estimate the women died between midnight and 6 A.M.

Two of the prosecution's most crucial witnesses took the stand on June 1. DeSanto gambled that the airport gift shop employees would be his star witnesses. He hoped they would identify Roger as the man who carried a small wicker suitcase and bought a suede garment bag the morning of the murders. The night before, DeSanto had met with Sandra Schwartzbauer and Joanne Kelly to discuss courtroom strategy. He wanted to try a technique Waller had picked up from FBI Special Agent Bob Harvey. On the witness stand, if either woman could recognize Roger in the courtroom, she would signal DeSanto by folding her arms. If the women failed to cross their arms, DeSanto would avoid asking them whether they saw the man from the gift shop in the courtroom.

As each woman took her turn on the stand, DeSanto sat nervously and waited for the signal. First one and then the other woman folded her arms and pointed to Roger as the man each of them had seen June 27 at Minneapolis-St. Paul International Airport only hours after the murders. Roger showed no emotion or reaction as each woman singled him out.

DeSanto began by asking Schwartzbauer, "Do you recognize Mr. Caldwell as that individual you saw in the gift shop that morning?"

"Mr. Caldwell's a little thinner, but he has in general the same features," she said.

"Do you have any doubt as you sit here in the courtroom that this is the man that you saw that morning?"

"No sir, I don't have."

More than relieved, DeSanto was ecstatic. The eyewitness testimony of the two women quashed Marjorie's attempts to give her husband an alibi. When both women had given the signal and identified Roger, DeSanto was convinced his case was nearly won.

But on cross-examination Thomson vigorously attacked the women's credibility. Gesturing dramatically toward each woman, Thomson angrily reminded jurors these witnesses had failed to positively pick out his client in two previous photo lineups. Thomson succeeding in extracting an admission from Kelly and Schwartzbauer that they'd seen Roger's picture in the news—the photo that Duluth police had released to the news media at the time of Roger's arrest. A disgusted Thomson threw the photo down on the counsel table in DeSanto's direction. The picture had been plastered across the front page of the daily papers and aired on nightly newscasts around the state. "Who else would these women pick out as the murderer?" Thomson sarcastically asked the jury.

"I was able to establish that they had seen the picture in the paper. The descriptions that they gave before they couldn't remember. I think they were overanxious to help," Thomson recalled. "He was sitting there. He was obviously the guy." Of course, Kelly and Schwartzbauer had seen the photo before it was in the paper, as part of a photo line up.

As hard as he tried, Thomson could not shake the women's testimony. His client was the man they remembered seeing in the gift shop. That night the news media played up the eyewitness identification. Roger had been sighted in Minnesota with incriminating evidence the day of the murders. It was the only direct evidence linking Roger to Minnesota at the time of the murders.

The intense pressure of the trial, impossible to escape, wore down Waller, prosecution second chair Mike McNabb, and especially DeSanto. Every morning after arriving at the courthouse, DeSanto headed for the bathroom and threw up. Although it hadn't helped during his own testimony, Waller kept jogging to try to relieve the continuing stress of the trial. McNabb read books. DeSanto sought comfort in soothing music. But the trial schedule left little time for decompression.

At the end of each day's testimony, Waller, DeSanto, and McNabb would put away their documents and exhibits, stuff their fat leather briefcases, lug them downstairs to the car, and head back to the motel. Every evening they watched the local six o'clock news, then grabbed dinner, often at the Holiday Inn. By trial's end, they'd memorized the restaurant's menu and sampled every entree, even the liver and onions. For a culinary change of pace, once a week the men alternated between a Chinese restaurant and a barbecue joint down the highway.

After dinner, they interviewed upcoming prosecution witnesses at the card table in DeSanto's room. They got to bed anywhere from midnight to 2 A.M. Their morning ritual was to rise at 6 A.M., grab a cup of coffee at the restaurant, and arrive at the courthouse by 8 A.M.

On Friday afternoons, they'd review the week's testimony, talk over upcoming witnesses, and rate their progress over a cold beer. Most weekends Waller drove home to

Duluth to spend time with his wife and two young children. Bringing home a week's worth of dirty laundry in his suitcase, Waller would return Sunday night with clean clothes for another week. McNabb was also married and went back to St. Paul every Friday—his room wasn't paid for through the weekend. Whatever belongings he left behind had to be moved to Waller's and DeSanto's rooms.

DeSanto was single and dating Lana Eckenberg, a legal secretary in Duluth. They'd been introduced three years earlier by her boss, who had arranged for Lana to deliver legal documents to his friend DeSanto. The couple had started thinking about marriage, but DeSanto wanted to wait until after the trial. In fact, during the long trial, he only averaged one weekend a month at home. His routine weekends in Brainerd always included work and watching sports on TV on Saturday afternoons. Saturday nights he stayed in his room or took in a movie. Sunday mornings he attended the Catholic church near the motel. He spent Sunday afternoons and evenings preparing for the week ahead.

The three-month trial took a physical toll on the three men. McNabb, who had suffered a back injury during law school, found the heavy boxes and briefcases aggravated his back. Waller and DeSanto lost more than twenty pounds each. DeSanto developed a bladder infection from the stress; it was so painful he had to leave court one morning to see a doctor. He was back in court that afternoon.

"How would we get up fresh each day? It was fear that got me up each day," DeSanto recalled. "I was so frightened I wasn't going to get the job done that had to be done, that my adrenaline would get going. But we were drained at the end of each day, each week. There was never a real rejuvenation."

Judge Litman and his court reporter, Don Macheledt, also fought the grinding routine of the long trial. Each night after going out for dinner, the two men made use of the hotel's swimming pool or spa. Wednesday nights, they treated themselves to crab legs at a local restaurant. Every Friday afternoon they packed their suitcases for Duluth, returning to Brainerd on Sunday afternoon. Judge Litman recalled it was "like being a traveling salesman."

Even Memorial Day weekend provided no respite from the rigors of the case. DeSanto, Waller, Thomson, and Roger flew to Denver over the Memorial Day break to take a videotaped deposition of trustee Tom Congdon on Friday, May 26. Unable to testify in person because of a recent heart attack, Congdon was an important prosecution witness because he could detail firsthand the Caldwells' troubled finances. After all, he'd written a personal check only eight days before the murders to help the couple avoid eviction from their hotel.

Halfway through the trial, on June 1, Rick LeRoy was scheduled to testify about Roger's whereabouts at the time of the murders. Rick had refused to be interviewed after his initial statements and interview with Duluth police. DeSanto considered him a hostile witness.

DeSanto first questioned Rick about the crumpled note from Roger that police recovered from a wastebasket in LeRoy's room at the Holland House the week after the murders.

DeSanto asked, "And did you find anything on your bed at that time?"

"A note and some money," said LeRoy.

"Had you ever received a note, a written note from him that said 'Love, Dad' on it?"

"Not that I can remember."

"On that day, Saturday, June 25, did you see Roger Caldwell at all?"

"Not that I can remember."

"Did you see your mother that day?"

"Not that I can remember."

"Directing your attention to that day Sunday, June 26. Did you see the defendant Roger Caldwell on that date?"

"No."

"Did you see your mother on that date?"

"No."

DeSanto asked LeRoy the last time he had seen Roger prior to Monday, June 27, when Rick claimed to have seen his stepfather between 7:30 and 8 P.M. at the Holland House Hotel.

"I think it would be Wednesday the twenty-second," said Rick.

When Thomson cross-examined LeRoy, he prodded the young man's memory. LeRoy testified that when he was out late, he usually looked in on his parents in their adjoining hotel room.

"Have you had an occasion to look into the bedroom at night when you come back?"

"Yes."

"Okay. Did you see him in there then?"

"Yeah. They were usually sleeping then."

"Okay. And did you look into the room on Thursday night?"

"I usually looked in every night when I came home to see if they both were there, yes. I honestly don't remember Thursday night."

"You remember the Sunday night?" asked Thomson.

Rick LeRoy told jurors he had looked into Roger and Marjorie's bedroom Sunday night after returning home.

"Were they both there?"

"Well, it looked like to me there were two people sleeping in bed," LeRoy replied.

DeSanto bristled. This latest statement came as a complete surprise. LeRoy had never told police he'd seen his stepfather Sunday just before the murders. Now, a year later, he was trying to give Roger an alibi.

LeRoy acted cocky and defiant on the stand as DeSanto began his terse redirect, attacking the boy's credibility.

"Did you see Roger Caldwell in that bed?" demanded DeSanto.

"Identify him by looking at him?" asked LeRoy.

"Right," said DeSanto, impatient for LeRoy's response.

"I seen some hair. It looked like him."

"What did you see when you looked at the bed?"

"Two bodies."

"You actually saw two bodies?" DeSanto asked incredulously.

"Well, two lumps under the covers."

DeSanto abruptly ended his examination. LeRoy was obviously not going to recant his story. Better to let the jurors weigh the boy's defiant behavior rather than risk more damaging testimony. "No further questions, your honor," DeSanto concluded.

Looking back with twenty-five years of additional experience, DeSanto has said he should have then gone through every line of Rick's previous statements and grand jury testimony to emphasize that Rick had never mentioned seeing Roger that Sunday night before—and made it clear to the jury that DeSanto believed Rick had committed perjury.

But the prosecution scored points with testimony by Bertha Huskins, desk clerk at the Holland House Hotel. When DeSanto showed Huskins the suede garment bag purchased by Yagoda and Greene at the Twin Cities airport, she identified it as identical to Roger's, which the prosecution alleged had been bought the morning of the murders. "There is no difference," Huskins said.

Huskins also recognized Roger's handwriting on the envelope—postmarked June 27, 1977, Duluth, Minnesota—that had contained the gold coin. She said she had noticed the envelope when filing the Caldwell's mail.

During the trial's tenth week, one of the key Colorado investigators, Sergeant Randy Gordanier of the Golden Police Department, took the stand. During questioning by DeSanto, Gordanier said his investigation showed Roger was an avid coin collector—a motive for stealing the gold coin—but this assertion was based only on Roger's divorce settlement.

On cross, Thomson tried to downplay Roger's interest in coin collecting. He told jurors the coin collection was small and insignificant. He held up a copy of the divorce settlement and read out loud for jurors' benefit.

"The respondent shall have his stamp and coin collection and shall turn over to [daughter] Christi Lynn her coin collection. Was that ever brought to your attention before?" Thomson asked Gordanier.

"No, it wasn't."

"Now just so nobody's misled by that statement. Do you have any evidence [other than the settlement] that Roger Caldwell ever was a coin collector?"

"Not to my knowledge, no."

"Okay. And that statement does not say that he's a coin collector, does it?"

"No, it doesn't"

"Okay. Now, so no one is confused by the statement in this divorce paper. Did anybody ever ask you as a sergeant with the Golden, Colorado, Police Department to ascertain what was meant by this coin collection?"

"No."

"Were you ever instructed by Mr. DeSanto, here, or anybody from the Duluth Police Department, to ascertain exactly what was meant…by a coin collection?"

"No."

"Did you ever contact Mr. Caldwell's former wife to determine that?"

"No, I did not."

"Or his daughter that's mentioned?"

"No."

Thomson had gone hard on Gordanier, but DeSanto wasn't worried; he didn't think the jury would be swayed by finding out that Roger's daughter also had a coin collection. The important thing was that the divorce papers had clearly stated that Roger had one.

As the trial dragged on, the defendant continued to sit impassively next to Thomson. Even before the trial, it had quickly become apparent to Thomson that Roger would not be much help in his own defense. "Roger was very taciturn about the case," Thomson recalled. "He loved to talk about other things, like raising horses." But there wasn't much for the attorney and client to confer on—Roger had little to say except to declare his innocence.

Even the jail guards found Roger listless and withdrawn. Aside from Thomson, he had few visitors. None of his immediate family in Pennsylvania visited him. Marjorie had visited him just twice and both times she had an attorney accompanying her.

Roger had been prescribed tranquilizers, but he secretly stopped taking all but one of the five pills he received daily. He was stockpiling pills, perhaps for a suicide attempt if he were found guilty. Midway through the trial, his cellmate Larry Roloff caught on and alerted the jailer, who found 122 pills in a small brown bag Roger kept in the cell. Roger explained that he didn't always require five pills a day. But from then on, deputies watched to make sure he took every pill.

The last of the state's presentations focused on technical evidence—blood, hair, and fingerprints—keeping the evidence that linked Roger to the murders fresh in jurors' minds.

Investigators had found fingerprints in seven areas of the murder scene, but only three had useful detail. They lifted a small print from the base of the brass candlestick used to bludgeon Velma Pietila. That print, while too poor to identify, had sufficient detail to eliminate it as Roger's. The state maintained that the print had likely been left by one of the household servants while cleaning.

That left the prints from the nurse's bathroom, the only prints with sufficient distinguishing features for identification, which had still not been matched to anyone. The breakthrough came only days before DeSanto rested his case. In testimony June 16, John Douthit of the Minnesota Bureau of Criminal Apprehension publicly identified the mystery prints.

Douthit said the print on the bottom of the nurse's bathroom door belonged to nurse Sylvia Maki. He identified the left palm print on the sink in the bathroom as that of the chief investigator, Sergeant Gary Waller. The state crime lab had expanded the print comparisons to include all the officers who had gone to the mansion in the days after the murders. Douthit had broken the news to DeSanto and Waller earlier that morning. When Waller learned the print belonged to him, he avoided the courtroom the rest of the day—not only out of personal embarrassment, but to deny Thomson the chance to theatrically point him out in court to discredit the investigation. He was sure he had made the print when he leaned forward to look at the bloodstain on the wall behind the towel bar.

The impact of the print identification also concerned DeSanto. Obviously, the revelation fueled Thomson's claim of a careless police investigation. He was certain Thomson would argue that despite extensive comparison, police had found no prints of Roger's at Glensheen. DeSanto wanted jurors to remember that the absence of identifiable prints at the murder scene didn't rule out Caldwell as a killer. Some prints were simply too smudged or incomplete to identify.

Right in the middle of Roger's trial, Thomas Welch received an unexpected visit from Marjorie at Marquette National Bank. She told him she had cancer.

"Will the trust pay for my cancer treatment?" she asked.

"You have cancer?" Welch asked, surprised by the sudden news.

"Yes, the doctor told me I have cancer."

Welch told Marjorie that if she had cancer, of course, the trust would cover the cost of her treatment. "The trust is set up for those sorts of things," he assured her.

"Well, you'll probably have to be paying a substantial sum," Marjorie said before leaving.

Several weeks later, Welch got a medical bill for close to $30,000 but the letterhead indicated the bill was from a plastic surgeon. Welch wondered what a plastic surgeon could do to treat cancer. Two days later, Welch received a bill from a Minneapolis hospital for another $30,000.

Welch decided to call the doctor. "I've got this bill and I have some questions. What treatment did she go through?"

"I can't tell you that," the doctor said, because he needed Marjorie's consent to release the confidential information.

Welch said that he couldn't pay the bill without knowing what it was for. "Was this elective cosmetic surgery?"

There was silence on the phone. Then the doctor said, "I'll answer that if you'll answer a question for me." The two men had a deal.

Yes, the doctor said, Marjorie had undergone elective cosmetic surgery. "My patient's name is Marjorie LeRoy. Is she the same as Marjorie Caldwell?"

"Yes, she is," Welch said.

"Oh shit," the doctor said as he realized his patient's true identity.

"You didn't alter her looks, did you?"

"No. She came in and said 'I have one last chance to make the Olympic equestrian team.'"

Marjorie told the doctor she wanted to compete on the U.S. equestrian team at the 1980 summer Olympics in Moscow, and he had given her what she asked for—body tucks. Welch informed the doctor, hospital, and Marjorie that the bills would not be paid by the trust.

"Marjorie went ballistic," Welsh recalled, which wasn't an uncommon response for her.

As Marjorie tried to con her trust officer, she was also conning her husband and his family. Roger's sister-in-law Clara wrote him a letter on June 19, extending her sympathy for Marjorie's "cancer" surgery:

I was really sorry to hear about Marj's operation. From her description she must have incisions all over her body. I'll bet it was awfully difficult to sleep or rest comfortably. I'm writing to her today but tell her when you see her that I wish her a swift recovery. I do hope she doesn't have to have chemotherapy.

In the eleventh week of the trial, Patricia Rutz, the handwriting expert with the Boulder district attorney's office, took the stand. Rutz told jurors her comparisons of Roger's handwriting samples with the writing on the envelope addressed and mailed to him in Colorado showed they were written by the same person. Specifically, Roger had frequently written "Golden" with a large lower case "g" followed by an "a" which was then corrected to an "o". This was exactly how "Golden" was written on the envelope. Rutz also pointed out that "Roger S Caldwell" on the envelope was written exactly like Roger had written his signature for many years before 1977.

Thomson approached the enlarged photographs mounted on cardboard that Rutz had used to explain her conclusions to jurors. He pointed out variations between the handwriting samples and asked Rutz how they could have been made by one person.

"No one ever writes the same letter or word the same way twice," she answered. But, she clarified, such differences were insignificant, and it was her firm opinion that Roger wrote his own name and address on the envelope.

Steven Sedlacek, the fingerprint expert with the Colorado Bureau of Investigation, followed Rutz on the stand. Thomson, during earlier cross-examinations, had portrayed the fingerprint evidence from Glensheen as weak. DeSanto now asked Sedlacek, "Is it unusual, for instance, to process a crime scene and not find any latent prints?"

"Oh, no, sir," Sedlacek replied, and quoted from a five-year study by the International Association of Identification and the International Chiefs of Police Association.

"In eighty-five percent of the criminal cases where latent prints were developed, the person who was considered a suspect in that crime's prints were not found." In fact, then, it was unusual for a suspect to leave identifiable prints behind.

But the crux of Sedlacek's testimony was his examination of a partial print found on the flap of the envelope containing the gold coin. After processing the print with the chemical ninhydrin, Sedlacek had compared it with a known print of Roger's. As jurors studied enlarged photos of the two prints, Sedlacek said he believed Roger's right thumb made the print on the envelope. He found in excess of eleven points of comparison, he testified, more than the CBI required for identification.

Thomson didn't usually attack fingerprint evidence, but the prosecution's chart convinced him that the identification points didn't match. During a recess, he reviewed the photographs and, using a ruler, measured the two prints and their characteristics. "No way did they match," Thomson recalled years later.

On cross-examination, Thomson challenged Sedlacek about visible differences between the print enlargements. "It would appear to the untrained eye if you take the inked print and measure the distance, as you've indicated here, between those two ridge endings, that there is a considerable difference between the two photographs. Can you explain that to me?"

"This is probably done in the photographic process in enlarging," Sedlacek responded. "They may not be quite the same scale…. But yes, you have considerable variance." However, Sedlacek insisted the print characteristics matched.

That evening, Thomson went to work to find his own fingerprint experts. Sedlacek said that the disparity had to do with the distortion on the photographs. "Which is just total B.S. and he made that up right on the spot," Thomson said.

But the prosecution's case against Roger turned on more physical evidence than a fingerprint. DeSanto next called Wallace Sorum, a microanalyst for the Minnesota Bureau of Criminal Apprehension. He testified that three significant hairs had been recovered from Glensheen. Investigators had found two on the Oriental carpeting on the landing beneath Velma Pietila's body and the third in the sterile sheet used to wrap and carry the nurse's body from the mansion.

At the time of the murders, before DNA tests, fingerprints were "individual evidence" while hair and blood were considered "class evidence." Forensic science had not advanced enough to determine if a hair came from a specific person. An expert could only compare physical characteristics under a microscope and say the hair strands "compared favorably." According to Sorum's analysis, the three strands of hair were "mirror images" of Roger's head hair samples. Sorum also testified that the other hairs at the crime scene, including a single strand on the landing, a blond hair on the staircase, and a single strand found in Velma Pietila's hand, were consistent with Pietila's hair. He had only microscopically examined that one hair from her hand; there were more, but Sorum had felt the one he selected for the microscope was representative. This decision left an opening for the defense to make claims about the remaining hairs from her hand.

Sorum's testimony had been damaging to the defense, so over the weekend that followed, Thomson withdrew the hair evidence and flew to Milwaukee to meet with Dr. Kenneth Siegesmund, a forensic scientist who claimed several specialties, including hair matching. In Siegesmund's opinion, the hair found in Velma Pietila's hand was neither hers nor Roger's. "I'm thinking I was going to run a Perry Mason in this case. If it wasn't her hair and it wasn't Roger's, it had to be the assailant's," Thomson recalled. He instructed Siegesmund to prepare a chart showing the hair evidence and how the hairs failed to match up with Roger's.

Following Sorum's testimony, DeSanto called Alvin Hodge, a forty-five-year-old FBI serology expert from Washington, D.C., who bore a striking resemblance to actor Ernest Borgnine. Hodge testified about his examination of bloodstains on thirteen items investigators recovered from Elisabeth's bedroom. Bloodstains found on the pink satin pillow case used to smother the heiress and on the corner of the bedspread nearest her left arm were "consistent with the defendant's blood," said Hodge. These stains matched Roger's blood type and were similar to his blood enzyme grouping. Both victims and Roger had type O blood, but Caldwell had a different enzyme in his blood. He had enzyme group B while the two women had enzyme grouping BA.

DeSanto wanted the jury to understand the probability that the bloodstains would be consistent with the defendant's blood. "It's been testified earlier that in general the group O is found in about forty-two percent of the general population. Do you accept that figure as authoritative?" asked DeSanto.

"Yes. Forty-two to forty-five percent," said Hodge.

DeSanto next asked Hodge what percent of the population had the same blood type and enzyme group as the defendant. "Well, it's a straight multiplication: forty-two percent times thirty-six percent, which gives you roughly fifteen percent of the population," Hodge told jurors.

But Thomson pounced on Hodge's findings. Using the same figures the jury had heard during direct examination, Thomson forced Hodge to admit the bloodstain comparisons were inconclusive.

Given Hodge's estimate that forty-five percent of the population had the same blood type as Roger and the victims, Thomson said, "Say there are two hundred million people in America. That would be consistent with ninety million people?"

"That's correct."

"Including Mr. Caldwell and whoever else the other ninety million people in America that have Type O?" Thomson looked toward the jurors. "Which would mean perhaps half of the jury sitting in this box has Type O, is that correct?

"Yes."

If jurors accepted Hodge's estimate that thirty million people had the same blood and enzyme grouping as the defendant, Thomson asked, would it be fair to say that that the bloodstains could have come from any of those millions of people?

"Yes," Hodge conceded, he could not eliminate any of those thirty million people, but that was presuming that all of them had been at the crime scene and bleeding.

The state's final witness testified for jurors via his taped deposition. Tom Congdon described for jurors the desperate finances of Roger and Marjorie in the months leading up to the murders. Less than two weeks before the murders, Roger had asked for $250,000 to hire an attorney from F. Lee Bailey's firm to defend him and his wife against creditors and threatened lawsuits. The defendant had confided just days before the murders that he and Marjorie were using expired credit cards and bad checks to live.

While the prosecution had been wrapping up its case, Roger had received another letter from Marjorie. It was more succinct than her previous one, but just as self-centered. She wrote on June 21:

> Dear Rog,
>
> After gas and 2 quarts more oil I only had 65 cents left so couldn't get a paper. Did you mention visiting to Doug because Ron says Doug says wait till after the jury decides! The news in the paper is hard to learn from because it is always so slanted for DeSanto. Wrote a quick note to Clara [Roger's sister-in-law] but haven't heard back yet. What a crazy thing for both of us in one season! Back to the doc every third day but all seems to be going well. Rick is also doing quite well in spite of all the humid weather. The crazy little dog runs around like a skitter bug but she really is cute. Rick is afraid he will step on her! All my love, Me

The timing of the defense's opening statement, the one-year anniversary of the murders, was not lost on the prosecution or victims' families. Jennifer and Chuck Johnson and DeSanto's parents sat among the courtroom spectators on June 27, when the defense began to present its case.

Thomson only spent thirty minutes giving his opening statement, and he began it with a quip: "As the old lumberjack said when he was talking about his pancakes, he said, 'no matter how thick I make them, there's always two sides.' And we are now to present the defense side."

The defense planned to call only six witnesses. Jurors would hear expert testimony that key physical evidence—hairs recovered at Glensheen and

the handwriting on the envelope—did not belong to the defendant. The defense's hair expert, Dr. Kenneth Siegesmund, would testify that hair found clutched in Velma Pietila's hands did not come from her or Roger, but from "a totally independent source." The jury would also hear again from the manager of the Radisson Hotel in Duluth, Thomson said, to establish that envelopes like the one used to mail the gold coin were available only in guest rooms or at the front desk.

The defense would show, he said, that Roger was himself a victim—of an elaborate frame that included planted evidence in Minnesota and Colorado.

"We will demonstrate clearly Mr. Caldwell's innocence and I will, at the conclusion of the evidence, ask at your hands verdicts of not guilty on the grounds that there is no substance to either one of these charges," Thomson concluded.

Larry Jackson, one of the hundreds of people who called Duluth police after the murders with information, took the stand as the defense's lead witness.

He testified that he drove by Glensheen around 1:30 the morning of the murders. While on his way home from a hospital emergency room, where he had been treated for a rib injury suffered earlier in the day, he drove east on London Road. By Lakeside Cemetery, just west of Glensheen, he met another car traveling in the opposite direction. Jackson said he caught sight of a man near one of the estate's gates, illuminated by his and the oncoming car's headlights.

"I saw an individual standing about two trees from the Congdon estate," Jackson told jurors. He described the man as approximately six feet tall with long, shaggy blond hair, wearing blue pants and a cutoff jean jacket. The man made no attempt to hide, Jackson told the jury, during the four or five seconds the car headlights were trained on him.

Jackson arrived at home around 2:30 A.M., but waited to report the strange sighting to Duluth police until the next morning. Although he spoke with officers on two occasions in the weeks after the murders, Jackson testified police did not contact him after that. A year later, when Roger's trial began and he still had not been called back by police, he called Thomson, he said, "to see if the information would be of use."

During cross-examination, DeSanto attacked the significance of Jackson's reported sighting. Nothing DeSanto had read in the police interviews convinced him that Jackson had seen a possible murderer. A stranger on a warm summer night on a well-traveled thoroughfare—the defense was blowing smoke.

"The stretch that you're talking about is forty miles an hour that goes in front of the Congdon estate, as you've indicated?" DeSanto asked, wanting to emphasize Jackson would not have had long to look at the man.

"Yes."

"And of course it was dark so you had your lights on?"

"Yes."

DeSanto asked Jackson for a more precise location of the blond stranger. Jackson told jurors that the man stood approximately eight to ten feet away, near the sidewalk in front of Glensheen. In rebuttal testimony, DeSanto would have to reemphasize the physical evidence and motive linking the defendant, not some blond stranger, to the murders.

Following Jackson, Thomson called Congdon attorney Barney Johnson, who detailed Elisabeth's monetary gifts to her grandchildren, then Dr. Arden Anderson. The Brainerd doctor told of examining Roger at the Crow Wing County Jail during jury selection.

"As it regards to his mouth and face, what did you observe?" Thomson asked.

"He had some cold sores on his upper lip, four of them to be exact," Anderson testified.

DeSanto passed on cross-examination; while not wanting to lend credibility to the doctor's observations, he didn't have the evidence to dispute them.

Thomson had already decided Roger would not testify in his own defense. "Unless you really have to put a defendant on, unless it will really help a case, I've seen more cases lost through cross-examination," Thomson said. "I just didn't think in my view Roger would have helped himself." Roger had remained emotionless and passive throughout testimony and Thomson had no way of knowing what his client might say under fire, especially since Roger had been reluctant to discuss his case.

Thomson also would not call his own fingerprint expert. With only a few days lead time, he had failed to find an expert to refute Sedlacek's testimony. But hair expert Dr. Kenneth Siegesmund did succeed at overwhelming jurors with scientific evidence. The defense's fourth witness listed impressive credentials—associate professor of anatomy at the Medical College of Wisconsin and director of research for the Glendale Crime Laboratory. No one would have guessed from his testimony that he had arrived in Brainerd unprepared. "I picked him up at the airport and he hadn't done a damn thing. He hadn't made a chart," Thomson recalled. So Thomson stayed up all night with Siegesmund to ensure his chart and testimony were ready for the morning.

Siegesmund challenged testimony by the state's witness, Wally Sorum, about the two hairs found on the rug near Velma Pietila's body and the one in the sheet that wrapped her body. Siegesmund testified that although hairs vary between individuals, the diameters of hairs from a particular head will be similar. However, he cautioned, hair analysis was not an exact science.

"By present technology is it possible to say that two hairs definitely came from the same head?" Thomson asked.

"It's not possible with today's technology."

"Is it possible to say that two hairs did not?"

Siegesmund said yes, hair analysis could be used for the process of elimination. He told jurors that he analyzed the hair evidence using a light microscope and electronic scanning microscope, which magnified hair strands five-hundred times. The diameters of the shafts of the hair samples he examined were much larger than those known to be Roger's, he testified. There was too much variation in pigment density and distribution for the hairs to come from the same person. He told the jury that after his examination of the hairs using the powerful electron microscope, he was "absolutely certain" that the hair in question did not come from Roger.

Siegesmund also said that the hairs found in Velma Pietila's hand had come from an unknown individual, not Pietila. He told jurors the hair strands were light brown or blond. He left the impression that the hair could have come from the mystery man spotted outside Glensheen the night of the murders.

But the doctor's credentials were not above question. On cross-examination, DeSanto went after Siegesmund like a bulldog. DeSanto immediately challenged the impressive-sounding position of director of research at the Glendale crime lab. Siegesmund acknowledged that the lab was actually the basement of the Glendale police station and had no full-time employees.

Siegesmund also confirmed that the defense had found him through a national referral company called Technical Advisory Service for Attorneys, which lines up technical experts to testify at trial. His expert testimony carried a $300-a-day price tag, plus expenses.

"Your prior testimony with regard to hairs is exclusively, and has been exclusively, for the defense, is that right?" asked DeSanto.

"That's correct."

"And in addition to examining hairs, which you've indicated, you also do work in fingerprint analysis, do you not?"

DeSanto then ticked down the list: firearms analysis, blood analysis, hair analysis, and paint analysis. Siegesmund did analysis in each category.

"You do a little bit of everything, is that correct?" DeSanto concluded.

"That is correct," said Siegesmund.

When asked whether it might have been advisable to have more than two of Roger's head hairs for comparison purposes, Siegesmund admitted, yes it might. He had also only examined a sample of two head hairs from Pietila. Not a very large sample from which to make sweeping judgments, DeSanto said.

The final witness for the defense was handwriting expert Ann Hooten of Minneapolis. Before taking the stand, she handed each juror a copy of the handwritten address in dispute and several of Roger's known handwriting samples. These were accompanied by a plastic magnifying glass with her name embossed on the handle. The opportunistic advertising amused Judge Litman.

Hooten disagreed with state's witness Patricia Rutz on the authenticity of the hand-addressed envelope. She labeled the envelope, a key piece of evidence for the prosecution, a forgery.

"Could you explain to the jury if you will, why you do not believe it is the handwriting of Roger Caldwell?" asked Thomson.

Hooten claimed that signs of forgery were readily apparent—hesitation marks, tremors, alterations, overwriting, and patching. Someone familiar with Roger's handwriting had addressed the envelope. "It is my opinion this is a simulated forgery of Roger Caldwell's handwriting," Hooten testified.

But the prosecution had prepared for Hooten. Once they had learned she would testify, Waller and McNabb had called the Minnesota Bureau of Criminal Apprehension for leads on her background and testimony in other cases. They discovered that Hooten was the only American handwriting expert in the 1978 Howard Hughes forgery case to testify that the so-called "Mormon Will" was genuine.

During cross-examination, DeSanto attempted to discredit Hooten's record and impressive credentials. He pointed out for jurors that she had believed the Mormon Will was authentic. The majority of experts called to testify in that case had disagreed with her, as had the jury.

Yes, she had made mistakes. No expert is perfect, Hooten answered. But she said the writing on the envelope had many inconsistencies compared with Roger's writing. It's a fake, she maintained.

The state's rebuttal testimony was designed to counter the defense's attack on the hair and writing analysis. Samuel Palenik, of the Walter McCrone Institute in Chicago, disputed the hair testimony of Dr. Siegesmund, challenging his methods of taking hair measurements. Palenik directly disagreed with Siegesmund's conclusions that the diameter of hair varies only ten to twenty percent. Hairs can vary as much as one hundred percent in diameter, he told the jury, before shooting down the electron microscope's accuracy in comparing hair samples. According to Palenik, this type of microscope is useful only in observations of the outside of hair strands.

St. Paul police detective Robert Morehead took the stand on Friday afternoon, June 30, to challenge the reliability of Hooten's opinion on the handwriting. He told jurors Hooten had been mistaken in a check forgery case he'd investigated. She had testified as a handwriting expert that a check, later proven to be a forgery, was authentic. Along with the earlier information on the Howard Hughes case, Morehead's testimony damaged Hooten's credibility.

"The people of the state of Minnesota rest their case," DeSanto told the court, using the language Waller had suggested. They wanted to convey that the prosecution worked for justice for the people—not some faceless machine trying to frame an innocent man. After eight weeks of testimony and 109 witnesses, Roger Caldwell's trial was nearly complete. Only closing arguments remained—the final showdown between prosecution and defense.

Photo Gallery

Clara Hesperia Congdon, 1854 – 1950.

Chester Adgate Congdon, 1853 – 1916.

Glensheen as seen from the estate's gardens. Construction on the mansion began in 1905 and was completed in 1909. Elisabeth was the only one of the Congdons' seven children to live in the mansion her entire adult life. Today Glensheen is open to public tours (see page A33).

Chester Congdon holds up son Robert as daughter Elisabeth swims nearby while the three enjoy an afternoon playing in Lake Superior off Minnesota Point (Park Point) in Duluth.

Elisabeth Mannering Congdon in her schoolgirl years (left) and as a young woman (right).

The Congdon family yacht, Hesperia (after Clara's middle name). The fifty-two foot wooden craft was damaged by fire in 1916 and never repaired. In newspaper interviews, Marjorie claimed she and her sister Jennifer enjoyed outings on the yacht, but it was destroyed sixteen years before her birth. (She also claimed to have hidden vegetables in Ming vases at Glensheen, but the Congdon estate never owned any vases from the Ming Dynasty.)

A box that once contained Congdon pears sits in Glensheen's milk room. The estate was nearly self-sufficient (gardens and greenhouses produced vegetables and fruit) and included a pair of dairy cows, whose milk the staff used to make a variety of dairy products.

A blurred postcard of Westhome (also known as "Congdon Castle"), the Congdon estate in Yakima Washington, which Chester Congdon developed into a 375-acre cattle ranch and orchard with apple, cherry, pear, and peach trees. Westhome is built of native basalt stone on the side of a hill overlooking the orchards. It was also distinctive for its indoor swimming pool, the first in the region.

Swiftwater Farm, Elisabeth Congdon's summer home (actually a remodeled farm house) located in northwestern Wisconsin on the Brule River. Elisabeth visited "The Brule" every weekend during the summer, including the Sunday before she was killed.

Marjorie Congdon (first row, last on right) in her sophomore year of high school at Dana Hall, a private boarding school for girls in Wellesley, Massachusetts.

Elisabeth Congdon (left) and her oldest daughter, Marjorie, on the day she wed first husband Richard "Dick" LeRoy in June 1951. The ceremony was held in the living room at Glensheen.

Groom Dick LeRoy stands by as his bride tosses her bouquet from Glensheen's main stairway balcony, where the battered body of nurse Velma Pietila would be discovered twenty-six years later.

Dick LeRoy and Marjorie Congdon's wedding party at Glensheen, including (right to left) the groom's mother, Beth LeRoy, the bride's mother, Elisabeth Congdon, the groom, his bride, best man and Congdon cousin Chester d'Autremont, maid of honor and bride's sister, Jennifer Congdon, and Congdon family members and friends: John Garver, Helen Moore, Jim McLeran, Anne Paine, Russell Moore, Caroline Lewis, Jim Voss, and Betsy Congdon.

The LeRoy family enjoys an afternoon outing, including roasting marshmallows, at Wabun Park in Minneapolis in the early 1960s. From left to right, Dick, Peter, Heather (in front of Peter), Marjorie, Rebecca, Ricky, Stephen (behind Ricky), Suzanne, and Andrew.

Velma Pietila, the valiant nurse who struggled in vain to stop the intruder who killed her and Elisabeth Congdon and made off with Congdon's jewelry.

Elisabeth Congdon a few years before her death, wearing a brooch that was stolen the night of her murder and was later found in her daughter Marjorie's hotel room.

Miss Elisabeth (front row center) surrounded by her nursing staff, clockwise from left: Mildred Garvue, Velma Pietila, Marie Johnson, Mildred "Miss K" Klowsowsky, Sylvia Maki, and Joyce Loberg. Loberg was supposed to have worked at Glensheen on June 27, 1977—the night of the murders—but Velma Pietila agreed to take her place so Loberg and her family could visit relatives in Iowa. Oddly, Loberg died exactly twenty-seven years after the murders, on June 27, 2004.

Right: During a LeRoy family visit to Glensheen in 1958, Marjorie secretly removed this small oil painting by Henri Harpignies (1819-1916) from the library and sold it to the Beard Art Gallery of Minneapolis. The Congdon Office and Dick LeRoy then traced the painting to Newhouse Galleries in New York City. The Congdon Office paid the gallery, and the painting returned to Glensheen; it once again hangs in the mansion's library.

May 23, 1977

To Whom This May Concern:

    RE: Richard Leroy

In reference to my letter dated June 26, 1976, all of the conditions outlined are still true and in many ways have been intensified. In addition, the following changes have developed since that time. The cystic fibrosis, which was latent a year ago, is now an active and real problem. His physical limitations are more pronounced and his vocational field has now narrowed to agriculture or some other form of out-door endeavor. He showed an interest in veterinary medicine, which I have encouraged, but have also had to remind him to confine his thinking to large animals, so as to minimize his time in the office. His college studies would require longer than average time due to his inability to carry a complete schedule of classes plus his frequent hospitalization. Summer school and private tutoring could be required or possibly extending his normal schooling by two or more years.

His parents desire to operate a boarding stable is an excellent idea which could provide Richard with precisely the type of atmosphere which I deem medically necessary for his continued health and well being.

Richard is presently on an experimental drug which is provided to us by the F.D.A. Due to the uniqueness of his condition and his reactions to various treatments and medications there is substantial motivation for using his case for publication in medical journals, with his parent's permission, of course.

The experience that I have had in letters and phone conversations with his trust officers or any members of his family, aside from his parents, have proven in the most part to be fruitless. It is my understanding that his step-father has provided him with his horses, Motorcycle and automobile. Richard knows that his grandmother could, and would, provide financial assistance to him if she were legally able. Unfortunately Richard feels both unloved and unwanted by anyone other than his parents.

H Chai

Hyman Chai, M.D.
Director
Clinical Services and Research

Left: The letter, supposedly from Rick LeRoy's doctor at the National Asthma Center, that Roger presented to the Congdon Trustees as evidence that he and Marjorie needed $750,000 in order to build a ranch custommade for Rick's condition. The trustees turned Roger down. They learned the Caldwells had forged the letter on stationery stolen from the National Asthma Center. The Center had diagnosed Rick's asthma as moderate, not life threatening. Roger had typed while Marjorie dictated every word.

Crime scene: the top of Glensheen's main stairway, where Velma Pietila began her struggle with the intruder. This photo was taken from a spot directly in front of the table that held the brass candlestick the intruder used to kill Pietila. Her body was found arranged on the window seat, evidently moved there after she was killed.

Duluth Police Officer Barry Brooks attempting to place his arm through the window Roger Caldwell claimed he broke to gain access to Glensheen. Lead Detective Gary Waller and Prosecutor John DeSanto both now believe the window was broken to mislead investigators.

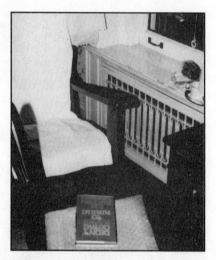

One of the murder weapons: the brass candlestick as police found it, standing upright on the main stairway landing's bloodstained carpet, near Velma Pietila's body. The second murder weapon, a satin pillow, was found covering Elisabeth Congdon's face.

In the nurse's room, where Velma Pietila sat reading I Didn't Come Here to Argue by Peg Bracken while eating a late meal before being attacked. A thermos that Pietila had used to prop up the window was removed by police prior to the photo. Sloppy police work would become an issue at trial.

The memorabilia case in Elisabeth Congdon's bedroom, from which a 1,700-year-old Byzantine coin was stolen on the night of the murders.

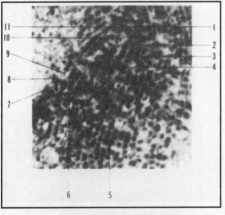

The envelope mailed to Roger Caldwell from Duluth to the Holland House Hotel in Golden, Colorado; a 1,700-year-old Byzantine coin (below) stolen from Glensheen was found inside. The envelope was tested for DNA in 2003 and was found to be consistent with a known sample from Roger Caldwell (see the epilogue for a complete analysis of new the DNA evidence). Expert handwriting analysis by a prosecution witness indicated the handwriting on the envelope matched Caldwell's; defense expert witnesses contradicted those claims.

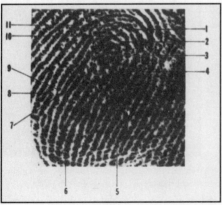

The latent print found on the envelope (top) and Roger Caldwell's inked right thumb print (bottom). Detective Gary Waller, a latent print expert, didn't think the prints matched, but prosecutor John DeSanto elected to present the evidence at trial anyway, which eventually hurt the murder and conspiracy case against Marjorie Caldwell. The fingerprint evidence was part of the Minnesota Supreme Court's decision to grant Roger Caldwell a new trial, which in turn led to his bargain for release in exchange for a confession.

The 1,700-year-old Byzantine coin (below), shown actual size. Murder victim Elisabeth Congdon kept the coin in a memorabilia case in her bedroom alongside other artifacts she collected during her travels abroad.

Jewelry stolen from Glensheen and found in a pantyhose container in Roger and Marjorie Caldwell's Bloomington, Minnesota, hotel room. Marjorie claimed the pieces were actually duplicates of her mother's jewelry that Elisabeth had had made for her. At Marjorie's trial, her defense claimed this evidence (and the basket and garment bag, below) was planted as part of an attempt by the Duluth Police and the Congdon family to frame her.

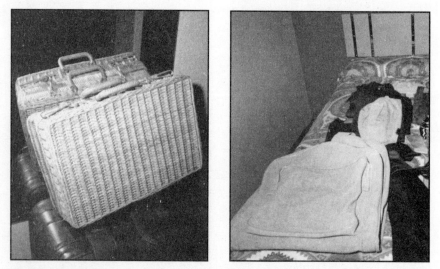

The wicker basket (left, leaning against a mirror) stolen from Glensheen and a suede suit bag (right) identical to one purchased at the Minneapolis-St. Paul International Airport the morning of the murders, both found in Roger and Marjorie's hotel room in Bloomington.

Marjorie Caldwell being questioned by police in a Bloomington, Minnesota, hotel room. Police had searched her room and found jewelry matching items stolen from Glensheen. When confronted with the evidence by Detective Gary Waller, Marjorie explained that the pieces were duplicates Elisabeth Congdon had had made as gifts for Marjorie. Although her civil attorney, David Arnold, told her over the phone to keep quiet, she continued to speak to the police without an attorney present and after being read her Miranda rights.

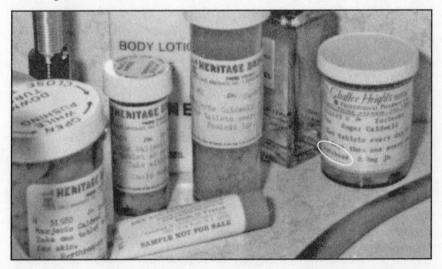

Various prescription medications lined the bathroom vanity of Roger and Marjorie Caldwell's hotel room at the Holiday Inn in Bloomington, Minnesota, including a prescription made out to Roger for Antabuse (white circle), an alcohol aversion drug that was supposed to help him control his drinking.

June 24, 1977

I, Marjorie Congdon Caldwell do on this day
of June twenty fourth, nineteen hundred and
seventy seven give and bequeth to my
husband Roger Sipe Caldwell all the cash
benefits due to and or accruing to me from
the Chester A. Congdon trust that must dis perse
all principel to the children of his heirs
within three calender years from the date of
death of the last surviving child of his,
namely, Elisabeth Mannering Congdon. This
bequest is made as a deed of gift with no
restrictions as to use, or any restrictions arising
from a state of divorce, seperation, my death
or any other conditions or restrictions. I do this
with the full knowledge that this document
is irravocable under any circumstances or for
any reasons whatsoever and that said document
shall be binding also upon my executors, heirs
or beneficiaries.

           Marjorie Congdon Caldwell

Subscribed and sworn to before me this
24th day of June, 1977, by Marjorie
Congdon Caldwell, who personally appeared
before me.

Notary Public, Arapahoe County, State of
Colorado (My commission expires 3/10/79)

     I certify that I have read the above this 24th day of
June 1977, and that I approve of the contents thereof.

            Roger S. Caldwell

Marjorie Caldwell's handwritten will dated June 24, 1977—three days before her mother, Elisabeth Congdon, was discovered smothered to death—giving Roger Caldwell a portion of the inheritance Marjorie would receive after Elisabeth's death. As part of the theory that this document set the crimes at Glensheen in motion, Prosecutor John DeSanto referred to the will as a "murder contract"—the carrot that led Roger Caldwell to commit two murders.

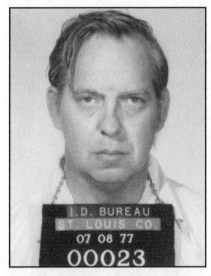

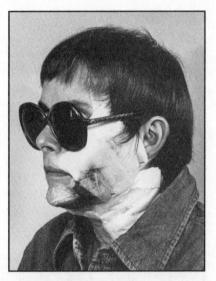

Roger Sipe Caldwell's mug shot, taken shortly after his arrest for the murders of Glensheen nurse Velma Pietila and his mother-in-law, heiress Elisabeth Congdon. When officers explained to Caldwell that he was being placed under arrest for the murder—while he was being hospitalized—he replied simply, "Oh."

Marjorie Caldwell, bandaged after an alleged attack. She claimed a man dressed as a police officer (and resembling detective Gary Waller) slashed her with a razor. Her examining physician said the wounds appeared self-inflicted. She insisted that a *Duluth News-Tribune* photographer take this photo.

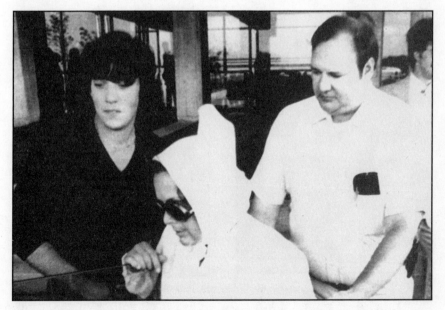

Marjorie Caldwell at the Dakota County Courthouse in Hastings, Minnesota—accompanied by her youngest son, Ricky (left)—being escorted to her trial for conspiring to murder her mother.

Gary Waller, Duluth police detective and chief investigator of the Congdon/Pietila murders. After leaving the Duluth Police department, Waller served as St. Louis County Sheriff from 1986 to 1999. He now operates a consulting service doing organizational and facility assessments.

St. Louis County Prosecutor John DeSanto, who tried both Roger Caldwell and Marjorie Caldwell. Marjorie Caldwell's case was the only murder trial he ever lost. DeSanto is now a trial court judge with his chambers in Duluth, Minnesota.

Well-known Minnesota defense attorney Ron Meshbesher, whose experience won Marjorie's acquittal. He later represented her at her Minnesota arson trial; she was convicted.

St. Paul defense attorney Doug Thomson, who defended Roger Caldwell and later negotiated his prison release in exchange for a confession to the Glensheen murders. He died May 2, 2007.

Above: Marjorie and Wally Hagen's home in Ajo, Arizona, where Wally was found dead when authorities came to escort Marjorie to prison. Since this photo was taken the house has been slightly remodeled and painted.

Below: The side of the Hagen's Ajo, Arizona, home. Note that the windows have been removed and the openings sealed over with cement. Marjorie so disliked her neighbor Mark Indvik that she had this work done so she no longer had to look at his house. She was later cought by Indvik, a U.S. Border Patrol officer, and the Ajo police while attempting to set fire to Indvik's home.

Helen Hagen in her younger days when she, like Velma Pietila, worked as a nurse. Helen died unexpectedly in her nursing home bed in 1981. Nursing home staff said Marjorie hand-fed her the night before she slipped into a coma. She died just a few days later.
(In 1974, Elisabeth Congdon mysteriously fell ill after Marjorie hand-fed her homemade marmalade.)

Wally Hagen, who married Marjorie shortly after his wife Helen's death. After marrying Marjorie, Wally became estranged from his family. He waited for Marjorie for nearly two years as she served a short prison term for the arson of the Cranberry House, their home in Mound, Minnesota. Hagen died in his home the morning Marjorie waited for authorities to take her to prison for arson.

Marjorie Hagen's prized antique stove, photographed by police the day her third husband, Wally, was found dead in their home in Ajo, Arizona. The flexible gas line (in white circle) was found near the stove, unattached. Police suspect Marjorie used a garden hose to transfer gas from the stove to Wally in his bedroom. Wally's official cause of death was listed as an overdose of propoxyphene, a barbiturate found in his blood. Gas dissipates in the body, leaving no evidence behind. His death was not ruled homicide or suicide, but "undetermined."

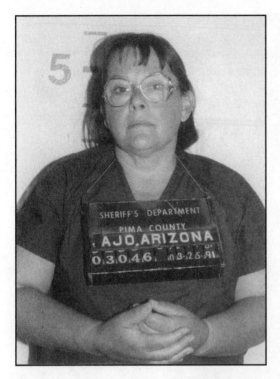

Marjorie (Caldwell) Hagen at the time of her arrest in Ajo, Arizona. She was arrested outside her neighbor's house where she had left a kerosene-soaked rag burning in a pried-open window. She was convicted of insurance fraud and attempted arson and was thought to be responsible for a rash of fires that occurred in Ajo during the time she and her third husband, Wally Hagen, lived there.

Before authorities came to take Marjorie to prison the day after her sentencing, they received a call from Wally's son Tom. Marjorie had called Tom in Minnesota to tell him Wally was dead. A joint suicide note, primarily written by Marjorie, claimed they had a suicide pact. Marjorie apparently couldn't go through with her end. Murder charges were dropped due to lack of evidence.

An apparently pleased Roger Caldwell leaving the St. Louis County Jail (followed by reporter Mike Simonson) after the Minnesota Supreme Court's decision on August 6, 1982, to grant Roger a new trial based on evidence raised at his wife's trial.

On July 5, 1983, he avoided trial and further prison time by providing the authorities a confession. Officials had hoped his confession would implicate Marjorie Caldwell. Unfortunately, the confession shed no new light on the case.

Caldwell returned to Latrobe, Pennsylvania, his hometown. He had trouble finding steady work and began drinking again. After making several failed attempts to sell his "real" story to Elisabeth Congdon's other surviving daughter, Jennifer Johnson, he committed suicide on May 18, 1988.

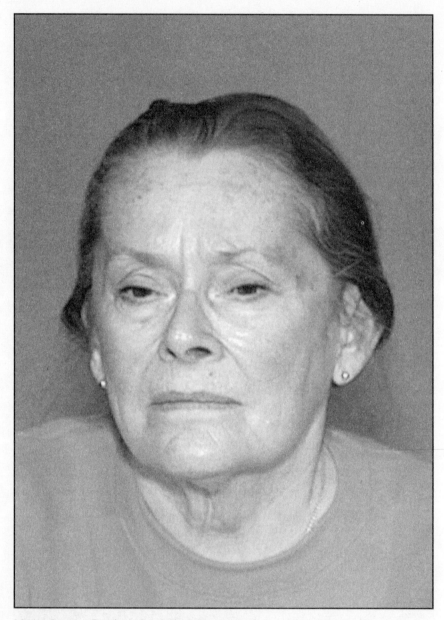

Marjorie Bannister Congdon LeRoy Caldwell Hagen in 2002, taken at the Arizona State Prison Complex-Perryville in Goodyear, Arizona, a western suburb of Phoenix. All of Marjorie's attempts at parole met with resistance from various family members, and were denied. She was eventually released on January 5, 2004, her earned release date based on her behavior while incarcerated (her sentence didn't officially expire until 2007, but she could not be held beyond her earned release date). While seeking parole, Marjorie's early-release plans indicated she would relocate to Tucson; now, however, she is free to move wherever she chooses, without supervision. She claims to have saved about $1.2 million while in prison.

The Santa Cruiz unit of the Perryville State Prison complex in Goodyear, Arizona, where Marjorie Congdon LeRoy Caldwell Hagen served a large part of her ten-year prison term for arsons in Ajo, Arizona.

Cell #110 on Cellblock A, where Marjorie spent her last few years in prison. The photos on this and the previous page were taken just hours after Marjorie was released from prison on January 5, 2004.

Top: A concerned-looking Marjorie Hagen carries out her belongings as she spies reporters attempting to document her release as she walked out of Perryville just after 9 A.M. on Monday, January 5, 2004.

Middle: Marjorie turns on the charm as she greets her hired driver. Hagen wore a salmon-colored sweater and khaki pants—along with her trademark large glasses—and looked fit and spry.

Bottom: Minutes later, inside a hired white Crown Victoria, Hagen ducked down to avoid TV crews waiting at prison exits as her driver sped out of the parking lot; reporters followed. The car entered the highway by passing other vehicles on the shoulder of the entrance ramp and was last seen headed toward Tuscon at speeds of over 100 miles per hour. One Ajo resident believes he saw Hagen riding in a van on the streets of his town later that day, and the Ajo Fire Department was called to three fires that day and the next, one in the Catholic church Marjorie had attended before going to prison. None were determined to be arson.

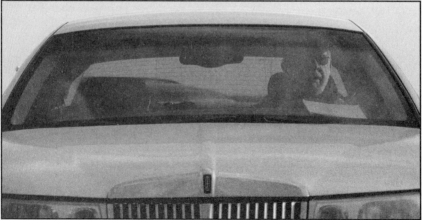

CHAPTER 16

Closing Arguments

BEFORE THE ATTORNEYS SQUARED OFF to give their closing arguments, another drama unfolded behind closed doors in the chambers of Judge Jack Litman. Litman met with juror Rosemary Robison shortly before 9:15 A.M. on July 5, 1978. A supervisor at Brainerd's North Country Outerwear, Robison had worked an hour or two almost every day since the start of the trial.

Several days earlier, an anonymous woman had mailed a letter to and telephoned the Crow Wing County Sheriff's Department, claiming Robison "had been telling everybody at work that [Roger Caldwell] is guilty ever since the trial started." The woman said her mother worked with Robison.

Judge Litman was concerned about possible grounds for appeal. After all the time and money everyone had invested, he wasn't about to risk it.

He told Robison, "I'll ask you once again to search your memory since we've been here and since you've been at work, whether you've ever given any indication to anyone at all, including any members of your family, as to whether or not you have some preconceived notion of the guilt or innocence of Mr. Caldwell?"

"Your honor, I really don't remember saying that the man was guilty, 'cause I don't come in with that feeling," Robison said. She then assured Judge Litman that when her coworkers talked about the case around her, "I walk away from it."

Judge Litman then asked Robison if she could continue as a juror and keep an open mind. She responded, "I'd still sit there with an open mind."

The judge next met with Thomson and DeSanto and asked for their comments. Both said they would defer to the court's judgment.

Judge Litman was quick with his decision. "Because of the seriousness of the report submitted, together with an accompanying letter and the fact that the person had called at the office in person, as opposed to the usual type of crank phone call or letter, the court feels the interests of justice would best be served if Mrs. Robison was excused as a juror."

Robison was replaced by the first alternate, another woman, so the gender makeup of the jury remained unchanged. DeSanto couldn't help but think of Fern Swartout, dismissed during jury selection. He couldn't remember another case in which he'd lost two jurors, especially ones he considered favorable to the prosecution.

DeSanto and Waller had driven to the courthouse earlier than usual on July 5, the day set for final arguments. The stagnant air dripped with humidity. Even in the relative cool of the morning, the heat rippled off the asphalt and could soak a person in perspiration. They spoke little, not even of the weather, as DeSanto continued to mentally rehearse his argument. Waller had assisted DeSanto by taking notes throughout the trial, keeping track of the inconsistencies in the defense's case, tough questions raised on cross, and testimony that seemed to have an impact on jurors. The night before the two men had stayed up late reviewing their notes—fifty yellow legal pads worth—and preparing for the culmination of the case that had consumed them for more than a year.

The Crow Wing County Courthouse, even with a stiff wind blowing in the windows, felt like an oven. The temperature soon pushed into the nineties. As Waller sat down in the front row, behind DeSanto at the counsel table, he felt his slacks stick to the wooden bench. When he stood later that morning, he found the combination of sweat and blistering heat had melted the varnish onto the back of his pants.

News media and spectators jammed the courtroom, standing in the doorway and pouring into the hall once all the seats had filled. The setting and sweltering temperatures reminded Waller of the courtroom scene from the movie To Kill a Mockingbird, when Gregory Peck's character, Atticus Finch, delivers his final argument in defense of his client, a black man accused of molesting a white woman. Like its movie counterpart, the Brainerd courtroom's dark wood gave it an air of formality. The heat magnified the anticipation, anxiety, and tension to almost painful proportions.

His perspiration-soaked shirt clinging to him, John DeSanto—pumped up, nervous, and uncomfortable—began his closing arguments. He wanted to seize the opportunity to show the jury the confidence he had in his case, to make all the evidence fit together. He'd slept maybe two hours, tops. Not the type to rehearse in front of mirrors, he had his outline ready. Contrary to trial manuals that recommend writing closing arguments before the trial starts, DeSanto had waited until that morning.

Dressed in a conservative three-piece navy blue suit with gray pinstripes, DeSanto had chosen a red, white, and blue tie to add a patriotic touch. He placed the podium a few feet nearer to the jury than during opening statements. After three-and-a-half months, he knew the jurors well enough to get a little closer. DeSanto looked over at Dale Brick, the juror he was convinced would be chosen jury foreman, and then located his parents, seated in the back row.

He gripped the podium with both hands, took a deep breath, and then began his summation by telling jurors he didn't want to bury them in facts. But in a circumstantial evidence trial, he needed to make sure they remembered the crucial evidence. By law, a guilty verdict demanded jurors find the evidence so compelling that guilt is the only logical conclusion.

DeSanto motioned toward the exhibit table and urged jurors to use the state's exhibits in their deliberations and consider where incriminating evidence had been recovered. "Compare, ladies and gentlemen, the handwriting on the envelope and the printing on the card on the suede bag with the known handwriting…[and] printing of Roger Caldwell…a comparison…that will lead to an inescapable conclusion," DeSanto said. He then emphasized how a cash register receipt found in the defendant's hotel room matched the kind of receipts issued by the Minneapolis-St. Paul International Airport gift shops.

"Use the documents that were found and seized from the defendant's safety deposit box in Golden, Colorado," DeSanto urged jurors. "The inference and only proper and reasonable inference in the difference of these two documents…is that this will was written by Marjorie Caldwell on June twenty-fourth in a desperate attempt to persuade the defendant, Roger Caldwell, to go to Duluth, Minnesota, to commit murder."

In opening statements, attorneys must only present the facts. But closing arguments give each side an opportunity to present their theories of the case. DeSanto returned to the analogy that got him in trouble during opening statements. DeSanto called the will, "the carrot that persuaded Roger Caldwell to commit murder. The last-minute concession to the defendant. That's why it's not typed [but is] handwritten and dated June 24th, while the power of attorney is not."

He anticipated Thomson would place great emphasis on the concept of reasonable doubt. Jurors would likely be instructed by Thomson that a single reasonable doubt required them to find the defendant not guilty. DeSanto wanted to erase any doubts. But first he gave them the prosecution's definition of reasonable doubt. "You have no reasonable doubt as to the defendant's guilt if you are morally certain of your verdict. What that basically means, and a commonly used analogy is, if you can look yourself in the mirror and say, 'I know he's guilty based on the evidence and I can live with that verdict,' you will have no reasonable doubt."

The deaths of Elisabeth Congdon and Velma Pietila were brutal and premeditated, DeSanto continued. He held up the brass candlestick. Remember jurors, he said as he banged it loudly against the podium, the murders were committed by a man of above-average strength. Several jurors flinched. DeSanto had their attention.

The prosecutor continued: "The evidence shows rationally and conclusively that there must have been first a struggle between the murderer and Velma Pietila. That Velma Pietila used her shoe—the one with the heel that had come off it—the heel pad off it, and take a look at that when you get back to the jury room, to defend herself. That that shoe was turned against her as she tried to protect herself from that beating…that one of the nails on the bottom of the shoe caused a cut on the lip of the defendant, Roger Caldwell, and the cut on the middle finger of his left hand."

DeSanto reminded jurors that after Velma Pietila was beaten to death with the candlestick, it was Elisabeth Congdon's turn to fight for her life. "[Elizabeth Congdon] had struggled, ladies and gentlemen. The bruise on her left arm indicates a struggle. The skin rubbed from her nose indicates a struggle and all of this goes to the additional elements of premeditation and intent to kill.

"[T]he defendant [had] time to wash up in that bathroom, to change clothes, to take the Pietila car and get to that airport by 6:35—and that ticket tells you [when] that car got there—[even if he went] forty miles out of his way, for a man unfamiliar with the...route to that airport. We gave you all the evidence, ladies and gentlemen. We didn't hide that fact that there were forty unaccounted for miles on that odometer of Loren Pietila['s car] and Mr. Thomson will remind you of it, I'm sure. How many of you have driven to Minneapolis and gone a little bit out of the way, taken the wrong exit? You only have to go twenty miles out of the way to put forty miles on the odometer."

DeSanto lingered on the most damaging evidence pointing to Roger's guilt. His star witnesses, the two women at the airport gift shop, had identified the defendant in court.

"This case is primarily a circumstantial evidence case. Not exclusively a circumstantial evidence case, because we have the direct evidence of the deaths. We have the direct evidence, ladies and gentlemen, the positive identification by two women of the defendant at that airport on the morning of June 27, 1977, purchasing this bag," DeSanto continued, holding up the suede suit bag.

He rebutted Thomson's suggestion that Vera Dunbar had mailed the self-addressed envelope containing the gold coin to Roger Caldwell. "Isn't it interesting that the question to Mrs. Dunbar was, 'Mrs. Dunbar, don't you recall Roger Caldwell going into the Radisson Hotel, getting an envelope, and giving it to you?' 'No', was her answer—because it didn't happen.

"But I submit to you the defense knows that's Roger Caldwell's handwriting or the question would never have been asked to try and plant that seed that, sure enough, there's a big frame here and Vera Dunbar sent this. It wasn't Vera Dunbar's print on that envelope, ladies and gentlemen. Now, interesting, now that after Vera Dunbar denied it and the other people in Duluth, Barney Johnson, Bill Van Evera, the other people that saw Roger Caldwell during his May visit denied seeing that, all of a sudden in midstream the defense thinks they can convince you now it's not Roger Caldwell's handwriting."

DeSanto believed that Thomson had made a serious error in judgment when he suggested Dunbar had sent the letter. It undermined the defense's later claim that the handwriting was forged. The jury could see that the defense was trying to have it both ways—claiming a frame whether it was forged or not.

"But no one will ever tell you not to use your common sense, and your common sense dictates one conclusion, that same conclusion, ladies and

gentlemen, that this is Roger Caldwell's handwriting. Roger Caldwell mailed this envelope from Duluth as it had to be mailed to get that postmark between 5 P.M. Sunday June 26 and midnight on Monday June 27." DeSanto misspoke when he said "midnight on Monday June 27." He had meant "before midnight Tuesday June 28." The jury understood this and his point: the letter placed Roger in Duluth at the time the murders occurred.

DeSanto continued to refute Thomson's allegations that Roger had been framed and ran down the list of defense witnesses. He dismissed the defense's hair expert as a hobby cop. He attacked Ann Hooten's testimony that someone had skillfully forged the writing on the envelope, his face getting progressively redder.

"No one in Duluth even knew Roger Caldwell before May 25, 1977.... Who in heaven's name, ladies and gentlemen, is the defense going to say knew the defendant's handwriting well enough to make that simulated or copied forgery? Steve LeRoy, who first met the defendant, Roger Caldwell, on June 30, just before the funeral, at the Radisson Hotel? Peter LeRoy, who also first met and saw the defendant on June 30? Barney Johnson, who met him for the first time on May 25?

"Was it Bill Van Evera, who also only met and saw the defendant the first time on May 25 and received nothing from him? Vera Dunbar? I'll let you judge her credibility. Nurse Klosowsky, who happened to see the defendant that day on his visit on May 25? Mildred Garvue? Maybe even Elisabeth Congdon herself? That's how absurd we get when we got to this frame.

"Why keep the flight bag? Why in heaven's name even buy the flight bag? Stupid, but I submit to you ladies and gentlemen, the undoing of Roger Caldwell. I submit to you there is no way he could have anticipated the meticulous, painstaking work of the Duluth Police Department and the people who did this investigation. There is no way he could have anticipated they would find the receipt he took from his bag and put in his hotel room.

"No matter how hard the defendant and Mr. Thomson have tried to rid Roger Caldwell of this bag, it's like the damn spots on MacBeth's wife's hands. She couldn't get rid of them. The one critical error that Roger Caldwell made, which will prevent him from getting away with murder, because he's been positively identified by two people as the purchaser.... Because Bertha Huskins testified she has no doubt the defendant or Ricky [LeRoy] was carrying this bag. [Because the] receipt for that bag was in the defendant's hotel room in Duluth."

DeSanto often became emotional during closing arguments. Sometimes, when that happened, he made mistakes, saying things he shouldn't. Referring to the cold sore on Roger's lip that was visible on the day the Pietilas testified, DeSanto slipped. "The prosecution doesn't come in here and write scripts and hand out roles. They take the witnesses as they get them. They take the evidence as they get them, as it comes in. We do not manufacture evidence, which I submit is more than you can say for the defense."

Thomson jumped to his feet in protest. "Just a minute!"

"Approach the bench, Mr. DeSanto," Judge Litman ordered. With the two attorneys before him, Judge Litman refused the defense's motion for a mistrial. But he told DeSanto in no uncertain terms, that his comment was out of bounds. Then Judge Litman turned toward the jury box and said, "There's been an objection by the defendant to the use of the words 'manufactured evidence.' The court is sustaining that objection."

Judge Litman instructed jurors to disregard the statement.

DeSanto went on to sum up his assessment of the defense's frame theory. "To believe this case is based on a frame is outlandish," he said. "That requires a lack of integrity of the police and every person involved, perhaps including myself. There isn't enough money in the world, much less the Congdon estate, to buy such a frame."

In reviewing the evidence, DeSanto admitted the state's case had holes—the absence of Caldwell's fingerprints in Glensheen and no proof of Caldwell's transportation. But he reminded the jury again, "Eighty-five percent of all crime scenes do not have fingerprints of the suspects or perpetrator."

As for the state's inability to place Caldwell on a plane despite three-hundred hours of investigation, DeSanto said, "I submit to you exactly how it was done by Roger Caldwell, if he took a commercial airline. And exactly the same thing the Caldwells did when they came on June 28th for the funeral. They bought tickets for North Central and flew on Western, and then switched to North Central from Minneapolis to Duluth, as Western doesn't go to Duluth.... If you were going to commit murder, would you buy a ticket directly to the point of destination?"

DeSanto reminded jurors, "For you to acquit Roger Caldwell of murder—of two counts of murder in the first degree—you are going to have to disbelieve, ignore, or explain away all of the following: the positive identification of the defendant by two people as the purchaser of a suede bag at the airport, the card on the carry bag being the defendant's printing, the receipt for that carry bag purchased in the defendant's Radisson Hotel room, Bertha Huskin's positive identification of that suede bag as the one carried by Ricky from the hotel when the Caldwells went to Duluth on June 28th, the payment for the bag with three twenty dollar bills [after receiving numerous twenties for pawned jewelry], the defendant's right thumb print on the Radisson envelope postmarked in Duluth on June 27, 1977, the defendant's handwriting on that very envelope.

"All the evidence of motive, including the June 24, 1977, will by Marjorie Caldwell to the defendant for payment upon [Elisabeth's] death of two-and-a-half million dollars of her inheritance.... You'll have to ignore, explain away, or disbelieve all the evidence of the defendant's desperate shortage of money in June of 1977 and his request to Tom Congdon as late as June 18, 1977, of $80,000 just to stay out of jail.... The evidence of the defendant's interest in and knowledge of the Congdon Trusts." The jurors would also have to ignore the jewelry stolen from Elisabeth's body and bedroom as well as the wicker case stolen from her bedroom closet—the case and most of the jewelry was found in the Caldwells' room at the Holiday Inn.

DeSanto then urged the jurors to consider the evidence that had brought Roger to trial—no quirk of fate: "Twelve of you by your verdict must declare the truth and the truth is only this. The defendant Roger Caldwell is guilty."

His closing argument over, DeSanto felt exhausted, relieved, and pleased by his performance. He received kudos from Waller and McNabb, who told him, "There's no way he can beat that," and "You've got this won." His closing argument had lasted past noon and DeSanto felt starved; he really hadn't eaten since the previous afternoon. The three men, joined by Waller's wife and DeSanto's parents, girlfriend, brother, and sister-in-law, walked down the street to a nearby café for lunch. They talked about their dinner plans, going for a swim at the hotel pool, how the Minnesota Twins were doing—anything but the trial and closing arguments.

Thomson gave the jury his final summation after lunch—a dramatic four-and-a-half hour speech. The hot weather continued and for the first and only time during the trial the defense attorney removed his suit jacket.

Alternating between quiet persuasion and emotional pleas, Thomson painted his client as an innocent victim of a frame. He attacked the Duluth Police Department for sloppy investigation and for zeroing in on Roger as the prime suspect almost immediately.

Roger Caldwell was powerless, Thomson argued, pitted against the resources and money available to the prosecution. He began with an impassioned statement he repeated throughout his summation—Roger Caldwell deserved nothing less than the presumption of innocence.

"That is a very, very chilling title, 'the State of Minnesota versus.' On the side of the prosecution you, indeed, have all the resources and all the facilities of organized government and they're brought towards one end.... Time unending and money unending all directed towards one goal and that is to bring the prosecution to a successful conclusion. And what does an American citizen, a Roger Caldwell, John Doe, Mary Smith, what do they have to combat the onslaught of organized government when the finger points and your freedom is at stake?"

Thomson worked the jury masterfully. He stood at the lectern facing the jurors, making sure he had eye contact. Then he answered his own question. "There's only one thing and that's the presumption of innocence."

He openly scoffed at the prosecution's suggestion that the investigation had been widespread. Clearly the Duluth Police considered Roger the prime suspect even before investigators removed the bodies from Glensheen, Thomson argued. Someone directly or indirectly responsible for the murders contacted the police and told them, "There's your man." The defense implied a family member called in the tip. At that point, Thomson contended, police began to focus the investigation exclusively on Roger.

"We all like to sit back and comfortably feel that criminal investigations are conducted in the reasoning process of a Sherlock Holmes. When Sherlock Holmes comes in and reviews the crime scene and makes these different deductions and then arrives at who the suspect is. But that is an entirely different approach than having a suspect and then trying to build a case around him.... They didn't want to see the whole picture," Thomson declared, "because they were afraid that whatever they saw would not point to Roger Caldwell."

If they found only one bit of evidence inconsistent with guilt, the jury was obligated to find his client not guilty, Thomson argued. Waxing philosophical, Thomson quoted from Sir Francis Bacon and Abraham Lincoln, cautioning jurors to carefully interpret circumstantial evidence. "Lincoln said there's not much substance to an inference on an inference. It's trying to make soup out of the shadow of a dead pigeon that died of starvation."

Thomson fixed his gaze on jurors as he told a story illustrating the problem of evaluating circumstantial evidence. He said the story, borrowed from a veteran attorney in Montana, had haunted him since he'd taken on Roger's defense. In fact, the "blueberry pie" story is a chestnut, well known in defense circles for its usefulness in circumstantial evidence trials.

The story goes this way: A farmer loved blueberry pie very much. One day his wife baked a pie and set it on the kitchen windowsill to cool. A neighbor boy snuck in the farmhouse and ate the whole pie, then spotted the farmer coming towards the house. The boy grabbed the family's puppy and rubbed its muzzle in the pie tin, leaving traces of pie around the puppy's mouth.

DeSanto looked back at Waller and rolled his eyes sarcastically to indicate that Thomson was playing with the jury's emotions. Waller nodded his head slightly and rolled his eyes in agreement. Thomson continued. The hungry farmer returns home to find the puppy and empty tin, then takes the dog outside. DeSanto found himself silently pleading, "Please don't kill the puppy. Please don't hurt the puppy." He could only imagine what jurors must have been thinking. The angry farmer kicked the puppy to death, Thomson's story concluded. Some of the jurors had tears in their eyes.

Thomson told the jury that motive alone does not provide sufficient proof for conviction. "Do not condemn a man because he has a motive to do a criminal act.... Motive will not supply evidence." None of the physical evidence linked Roger directly to the murders, Thomson argued. "The Pietila auto, the jewelry, the wicker case, the envelope with the coin, the garment bag, and Marjorie's will was found. Not one of these items was found on or near Roger Caldwell." Even the so-called murder contract proved nothing, Thomson said, except that the defendant was a patsy. Roger was a pawn for Marjorie, and still might be, but he's no murderer, Thomson insisted.

Thomson reviewed the individual items of physical evidence recovered from the mansion, saying they eliminated his client as the murderer. He attacked police investigators for failure to analyze strands of hair found clutched in Velma Pietila's hands. Thomson said police refused to follow through on this evidence, and concentrated on hairs recovered from a rug and sheet used to wrap the nurse's body. "They knew it was not Roger Caldwell's hair. They knew it was not her hair.... What's the conclusion? Somebody killed her other than who they had under arrest."

Thomson reminded jurors that Duluth police had ignored Larry Jackson, the Duluth resident who saw a blond-haired man outside Glensheen around the time of the killings.

He continued to attack the prosecution's case by criticizing investigators for failing to analyze all available fingerprints. "A double murder. One of the most prominent citizens in Duluth. They've got identifiable fingerprints. One is a palm print on the very sink where the murderer washed up. It's an identifiable print and they don't try to identify it with anybody until you've been selected as jurors. Now that is an actual fact. That's what happened. There were other fingerprints that they never tried to match up. The heck with it. We're not interested in anybody but Roger Caldwell.

"Now what could be more crucial, more important than the identifiable print on the sink where apparently the murderer washed up. We don't know how many prints were found in that house that are identifiable, because they don't have any inventory of prints."

Thomson challenged the blood evidence against his client—or lack of it. "Now I think it would go without question that whoever the murderer

was, murderer or murderers—and I'll get into that in a minute—would have been inundated with blood. And I think one of the people that [was] examined said yes...that was true. [W]ith this close proximity...to the victim...you would have to be...drenched in blood. There is nothing that was ever examined that was ever owned by Roger Caldwell, any type of trace evidence, blood, glass, anything that could have come from that home and they absolutely searched everything the man owned," he vigorously reminded jurors.

The court took a short break. Out in the hallway, DeSanto, Waller, Ernie Grams, and Grams' wife, Betty, agreed the prosecution was getting beaten up. So far, Thomson had poked large holes in the state's case, accused police of bias and a frame-up, and asked jurors to apply common sense to murder, often the most irrational crime.

"Thomson kicked the shit out of us during the first half of his closing argument," Waller recalled.

After the break, Thomson presented his theory that the real killers—also familiar with Glensheen and therefore able to gain entrance—could have been Marjorie's two oldest children, Stephen and Peter, conspiring with their mother to kill Elisabeth. After all, Thomson pointed out, Stephen had visited his grandmother the weekend before the murders at Swiftwater Farm.

"On June 20, 1977, Stephen LeRoy calls his grandmother and wants to set up an arrangement to meet at the Brule that weekend. He had not visited his grandmother for over seven months.... Three days after this, Marjorie Caldwell writes this out in her handwriting," Thomson said, motioning toward the will found in Roger's safe-deposit box.

It took more than one person to subdue and murder Velma Pietila, Thomson continued, and these persons were known to the household staff. "The murderer or murderers went through the front door because they were recognized.... And I suggest to you there was more than one, maybe more than two, but at least two. I think it's reasonable from the evidence that Mrs. Pietila was struck by more than one weapon.

She was struck by a candlestick holder [sic] and a shoe and possibly a flashlight, which would be consistent with more than one person."

After murdering Velma Pietila and Elisabeth Congdon, the killers had a second mission—to frame Roger Sipe Caldwell. The murderers then probably sat back and smiled, Thomson said. Duluth police, so eager to solve the case, may have played into the hands of the real killers. Maybe police had been tipped off to the evidence in the Caldwells' hotel room in Duluth, Thomson claimed, because someone had planted it there.

"It was conceivable to me that maybe Stephen LeRoy came to the police department with the receipt and said, 'Look what I found in the hotel room.'" Thomson told jurors, although this contradicted Waller's testimony about discovering the receipt in the hotel room.

Finding the wicker case and jewelry in the Caldwells' Bloomington hotel room made no sense—after all, they had no reason to bring the jewelry to Minnesota. "The mission of the murderers was to point the finger at Roger Caldwell," Thomson argued. The Pietila car was found at the Minneapolis-St. Paul International Airport because the real killers wanted police to think the murderer came from out of town.

Thomson told the jury Colorado authorities seized the envelope containing the gold coin and addressed to Roger because someone had tipped them off. "Bam, bam, bam they had that thing analyzed and searched and they found the coin."

He dismissed prosecution witness Patricia Rutz's testimony that Roger had addressed the envelope. He argued that the use of the word Mister proved someone else addressed the envelope.

"How many men ever write to themselves and use the word 'Mister?' You just don't do it. You use your name. This envelope has 'Mister.' If Roger Caldwell were going to write something to himself, it's an uncommon thing to do."

Jurors could either go with the state's version of the crime or his theory that Roger had been set up by his own wife and stepsons. The evidence makes no sense, Thomson argued, it's just a hodgepodge. "But if you cast the light of a motive to frame Roger Caldwell upon the evidence every piece of it makes sense…. I submit that Roger was a patsy for Marjorie and never ended being [the patsy], and probably, as he sits here now, unbeknown to him, he is."

In a voice hoarse and strained by a summation that filled 107 pages of court transcript, Thomson concluded: "If you rush to this courtroom with a verdict of not guilty, Roger Caldwell will win, I suppose, to the extent that he prevails here. But more important than that, ladies and gentlemen, maybe much more important than that, that the people of the state of Minnesota will also win because you will have done justice to an American citizen."

Waller later said, "He walloped us on the problems we'd had with the investigation and our inability to look at anything other than what we'd hypothesized as to how the crime had happened. But when he came out with his theory during the second half, it was a critical error."

"If you're going to argue frame-up, then you've got to give the jury a reason for the frame," Thomson said of his strategy. "I'm sure that somebody had to gain entrance through that front door and somebody that they knew, you see.... It was made to look like a forced entry later."

On July 5, at 8:47 P.M., final arguments over, the jury of five men and seven women received the case. They would begin deliberations the next morning in a third-floor room without air-conditioning. Judge Litman gave jurors the option of deliberating in the courtroom if the jury room became too stifling.

The defense and prosecution teams, with the exception of Roger, retired to the Holiday Inn. The jurors, now sequestered, dined in a corner of the motel's restaurant. Waller and DeSanto felt too exhausted to leave their rooms. Judge Litman and court reporter Don Macheledt continued their stay at the Holiday Inn. Even Thomson moved from his cabin into the Holiday Inn for jury deliberations.

As DeSanto, Lana, McNabb, and Waller and his family watched the ten o'clock news, they switched from channel to channel to catch each station's coverage of final arguments.

On July 6, 1978, exactly one year after his arrest for murder, Roger waited as jurors began to deliberate his future. As DeSanto had guessed, they elected as foreman Dale Brick, the fifty-one-year-old vocational school supervisor.

Early in the morning, jurors sent Judge Litman a written request for a fan in the jury room. The note met no resistance from the attorneys. Shortly before 9:30 P.M., July 6, the bailiff delivered another note from jurors. This time the judge called De-Santo, McNabb, Thomson, and Caldwell into chambers. The request: "We would like the rules governing our decision on circumstantial evidence read to us again. In the morning at 9 would be fine."

Judge Litman showed DeSanto and Thomson the court's typewritten instructions on circumstantial evidence. DeSanto read over the intended instructions and told Judge Litman, "I've reviewed them and see that as appropriate." Thomson, however, once again asked the judge to include the phrasing "if one or more circumstances found proved are inconsistent with guilt or consistent with innocence, then a reasonable doubt as to guilt arises."

Judge Litman denied the defense's request, and read aloud the instructions jurors would receive the next day: "[Circumstantial] evidence may be of the highest and most conclusive kind of proof. But in order to reach a conclusion beyond a reasonable doubt on circumstantial evidence, all circumstances proved must be consistent with that conclusion and inconsistent with any other rational conclusions."

While DeSanto drove back to the motel, Thomson decided to visit his client. Instead of talking in an open cell near the jail lobby, as they had in all their previous meetings, Thomson walked back to Roger's cell.

Roger stood off to one side as Thomson looked around, surprised by what he saw. Roger behaved as if he was showing off his home. He had decorated his cell like an apartment, said Thomson. "He had things on the walls, old newspapers. He had a coffeepot. And the thing that kind of struck me strange was that you're sitting there on trial on a first-degree murder case and hope you're going to win. You certainly don't try to dig in."

Back at the motel, DeSanto nervously passed the time with Lana, his family, the Wallers, and McNabb. But by Friday afternoon, DeSanto had waited longer than he had for any other verdict, and neither talking nor swimming could cut the tension. That afternoon DeSanto's close friend Greg Larson, who had worked under DeSanto as a prosecutor in St. Louis County and was now an attorney in Little Falls, Minnesota, arrived in Brainerd to lend his support.

Friday night, Thomson, DeSanto, Waller, and Larson drank together at the Holiday Inn bar and dissected the deliberations. The jury's decision to deliberate another day buoyed DeSanto. In a complex, circumstantial evidence case such as this one, it meant jurors were taking time to analyze the evidence. Thomson felt edgy and said so. "This case has now turned into a pumpkin," he announced gruffly, referring to *Cinderella*. But no one knew which side held the pumpkin and which would fit the glass slipper.

The press had put their money on Thomson to win, and one reporter told the defense attorney he couldn't understand what was taking the jury so long. "The only thing that alarmed me a little bit was that all the press corps thought Roger was going to be acquitted. And that's always the kiss of death," said Thomson, referring to the superstitious attitude trial attorneys have about jury verdicts.

DeSanto slept fitfully, unable to concentrate on anything but the trial. It didn't help knowing that the twelve people who would make the fateful decision were sleeping in another section of the motel.

Everyone involved spent a hot, tense Saturday wondering what was happening in the jury room. The group hung out poolside, swimming and sunbathing. DeSanto's parents had returned to Duluth for Jeno Paulucci's sixtieth birthday party that night. DeSanto and Lana had just finished swimming when the bailiff called, shortly before 4 P.M. After seven ballots, the jury had a verdict.

After three months, instead of being able to rush to court, it angered DeSanto that he had to take time to dry his hair and dress. Before he left the room, the prosecutor sat on the bed for a moment, and said a short, silent prayer. Then he, Waller, and McNabb drove to the courthouse.

The courtroom was uncomfortably still. A handful of spectators whispered in anticipation as the prosecution and defense took their positions at the counsel table. Reporters scrambled into their usual seats. The courtroom crowd would grow as the news continued to make the rounds in downtown Brainerd.

At 4:25 P.M., July 8, the wait ended, two-and-a-half days after it began. As jurors filed into court, Thomson and Roger tried to read their faces. DeSanto noted that the jurors avoided both men's gaze. Judge Litman turned to the jury box.

"Ladies and gentlemen of the jury, have you reached your verdict?"

"We have, Your Honor," said foreman Dale Brick, as he handed the verdict slips to the court clerk who then passed them to the judge.

Judge Litman read silently, then returned the slips to the clerk to read aloud. On the first count for the murder of Elisabeth Congdon, "We the jury impaneled and sworn to try the guilt or innocence of the above-named defendant, find Roger Sipe Caldwell, guilty." DeSanto turned back to Waller and McNabb and gave a thumbs up.

Roger Caldwell leaned forward, looked at the jury box and firmly said in a low voice, "You're wrong."

It was the first time Caldwell had spoken during his trial. He then settled back down in his seat, silent beside Thomson, for the reading of the second count for the murder of Velma Pietila. Guilty. Judge Litman asked the clerk to poll jurors one by one, asking whether their guilty verdict was correct.

Guilty, guilty, guilty—eleven jurors solemnly affirmed their decision until the twelfth juror took her turn. Margaret Soyet, a retired resort owner who'd replaced Rosemary Robison just before final arguments, broke down sobbing. For several seconds she couldn't answer.

DeSanto froze. Eight weeks of testimony, 109 witnesses, more than 500 exhibits—and now it came down to one person. Finally, unable to meet Roger's eyes, tears streaming down her face, Soyet choked out the word—"Guilty."

Pandemonium broke out as reporters swept down the aisles in a hurry to reach the hallway phones first. Waller was reminded of the journalistic frenzy in the classic film *The Front Page*.

Under Minnesota law, first-degree murder carries a mandatory life sentence. Roger would serve his terms either consecutively or concurrently. At the defense's request, Judge Litman delayed sentencing until Monday, July 10.

DeSanto and Waller shook hands with Thomson. The prosecution team rode an emotional high, but at the same time felt completely exhausted from the efforts the trial had demanded. Vindicated after months of defense charges that Roger had been framed, DeSanto had to compose himself before speaking with reporters on the courthouse steps.

"I had a lot of mixed emotions," DeSanto recalled. "It's hard to see anyone convicted of murder and going to prison for life. I was elated—it was the verdict I'd worked hard for—but I wasn't happy that Roger Caldwell had ruined his life so completely."

Jury foreman Dale Brick had been crucial to the outcome of the trial. DeSanto had believed Brick would be the jury's choice for foreman because he struck the prosecutor as a leader and a man who, if personally convinced of guilt, would try to convince others. Apparently he had persuaded several of the other jurors unsure of Roger's guilt to vote for conviction.

Judge Litman later said that Roger's failure to take the witness stand might have been a decisive factor in his conviction. "I don't think I heard ten words out of Roger's mouth," he recalled. "I've always had a theory that when you have a dead body, the defendant has to give some sort of explanation."

Outside the Crow Wing County Courthouse, jury foreman Dale Brick told a throng of reporters, "I just want to forget about this as soon as I can.... It was a very hard thing to have to do—probably the hardest thing I ever had to do."

DeSanto talked briefly with reporters on the courthouse steps. "Step one is over," he said. When asked if he would prosecute Marjorie, he replied, "Step two."

Then Waller, DeSanto, and McNabb returned to the Holiday Inn, where they found friends and relatives in their rooms ready to celebrate. Motel staffers delivered complimentary bottles of champagne and relayed congratulatory calls and telegrams from Congdon relatives, Colorado law enforcement, their bosses, and others. News reporters kept stopping by DeSanto's, Waller's, and McNabb's rooms for one more quote or sound bite.

Waller, McNabb, and their wives spent the evening at a steak fry in their honor thrown by Crow Wing County Attorney Steven Rathke. The two men planned to remain in town until Monday morning's sentencing. Meanwhile, Judge Litman contemplated a long vacation with his wife and good fishing at the couple's cabin in Canada.

DeSanto and Lana had made plans to drive to Duluth that night to attend Jeno Paulucci's birthday party. Waller was extremely disappointed at not being able to celebrate with his partner. "I told John he was leaving behind all the people that had helped him through the trial to celebrate without them," Waller recalled. But DeSanto said he'd committed to the party and promised his parents he would attend.

DeSanto and Lana left Brainerd around 6 P.M. The biggest win of his career left him elated—and determined to arrive in Duluth by 7 P.M., when the party started. Despite the distance of more than one-hundred miles on country roads and protests from Lana about speeding—up to one-hundred miles per hour—they almost made it on time.

The party had already begun as the two pulled up at the Hotel Duluth, an elegant, historic hotel on Superior Street in downtown Duluth. As the couple walked into the ballroom, conversation ceased and everyone stood up and applauded DeSanto. At one table, DeSanto spotted then Vice President Walter Mondale among the congratulatory partygoers.

On the morning of the sentencing, Doug Thomson once again took his client into the judge's closet. This time they quietly discussed a sentencing offer by the prosecution. DeSanto would ask the judge for concurrent rather than consecutive life sentences if Roger would come clean about his wife's involvement in the murders. That meant Roger would be eligible for parole in seventeen-and-a-half years instead of thirty-five. The two men said they weren't interested. Thomson told the court he would appeal the verdict.

Among the small group on hand for sentencing were Jennifer and Chuck Johnson, who had flown in from their home in Racine, Wisconsin, with their six children. Having missed the verdict, Jennifer and Chuck wanted to see their brother-in-law punished. Roger, dressed in a dark suit and tie, stood silently in front of the bench, his attorney at his side. Marjorie remained absent, as she had been throughout the trial. She waited to see if she would be indicted in her mother's death.

Before pronouncing sentencing, Judge Litman asked Roger, "Do you have anything to state at this time?"

Roger, looking somber and subdued, quietly responded, "Only that I am not guilty of these charges." It was the second time he had spoken.

Judge Litman then pronounced the mandatory life sentence and ordered Crow Wing County Sheriff's deputies to escort Roger Caldwell to the state penitentiary in Stillwater, Minnesota. He grimly characterized the double killing as "the murder of two, elderly, defenseless women."

Before he announced his decision on how Roger would serve his life sentences, the judge repeated a description of the crime used throughout the trial as "brutal, heinous, awful, and awesome." Finally, Judge Litman decried, "It is therefore the conviction of this court that based upon the two findings of guilt, as well as the nature of this crime, that the court does hereby order that these sentences, which the court has imposed, shall run consecutively."

Sheriff's deputies ushered a handcuffed Roger Caldwell out of the side door of the courthouse to the jail next door. His sentence required him to serve at least thirty-five years in prison. Before day's end, he would don prison dungarees and call a six-by-nine-foot cell home.

CHAPTER 17

Marjorie's Turn

O N THE MORNING AFTER ROGER CALDWELL BEGAN SERVING two life sentences for killing Elisabeth Congdon and Velma Pietila—Tuesday, July 11, 1978—Duluth police arrested Marjorie Caldwell on murder and conspiracy charges in Duluth.

Informed of the charges, her Minneapolis defense attorney Ronald Meshbesher advised her to cooperate. She had flown from the Twin Cities to Duluth for the arrest, accompanied by her son, Rick, and Meshbesher. The forty-six-year-old Meshbesher, one of the Upper Midwest's top criminal lawyers, had a reputation for being competitive, organized, biting, clever, resourceful, and persuasive. He was convincing enough to have won acquittals in thirteen of the fifteen murder cases he had handled, and experienced enough that F. Lee Bailey had recruited him to help defend a doctor accused of strangling his wife. Meshbesher's meticulous appearance added to his commanding presence in the courtroom: designer glasses, full, neatly groomed beard, wavy dark brown hair flecked with gray, monogrammed shirts, and tailored three-piece suits.

Meshbesher had wanted to be an attorney as far back as he could remember. His father, Nate, worked as a lighting salesman. He had quit school to support the family and grew frustrated at never having had the chance to become a lawyer. That didn't stop him, however, from becoming a self-made legal expert whom people sought out for advice. "He knew everything about the law, knew all the players at the county courthouse," Meshbesher remembered.

Early on, Meshbesher wanted not just to be an attorney, but to "be a trial lawyer." At age eighteen, instead of spending Memorial Day relaxing with family and friends, Meshbesher was at the Hennepin County courthouse, watching closing arguments in a tax-evasion case of a major gangster.

But Meshbesher hadn't planned to make a career out of defending criminal suspects. Back in 1968, fresh out of the University of Minnesota law school, he had worked as a criminal prosecutor for Hennepin County. When he went into private practice three years later, however, he switched sides. Defending the people he had once helped prosecute, Meshbesher discovered how much he enjoyed helping clients win their freedom.

Upon arrival in Duluth, Marjorie surrendered to St. Louis County sheriff's deputies. During booking she underwent a strip search. Officer Donetta Wickstrom saw that Marjorie had scars all over her body—they were from the body tucks she'd gotten during Roger's trial. When Wickstrom asked about them, Marjorie claimed she'd had lymphatic cancer. Wickstrom also asked for a handwriting sample, which Marjorie voluntarily provided. When Meshbesher found out about the handwriting sample he asked for it back; Wickstrom refused. The sample helped police confirm it was Marjorie's writing on the so-called murder contract. Marjorie was arraigned at about 10 A.M. before St. Louis County Court Judge David Bouschor. The defendant, wearing a navy pantsuit, large round sunglasses, and short, straight hair with ragged bangs, appeared relaxed and unconcerned. She looked too confident, DeSanto thought, for a woman making her appearance on first-degree murder and conspiracy charges. She kept whispering to Meshbesher throughout the proceedings. When asked for her correct age, forty-seven-year-old Marjorie lied, saying she was two years younger than the date listed on her birth certificate.

Judge Bouschor granted an unusual request by Meshbesher to seal the police complaint against Marjorie. In addition, he issued a gag order to prevent either side from talking to the news media. "Both parties are concerned, as you know, about giving this woman as fair a trial as we can give her," Bouschor said.

According to the complaint, the case hinged on contradictory statements Marjorie had made to investigators and acquaintances about her husband's whereabouts the weekend of the murders. The complaint cited "confusion" in Marjorie's explanations regarding jewelry stolen from Glensheen and recovered in her Twin Cities hotel room. The complaint also mentioned the will, written and signed by Marjorie, that promised Roger $2.5 million of her expected $8.2 million inheritance.

Judge Bouschor released Marjorie on $100,000 bail after scheduling her district court arraignment for July 20. Marjorie returned to the Twin Cities with her son and attorney to await her next court appearance.

The judge's decision to seal the criminal complaint drew strong objections from news media statewide. The issue of free press versus fair trial came to a head that Friday, July 14, when Judge Bouschor heard arguments by both sides.

Attorneys representing the Minneapolis and St. Paul newspapers, the *Duluth Herald* and *Duluth News-Tribune*, the Associated Press, and the Minnesota Newspaper Association argued that closing the file violated the First Amendment and the public's right to know. The defense failed to meet Minnesota Supreme Court guidelines allowing files to be sealed only when all other options to ensure a fair trial are inadequate, said the media lawyers.

Meshbesher argued that "massive and pervasive" publicity threatened Marjorie's right to a fair trial. He said if the publicity continued, even a change of venue and a thorough juror selection process wouldn't guarantee that right.

Judge Bouschor ruled for the media. The file was public record. However, he decided to keep the file closed until Meshbesher's appeal to the Minnesota Supreme Court.

One week later, the Minnesota Supreme Court opened the criminal complaint to the public. The justices said Marjorie had failed to demonstrate "that she is entitled to the extraordinary relief requested."

On August 17, 1978, a St. Louis County grand jury handed down its indictment charging Marjorie with two counts of first-degree murder and two counts of conspiracy to commit murder in the deaths of Elisabeth Congdon and Velma Pietila. The following day, Marjorie pleaded not guilty. Normally, defendants entered their plea at the omnibus hearing, when the judge determines what evidence will be allowed at trial. But Meshbesher wanted to speed things up, and he requested that the trial begin within sixty days.

DeSanto was happy to oblige. He had gone through the routine once before and found it beneficial for the state. Typically a case quickly tried benefits the prosecution. As a case gets older, witnesses move away, die, change their minds, or forget evidence. But DeSanto thought Meshbesher was playing for sympathy. He intended his request for a speedy trial to signal to the public and media his client's innocence. DeSanto knew Meshbesher still needed transcripts from Roger's trial, and they still hadn't argued the change of venue motion. The defense couldn't possibly prepare in sixty days.

Roger feared for his life in the state prison in Stillwater, Minnesota, a high-security institution resembling a stone fortress, ringed with barbed wire and security towers. He began to write a book about the murders, he said, giving his version of what had really happened.

"I may not get out of here alive," Caldwell told his friend David Arnold several months into his life sentence. He had received no overt death threats, he said. But he told Arnold he had a bad feeling that "it was in the best interest of some people if I don't survive prison." He asked Arnold, still his informal legal advisor, to draw up a will.

Arnold tried to reassure Caldwell, saying that the greatest security he had was that no one knew whether he had a statement hidden or secured away. "Nobody knew if I or some friend of his or somebody at the prison [was] holding something in a vault somewhere," Arnold said years later. But Roger's concern didn't surprise him. Arnold had asked himself whether he might also be in danger from those who assumed he knew more than he did.

Despite his initial fears, Roger had adjusted to prison life in the months since his sentencing. He let his gray hair grow long enough to stick out awkwardly from his prison-issue cap. To a casual observer, he could have been an aging hippie or vagrant. He was cooperative and deferential toward prison staff. As a result of his good behavior, prison officials allowed him frequent access to the phone. Whenever Arnold visited, the two men met in the captain's office.

Ironically, in the prison's hierarchy, other prisoners held Roger in high regard, whether out of fear, respect, or age considerations. He had virtually replaced T. Eugene Thompson, the attorney convicted of having his wife murdered, as the prison's most notorious killer. Roger described the prison's caste system to Arnold during one of their meetings. "He said believe it or not, there's a certain society in here," Arnold recalled. "[And] the cons have great respect for age." This explained Roger's new look, Arnold said. "If they [the cons] came up behind someone, instead of just whacking them over the head, if they saw the gray hair, they'd be less likely to whack them over the head."

But as long as his wife's innocence in the case remained unsettled, Roger would not rest easy. Anything can happen in prison, and anyone could get to me if they really wanted to, he grimly told Arnold.

In early September, one month before his wife's omnibus hearing was scheduled, Roger gave an exclusive interview to the St. Paul Pioneer Press. He told reporter Jeffrey Kummer that he and Marjorie were innocent. "My wife had nothing to do with the deaths of those two women. I know that for a fact," Roger said. Professional killers, hired by people close to the Congdon family, were responsible for the murders. "The murders were done in a flamboyant fashion designed to attract attention and frame me at the same time," he insisted.

Roger's statements inspired his brother, David, a police officer back in Pennsylvania. In a September 17 letter he wrote:

> Dear Roger:
>
> I got the Duluth papers last week, the ones where you spoke out about not being guilty and about Marge, etc. I wanted to write and say I think you did the right thing, it's my opinion it's time to say what's on your mind, not just you but maybe all of us.
>
> I want to know a couple of answers if you don't mind telling me, I've heard from [Lou Reidenberg] that the jury was never even sworn in. Is this so? And how do you account for that, wasn't this point brought up by Thomson? (if it's true).
>
> Also what is the talk in the paper about a 2 1/2 million dollar will Marge made out to you a few days before the murders?
>
> Roger I don't want to be nosy, I intend to start trying to help but I want to know what I'm talking about.
>
> David

During Marjorie's omnibus hearing in October, Meshbesher attempted to discredit the police investigation and evidence. He accused Duluth police of illegal search and seizure of the evidence DeSanto would use to prosecute his client. Police had also wrongfully used a grand jury subpoena to obtain Marjorie's bank and car rental records in Colorado, Meshbesher argued. DeSanto insisted the evidence had been gathered legally, and revealed a pattern of check and credit card fraud. Judge Bouschor said he would rule on this and all other pretrial motions within a month.

That same day, Glensheen's new owner toured the house and grounds. Chester Congdon had willed the mansion and grounds to the University of Minnesota upon his last surviving child's death. Now the university's board of regents and a media entourage, escorted by Vera Dunbar, inspected the estate. The tour agenda did not include a look at Elisabeth's bedroom and the front staircase, where Velma Pietila was found.

Duluth police continued to cordon off parts of Glensheen in case the jury needed to view the murder scene.

Although Roger had made a point to proclaim his wife's innocence in the exclusive interview, Marjorie had yet to visit him since he was sent to prison in Stillwater. She had told Roger that Meshbesher would not permit it, but a letter from David Arnold in November 1978, hinted at Roger's doubts.

> I have had some difficulty in trying to "get your message through" to Marge. I finally received a return call from Ron Meshbesher, and he indicated that Marge would not be seeing you, on his advice. I indicated to Ron that if that was the case, you wanted to know precisely what the legal reasons were for her not being able to see you. Ron suggested that you call him at your convenience and he would be pleased to discuss the matter with you.

As expected, the defense wanted the trial held in another city and the prosecution wanted to remain in Duluth. As it had done in Roger's trial, the defense based its arguments on a research survey designed to show that most citizens of Duluth were prejudiced against Marjorie.

Meshbesher hired Ronald Anderson, an associate sociology professor from the University of Minnesota, to randomly survey 208 people in St. Louis County. During the November 7, 1978, hearing, Meshbesher presented Judge Bouschor with photocopies and transcripts of news media reports and the professor's findings. According to Anderson's survey, ninety-seven percent of the people interviewed knew that Roger had been convicted. Two-thirds of the potential jurors said Marjorie was guilty. Only eight percent said she was not—the rest weren't sure. Anderson's research also included national data showing that there is less prejudice toward a criminal defendant in geographic areas with people of diverse socioeconomic backgrounds.

DeSanto attacked the defense's change of venue motion using the same poll results. The survey showed that thirty-six percent of the respondents felt they could be impartial jurors—a sufficient jury pool. Sixty-eight percent of those surveyed believed Marjorie could be tried fairly in St. Louis County.

On December 6, 1978, Judge Bouschor denied the defense's request to move Marjorie's trial. "People throughout the state have been constantly bombarded by the news media and it would be very difficult to find anyone who has not heard something of this case. It is the court's duty to see that the defendant has a trial by a jury which is fair and impartial, not by one that has never heard of the matter," Bouschor stated in his ruling.

But Meshbesher wasn't about to concede the trial's location. He appealed Bouschor's decision to the Minnesota Supreme Court, which heard oral arguments on Marjorie's requested venue change shortly before Christmas. While Meshbesher argued that extensive news coverage in Duluth made prospects for a fair trial "nearly impossible," DeSanto argued that changing the venue to the Twin Cities "does nothing to reduce the amount of pretrial publicity."

In January 1979, the Minnesota Supreme Court moved Marjorie's trial to Hastings, Minnesota, a small city built along a rock ledge overlooking the Mississippi River about fifteen miles southeast of St. Paul. The court's decision echoed Meshbesher's arguments that the Twin Cities area was more suitable because of its heterogeneous population. Potential jurors would be drawn from Dakota County, a rapidly expanding county whose nearly 200,000 residents lived in four of the Twin Cities' newest suburbs.

The Supreme Court's decision angered DeSanto—he believed it gave his opponent a clear advantage. Meshbesher's home and office were in Minneapolis. While Meshbesher lived 40 miles from Hastings, DeSanto faced a 175-mile drive. As for pretrial publicity, four daily newspapers, four TV news stations, and plenty of radio stations served the Hastings community.

The *Duluth News-Tribune* sided with DeSanto in a stinging editorial. "Dumb change of venue," read the headline, and the column started, "Someone must have turned out the lights at the Minnesota Supreme Court. If ever the court made an unenlightened decision, it was Thursday."

DeSanto began searching for a house to rent in Hastings. During Roger's trial, he and Waller had spent three months in adjoining rooms at a Holiday Inn. But a year later, DeSanto's newly elected boss, Alan Mitchell, was sympathetic to cramped quarters and willing to pay for roomier accommodations.

Back in Duluth, tired of his cramped apartment, DeSanto showed Lana a house he wanted to bid on. She told him, "It's kind of big for a single guy."

"Well, you'd be living there too," DeSanto replied.

"Is that a proposal?"

"I guess you could consider it one."

So much for a romantic marriage proposal, thought Lana. The couple planned to get married in a formal ceremony at St. Michael's Catholic Church in Duluth, where DeSanto had always attended church with his family. They decided to wait until September, however, after Marjorie's trial.

DeSanto found a house in rural Hastings that the prosecution team could live in for the first month of trial. The team this time around consisted of DeSanto, Waller, and Mark Rubin as second chair. For the remainder of the trial, DeSanto rented a three-bedroom furnished rambler from a retired couple who spent February through May in their trailer home in Florida. The large finished basement became the prosecution's work space. DeSanto moved in several four-drawer file cabinets, a folding table and chairs, and an easel to map out trial strategy and exhibits. Throughout the trial, DeSanto kept a diary. He made his first entry the day before jury selection began:

Sunday, April 1

No April Fool's tricks played by the defense. Left Duluth at 3 P.M. Arrived at rented house…around 6 P.M. Exactly 176 miles from courthouse to my new home in Hastings. Ed McLean of the Duluth Police Department followed me here and has spent the evening putting a burglar alarm system into the house to make sure that no tricks will be played by the defense. Work on voir dire for tomorrow. Anxious and nervous about opening the case tomorrow.

Built on a rural hill several miles west of downtown Hastings, the concrete structure of the Dakota County Courthouse presents a severe and charmless façade. The courtroom selected for Marjorie's trial had low ceilings, no windows, blond wood, and lots of chrome. Jurors sat in bright yellow vinyl swivel chairs. A railing separated the counsel table from the spectator section—seventy-nine chairs reserved for reporters and visitors.

This time DeSanto grabbed the choicest seat, nearest the jury box. He also had his assistant prosecutor, Rubin, sit in the first row of the spectator section rather than with him. He wanted jurors to see the three-person defense team and the solitary prosecutor seemingly outgunned.

Meshbesher didn't dispute the seating arrangement. Marjorie would sit on the far side of his assistant defense attorneys, Frank Berman and Carol Grant. Marjorie contrasted starkly with her docile husband. Unlike Roger, she refused to sit still or remain quiet in court, and Meshbesher didn't want her to disturb him with her loud whispering and note passing.

"I needed a buffer. And I had to keep her under control because she was a loose cannon," Meshbesher recalled later. "She passed notes to Frank Berman. I said, 'Do me a favor, Marge. I don't want to hear from you.'"

Meshbesher described Marjorie as "a real character, and a very, very difficult client. I think she respected the fact that I was tough and I told her what had to be done. And I would not allow her to control how I was going to try the case."

On April 2, Judge Bouschor began jury selection by briefly addressing the sixty-five prospective jurors who stood attentively at the rear of the courtroom. Bouschor, with three years' experience on the bench, was presiding over his first murder trial. A genial man, Bouschor had a round face and thinning blond hair that complemented his soft-spoken and low-key manner. He had little use for courtroom formalities. He didn't require attorneys to stand when they addressed him. Jurors often took their seats before he took his. Bouschor even liked to slip in an occasional quip.

He had known the Congdon family since his childhood. His parents had been patrons of the Duluth Symphony and had seats behind Elisabeth Congdon and her mother, Clara. Bouschor's mother and later his wife had attended teas for the symphony association that Elisabeth held at Glensheen. Neither the defense nor prosecution was aware of Bouschor's relationship with the Congdon family, so the issue of recusal was never raised.

Bouschor had not been the original trial judge. The previous winter when the district judges had drawn straws to decide who'd preside at Marjorie's trial, Judge Luther Eckman came up short. DeSanto, however, was concerned a long trial would be too stressful for the semiretired judge, and filed a notice to remove Eckman. The courts assigned Bouschor to take Eckman's place.

Both prosecution and defense predicted it would take three or four weeks to pick twelve jurors and three alternates. Dakota County officials had prepared for the worst. They had six pay telephones installed for reporters, hired an extra bailiff, and roped off an area in the hallway outside the courtroom for overflow spectators.

Even that first day of jury selection, spectators noticed the obvious difference in courtroom styles—and personalities—of the prosecutor and defense attorney. DeSanto's passion for massive amounts of evidence and for pinning down defendants on details had continued to help him win cases. He had won four since Roger's conviction. DeSanto continued to drive his rust-colored Toyota Celica, but in the months since Roger's conviction, he had added personalized license plates that read "STATE-V" as in "State of Minnesota versus the defendant." He was serious and straightforward with prospective jurors, but at times still appeared a little unsure of himself.

Meshbesher, in contrast, acted supremely confident, and his string of successful cases only fed an already healthy ego. When he asked prospective jurors if they had heard of him, most said yes. They had heard he was a good attorney—and well-prepared. He had a battery of lawyers and private investigators working on the case outside of court.

But Meshbesher wanted to avoid coming off like a high-priced hired gun. So he took time to joke with panelists, putting them at ease. DeSanto admired how quickly his opponent evaluated and established rapport with each prospective juror through a series of rapid questions. What kind of hobbies do you enjoy? What kinds of books and magazines do you read? Whether it was knitting or motorcycles, Christian Life or Playboy, Meshbesher seemed genuinely interested. He specialized in picking juries.

Meshbesher also never shied away from the publicity surrounding many of the cases he handled. The first morning of jury selection reporters rushed Marjorie as she arrived at the courthouse. One photographer tripped and fell directly in front of her and she had to step around him. But while the news media filled the front rows, many courtroom seats remained empty despite predictions of heavy turnout.

The jury pool consisted of noticeably more women than men. Many of the men summoned said they couldn't serve; they were farmers who couldn't afford to sit in on a two- or three-month trial that would interfere with spring planting. As a result, there were only 65 people on the jury panel instead of the intended 125. DeSanto noted in his diary that only one person on the panel raised his hand that he had not heard of the case before.

As in Brainerd, DeSanto's assistant would help with legal briefs, research, witness interviews, note taking, and investigation. Mark Rubin, just twenty-four, already had a reputation as a skilled legal researcher. He had interned with the St. Louis County Attorney's Office and now worked as an assistant county attorney in a branch office in northern Minnesota. Rubin also looked somewhat like the chief prosecutor. The two men were about the same height and both had brown hair, mustaches, and wore glasses.

But the similarities ended there. As housemates, DeSanto and Rubin were a bit of an odd couple. Rubin complained that DeSanto left the water running when he brushed his teeth. Stop wasting water, Rubin would yell. DeSanto slept fitfully and paced the house at night; Rubin slept soundly. Rubin often tried to interest DeSanto in a game of tennis or a jog around the neighborhood. He gave up after several weeks. Still, the two got along as well as could be expected under the circumstances. A regular performer in high school musicals and talent shows, Rubin played guitar while he and DeSanto sang songs on the back patio to unwind at night. Rubin, a family man with a one-year-old son, drove over 190 miles to his home in Virginia, Minnesota, each weekend—a four-hour commute one way.

As DeSanto's associate, Rubin's first job was to assist with the screening of the sixty-five prospective jurors. DeSanto relied on Dakota County law enforcement and the local county attorney's office for background checks of the jury panel. Their investigation provided the basics: whether a juror had ever been in trouble with the law; his or her marital status, type of job, number of children; and where he or she lived. But the research was not as extensive as it had been at Roger's trial—DeSanto lacked the insights of the local postman.

The state did, however, have a wish list. It included bankers, store owners, horse breeders, and henpecked, conservative, middle-aged men. The prosecution also looked for jurors likely to be turned off by a domineering, bossy woman like Marjorie and unimpressed by her wealth. DeSanto's blacklist included young women, engineers, mathematicians, loners, activists, people with marital problems, teachers, athletes, social workers, and overbearing wives. He believed this last group could possibly sympathize with Marjorie's assertive, controlling behavior.

Many of DeSanto's questions concentrated on how well prospective jurors understood the law regarding conspiracy and circumstantial evidence. He used the analogy of a bank robbery. Not only is the driver of the getaway car as guilty as the robber, but if someone else drew a map of the safe's location, that person would be liable for aiding and abetting a crime, and just as guilty.

The defense looked for an intelligent jury with a twist. Meshbesher particularly wanted intelligent homemakers who liked to watch soap operas. "We were looking for smart women who had a romantic bent, who had read romantic novels, murder mysteries preferably, and soap operas and all of that," he recalled. "Because this was a soap opera." He wanted to avoid engineers, computer programmers, bankers, and accountants—people he considered too rigid.

Jury selection proceeded. On Tuesday, April 3, one of sixteen jurors questioned was selected. The following day two more were chosen. During one of the breaks on Wednesday, Marjorie unexpectedly approached DeSanto at the prosecution counsel table. Throughout the trial, Marjorie would often attempt to have some informal conversation with the prosecutor in the courtroom. Each time made DeSanto uncomfortable because he did not want jurors to observe him apparently socializing with the defendant.

"Would you prosecute someone if you knew they were not guilty?" asked Marjorie.

"No, I would definitely not," DeSanto replied. Marjorie then returned to the defense counsel table and loudly informed Carol Grant that "DeSanto would prosecute his own mother."

On Thursday, the attorneys selected one more juror. The woman, who was to be divorced the next day, had two daughters, ages eleven and twelve. DeSanto felt uncertain of her, but he only had six peremptory challenges left. The attorneys selected one more juror on Friday.

Waller had remained in Duluth for the first week of jury selection, arriving in Hastings on Sunday, April 8. In his new job as head of the tactical investigations unit, his responsibilities included supervising four officers. The unit, which carried out undercover surveillance and sting operations, was busy trying to crack a burglary ring. Additionally, once testimony began, Waller would be sequestered, and not permitted to sit in the courtroom until after he took the stand. DeSanto didn't want Marjorie's trial to be a repeat of her husband's, so he changed the order of witnesses. Waller no longer had to testify first.

When the three men stayed together at the house, it was like life in a college dorm. They had to take turns in the bathroom. They complained about each other's messes. They lived out of suitcases and their refrigerator remained sparsely stocked. The three ate out most nights. Once in a while they would grill burgers on the backyard patio for a change of pace. Their favorite restaurant in town was the Bier Stube, where they usually ordered the house specialty, steak sandwiches smothered in onions and mushrooms.

As jury selection plodded along, juror number four, Jane Estes, told the court she couldn't remain on the jury. Her employer at a local printing company refused to pay her for jury duty unless she worked the night shift during the trial. She needed the money and told the court it she would have difficulty remaining alert during the trial if she worked nights.

Judge Bouschor had previously let several people off the jury because of financial hardship, and DeSanto felt sure he would excuse Estes. Since he had accepted Estes with reservations, DeSanto was relieved. But then Meshbesher announced the existence of a special fund to reimburse people in similar situations. The fund would make up the difference between an employee's wages and what the state paid the jury duty. The fund had been set up by the Criminal Courts Bar Association of Minnesota.

"I've never heard of such a fund or organization," DeSanto protested. "Who belongs to it? Who contributes to it?" he asked. Meshbesher assured them of the fund's legitimacy; its contributors included a number of state criminal defense attorneys. DeSanto agreed to this special arrangement only if approved by the judge. Bouschor said Estes wouldn't know the money came from a defense-sponsored fund. The county clerk's office would issue her a check for the difference between her regular paycheck and jury pay. Juror four remained on the panel. (Only months later would DeSanto learn that the fund at that time had just five members—and two were Ron Meshbesher and Doug Thomson.)

DeSanto continued to make entries in his diary:

Monday, April 9

Selected one juror approximately 40–45 years of age. Worried about her ability to convict, but at the same time she did express an opinion that it would be hard to believe that a wife was not involved with Roger Caldwell if he's guilty. The day ended with Marjorie Caldwell indicating to me that she didn't think it was fair that her inheritance tax dollars are going to pay me to prosecute her for these murders. I indicated that justice works in strange ways.

Tuesday, April 10

Our last juror questioned and selected today…is 25-year-old Catherine Sportelli, who is a mother of two children ages two and three and wife of…an electrician. Mrs. Sportelli was very concerned about being on the jury during the summertime…. I personally think the woman was put upon by being required to stay on the jury. However, I couldn't afford to use a peremptory challenge on her and there were many good factors about her. Primarily that she respects authority and thinks it is most important to teach [children] not to be sassy toward people or adults. This of course will be very important in this case where we have a disrespectful daughter who murders her mother. The other big plus about her was she is very familiar with and close friends with Eagan police officers and her uncle is a highway patrolman. Her girlfriend's husband, who is an Eagan police officer, thinks the defendant is guilty.

Juror Sportelli (who was reluctant to serve because it would be difficult for her to maintain her in-home day care business if chosen, especially during a long trial), recalled her initial impressions of the two attorneys. "DeSanto came across as being very nice. He also came across as being new at it, a beginner. You could tell he wasn't as polished as Meshbesher," she said. "Meshbesher came across as having done this a lot before, more experienced."

As for Marjorie, Sportelli was somewhat surprised by the defendant's appearance. "She was never in a suit or a dress, always pants. She wore casual clothes. Her hair was not really taken care of. No makeup. Big round glasses. She came across as being very plain. I don't remember thinking she was making an effort to present herself at her best."

Sportelli also recalled Marjorie's demeanor in the courtroom—never still, nervous energy in motion. Marjorie continually scribbled notes, scrutinized each witness, and whispered asides and passed notes to her attorneys. She also showed little emotion or response to the testimony, Sportelli said.

Thursday, April 12

Selected two jurors today. Thirty-nine-year-old, second man on the jury, works for the government at Fort Snelling as a mechanic, and 31-year-old woman, once divorced and now remarried, an LPN and medical supply company secretary. Only juror so far who has known of and been to the Broadmoor Hotel in Colorado Springs. We have tomorrow off because it's Friday the 13th and Good Friday. We'll resume again next Monday. Now I have 10 jurors. …I am at this point not too pleased with the jury.

Monday, April 16

Marjorie showed up in court today, the day after Easter Sunday, with a new hairdo. Short and curly hair. She was also wearing a bright yellow v-neck sweater and bright yellow pants. She looked like a canary with new wings.

Tuesday, April 17

Had a day off because Ron Meshbesher had some oral surgery to be done. First beautiful day of the spring. Got up to 65 degrees. Took the afternoon off after working the morning with Gary Waller on a new order of witnesses to keep Meshbesher off guard. Went to the Twins opening game with Charles Bernsen of the *Duluth Herald* and News Tribune and my brother. Beautiful afternoon despite shortage of beer and hot dogs. Twins had record opening day crowd of 37,000 people to see the Twins take on Rod Carew and the California Angels [in Carew's first game against the Twins, his former team of many years].

One week later, after twenty-two calendar days, DeSanto and Meshbesher completed jury selection. The jury included ten women and two men, plus alternates, two female and one male. DeSanto disliked having so few men, whom he thought would be harder on Marjorie. The large proportion of younger, blue-collar jurors also made him uneasy. He believed these jurors would tend to be less sympathetic to the elderly victims. The panel reflected the county's demographics, however. Most jurors were in their twenties and thirties, the oldest fifty-six. They included several homemakers, a mechanic, a bank clerk, a records clerk, a printer, and an assembly worker.

Tuesday, April 24

Selected the last alternate, 45-year-old woman. Likes horses, always wanted to be a nurse. Spent the afternoon marking exhibits. Meshbesher and Berman present, Waller, me, Cox and [court reporter] Damos Grebanowski. Some chiding going on between counsel during this time when Ron and Berman were showing a picture of the house Marjorie intended to purchase. Ron stated that if we would dismiss the case he would agree to have Marjorie remain in that house in Colorado for the rest of her life. Kiddingly accepted. Best line of the day, however, was when I referred to the will written by Marjorie on June 24 as a will. Ron got upset saying that's not a will, but a document. …I intend to refer to [it] in final argument as a contract to commit murder.

CHAPTER 18

The Woman Behind the Man

JOHN DESANTO DELIVERED HIS OPENING STATEMENT in a courtroom packed with news reporters and spectators, including his parents, Bill and Hazel DeSanto. His mother even rented an apartment in Hastings so she could attend daily. Marjorie's trial, like her husband's, attracted a small group of daily spectators, mostly older women who liked to recite the detailed evidence and weren't shy about rooting for the prosecution or defense. Marjorie's side included the Hagens, old skating friends who had offered their support to her since Elisabeth's murder. One woman baked DeSanto a rhubarb pie.

DeSanto's two-and-a-half hour opening statement depicted Marjorie as the "woman behind the man" who murdered her adoptive mother, the woman who, in exchange for her mother's death, promised her husband a $2.5 million cut of her inheritance. DeSanto reviewed evidence and testimony jurors would hear, much of it a repeat of Roger's trial. To prove Marjorie's involvement in the murders, he first needed to establish her husband's participation.

He argued that the defendant's "complex web of inconsistent statements and lies" lay at the heart of a murder conspiracy. He described the Caldwells' lifestyle: "purchases of many other expensive things in the months...immediately preceding the murders, purchases, ladies and gentlemen, without financial resources. A lifestyle which is typified by Roger and Marjorie spending a holiday at the Broadmoor Hotel in Colorado Springs, Colorado, in February 1977 and running up a bill of $6,000 in one week. All at a time, ladies and gentlemen, that Roger Caldwell is unemployed and when the defendant is receiving much less than the...necessary funds from the Congdon Trusts, at a time, ladies and gentlemen, when Thomas Congdon has to go to the Holland House on June 19, 1977, and pay $400 to keep the Caldwells in their rooms."

DeSanto described Marjorie's selfish relationship with her mother. "The defendant was a very demanding person of her mother, often insolent, often rude; ...the defendant was a constant source of emotional upset to her mother because of her spendthrift propensities, which have been lifelong."

DeSanto explained that the prosecution's new evidence would include "a statement made in January 1977 at the Table Mountain Ranch, by the defendant that 'the only way out of my financial mess or troubles is my mother's death.'"

Throughout DeSanto's opening remarks, Marjorie listened intently and took notes. Just shy of five feet tall, she had her feet propped on two concrete blocks provided by the court after she complained her feet couldn't touch the floor. One of her books sat on the table. An avid reader, she always seemed to have a book with her, and told one courtroom spectator she enjoyed a good mystery.

After DeSanto's remarks, Meshbesher told Judge Bouschor the defense would make its opening statement after the state rested. The defense still hadn't hinted at its strategy or whether Marjorie would testify on her own behalf.

DeSanto decided to lead off with the Glensheen household staff, hoping to throw Meshbesher off-guard, especially after the news media reported that Waller would testify first. Hazel Conger, Glensheen's sixty-seven-year-old maid, took the stand first. Under questioning by DeSanto, Conger testified about the $345,000 loan that Marjorie had tricked her mother into guaranteeing in 1974, saying that she saw a signature by Elisabeth that she never witnessed her employer write. She also testified about the phone call she had answered on Friday night, June 24, which she had assumed was Marjorie. She then established that Marjorie visited her mother very little after moving to Colorado in 1975.

When Meshbesher took his turn, he got Conger to acknowledge that she thought that relations between Marjorie and her mother were fine. Conger also testified that Marjorie had made a number of needlepoint cushions and a large rug as gifts for her mother.

Her testimony was followed by that of other Glensheen employees, including cook Prudence Rennquist, who repeated for these jurors the story of her poodle Muffin's excitement in the middle of the night. DeSanto and Meshbesher asked each employee for comments on the relationship between Elisabeth and Marjorie. While DeSanto attempted to show evidence of a troubled relationship, Meshbesher countered with questions designed to portray Marjorie as a loving, caring daughter, incapable of conspiring to murder her own mother.

Thursday, April 26

Meshbesher's cross-examination was quite intense. Immediately tried to make the Congdon mansion very clean and tidy, going to any prints in the house being that of the murderer and ultimately to the print found on the candlestick.... Meshbesher also established through Hazel that all the towels in the nurse's bathroom were white towels contrary to finding blue and yellow towels in the bathroom after the murders. Have to believe that Roger Caldwell used the white towels to clean himself up and then took the colored towels from a drawer in the nurse's room and put them there.

On Friday, April 27, chauffeur Richard Kartes testified that Elisabeth took along the small and large wicker baskets to the Brule on June 24, 1977. Kartes also testified that he was "positive" that he had taken both wicker baskets out of the car upon returning to Glensheen on June 26. Nurse Mildred Klosowsky bolstered his testimony. Klosowsky testified that the wicker baskets accompanied Miss Congdon, Kartes, and

Conger to Swiftwater Farm. She told jurors that after they returned to the mansion on Sunday afternoon, Conger placed both baskets in Elisabeth's bedroom closet.

Meshbesher's cross-examination of Kartes and Klosowsky seemed to suggest the smaller wicker basket, reported missing from Glensheen after the murders and recovered from the Caldwell's Bloomington hotel room, was planted. Both Glensheen employees acknowledged that they had never seen the smaller wicker case prior to the weekend of the murders, despite having worked at the mansion for many years, and having taken frequent trips with Elisabeth.

Friday, April 27
More witnesses. Not too eventful a day....

Glensheen chauffeur Dick Kartes told jurors that Marjorie Caldwell saw her mother infrequently. But during cross-examination, he testified that Elisabeth Congdon liked to visit Marjorie Caldwell in Minneapolis. Employees also told the jury that Marjorie Caldwell called her mother about once a month.

Monday, April 30
Marjorie pulls her first day off during the trial. Meshbesher had called Judge Bouschor about 7:45 A.M. to say…Ricky had called him and told him that Marjorie had a high temperature and had been throwing up all night. Judge Bouschor called our house talking to Waller about 8:20 A.M. to tell us there would be no court today. Very maddening. Intend to present a motion to court requiring the defendant to submit a doctor's diagnosis before letting her out of a day of trial. Since it costs the county of St. Louis so much each day she is not here. I interviewed police witnesses at the motel with Waller. Came back, went to bed pretty early, about 11:30. Waller came back after being out for a few drinks with the other police officers about 1 o'clock. He woke me up very excited. He had been looking through the wallet taken from Roger Caldwell at the time of his arrest because Meshbesher, Berman, and Grant had been very interested in the wallet during the day. Because incidentally we permitted the defense to review all state's property during Monday when we didn't have court. Waller found four postage stamps identical to the kind of stamps placed on the envelope with the coin in it.... We are very confident that when we bring these stamps to the BCA they can make a physical match…to the perforations on the stamps on the envelope. We sure hope so. Even if not, these are identical stamps to those on the envelope. Digging a further grave for the defense. During the review of exhibits, Meshbesher not very complimentary of Marjorie saying he sure would miss her at lunch that day and commenting about her horniness since Roger in jail.

On the following day, Tuesday, May 1, Waller delivered the Radisson Hotel envelope and Roger's wallet with its entire contents, including the stamps, to the BCA Laboratory. The stamps would be examined microscopically by analyst Wally Sorum. In the courtroom, DeSanto next put Duluth police officers on the witness stand. Canine officer Jerome Larson testified that his German shepherd tracked a trail consistent with the prosecution's theory of the killer's route to Glensheen in reverse, from Elisabeth Congdon's bedroom downstairs to the broken basement window and finally out to one of the creeks on the estate. Larson also testified that the dog did not go through the open window out of his concern for preserving the crime scene. When cross-examining Lieutenant Nick Radulovich, however, Meshbesher got him to contradict Larson's testimony. Radulovich not only testified that the German shepherd had climbed through the window and that Larson followed the dog, but that he had gone through the window before either the dog or Larson. Meshbesher was continuing to build on a theme: Duluth police had made critical errors in maintaining the integrity of the crime scene.

The prosecution and defense were both interested in testimony focusing on the cook Prudence Rennquist's poodle. DeSanto hinted that the dog could have kept barking even after the murderer fled Glensheen. The defense maintained that Muffin barked until nearly 5 A.M. because the murderer was still in Glensheen. That would have made it virtually impossible for the killer to have caught the morning flight from Minneapolis to Denver, as the state argued.

DeSanto asked officer Chris Kucera, the first officer to arrive at the murder scene, for his dog expertise. A former poodle owner, Kucera could tell jurors only that the dog might bark. The news media poked fun at the prosecution that night for its "dogged" line of questioning.

Officer Kucera also testified about the room-to-room search he conducted of Glensheen hours after the murders. He told jurors he didn't disturb the physical evidence and left the crime scene as he found it. But Meshbesher went on the attack during cross-examination. Under rapid fire questioning, the officer admitted he had used the toilet and washed up in the sink in the nurse's bedroom the second day of crime scene processing.

"So everything wasn't left the way you found it. And we don't know what else may have been altered," Meshbesher said, referring to the bathroom blood samples and fingerprints that had yet to be collected when Kucera slipped up.

The long days left DeSanto, Waller, and Rubin little time for relaxation, fun, or housekeeping. They had no time to socialize, even when Duluth police officers drove down to testify. They bought few groceries except for an occasional loaf of bread, box of cereal, or hot dog. When testimony concluded each day, the three went out to eat, returning in time for the 10 P.M. news. Usually in bed by 2 A.M., DeSanto was the first one up at 5:30 A.M. and first in the shower. They always arrived at the courthouse by 8 A.M.

Tuesday, May 1

Kind of down after the end of this day. Meshbesher continued to poke holes in investigation. He is doing excellent job of cross-examination.

Wednesday, May 2

Spent whole day with ID technician Bob Cox and the last 20 minutes with officer David Cismoski. Strenuous cross-examination of Cox on preparation of a photo log. Cox stated that the photo log that we had was prepared within a year of the homicides, when in fact it was only prepared a month or so ago from prior logs. Presented a true ethical problem which caused me much stress that night when interviewing next witness Bob Gracek with Bob Cox as to how we were going to handle it.

But DeSanto still felt he had ended Wednesday's testimony on a high note. He had called Cismoski to testify about sound experiments Cismoski and Waller conducted. With Waller in Rennquist's room, Cismoski had gone up and down the stairs and made noises in the hall to determine how the sound carried, since Rennquist had not heard anything the night of the murders. Among other things, it was determined that the first three stairs from the landing to the second floor squeaked loudly enough to be heard in the nurse's room. This could have been what drew Pietila to her death. On cross-examination Meshbesher got Cismoski to admit that when he had spoken loudly near the nurse's room Waller, then located in Rennquist's room, had been able to hear him. On redirect, DeSanto asked Cismoski just one question. "Did you give Sergeant Waller time to fall asleep when performing these sound and noise experiments?" Waller had been wide awake and listening during the experiments, while Rennquist had slept until her dog woke her up by scratching at her arm and barking at nearly 3 A.M.—at which time she might have already slept through the entire attack. Cismoski answered no, and DeSanto's point was made.

On Thursday, Meshbesher continued to attack the police investigation as sloppy and careless. Police weren't sure when some pictures were taken or by whom. One batch of film taken the day of the murders had been destroyed during processing. But during questioning by DeSanto Bob Gracek told jurors most of the missing photos had been reshot. The month before Marjorie's trial, police had compiled a new, detailed photo log.

Meshbesher's theory, however, maintained that some items had been moved for the camera. He suggested the wicker basket reported stolen from Glensheen—and supposedly carried by Roger—had never left. Without complete original photographs, DeSanto stood helpless against the defense claim that missing photos would show the wicker basket in Elisabeth's closet.

Thursday, May 3

Meshbesher made more points about the photo inventory made within the last month by the identification bureau. However, the media stated that Meshbesher brought this out on cross-examination. That is incorrect. I brought it out on direct examination. On cross, however, Meshbesher did get an admission from Gracek that he was unable to match the palm print lifted from the sink with the inked palm impression of Gary Waller's left hand. More anxiety as the defense continues to nibble away at the investigation.

Monday, May 7

Got to court early today about 8 o'clock because wanted to prepare and line up many new exhibits which will be offered through officer Barry Brooks' testimony. Gary Waller came back as he is going to testify this week. Barry Brooks arrived at the courthouse to find it dark and only to have the day canceled because of a power outage at the government center. All the day did was build up pressure on Gary. Hope neither one of us reaches a breaking point before this trial is over. Certainly no one will ever appreciate the pressure we had to shoulder and today it almost seemed too much. Gary very worried about Meshbesher questioning his integrity. We both ran a mile and a half. Sure will be glad when this is all over regardless of verdict.

Tuesday, May 8

A little apprehensive about having put in too much including…fibers from the [Virgil] statue [to the left of the dresser with the candlesticks], etc., through Barry. But on the other hand, I'm trying to show thoroughness of police investigation and collection of evidence regardless of significance at the time. Spent 'til two A.M. with Gary Waller going over his testimony. Gary's very nervous, apprehensive, and uptight. I know he'll make it.

Determining the right amount of evidence was a common concern for Kitchen Sink DeSanto. "Good police work involves collecting anything and everything at the start of an investigation," DeSanto recalled later. "As the pieces of the puzzle start to come together, what is less relevant to the case may be unused by the prosecution. But as Gary and I have learned and taught, based

primarily on our experience in this specific homicide case, we believe that it's better to be accused of a 'frame' because you have too much evidence than be accused of being incompetent because of failing to collect pieces of evidence."

A tired and tense chief investigator took the stand Wednesday afternoon, the twenty-ninth day of trial. Waller had skipped a good night's sleep, breakfast, and lunch due to nerves and rehearsing his testimony with DeSanto. At least Waller was familiar with the witness chair. During jury selection, when he had wanted to get the feel of the courtroom and how to play to jurors, he sat in it to see how it felt.

Much of Waller's three days of testimony focused on Marjorie's inconsistent statements to police and her handwritten will, which the prosecution had dubbed a "murder contract." He told the jury this legal document promised Roger $2.5 million from the Congdon family trusts.

Waller described his interrogation of Marjorie about jewelry stolen from Glensheen and recovered in her Bloomington hotel room eight days after her mother's death. Waller said she claimed all the items, including a gold watch and a diamond-and-sapphire ring, were duplicates. Many of the earrings found were clip-ons, however, Waller told jurors, and Marjorie had pierced ears.

Waller detailed the different stories Marjorie told police about Roger's whereabouts at the time of the murders. He said her first story placed Roger with her at the laundromat the morning of the murders. But the owner told police he never saw Roger on June 27, Waller testified. Other false alibis she gave claimed that Roger had taken Rick LeRoy to the mountains to avoid the media and that she'd dropped her husband off at an attorney's office in Denver.

Jurors learned that more than one hundred Congdon family members stood to benefit from Elisabeth Congdon's death, but the two people who would receive the largest share of money were her adopted daughters, Marjorie Caldwell and Jennifer Johnson.

The following day, during his cross-examination of Waller, Meshbesher immediately went after the investigation. He attacked the legality of subpoenas Waller had used to obtain evidence against the Caldwells in Colorado. DeSanto loudly objected and the two attorneys approached the bench.

Meshbesher said he intended to show that Sergeant Waller was "part of a conspiracy" to illegally obtain evidence against his client. Judge Bouschor then reminded the defense that counsel had argued and settled the issue before trial. But like many whispered conferences at the bench, Meshbesher made sure to project his voice loud enough for the jury to hear.

"I was shocked—it took me by surprise," Waller recalled. "I knew I had to maintain my composure on the outside for the jury. But inside, it felt like I'd been suckerpunched. That's the effect of a public attack on your reputation, when you've done everything you can to maintain integrity and pride in your career."

Meshbesher returned to the witness. He tried to throw Waller off guard about his conversation with Marjorie at the Holiday Inn the night before her husband's arrest.

"Marjorie lied to you, didn't she?" Meshbesher asked. Though tempted to agree, the defense's sudden candor surprised Waller, and he said nothing. Meshbesher again insisted that his client had lied—but she lied not because of a guilty conscience, but out of fear and because she didn't know what to do.

Waller refused to concede anything. He told jurors that when he showed her jewelry identical to items stolen from Glensheen, Marjorie repeatedly responded, "This is mine. My mother has one just like it." She said she had "ripped off" a silver picture frame from the mansion at her mother's funeral.

Next, Meshbesher hammered away at police negligence during the crime scene processing and investigation. He charged that Waller and the officers he had supervised had made critical mistakes. Why hadn't a detailed photo inventory of the crime scene been kept? Meshbesher asked. Instead, Duluth police had relied on information, including the date, time, and location, written on the back of each photograph. Waller could not deny that inventories made the best method of photo identification.

"Did you ever see an inventory of photographs other than the one that has been prepared about a month ago?" Meshbesher asked.

"No, I have not," said Waller.

"You had never seen one, yet you were the chief investigating officer of this case, right?"

"That is correct."

"In fact to your knowledge such an inventory never existed?"

"To my knowledge, no, sir."

"Aren't these identification people that prepared the photographs working under you?"

"They were at the time."

"Yet you state now that at no time prior to the preparation of exhibit 492 had you ever seen an inventory or list of photographs of this case, right?"

"Right," said Waller.

Meshbesher fired off questions in a confident, direct style reminiscent of a rifle—and most hit their mark. For added discomfort during his cross, Meshbesher liked to stand several inches behind the witness's shoulder where they couldn't see him. Some prosecution witnesses said they could feel the defense attorney's breath on their neck.

When Meshbesher turned his attention to the collection of evidence, he accused police of placing evidence in unsterile paper bags, making it sound as if officers had used grocery sacks from home. Waller angrily responded that only new brown paper bags were used to hold the sterile stretcher sheets in which the bodies had been wrapped. Police preferred paper to plastic bags—since paper breathes, bloody material wouldn't putrefy.

Waller gritted his teeth when Meshbesher again attempted to embarrass him with a loud reminder of another police screw-up. They had overlooked a piece of evidence—Velma Pietila's watch—for nearly two years. The watch read 2:50 in photographs police took at the autopsy. But investigators failed to notice the time and check whether the watch could have stopped around the time of Pietila's death. Unfortunately for Waller, Meshbesher had made the catch during pretrial preparations.

Meshbesher's overall strategy was to discredit the police investigation and the evidence, particularly against Roger. By raising doubts about Roger's case, the defense hoped to create doubt about the alleged murder conspiracy between Marjorie and her husband. Not only did the state have to prove the elements of the crime, the conspiracy charges required them to show that the defendant actively planned her mother's death.

By Friday, nearing the end of cross-examination, Waller could barely conceal his growing hostility toward the defense. Meshbesher used the standard defense line, "I've only got a few more questions." Waller braced himself. "When you hear that, you can anticipate the garbage coming at you."

Meshbesher persisted in trying to get Waller to confirm that police had never documented the photos taken of the remaining wicker suitcase in Elisabeth's closet, implying that the photos showing just one suitcase could have been staged at a later date. Waller said he would have to check his files before answering, much to Meshbesher's exasperation. The defense attorney wouldn't get an answer before lunch.

At the noon break, Waller went downstairs to the courthouse basement cafeteria for a cup of coffee. Too nervous to eat, he decided to work through lunch. But first he wanted to greet his wife, Pat, who had driven down for his testimony. As he looked over the crowd, he caught Marjorie's eye. She sat at a table with her entire defense team. Spying Waller, she jumped up, waved, and called out for him to come and eat with them. Meshbesher shook his head and had to yank his client back down. Later that day, he asked Waller, "Can you believe her? She wanted you to eat lunch with her!" Waller didn't respond, but thought, "Yeah. It's like asking the enemy to join you in your foxhole."

Friday, May 11

Finished with Gary about two o'clock in the afternoon. Feel pretty good about his testimony. Meshbesher brought out for the first time Tom Cong-don's hiring of private investigators Furman and [Furman's associate Gary] Fick.... Meshbesher commented to me at the end of Friday that Waller did a good job. Marjorie her same old flaky self. At the break in the morning she asked Gary about his children. He tried not to talk to her but couldn't avoid it. Then at lunchtime in the cafeteria she asked Gary if he wanted to join them at their table. Finished Friday with Dr. Goldschmidt. No tears from Marjorie.... Meshbesher tried to establish time of death from the freshness of the blood on the staircase. [Goldschmidt] wouldn't let him. Reestablished on redirect that [Goldschmidt] was certain that EMC had died from suffocation, that it took four to ten minutes. And on recross he stated that this was really only a guessing figure because it's hard to tell how long an 80-year-old woman who's a semi-invalid having suffered from a stroke years before could actually struggle for her life with her murderer.

Saturday, May 12 and Sunday, May 13

All weekend constant job of reviewing notes and testimony trying to plug holes that Meshbesher creates. Constant anxiety even while relaxing at my brother's place for Mother's Day dinner with my parents, my brother and sister-in-law Vicki on Sunday, May 13. Idea to change order of witnesses around. Good to keep Meshbesher guessing as to who's next. But even more importantly, it breaks the monotony of presenting the same evidence for a second time. Presenting it in a new and different way. This somewhat challenging. For instance, the idea of presenting the crime scene through individuals rather than mostly through Gary Waller has worked out very well.

Monday, May 14

The Pietilas testified. Jim Pietila was unreal, although the media didn't emphasize that the meeting of the Caldwells at the Pietila home had Roger very apprehensive about going there and tugging at Marjorie's sleeve to leave.

Sparks flew between the prosecution and defense on Thursday, May 17, during testimony from Wilma Farley, a waitress at the Holland House Hotel coffee shop. Farley and another waitress, Jan Mynheir, both had told Duluth police they saw Roger and Marjorie in the coffee shop at around 6:30 A.M. Sunday, June 26. Farley testified that when she waited on the Caldwells, Marjorie "told me they were in a hurry because they had to get to the airport."

On cross-examination, Meshbesher attacked Farley's credibility, demanding to know why her testimony differed from statements she originally gave to police. Farley maintained that any differences should be attributed to police error in taking down her statement. Under persistent questioning by Meshbesher, Farley retorted, "I'll take a lie detector test," to which the defense responded that maybe the Duluth police should as well. This drew an angry objection from DeSanto who said that Meshbesher was inserting an editorial comment in his cross-examination. When Mynheir testified she overheard Marjorie talking with Farley, Meshbesher insinuated that the two waitresses had collaborated and concocted a story. DeSanto loudly objected to this line of questioning by Meshbesher as being "repetitious and argumentative."

Meshbesher's birthday fell on Friday, May 18. Marjorie baked a chocolate cake that she brought to court and carved up at the counsel table. Marjorie took a piece back to the judge in his chambers. She then approached the prosecutor and said, "John, why don't you have a piece?"

"Are you kidding?" DeSanto said, refusing the offering.

"Don't worry," Marjorie replied. "There's no marmalade in it."

DeSanto prided himself on knowing the state's witnesses. He had taken whatever time necessary to review their testimony and help each witness anticipate possible questions from Meshbesher. So when Marjorie's personal attorney, David Arnold, testified on May 21, the prosecutor didn't expect to hear something new.

Arnold's testimony started routinely enough. He told jurors that Marjorie owed more than $1 million before the murders. Her extravagance included $6,000 to reserve skating rink time for her children, a $7,200 custom-made horse pin, and horses worth between $4,000 and $20,000. Her finances remained dismal after her move to Colorado in 1975.

Arnold also acknowledged that in 1974 Marjorie had signed a document admitting she had tricked Elisabeth into guaranteeing a $345,000 bank loan at Marquette National Bank, which Marjorie later defaulted on. But during questioning by Meshbesher, Arnold said that Marjorie had signed the document on his advice. She "absolutely denied ever using false pretenses," to get her mother to cosign the loan, Arnold testified.

During cross-examination, Arnold also said Marjorie had a number of jewelry pieces identical to Elisabeth's. On redirect, DeSanto challenged Arnold about Marjorie's claim that the items seized from her hotel room were duplicates of her mother's.

"Did you personally ever see any of Elisabeth Congdon's jewelry pieces?" DeSanto asked.

"Not other than what she was wearing at the time of my two visits with her," said Arnold.

"On either of those visits, did you notice anything that Miss Congdon was wearing that was a duplicate of or similar to anything the defendant had shown you?"

"I have no recollection."

"What is your sole source of information that the defendant's jewelry, some of these jewelry items shown you, was a duplicate, were duplications of her mother's?"

"Two sources."

"Who was that?"

"Marjorie and her former attorney."

But also on cross, Arnold unexpectedly testified that Marjorie had a warm and loving relationship with her mother. She "loved her mother and never spoke an unkind word about her," Arnold told the jury. "She was especially grateful to Miss Elisabeth for adopting her when single-parent adoptions weren't easy." DeSanto had not expected Arnold to characterize Marjorie as a loving daughter. DeSanto found it difficult to read the jurors' faces, but he noted the rumblings among the courtroom spectators.

DeSanto couldn't wait to go after Arnold in redirect, and in his anxiousness his right leg twitched under the table and his foot tapped against the floor.

"How many times total in your lifetime did you see the defendant together with her mother?" DeSanto asked.

"Once," said Arnold.

"That was that forty-five minute meeting in your office?"

"In my office, yes."

Monday, May 21
Seem to be constantly beating our head against the wall. No matter what we do, Ron seems to tear it down effectively. Felt today was a good day in that I got out the June 24 document giving Roger two-and-a half million dollars could be a contract. Yet the news media only picked up that it was probably to protect Roger from financial insecurity if he had to take over Marjorie's debts upon her death.

On May 22, DeSanto called Marjorie's cousin Tom Congdon to testify. DeSanto moved quickly to have Congdon explain why he hired William Furman, the private detective who had defrauded him out of $15,000.

"On that day of June 27, 1977, did you contact a man by the name of William Furman?" asked DeSanto.

"Yes," Congdon answered.

"How did you get his name?"

"I got his name or the name of his organization from the Denver Police Department."

"Would you tell this court and jury why you contacted Mr. Furman and decided to hire him?"

"I had a personal concern for the security of my family…and I had already felt the Caldwells were under some suspicion and I had reason to feel that, either directly or indirectly, they could be even considered dangerous."

DeSanto couldn't interpret the jury's response, but he hoped to convince them this witness had no role in any effort to frame Roger or Marjorie. Indeed, he was a victim. After all, Congdon had saved the check stubs from all his financial dealings with Furman. It was unlikely that a man intent on a frame-up would have kept evidence showing exactly how much he had paid Furman.

Congdon testified about the Caldwell's financial problems. He told jurors Marjorie Caldwell had received more than $2 million from the Congdon family trusts over five years. Yet, by 1974, she owed $1.1 million and badgered trustees for more. He described how in August 1975 Marjorie demanded more than $200,000 to refurbish her house in Denver, claiming Rick's asthma required a specially designed house. When trustees refused, Congdon said, "Marge was very angry and said that if her son Ricky died as a consequence, [Congdon cousin and Boston physician] Terry d'Autremont and I would be responsible for his death."

"Would you relate to the jury with as much detail as you can recall the conversation you had with the defendant at the time [of the murders]?" asked DeSanto.

"Marjorie, as I say, called me and was upset," Congdon began. "She asked if I had heard the news and I said, 'yes.' She said I was the first family member she had contacted. She said she had received a call from David Arnold here in Minneapolis, who had given her the news…Marge expressed her concern. She also described what she said she and Roger were doing the afternoon and evening before.

"She said they had been out looking at real estate, at prospective land or ranch property to purchase. That they had been so late at this that they hadn't finished dinner until ten o'clock Sunday evening. And that she had wished to telephone her mother at that time, but that Roger said to her, 'Look, it's ten o'clock here, it's eleven there, in the Middle West. It's too late to call your mother.' And she said, 'Oh, now I can never call her again.' [Then she asked], 'What was mother doing in Duluth? She was supposed to stay at the Brule place until the Fourth of July.' Marge also went on and asked that I make certain arrangements. She also asked…[w]hat details did I know, what was the condition of the bodies, did anyone suffer?"

But when it was Meshbesher's turn for questions, he tried to advance his claim that Tom Congdon was part of a frame-up. The defense's theory maintained that private detectives hired by Congdon and Duluth police gathered and planted incriminating evidence against Marjorie and Roger. Congdon admitted that Furman had told him about a "military device" he used for eavesdropping. But he insisted he never told Furman or his associates to do anything illegal, including planting evidence.

Meshbesher produced the rough handwritten notes Congdon had made during his conversation with Marjorie the morning of the murders. He stopped after each notation and questioned its meaning.

"'We had been out looking for a place to live,' right?" Meshbesher asked.

"Right."

"It doesn't say that Roger and she had been out, did it?"

"She had said that."

"You quoted her exactly and you put quotation marks around it and it says, 'We had been out looking for a place to live.' Doesn't it say that?"

"It says that."

"Okay."

"But this is not a ten-minute conversation right here. These are notes."

"But you put in quotes to mean that was the exact words she used, right?"

"Yes."

"Isn't that why you use quotes: you have a couple of college degrees and you know what quotation marks are for, right?"

DeSanto objected: "Your honor, I object to this line of questioning. It's argumentative."

Judge Bouschor sustained the objection, suggesting to Meshbesher that he ask the questions without being argumentative.

The defense's nitpicking, designed to raise doubts over the accuracy of Congdon's notes, filled six pages of court transcripts. But DeSanto felt it had been "a truly up day," noting in his diary that the "overall impression of Congdon very positive, according to news media."

On Wednesday, May 23, Marjorie's riding instructor, Dion Dana, testified the Caldwells had talked many times about breeding horses. Marjorie had "a very definite desire" to own her own ranch, Dana said. She had even helped the couple design their ranch so Roger could take something on paper to show Congdon trustees when requesting a loan. But the Caldwells failed to tell her that their loan request of $750,000 had been rejected by the trustees.

On cross-examination, Dana testified Marjorie stopped by her house several hours after being informed of her mother's death. "She was very upset...in shock. She was repeating herself. She was very confused."

Wednesday, May 23
Things picked up with a call from Bill Furman to Mark Rubin. He's concerned that two men have been following him for at least a few weeks. He supposedly dragged one guy out of the car as he was following him and the guy said he had been hired by somebody in Minneapolis. Furman also indicated to Mark that [assistant defense attorney] Berman has been looking for Gary Fick and has threatened Fick's mother that if she doesn't produce him they will subpoena her to the courtroom to testify where he is. Furman, according to Mark, seems genuinely concerned.

Hair and blood expert Wally Sorum took the stand on Tuesday, May 29. He had examined hairs recovered from Glensheen; two from the Oriental rug near Velma Pietila's body and one from the stretcher sheet used to carry her body were "mirror images" of, and compared favorably with, samples of Roger's hair, Sorum testified.

Sorum also told jurors that bloodstains found on Elisabeth's bedspread and pillowcase matched Roger's blood and enzyme group. Meshbesher, reusing Thomson's line of attack, pointed out that forty-two percent of all people in the United States had the same basic blood type as Roger Caldwell. He ignored the fact that the enzyme group narrowed the pool of possible matches to approximately fifteen percent.

Throughout the trial, Marjorie couldn't stop talking to people, even those she should have avoided—reporters, spectators, witnesses, and the prosecution. Meshbesher recalled, "Right at the beginning I told her, 'Do not talk to the media, keep your mouth shut.' All of a sudden I pick up a paper, the front page is a story about an interview she gave to some reporter. I called her and said, 'What the hell's going on? Are you nuts?' And I realized that she would never listen to me."

As the St. Paul Pioneer Press reported one Sunday, "During breaks in the trial, [Marjorie] chats freely with reporters and spectators discussing everything from her love of reading, to her mother Elisabeth Congdon, to her fondness for 'Hägar the Horrible,' a newspaper cartoon she faithfully follows." She persisted in trying to converse with the prosecution team, asking about Waller's kids and making comments about the trial to DeSanto and Rubin.

Marjorie also solicited money to save horses from being destroyed. The money went to an organization that cared for injured and old horses. She even asked David Arnold and DeSanto for donations. DeSanto had Judge Bouschor remind Marjorie that she wasn't in court to make friends with the prosecution or solicit money for personal causes.

Tuesday, May 29

Many, many decisions to make now with regard to who to call. Should we call Fick and Furman? Should we call call Donetta Wickstrom regarding the plane investigation? Should we call the people in Room 802 [the Radisson hotel guests across the hall from the Caldwells who could testify they saw no one suspicious going into the Caldwells' rooms, in order to counter claims of evidence planting] or should we save this for rebuttal? Very difficult decisions. Discussions with Rubin and Waller. Don't want to leave any gaping holes, but at the same time should now focus on positive evidence.

The sixtieth and sixty-first witnesses were Sandra Schwartzbauer and supervisor Joanne Kelly from the Minneapolis-St. Paul International Airport Host gift shop. During Roger's trial, each woman had pointed to him as the man who bought a suede suit bag minutes after the shop opened at 6:35 A.M. on Monday, June 27, the morning of the murders. Both women again identified a wicker suitcase as similar to one the man had brought into the shop. Schwartzbauer said she remembered it clearly because she and the man tried to fit the suitcase into the suit bag. DeSanto also asked the women to describe the wallet the man carried with him, establishing that the wallet the man had was the same as Roger's, which would later be entered as evidence.

Meshbesher intended to show he had learned from Doug Thomson's mistake at Roger's trial, when Thomson couldn't budge Schwartzbauer and Kelly from their eyewitness identifications. Waiting outside the courtroom for testimony to resume, Meshbesher—dressed in a light green suit—told DeSanto and Waller, "I've got my surgical greens on today."

During cross-examination, Meshbesher pulled out a small wicker case almost identical to the one the prosecution had entered into evidence. The only visible difference was that the second case had brown, not beige, handles.

"Isn't it true that this wicker suitcase with the brown handles looks more like the one you saw the man carrying?" Meshbesher asked Schwartzbauer.

"Yes," she said. Meshbesher implied that if the wicker case was different from her earlier recollection, then maybe the man was, too.

Both women admitted being unable to pick out Roger when first shown his photograph a week after the murders. This also meant that the women had seen his photograph before they identified him in court.

Meshbesher hammered away at differences between Schwartzbauer's description to police of the man in the gift shop and Roger's appearance at his trial in Brainerd. She initially described the man as weighing about 185 to 195 pounds, with curly sandy-blond hair. Roger Caldwell had straight, gray-brown hair and weighed twenty pounds less.

However, during redirect by DeSanto, both women stuck by their identification of Roger. At day's end, DeSanto felt relieved his witnesses had survived Meshbesher's barrage.

Perhaps the trial's most dramatic moment took place Friday, June 1—but it was all behind the scenes. The prosecution was going to introduce Roger's wallet into evidence through testimony by Duluth Police Detective Jack Greene. Detective Greene had retrieved Roger's personal possessions at the Hennepin County jail and brought them to the St. Louis County Jail after Roger's arrest. The wallet had only become significant since Waller discovered the enclosed stamps; at the first trial DeSanto hadn't even offered it into evidence. The stamps had been examined by Wally Sorum on May 3. Sorum's report had come back on May 7, stating: "Examinations indicate with virtual certainty that the stamps on the letter were not at one time directly connected to the stamps from the wallet. However, this analyst cannot eliminate the possibility that the above stamps were once part of the same 'roll.'" It was not what Waller and DeSanto had hoped for, but they were certain the stamps would still have an impact.

At about 9 A.M., DeSanto sent assistant Mark Rubin to the evidence vault. His responsibilities each morning included setting out the exhibits for that day's witnesses. He prepared Roger's wallet—after the tests the stamps had been returned to their original location in the wallet, which was then placed back in evidence. Defense attorney Frank Berman accompanied him in the vault. "Going to call Greene next?" Berman asked. "You'll have to ask John," Rubin said. Both men left, and Rubin returned to the prosecution's makeshift office adjacent to the courtroom, where DeSanto and Waller were discussing the day's witnesses and testimony.

Less than five minutes later, the court clerk approached Rubin and said, "You should go back in there. Frank Berman is in there alone." Both sides had agreed that a member of the defense and prosecution must be present when anyone from either side entered the vault. But Berman had left by the time Rubin arrived. Since testimony would start soon, Rubin decided to bring the wallet out to the counsel table.

DeSanto was busy reviewing Detective Greene's statements when Rubin returned, looking panicked. "I can't believe it. It's gone. The wallet's gone," he told DeSanto.

"Mark, you must have misplaced it. Are you sure you looked everywhere?" DeSanto asked, trying to remain calm. "Go look again."

Rubin searched the evidence vault thoroughly. "It's not there," he told DeSanto. "It was right inside the door and now it's gone."

By now, DeSanto was alarmed. He called the court clerk and bailiff to join their search. But the wallet, in place minutes earlier, had vanished.

Waller urged DeSanto to demand that Judge Bouschor stop the trial. He wanted the sheriff's department, responsible for courtroom security, notified so they could search everyone in the courtroom. DeSanto hesitated, not wanting to jeopardize his reputation and credibility with the court by making serious accusations without proof. He approached the judge's chambers, where Bouschor sat reading at his desk.

"Judge, the state isn't prepared to proceed," DeSanto said. "We have a piece of evidence missing. Besides, I believe it's been stolen."

"What?" Bouschor responded. "Get Meshbesher in here."

With the defense attorney present, DeSanto repeated the news. "We're missing a wallet from the evidence vault. Mr. Berman knew about this—"

Meshbesher jumped in. "You're not accusing us of stealing?"

"All I know is that the wallet's missing," DeSanto replied curtly.

Bouschor cut both men short. He wanted to keep the trial moving, so he refused DeSanto's request for a delay until someone found the wallet. He tabled further discussion until the following Monday.

When DeSanto informed Waller, Waller again told DeSanto they should call the police. "But [John] said, 'I'll talk to the judge again this afternoon.' By then the wallet was gone."

Years later, DeSanto agrees. "I should have stopped the trial right then and there. I should have refused to proceed and drafted a search warrant. But I was too timid."

Bouschor instructed DeSanto to call his next witness, so detective Greene took the stand late Friday morning. A solidly built man with a potbelly, graying curly hair, weathered face, and bright eyes that softened when he smiled, Greene looked the part of the stereotypical Irish cop. His testimony avoided any reference to the wallet, which Greene could not describe from memory. Greene identified the wicker suitcase as "the first thing I saw" when he entered the Caldwells' hotel room in Bloomington.

Monday morning, the prosecution and defense regrouped in Judge Bouschor's chambers for further discussion of the missing evidence. Both sides insisted the conversation be on the record.

DeSanto went first. "We do have a piece of evidence, a wallet of Roger Caldwell's, that was seized from him at the time of his arrest, which is no longer in state's property," he told the court. "Over the weekend, we have been unable to locate it. We have checked everywhere, my associate Mark Rubin and I, with the assistance of clerk Judy Gilbert, and we just haven't found it.

"I, at this time, intend to make no accusations, but it does present a problem because it is an important piece of circumstantial evidence. And I would ask the court for either a continuance…so that counsel on both sides can sit down and make a thorough search of everything, to either find that wallet or, if that cannot be done…I would ask if defense counsel would agree to a stipulation that the wallet that was seized from Roger Caldwell was, in fact, a black single-fold standard wallet, which was a wallet like that described by clerk Sandra Schwartzbauer…as being in the possession of the man who purchased the suede bag on the morning of Monday, June 27, 1977."

Meshbesher responded. "I want to put this on the record, too, that this matter came up last Friday; and as an accommodation to the prosecution we searched all of our briefcases. ...[W]hat I want to do now, to avoid any inference or insinuation whatsoever about evidence, I will return the key that I got. I'm sorry I even got the damn thing and I want that now on the record, the key to the room where the exhibits are being stored."

But Meshbesher argued that the missing wallet was a bi-fold, and refused the prosecution's stipulation. DeSanto was livid. He could not corroborate Sandra Schwartzbauer's description of the wallet in court, because now the defense attorney claimed the missing wallet was of a different design. You know that's not true, DeSanto yelled at Meshbesher. But the defense attorney insisted DeSanto was mistaken. When Detective Greene resumed testimony, he again avoided specific references to the wallet, which no one ever found. Its disappearance remains a mystery.

Monday, June 4

Whole new ball game. Reemphasized to court that defendant should not be talking to press. Got the judge to tell Meshbesher to tell her not to do so. Emphasized to Meshbesher that the prosecution would not be talking to Marjorie anymore and did not want her talking with us. Monday spent mainly with testimony of Jack Greene.

During cross-examination, Greene said he had never opened the wicker case to see if it contained anything. Meshbesher hinted that the jewelry found a short time later might have been planted by Duluth police or with their consent. Meshbesher would go on to make further accusations against Greene.

Meshbesher produced a transcript of the tape-recorded conversation between Greene and Tom Congdon two days after the killings. Facing the jury, Meshbesher read aloud a quote of Congdon's from the transcript.

"And if you want," Meshbesher read, "I can give you how this Furman can be reached.... And I say he is doing some things that I don't think sometimes you guys are allowed to do."

Then he read Greene's response. "I'm sure and we won't even talk about those."

Meshbesher, pausing for emphasis after this exchange, turned back to his witness. Greene knew what the defense was implying; Duluth police had condoned the use of electronic surveillance equipment.

"Why did you close your ears to what Mr. Furman might have been doing?" Meshbesher asked. "Aren't you supposed to be concerned about persons in Duluth who are violating the law?"

"It wasn't my place to tell Mr. Furman what to do," Greene said. "If he's like other private detectives, he'd have told me to go to blazes." Besides, Greene added, why would he record a conversation in which he was going to make incriminating statements?

Tuesday, June 5

Cross-examination of Jack Greene very hard on his statement to Tom Congdon.... Believe it came off pretty well. More hard fast lies [exposed] by Marjorie's best friend for some years, Mannette Allen. Prosecution's case picking up steam. Finished with Dr. Bagley who finally got in that the defendant was always very demanding toward her mother and rude as a child.

Wednesday, June 6

Started off the day with court striking from testimony and asking the jury to disregard that the defendant was rude as a child, leaving that she was demanding in her relationship between herself and her mother. Presented only half day of testimony, that of the Spencers. Very damaging. More lies [of Marjorie's exposed]. Things really picking up. Intended to put Bob Vathing on the stand. Had to quit at noon, however, because Marjorie had a doctor's appointment for some kidney examination.

Thursday, June 7

The court ruled in chambers that [Carte Blanche director of security] Arnold Peller's [forged] card testimony is admissible. Meshbesher became very irate and we are going to the Supreme Court Friday morning, June 8. I don't believe it's appropriate but we have to go anyway. Hope we come out all right.

On Friday morning, the Supreme Court upheld Judge Bouschor's ruling by denying Meshbesher a hearing on the admissibility of Peller's testimony. The trial, in its eleventh week, could continue.

The courtroom buzzed when Marjorie's oldest daughter took the stand. Suzanne LeRoy, shy and visibly nervous, avoided her mother's stare. The twenty-four-year-old nursing student spoke softly during testimony, describing her mother as a spendthrift with outrageous habits such as buying each of her seven children a horse for Christmas one year. "She just kept buying more and more," Suzanne testified of the 350 riding outfits she and her sister Heather had each gotten from Marjorie. Juror Sportelli recalled that during her children's testimony, Marjorie showed glimpses of emotion curiously absent during the rest of the trial. Her usual demeanor, which Sportelli described as "matter of fact," was replaced by flashes of anger. "You could tell Marjorie was displeased with what her children were saying," Sportelli said. "She was irritated, uncomfortable."

Suzanne recounted how, in 1970, her mother had forced her to call and demand money from her grandmother. She told jurors that incidents like this were not unusual—her mother frequently asked Elisabeth for money. When Marjorie took out a $100,000 loan in 1972, she told Suzanne she planned to repay it with her inheritance. "Grandmother won't be living that much longer. So I can pay it back," Marjorie said, five years before her mother's murder.

Marjorie showered her children with presents in exchange for their loyalty and affection, Suzanne testified. She said that during her late teens, her mother's actions had forced her to move out of a guest house on her mother's house in Marine On St. Croix, Minnesota. Suzanne said she left after only one month when she discovered Marjorie listened in on her phone calls and read her mail.

Friday, June 8

Friday afternoon was spent with testimony from Richard Heimbach regarding positive identification of Elisabeth Congdon's strawberry dome ring. Arnold Peller's damaging testimony concerning a credit card issued to E.M. Congdon at 7650 Rosemary Circle South in Littleton, Colorado and the beginning of Suzanne LeRoy's testimony. Very damaging about her mother constantly going to Duluth to demand money from Elisabeth Congdon and seeking money from her time and time again. Elisabeth Congdon would state "We'll see." ...This next week should be a good one. Many witnesses from Colorado and more people locking in Marjorie. It will be a four-day week and then a five-day weekend. Much welcomed.

Monday, June 18

Meshbesher still trying to get me to call Furman, Fick, and Gary Dolan, whoever he is. I don't intend to fall into the same trap he has led other prosecutors into. Calling witnesses for him. He has indicated that his client has no money to return witnesses to Minnesota for testimony.

The night before latent print expert Steven Sedlacek hit the stand, DeSanto showed Waller the enlarged photo of the print on the envelope. Waller hadn't seen the blown-up print before. He had wanted to avoid being pegged as the fingerprint expert; any identification he made would be dismissed by the defense as biased. But Waller knew a fragmented print when he saw one. "It's not clear enough, John. I think it's unidentifiable," Waller said. He advised DeSanto the print showed fewer points of identification than Duluth police preferred.

But DeSanto decided to rely on Sedlacek's opinion. Sedlacek was a pro. On the stand the next day, Sedlacek, as he had at Roger's trial, testified that the thumbprint on the envelope belonged to Roger. In a surprise tactic during his cross-examination, Meshbesher asked Sedlacek to reexamine the original print. Meshbesher deliberately ignored the prosecution's chart, a blown-up photograph of the print used at Roger's trial. This forced Sedlacek to analyze a thumbprint developed two years earlier. He admitted the print had faded over time, the result of a chemical reaction between the ninhydrin and the amino acids in the perspiration that had left the print. Even with a magnifying glass, the thumbprint ridges had faded to a point so faint Sedlacek acknowledged no one could identify them.

It was a bit of a defense stunt, but less than a week later, while the defense presented its case, it would appear to have been a bad omen.

Sixteen-year-old Richard "Rick" LeRoy, Jr., took the stand as a hostile witness for the prosecution. Rick testified that his stepfather was an alcoholic who would go off for days at a time on binges. "Mother told me he was an alcoholic before they got married," the boy told jurors.

"I was afraid of him when he was drinking," he testified. When Roger was drunk, he would often become violent, Rick said. "My mother and I would leave. We'd go to a motel for the night just to get away."

He also described for jurors the incident in January 1977, when Roger struck him with a tire chain. Roger was arrested on assault charges, but officials dropped the charges when he agreed to go through chemical dependency treatment. However, Rick said, the treatment didn't work.

During cross-examination, Rick recalled another incident at a Denver horse show when the Caldwells got into a terrific argument. Roger held up a piece of paper, Rick testified, which supposedly gave him power of attorney for his wife's estate. "He said she better sign this piece of paper or he'd walk out then and there. Mom started crying and stormed off." A document giving Roger the power of attorney had been found along with the so-called murder contract in Roger's safety deposit box.

Thursday, June 21
Most of the day with Rick LeRoy. No lumps in the bed this year. This year's defense is Roger out on one of his drunk binges.

During the three-month trial, DeSanto made it back to Duluth only four times. Most of the details of his September wedding he had left up to his fiancée, including their engagement announcement in the Duluth newspaper. The grinding trial routine was broken on a few occasions when the trial adjourned for the day because Marjorie claimed to be ill. One time, DeSanto, Waller, and Rubin drove to the Twin Cities in a severe thunderstorm just to see a new movie, Escape from Alcatraz. On another day off, the men drove to Minneapolis to watch Doug Thomson try a murder case. No matter what they did, they couldn't seem to leave their work behind.

Nearing the end of the prosecution's case, Colorado horse trainer Judith McCoy took the witness stand. She testified that months before the murders, Marjorie had told her, "The only way I'm going to get out of this financial mess is if my mother kicks the bucket."

DeSanto rested the state's case on June 26, 1979, after calling 112 witnesses over eight weeks. Meshbesher would start his case the following day with Duluth police officers Waller, Grams, Yagoda, Greene, and Cox, and BCA lab analyst Wally Sorum. DeSanto noted in his diary that "Waller had a sleepless night last night as I'm sure all the cops did." The next day was also the second anniversary of the murders.

CHAPTER 19

Fool if You Think It's Over

MARJORIE AND ROGER CALDWELL WERE ALSO VICTIMS—victims of a frame, Ron Meshbesher told jurors in his opening statement. He suggested they had been set up by the "Colorado Connection," comprised of Denver private investigator William Furman, the detectives who worked for Furman, and Colorado Bureau of Investigation Agent Bob Harmon. Furman or an associate was in each location where police found critical evidence against the Caldwells, Meshbesher told jurors. "They just happened to be there," he said. "This was no coincidence."

Meshbesher kept his remarks brief, as he told jurors "you're basically familiar with the issues, testimony, witnesses, and what this case is all about." Despite courthouse rumors that Marjorie would take the stand, neither DeSanto nor Waller expected Meshbesher would allow her to testify. But Meshbesher gave no clue in his opening statement.

The known list of defense witnesses was relatively short—less than half of the 112 witnesses called by the prosecution. Meshbesher said he planned to call a handwriting expert who would refute testimony that Roger addressed the envelope containing the gold coin, a Duluth police officer who unsuccessfully tried to place Roger on an airplane the weekend of the murders, private investigator William Furman (who had been hired by Tom Congdon), and the Twin Cities airport police officer who found an unaccounted for parking ticket the morning of the murders.

Before calling the first defense witness, Meshbesher put rumors to rest by informing the court that Marjorie Caldwell would not testify. Even the most casual courtroom observer could see she liked to talk. While Meshbesher had made up his mind as soon as he heard the prosecution's case, the final decision belonged to his client. Strategically, the defense gambled either way. By not testifying, Marjorie might leave jurors speculating about what she had to hide. But if she took the stand, Meshbesher would have little control over what she said, as he had confided to DeSanto. He was relieved when she finally gave in to his recommendation.

"Either she's the greatest actress in the world or she really wanted to take the witness stand," Meshbesher recalled. "Because I had a knockdown, drag-out session with her in my conference room the day she agreed not to testify." He and assistant counsel Frank Berman spent three hours grilling Marjorie the way they said she would be cross-examined in the courtroom before sitting back down. She told Meshbesher, "I haven't listened to everything you've said, but I'm going to listen to you."

Meshbesher's strategy involved showing his client's innocence by attacking the evidence used to convict her husband. On July 2, he delivered a near knockout punch, suddenly producing a surprise alibi witness. Under the rules of discovery, the defense provides the prosecution with statements of all witnesses they plan to call before the trial begins. But DeSanto received Candace Byers' statement minutes before her testimony. On the stand, Byers would testify she saw Roger at the time the prosecution contended he was en route to Minnesota. If Roger had an alibi, then so did Marjorie in her role as coconspirator.

Caught off guard by the defense tactic, DeSanto angrily confronted Meshbesher. But Meshbesher was matter-of-fact about his next witness. Wasn't her name on the prosecution witness list? Then how could she really be a surprise?

At that, DeSanto jumped to his feet to address the court. "Your Honor, this is completely unexpected. The prosecution requests a day's recess to interview this witness and review her statements."

Judge Bouschor agreed to delay the start of the day's testimony for twenty minutes. A livid DeSanto said nothing—he didn't want to antagonize the court. Instead, he met with Byers in the county attorney's office next door and challenged her convenient memory. During the interview, the court reporter continually ducked his head in to say Judge Bouschor was "ready to go." DeSanto could see that Bouschor wanted nothing to slow down the trial's progress. "Today I would stop the trial," DeSanto said later. "Now I would appeal the discovery violation and insufficient time to prepare. Bouschor prevented us from a real chance to challenge Byers' statement."

For the prosecution, this was strictly damage control time. Byers, a twenty-five-year-old former waitress at the Holland House Hotel, originally told Colorado law enforcement that she didn't see the Caldwells the day of the murders. She had even put it in writing.

Now, nearly two years later, she testified she had seen Roger in the lobby of the Holland House Hotel about 10 P.M. Sunday, June 26. She spotted Caldwell when she was in the lounge "sneaking a beer" during her shift. Byers testified she knew she saw Roger on Sunday, June 26, because the bar was closed and she had to jump over a fence to draw a beer.

DeSanto could tell Byers' testimony had made a strong impression on the jurors. By the time it was his turn to cross-examine, DeSanto, who rarely moved while at trial, paced briefly about the courtroom before sitting back down. Why, he demanded loudly, had Byers told police the week after the murders that she hadn't seen the Caldwells? "I was real nervous when I was talking to them. I just wanted them to leave," she responded.

DeSanto turned to Byers, his voice taking on a harder edge. Why then hadn't she reported her change of mind to authorities? Byers replied she "hadn't put the dates together" until recently. She claimed not to have realized the importance of seeing Roger and told no one until two of Meshbesher's associates interviewed her in April. DeSanto's left leg twitched under the counsel table. He hoped jurors couldn't see his leg, but he wanted them to notice the incredulous look he shot Byers.

If the jury believed Byers' story, then it was impossible for Roger to have made the round trip from Colorado to Minnesota as the prosecution claimed. DeSanto continued to push Byers, trying to discredit her testimony. But she refused to back down in any way.

That left the prosecution with two options. DeSanto could trot out an alternative murder theory for jurors or he could stick by the account he had presented in Brainerd—and now again in Hastings—and hope jurors would discount this new evidence. Although he had two options, DeSanto had no choice. He believed Roger committed the murders and Marjorie acted as his accomplice. But by sticking to his theory he risked that the jury might decide to give Byers' testimony enough significance to throw out the rest of the prosecution's evidence.

Back at the rental house, DeSanto said aloud what the others were thinking. "That woman is lying. She got up there and told a pack of lies," he said. "And I'm afraid the jury bought it."

DeSanto wrote in his diary that night, "The case is really looking bad as of right now. Certainly he's created a reasonable doubt unless the jury disbelieves Byers."

Byers' testimony prompted attorney David Arnold to write Roger and fill him in on the startling revelation.

> Dear Roger,
>
> I presume by now, that you have heard the somewhat heartening news of the "surprise" testimony of a witness in Marj's case, who remembers seeing you at the Holland House on June 26th (at about 10 P.M.). Obviously, the testimony came as a shock to the prosecution, and I presume that the witness will have to withstand significant inquiry into her credibility and recollection. However, assuming the testimony to stand unchallenged, it would seem that it should be of great significance in not only Marj's case, but certainly used in an effort to secure a new trial for you. Apparently, much credit for investigation in Marj's matter goes to Frank Berman. He had made several trips to Colorado in investigation of the matter.

On learning Meshbesher planned to recall him as a witness, Waller nearly lost it. He was so worn out from his last go-round with Meshbesher's tough cross-examination, he threatened to leave. "He's not going to do this to me again, John," he told DeSanto the night before his testimony. After his experience on the witness stand in the two Caldwell trials, Waller would refer to what he called "post-Caldwell syndrome"—any other trial testimony seemed easy in comparison.

During Meshbesher's pointed questioning, Waller acknowledged he knew private detective William Furman had been investigated by Colorado authorities in the past. But Waller reminded jurors that Tom Congdon had hired Furman after getting his name from the Denver Police. Yes, Waller said, he and Furman had met twice, once in Denver before Roger's arrest and once prior to Roger's trial. Not sure what Meshbesher was trying to imply, Waller emphasized that he had distrusted Furman from their initial encounter. When he realized Furman was swindling Tom Congdon, Waller said he immediately reported him to Inspector Grams.

Waller couldn't wait to get off the witness stand. He would remember most the feel of Meshbesher hovering over his shoulder, "so close, like an animal waiting to pounce."

Next, the defense called Officer Donetta Wickstrom, who testified about unsuccessful efforts by Duluth police to pin down Roger's transportation to and from the murder scene. Wickstrom told the jury that despite three-hundred hours of investigation, police could not link him to any airline flights between Denver and Minneapolis-St. Paul the weekend of the murders. Meshbesher wanted jurors to reach one conclusion: Roger was in Colorado on June 26 and 27.

Ray Halgren, a police officer at the Minneapolis-St. Paul International Airport, testified that he found the parking ticket assumed to be from the stolen car driven by Roger the morning of the murders. The car keys had been found in a trash can in the short-term parking lot. Halgren told jurors that he later discovered a parking ticket stamped 6:35 A.M. in the same garbage can, but underneath the plastic liner, not inside the garbage bag where the keys had been discarded. Since the ticket was discarded in such an unlikely place by a murderer in the midst of his getaway, Meshbesher wanted jurors to conclude it had been planted.

Meshbesher then called one of the defense's most important witnesses, fingerprint expert Herbert MacDonell. Professor of scientific and criminal investigative procedures at two upstate New York colleges, MacDonell testified about the thumbprint on the envelope containing the coin.

MacDonell held up two fingerprint charts, the same ones used by the prosecution's print expert, Steven Sedlacek—one an enlargement made from a negative of the photographed print in question, the other a photo enlargement from Roger's fingerprint card.

MacDonell told jurors he found unexplained differences between the two photos.

"We have two discrepancies," MacDonell told jurors. "We have an area on the thumbprint which does not show up in the latent. We have an area of the latent print which does not show up in the thumb. And both are good discrepancies."

MacDonell stated that these discrepancies included the presence of a scar in the print found on the envelope. This scar, however, did not appear in the prints taken at the time of Roger's arrest. Meshbesher asked his witness for his professional opinion on the origin of the thumbprint.

"I concluded that the fingerprint in the evidence photograph, the latent print developed with ninhydrin, is not a print that could have been made by the thumb of Roger Caldwell."

DeSanto was indignant. The measurements were skewed, as MacDonell pointed out to the jury, but DeSanto knew the enlargements had not been blown up to identical proportions and one of the prints had been turned slightly. Sedlacek had told him this during Roger's trial and now it was too late to think about why he hadn't insisted on new, accurate enlargements.

"Couldn't these so-called discrepancies amount to nothing more than differences between the charts?" DeSanto asked MacDonell. But MacDonell was sure of his testimony: the points did not match up; the print was not Roger's.

Sunday, July 8

10 p.m. Mark got back about 9 p.m. Waiting for Furman and his attorney Scott Robinson to arrive at the motel here about 11. Hope to talk to him tonight. Unique problem. Will he take the Fifth Amendment, will he tell the whole truth, will he be subject to any further criminal liability in other jurisdictions? Exactly what has he lied about with regard to his reports[?]...[Regardless] he clearly did not plant any evidence because he wasn't available to do so. His agents evidently were not present in either Duluth or Minneapolis at the Holiday Inn.

To say the defense had subpoenaed private investigator William Furman would be an understatement. Meshbesher had hired a private investigator in Colorado to chase him down. Although it took several months, the investigator finally tracked Furman to a Denver bowling alley. He was wearing a disguise.

Furman's private attorney, Scott Robinson, accompanied him to court and insisted on a meeting with Judge Bouschor and the other attorneys in chambers.

"It seems to me there is an issue here, from what I hear about the case, whether or not Furman planted evidence. He can testify about that. He can testify about that truthfully without taking the Fifth, but there are going to be some situations where if asked about his report to Tom Congdon, he's going to have to take the Fifth," Robinson informed the group.

DeSanto could hardly believe the nerve of Furman's attorney, setting conditions on his client's testimony. The prosecution had tried unsuccessfully to persuade Judge Bouschor that a man who continually invoked the Fifth Amendment would fail to enlighten jurors. That was why DeSanto had never called Furman to testify at Roger's trial. Now Meshbesher continued his Furman strategy in the discussion of where Furman's attorney would sit. Meshbesher wanted jurors to link the disreputable Furman's actions with the prosecution.

Meshbesher began, "There is a little chair behind Mr. DeSanto."

The judge interrupted, "There's another chair behind you."

Meshbesher continued, "Where Mr. Rubin used to sit."

Mark Rubin chimed in, "I think it would be best if he sat on the other side, your honor."

Meshbesher broke in, "The other side of what? I don't want him on any side of the counsel table. He's not affiliated with the defense."

DeSanto reminded the judge, "He's being called by the defense, your honor."

The judge allowed Robinson to sit in the front row behind the counsel table, on the right side of the courtroom facing the bench.

A large man, Furman weighed about 225 pounds and stood over six feet tall, with dark curly hair and a mustache. He wore a dark sport coat and a wide collared white shirt with several buttons open to reveal a heavy gold medallion in the middle of his hairy chest. The former trucker and bus driver told jurors he'd been trained in private investigation by an investigator by the name of Lawless.

Furman testified he'd been hired by Tom Congdon the day of the murders because Congdon feared for his family's safety. He wanted security for himself and his family at home. Furman said he traveled to Minnesota just once and denied being in Minnesota in the days after the murders.

"You didn't come to Minnesota on June 29th?" asked Meshbesher.

"No, sir," said Furman.

"Did you send a man to Minnesota?"

"I take the Fifth Amendment on that sir, on the ground it might incriminate me."

The private detective continued to hide behind the Fifth Amendment's protection against self-incrimination, afraid to answer questions about his supposed investigation of the Caldwells since he risked fraud charges for cheating Congdon. Meshbesher, aware that Robinson was trying to maintain eye contact with Furman in order to signal him on how to answer each question, took pleasure in occasionally standing squarely in the way. That left Furman on his own to decide when to take the Fifth.

Meshbesher continued questioning his witness. "Have you ever been to Duluth, Minnesota?"

"Have I ever been personally to Duluth? No, sir."

"Did you ever tell anybody that you had stayed in the lobby of the Radisson Hotel in Duluth on June 29th and 30th?"

"I take the Fifth on that, sir."

Meshbesher got Furman to admit he had been in Reno, Nevada, several weeks before June 27, 1977; the defense even had records to prove it. This allowed Meshbesher to insinuate that Furman may have been at Glensheen at the time of the murders or just after the murders. A matchbook from Reno, Nevada, had been found on the beach behind Glensheen during "Operation Clean Sweep," and it had been entered into evidence, much to DeSanto's dismay.

Furman said he visited Minnesota on August 11, 1977, when he stayed at the Bloomington Airport Holiday Inn.

"Who did you see on August 11th when you came to Minnesota?"

"I didn't see nobody, sir. We checked into the Holiday Inn Airport. I can't remember the exact location, sir."

"Who is 'we?'"

"I'll take the Fifth on that, sir."

"You didn't talk to anybody that was in Minnesota in connection with some business here?"

"I'll take the Fifth on that, sir."

"How long did you stay at the Holiday Inn in Bloomington?"

"One night."

"What was the purpose of that trip?"

"I'll take the Fifth on that, sir."

Meshbesher asked Furman about his conversation with Tom Congdon at the time Congdon hired him, which Congdon had repeated for Detective Greene in the taped phone conversation on June 29.

"Did you ever tell Tom Congdon that you were going to use some police methods that police were not allowed to use?"

"No, sir."

"You deny telling him that?"

"Yes, sir."

Meshbesher tried to reinforce his frame theory by raising questions about Furman's presence when police discovered key evidence against the Caldwells in Colorado.

"Were you present at the Holland House when an envelope containing a gold coin…was shown to police officers?"

"Yes, sir."

"Where were you at that time?"

"I was standing with, I believe, Sergeant—the police department from Golden, and Bob Harmon from CBI."

"Had you at any time gone through personal documents and papers belonging to Roger Caldwell and Marjorie Caldwell?"

"They would not let me enter into that room, sir."

"Did you ever go through any personal papers of theirs?"

"I went through the trash that the owner had thrown out."

When it came time to cross-examine Furman, DeSanto stood up at the counsel table and began to ask questions in a near yell. Furman's testimony so angered DeSanto that his face went red and his breathing became labored.

He grilled Furman about his supposed trip to Minnesota on August 11, 1977. Furman admitted he'd been fired by a Congdon family member that same day, after he'd already received more than $15,000 from Tom Congdon. He said he'd filed a report with Congdon just two days after the murders detailing his surveillance of the Caldwells. DeSanto, his gaze fixed on Furman, waved a copy of one of Furman's reports for jurors to see.

"Mr. Furman, your report to Tom Congdon dated August 13, 1977, is a fraud, isn't it?" asked DeSanto.

"I take the Fifth on that, sir," Furman responded.

"In fact, Mr. Furman, isn't it a fact that your trip on August 11, 1977, to Minnesota was to check out and make sure the places you put in your report August 13th would be reasonably accurate?"

"I take the Fifth on that, sir."

DeSanto moved from the question of fraud to the bigger issue of planted evidence and a frame of the Caldwells.

"Have you ever planted evidence in this case for anyone?"

"No, sir."

"Have you ever been in the rooms of the Caldwells that they rented at the Radisson Hotel in Duluth, Minnesota, between June 28th and June 30th, 1977?"

"No, sir."

By day's end, the state's case had suffered a setback. DeSanto tried to read the jurors' faces. He hoped they didn't believe Furman had planted evidence or had been involved in a conspiracy to frame the Caldwells. But how could they trust a guy who took the Fifth Amendment so many times it made newspaper headlines the next day? "Detective silent 59 times at trial" the Minneapolis paper read. The pit in his stomach told DeSanto he had started to believe he could lose this case.

DeSanto made a short and sarcastic entry into his diary that night: "Furman testified. Had a good day for the prosecution."

Meshbesher's defense strategy throughout the trial involved presenting evidence that contradicted earlier testimony by prosecution witnesses. On Tuesday, July 10, handwriting expert Ann Hooten took the stand and testified about the handwritten address on the envelope containing the coin. Hooten, like prosecution handwriting expert Pat Rutz, had appeared at Roger's trial in Brainerd.

In a repeat of her Brainerd testimony, she told jurors that Roger did not write the address on the envelope mailed to the Holland House Hotel. She had examined the envelope under a microscope and analyzed photographic enlargements of the address, and she dismissed the writing as a "freehand copy." She said the writing showed hesitation marks, erasures, tremors, and other obvious signs of forgery.

During cross-examination, DeSanto asked Hooten whether these marks couldn't have been made by an alcoholic. Only someone intent on copying Roger's handwriting could have made those mistakes, she replied.

DeSanto listed mistakes she had made in prior handwriting analyses. As he had at Roger's trial, he mentioned the Mormon Will, allegedly drawn up by reclusive millionaire Howard Hughes and later proven a forgery. Hooten replied that she could not recall ever pronouncing handwriting as genuine that later turned out to be forged. This was different from just a year before when, during cross-examination and pressed about the Mormon Will, she had admitted to making mistakes.

Dr. Hyman Zuckerman, a Denver physician, testified on Wednesday, July 11. Meshbesher called Dr. Zuckerman to bolster the defense's claim that Marjorie had nothing to do with the murders, and neither did Roger because he had been drinking heavily around the time they occurred.

Dr. Zuckerman had first treated Marjorie in 1975 after a horse kicked her and, on another occasion, in April 1977, when she claimed another horse crushed her against a wall. She had later confided to Dr. Zuckerman that a drunken Roger had beaten her. Dr. Zuckerman testified that Roger had been hospitalized for his alcoholism in Denver in January 1977. The doctor had prescribed Antabuse for Roger.

Prosecutor DeSanto had said in opening statements that Marjorie behaved strangely when she shopped for a million-dollar ranch and signed purchase agreements on two properties only hours after she learned of her mother's murder. To try and persuade jurors that Marjorie's response to her mother's death was normal, Meshbesher called Minneapolis "grief therapist" Richard Obershaw to testify. DeSanto challenged Obershaw's standing as an expert witness, pointing out that he was a Twin Cities funeral home director, not a psychologist, but Judge Bouschor allowed his testimony.

"Is there such a thing as a normal response to death?" Meshbesher asked.

"I don't believe so," Obershaw replied.

The "normal" reaction to news of a loved one's death "runs the gamut," Obershaw testified, from simply crying or sitting in a corner to screaming. Obershaw related that one client cleaned house at two in the morning right after she learned of her husband's death.

On cross-examination, DeSanto challenged the validity of Obershaw's expertise on Marjorie.

"Have you ever counseled or talked with the defendant Marjorie Caldwell?" DeSanto started.

"No, sir. I'm sorry. I said 'good morning' to her at the table," Obershaw responded.

"Do you know of any of the facts of this case personally?"

"Some parts I have read in the newspaper, yes."

So much for experience, DeSanto thought. In his closing he would refer to the so-called "grief therapist" as a mortician.

Walter Rhodes, a sixty-three-year-old fingerprint expert and former head of the Minnesota Bureau of Criminal Apprehension's latent print division, took the stand next. He told jurors the fingerprint on the base of the brass candlestick had insufficient details for identification. More importantly, no one could positively trace the thumbprint on the envelope. After Roger's trial, Thomson had told Meshbesher he was convinced the print did not belong to his client. Meshbesher had heeded the advice to go after the thumbprint.

"Do you have an opinion as to whether or not the fingerprint that was said to have come from the envelope was Roger Caldwell's right thumbprint?" asked Meshbesher.

"Yes, I have an opinion," said Rhodes.

"What is your opinion?"

"My opinion is from what I can see, [there are] characteristics in the latent print I cannot find in the inked print."

"Does that mean it was not his fingerprint?"

"That is my opinion."

Rhodes compared eleven identification points on the charts of the inked and latent thumb prints. He agreed with Sedlacek's testimony that the characteristics of the latent print matched the inked print on only three points of identification. Rhodes' assertion was that the latent print was so poor it was impossible to determine anything. "Mr. DeSanto, I wouldn't come to court with a latent print like this," Rhodes said.

DeSanto wanted to put an end to the battle of experts. As soon as the day's testimony ended, Waller tracked down George Bonebrake, former head of the FBI fingerprint laboratory in Washington, D.C. DeSanto then phoned Bonebrake and asked him to fly out to Minnesota to evaluate the print—Bonebrake would be the prosecution's rebuttal fingerprint witness.

Early the evening of July 11, DeSanto and Rubin met Bonebrake at the Minneapolis-St. Paul International Airport. After they arrived back at the house, Bonebrake was anxious to get to work. He spread out the latent print and the inked print side by side on the kitchen table. "Just leave me alone here and I'll give you my opinion in an hour or so," he told the two men.

Like expectant fathers, DeSanto and Rubin marked time by nervously pacing in their basement office. Shortly before 11 P.M., Bonebrake called them upstairs. "In my opinion, this is not Roger Caldwell's print," Bonebrake said.

For several seconds, DeSanto could only stare in disbelief, until the news sunk in. "Son of a bitch," DeSanto said. DeSanto and Rubin pressed Bonebrake about his opinion. Was he positive that the print couldn't have been made by Roger? Yes, Bonebrake said, positive. This was a major setback, especially so late in the trial. Ethically, DeSanto would have to inform Meshbesher of Bonebrake's findings. Rules of criminal procedure required that exculpatory evidence—any evidence that might point to a defendant's innocence—be turned over to the defense.

DeSanto and Rubin dropped Bonebrake off at his motel after midnight. DeSanto was silent as he and Rubin drove back to their rental house. Once inside, DeSanto collapsed onto his bed. "I can't believe we lost the fingerprint," DeSanto said. Neither of the attorneys could sleep, so DeSanto and Rubin walked the deserted streets of residential Hastings for the next few hours. What should have been a beautiful summer's evening had become a countdown to what DeSanto feared would be the final unraveling of his case.

Bonebrake's testimony would severely damage the prosecution's case, particularly coming on the heels of Byers' alibi claim. What convincing evidence did the prosecution have left? They had the "murder contract." But DeSanto, his confidence badly shaken, could only wonder what the jury would think and whether he could still convince the jury to convict Marjorie. After Rubin and DeSanto returned to the house, Rubin called and woke Waller up at home in Duluth, asking him to come support DeSanto. "John's in bad shape. He's having a real rough time," Rubin said. "We need you down here as soon as possible."

Wednesday, July 11

Much consternation, indecision as to how to approach this situation. Drove Bonebrake back to his room intending to put him on a plane this morning. Then called back telling him to wait in his room until I had made a record notifying defense counsel of his findings and permitting defense counsel to call him as a witness if they wished. ...Mark prepared most of the night to cross-examine psychologist June Tapp regarding eyewitness identification and its frailties. Got up early this morning prepared for Steve LeRoy. Frustration remains permanently at this time because as I prepared for Steve LeRoy's cross-examination I realized that last year [at Roger's trial] he was the [defense's] scapegoat and the murderer and the framer with his mother and Peter LeRoy. This year, of course, the defense is different. And now Tom Congdon and the Furman/Fick/Dolan gang are the defense scapegoats. I hope the jury can see through this but I'm not quite sure they will.

The morning of July 12, Meshbesher called Bonebrake to testify for the defense. Although the fingerprint had nothing to do with Marjorie's guilt or innocence, its misidentification became a turning point in the trial, raising doubts about the prosecution's other evidence.

"The fingerprint cast a shadow over all of the case because DeSanto kept emphasizing 'this important piece of evidence,'" Meshbesher recalls. "When that thing just blew up in his face, he had egg on his face for the rest of the trial. I don't think he ever recovered."

The defense wasted no time in questioning Bonebrake, while DeSanto, his expression pained, looked down at the counsel table.

"When did you get here?" Meshbesher began.

"Yesterday evening." said Bonebrake.

"You visited with Mr. DeSanto, did you not?"

"Yes, sir. I did."

"And he showed you all the fingerprint evidence in this case, did he not?"

"He showed me several items, yes, sir."

"He showed you specifically the fingerprint card for Roger Caldwell?"

"Yes, sir."

"And he showed you an envelope?"

"Yes, sir."

"And he also showed you a contact fingerprint, or contact print of a fingerprint—there."

"Yes, sir."

"After your comparison what did you conclude, whether or not the latent print and the inked print were the same?"

"It was my opinion they were not the same."

"They were from different people?"

"That is correct, that the latent print was not made by the same finger that made the right thumb print on the fingerprint card bearing the name Roger Caldwell," Bonebrake concluded.

Following Bonebrake's testimony, the press corps eagerly awaited Doug Thomson's reaction. He rewarded them with a front-page story. Thomson told reporters that the discredited fingerprint was so significant he planned to petition the Minnesota Supreme Court for a new trial for Roger.

By the time the court recessed that afternoon, Waller had returned to Hastings. Rubin told Waller that he needed to help pull DeSanto out of his funk. Even Judge Bouschor had observed the prosecutor's dark mood. In trial notes for the day, he wrote, "John down in the dumps."

Over dinner, and later sitting out in the living room until early morning, Waller argued that they hadn't yet lost. "When the print went wrong, it was like somebody had died," Waller said. "That's the kind of grieving [John] went through. I told him there was a lot of other evidence that he still had, like the murder contract, the lies, the jewelry. He had a tremendous amount of evidence left."

Juror Sportelli said years later that the jurors, too, did not think that the prosecution's case was lost when the fingerprint evidence was discredited. "We had so much evidence to review," Sportelli recalled. But after the print went bad, Sportelli said she and the other jurors noted that DeSanto seemed "to struggle more," and that his confidence had been shaken.

On the morning of Friday the thirteenth, the defense rested its case, having called fifty-five witnesses. DeSanto took his turn for rebuttal testimony.

He recalled Tom Congdon. He wanted to convince jurors that Congdon had nothing to do with any frame-up or plot to plant evidence against the Caldwells. Congdon reminded the jury that Furman had bilked him out of thousands of dollars. DeSanto summarized for his witness; Congdon's decision to hire Furman was a mistake, but certainly not sinister.

The state also recalled Golden, Colorado, Police Sergeant Randy Gordanier to testify about his two interviews of Candace Byers following the murders. The first interview had taken place on July 1, 1977, when Byers advised Gordanier that "she had not seen Roger and Marjorie Caldwell since June 25th," the weekend of the murders, Gordanier testified.

Gordanier had interviewed Byers a second time on July 9.

"On the date of July 9, 1977, did Mrs. Byers indicate that she had seen Roger Caldwell at all on Sunday, June 26, 1977?" DeSanto asked.

"No, she did not." Both times, Byers had said she had not seen Roger Caldwell during the critical time period preceding the murders.

By Friday afternoon, testimony came to a close. DeSanto had his work cut out for him regarding closing arguments—he had to recover from Furman, the fingerprint, and Byers.

As testimony concluded in his wife's murder conspiracy trial, Roger wrote back to David Arnold about Byers' surprise revelation.

> Dear David,
>
> Since my imprisonment, of over a year ago, corresponding with various members of my family has been my greatest joy, it is true that I was also in jail for over a year as well, but on the advice of my attorneys, (and I have always obeyed the advice of my attorneys) I didn't write to anyone, lest my writing be misunderstood, or worse. I make mention of this only by way of explaining my style in response to your thoughtful letter of twelve days ago.
>
> Yes, you're right, of course, in presuming that I had heard the "heartening" news of the witness in my wife's trial that testified to having seen me in Colorado at nearly the same time that the murder was committed for which I have been so unjustifiably persecuted. Naturally I would expect that this eye witness identification by someone familiar with my appearance would override the obviously mistaken identification of the imbecile girls at the Twin Cities airport, who, a year after the fact, and with constant pressure from the prosecution, confused me with someone else. As pleased as I am that this witness has now come forward, I'm still regretful that she didn't do so over a year ago.

Closing arguments began July 18 shortly before 9:30 A.M. in a packed courtroom. Under Minnesota law at that time, the state went first with no opportunity to rebut the defense's closing argument. The only choice the prosecution had was how long to make the final summation.

"What the defendant is charged with doing, really, is entering a criminal agreement with Roger Caldwell to commit a crime, that being the murder of Elisabeth Congdon," DeSanto told the jury.

Added together, the circumstantial evidence linked Roger and Marjorie to the murders. The handwriting on the envelope mailed to the Holland House, the gold coin inside stolen from Glensheen, the gift shop receipt found in the Caldwell's Duluth hotel room, the jewelry recovered in their hotel night stand, and the suede bag on the hotel bed in Minneapolis—all were pieces of this murder puzzle.

In a circumstantial evidence case, jurors should consider all the facts. DeSanto told the jury that unless they could reason away the circumstances, a guilty verdict is the only logical conclusion.

The facts included incriminating evidence like the wicker basket and jewelry stolen from Glensheen. He suggested the defendant must have been aware her husband had taken the basket because she lied to Mannette Allen about the basket, saying, "You know how I am about mother's things, whenever I see something I like I take it, not that I steal it."

So much for the defense's claim, DeSanto said, that the "Colorado Connection" had planted the wicker basket and jewelry in the Caldwell's hotel room. The defendant, DeSanto reminded jurors, had also "told Sergeant Waller and the people present on July 5th that the blue container was hers, the jewelry was hers."

There was blood and hair evidence recovered at the crime scene that matched Roger. DeSanto attacked the defense's argument that thirty million people shared the same blood type. Of the thirty million, only Roger had evidence against him.

As for motive, the Caldwell's extravagant, spendthrift lifestyle had brought them to bankruptcy and desperation in the months and days preceding the murders: "The defendant's purchase and negotiations for land with Fran Beyer in June of 1977…the Caldwell's purchase and default regarding Pine Valley Farms in November of '76 and the early part of '77…the defendant's looking for more property on June 27, 1977, the date Elisabeth Congdon is murdered, including a $1.3 million place."

Meanwhile, on Marjorie's relationship with her mother, DeSanto argued, "I submit the evidence shows that the defendant used her mother, and whatever respect there was in the years immediately preceding the murders was a token respect…for the only person that could satisfy her spendthrift desires, a token respect for her mother's purse strings."

DeSanto acknowledged, as he walked closer to the jury box, the state could not show how Roger got to and from Duluth. "The defense would have you believe in this case, and this is a highly-celebrated case, that this is really unusual. Well, ladies and gentlemen, I submit to you in most burglaries, rapes, robberies, you don't know how the defendant got to and from the scene unless you catch him right at the scene.

"How are they generally found?" he asked jurors. "By something left at the scene like blood and hair and also by the fruits of the crime. The money taken in the robbery, the loot taken in the burglary, the jewelry taken from Elisabeth Congdon's body and from her bedroom, and the wicker basket taken from her closet."

The state had made a big mistake, DeSanto told the jury. The prosecution had failed to prove the thumbprint on the envelope belonged to Roger. The prosecution's fingerprint expert made a mistake; he had misidentified the print. But, DeSanto said emphatically, the rest of the case remains strong. "The absence of Roger Caldwell's right thumbprint on this envelope does not acquit Roger Caldwell, does not acquit Marjorie Caldwell."

As DeSanto tried to attack the defense's frame-up theory, he started anticipating the defense's arguments, telling jurors what he thought Meshbesher might say. Years later, he would admit, regrettably, that he felt like the underdog—and it showed. "I was more worried about what jurors would think of Meshbesher and what he might say, than the evidence."

DeSanto couldn't conceal his anger. The defense would claim that the Caldwells had been set up after Tom Congdon hired Furman and his Colorado associates Fick and Dolan to plant evidence. Duluth police were supposedly part of this frame, whether duped or not, because they'd zeroed in on the Caldwells from the start. Ridiculous, DeSanto argued, his face grimacing in disgust.

"Please clear away the smoke. Look at the evidence. Would Thomas Congdon coordinate a frame by paying William Furman with checks? Absurd. Would he take notes of the number of Furman and the name of Dolan and give them to the defense so the defense could use them in cross-examination?

"A frame…would require not only the Congdon money, but…all the money in the world. It would require the police to know exactly and to be in cahoots with everybody that is planting this evidence so they would know when and where to go get it." He hit hardest on Meshbesher's allegation that because Furman took the Fifth Amendment fifty-nine times on the stand, he must be a murderer or a planter of evidence. "There were certain times he was not frank, open, and honest," DeSanto admitted to the jury, but there was a reason for that—Furman had defrauded Congdon of $15,000. Most importantly, Furman was hired after, not before, the murders.

If Furman and his associates were unbelievable, then why accept their word that they traveled to Minnesota to tail the Caldwells—or, as Meshbesher charged, to plant evidence? DeSanto argued, "They didn't even have, or Furman didn't even have, the correct room number the Caldwells were in at the Radisson in Duluth."

Meshbesher leapt to his feet. "I object to that. There is no evidence of that, your honor."

Judge Bouschor responded, "Well, we'll leave that up to the jury to determine what the evidence is."

DeSanto continued, "The evidence presented by Mr. Meshbesher himself…shows that Furman was at the Holland House Hotel between July 1 and July 5 when he's supposedly planting evidence at the Bloomington Holiday Inn."

The circumstantial evidence that tied the case together was Marjorie's assignment of inheritance, DeSanto said. "I submit to you that the consideration that Marjorie Caldwell received from Roger Caldwell, in return for her assignment of money to him, was murder. And, as David Arnold stated at the very end of his testimony, [regarding] the document itself, 'In what other kind of legal document do you generally see two parties involved in it and their signatures on it?' Answer, 'In a contract.' A contract for murder, ladies and gentlemen. The state's evidence has overwhelmingly proven that in fact, Marjorie Caldwell was the woman behind the man who committed these murders," DeSanto said. "She persuaded Roger Caldwell to murder in return for an irrevocable assurance of at least…$2.5 million."

Wednesday, July 18
Gave final argument from 9:30 'til noon with one break at 11 o'clock, from 1:30 'til 3 and then from 3:20 'til 5:10. Meshbesher to give final argument tomorrow. Feel confident after final argument. Also relieved. Here with Gary and Pat Waller, Mark and Lana. Just before going to Steamboat Inn for dinner, received call from Duluth Police Department. Some kook identifying himself as RK102 called KDLH [radio] in Duluth saying he had committed the Congdon murders, that the Caldwells were innocent, that he did so for food, didn't mean to harm anyone.

The next day's final arguments by the defense went until 8 P.M. DeSanto later said Meshbesher's closing statements were so persuasive he had a sinking feeling as he listened. A skilled communicator, Meshbesher's down-to-earth oral presentation and careful dissection of the evidence would have raised reasonable doubts for DeSanto if he'd been a juror.

"I'm going to deviate from the opening I had originally planned because I think the argument of Mr. DeSanto calls for it," Meshbesher told the jury. "I think the first time I heard the word ad hominem was in a speech class in college, and I think if you all recall, that is an argument that is geared to the personality rather than to the subject matter…it's an appeal to prejudice rather than reason."

Looking toward the jury box, Meshbesher said that he'd felt like he'd been the one on trial and urged jurors not to hold his personality against Marjorie. "I told you at the beginning I sometimes get a little bit tough, but you'll find that paid off in this trial. I got tough with that fingerprint expert and because I persevered, I got that negative from Colorado and but for that negative, Mr. DeSanto would be here today, or yesterday, telling you that this was Roger Caldwell's fingerprint, as he did in his opening statement. And you bet his face is red. Am I accusing him of being a coconspirator? He was duped and he was duped by an incompetent, opinionated fingerprint examiner, but he goes on and [implies the defense] accuses everybody in the police force of being involved in this frame-up, and that just is not the case."

Meshbesher told jurors not to be sucked in by DeSanto's efforts to portray the State as the underdog in the criminal prosecution because DeSanto was in fact accomplished, well-trained, and well-educated. Then Meshbesher ticked off a list of alleged errors and bad decisions by the Duluth police for jurors to ponder: "We did not make up a photo inventory a month before trial; we did not tell Jan [Mynheir] and Wilma [Farley] to redo their statements so they would jibe; we didn't have a witness whose arm got bigger four months before trial so it couldn't be measured," he said, referring to Duluth police officer Barry Brooks. The officer's arm, which had reached through and unlocked the suspected entry window in an experiment right after the murders, had since grown too large to make that possible.

He vehemently warned the jury against putting too much trust in the state's government witnesses. Citing the Skylab fiasco when a section of the U.S. space station crashed to earth in Australia, and the tragic fire that killed three Apollo astronauts in their spacecraft, Meshbesher said harshly, "These are the geniuses of our time.… These experts are not always right. In fact, I proved to you, as I have never seen it proved in a courtroom before, that an expert fingerprint man was dead wrong."

As his opponent had done during jury selection, Meshbesher used a bank robbery analogy to help explain the elements necessary for a conspiracy conviction. "You ask yourself, was [it] proved beyond a reasonable doubt that [Marjorie] aided, abetted, or conspired with Roger Caldwell? If she did so innocently, that is not enough.

"If someone comes to your house and says 'I need a ride to the bank' and you give him a ride, and that person goes in and robs the bank, you are not guilty," Meshbesher said. "Yes, you aided and abetted a robber, but you had no idea a crime was going to be committed."

Now change the circumstances, he told jurors. If the person told you beforehand and you agreed to act as a lookout, you are a participant, an accessory. You are "guilty as all get-out," said Meshbesher.

His eyes fixed on the jury, Meshbesher argued that police had destroyed evidence, perhaps intentionally. The glass pane had been repaired before further tests could be conducted, particularly to determine if Roger's arm could reach through the hole. "They saved everything in this case. We could have a rummage sale with some of the stuff they saved…stuff that was insignificant. Yet the window pane is destroyed." Jurors couldn't miss his tone, thick with sarcasm.

The litany of police mistakes continued. How could investigators for two years have overlooked Velma Pietila's watch, which had stopped around 2:50 A.M.? he asked. Prudence Rennquist's barking dog verified the time, he told jurors. "The dog started barking at 2:50 in the morning," said Meshbesher. "The dog was right, wasn't he? They are trying to minimize the credibility of the dog now." The dog continued to bark until 5 A.M., a signal that the killer was still in the mansion, Meshbesher argued.

This is further proof, he told the jury, of a conspiracy. If Roger was still in Glensheen at 3 A.M., he had to do a lot of running around to make it to the Twin Cities airport by 6:30 A.M. Only a fool would speed and risk being stopped by the highway patrol. "But," Meshbesher added, "if there were a couple of people in conspiracy with a frame-up, one in Minneapolis and one driving a car down earlier, it makes a little more sense."

The baggage claim tickets, the airport parking ticket, and particularly the gift shop receipt were all too easily found, Meshbesher insisted. "No one ever…suggested that the Duluth Police are involved in this frame-up," he said. "I think they were duped, tricked, or deceived by some people who had planned this thing for some time, and the evidence justifies it. All they had to do was give that receipt and it led [police] on their merry way."

Meshbesher fingered private detective Bill Furman, conveniently present when-ever officers found crucial evidence, as one of the conspirators. When Bertha Huskins discovered the envelope containing the gold coin in the Holland House mail, Furman was there. Furman or his men were supposedly in Minnesota when authorities recov-ered the wicker basket, stolen jewelry, and garment bag from the Caldwell's hotel room. "Nice clean package, you know," Meshbesher added. "Even Agatha Christie doesn't make the clues that obvious."

Meshbesher hammered away at the blood and hair evidence. Thirty million people share Roger's blood type, he reminded jurors. As for hair evidence, why had police been unable to explain the identity of a blond hair recovered from the mansion's central staircase? Could it be the mysterious blond stranger who passerby Larry Jackson had reported to police? "Their expert told you that the blond hair at the scene wasn't dyed. Now, who had blond hair around there that wasn't dyed?"

Meshbesher continued, "[I]n Mrs. Pietila's hand, there was some black hair. Her husband came in and said she never had black hair.... Now, whose black hair was that? Because Roger Caldwell did not have black hair either. Where did that black hair come from...?"

Marjorie Caldwell may be a liar, she may have told inconsistent stories to police and friends, but she's no murder conspirator, Meshbesher emphasized. "Marjorie...has a tendency to tell little white lies. They don't mean a thing," he said.

Sure his client grew up "with a silver spoon in her mouth," Meshbesher said. But he hoped the jury wouldn't hold her wealth and spending habits against her. "Everyone has little idiosyncrasies we revert to at times," Meshbesher continued. "Some people drink, some can't stay away from bingo games. Some, like Marjorie Caldwell, go on shopping sprees."

The state's so-called murder contract, he told jurors, was simply a will to ensure Roger wouldn't be saddled with his wife's debts. Marjorie had signed the document very reluctantly, he claimed, because it gave her husband control, and a major share of her inheritance.

According to Meshbesher, there were two plausible theories which maintained his client's innocence and explained the evidence. The first theory held that the "Colorado connection" of Tom Congdon, CBI Agent Bob Harmon, and private investigator William Furman and his associates framed the Caldwells. The defense alleged this group had orchestrated the planting and discovery of crucial evidence and, at the very least, duped Duluth police into fingering the Caldwells as suspects.

Under theory number two, Roger had committed the murders on his own. His incentive: the documents drawn up by his wife giving him power of attorney and a share of her inheritance. But Marjorie, of course, had no prior knowledge of her husband's plans and therefore, the jury couldn't find her guilty of conspiracy.

Meshbesher told jurors that no matter how someone labeled the assignment of inheritance, whether as "a nice business arrangement" or "a contract for murder," he could explain it easily. He alleged that "Roger was lying to Marjorie [when he requested $750,000 from the Congdon trustees], and [told her] that it was accepted by the trustees." The only people who could have confirmed this were Roger and Marjorie, neither of whom had testified. Certainly nothing in the testimony of Tom Congdon indicated that Marjorie was expecting to receive $750,000 from the trustees. "I think he had to tell her that because that was added incentive to get her to sign that assignment because if the money was coming forth, he claimed he needed some security to protect himself from creditors and the disposition of those funds and the incurring of additional debts by way of real estate and the building of this horse ranch. After the assignment, nobody ever sees Marjorie and Roger together again until the 27th of June except, if you want to believe it, Wilma Farley and Jan Mynheir."

Meshbesher portrayed his client as a loving daughter who had a warm relationship with her mother, and spent "untold hours" making numerous personal items, including needlepoint gifts, for Elisabeth. While Meshbesher acknowledged Marjorie was too financially dependent on Elisabeth, he asserted she had been brought up that way. "She was given everything. Her mother was never married. She adopted two children and gave them the world, if money is the world. I'm convinced it didn't help in this case."

Meshbesher reminded jurors that there were two significant pieces of evidence missing—no proof that Roger flew between Colorado and Minnesota on the day of the murders, and no fingerprint of Roger's on the envelope containing the coin. "I think we broke open this case because we called in Herbert MacDonell…and he shows you graphically why [it's] not the same print," he said. "Well, I figure maybe you'd be a little suspect of this guy from New York, so I locate a local person, Walter Rhodes,…and I said 'What do you see at that point?' 'I don't see nothing,' he said, 'nothing,' and then he says that the funny thing is that the guy had three points where there is only one. That is an awfully bad mistake."

Meshbesher reminded jurors that Sedlacek had disagreed with defense expert MacDonell, "after MacDonell went over that print point by point. It's either a mistake, or he's lying. Those are the only two explanations."

"Now, Mr. DeSanto tells you, with red face, he said that the fingerprint was false, as though that makes it go away. It is still there, ladies and gentlemen…. The phony fingerprint alone is a reasonable doubt."

Near the end of his closing, Meshbesher summed up his case. "There is no motive for a killing for a woman who can't get the immediate cash if she gives a lion's share away to a drunken husband. There is no transportation connection between Colorado and Denver for a killer who had to be on one of two flights, if that is the man. The baggage tickets, the lack of the interline tickets, the wicker basket, the empty closet, they are all positive proof of a frame-up, and we don't have to give you positive proof. We just have to raise it to a reasonable doubt."

Looking back, DeSanto has thought that he didn't emphasize the baggage tickets enough. The claim tickets found in the Duluth Radisson Hotel room were numbered consecutively with those still on the suitcases in the Holiday Inn in Bloomington. The garment bag had one of those consecutive tickets, further linking it to Roger via the Radisson room. There was no way Furman could have planted consecutive baggage tickets from the same flight in the two locations.

Meshbesher implored jurors, "You have got to be morally certain that Marjorie Caldwell plotted the murder of her mother before you can find her guilty. I don't want any sympathy. I want a clear analysis of the facts."

Meshbesher was visibly drained and his voice hoarse as he thanked the jury and finished his closing arguments around 8 P.M. After sixteen weeks of testimony, the case finally was in the jury's hands. But before the jurors retired to the jury room shortly before 9:30 P.M., Judge Bouschor read them thirty-six pages of instructions and, since there were four charges and two possible verdicts for each charge, eight different verdict forms.

After the long day, DeSanto was not surprised when jurors ate dinner then retired to their hotel without deliberating. Juror Sportelli recalled being driven on a bus to the hotel as reporters tried to follow the group, hoping for at least a photo opportunity. That first night jurors slept in what Sportelli described as a "dive," with dripping air conditioning units and bugs. "We were so tired that once we got to our rooms we just wanted to go to bed," she said. "But one of the bailiffs gave someone hell for putting us in a dive, so after that we stayed at the St. James Hotel [a quaint, historic landmark hotel] down in Red Wing."

That evening, while DeSanto and Meshbesher had waited in the hallway outside the courtroom to see what the jury would do, DeSanto told Meshbesher, "You know that Furman didn't do it. He's the fictitious villain."

It was a common defense tactic to misdirect a jury.

"But this time I had a real person," Meshbesher said. "I had him in the flesh and blood." Furman was the biggest "gold mine I've ever found in a criminal case," he said. DeSanto wanted to punch Meshbesher in the nose.

Friday, July 20

[After the jury was sent out] they elected a foreman, which I found out this morning is Larry Smith. They started deliberations this morning at the courthouse. Went to the courthouse at 8 o'clock this morning. Went through exhibits with Judy Gilbert, Ron Meshbesher and Frank Berman. Carol Grant and Marge Caldwell were both present. Now just sit and wait and wonder. Waiting now for [Duluth television reporter] Holly Ramstad to show up for an interview.

Friday morning as the jury started deliberations, Roger kept his transistor radio on in his prison cell for word of his wife's fate. Marjorie remained hidden away on the second floor of the Dakota County government center where she tried to sleep and read books. That afternoon, standing near Meshbesher outside the courtroom, Marjorie acknowledged to reporters she was extremely nervous about the verdict. "I feel like a woman who has been in labor for nine months and now wants to see if the baby's normal or not," she said. At their rental house, Rubin, the Wallers, and De-Santo and Lana hung out and talked nervously, jumping each time the phone rang. After a barbecue dinner, the group sat in the living room listening and singing along as Rubin played guitar. It helped ease the tension—a little.

Saturday morning shortly before eleven, the phone rang. The verdict was in. The three men said nothing—they didn't have to. The jury had been out less than two days and deliberated less than ten hours. Hardly time to go over the evidence in detail. The mood was somber as they drove to the courthouse in Waller's squad car. Lana, Pat Waller, and DeSanto's parents would meet them in the courtroom.

When they arrived at the courthouse, DeSanto—with a nervous stomach —went directly to the bathroom. While Waller and Rubin waited in the hallway outside the courtroom, Meshbesher walked up.

"Where's John?" he asked.

"He's just in the bathroom," Waller said.

Meshbesher snapped, "I'm getting too old for this shit," and wheeled around. The strain had gotten to everyone in the trial.

Judge Bouschor and his court reporter had been notified at the Perkins restaurant where they were having lunch. They rushed back to the courthouse, where Meshbesher approached Judge Bouschor. "Give me a few minutes before you start," the defense attorney requested. "Margie's pretty shaken up." Bouschor agreed not to bring the jury in right away.

By the time the jury filed in a little after 11 A.M., reporters had filled the courtroom. Several jurors smiled and talked nonchalantly, DeSanto noted, and they looked over at Marjorie—not a good sign for the prosecution. Marjorie sat tensely, her arms folded tightly against her chest, surrounded by her attorneys. Meshbesher later said he could hear his heart pounding.

DeSanto tried to remain optimistic, despite a sinking feeling that his case might be headed for total collapse. There had been unpleasant surprises toward the end of the trial. Evidence, most notably the thumbprint, had soured, and several witnesses had changed their stories. Waller's pep talk after the Bonebrake loss had helped. But now, after a year of preparation, a four-month trial—the longest criminal proceeding in Minnesota history at that time—and more than $1 million in court costs, Marjorie's case was seconds away from being resolved.

"Ladies and gentlemen, have your reached a verdict?" Judge Bouschor asked.

"We have," responded jurors.

Court clerk Judy Gilbert read the verdict. In the first count, first degree murder in the death of Elisabeth Congdon, "we the jurors find the defendant, Marjorie Caldwell, not guilty." In the second count, first degree murder in the death of Velma Pietila, not guilty. DeSanto, Waller, and Rubin remained hopeful for the conspiracy charges. But then came a third and fourth "not guilty" of conspiracy to murder Elisabeth Congdon and Velma Pietila. Not guilty on all four counts—Marjorie would leave the courtroom a free woman.

A mixture of cheers and gasps erupted from courtroom spectators. Hazel DeSanto had tears in her eyes. "It was a very emotional time," Sportelli recalled. "I remember crying with relief. After sixteen weeks the trial was over."

As the foreman announced the verdicts, Marjorie's supporters stood up and applauded. DeSanto, Waller, and Rubin stood stunned; their family members sat silently in disbelief. Waller and Rubin didn't move, but DeSanto slumped forward, fighting a sudden urge to throw up. Marjorie broke down, sobbing out loud. A teary-eyed Ron Meshbesher hugged his client and wiped away tears before walking over to shake DeSanto's hand. "Regardless of the way it turned out, you did a good job," Meshbesher said. Then Meshbesher pushed his way through the spectators to Waller and Rubin. "He told me it was professional, it wasn't a personal thing, and that we had done the best we could," Waller remembered.

According to newspaper accounts, when Marjorie's son Rick heard the verdicts while standing in the hallway outside the courtroom, he let out a holler, ran outside, jumped in Meshbesher's gray Cadillac Seville, and drove in tight circles around the courthouse parking lot.

Before Marjorie left the courtroom, several jurors came up to embrace and congratulate her. Some jurors would stay friendly with her in the months that followed, and would have lunch with her on a few occasions. One of the alternate jurors even attended Rick's wedding.

Sportelli later said she thought the defense did a good job of poking holes in the state's evidence and that the prosecution failed to prove Marjorie was involved. "I think we were comfortable with our decision," Sportelli said, "but a little frustrated at the same time because there were so many questions that were still unanswered." Jurors were not allowed to hear about the drugged marmalade incident. "That would have been pretty big," Sportelli said.

Twenty-one-year-old juror Jacquelyn Schneider, when interviewed by reporters, said Muffin, the poodle, "had a lot to do with" her decision to acquit Marjorie. Schneider believed that the dog barked from 3 A.M. to 5 A.M. the morning of the murders because the intruder was inside Glensheen that entire time. That meant, as Meshbesher had argued, that there was no way someone could drive to the Minneapolis-St. Paul International Airport in time to arrive around 6:30 A.M.

Juror Eileen Muich, thirty-one, told reporters that she became convinced Roger could not have committed the murders and therefore, Marjorie could not be guilty. "There was nothing connecting him with the house at the time of the murders." She was also believed banker John Hannigan when he said he saw Roger at about 9:30 A.M. the morning of the murders.

As Marjorie left the courtroom, reporters engulfed her, demanding to know how she felt. "A little wobbly in the knees," she said. Marjorie had no news on her immediate plans except to go home and feed and let out her cat. She lost no opportunity to blast the Congdon trustees. "I don't know what my finances are," Marjorie said. "The trustees have held up every dime."

Meshbesher told reporters that the discredited fingerprint was the key evidence in his client's favor. "The turning point was the fingerprint—exposing the fingerprint as a fraud," said Meshbesher.

Waller and DeSanto retreated to the bathroom to get some privacy from the media and spectators. Rubin guarded the door so no one else could enter. As Waller and DeSanto stood alone in the bathroom, they had little to say. For any attorney, losing that first murder case is tough, especially such a well-publicized one, and John was overcome with emotion. Twenty minutes later, finally composed, the trio stoically walked out the front door of the courthouse to face reporters.

"Was it worth it?" several reporters asked DeSanto.

"Of course it's worth it. I'd do it again if I had to," he responded. "I think the jury said we didn't prove Marjorie Caldwell did it. I have no doubt whatsoever that Roger Caldwell is guilty."

Minutes later, DeSanto and Lana left the courthouse to drive back to the house, followed by Waller and Rubin. While the grueling four-month trial didn't go the way he'd hoped, there was one bright spot for DeSanto now that the ordeal was over. He and Lana could finally get married.

In Waller and Rubin's car, a familiar song played on the radio—"Fool if You Think It's Over." I'll never get over this case, Waller thought. For Waller, DeSanto, and Rubin, the homecoming felt more like a wake. No one said much that night at dinner, each person lost in thoughts of what-ifs and why-nots.

Across town, the jurors celebrated at the Mississippi Belle restaurant, where they had shared many meals over the past three months. Marjorie and her defense team were among those invited as guests of honor. But Marjorie and her attorneys celebrated at Meshbesher's brother's house instead. Meshbesher celebrated one of the biggest victories of his life that night. "It may have been the biggest because public attention was focused on it so much," said Meshbesher. "And people didn't think I was going to win it."

In his prison cell Roger heard the news on his radio. He told the St. Paul Pioneer Press that his wife's acquittal made him "extremely happy, ecstatic, elated, and any other adjective toward joy." Caldwell was optimistic that the fingerprint testimony and Byers' alibi statements would mean a new trial for him.

Sitting alone in his room late that night, DeSanto continued the entry he had started hours before.

Saturday, July 21
Tried to call Meshbesher at his office and congratulate him. Early afternoon. Later tried to call about 5:30, 5:45 at his home. He wasn't there. Tried his brother's. Couldn't reach him. Will try again on Sunday.

If Marjorie had been convicted, much of the evidence used in her and Roger's trials would have remained in Dakota County. But her acquittal meant that the prosecution would have to return the evidence to Crow Wing County, site of Roger's trial. On Sunday, DeSanto and Waller boxed up volumes of notes, interview statements, police reports, and transcripts, then drove it all back to the Brainerd courthouse. Marjorie later told reporters she spent the afternoon at St. Paul's Como Park Zoo and treated herself to a bag of White Castle hamburgers.

DeSanto's final diary entry was made the next day:

Monday, July 23
Cleaning up. Getting ready to move back. Picking up all the notes for final argument from the floor to throw away. Hundreds of pages of notes.

In the weeks following Marjorie's trial, DeSanto's life slowly began to return to a more normal rhythm and routine. The outrage had given way to plain disappointment and a twinge of sadness at the verdict that set Marjorie free. DeSanto closed on the house in Duluth that he had shown his fiancée the day he had proposed. They had to decide on the final details of their wedding. Back at the office, his new caseload included another murder.

CHAPTER 20

Husbands

MARJORIE NEEDED A MAN IN HER LIFE. She found happiness whenever she found a man she could dominate, yet count on to protect her against creditors, family members, and the world at large. She expected marriage to be passionate and all consuming, and if she smothered at times, she did so in the name of love. But when a man could no longer keep up with her demands, Marjorie moved on. A few months after Roger's guilty verdict, she had become involved with Wallace "Wally" Hagen, a seventy-year-old retired electrician from Minneapolis. Wally, a silver-haired ladies' man twenty-three years her senior, prided himself on his lean, muscular frame built by years of physical labor. Wally and Marjorie had a problem, however. Although Roger was safely away in prison, Wally's wife wasn't. And she had no plans to leave.

Helen Hagen had been a friend of Marjorie's since the early 1960s, during Marjorie's marriage to Dick LeRoy. Helen and Marjorie had met at the Ice Center, where their children took figure skating lessons. The Hagens had three children, Dick, Tom, and Nancy; only Tom and Nancy skated.

Marjorie and Helen were alike in many ways. They pushed their children to excel, challenged their children's coaches, and spent countless dollars and hours to help ensure success. Fortunately for the women's friendship, Tom and Nancy, pairs skaters, didn't compete with the LeRoy children.

Helen and Marjorie saw a lot of one another in those years, not only at the lessons and practice sessions, but at competitions as well. As Stephen LeRoy and Tom and Nancy Hagen advanced to compete regionally and nationally, their mothers stayed by their sides. However, the Hagens and LeRoys socialized very little away from the rink, except for the occasional breakfasts with all the kids after the morning practice. At that time, Wally hardly knew Marjorie.

"The fathers worked. The mothers schlepped the kids to the rink," Nancy explained.

Despite Olympic hopes, the Hagen children quit skating; Tom's decision to get married after college had ended the brother-sister team. Marjorie and Helen communicated only infrequently in the years that followed—until the time of Elisabeth's murder.

"When I told Mom of [Elisabeth's] death, Mom somehow got in contact with Marge," Nancy recalled. "Through whom or how I don't know."

Marjorie turned to her old friends for support after her husband's arrest and during the murder trial. The Hagens invited her to stay at their house until they helped her find an apartment. Marjorie confided in the Hagens that she was broke. The couple began taking her out for dinner. "My folks gave Marge money," Nancy said. "We gave her clothing for the kids."

Marjorie told the Hagens that Roger was innocent and that the jewelry, garment bag, and other evidence against him was a frame-up. Marjorie insisted that Roger was in bed with her at the time of the murders. She reminded the Hagens that Ricky had testified he saw a head in bed next to her at the Holland House Hotel early June 27. The Hagens readily accepted Marjorie's story.

After his conviction, Roger began to reconnect with his past as well. He received a letter from his parents in January 1979, in which they included news of his three children, Caren, Scott, and Christi. Caren was looking for work in her field of anthropology, Scott was playing the piano for a living and writing music, and Christi and her husband had bought a house. They "were all upset when you were found guilty, as they were so sure you would be acquitted. Roger, they really do care about you and hope you will soon be free," his parents wrote.

Estranged from his children for years, Roger eventually tried to reconnect with them. He began regularly corresponding with daughter Christi, who enjoyed swapping jokes with her father. Roger had also begun to fancy himself a writer while in prison, and Christi was not afraid to poke fun at this, as shown in this May 6, 1979, letter:

> Daddy-do-day-day!
>
> I loved the Monty Python cartoon. The other cartoons were also cute. Your poetry… what can I say? It's a good thing you never had to make a living on it! Just kidding.
>
> Thanks for the histories on the family names. That's something you might make a living at, you know. Please continue the histories and the book reviews and even the poetry.
>
> If you can write poetry I suppose I can try. Here's something I thought up regarding your unfortunate situation:
>
> > Oh Father dear,
> > It would appear,
> > You've taken a long walk
> > Off a very short pier!
>
> Isn't that awful? It's the best I can do!…Enough of this drivel! Health and Prestige!
> Love, Christi

In one of his "rambles and starts of things," Roger wrote that he wondered "if there's anything in this blue-eyed world that's worse than a sarcastic finger-pointing daughter that giggles and snorts over her own reluctant agreement with her dear old dad because his warped viewpoints are so similar to hers, and she knows full well how she's arrived at her own opinions, by reading deep thinkers like Erma Bombeck. I'd suppose one thing worse would be having a daughter with no sense of humor at all. I'm very fortunate though, in that both of my daughters have demonstrable wit."

Years before, when Roger learned that Scott was gay, he had been angry and refused to accept it. Once, in a drunken stupor, he denounced Scott to his brother Howard Jr. as his "no good queer son." But time and circumstances had apparently softened Roger's outlook. After Scott first contacted him in prison, Roger wrote back that he had thought about writing before, but had waited for his son to make the first move toward reconciliation:

> Like you apparently, I'm somewhat at a loss for words too. How to actually begin something that I've done many times while I was wool gathering, presents me with approximately the same difficulty that you seem to have had in getting your letter off to me.... You'd no way of knowing that I'd be so absolutely delighted to have you write to me.
>
> Although you didn't say so directly, I still got the impression that you'd like us to try getting reacquainted. Not being at all sure how I might feel about it, you thought perhaps it would be better to see what my response to your friendly inquiry was before making any commitment. If that's right, I certainly can't fault your judgment.
>
> I'd be pleased, even happy, to "talk" with you about anything you'd care to bring up, and answer all and any questions that you may think I'm able. I'm neither reticent or shy...actually I'm more inclined toward being plain-spoken, irreverent, and cynical. I fancy myself a wit, but Christi would quickly tell you that I'm only half-witted.
>
> Thank you for writing to me; I'm just tickled pink to have heard from you.

Caren, however, remained estranged from her father while he was in prison. As one relative put it, "Caren disowned her father," and did not want anything to do with him.

Later in May 1979, Roger had offered Christi and her husband, Tim, all his "worldly possessions"—furniture and other items that he had left in storage when he entered prison. Christi wrote back with bad news that seemed like a refrain from his history with Marjorie. The items had either been sold or discarded by the moving and storage company a year earlier to pay off an outstanding $1,200 bill. The news in particular disappointed Christi, who had hoped to sell some of the furniture to raise money to visit her father.

Roger's family was hopeful about what Marjorie's acquittal might mean for him, as his father, Howard, noted on Monday, July 30, 1979:

> Well that was sure good to talk with you last week July 21…and to know you are in good with the world or so it looks to me, you should be as you did nothing to be in prison and we are so happy that Marge did so good in her being found not guilty.
>
> Marge's lawyer sure is a good one…with what he, Marge's lawyer, brought out for you that you was nowhere up at Minnesota. I won't go in for that, you know what I am talking about.
>
> We have had no papers from [your brother] Dave for a week or 5 days about you and Marge, but will catch up one of these days. Mom and I think it will turn around for you

now and they will get you out and free, now you know you are a lot better off without drinking. So please don't ever drink again.

Others connected to the case tried to get on with their lives. On the afternoon of November 3, 1979, as the last of autumn's crimson and gold leaves dusted the ground, John DeSanto and Lana Eckenberg were married at Duluth's St. Michael's Catholic Church, DeSanto's childhood parish. About four hundred people attended the formal ceremony. The wedding party included groomsman Gary Waller and usher Mark Rubin. Waller's daughter, Bridget, served as the flower girl. They held the reception downtown in the ballroom of the venerable Hotel Duluth, site of Jeno Paulucci's birthday party and DeSanto's celebration of Roger's conviction. The DeSantos honeymooned in Florida at New Smyrna Beach, just south of Daytona Beach. They stayed in Paulucci's beach front condominium, spending lazy days in the sun. DeSanto considered the Congdon case closed. And it was—for the time being.

Besides corresponding with his family, Roger still kept in touch with David Arnold, who visited him in prison. Roger counted Arnold as one of his few friends, someone who didn't judge him based on his past, someone willing to give his future the benefit of the doubt. Roger wrote Arnold on December 13, 1979:

> You probably never will fully understand the pleasure I received today in just seeing that the envelope that I was being handed had been sent from your office. Creeping paranoia being what it is, I had just about convinced myself that I'd never be hearing from you again either. Oh yes, I correspond weekly with genetic members of my family, but I seldom ever get mail from anybody else any more. Even the cranks and the Jesus freaks have long since forgotten me, and doubtless have turned their effort toward some other poor victim. The adage…out of sight, out of mind…never had any real meaning for me until after my arrest.
>
> Your mentioning of Marge in such a casual way indicates that her charm is still very much intact, and I would assume along with it, her powers of persuasion as well. She does have a way of making folks want to believe and trust in her, even when they know full well that she is one of this world's truly great congenital liers [sic]. She surely must possess something magical, a quality that I've never seen in any other. After all, like yourself, I'm not anxious to admit to some inherent character weakness any quicker than anybody else is. But I shouldn't be picking on her, I guess, after all, even if I didn't really know what I was getting into when I married her, it sure didn't take me very long after that to figure things out. Boy, what a surprise!

Marjorie's charm had certainly worked on the Hagens, who had continued to stand by her, attended her trial, and cheered her acquittal. But by 1979, Helen began suffering memory lapses and having trouble speaking. Doctors diagnosed her as showing symptoms of Alzheimer's disease, then known as senility. During 1979 and early 1980, Helen reported unusual suspicions and incidents to her children—each involving Marjorie. But at the time, Helen's family dismissed her allegations as paranoia attributable to her disease.

Helen told Nancy that Marjorie had stolen her wedding rings after Nancy had them reset. "Mother and Dad went over to Marge's and showed the rings to her," Nancy recalled years later. "Marge asked Mom to take the rings off and she put them on. Mother told me, 'Marge took them and she never gave them back.' I asked my Dad, who says, 'No, it's one of those fantasy stories of hers again.'"

Nancy said, "My mother, for a good year and a half prior to her death, kept telling me my Dad was having an affair with Marge—and I didn't believe her." After her mother's death, when her father and Marjorie's relationship emerged, Hagen backtracked. She discovered that Wally had left her mother at the grocery store on a regular basis. Wally would leave Helen in an aisle and disappear for two hours. In the meantime, the store manager would get her a chair, where she'd sit and wait for Wally to return. Sometimes he had left Helen at home. He met Marjorie regularly at a nearby Country Kitchen restaurant at one or two o'clock in the afternoon.

As the Alzheimer's progressed, Helen had great difficulty with her speech. Her daughter recalled that, particularly around people she didn't know well, Helen stuttered so badly that she couldn't communicate.

Nancy worked two jobs to help her parents with the mounting medical bills. Divorced at the time, she sold her diamond engagement ring to raise money. She also decided to return a five-piece pewter set Marjorie had given her as a wedding present, but had some trouble getting a refund at the downtown Minneapolis jewelry store where Marjorie had purchased it.

The sales clerk snatched the tea set and excused herself to get the store manager, leaving Hagen to wonder what was going on. The store manager emerged and told Hagen, "This pewter set belongs to us. We will issue a store credit." When Hagen said the set belonged to her, the manager told her Marjorie had never paid for it. He then added that "Mrs. LeRoy left Nicollet Avenue with over $500,000 worth of credit card debts." The wedding present was hot.

On March 3, 1980, Helen was hospitalized at Abbott Northwestern Hospital in Minneapolis for complications from Alzheimer's disease and diabetes (she had been previously diagnosed as diabetic). Helen had difficulty swallowing, she wouldn't take fluids, and she had digestive and speech problems. She was released several weeks later and admitted to Twin Birch Nursing Home in Mound. Nancy had moved into her parents' house and was helping make the mortgage payments.

On the day of her admission, Sunday, March 23, Helen arrived in excellent physical condition—except for the effects of the Alzheimer's. Her family visited her often those first few days. When Nancy stopped by on Wednesday night, March 26, Helen was a little incoherent, but able to sit up in bed and talk with her daughter. It thrilled her to find her mother cognizant enough to recognize her and carry on a normal conversation. Helen was having trouble moving her arms however, so Nancy fed her dinner, baked chicken and spaghetti. She stayed about an hour and a half, leaving around 7 P.M.

Shortly before eleven on Thursday morning, March 27, the nursing home called Nancy at work to notify her that Helen had gone into a coma. Nancy was stunned. She drove her father to the nursing home. On the way, they talked about the possibility that Helen might die. If death was inevitable, they decided against placing her on life support.

After Nancy and her father arrived at the nursing home, they hurried to Helen's room. No one on the medical staff could explain what had happened to Helen. Nancy watched as a nurse tried to provoke some response from Helen as she inserted a thin needle into Helen's foot. Helen didn't flinch.

As the nurse worked on her mother, Nancy glanced down at the medical chart posted at the base of her mother's bed. A handwritten notation caught her eye. In case of an emergency, the nursing home was to call Marjorie LeRoy, daughter of Helen Hagen. Nancy's name had been scratched out.

Nancy immediately informed the head nurse, "Marjorie Caldwell is not Helen Hagen's daughter. I am." The nurse told Nancy that Marjorie had been in the previous night to visit Helen. During the visit, Marjorie had fed Helen from baby food jars, the nurse said.

"I just attributed that to Marge's way of being helpful," Nancy said. "She's a very pushy woman. I mean she tries to take control of things." Nancy, of course, did not know about the marmalade incident.

From the nursing home, Nancy called her mother's physician to advise him of Helen's condition. He told Nancy he was surprised to hear that Helen had slipped into a coma. Aside from the brain deterioration caused by the Alzheimer's, Helen's physical condition had been stabilized, the doctor told her.

Helen never came out of the coma. She died on Palm Sunday, March 30, 1980, one week after entering the nursing home. Helen's death baffled her doctor. In his experience, a patient in Helen's condition and age—she was sixty-three—should have lived twelve to fifteen more years. The Minnesota Bureau of Criminal Apprehension investigated Helen's death, but no charges were ever filed.

The autopsy failed to illuminate a precise reason for the swiftness of Helen's decline, but confirmed the diagnosis of Alzheimer's disease and the debilitating effects of diabetes. The doctors, also unaware of the marmalade incident, didn't have any reason to generate a toxicology report, unfortunately; an overdose of meprobamate—the drug that Marjorie was suspected of putting in the marmalade which she fed her mother in 1974—can induce coma, as can other drugs, such as barbiturates. The coroner listed pneumonia brought on by dehydration as the official cause of death. The autopsy also revealed the presence of protein rich fluid in the lungs, a possible sign of early pneumonia. Helen's funeral was held on Wednesday, April 3, at the Union Cemetery in Mound, located near the house where she had raised her children. After a simple graveside service, Helen's remains were buried alongside a plot designated for Wally. Nancy had paid for the plot; Wally claimed he didn't have the money. Wally and his children donated Helen's brain to the University of Minnesota for Alzheimer's research.

The day of Helen's funeral, the entire family and Marjorie sat in the Hagen's living room and Nancy, executor of her mother's estate, read the will. Their mother's will stated that the real estate she owned, including the house and three other lots, was to go to her children. Her husband Wally could continue to live on the property until his death, at which time the house would go to Nancy.

A week later, Nancy recalled, "all hell broke loose." She was in the living room reading when Wally confronted her, his voice hard and callous.

"You know I'm going to tell you right now I hated your mother for the forty-three years I was with her."

"Then why did you stay with her, Dad?"

"Because of you kids."

"Dad, I'm thirty-six years old. I've been out of the house twenty years. Can't you give a better reason?"

Wally couldn't or wouldn't answer his daughter's question. Instead, he turned his back on Nancy and hurriedly walked out the door toward the car parked outside, where Marjorie sat waiting.

Wally and Marjorie's relationship quickly grew more openly intimate. Wally began spending nights at Marjorie's house. He said he didn't care what anyone thought of his involvement with another woman so soon after his wife's death. He was clearly infatuated with Marjorie. But his children were more concerned, however, by their father's mood swings, which included unprovoked fits of anger. And the children soon learned that Marjorie had begun pressuring their father to settle the estate and liquidate all of Helen's property.

Following the outcome of Marjorie's trial, Roger had petitioned for a new trial; the request had received two hearings in Duluth District Court before Judge Litman, one in September 1979 and another in February 1980. Roger had asked for a new trial based on new evidence that included the alibi testimony of Holland House waitress Candace Byers and the discredited thumbprint on the envelope. Three jurors from Roger's trial had made headlines when they publicly stated that he deserved a second trial because of new evidence presented at Marjorie's trial. "If the fingerprint had been disproved at Roger Caldwell's trial, I don't believe I would have voted the way I did," said juror Minna Wallin. "I feel he's been framed. But I could be wrong. Maybe I'm trying to ease my conscience." The other two jurors supported a new trial to get all the evidence presented, but clarified that they were not implying that Roger was innocent.

Judge Litman denied Roger's request for a new trial on April 21, 1980. The judge did not believe that if the jury had heard the new evidence brought out at Marjorie's trial that it would have made a difference. Doug Thomson appealed Judge Litman's ruling in the Minnesota Supreme Court on May 30. The following month Roger wrote Arnold:

I'll not let the bastards beat me. They'll never, any of them, ever have the satisfaction of even being able to THINK that I've given up with my intention of winning, and beating THEM within the confines of their own system, becoming freed again myself, and in time seeing that those who have had a hand in my having been mistreated like this, seeing that somehow each one of them is made to pay for the wrong that's been done.

One of Helen Hagen's best friends surprised Nancy with a phone call, telling Nancy that Wally had just visited her unexpectedly. Wally had asked her to swear under oath that Helen was crazy when she made out her will. The friend refused. She told Nancy, "I was very shocked when Wally asked me if I would testify that Helen was not rational. She was always perfectly rational and good company whenever I was with her; we had many good times together."

Wally asked his son Tom to sign over his inheritance rights to his mother's estate so Wally would be the one to divide up the property. Tom recalled, "I asked a lawyer, I said 'Look, what is the situation here. We don't want to screw my Dad out of anything.' And the lawyer replied, 'You cannot sign over your inheritance rights to anybody.'"

Tom called and confronted his father. "Dad," he said, "you're lying to me. I know why you're lying. You guys want to try and protect your interest, what you consider your interest. I have to protect what I consider my interest…and let the chips fall where they may." Wally called his son back later that day and told Tom, "I don't have a son and I don't ever want to talk to you again as long as I live."

Likewise, Dick Hagen was angered by a visit from Marjorie's son Rick, who dropped off a release form for him to sign that would relinquish control of the property to his father. Dick refused to sign over his inheritance rights. Wally reacted the same way as he had with Tom. He never wanted to see or talk to Dick again. "If you want to talk to me, contact my attorney," Wally said. Within a month of Helen's death, Wally packed his clothes, moved out of the family home, and moved in with Marjorie.

Nancy later told authorities that after her father moved out, "Marjorie almost convinced me that I was crazy." Arriving home at night she would find the lights on or the doors open. Sometimes she received phone calls in the middle of the night and an anonymous caller would tell her, "We're out to get you."

Nancy's brothers were skeptical at first, but that changed the night her home was burglarized. Nancy had arrived home at 11 P.M. to find the house open, all the lights on, and the dogs running free in the yard. The house had been ransacked. Drawers had been opened and their contents dumped and scattered. The few family photographs they had were destroyed or missing. Helen's will—along with numerous receipts and invoices—had disappeared. Nancy had saved the paperwork in order to be reimbursed for the more than $50,000 she had spent paying her parents' medical and other bills (she had mortgaged her house to help out). Nancy eventually learned that the money she had given her father had gone to Wally's and Marjorie's needs because, as Wally later said, Marjorie had told him that his wife's care and medical bills were not his responsibility. Nancy has always believed that Marjorie was responsible for the break-in.

Nancy made no effort to hide her distrust of Marjorie, but her father wouldn't hear a bad word about his new companion. No doubt Marjorie was also aware of how Wally's daughter felt about her. In the months after Helen's death, Marjorie tried to pit the Hagen children against one another. Marjorie and Wally told Dick and Tom that their sister was being irresponsible with the money their mother had left behind and charging on Helen's credit cards—both lies. Marjorie's bogus accusations described actions typical of her own behavior.

Nancy moved out that summer and within a week Wally and Marjorie had cleaned out the house and sold the furniture. Eventually the estate was divided up: Wally received about $40,000, Tom and Dick got about $9,000, and Nancy got slightly more, because of the money she had paid to cover her father's bills.

While Marjorie's relationship with Wally grew more serious, Roger languished in prison, hoping for a new trial. Arnold wrote on November 13, 1980:

> Dear Roger:
>
> I continue to marvel at your ability to stimulate a wry smile from me upon reading your correspondence. The smile does not relate to your plight of incarceration, but rather in response to your ability to use the King's English to extract even the minutest wry humor. Your correspondence often leaves me with the feeling that you and Mt. St. Helens may share a common attribute, that is, your ability to camouflage the seething inferno below. Unlike St. Helens, you have apparently learned the magic of withholding any eruption.

Roger still seemed upbeat in June of 1981 when he wrote Arnold that he was celebrating his first year of not smoking. In the same letter, Roger noted that he had once again been the lead item in the local news:

> I've no way of knowing if you had heard about my clumsiness or not...I stumbled and fell on the stairs, cracked my forehead enough that I took some stitches, and this was enough of an incident to become the lead-off story on the ten o'clock news over channel five last Saturday night...so you can tell what kind of a news day they must have had.

The next month, however, his ability to "withhold any eruption" would be tested. On July 21, 1981, he wrote a letter to Thomson with some disturbing news:

> Last Wednesday Dave Arnold came out to see me. My wife had requested him to tell me that she wanted a divorce. As is usually the case with her, she wanted it accomplished in an underhanded, secretive, and in all likelihood an illegal manner. Arnold told me that he tried to reason with her, advising her that not only were her methods wrong, but that a divorce at this particular time would probably be detrimental to her as well as to me.
>
> Now you know as well as I, as well as anyone of good judgment knows who has ever spent more than an hour's time with her, that she's unstable and prone to bizarre thoughts and actions, particularly whenever she's been denied something, even trivial things...which is my reason for writing you.
>
> Without knowing any more than what passed onto me by Dave Arnold, I would expect that she has conjured up unimaginable dreams based upon what she would do once her

plan was accepted. Refusal will likely drive her to God knows what kind of berserk activities, none of which can possibly be beneficial to me.

Perhaps you and I should discuss the ramifications of her request before you submit your final brief, on my behalf, to the state Supreme Court?

Marjorie Congdon Leroy Caldwell married Wally Hagen on August 7, 1981. She hadn't bothered to divorce Roger, so she applied for a marriage license in North Dakota, where no one recognized her or her name—which she gave as LeRoy. The newlyweds continued to live in Marjorie's house, which they shared with Rick when he came home from college.

Wally's children doubted love had much to do with Marjorie's marriage to their father. "Marge needed my dad for his credit rating," Nancy later said. "My dad has always needed to have a female." She said she'll never forget when she learned of the marriage. After many months of no contact, Wally surprised her by just walking into the bathroom as she got ready for a friend's wedding. Wally picked up his five-year-old grandson, Michael, looked at his daughter, and said, "I just want you to know I married Marge yesterday." Then he set Michael down, who had been thrilled to see him, walked out the door, and drove off with Marjorie.

Wally's younger son Tom noted that besides their mutual attraction to his father, his mother and stepmother also shared a similar trait. "My mother was a dominant woman. And Marge is a dominant woman," Tom Hagen said.

Bigamy wasn't Marjorie's only legal trouble. Five of her children—Suzanne, Peter, Heather, Andrew, and Rebecca—had legally challenged her right to share in the Congdon inheritance. The history of this suit stretched back to before either of the trials. Jennifer Johnson recalled that after the murders "Everybody said it was Marjorie. I don't know of anyone in the family who thought it wasn't."

In August 1977, trustees Salisbury Adams, Thomas Congdon, and Bill Van Evera had gone to probate court to challenge Marjorie and Jennifer's inheritance from their mother's estate, noting that Chester Congdon's will did not provide for adopted children. This had been done with Jennifer's knowledge and cooperation; the sole intent was to keep Marjorie from getting any money. The probate judge, however, had determined that Marjorie and Jennifer were entitled to their inheritance.

That was when her children, except Stephen and Rick, had filed a civil lawsuit against Marjorie in St. Louis County probate court. After her acquittal, her three daughters had continued to contest her eligibility and requested a probate hearing to determine whether she was involved in the murders. Minnesota law prohibited a person who feloniously and intentionally killed another from sharing in the victim's estate. Although Marjorie had been acquitted of criminal charges, her possible involvement could again be raised in a civil trial, where the standard of proof was "a preponderance of the evidence" as opposed to "proof beyond a reasonable doubt."

Until the dispute was settled, Marjorie's portion of the family trusts was being kept in a special account. In an interview in August 1979, Marjorie claimed to be virtually destitute. "My dishes and blankets are only through the courtesy of friends," she said. She also reinvented her natural parents, saying that they were "two fourteen- and fifteen-year-old farm kids of French and Irish descent." Acknowledging that she had spent a lot over the years, she said she "never had learned how to handle money. I wasn't prepared for it." She told the *Duluth News-Tribune*, "I'll be damned if I'll be put up to a guilt trip for spending it on my kids." However, in the same interview, Marjorie said she now realized that some of her children were "selfish little pigs" who kept demanding more. She sharply criticized her children for challenging her right to collect her inheritance. "Obviously, I gave them too damn much," Marjorie said. As with her accusations about Nancy being irresponsible with money, Marjorie's portrayal of her children's greed sounded more like a description of herself.

In August 1981, the Minnesota Supreme Court ruled that the lawsuit was valid. Despite Marjorie's acquittal on murder conspiracy charges in Hastings, the LeRoy children could try to prove their mother's involvement. If their efforts to disinherit her succeeded, Marjorie would lose her share of Elisabeth's estate and her children stood to inherit about $3.2 million.

The civil suit had already exposed perjured testimony given at Marjorie's trial. Richard Solum and Alan Eidsness, the children's attorneys, had traveled to Colorado in 1980 to reinterview key witnesses from the criminal trials about the Caldwells' activities. The interviewees included former Holland House Hotel waitress Candace Byers, the last-minute, surprise witness for the defense at Marjorie's trial. Byers had told the jury she saw Roger coming down the stairs into the Holland House lobby around 10 P.M., Sunday, June 26. The jury's acquittal of Marjorie indicated they considered Byers a plausible witness.

But Byers said something different in 1980. Maybe she was mistaken, she said, about having seen Roger just hours before the murders. Solum and Eidsness could hardly believe their ears. Byers was the only person—other than Rick, who had claimed at Roger's trial to have seen "some hair" and "lumps under the covers" that he took to be his stepdad—who claimed to have seen Roger during the twenty-four hour period leading up to the killings. A recantation would boost their clients' civil case by destroying Roger's new alibi.

Solum returned to Colorado in November 1981, to reinterview Byers. This time he asked her for a written statement on why she testified as she did in Hastings.

During Marjorie's trial, Meshbesher's investigator Vincent Carraher and attorney Frank Berman had questioned Byers at length. The two men wondered what she remembered about the weekend of the murders. They asked if it was possible she might have seen Roger at the Holland House on June 26. When she wasn't certain she recalled seeing Roger, the two men told her to think hard, because they needed her help to prevent further injustice to the Caldwells. Byers told Solum that Carraher and Berman then led her to believe Roger was ill and dying in prison for a crime he didn't commit.

During persistent questioning by Carraher and Berman, Byers told the two men she now remembered seeing Roger at the hotel about 10 P.M. on Sunday, June 26. Although Carraher and Berman then told Byers her sighting wasn't that important, they extracted a promise that she wouldn't talk to anyone else.

As Solum's deposition continued, Byers said that after the defense team brought her to Hastings, they rehearsed her testimony, rephrasing answers they didn't like. They told her to be positive about her sighting of Roger.

Byers now told Solum she felt more comfortable with her original story and the statements she gave police the week after the murders. The two statements indicated that Byers didn't see Roger, Marjorie, or Rick on Saturday, June 25, or Sunday, June 26.

Byers concluded the deposition, saying she believed she misled the jury in Hastings and had been troubled by this for some time. She told Solum it relieved her to finally tell the truth and get this information off her chest. In short, Byers admitted to perjury.

In yet another twist, even though Byers had now admitted in writing that her key testimony had been false, the Minnesota Supreme Court had already agreed to hear Roger's new trial appeal—which had, in part, been based on the alibi Byers had given him. On October 2, 1981, Doug Thomson delivered the news to his client. Oral arguments in the appeal had been set for November 3, 1981, before the nine-judge panel. However, Thomson wrote, Roger's request to be present would not be honored as the Supreme Court did not permit defendants to attend. Other things were not going well for Roger; rumors of Marjorie's bigamy had started to spread.

On December 24, 1981, Arnold wrote Roger:

> After our last visit and my disclosure to you of Marge's request of me, I tried to reach her to convey your response. She has not seen fit to respond to my telephone calls or letters. However, at your request, I did advise both Doug [Thomson] and Ron [Meshbesher] of the matter and they were "shocked" to say the least. Shortly thereafter, at lunch, I was advised by one of my associates who attends the same church that Marge does, that an announcement of the marriage of Marge to Wally was made in church. After the services, they presided at a "coffee" gathering. Disbelieving that Marge had in fact secured a divorce without apparent word to you (presumably you would have advised me), I checked the Hennepin County records and found no indication that she had in fact been married. Ron denied any knowledge of the occurrence and in fact was speechless when I inquired as to the veracity of the allegation. He indicated that he had been unable to contact her since she failed to return any phone calls or respond to any written communication also.
>
> After receiving several telephone calls from Tom Welch, since he had also heard the "rumors," he called to say that Wally had confirmed in person that they were not married. It would therefore appear that the announcement of "marriage" was made for the purpose of appearance rather than having any basis in fact.

Even with her history, Marjorie continued to fool people, and Wally was obviously playing along.

When Gary Waller learned of Byers' latest story, he contacted the FBI about getting involved in the case. He asked Special Agent Robert Harvey to assist in obtaining a new statement from Byers. The perjury had occurred as part of a murder and conspiracy case with multi-state jurisdiction, Waller reminded Harvey. On January 7, 1982, Special Agent Harvey obtained a waiver from officials in Dakota County, where Marjorie Caldwell's trial was held. Byers was guaranteed immunity from prosecution, despite having lied under oath.

Six days later, FBI Special Agent Harvey telephoned Byers in Denver. Arrangements had been made for a conference call; Detective Waller listened in at Duluth Police headquarters and Solum from his Minneapolis law office. This time, Byers went even further than she had during her previous conversation with Solum. She admitted she'd lied about seeing Roger on the staircase at the Holland House Hotel on Sunday evening, June 26, 1977.

Before Harvey hung up the phone, he'd made one thing clear to Byers. The FBI wanted her recantation in writing. So the following week, on January 21, Harvey interviewed Byers in her Denver home and obtained the following signed statement:

> I was employed at the Holland House in Golden, Colorado, May of 1977 until about February or March, 1978. I was employed as a waitress and through my employment I met Roger and Marjorie Caldwell and Ricky LeRoy who resided at the Hotel and often ate in the coffee shop and I served them numerous times. My normal workdays were Friday, Saturday, Sunday, Monday with the next two to three days off.
>
> On July 2nd, 1979, I appeared in State Court in Hastings, Minnesota, as a witness for the defense. I testified under oath that I had seen Roger Caldwell in the staircase leading into [the] lobby from upstairs at the Holland House about 10 P.M. on the evening of June 26, 1977, which is a Sunday. This statement was not true and my testimony in that matter was untruthful.
>
> I know now that my testimony in Hastings, Minnesota, misled the jury and court proceedings in the Marjorie Caldwell case.
>
> My testimony to seeing Roger Caldwell has been bothering me since the time I gave it and I even wanted to tell the truth prior to going on the stand, but I didn't.
>
> I am very confident that I can and did tell the truth about not seeing Roger Caldwell on the evening of Sunday, June 26, 1977, and furthermore I had not seen him after I served his stepson, Ricky LeRoy, either Friday or Saturday prior to June 26, 1977. I remember several days later that I had observed a newscast about the murders and I thought about not seeing Roger or Marjorie Caldwell around for about a week.

Besides her signed statement, Byers gave Harvey additional information about her testimony in Hastings. She had picked up a prepaid airline ticket at the Denver airport and flew to Minnesota the night before she would take the stand. Berman met Byers at the airport and drove her to her hotel. There she met with Berman, Meshbesher, and attorney Carol Grant. They all reviewed her testimony over dinner.

Byers told Special Agent Harvey that Meshbesher never asked her if she had seen Roger on June 26. Instead, he asked, "When you saw Roger Caldwell on June 26, 1977...." They instructed Byers not to say she thought or she believed she had seen Caldwell, but to be positive. If she wasn't positive on the stand, Byers recalled, Meshbesher said that "ogre" prosecutor John DeSanto will "cut you apart."

But despite its significance for discrediting Roger's alibi, Byers' recantation changed nothing in Marjorie's case. The statement became part of the official evidence, but a retrial would have been double jeopardy—having once been tried and acquitted of her mother's murder, Marjorie could never be tried for the murder again, at least in criminal court.

Waller and DeSanto remained convinced that Marjorie had been involved in her mother's death, and now Byers' statement helped solidify that belief. If they had spoken at that time with Helen Hagen's children, they would have suspected, as Helen's children did, that Marjorie had now also gotten away with killing someone else's mother.

CHAPTER 21

A Killer Goes Free

I DO THINK OF YOU OFTEN, PROBABLY EVEN DAILY, frequently in connection with what my wife (of six years now) might be doing and what new escapades she might have involved herself with," Roger wrote Arnold early in 1982. They still awaited the Minnesota Supreme Court's decision on a new trial. Roger was hopeful, but skeptical that his life would change for the better no matter what the high court's decision. He continued:

> I've wondered too if I'm still as welcome as I once was to call upon you for help if I might need it. Who knows, I could "be on the streets" soon, as they say in here, and as you can well imagine I'd be in terrible need of assistance for at least a short while. Nothing has changed with me in that regard. I still am without friends anywhere in Minnesota, and I'd be floundering around pretty badly if not offered a hand by someone. I don't even have anywhere that I could spend the night.
>
> Even though it is one option of the [Supreme Court], I'm really not expecting my physical personage to find itself completely freed by them. It's far more likely that I'll find myself in another jail cell somewhere awaiting the pleasures of those good people of Duluth, MN.

Arnold wrote Roger in April:

> I continue to be amazed at how slow the wheels of justice do grind. I look each Friday in our Supreme Court Decision periodical for the Court's Order granting a new trial in the matter. Hopefully, that will be shortly forthcoming.
>
> Strangely enough, Marge seems to have drifted into the sunset at least in terms of her occasional visits with me. I am also led to believe that she does not stay in contact with any of her numerous attorneys, but prefers to live a very quiet life in Mound, MN. Since she attends the same church as one of our associates, I do periodically receive little newsy tidbits, all of which I quickly discard as mere rumor.

Arnold renewed an offer he had previously made to Roger. If he was released from prison, Roger could stay with Arnold and his family in the Twin Cities. "It goes without saying that the welcome mat is still out for you as soon as you are able to take us up on the offer and we'll do all that we can to reacquaint you with many of the joys of freedom that we take so much for granted," he wrote.

Meanwhile, Marjorie's new husband was getting into the act. Wally had an expensive ruby he had purchased for $500 while working in Venezuela in the late 1950s. Wally told the North Star Mutual Insurance Company he lost the ruby at the Shrine Circus in March 1982. Although the ring had never been insured previously, Wally had recently taken out a floater policy. He told the insurance adjuster that the ring had been appraised at $16,000 the week before. Nancy Hagen Kaufmann recalled years later that Marjorie pressured the adjuster to pay the insurance claim because she and Wally needed the money to buy property. The insurance company paid Wally $11,100.

That summer, in July 1982, Marjorie and Wally visited Swiftwater Farm, resulting in a complaint filed with the Brule County Sheriff by Peter LeRoy. He called the sheriff's department after he observed the Hagens moving furniture out of the guest house and caretaker cottage. A sheriff's deputy made Marjorie and Wally return the furniture.

That June, Arnold wrote Roger, "I couldn't help but think that it's almost been 5 years of incarceration for you. June does not hold many happy thoughts for me.... I am hopeful that I will be out to see you soon and in the interim, our Supreme Court will rule on the matter of your pending appeal. Take care and keep the faith."

Roger replied to his "dear good friend David:"

> I'm tired, so I shouldn't be writing I guess. Weary actually; in no fit state to think sensibly on any subject. You see, yesterday was the fifth anniversary of my engagement and I'm afraid that I tended to sulk a bit. This Saturday will be the anniversary of my being brought to prison—four years ago now—and I suppose I'll probably get sulky again then too. Too bad about me, huh? One might have thought I'd have adjusted better by now and grown more philosophic toward my situation or, at least, maintained this facade of sarcastic humor just a bit longer. But I haven't. GOSH! I sure hope I haven't let anyone down....
>
> And please don't feel that you need to apologize for not being able to find time to come out here and "visit" with me.... Not to worry! Really! Plenty of time for visiting later on, once I'm out and under more favorable circumstance. Just knowing of your willingness to help me after I've gained my freedom again, more than compensates....
>
> You signed off your letter by asking me to "take care and keep the faith" so I'll assure you that I'm as careful as I know how to be. Faith? Sorry. I've none. That's been taken from me too. But come see me when you can. Until then my friend.

John and Lana DeSanto celebrated the birth of their first child, Amy Lee, on July 22, 1982. DeSanto had lightened his case load so he could take two weeks off to help care for the baby. Less than two weeks later, John and Lana were getting used to their daughter's demands to be fed every four hours. Early the morning of Friday, August 6, they'd expected to be awakened by Amy's crying, not the shrill ring of the bedroom telephone.

DeSanto glanced over at the alarm clock on the night stand as his wife groggily answered. It read 1:30 A.M. His wife said, "Just a minute. He's right here." Probably the police or sheriff's department, he thought, calling about a search warrant.

Lana handed the phone to her husband, the cord stretching tightly across the bed. The night copy desk editor for the *Duluth Herald* was on the line. "Are you going to retry Roger Caldwell?" he asked.

"I don't know," DeSanto answered, surprised by the question.

"What is your reaction to the Supreme Court's decision?" the reporter continued.

"What decision?" DeSanto asked, still not comprehending the reporter's line of questioning. The Minnesota Supreme Court had been deliberating Roger's appeal since winter. Although a lengthy deliberation usually doesn't bode well for the prosecution, DeSanto hadn't worried. Surely, they had gathered enough other evidence—hair and blood, the gold coin, and handwriting analysis—to sustain the conviction.

But the reporter told DeSanto he had a copy of the court's decision, which would be announced later that morning. The Supreme Court had overturned Roger's conviction and ordered a retrial. The court cited the controversial fingerprint on the envelope as the main reason it overturned the verdict.

The news stunned DeSanto. He hadn't even received his courtesy copy of the court's opinion. Usually each side would receive notice on Thursday, the day before the court officially announced its decisions. He sat speechless for a minute. "No comment until I've read the Supreme Court's opinion," DeSanto said crisply, then slammed the receiver down in disgust. Then he sat shaking, frozen on the side of the bed. Lana, now wide awake, saw her husband's ashen face and stricken eyes. Bad news, she thought, someone in John's family has died. "John, what's the matter?" she asked. "Who was that?"

He slowly got up and knelt down in front of her at the side of the bed. "The Supreme Court reversed Roger Caldwell's conviction," DeSanto told his wife, unsuccessfully fighting back tears. Lana put her arms around her husband and cried with him, trying to console him.

Minutes later, despite the late hour, DeSanto called his parents. He didn't want them to learn the disappointing news from the morning paper. "I'm so sorry. Don't worry, everything will be okay," his mother advised. "Get some sleep. We'll talk with you in the morning."

DeSanto also phoned Waller. Although used to having his sleep interrupted, he wasn't prepared for the news. "Oh, shit. I can't believe you and I have to go through this again," Waller said.

Both men slept very little the rest of the night. For DeSanto, daughter Amy's nocturnal feedings came as a welcome distraction. After two long trials and two years of appeals, DeSanto knew the case would never be completely behind him. But he hadn't anticipated a new trial for Roger. At the moment, he couldn't stomach the thought—he was too tired and disheartened.

Several hours later, a restless DeSanto and his wife took Amy out in her stroller down to the park near their house. As they walked along the Lester River, DeSanto told Lana he was thinking about quitting his job. He had worked so hard only to have a conviction overturned on a technicality. But it wasn't just the professional disappointment. He also had sacrificed precious time with his family, and now he had a baby daughter to think of.

"I don't care what you do. It's all right if you want to collect garbage or whatever it takes until you can be trained for something else," Lana told him. "It's just not worth it to see you going through what you did today." By the time he returned home, DeSanto began weighing his career options.

Waller got up earlier than usual, around 5 A.M., and ran twice his usual distance. But the workout only partially diffused the stress and anxiety. He didn't feel like talking to anybody about the Caldwell investigation.

Later that morning, the Supreme Court released its decision.

"The fingerprint expert's testimony was damning—and it was false," Chief Justice Douglas Amdahl wrote. "If, as we must assume, the jury believed that the fingerprint was [Caldwell's] and that therefore he must have been in Duluth at the time the murders were committed, it relied in part on the totally incorrect evidence in finding [him] guilty.... If it had been proven that it was not his during the trial, investigators would have had the chance to prove whose it was."

In other words, the court said the jury might have acquitted Roger if the fingerprint had not been evidence against him.

"Under the unusual circumstances of this case, where the uncontroverted testimony of the state's expert substantially proves to be incorrect, and the testimony was the basis of the only circumstantial evidence tending to establish that the appellant was in Duluth on the date of the murders, appellant is entitled to a new trial," the Court said.

Several weeks later, the chief justice called DeSanto to apologize for the lack of notice and the media leak. He told DeSanto he should have received a courtesy copy and said the *Duluth Herald* would no longer receive theirs.

But there was still more coming back to haunt DeSanto. During his closing arguments at Roger's trial, DeSanto had referred to Roger's cold sore as "manufactured evidence," which had drawn an objection from Thomson and directions to the jury from Judge Litman to disregard the statement. Because of this, the Supreme Court decision had referred to his closing as including misconduct; in response, the Lawyers Professional Responsibility Board, acting on its own without a complainant, would soon issue DeSanto a reprimand.

As the news of the retrial became public, Waller remained unavailable for comment and wished he had fought harder to discourage DeSanto from using the fingerprint evidence. Waller's remorse paled in comparison to the consequences suffered by prosecution and defense experts: Steven Sedlacek and Ronald Wellbaum had their latent print examiner certification revoked by the International Association of Identification. Sedlacek also lost his job with the Colorado Bureau of Investigation.

Learning about the involvement of Wellbaum had been an ironic surprise for the prosecution team. Wellbaum, a retired fingerprint expert from the Minneapolis Police Department, had been hired by Thomson during Roger's trial, but had declared the envelope print a match to Roger. The rules of discovery only required the prosecution to turn over exculpatory evidence to the defense, as DeSanto had done at Marjorie's trial; there was no requirement for the defense to disclose incriminating evidence to the prosecution. So the defense's fingerprint match would only be exposed after an appeal on the basis of the fingerprint having been thrown out—it was a strange echo of the Byers testimony turnaround.

For his part, Waller believed the court foolish for overlooking the other evidence, like Roger's lack of alibi, Marjorie's lies about his whereabouts, and the stolen jewelry. Waller felt deflated and tired as he sat listening to his boss, Inspector Grams. The inspector, agitated and angry, would not let this reversal stand. "You want to go through the whole goddamn thing again," thought Waller wearily. "Easy for you to say." After all, Grams wouldn't be the one back in the hot seat.

Across the courtyard, calls from the media swamped County Attorney Alan Mitchell's office. Reporters tracked DeSanto down at home, requesting interviews at his house. Twin Cities television station WCCO-TV asked him to come on the 6 P.M. news for a live interview. Doug Thomson has already been booked, the reporter told him. Our company plane can pick you up and fly you down here this afternoon, she said.

That evening anchor Dave Moore interviewed DeSanto and Thomson in the WCCO-TV studios. DeSanto recalls Thomson saying he was overjoyed by the high court's decision. In response, DeSanto assured Moore and viewers the county would retry Roger Caldwell. After the show, DeSanto learned the company plane was unavailable and he'd have to fly back on a commercial jet the next morning. DeSanto consoled himself that night with a free ticket to a Minnesota Twins game. The Twins won.

"We are all, of course, very happy and relieved with the news you phoned to us last evening," Roger's brother, David, wrote Roger on August 6. "I was really wondering if that would be their decision or not. I guess whoever got to the others involved in your frame-up couldn't or didn't get to the Supreme Court judges. You were again right— 'somewhere out there in black robes there sits an honest concerned person.'"

The Monday after the court's ruling, Waller and DeSanto met for lunch at Sir Benedict's Tavern on the Lake, located on London Road in the shadow of the Kitchi Gammi Club. Waller and DeSanto were still in disbelief over the court's decision, and the dimly-lit, English-style pub offered privacy and a view of Lake Superior. The two men had to concede they faced a no-win situation. They had to decide whether to take the case to trial for a second time or to try to work out a plea agreement.

"We didn't feel we could reconvict Roger Caldwell," DeSanto said. "Almost immediately, we decided to approach our bosses with a plea negotiation proposal. But it was the people above us who would make the bottom line decision. That was kind of disturbing. We could offer our suggestions, but the decision wasn't ours."

Come up with a list of pros and cons, County Attorney Mitchell instructed De-Santo. Inspector Grams reluctantly gave DeSanto the go-ahead. They knew they had to begin discretely scoping out defense attorney Thomson's willingness to consider a plea bargain.

Three weeks after his conviction was overturned, officials transferred Roger from the state penitentiary to the St. Louis County Jail in Duluth. The following Monday, Thomson was in court asking the judge to free his client without bail to await the re-trial. In support of his request, Thomson cited his client's "exemplary" record of good behavior in prison, the absence of prior criminal convictions, and Caldwell's strong family ties.

DeSanto said the county had no objections to Caldwell's being out if he remained in Minnesota and reported weekly to a probation agent. "Continued incarceration…in the St. Louis County Jail will continue to increase the already exorbitant public ex-pense of these proceedings," DeSanto told the court. He didn't say that the move was strategic.

DeSanto and Waller knew Roger's old pattern of drink and talk. They believed that once freed, he would eventually get drunk and perhaps confide in a drinking buddy about the case. Police would tail his activities and interview his acquaintances. Secondly, with Roger out, there would be less pressure to quickly reschedule the second trial; DeSanto wanted to use Marjorie's testimony from the upcoming civil trial if they had to retry Roger.

Thomson recommended Roger be placed in the custody of David Arnold, in Minneapolis. This single item drew strong protest from DeSanto. Although Arnold was no longer formally retained as Roger's attorney, clearly Roger still relied on him for legal advice, and DeSanto planned to call Arnold as a prosecution witness if there was a retrial. DeSanto argued it was inappropriate for the defendant to stay at Arnold's house. The judge took the motions under advisement.

Wednesday afternoon, September 1, 1982, District Judge David Bouschor an-nounced his decision. He granted Roger supervised release and placed him in David Arnold's custody. Roger would be free for the first time in five years.

During his years in prison, Roger had kept a diary using various donated pocket-sized appointment books. He kept track of important dates regarding his appeal, his visitors, mail received, letters he'd written, and, after several years, days when nothing notewor-thy happened. Those days he marked with a single notation, "Zip!" Roger also collected and wrote poems and limericks (some bawdy), extensively researched druids and Celtic art, and memorized the terms of all the U.S. presidents. His prison writings included numerous notecards and pieces of paper with the definitions of words grouped to-gether in the dictionary, and he traced some words back to their roots. Roger noted that "it wasn't any accident" that the words conjunct, conjugal, conjoin, and conjecture were so close together in the dictionary. He defined them as: a close association; between a husband and wife; combine and unite; and inference and guess, respectively—a synopsis of his relationship with Marjorie.

His diary showed his dark moods more than did his correspondence. One undated entry reads:

> Daily I'm assaulted with taunts and jeers from calendars and mirrors that persist in reminding me that gravity pulls on flesh just as it does on hour glass sand. Not that a loss of physical youth means so much—though the losing of it does rankle—what eats at me more is a ceaseless niggling that insists in reminding that I've joined the trailing edges of life's second stage—regardless of how involuntarily…. Physiologically, in spite of these years of incarceration, it would seem that nothing of a deleterious nature has occurred…. I'm not able to be as generous when it comes to a discussion about the relative state of my thought processes, for in these my bitterness has grown in proportion to the increased awareness I have of the irreplaceability of time.

But his private writings also included much lighter fare. Roger created a character he called "Elmo Sqeeg: Master Detective," a sort of low-life, senior James Bond he described as "quick as a fox, a somewhat tattered, and perhaps arthritic fox" who, after doing a backward somersault landed on "his one good remaining leg." One rambling tale began:

> When we last left Elmo Sqeeg: Master Detective, he was recovering from wounds received during the "Crippling Chiropractic Caper," when, as you recall, he was viciously attacked by an enraged herd of near crazed chiropractors…. Elmo, you will remember, had uncovered an organized plot by the chiropractors to further feather their own nests by dislocating tibias from fibulas in large numbers of their geriatric patients, thus requiring them to rent or purchase prosthetic devices.

Roger had been working on a more serious book as well. He spoke with Arnold and his brother David about the project. Roger hinted that the book would be a disguised version of the Glensheen murders that people familiar with the case would be able to see through. In his prison correspondence, he noted that he planned to contact a book publisher. At one point he wrote Arnold:

> For some time you and I have talked, off and on, about what I might possibly say if I ever did decide to publish. As you know, I've attacked the making of this decision in the same fits-and-starts manner that I do most things, which only resulted in frequent false starts that didn't seem to fit. Regardless of the approach that I took somebodies [sic] viewpoint kept getting overlooked and it seemed that I (oddly enough) placed excessive emphasis on my own. GOOD NEWS AT LAST!! I've hit upon a device that's working very well for me, and one that I'm comfortable with, too. Your peculiar sense of humor will, I'm sure, cause you to read "real people" into various fictionalized characterizations that I've made, but when a novel based in a certain location and time period also seems to tie-in with one of the most publicized crimes of that area…well, I suppose folks will jump to conclusions; particularly when they've seen who's written it.

Following his release from prison, his personal items—including correspondence, po-ems, short stories, articles, and research—were gathered together in three boxes and a black satchel and forwarded to Arnold. Years later, a search of the documents contained in the boxes and satchel produced no manuscript of a novel depicting events similar to those that occurred at Glensheen.

However, among the documents Roger collected in prison was a copy of a chapter from a 1981 book, *A Tremor in the Blood, Uses and Abuses of the Lie Detector*, by David Lykken, an emeritus professor at the University of Minnesota. Chapter 21, "A Body on the Stairs," contained a fictionalized version of the Glensheen murders set in a Duluth mansion on London Road. In the fictional account, a night nurse and the bedridden mistress of the house, Victoria Haverstock, a wealthy widow of a mining executive, are murdered during the night. The nurse had been bludgeoned to death and the widow smothered with a pillow. Many years earlier, the widow had decided to become a single mother, and adopted a baby girl. The widow had provided her daughter with every in-dulgence money could buy. In the end of Lykken's fictionalization, the adopted daugh-ter, Merry Bell Plunkett, the daughter's husband, and one of the daughter's sons were tried and convicted of conspiracy and first-degree murder. It can only be imagined what Roger thought of this version of the story.

His collection of book excerpts also contained a page from A.C. Bradley's literary review of Shakespeare's play *Anthony and Cleopatra*. In the few pages Roger saved is this passage: "He is under no illusion about her, knows all her faults, sees through her wiles, believes her capable of betraying him. It makes no difference. She is his heart's de-sire made perfect. To love her is what he was born for. What have the gods in heaven to say against it? To imagine heaven is to imagine her; to die is to rejoin her. To deny this is love is the madness of morality. He gives her every atom of his heart. She destroys him." It isn't difficult to imagine who Roger had in mind.

After the court had announced Roger's release, reporters jammed the steps and side-walk outside the county jail waiting for him to emerge. Twin Cities reporters jostled alongside the local news media, all hoping for the best photo, quote, or sound bite.

Gail Feichtinger, a *Duluth News-Tribune* crime reporter at the time, asked the jailer to deliver a note to Roger. "I had just two short questions I had hoped to ask you," the note said. "What you missed most in prison and were looking forward to doing after your release? And if it will be hard to readjust?"

Minutes later a sheriff's deputy returned with the note. Roger had circled the question about what he'd missed most and drawn a line to the bottom of the page where he'd written "Baskin-Robbins" and signed his name.

The reporter sent the note back offering Roger a pint of of his favorite ice cream in exchange for a brief interview. He responded "mocha almond fudge."

But less than ten minutes later, Thomson arrived in his Jaguar to pick up his cli-ent. Both men emerged from the jail a short time later. Roger carried his personal effects in a brown grocery bag tucked under his arm. Dressed in blue jeans, a navy windbreaker, and brown suede shoes, he looked subdued and ill at ease. He refused to answer the rush of questions shouted out, but managed a slight smile for the news photographers.

Thomson, immaculate as usual in a three-piece, pinstriped suit, talked briefly with reporters. "There's a certain amount of ecstasy when your client obtains his freedom after five years of agony," said Thomson. The two men left for Thomson's law office in downtown St. Paul shortly before 3 P.M.

During Roger's incarceration, Arnold had visited his former client three or four times a year and talked with him by phone every couple weeks. Roger had been a loner, Arnold recalled, as much as a man can be while surrounded by inmates and guards. Aside from Arnold, Roger only received visits from his brother Jack and sister-in-law Clara, who occasionally drove from Rock Island, Illinois, to see him. Marjorie had long ago stopped visiting her husband behind bars and had been married to Wally Hagen for over a year.

Days before his release from jail, Arnold had received a call from Roger. "Guess what? Your wish is coming true," he told Arnold, referring to Arnold's long-standing offer to "come spend a little time with us when you get out."

Arnold mused about the timing of Roger's release as he drove over to St. Paul to pick up his house guest. This was his wedding anniversary. So much for a private, intimate dinner on the town with his wife, Kari.

Arnold lived in Minnetonka, a well-to-do Minneapolis suburb best known for its large lake, fancy yachts, and pricey shops and restaurants. But it was also a community of quiet neighborhoods and residents who valued their privacy. Arnold hoped the location of his house—on a cul de sac—would discourage reporters.

Arriving home, Arnold introduced Roger to his wife and four children before showing him his room. Arnold and his wife had already talked about arrangements for their new boarder. He would sleep in one of their sons' rooms. They would not give him any special treatment, but would expect him to participate in whatever activities the family had planned.

"We had introductions. Then I remember it was a nice day, and he was sitting out on the porch and we kind of left him somewhat alone for awhile," Arnold recalled.

That night, the Arnolds celebrated their anniversary with a formal family dinner; Roger sat at the head of the table. He looked at his place setting and said in a mock-serious voice, "Oh shit. I suppose we're going to breach the terms of the release order."

"What do you mean?" Arnold asked.

Caldwell held up his knife dramatically. "It says I can't have any weapons in my possession," he said. The family chuckled, and any remaining awkwardness dissolved. "Roger was a very soft-spoken, quiet, and sociable individual," Arnold later explained. "There was no conscious association of Roger that night with the 'murderer' of the taboids. [So] there was no uneasiness prior to the conversation and the irony seemed laughable."

As the Arnolds and Caldwell ate, they tried to ignore the barrage of phone calls, knocks at the door, and doorbell ringing. Arnold remembered "People wanting to talk to him and creeping up the driveway and standing on the front steps. And having the lights blaring from the TV cameras at ten o'clock at night photographing the house." The news trucks and cars parked in their driveway and lined the street. Arnold could sit in the family room and look out down his long driveway and see the reporters as they approached the house.

Later that evening, Arnold spoke with a reporter who asked what Roger's immediate plans were and how he was taking his new freedom. "He was very pleased to be out and was appreciative of the fact he now has the opportunity to reenter society somewhat and catch up on the last five years. He plans to just relax and draw his thoughts together for the next several days," Arnold said.

As Arnold recalled later, it wasn't long before Roger was puttering around the house. "He really fit in beautifully. He made himself completely at home."

The day after Roger's release, the news media hungered for any information on his activities. Feichtinger recruited a University of Minnesota journalism student in Minneapolis to deliver a pint of ice cream to Arnold's home. Late that afternoon, the reporter phoned the house to see if the ice cream had arrived.

"Arnold residence," a voice answered.

"May I please speak to Roger Caldwell?" Feichtinger said before realizing that the soft-spoken, halting voice belonged to Roger. Roger said the ice cream had been delivered and thanked her and the *Duluth News-Tribune*.

Although Roger refused an in-person interview, he didn't mind talking on the phone. He said he was glad to be out of prison. But he didn't feel free. "Prison is a state of mind," he said, "more than your state of confinement."

He said, "I'll remain in prison regardless of how pleasant the surroundings. I'm in a very comfortable jail at the moment, surrounded by very congenial, generous, goodhearted people." He insisted on his innocence saying, "I'm still accused of crimes I haven't committed. I'm accused of things I haven't done and I'm very uncomfortable about it."

His plans for the future were uncertain, he said. "I have no job. I have no income and I have no plans of looking for a job. I'll probably just sit and read…and correspond with people." Roger said he was shy, and the amount of publicity his case had generated upset him. "I'm a private person not a public person. I'm truly a simple man," he told Feichtinger.

Over the next few months, Roger once again became a private person. He loved to sit alone, seemingly lost in thought as he stared out a window. Arnold recalled that Roger liked to sit out on the porch reading westerns and mysteries from the Arnolds' library. Roger liked to talk about his family, particularly his kids. But the image most vivid in Arnold's mind is that of Roger tagging along after his wife, pitching in to help with household chores.

"He took charge of the kitchen," Arnold remembered. "He would clean things up. We had never had our cupboards so organized. He would take glasses out of the dishwasher and he'd put them in descending order of height.... Kari was forever looking for things because he'd always put them where he thought they were supposed to be, not where she would put them."

The Arnolds found it surprisingly easy to treat Roger as if he were part of the family. He ran errands with them, went shopping, took walks around the neighborhood, and even accompanied them to parties. There was occasional awkward small talk—at one backyard barbecue, a woman asked Roger, "So you like being out better than being in prison?" Arnold said, "It was so stupid that we all burst out laughing." But Arnold recalled that their friends happily donated clothes, since Roger had arrived at the Arnolds with only the bare essentials—the clothes on his back, a few belts, a fan, some letters, a comb. Arnold's barber even gave Roger free haircuts.

That summer, during a trip to the Arnolds' cabin near Alexandria, Minnesota, Roger told Arnold his theories of the murders. He blamed Tom Congdon and Bill Van Evera for framing him, which didn't surprise Arnold, given Roger and Marjorie's animosity toward them. "Under Roger's first scenario, either Tom Congdon planned it or [Furman and Fick] thought, gee, this would be a nice touch, and kind of ad-libbed," said Arnold. "Or under his second scenario, it's more conceivable that Bill Van Evera may have had some involvement in...directing these guys to plant evidence. [Not] that Bill Van Evera had done anything directly."

Later that fall, Roger asked the court if he could go visit his brother and sister-in-law in Rock Island, Illinois. Roger's sister-in-law Clara and brother John, a history professor and the head librarian at Augustana College in Rock Island, were happy to have him stay with them. The Arnolds supported Roger's trip, which the court approved. "You know it's just like fish and relatives get old or smell after a few days," Arnold recalled in jest.

After his visit to Rock Island, Roger flew to his hometown of Latrobe to visit his elderly parents for an extended stay. The judge assigned to retry the case granted the request without DeSanto or Waller's knowledge. DeSanto didn't even know Roger had left the state until he happened to call Roger's probation agent several months later. "How's Roger doing these days?" DeSanto asked the agent.

"Oh fine. He's in Latrobe, Pennsylvania, but he's been staying in touch," the agent replied.

"What?" DeSanto shouted. "What is he doing back there?"

The agent explained, "He asked if he could go back for the holidays. I talked with the judge and he didn't have any objections if I didn't. We didn't think anyone cared."

So much for DeSanto and Waller's surveillance plan. The judge had shot it to hell and they hadn't even been notified. "If I'd known I would have objected," DeSanto said later. "I was distressed and angry." They couldn't understand how a convicted killer warranted such special consideration. He was not only free, but free to go wherever he wanted.

CHAPTER 22

Fire Starter

MARJORIE AND WALLY HAGEN SOLD THE CRANBERRY HOUSE, a home they owned in the Minneapolis suburb of Mound, to Gerane and Clayton Kulseth. The Kulseths planned to move into the house on Wednesday, September 15, 1982. Instead, Gerane received a phone call from her sister, Shelly, at 8:15 that morning after Clayton had left for work. "Your house is on fire," Shelly told Gerane.

The Kulseths had spent $89,000 for the Cranberry House—more than they had planned, but the house was worth it. The two-story wood frame structure dated back 125 years and was listed on the National Register of Historic Places. The house's red exterior gave the Cranberry House its name. Marjorie herself had decorated the interior walls with rosemaling, the Scandinavian style of painting floral designs. The Kulseths had planned to open an antique shop in the house.

The previous night the Kulseths had gone out to dinner with the Hagens and the Mallimakis, the couple who had owned the house before the Hagens. Marjorie had insisted that they all get together before the Kulseths moved into the Cranberry House. The three couples had eaten hamburgers at the Ox Bow Restaurant, and then the Kulseths and Hagens stopped at the house on the way home. Wally said he needed to clean out a few items left in the garage. He gave Clay Kulseth a house key, saying the Kulseths now had all the keys. The Kulseths and Hagens left the house together at around 9:15 P.M.

The next morning, just after 6:40 A.M. Wednesday, the fire was reported. Five hours later, firefighters had extinguished the blaze, but not before it had consumed the Cranberry House.

The day after the fire, investigators from the State Fire Marshal's Office and BCA searched the charred remains, looking for the cause. Their initial suspicion of faulty wiring quickly changed upon closer inspection of the scene.

The outer shell of the house was still standing, but eighty percent of the interior had burned. Next to some wiring, which ran adjacent to the first-floor fireplace, investigators found a stack of old newspapers and signs of flammable liquid burn patterns they believed were made by gasoline. Because arson fires often share many of the characteristics of accidental fires, this was key evidence. On the second level, investigators found a hole burned in the middle of the floor; more burn patterns surrounded the hole—two fires had been started.

Curiously, the locked windows showed no signs of forced entry and the doors were securely locked. The first firefighters on the scene told investigators they found no broken windows when they arrived. Whoever started the fire had a key.

Questionable fires had surrounded Marjorie before. In 1966, during her marriage to Dick LeRoy, the family's garage had burned. Investigators attributed the fire to teenagers smoking, but several of Marjorie's children later swore that Dick said Marjorie claimed items on the insurance claim that Dick had never seen before. Other family members and neighbors had their own suspicions. After all, when guests of the LeRoy wedding in 1951 failed to receive thank you notes, Marjorie later told friends and relatives that she had placed all the notes in the mailbox, but the mailbox had been destroyed by fire.

Marjorie's connection to fire became even more apparent less than two weeks after she moved to Colorado in 1975. "Homestead," her house in Marine On St. Croix, Minnesota, burned to the ground on the morning of May 12. Thomas Welch recalled an earlier visit to the property that he dubbed Disneyland because of its extravagant furnishings: "I went out there and got a tour. The sprinkler heads were little statues made in Italy. They were little squirrels and rabbits. And when you were wandering out in the garden, the music speakers were up in the trees and were disguised as bird houses." A long, tree-lined brick driveway led to the house, and a fountain adorned the backyard. Marjorie had filled the house with antique furniture and a custom fireplace. Expensive hardwood covered the floors throughout the house. All the hardware, including the bathroom faucets, was gold. The "Homestead" was worth about $1 million, but Marjorie had only insured the house for $287,000 and its contents for an additional $143,000.

Minnesota State Fire Marshal Ronald Sockness surveyed the damage and determined that the fire had broken out in the basement. But the basement was so badly gutted he couldn't take samples, making pinpointing the exact cause and origin of the fire nearly impossible.

Several days later, when Sockness interviewed Marjorie by phone, she said she was in Colorado when the fire occurred and had no idea how the blaze could have started. The house had recently been remodeled, she said, implying that the work of Michael Billingsley, her contractor and one-time fiancée, was the cause.

Sockness contacted Billingsley to see if bad electrical wiring might have caused the fire, but Billingsley assured him new wiring had been installed. Sockness also learned that Marjorie still owed Billingsley and his subcontractors $100,000.

Fire investigators obtained Western Airlines records that showed that Marjorie had made round-trip reservations from Denver to Minneapolis for May 11. Her departure time was 8:45 P.M., with arrival at the Minneapolis-St. Paul International Airport at 12:02 A.M., six hours before the fire began. She returned to Colorado on Flight 701, which departed Minnesota at 7:50 A.M., about two hours after the fire started.

According to Hertz rental records, Marjorie rented a Cougar after midnight May 12 under the name Mrs. R.W. LeRoy. The rental agent positively identified Marjorie as the person who rented the car. Mileage on the car totaled seventy-four miles—the exact mileage from the airport to the house and back.

Investigators later learned that Elizabeth Oakerland, a childhood friend of Marjorie's, had seen her at the airport the night before the fire. Oakerland told authorities that as Marjorie approached, Oakerland said Marjorie's name aloud and their eyes met, but Marjorie walked right by, giving no sign of recognition. Billingsley told Peter LeRoy that he saw Marjorie carrying furniture from the main house to the guest house the morning of the fire. He also said a gas can was missing from the garage the next day when he returned to the house.

The Washington County Sheriff's department, which had received the first report of the fire, decided to reinterview Marjorie. Undersheriff Scott Kline talked with Marjorie at her Denver home. In her statement to Kline, Marjorie had difficulty remembering dates and times.

"Were you at any time at 14990 Norrell on May 12 of 1975?" Kline asked.

"What's May 12?"

"It's a day of the year, a Monday, May 12."

"Yeah, but it's not ringing a bell."

Kline pressed her about her memory lapse. "It's the day of the fire of your house."

"No. I was there on what I think was the fourteenth. I think it's Wednesday. I was not there on the twelfth."

"All right. Were you in the state of Minnesota?"

"If I was, my body was there and the rest of me was here, because I was on the phone at ten o'clock at night with a friend." Marjorie then told Kline she and her son Rick had gone to a Denver medical center earlier that day for more asthma-related tests.

But she had a different story for her friend Ruth McDermott, whose son, Patrick, had been at the LeRoys the day before the fire. Months later, Marjorie had complained to McDermott that investigators blamed her for the fire, and planned to bring charges against her. "On that night, Pat, Rick, and I were watching 'Romeo and Juliet' on television at that time," Marjorie said. In reality, Patrick had ended up spending the night at the LeRoys' apartment because Marjorie had gone out and not returned home.

Marjorie's insurance company was also interested in the arson investigation, particularly because her policy had expired. Arson law at that time didn't prevent someone from burning down his or her house. The law regarded such fires as pranks, unless the homeowner financially benefitted or the fire caused injury to a person. Since Marjorie's policy had lapsed and she had not filed an insurance claim, no crime had occurred. Marjorie received no money for the loss of her million-dollar home, and Minnesota authorities closed the case, albeit reluctantly.

In the fall of 1976, the First National Bank in Englewood, Colorado, experienced several fires. Marjorie had overdrawn her checking account and the bank had closed it in March. She also had a $4,000 loan over which the bank had threatened legal action; Marjorie had sold the car that was supposed to be security for the loan. On September 29, a fire broke out on the fifth floor of the bank. Robert Kinch, assistant vice president, recalled that Marjorie had visited the trust department around the time the fire broke out.

Tony Ortiz, night janitor at the bank, said he and his wife, also a janitor, had gotten off the elevator on the fifth floor of the bank building around 8:30 P.M. They spotted a rug and wallpaper on fire in the hallway leading to the restrooms. Ortiz doused the fire with an extinguisher while his wife alerted night foreman James Wilkins. Wilkins told arson investigators that after he heard the elevator emergency bell sound, he ran to the ground floor elevators. When the doors opened, a woman stepped out, smiled, and told him that there was a fire on the fifth floor. He described the woman as short with cropped brown hair and glasses.

She was back early the next morning, September 30, waiting for the bank to open. Shortly after 9 A.M., as bank guard Corky McHugh sat at his desk facing the central staircase, he saw a woman coming around the corner from the hall leading to the restroomswhere another small fire was soon discovered. "She ran around the corner and up the stairs taking two at a time. She was running like hell," he recalled. "She was dressed in dark-colored clothes. She was carrying a light-colored purse.... She wore glasses, large lenses. She had short dark hair, close to her head." As she left the bank she mentioned to bank employee Eugene Lamont, "Sure is lots of activity this morning."

Investigators determined that the fires were set by placing small pellets used to ignite fireplace logs underneath the carpeting and a couch. They interviewed Marjorie, who admitted being at the bank, but insisted that she had been there on business. The case was eventually closed with no charges filed.

After Marjorie's return to Minnesota in 1977, a series of suspicious fires involving houses she was trying to buy or sell brought her more unwanted attention from investigators. In late summer 1979, a house she'd agreed to buy flooded on the day the down payment was due. Marjorie told police she'd gone by the house to plant flowers and when she looked inside, the faucets had been left on and water was overflowing onto the floors.

The owner lowered the selling price, extended the down payment deadline, and replaced the waterlogged floors. But on September 4, the day before closing, fire destroyed the house. That morning, the investigator for the state fire marshall's office noted that the fire had burned very low, unusual for most house fires. Since flames naturally travel upward, low burn damage indicated an accelerant had been poured on the floor. As the investigator dug through the ashes and charred debris, he found "alligatoring"—the fissure-like, telltale patterns that an accelerant such as gasoline leaves behind.

Hours after the fire, Pat Shannon, an agent with the Minnesota Bureau of Criminal Apprehension, arrived at the scene and began talking with the fire marshal when a woman drove up in a gray Renault. She looked extremely agitated and practically jumped out of her car.

"My God, what happened to my house?" the woman cried out as she rushed toward the two men. "What's going on? Who's in charge here?"

The fire marshall pointed at Shannon, who asked the woman to identify herself. She said her name was Marjorie Bannister. "I'm the one who's going to buy this house."

"Well, it burned down last night," Shannon said.

"Oh, that's horrible," the woman responded in a slightly raised voice, as she rushed on. "It's a beautiful house. It's just beautiful. Oh, this is the worst thing that ever happened to me in my life."

Up close, agent Shannon recognized her from the publicity surrounding her murder trial earlier that summer, but he played along. "You're Marjorie Bannister."

"Yes. Oh, this is terrible. We were just going to close…when was it? Today or tomorrow? I love this house."

"How did you happen to come to the house today?" Shannon knew she had not been notified of the fire.

Marjorie said she was on her way to an appointment when she first saw the police cars and then the condition of the house. "I almost ran off the road into the ditch," she told Shannon. He asked to get a statement from her that afternoon at the police station.

While he waited for her to arrive, Shannon phoned Gary Waller in Duluth to verify his suspicions as to Marjorie's real identity. "Do you know a Marjorie Bannister?" Shannon asked. Waller replied simply, "What did she do now?"

But an hour later, Shannon got a message from police headquarters that Marjorie had canceled. She was suddenly "tied up." So that night Shannon phoned her at home and asked to drop by. "Pat, I'd love to have you come over. I want to talk to you, but my dog is sick," she said. "Throwing up all over the place." Shannon suggested that they could talk outside, but she demurred. "Oh, it's late. You know, maybe we could do it some other time. Could you call me tomorrow?"

The following day, when Shannon and a police officer drove out to Marjorie's house, she had nothing to say to them. She had been on the phone with Meshbesher, and he didn't want her talking to the police. State and fire investigators also learned that Marjorie had signed papers canceling her purchase of the house, putting her financially in the clear. An arson investigation involving Marjorie so close to her acquittal demanded that investigators put together a solid case—and they didn't have one. Within weeks of the fire, Shannon dropped the investigation for lack of evidence.

Three years later, Marjorie had remarried, and fire had damaged a house she planned to buy. On May 5, 1982, a blaze broke out in the garage of the house, two days before closing. This was the fourth time the closing date had been moved back. The Hagens owed $500 in earnest money, and were due to make a down payment on the property.

A neighbor who lived across the street from the house told authorities he saw a small foreign car at the site about half an hour before the fire was reported. He believed the car's driver spotted him, and the car sped away. Marjorie drove a small foreign car at that time.

On May 6, the Hagens said they still wanted to buy the house, but for a reduced price. The owners rejected the offer.

Again, BCA Agent Shannon was investigating Marjorie and a suspicious fire. But given the publicity that would follow any charges involving Marjorie, Shannon for the second time refused to settle for less than an airtight case. "At best, arson is a long shot," said Shannon. "And after her murder trial, it might have looked like we're picking on her."

After the Cranberry House burned in the fall of 1982, the circumstances surrounding the fire had an all-too familiar ring for Shannon. He noted several marked similarities between this fire and the two previous ones connected to Marjorie. The houses were unoccupied at the time of the fire, each fire had been set with an accelerant, and all had occurred at night. But perhaps the most significant pattern was that all three fires happened shortly before real estate payment deadlines Marjorie didn't have the money to meet.

Outwardly, Marjorie seemed like anyone's middle-aged next-door neighbor—a chatty, extroverted woman who enjoyed antiques, needlepoint, and murder mysteries. But she was also one hell of a strange woman, Shannon thought. Apart from standing trial for her mother's murder, she apparently started fires.

BCA Agent Ray DiPrima, also an experienced arson investigator, worked closely with Shannon on the case. The investigators learned from the Mallimakis that the Hagens had bought the Cranberry House on a contract for deed. The purchase agreement included nothing unusual, but the $36,832 balloon payment the Hagens still owed came due in four months.

Several weeks later, search warrant in hand, Shannon and DiPrima and several Mound police officers—including Herman Kraft, an old acquaintance of Wally's—visited the Hagens at their new house. DiPrima and Shannon wanted to look for purchase agreements, insurance records, promissory notes—any documentation on the house that had burned. Among the other items of evidence listed in the warrant were keys for the Cranberry House.

"When you have an arson case like this, it's a very private crime," DiPrima said. "Where you sneak out in the middle of the night and splash some gas and light a match and if no one sees you then it's up to the investigators to put it back together. You're looking for pieces of circumstantial evidence."

DiPrima wore a hidden microphone under his shirt to tape record the conversation. As investigators walked up to the open basement door and called out for the Hagens, Wally came around the corner, clearly not pleased to see them.

Wally's white hair and beard reminded DiPrima of Rip Van Winkle. He stood blocking the door; the investigators looked past, unable to see Marjorie. "Marjorie's not home," Hagen told the agents.

Shannon began, "Ah, my name's Pat Shannon—"

Hagen broke in. "I'm the guy that's madder than hell. You've gotten me all upset when you start picking on my wife."

Shannon calmed Hagen down by explaining that the Hagens' insurance company pressured him to wrap up the investigation and he just wanted to ask a few questions.

Hagen said that there had been four keys to the house. He and Marjorie each had one, Marjorie's son Rick had the third key, and they had given the fourth to the milkman. When Shannon pressed him on whether all four keys had been turned over to the new owners, Hagen insisted, "I'm quite sure they should have four keys."

The investigators asked Hagen to tell them what he and Marjorie had been doing the morning of the fire.

"It was a Wednesday. So [Marjorie] got up. She probably got up here at seven o'clock and had, and fixed breakfast. She never leaves without fixing breakfast for me." Wally said his wife hung around the house that morning until about 8 or 8:30, when she went to her quilting group in Osseo, a nearby Minneapolis suburb.

About ten minutes into the interview, Marjorie returned home wearing her large round sunglasses and carrying a big leather purse. Marjorie intensely disliked Agent Shannon after a conversation the previous week.

"Out, out. I mean it. You come back here with a court order that's signed," she spat as she stepped toward Shannon, her face flushing red.

Agent DiPrima quickly moved between Shannon and Marjorie, and held up the search warrant. But that failed to calm her.

"I've had friends calling, telling me the things you are saying." Marjorie jabbed her finger toward Shannon. "And the things you are making, making remarks to, and I don't want you in my house."

"We have to have one final question, Marge, and we could wrap this thing up. You want to settle the things up with the insurance company?"

"I won't settle with the insurance company. I had a contract. A contract. We do. What do you want?"

"Just wanted to know where you were that morning?"

"I was here in bed and my husband can tell you that."

"So you were here in bed at seven-thirty in the morning, eight o'clock in the morning?"

"I was here until I left to go quilting. I imagine I left between eight and eight-thirty. That's the time I usually do leave. And then I was in Osseo."

"And how long did you stay there?"

"I was there 'til I came back here."

"Okay. And what time was that? Around twelve o'clock or one o'clock?"

"Whatever time my husband says. I don't keep track of time. I imagine it was around twelve o'clock."

The agents encouraged their suspect to talk, a strategy commonly used in arson investigation. Shannon and DiPrima tried to catch Marjorie in as many lies and inconsistencies as they could get on tape.

Marjorie told investigators that on her way to her quilting group, she stopped at the Mound Public Library to drop off an overdue book. Near the library, she saw water trucks and encountered a roadblock. But she insisted, "you couldn't see fire," and she had no idea the Cranberry House was burning.

She returned home and had lunch with her husband shortly after noon, still unaware of the fire. Marjorie only learned of the fire when her husband told her the bad news after lunch.

"Did you turn all of your keys in to the Kulseths?" asked DiPrima.

"Yes."

"On the evening of the fourteenth of September?"

"No, we gave some to them at closing." She also insisted that she and Wally had retained one key after the closing, and Wally had given it to the Kulseths the night before the fire.

During the search of the Hagens' house, investigators found a Century 21 folder containing various documents. When Marjorie saw the officer holding the papers, she screamed, ran up, and grabbed a document out of his hands. Marjorie then took the document—the certificate of her marriage to Hagen—and shoved it down her pants as Shannon and DiPrima looked on.

Marjorie called her attorney's office to complain about the search. The agents are "ransacking the house and trying to take my marriage certificate," she complained. After she hung up, she went into the bathroom and slammed the door.

"You cannot go into the bathroom with that document in your pants." Shannon ordered her to come out.

"I have to go to the bathroom."

"What you really want to do is destroy that document," Shannon said.

DiPrima told Marjorie that the investigators needed to verify the document was a marriage certificate, and not evidence the search warrant allowed them to seize.

"I'm not going to pull it out. I don't have to show you. Believe me, it's not important."

After fifteen minutes of negotiations, Marjorie pulled out the certificate, but would only show it to Kraft, the only cop she trusted. Then she quickly put the certificate back down her pants for safekeeping. Months later investigators learned the reason for her paranoid behavior: the marriage wasn't legal.

During the systematic search of the house, officers found a set of keys. Shannon dispatched an officer to the Cranberry House to see if any of the keys fit. None did.

Toward the end of the search, Shannon discovered another key in an otherwise empty basket in the kitchen cupboard over the stove. He thought to himself, "I almost hope this isn't the key because sure as hell here I am, the case agent, finding the key. I have all these other people around and I find it in a bowl." Shannon didn't want anyone to think he had planted the evidence. His only witness was Wally, who continued to follow him around as he went from room to room and inventoried the house.

"Where is this key from?" Shannon asked Wally.

"Damned if I know," he replied. Neither did his wife.

It was late afternoon and everyone was tired. Shannon decided to test the key the following day, but not before he showed it to everyone present. He announced loudly, "I found this in the cupboard." Big deal, the other investigators kidded.

On his way home, Shannon stopped at BCA headquarters to drop off the evidence collected, which included sixty-eight documents. The following afternoon, agents Shannon and DiPrima visited the Cranberry House to try out the key, which opened the front door easily on the first try. Shannon turned to DiPrima and they shook hands, elated that the case against Marjorie was solidifying. "Can you imagine that? What a coincidence," Shannon said, shaking his head.

That same afternoon, Shannon and DiPrima reinterviewed the Kulseths. The Kulseths told investigators they had agreed to a special condition imposed by Marjorie. They had insured the house for its full value from the date of the closing to two weeks after possession, with the Hagens listed as the insured party in case of loss.

The Hagen case belonged to Dan Mabley, a thirty-three-year-old assistant prosecutor with the Hennepin County Attorney's Office in Minneapolis. He had the most experience prosecuting arson cases.

His legal career had started in 1977, twenty miles south of the Twin Cities in the Dakota County Attorney's office. Mabley specialized in white collar crime, bringing corporate embezzlers to justice. His office was right around the corner from the courtroom where Marjorie was tried for her mother's murder. During the trial, he occasionally looked in on the proceedings to watch John DeSanto at work.

After three years, a federal grant job opening for an arson attorney turned his career in a new direction. Hennepin County hired Mabley and trained him in arson investigation and prosecution. Since then, he had prosecuted dozens of circumstantial arson cases successfully.

"After you try a lot of burglaries, robberies, and even murders, seeing a case with circumstantial evidence makes everyone real nervous." But Mabley preferred taking his chances with circumstantial evidence over eyewitness reports. "The jury finds it more interesting and less likely to be subject to typical impeachment, and a number of human observations and errors. The real hard part about arson cases isn't establishing arson...it's establishing who did it."

Mabley soon learned from state investigators that Marjorie had a longtime association with house fires, stretching back to the 1966 fire at the LeRoys' Fremont Avenue home. Suzanne told arson investigators about the garage fire that occurred when she was about twelve years old. She was sitting inside the screen porch at the rear of the house when she noticed smoke coming from the garage. Suzanne notified her mother, who, without turning to look, said "Don't worry about it." After several minutes passed, Suzanne saw flames and again informed Marjorie. Marjorie repeated, "Don't worry about it."

On Saturday, January 15, 1983, the BCA notified Waller they were about to arrest Marjorie for arson and insurance fraud. From the Hagens' neighbors they had learned that the couple planned to take their Airstream trailer to Florida for a winter vacation sometime that weekend. Investigators had also been notified by the Hagens' insurance company that Marjorie's claim had been processed and a $16,615 check had been mailed. They'd drawn up another search warrant to include the check. Waller told the BCA that when they searched Marjorie's belongings, he wanted them to look for evidence never recovered in the Congdon-Pietila case. Among the items cited in Waller's search warrant was Elisabeth Congdon's charm bracelet.

"We were hoping they would find something that would be the nail in Roger's coffin—and close the door to bar Marjorie from inheriting," Waller said.

At 7:55 on a bitterly cold Sunday morning, BCA agents and local police arrived at the Hagens' house to serve their warrants. Back at the Mound Police Department offices, Waller and Yagoda cooled their heels, awaiting the outcome of the search.

Wally, wearing designer pajamas, a matching tasseled cap, and slippers, opened the door. BCA agents immediately served him copies of the search warrants. As Wally stepped aside, investigators moved past to the entrance of the couple's first-floor bedroom. They suddenly stopped in their tracks. Marjorie was struggling to the bathroom with the bed sheets loosely wrapped around her. She nearly mooned the agents in a fleeting moment of levity. Less than a hour later, her backside would be warming a jail cell bench.

Shannon and DiPrima waited outside the bedroom as Marjorie got dressed. This time they had brought a female investigator, Agent Joel Kohout, with them. For Kohout, finally meeting the "notorious" Marjorie was a bit of a disappointment. "It was almost anticlimactic to see her. She looked almost normal, kind of a dumpy housewife."

When Kohout informed Marjorie she was under arrest, she couldn't believe how nonchalant Marjorie remained. After being read her rights, Marjorie demanded to call her attorney. You have to wait until you're booked at the jail, Shannon told her. Instead, her husband called Meshbesher.

In the bedroom, DiPrima searched Wally's wallet. Inside he found the $16,615 settlement check dated two days earlier—the evidence they had come to find. They recovered no evidence from Glensheen. "I guess we were hoping for too much," Waller said. He decided this would be the last official effort.

Kohout handcuffed and escorted Marjorie to an unmarked squad car, drove her to the Hennepin County Jail in downtown Minneapolis, and had her booked. "During the ride to the jail, she was pleasant," Kohout recalled. Marjorie, seemingly unaffected by her latest crisis, chatted amiably with Kohout about the weather and recipes.

This changed after arriving at the jail. "She got very snippy with me and said she wanted to be booked under the name of Hagen because Caldwell was no longer her name and besides it was too well known," Kohout said. Marjorie's attempt at avoiding publicity didn't work. Her story led the local newscasts that night.

Back in the Hagens' kitchen, DiPrima asked Wally, "When did you learn about the fire?" Wally had warmed up after his wife's departure and even volunteered to make coffee for his uninvited house guests. Shannon swapped him a cigarette for a cup of coffee and a statement about his activities the morning of the fire. Gordy Swenson, a friend of the Hagens', came to the house to tell Wally about the fire between 10 and 11 A.M. Wally told investigators he decided not to go look at the house with Swenson, but instead waited for Marjorie to return. When she arrived around 2 P.M., he delivered the bad news, and they drove over to their old house.

Bingo, thought the agents, another inconsistency. Back in October, during their tape-recorded interviews with the Hagens, Marjorie had claimed that they had run errands and then driven by the Cranberry House with the Mallimakis. Their divide-and-conquer tactics with the Hagens were paying off.

DiPrima asked how Wally and Marjorie intended to pay the Mallimakis their $36,800 by January. Hagen claimed that he had sold the Kulseths a contract for deed at a ten percent discount.

That afternoon, at the adult detention center in Minneapolis, Meshbesher arrived to secure his client's release. She was soon freed on $20,000 bail, released on her own recognizance. Stay out of trouble, Meshbesher advised Marjorie before she left the jail.

Looking back, DiPrima said, "If you look at the fires, they were fires of vindictiveness. They were fires of need," he said. "She needed this. She was always hungry for cash. And I think that's what motivated her, is that she was living beyond her means and she needed more money.

"She's an amateur of course, because she's getting caught," he continued. "All the time, by God, she's got enough money she can buy herself out of it. So I think our position was we would do the most professional case we could. We went to such great lengths to lock that house up. We wanted to make sure that she couldn't say that there was a window open that someone could have come in. We went out and photographed every window."

As investigators made progress on the arson case, Marjorie made more news—but this time for bigamy. At the time of her arrest, she'd listed Hagen as her last name. Her attorney had told reporters that his client used the name to avoid unpleasant publicity. But the county prosecutor had publicly disputed that, saying he'd seen an out-of-state marriage license for Marjorie and Wally, which she had stashed in her pants during the BCA search. In the weeks that followed Marjorie's arrest, North Dakota authorities had quietly been investigating her latest claim to marital and financial bliss.

In April 1983, North Dakota officials were ready to act. The district attorney's office in Valley City, North Dakota, filed formal bigamy charges against Marjorie. According to their records, Marjorie had remarried two years before, but failed to mention her marriage to Roger, who as far as he knew had been serving his prison term as a married man. Doug Thomson and Ron Meshbesher also told investigators they had no knowledge of any divorce.

Marjorie, however, had identified herself as Marjorie LeRoy. The North Dakota courts had a copy of her divorce from her first husband, but no divorce decree for her second marriage. The evidence indicated Marjorie was still married to Roger when she wed Wally.

North Dakota authorities decided not to extradite Marjorie because of transportation and prosecution costs. Instead they made her a promise. If Marjorie Caldwell Hagen ever set foot on North Dakota soil again, she would be arrested—and bigamy was a felony punishable by up to five years in prison and a $5,000 fine.

There were, of course, other skeletons in Marjorie's closet. During the arson investigation Wally told Nancy over the phone he would go after her son if she told investigators anything about her mother's death. In the background Kaufmann heard Marjorie saying, "Tell her to keep her mouth shut or we'll take care of her."

The holiday season had arrived in Minneapolis. Despite temperatures that had plummeted since Thanksgiving, the Salvation Army rang bells on street corners. Tiny white lights adorned trees and glass skyways in downtown Minneapolis. Wreaths and bows trimmed streetlights and shops along the Nicollet Mall and animated store window displays distracted shoppers. But amid the holiday festivities, inside the smoke-blue glass tower of the Hennepin County Government Center, Marjorie once again tried to avoid going to prison.

As her arson trial opened in December 1983, the attorney who had defended her in her murder trial again stood by her side. Meshbesher quickly ushered her into the courtroom, pushing past the eager reporters and photographers. This time Dan Mabley, assistant county attorney, carried the boxes laden with police reports and witness interviews.

The tedious routine of jury selection had attracted few spectators. But for opening statements, the courtroom on the fourteenth floor of the government center was crowded. The housewives and retirees who would become regulars included several women who had been jurors for Marjorie's murder trial in Hastings and had kept in touch with her over the years. They constituted a small cheering section for the defendant.

Although Nancy Hagen Kaufmann faithfully attended the trial, and her brothers dropped in as work allowed, their father was conspicuously absent. He had undergone heart surgery the month before the trial and remained at home, recuperating. He would testify via videotape.

Both sides had sought the same kind of jury: well-educated, intelligent jurors who could follow the technical testimony from the evidence of technicians and fire investigators. The jury consisted of seven women and five men, with vocational backgrounds ranging from community volunteer to engineer to locksmith.

"Witnesses are going to take the stand and tell you…that there was no accidental cause to the fire," Mabley told jurors in his opening statement. He promised to leave the technical details of the fire investigation to experts and continued. "As they were negotiating the contract, the defendant…insisted that possession not be given to the Kulseths for two weeks after closing because [they] wanted to [finish] some wiring…and some touch-up painting.

"The day of closing the Kulseths…got an insurance policy and under that…if there was a loss…the Hagens would be paid for their interest in the property." Mabley said the evidence would show that Marjorie Hagen set her former house on fire and collected more than $16,000 in insurance.

Marjorie had told investigators a number of lies—proof of her guilt, Mabley argued. She had insisted that she and her husband had given all the house keys to the Kulseths the night before the fire. But BCA agents found a key to the front door in the Hagens' kitchen cupboard. When investigators had asked Marjorie if there was a gas can on the premises, she denied it, but, said Mabley, "her husband was standing right next to her and overheard the question and informed investigators that in fact they did have a gas can." He also informed jurors of the mysterious fires in September 1979 and May 1982 which had aroused the suspicions of BCA agent Pat Shannon.

Mabley concluded his remarks with a brief mention of the insurance settlement, made the day before the balloon payment the Hagens owed came due.

During a fifteen-minute recess, Meshbesher vigorously protested that the prosecution had alluded to other fires his client was suspected of setting and demanded a mistrial. The judge refused and ruled that evidence of the two previous fires could be presented.

Mabley had won an important battle. Both houses were vacant at the time of the fires and the fires freed the defendant from purchase agreements she'd signed. It was part of the pattern he wanted the jury to recognize.

Throughout the trial, Marjorie's friendly demeanor toward him surprised Mabley. The prosecutor had tried to avoid the traditional, navy blue lawyer's uniform—and Marjorie paid him high compliments. One day Mabley wore a tweed sports jacket and cable sweater vest, and at the morning break Marjorie walked up and admired the sweater. "Where did you buy it?" she asked. "I wish my son had one like that." Sure enough, she went out and bought one just like it. Another day, when he had a flare-up of tendonitis, Marjorie insisted on giving Mabley a new brand of aspirin she had brought back from Europe.

The state's first witnesses included Clayton Kulseth. He said Wally gave him some house keys including one he removed from his key ring.

"Did he make any statement about whether they had any more keys at that time?" Mabley asked.

"No, he said this is the master key, this is the last key that he had."

Clayton testified that after dinner the Kulseths left the Hagens at the Cranberry House at about 9:30 P.M. and visited Gerane Kulseth's sister, who lived nearby. About forty-five minutes later as the Kulseths drove home, they saw the Hagens driving in the direction of the Cranberry House. The couples waved at one another, and that was the last time the Kulseths saw the Hagens before the fire.

Knowing the defense's theory of the crime was that the Kulseths had ample opportunity and financial motive to set the fire, Mabley beat Meshbesher to the punch.

"Mr. Kulseth, did you set the fire?"

"No, sir."

"And did you engage in any planning to set the fire?"

"No, sir."

On cross, Meshbesher tried to dispel the Hagens' insurance settlement as a reasonable motive for torching the Cranberry House. He asked Kulseth if they had discussed the insurance policy with the Hagens at closing.

"I'm not sure," Kulseth said.

"And Mr. and Mrs. Hagen made no big point of finding out whether you had insurance and how much you had, did they?" Kulseth said they hadn't.

"In fact, as a result of your having the property underinsured, Mr. and Mrs. Hagen lost about $4,000 that they otherwise would have been entitled to under the contract?"

"That's true," Kulseth replied.

Next, the state called Gerane Kulseth, who testified that the Kulseths had received no insurance money after the fire. She said that though they did get the land, fire had gutted the house, forcing them to have it torn down. They rebuilt the house, but it was no longer suitable for the antique business she had planned to open. Meshbesher again asked about the homeowner's insurance and got the same answers.

The prosecution's strategy at this point was to establish inconsistencies in Marjorie's statements to police and fire investigators. Mabley's first step was to call to the stand Pharmacist Brian Hall, who worked at Snyder Drugs in Mound, where Marjorie said she picked up a prescription September 14. He testified that the store had no record of any prescriptions sold on September 14 or 15 to Marjorie or Wally.

Marjorie had insisted to investigators that she hadn't learned about the fire until she returned from quilting after noon, but Marlys Annis, one of the Hagens' former neighbors, testified she saw Marjorie driving near the scene about 8:20 A.M. Annis and her daughter had just passed the burning house and as they approached the next corner, Annis spotted a black pickup. "When this truck got to the stop sign I noticed that it was Marjorie and that her window was down, and I did not say anything first. But she asked me, 'What's going on down there?'"

Annis told Marjorie, "Your house is burning." Marjorie replied that she had sold the house two weeks before.

The prosecution put on evidence of the fire's cause through testimony from investigators for the Minnesota State Fire Marshal's Office. Jerry Babb had examined all the windows and doors the day of the fire and ruled out forced entry. It was clear to him that whoever started the fire had used a key.

James Hellerud testified that when he arrived at the scene he had been concerned about a possible electrical cause, but found no evidence of defective wiring. Instead, he saw flammable liquid patterns on both floors of the house. Mabley asked Hellerud to define the term for the jury.

"A flammable liquid pattern is an indication, usually on a floor surface, where a liquid is poured from one point to another and it leaves a pattern that is quite distinctive from anything else, any other burn patterns," Hellerud explained.

"What's your opinion about this fire as to its cause?"

"That the fire was accelerated by…an accelerant, probably gasoline."

During cross-examination, Meshbesher grilled Hellerud about his original findings on the cause of the blaze. Hellerud admitted he had listed "possible electrical" on the report he filed September 15, but testified that an electrical fire was no longer a plausible theory.

Meshbesher was on the attack, doing his best to convince jurors that fire investigators couldn't be certain the cause wasn't electrical. Why hadn't Hellerud and other fire investigators mentioned arson to begin with? Didn't arson become the cause only after they learned the owner of the house was Marjorie Caldwell Hagen?

David Petersen, a BCA forensic chemist specializing in arson and explosive analysis, testified about his analysis of fire debris. Petersen had received six samples from the Cranberry House from James Hellerud. Two were fire debris taken from the first floor, and the other four samples were standard controls of various liquids. He tested the two samples from the first floor for the presence of a liquid accelerant and detected the characteristics of gasoline.

On cross-examination, Meshbesher challenged the chemist. "But when you say something is characteristic of something, it doesn't necessarily mean it is something?"

"Well, legally it can't be gasoline as I found it because there are certain boiling point definitions that gasoline has to fit in the State of Minnesota, so I agree, it is not gasoline. However, if you took that same gasoline and evaporated it, then it would give you what I found," Petersen shot back.

Midway through the trial, Rick took the stand to testify about his mother's whereabouts early September 4, 1979, when an earlier suspicious fire had damaged a house his mother had agreed to buy.

The fire had broken out about 2:32 A.M.; Mabley needed Rick to admit that when he had returned home from college early on the fourth Marjorie was not home. But Rick could not with certainty remember the date he returned home—it was the third or fourth or fifth, he said.

During Meshbesher's cross-examination, however, Rick testified that he came home the morning of the fifth, twenty-one hours after the fire, because he now remembered registering for classes the next day at a local college.

On redirect, Mabley reminded Rick that he had originally said he was unsure about the dates, but Rick wouldn't budge. Mabley could do little else but move to the next name on his witness list, volunteer firefighter Roger Schaffhausen, who confirmed that based on his experience, the fire on September 4, 1979, was arson.

The state's witnesses also included Wally, who remained at home recovering from his recent heart attack. He testified via videotape that Marjorie was asleep in bed with him at the time the Cranberry House fire started. She got up around 7 A.M. and fixed him breakfast before leaving for her quilting class. After Marjorie came home he told her about the fire and they went over to look at the house. They didn't go in because they were concerned someone might see them and accuse them of setting the fire.

In his earlier statements, Hagen had said there were four keys to the Cranberry House, but in his taped deposition he said five. When Mabley questioned Hagen about who had keys, he answered that himself, Marjorie, Rick, the milkman, and the man who serviced their water softener.

Mabley got Hagen to say that his wife frequently checked books out of the library, then asked, "To your knowledge, did she ever have an overdue book?"

"Not to my knowledge," Hagen said.

So much for Marjorie's story that she returned a late book the morning of the fire. He moved on to the Hagens' activities the night before the fire.

Hagen testified that after dinner they and the Kulseths had left the house "about the same time" with the Kulseths "just ahead of me." He then said that he and Marjorie drove to a nearby drugstore so Marjorie could pick up a prescription; previous testimony had already discredited all this, and Mabley hoped this string of inconsistencies wasn't lost on the jury. He now turned his questioning to the payment the Hagens still owed on the house.

"That balloon payment was due January 15, 1983?"

"Approximately in there," Hagen replied.

"And at that time over $36,000 was due?"

"Right."

"Did you have $36,000 in September?"

"No." Aside from the $15,000 cash they had received from the sale of the Cranberry House, his pension, Marjorie's trust income, and Social Security, "nothing more" was coming in.

Meshbesher's cross-examination focused on the remodeling that the Hagens had done. They had painted, replaced plumbing, added a half bath, and built a false fireplace. He then asked about the rosemaling in the dining and living rooms.

"She did that by herself," Wally replied.

"When that was completed did she ever indicate great pride in that accomplishment?"

"She did."

Meshbesher stressed the unlikelihood that Marjorie would burn down a house she had so carefully worked to decorate. He moved on to the Hagens' morning routine.

"Did your wife ever fail, in the years you have been married to her, the last couple years, ever fail to fix breakfast for you while you were living with her?"

"She never has."

"Did she at any time the evening of the fourteenth and the early morning hours of the fifteenth up to seven or so in the morning, get out of bed?"

"No, she didn't."

"Are you prepared to state that she was in bed all night with you?"

"I will, yes."

Mabley decided not to push Hagen on the alibi he had provided for his wife. Instead Mabley would continue to expose his inconsistencies.

Mabley called Robert Flemal, owner of a Culligan water conditioning business. He said he had no memory of being given a key to the Hagens' house. When he needed to service their water softener he called ahead to arrange access.

BCA Agent DiPrima was also recalled to refute Wally's testimony. "During the videotape deposition I asked Mr. Hagen what time he got up the morning of the fire, and I believe he stated that it was between six-thirty and seven approximately, and specifically he said that seven-thirty and eight were much too late."

"Did you [previously] ask him when he got up the morning of the fire?"

"Yes, I did."

"And what was the first thing he told you?"

"First he told us he got up between seven-thirty and eight. On a later interview in January, he told us definitely that he got up at seven with his wife, Marjorie."

DiPrima testified that Hagen had told him there were only four keys for the Cranberry House.

"Did he ever mention to you that he had made five keys at one particular time, rekeying?" Mabley asked.

"No, he told us nothing about a rekeying," DiPrima said.

Following DiPrima, BCA Agent Shannon took the stand to testify about the front door key that he found in the Hagen's kitchen. Mabley, however, could not introduce the door into evidence to demonstrate that the key fit. The door had been lost while in storage at the Mound Fire Department.

"About three weeks before trial, it disappears and they were cleaning up the fire department because of this fund raiser they were going to have," Mabley later explained. "I sent them out to about five different garbage dumps…. It couldn't be found."

He had been furious. If the defense found out, it would make the investigation look sloppy. Mabley had to limit the amount of physical evidence introduced to avoid calling attention to the missing door, and concentrate on the key.

After Shannon told the jury that he found the key in the kitchen cupboard inside a basket, Mabley asked, "Did you show it to anybody at the search warrant scene?"

"I showed it to the defendant and her husband," said Shannon.

"And what was his response?"

"He said he didn't know."

"And what was her response?"

"She said she'd never seen it before."

Shannon noted that although officers found other keys at the house, Marjorie had precise explanations for each. The only key she didn't have an explanation for was the one recovered in the basket. When she saw the key she turned her back and walked away.

Shannon had tested the key the next day. "You go to the front door and it turned, it worked," he reported.

Shannon also testified that he reviewed microfilm of the names of people who took books out of the Mound Public Library system from July 30, 1982, through the day of the fire.

"And were you able to find any entry listing a book under the name of the defendant?" Mabley asked.

"No, sir."

During cross-examination, Meshbesher insisted that since the key wasn't tested the same day, there was no proof the key that opened the door was the same one agent Shannon found.

"Now did you compare the key with the other keys that you got from the Kulseths?" Meshbesher asked.

"Yes, sir," replied Shannon.

"Did they look alike?"

"Yes, sir."

"Exactly alike?"

"Not exactly, no."

Under further questioning, Shannon said the key was cut a little differently and was a different brand from the rest of the Kulseth's keys.

"It appears as though they were made at different times, doesn't it?" Meshbesher asked.

"Yes, sir."

The defense's insinuation was clear—investigators could have planted the key. Anyone familiar with Marjorie's murder trial might have wondered why people always wanted to frame her.

Marjorie was out on bail during the trial and returned to her Mound home each afternoon after testimony ended. Several times she called Meshbesher complaining of an upset stomach, implying the stress of the trial affected her. During court recesses, however, Marjorie seemed fine. She chatted with reporters and spectators or sat reading or doing needlepoint. At the noon break, she ate lunch with her defense team in the government center's cafeteria.

The trial proceeded into the defense phase. Meshbesher called Mound police officer Herman Kraft. Officer Kraft testified that he "took over the traffic detail" in the vicinity of the fire about 8:15 A.M. for approximately an hour.

"Did you ever see Mrs. Hagen that morning?"

"No, I did not."

Kraft explained he had met Marjorie several years earlier through Wally. "I've known Wally for many years…probably twenty-some years, twenty-five years," Kraft told jurors. "I got to know Wally and his sons and we'd have coffee on occasions when he'd come into the coffee shop, sit and talk."

Meshbesher asked about Wally's "reputation for truthfulness." This was important to the defense, given the discrepancies between the Hagens' testimony and what jurors had heard from the state's witnesses. Kraft testified that "I'd have to say that Wally has always been quite straightforward and a nice person to talk to." In his opinion, Wally was a truthful person.

Beginning a battle of experts, Meshbesher called Dr. Roger Upham, a senior consultant with a local testing laboratory whose work included arson analysis.

"Can you make any valid scientific conclusion whether or not accelerants were added to the already existing floor in this particular fire?" Meshbesher asked.

"On the basis of the evidence I have, I would say no."

On cross-examination, Mabley attacked Upham's experience. "What percentage of your work involves arson testing?"

"I would assume between ten and fifteen percent."

"You have to have experience with arson testing in order to interpret gas chromatograms."

"Yes, you do."

"You were aware, are you not, that Petersen is devoted to arson testing a hundred percent of the time?"

"Yes, I am."

But Meshbesher rallied in his redirect examination. He suggested the possibility that the control sample used by Dr. Petersen in his arson analysis was contaminated by gasoline.

"How would that affect any scientist's conclusion with respect to the results in this case?"

"I would expect that would make it very difficult to draw conclusions about the rest of the fire debris."

"If Mr. Petersen's testing process with respect to the control sample was done properly and you did your testing properly and you read your results properly, would you expect the same findings?"

"I would expect to see similar things, more [elements] in Mr. Petersen's than were in mine."

"And in fact you found more in yours, is that correct?"

"That's correct."

Mabley recalled Dr. Petersen to testify on rebuttal. Petersen started from the beginning: "To do the tests you use a gas chromatograph exclusively for arson analysis. A gas chromatograph is a machine that will take a liquid sample and break it up into its individual parts. If you had twenty-five items in a certain liquid it would break it up into all twenty-five items."

As a result of the tests he conducted on debris samples from the Cranberry House, he obtained chromatograms which identified several components that he again testified were "characteristic of gasoline." He told jurors he knew of no other chemical that shared those same characteristics.

The defense called Robert Carr, a professor of chemical engineering at the University of Minnesota, as a rebuttal witness. Carr had listened to Petersen describe the tests he had conducted. Carr now challenged Petersen's test methods, criticized his analysis of the control sample as being less complete than that of defense expert Upham. Although Petersen had testified that he found gasoline in the debris, Carr told jurors that the compounds present did not necessarily indicate gasoline had been present. He noted that finding the same substances as Petersen had, in both the control sample and the debris sample, would in his opinion "hinder a determination as to whether a foreign accelerant had been added to the debris sample."

However, on cross-examination, Carr admitted that he did not perform arson testing. He also acknowledged that he had used the gas chromatograph for identification of substances, and that the presence of gasoline could be identified with the instrument.

By the end of testimony, Mabley had become so discouraged by Meshbesher's aggressive cross-examinations he felt it likely Marjorie would walk away a free woman. The defense had made it seem as though Marjorie's past made her an easy target. Meshbesher had skillfully used witnesses to point out the illogic of Marjorie torching a house she had so carefully remodeled, and for a fairly insignificant payoff. From Mabley's perspective, his case had been on a downward slide for two weeks. But he was determined to try to turn it around with his closing statement.

Press coverage of the trial itself had been spotty, but for closing arguments more than a dozen reporters crowded in front of the railing, a place usually off limits to any spectators.

Mabley said investigators had looked for "the possibility of spontaneous fire or a cigarette fire and had checked out the house's heating system. They went through and did a thorough job and found absolutely no accidental cause...that would have explained the fire."

During his closing argument, as he turned and glanced at the defendant, Mabley involuntarily shrank back. Marjorie wore a fixed look of pure hatred, one of the few genuine glimpses of emotion he saw in her during the trial.

"Burn patterns indicated there was some kind of accelerant applied," he continued. Marjorie had the motive, means, and opportunity to set the fire. "This fire was set for a very specific purpose—to pay off a debt." He reminded the jury of the $36,832 the Hagens still owed on their former house.

"Who else would want to set a fire at the Cranberry House? We haven't heard any evidence about any vandals...[or] revenge motives against the Hagens or...any indication that this was a psychological fire. In fact, the fire investigators say that this fire had the characteristics of a fire for profit because of the fact it was accelerated and appeared to be somewhat planned, whereas a pyromaniac fire, revenge fires, and vandalistic fires tend to be [impulsive]."

Arson investigators found no signs of forced entry and, Mabley told jurors, they found a key fitting the front door in the Hagens' kitchen cupboard.

"The defendant said...all the keys...were turned over to the Kulseths. Well, that's not true. No matter which version of how many keys you believe...both of them said initially three, both of them changed it to four, Wally even went up to five. But the testimony is absolutely clear that the Kulseths only got two."

Mabley argued that Marjorie had the opportunity to set the fire. "It's only a seven-minute drive away, two-point-three miles, it would take a matter of minutes for her to drive over there and accomplish this and drive back [to her current home]. [No witness] saw anybody set a fire...but we do have the second kind of thing that investigators look for, and that's the fact that sometimes criminals will return to the scene of the crime to see what has happened.

"Well, in this particular case we do have evidence that she was there...approximately an hour-and-a-half after the fire was reported, so what does that mean to you? It means she went back to check on the progress of the fire, to see if she had accomplished what it was that she set out to accomplish."

Mabley reminded jurors of the previous house fires in 1979 and 1982. "I suggest that she uses fire as a way of solving immediate problems." He described the similarities: an accelerant was used in all of the fires, they occurred at night, at the time they happened the building or house was unoccupied, and each fire broke out around the time Marjorie owed significant amounts of money.

He concluded, "There's only one person who had an interest in setting this fire, and there's only one person who could have started the fire, and all the other evidence only points to one person."

Meshbesher's closing argument began with a quotation from *Alice in Wonderland*: "The King said, 'The evidence first and then the sentence.' the Queen said, 'No, the sentence first and then the evidence.' Alice said, "That's nonsense,' and yelled, and everybody got alarmed at what she said. The very idea of the sentence first and the evidence second." Meshbesher explained, "As I heard Mr. Mabley do a beautiful job in arguing these facts, I realized what you could do with words, and your whole approach to the case can color your viewpoint."

The original cause of the fire, Meshbesher reminded jurors, was listed as possible faulty wiring, even by a state fire marshal. He snatched up a document from the exhibit table as he explained. "This report is made at the end of the day.... It's made after all the firemen had gone in, including Mr. Babb and Mr. Hellerud, and done their examination of the premises.... 'Cause of fire, possible electrical, state fire marshall, Jim Hellerud.' Mr. Babb put that in and Fireman Platzer signed it."

Meshbesher argued that investigators changed their minds once they learned who Marjorie Hagen was—that her last name had been Caldwell. Her past legal troubles prompted officials to build a case against her.

There are so many differences between the other fires and this one, Meshbesher argued. If Marjorie supposedly sets fires for profit, keep in mind she didn't make a penny off those other fires. No eyewitnesses placed her at the other fires—the only evidence, Meshbesher continued, was that she had signed purchase agreements on the two houses and the fires occurred before closing. He cautioned jurors that even if they believed her responsible for those two fires, "that still doesn't mean she's guilty of this fire." Those investigations are closed, he told them, and shouldn't be part of your decision in this case.

"The finger of suspicion is pointed at Marge Hagen," Meshbesher reiterated, "and nobody else. Don't let them kid you.... They picked on Marge and made this evidence fit. Everyone agrees the fire got started around five-thirty, six in the morning.... [But] she's with Wally the whole time. If she's doing something to set up a fire then Wally's guilty, too. Why isn't Wally charged? Why? Because Wally's name was never Caldwell," he concluded, his voice full of outrage.

Meshbesher captured the attention of the press corps with a demonstration using the Kulseths' keys and the key discovered in the Hagens' house. He picked up the keys and walked to the jury box, standing only a few feet away from the jurors and the pack of reporters at the rail. Holding the keys up, he announced, "I've solved the case for you."

Mabley braced for the bombshell, wondering what Meshbesher was going to say next. Meshbesher pointed out that the Kulseths' keys were shaped differently than the one belonging to Marjorie. How could anyone believe that Marjorie's key opened the front door of the Cranberry House? he asked.

Mabley could see the reporters intensely taking notes. He looked at the jurors' faces and tried to read whether they believed Meshbesher. Whatever the impact of the defense attorney's statement, Mabley was powerless to say or do anything. Minnesota, alone among states, allows the defense the final word.

After a long day, final arguments finished, and bailiffs escorted the jury to dinner before jurors began their deliberations.

Only sixteen hours after deliberations began, the jury was ready to announce its decision. The relatively brief length of time the jurors had been out—and their serious demeanor—encouraged Mabley. Curious spectators and reporters filled the courtroom to near capacity.

Marjorie walked in with Rick and Meshbesher at her side. She sat subdued and silent as she took her seat at the counsel table. On the way to court, Marjorie confided in Meshbesher that she had a bad feeling about the verdict. Now she stared at the serious faces in the jury box and braced herself as the clerk began to read aloud.

"We, the jury, find the defendant guilty of arson in the second degree.... We, the jury, find the defendant guilty of defrauding an insurer." Marjorie's face registered no reaction or emotion. Meshbesher looked down at the counsel table as his assistant, Diane Wiley, reached over and patted Marjorie's hand. Wally's daughter Nancy, clenched her fist and exclaimed "Yes!" loud enough that several of Marjorie's supporters turned around and glared. As Marjorie left the courtroom with Meshbesher, she pointed at Nancy and said, in a soft but menacing voice, "I'll get you for this." Marjorie would be sentenced in three weeks.

As Meshbesher went over to shake his opponent's hand, Marjorie grabbed hold of Rick. They stormed out of the courtroom, trying to avoid the throng of photographers. But on her way to the privacy of a courthouse office down the hall, she stumbled and fell down. Marjorie immediately made a scene, yelling and blaming the closest photographer. "You tripped me on purpose," Marjorie screamed.

Meshbesher and Mabley talked to reporters in the lobby of the Hennepin County Government Center. Mabley had learned that one of the jurors, a former locksmith, had shot down Meshbesher's attempt to discredit the key evidence. The man explained to fellow jurors that master house keys don't look the same as the rest of the keys. No discrepancy; end of argument.

Meshbesher said he was considering an appeal. The use of evidence from two previous arson fires in which his client had been investigated severely damaged the defense's case, he told reporters.

Mabley was also contemplating Marjorie's future, one that might include prison. He told the press he might ask the judge to deviate from the sentencing guidelines and give Marjorie a stiff sentence, prison versus probation.

For those closest to the arson investigation, the verdict was justice long overdue—and a responsibility fulfilled.

DiPrima explained, "This woman had gotten away with murder.... I think of all the cases I've ever worked, I've never wanted to nail someone like I wanted to nail her. She's an evil person."

Shannon, who eventually left law enforcement, later said he would have stayed in the field if "there were more like Marjorie.... Dangerous, compulsive, and altogether just a real interesting hunt. A good criminal. Just one that every cop wants to track down and get a hold of."

That afternoon, DiPrima phoned Waller in Duluth with the news. Waller hadn't wanted to consider the possibility that she might go free again. The detective told Di-Prima, "She'll finally get a little taste of what she deserves."

The day before her sentencing, Marjorie again made front page news, this time for shoplifting. Security officers at an upscale grocery store discovered a $7.99 bottle of vitamins in her purse after she had passed through the checkout line. She got off with a citation.

The Hennepin County Government Center courtroom swarmed with spectators the morning of February 9, 1984. Meshbesher ushered Marjorie in. Wally sat quietly, distraught by the prospect of losing his wife to prison.

Marjorie's declaration of innocence did not impress Judge Robert Schiefelbein. Although the fire had not resulted in any deaths or injuries, the judge said it had endangered the lives of the firefighters at the scene.

"As Harry Truman said, the buck stops here. It's my duty to impose the sentence," Schiefelbein said. "...Ma'am, you stand convicted of a major economic crime involving $70,000, accomplished by a series of illegal acts committed by concealment and guile to obtain money and avoid the loss of money and property. The offense involved actual monetary loss substantially greater than the usual offense, and the minimum loss specified in the statute. Further, the offense involved a high degree of sophistication and planning and occurred over a rather lengthy period of time."

He sentenced Marjorie to two-and-a-half years in prison and fined her $10,000. The sentence was harsh—Minnesota sentencing guidelines recommended one-and-three quarters years' probation and no fine. Shrouded in a dark hooded jacket and her trademark oversized sunglasses, Marjorie refused to talk to reporters. Meshbesher said he would file an appeal. Taken into custody immediately after sentencing, Marjorie was free that afternoon on a $50,000 bond pending appeal.

In a somewhat unusual move, Judge Schiefelbein stayed Marjorie's sentence, pending her appeal. She would remain free for nearly two years, until the court upheld her conviction. She entered Shakopee Women's Prison, located just south of the Twin Cities, on January 25, 1985. The minimum stay at the prison was one year and a day; her sentence required Marjorie to serve at least twenty-and-a-half months. Roger was pleased when he heard that Marjorie had been convicted of arson. He told Arnold "at last she got caught."

CHAPTER 23

A Controversial Bargain

IN THE MIDST OF MARJORIE'S EXPANDING LEGAL TROUBLES—she had been arrested for arson in January and would soon be charged with bigamy—the spring of 1983 looked like the beginning of the end of Roger's problems with the law. A plea agreement that would save him the worry and time of another trial was taking shape. It had started in March, when DeSanto stopped by Thomson's St. Paul office, where he got a closer look at his competitor's taste and style. The decor, like Thomson, was polished and expensive. The cherry wood desk and credenza particularly impressed DeSanto.

"Nice office," he told Thomson, warming up to the real reason for the visit. De-Santo's boss had instructed him to see how serious Thomson was about a plea bargain. "Aren't we glad to go through this again?" DeSanto joked. Both men, however, knew the real question: "If I were to make an offer, what's the bottom line?"

"Minimal time or no more prison time," Thomson insisted. But he told DeSanto he wasn't optimistic about "selling" Roger on any agreement. Roger remained adamant—he was innocent and wrongly convicted.

That same spring, David Arnold accompanied Roger to a meeting with Thomson to discuss the retrial. "[Roger] was concerned about going to trial again. I remember his words exactly as we sat in Doug's office. 'I'm just as innocent now as I was the first time and I was convicted.'"

Weeks later, while attending a criminal justice conference in Minneapolis, DeSanto and Waller dropped in on Thomson. Time to assess the likelihood of a plea agreement versus a second trial, they told him. "A new trial—it's like eating cold oatmeal," Thomson responded. The defense would take as much of a risk as the prosecution. The only major difference this time around was the absence of the fingerprint evidence from the envelope. The men parted company with an understanding—they'd work out a plea agreement somehow.

As DeSanto and Waller drove back to Duluth, they rehashed their list of reasons for avoiding a retrial. The St. Louis County Attorney's Office would be up against terrible odds in a second trial. The rate of conviction in murder retrials is discouraging at best. The amount of publicity this case had attracted would make it hard to find twelve jurors in Minnesota who'd never heard of the murders or Marjorie's acquittal.

Several prosecution witnesses had died, including Merrill Hughes, the sheriff's deputy and crime lab technician who discovered the stolen jewelry in the Caldwells' Bloomington hotel room. Witnesses would testify from refreshed memory and would probably come off as rehearsed and stiff. Chances of a witness accurately recalling events from six years earlier were far less, and the opportunity for inconsistencies far greater. The defense would jump on every mistake, and there would be plenty of ammunition. Two grand jury transcripts, two omnibus hearing transcripts, two trial transcripts, and the original police statements meant seven different ways defense could impeach some witnesses.

A change of venue had also been granted, moving the trial to the Hennepin County Government Center in downtown Minneapolis. The trial judge apparently had no concern about the aggressive coverage the Twin Cities media had given the prior trials. The cost of a second trial would be significant for St. Louis County taxpayers—at least half a million dollars. But the biggest blow to the prosecution's case was still to come.

Rebecca, Heather, and Suzanne had continued to challenge Marjorie's right to the Congdon inheritance if she were found to have been involved in Elisabeth's murder. A civil trial had been scheduled to begin May 9.

As the trial date came and went, it became obvious that the suit would be settled out of court—bad news for DeSanto and Waller. Without the civil trial, they'd lost the opportunity to question Marjorie under oath about her mother's near-fatal drugging in 1974 and her activities the weekend Elisabeth died. At her criminal trial, Marjorie had avoided testifying. In a civil trial, she would have had no choice.

"When the suit folded, there was no incentive left for us to go through with another trial," Waller recalled. "We weren't going to get Marge's version. We would probably lose. Why put the county through the expense? Finally, why put ourselves through the misery again?"

The St. Louis County Attorney's Office prepared to offer a deal. In exchange for his confession of murder, Roger would serve minimal additional time in prison. DeSanto put the offer in writing in this May 17, 1983, letter to Doug Thomson:

> This office will permit Mr. Caldwell to plead guilty to two counts of Murder in the Second Degree in violation of Minnesota statutes 609.19 for the murders of Elisabeth Congdon and Velma Pietila and will dismiss the two counts of murder in the first degree presently pending against him in accordance with the following conditions.
>
> 1) Mr. Caldwell must admit his guilt of these two murders at the time of these guilty pleas
>
> 2) At the time of the guilty pleas, Mr. Caldwell must give a truthful and complete statement, under oath, indicating the involvement of these murders, the carrying out of these murders, and/or the covering up of his participation in these murders
>
> 3) For the two Murder in the Second Degree convictions Mr. Caldwell will receive two concurrent 111 month sentences to prison; assuming "good time" would be earned against these sentences Mr. Caldwell would actually serve 74 months at Stillwater

> Prison; since Mr. Caldwell was incarcerated from July 6, 1977, to September 1, 1982, for his original convictions of these murders, these 62 months already served would leave a remainder of 12 months to be served for the new Murder in the Second Degree convictions.

On May 17, Thomson mailed Roger a copy of the plea agreement to Latrobe, Pennsylvania, where he had been living since December 1982. "You have to make up your own mind what you want to do," Thomson told him. It was a roll of the dice either way—maybe he'd walk after a new trial or wind up with a life sentence. Eager to avoid another trial and possible additional prison time, Roger chose the plea, but objected to the remaining twelve months. Thomson negotiated with DeSanto until the twelve months were dropped pending a judge's approval for time already served.

Judge Charles Barnes, the newest judge on the district bench, had been assigned the case. He reviewed the letter and agreed to the conditions. The next step would be Roger's official on-the-record confession.

One more twist occurred before the civil lawsuit was settled. In mid-May Roger had written a letter from his prison cell to Duluth Probate Judge Robert Campbell. He told the judge he was entitled to a share of Elisabeth's estate: "I object to any proceedings held to make a final decision in these matters without consideration for my interests and request that the hearing be delayed until I can hire an attorney or perhaps you will appoint an attorney to represent me and protect my interests."

Judge Campbell ruled that Roger was not entitled to part of the inheritance and the final settlement of the LeRoy children's civil lawsuit came on July 1, 1983. Under the terms of a complex settlement, approved by a Duluth probate judge, Marjorie would receive a small fraction of the money left by her mother. The remaining millions would be divided among her children. The terms of the settlement required that one-third of the children's share be used to create a special fund from which their mother could draw income for the rest of her life.

The LeRoy children would also divide assets and income from a second trust, the Congdon Trust, valued at approximately $2 million. According to their grandfather's will, these funds could not be touched until twenty-one years after the death of his last child.

Before distribution of the funds, however, Marjorie's creditors, attorneys, and her children had to be paid. Creditors' claims totaled close to $400,000. Legal fees, including those for the murder trials, amounted to $1.3 million. Thomson received $100,000. Meshbesher took home more than $1 million and stock in St. Mary's Parish Land Company (one of the Congdon family businesses) and the Congdon orchards in Yakima, Washington. (The Congdon family later bought out Meshbesher's Congdon holdings).

On July 5, 1983, nearly six years to the day after his arrest for the murders of his mother-in-law and her nurse, Roger prepared for his confession.

Late that Wednesday morning, Roger, casually dressed in a blue shirt, gray slacks, and the navy windbreaker he'd worn the day of his release from jail, arrived at the St. Louis County Courthouse with David Arnold. Rather than use the highly visible main entrance, Arnold ushered Roger through the courthouse's rear door.

"I'll never forget the face of the secretary at the reception desk," DeSanto recalled. "No one knew this was going to happen. People started arriving and then Roger Caldwell walked in. Faces just dropped. I told the secretary, 'We'll be meeting in the library,' and walked away."

Arnold and Caldwell met DeSanto, Waller, Doug Thomson, Thomson's associate Bruce Meyer, and court reporter Don Macheledt in the small, wallpapered library of the county attorney's office. Over the next three hours, Caldwell gave a sworn statement—his confession to and version of the murders of Elisabeth Congdon and Velma Pietila. DeSanto had filled his yellow legal notepad with questions, which he checked off as Roger provided the answers.

But while Roger was more talkative than DeSanto and Waller could ever remember, he was as emotive as a bowl of Jell-O. He assumed complete blame for the killings without changing expression or meeting DeSanto's or Waller's eyes. Roger's insistence on calling the prosecutor "John" increasingly irritated DeSanto. "Don't you call me John. I'm not your friend," he thought, disgusted by the familiarity.

More importantly, Roger was vague—or said he couldn't remember—in response to several of DeSanto's key questions.

"You have stated that [you threw] the suede bag and the wicker basket...into the trunk of Marge's car when she picks you up at the restaurant?" DeSanto began. Caldwell nodded his head affirmatively.

"Is that right?" DeSanto prodded for a verbal response.

"Yes."

"Can you explain why you remember that but you don't even remember purchasing the suede bag or getting the wicker basket?"

"I can't explain it other than different levels of consciousness at one time or another."

"Well, back up from when you threw it into the trunk of the car. As you sit here now, when is the [first] time before that you recall the wicker basket and the suede bag?"

"Well, by the time I got back to Denver and got back downtown and got something to eat—time had passed and the anxiety of leaving Duluth was somewhat behind me and...."

"You had a few moments to think of why you took the coin."

"I didn't take the coin. I shouldn't say—I don't recall taking the coin."

"You are not denying taking the coin, you are just saying you don't—"

"—I am not denying it. I just have no recollection of it."

"Do you have any recall of it now?"

"None. And I have had five years to think about it."

DeSanto moved on to questions about how Roger got to and from Duluth, assuming Roger must have flown under an alias. "Do you have any recollection of what name you used—you're saying you don't remember?"

"I don't have any idea. I couldn't possibly remember," Caldwell said.

"Can you guess?"

"No, I know I couldn't."

"Mr. Caldwell, do you know that's kind of hard to believe that you don't remember the name?"

"Well, yes, I can understand for you almost how it's hard to believe, but as you well know with the investigation you conducted, I am an old drunk. I have been on the sauce for a long, long time. I have been treated professionally on two different occasions and have wandered in and out of Alcoholics Anonymous heaven knows how many times over the years. And in times of stress I mean I would maintain a glow all day, every day, seven days a week, year after year. Not just periodically, this was a constant ongoing thing. I am not trying to imply that drunkenness was my normal state and sometimes worse...."

"That's what you are attributing your failure to remember the name that you used to travel?"

"There were many things I don't remember throughout my lifetime that were near and dearer to me than a false name I would give at an airline counter. I don't recall names of uncles and aunts and nieces and nephews."

"You are saying you don't recall even purchasing the ticket, but you must have done it at the airport?"

"I have never dealt through travel agents. I didn't have any plan. I didn't—this was the most amateurish, slipshod thing, now that I have had years to ponder it."

"Well, how did you feel when you saw we were unable to put you on an airline, you're saying this is amateurish?"

"Dumb lucky. I know, I recall our trial, the three months you and I spent in court, vividly. I was quite sober at the time and I know through the evidence that you presented the lengths you went to to put me on an airline and the hours that were spent in trying to get me there and I couldn't imagine how [the police] missed me."

Years later, Arnold remembered sitting at the table waiting for the hammer to come down. Waiting for DeSanto and Waller to stand up and say "That's it. We're done." The ground rules were that Roger would tell the truth and provide details—and he wasn't doing so. In retrospect, Waller and DeSanto have said they should have walked. But it all came down to the bottom line: they didn't have the evidence to confront Roger about his omissions.

Thomson, too, shook his head over the convenient gaps in Roger's memory. He kept looking over at the prosecutor during the confession, convinced that his client "was going to blow the whole thing." But Thomson felt the prosecution desperately wanted to put the case to rest. During a break that morning, Thomson joined Waller and DeSanto in DeSanto's office. "Well, you guys believe in fairy tales, don't you?" Thomson scoffed. "Hasn't this been enlightening?"

Thomson told DeSanto and Waller that his client had been taciturn about the case from the day he agreed to represent him. "Now you know what I had to put up with the whole trial. Roger wouldn't talk to me. I couldn't get information out of him. I'd ask him a question and he'd answer by asking 'What does the report say?'"

Back in the library, Roger continued his story. He told DeSanto and Waller he took a cab from downtown Denver to Stapleton International Airport the morning of Sunday, June 26, 1977. Using an assumed name,

which he couldn't remember, he bought a ticket to the Twin Cities. From the Twin Cities, he traveled to Duluth by Greyhound bus, arriving that afternoon. He had some drinks at a bar, the name of which he couldn't remember, and later took a cab to a spot past Glensheen on London Road. After the cab driver let Roger off, he waited in Lakeside Cemetery just west of the estate until dark. Then he broke a window at the back of the mansion.

"After you break the window—this was always something that, you know, puzzled us during the investigation—did you reach all the way through to unlock the window or did you just reach the middle lock?" DeSanto asked.

"I reached all the way through," Roger said, supporting the state's theory that he had let himself in. Roger's attorney had maintained that it was physically impossible for Roger's arm to reach through the broken window without being cut. But until now, both sides could only argue arm measurements. DeSanto moved on to another unexplained piece of evidence.

"Did you have a nylon stocking with you?" A dark stocking had been wrapped tightly around Pietila's left wrist in an apparently aborted attempt to tie her up.

"No, no," Roger replied. "That's been a mystery to me all this time."

After breaking into the mansion, Roger said he walked past a pool table and found a set of stairs, which he assumed led to Elisabeth's bedroom. He did not know where her bedroom was, he said, because he and Marjorie had never discussed Glensheen's floor plan. He started up the stairs not expecting a confrontation because he assumed everyone in the mansion was asleep.

"The intent was burglary," Roger admitted. "I was surprised in the act of the commission of the burglary by the nurse who was totally unknown to me."

He said he saw Pietila standing on the landing between the first and second floor.

"What happens there?" DeSanto asked.

"She shouts and struck out at me."

"Do you recall with what?"

"No."

"Her fists, her shoe?"

He wasn't sure what Pietila had in her hands during their struggle, but he remembered leaving her unconscious on the landing.

"I then went on up to the second floor and, as I recall, she had let out a moan or something to indicate that she was still, if not awake or alert, but still making noises.... I found the candlestick and went back down and beat her with that to quiet her down."

"Then what happens, what do you do after that?"

"Well, that quieted her and there was a light on in a room. I poked in there, looked in and Miss Congdon was in there and I didn't wish to—she was obviously sleeping and I knew she was not a well woman, I didn't want to disturb her. I didn't want her to hear me for one thing and so I thought, well, better if I can obstruct her hearing. Anyway, I took the pillow and put it over her head, more to block out light and sound than anything else."

DeSanto said that the physical evidence, including Elisabeth's scraped nose, indicated that she put up a fight before she died. Roger said he didn't deny suffocating her, but he couldn't remember her struggling.

DeSanto tried to draw information from Caldwell. "At some time there must have been some resistance to what you were doing to her with the pillow."

"There probably was. I don't question that at all. I had just completed beating a woman and was in a state of frenzy, I would say, and my actions from that point on were rapid and I don't recall her struggling. I don't deny that. I may have been more firm in placing the pillow than I recollect."

"So at that time there must have been some intention on your part to do more than simply put a pillow over her head to shield out noises and light, isn't that true?"

"That was the intention. Whether or not I did more, I won't deny that perhaps I did. But the intention was never to kill the women."

Roger's attempts to sidestep responsibility for the murders frustrated DeSanto. "You understand, though, for the court to even accept a factual basis for this plea that there is going to have to be some admission on your part about what you did that resulted in her death?"

"Oh, I admit that."

After killing the two women, Roger said he was in such a state of terror he couldn't move fast enough to get out of Glensheen—or remember much of what he did next. He said he couldn't remember removing the ring and watch from Elisabeth Congdon's body, taking her wicker case from her bedroom closet, nor stealing the gold Byzantine coin and mailing it to his hotel in Colorado.

"Would Marjorie, your wife, have had an envelope self-addressed by you?" DeSanto asked.

"I don't know why in the world."

"How would your name and address get on Duluth Radisson envelopes?"

"Only if I put it there."

"The coin, was it any kind of a signal?"

"I don't have any knowledge of the coin."

DeSanto hoped to clear up another question—the mysterious calls to the Hyatt Regency Hotel in Indianapolis one week before and later on the day of the murders.

"Why, on the twentieth, a few days before the murders, why are you calling the— why do you get," DeSanto started, trying to carefully compose the question. "You call from your room to the Hyatt Regency in Indianapolis, why is that? These are facts that we just can't explain."

"No, I am not disputing what your investigation turned up. I don't know anything at about the Hyatt Regency in Indianapolis."

"Did you come through there at all?"

"No."

"Did anybody helping you come through there?"

"I have never heard of the Hyatt Regency in—I know where Indianapolis is. I lived there at one time, but I had no reason in the world to call them. Unless Marge made the call. The only thing I can guess—and this is one hundred percent new to me and off the cuff all I can guess—it had something to do with horse business that she was involved in. She was very horsey. And she was very, very astute. She knew what she was doing and knew people in the business and she called. But no, John, I don't have any knowledge of that at all."

After fleeing Glensheen, Roger said he drove fast to the Twin Cities and then took a commercial flight back to Denver. Again, he couldn't recollect the alias he used, one of the more significant holes in his story.

To DeSanto, it was inconceivable that an alcoholic like Roger could have carried out such a mission unassisted without being caught. He pressed for information about Marjorie's role, if any, in the murders.

"Now with regard to the murders of Elisabeth Congdon and Velma Pietila, would you state, in your own words, when the incident which led to those murders was first planned or discussed with anyone?"

"There was no plan of murder. And there was never any discussion with anybody. There was never murder intent."

But if Caldwell had gone to burglarize the mansion, how had he planned to get away with the stolen goods, DeSanto asked.

"I had no plan. I was drunker than a lord, without any—I had no plan. I had nothing. It was stupid…. I had no prior experience along those lines."

Upon Roger's return to Colorado, Marjorie had picked him up in downtown Denver. He said he didn't explain his disappearance to his wife because it wasn't unusual for him to go off on his own for days at a time. Especially when he and Marjorie quarreled, "I would simply get in the car and drive off and go somewhere and get bombed and be gone sometimes, many times overnight, sometimes two, maybe three nights."

"What reaction did Marjorie have when she picked you up at the restaurant?"

"Anxious, hurried. She had been real estating again. She had seen some properties and was telling me about them and wanting to hurry back to the animals."

"What did you say to her about where you had been?"

"Virtually nothing. She never had a great deal of interest. I told her something to the effect a session with the lawyer and I had been off tooting and she didn't want to hear about it. She didn't like listening to stories of drunks."

"Now, this is obviously after…she's been notified, by phone at least, of the death of her mother, correct?"

"Correct."

"Isn't there some conversation about the death of her mother?"

"She was—we went somewheres, as a matter of fact. She—what did we do? We went—she was just grief-stricken, is what she was."

"But that's inconsistent with what you just told us that she is worried about real estate."

"Well, it's having to know Marge and how her processes work. She was upset and yet controlled enough to want to continue what had been our routine and yet to be left alone without being left alone. To have someone with her without getting into a lot of detailed discussion over this and that and I mean it's a difficult thing to know unless you know Marjorie."

"You understand that if she is involved, whether it be before the fact or after the fact, at this stage she is not going to face any criminal consequences. She has the benefit of what we call the double jeopardy clause. Do you understand that?"

"Yes, of course I do. Yes."

"I don't want you to sit here with some kind of motive to cover up for her, to protect her. She is virtually home free, do you understand what I am saying?"

"Yes, John. I have no more reason to implicate her than I have not to implicate her."

"Is there any way she is involved before the fact or after the fact?"

"None whatsoever."

"Don't you think you're getting the short end of the stick right now?"

"I know I am getting the short end of the stick, but not financially. I never had any claim to it. I didn't marry Marge for her money. When I married her, I didn't even know she had money. I had never heard of the Congdons."

"Well, why is it then if you say Marjorie knew nothing about your going to Duluth, to Minnesota, why on the morning of Saturday the twenty-fifth does she say Roger went to—is going to Colorado Springs the next day, why does she do that?"

"To—trying to find a reason for what Marjorie ever has done is something that none of us are able to do, including me."

"Wouldn't you admit that that would point to some knowledge on her part, it's somewhat reasonable to assume she knows where you have gone when she—"

"No."

"—telling a false statement about where you are?"

"She would come up with an awful lot of spur-of-the-moment explanations for anything and everything to total strangers."

Near the end of the statement, DeSanto asked, "Have you ever talked with Marjorie since you got out of prison?"

"No, I haven't."

"Is that the truth?"

"That's the absolute truth. I haven't spoken to Marjorie."

"Have you been offered any money to protect her?"

"None whatsoever."

"OK, Roger, has Marjorie ever called you and asked you about this?"

"I haven't seen or spoken with Marjorie since approximately three weeks after her acquittal."

"Did Marjorie ever ask you after you were charged whether you did it?"

"No. That was never—that never came up. Marjorie at the time I was arrested and charged and for the months that I spent in jail here in Duluth, she visited with me, she brought me items. We talked as best we could under the circumstances, through the bars and what have you. She seemed to be standing by me and supporting me in every way she could. There was never any question that I was guilty. There was never any—never any from her."

Finally, at 3:45 P.M., DeSanto asked the last question.

"Who do you think is getting left high and dry now?"

"Me."

The confession filled ninety-two pages of court transcripts, but DeSanto and Waller noted one striking omission. There was no mention of remorse for the brutal murders, just Roger's admission he had been drunk as usual and had "assumed people were sleeping and I meant no harm."

After the confession, the group was almost ready to move to Judge Barnes' fourth floor courtroom. But first Thomson had one final stipulation for his client: No guilty plea without the prosecution's guarantee of no more prison time. Allowing for good behavior and five years already served, Thomson wanted his client to walk away a free man. DeSanto's boss, County Attorney Alan Mitchell, reluctantly agreed; Judge Barnes was not so agreeable. In his chambers, the judge told DeSanto and Waller he believed Roger should serve his remaining year. Realizing both sides were insistent, the judge reluctantly said he would abide by the plea agreement. But he wanted DeSanto to put on the record that the county attorney's office, police, and the victims' families supported the waiver.

Before the group entered the courtroom, Waller abruptly left the courthouse, headed back to police headquarters. "I didn't go to Roger's actual plea. I'd heard enough. I was disgusted with us. We hadn't learned anything new," Waller recalled. "He spit back at us the information in the police reports and what had been testified to. We should have been harder with him and Thomson."

In a nearly empty courtroom—most of the news media would not learn of the plea agreement for several hours—Roger took the witness stand for the first and only time in the case. In a soft voice, still avoiding direct eye contact with anyone, he gave a much-shortened confession and pleaded guilty to two counts of second-degree murder. In exchange for pleading guilty, he avoided a retrial on first-degree murder charges—and became a free man. Under the plea bargain agreement, Judge Barnes dismissed the remaining twelve months of incarceration and made Roger's sentence concurrent with the time already served. Five years after his arrest for murder, Roger was free.

Judge Barnes looked somberly at Roger, who'd resumed his seat beside Thomson at the counsel table. Behind the bench, the judge straightened, leaned forward, and said gravely, "What is done, is done. It's not my policy or province to lecture anybody and I'm not going to start today. I'm just saying the matter is at an end. Hopefully the parties, the families most directly involved in it, will recognize that at long last these matters are behind us."

Outside the courtroom, reporters had gathered. A Duluth reporter had spotted Thomson earlier, and had not been convinced by the assurances of a clerk of court that Thomson was there just for pretrial motions. As Arnold ushered Roger to the elevator he told reporters he was "relieved" the case was finally over. He didn't know what he would do next or where he would go. The story of his confession made front page news around the state, led the evening broadcasts, and went out on the national wire.

An emotionally spent DeSanto went home to his wife and daughter. He wanted to avoid reporters. Sixty-two months was not much of a penalty for murdering two people, but the killer's identity had finally been confirmed. "I was relieved that I wouldn't be putting them through another trial. And I felt good that the public now knew who committed the murders. But I was left with a kind of empty feeling. We really hadn't gotten the complete story. The guy was going to walk. He wasn't going back to prison," DeSanto said.

Thomson recalled somebody came up to him once and said, "I don't quite understand it. Roger denied he did it and ended up with two life sentences. Then he admitted it and they let him go."

That afternoon, Dale Brick, foreman of the jury that convicted Roger Caldwell in Brainerd, told a *Duluth News-Tribune & Herald* reporter, "With laws the way they are, anything can happen. I've tried to put the whole thing out of my mind. It was a job that I did and it's done."

Meshbesher's statement to reporters was that the plea bargain exonerated Marjorie from any involvement with the murders. The *Duluth News-Tribune & Herald* quoted him as saying, "Caldwell might have served another twenty-nine years, but now he's off scot-free. It's a strange cap to a strange case."

The public agreed with Meshbesher. As news of the plea agreement spread, calls and letters began flooding the St. Louis County Attorney's Office. The letters ran about three-to-one against the agreement. No matter what the reasons for a plea bargain, public opinion was that a killer had gotten away with murder—two murders.

The Reverend Patrick Schonbacher of Lester Park United Methodist Church was among community leaders who sounded off: "The wealthy may commit serious felonies, including murder, serve little prison time, and because the county attorney's office is unwilling to pursue the case further, be released. I believe your decision diminishes the value of human life, discredits the criminal justice system by the questionable practice of plea bargaining, and does the Duluth community a serious injustice by returning convicted felons into the community."

Letters to the editor at the *Duluth News-Tribune & Herald* also expressed public outrage. One person wrote, "I cannot believe the mutilation of justice that has just occurred in the state of Minnesota and Duluth. A murderer, a cold-blooded murderer, has just walked away from one of the most sickening crimes in Minnesota's history."

"Justice has been made a mockery of," said another.

There were mixed reactions from Congdon family members, all of whom had been contacted by the county attorney's office prior to striking the plea bargain. Stephen LeRoy said in a letter to the Duluth paper:

A sense of outrage runs into the depths of my soul. The practical expediency of the St. Louis County Attorney's office in bringing the Roger Caldwell matter to a 'conclusion' represents a grievous injustice.

Prosecutor John DeSanto claims the confession of Caldwell provided a definitive answer of who committed the murder of my grandmother and Velma Pietila, and thus vindicates the plea arrangements. His 'answer' showed me a drunkard who expressed no remorse over his actions, a spineless judge who backed down from the ministrations of a defense attorney who had nothing to lose and a district attorney who was attempting to vindicate [the] theories of the Duluth Police Department and his own office and took the easy way out rather than [face] the embarrassment of losing political stature over the prospect of losing a second trial.

…The feeble efforts shown by the St. Louis County Attorney's office, based on the fog-like set of assumptions in bringing this case to a close, has shaken the foundation of the Minnesota legal system. One wonders what sort of horrendous crime it will take for some vile creature to serve more than four years in jail. I can only hope that if DeSanto or Alan Mitchell have any further political ambitions the people of Duluth will rise up in anguished protest and strike them down!

LeRoy's letter angered DeSanto and Waller. They considered it self-serving and inappropriate. LeRoy had refused to take a polygraph for Duluth police, and they considered him the least helpful witness of all the Congdon relatives. But other family members also were unhappy with the plea agreement. Jennifer and Chuck Johnson felt that if Roger refused to answer key questions, there should be a new trial to get at the truth.

Tom Congdon, however, wrote to DeSanto in support of the plea bargain:

"I have become only aware late last week of the public ruckus following the plea bargain and confession of Roger Caldwell. I am disappointed—as I am sure you are—that Caldwell's confession did not cast still more light on all the events surrounding the two homicides. However, I certainly agree with you that a confession serves the public interest and is an important gain offsetting whatever considerations were given the accused...."

Years later, DeSanto said, "If I had to do it over I would have retried Roger Caldwell. I now believe that despite the negative impact of Marjorie's acquittal and Roger's reversal by the Supreme Court, we could have reconvicted Roger.

"When I reconsider all the issues now, I would not have plea bargained with Roger Caldwell. Since we weren't getting any new facts and Roger was fudging about the important accomplice information, how he got to and from the murders, and the coin, we should have insisted on a new trial," he said, shaking his head in frustration.

But if DeSanto had thought the plea agreement would put an end to the headlines and public debate, he was wrong. A month after Caldwell's confession, the Minneapolis Star and Tribune obtained a copy of Marjorie's deposition taken for the civil lawsuit. Back on February 7, Marjorie had given Richard Solum, the attorney representing her children, sworn statements about the murders. Marjorie's version differed substantially from her husband's confession. DeSanto hadn't seen the deposition before, because the suit was settled and Marjorie's statements weren't entered into the court record.

Marjorie had said in her deposition that on the morning of June 27, 1977, "I was asleep; when I woke up he [Roger] was there in the room with me." But Roger had confessed, "It was late morning [when I got back from Minnesota]. I took a shuttle bus...or a limousine [from the airport] to downtown Denver.... I went to a restaurant down there right on the main street on Colfax and I don't know what the side street is, but I frequented it often."

The so-called murder contract was another disputed piece of evidence. Roger had said the will was his wife's idea. However, Marjorie had claimed that Roger beat her and coerced her into signing the document.

Roger had confessed to taking the wicker basket right after the murders to carry the stolen jewelry. In her deposition, when asked if she had stolen anything from Glensheen on the day of her mother's funeral, Marjorie had said, "I took a wicker basket from the closet off the flower room."

DeSanto began reviewing the two sets of statements, contemplating whether to pursue perjury charges against Roger and Marjorie. The trouble was he wouldn't be able to prove which one was lying. "Someone is lying," DeSanto told the Minneapolis reporter who had contacted him for a comment.

Meanwhile, Roger contacted Doug Thomson. Since the plea bargain had finally resolved his legal troubles, Roger wanted to put his personal life in order—he wanted a divorce. Thomson recommended several divorce lawyers.

"The times he did call me were regarding his marital status with Marjorie," Thomson said. "…And whether or not he should get a divorce. I think [he had] the idea of maybe a settlement or something…. I think he felt that because she had money, because her [new] husband had money, that he was entitled to some." But for whatever reason, Roger never divorced Marjorie.

CHAPTER 24

Grave Secrets

Back home in Latrobe, Pennsylvania, Roger had had little cause to celebrate in the three years since his plea bargain. Just days after his plea the Latrobe Bulletin published a front-page story that put him back in the local news, a place he hadn't been since his high school football days. The story, which detailed the murders, ran under the headline "Ex Latrobe man free in bizarre case." Roger's mother, Cecile, reportedly collapsed after reading the story.

Roger's brother Howard Jr. challenged Roger after learning of the confession. "You confessed to murdering two women. Why did you confess if you didn't do it?"

"Were you ever in prison?" Roger replied. He told Howard it took him less than a minute to agree to the plea bargain. "I didn't murder those women, but the prosecution promised they'd let me out if I would confess to the murders. I would have done anything to get out of prison."

Howard recalled later that when he pressed his brother about the evidence used against him, Roger remained adamant that he was innocent and had been framed. Roger told him, "How stupid would it be for me to mail the coin to myself? If I wanted that coin I'd put it in my pocket. That's proof that someone was trying to frame me. People might think I'm stupid, but I'm not that stupid. The old woman was in bad health. All we had to do was wait it out. Why would I be stupid enough to kill those women?"

"I don't think he was all that excited to come back to Latrobe," Howard recollected. "He didn't know how people would treat him, whether he would be accepted. But he told me, 'Home is where you go and they have to take you in.' He had his mother and dad and brothers, people who could help him."

But it didn't turn out that way. Roger had counted on work at one of two local steel mills with family connections—his father had worked at American Locomotive Co. and his brother was personnel manager at Teledyne Vasco. Instead, Roger spent weeks job hunting before securing work as a bartender. The job lasted only as long as he stayed away from the bottle. In prison, Roger had been able to avoid the relapses, but less than six months after his release from Stillwater, Roger returned to drinking. He lost his bartending job and, with it, his prospects of future employment. Roger's brother David helped him get food stamps and money for housing. "I think he felt people looked at him as a murderer," his brother Howard said. "No matter how much he denied it, he was still a confessed murderer."

Having his family around did little to lift Roger's spirits. He was restless, depressed, and flat broke. He frequently ate meals at his parents' high-rise apartment, just blocks away from the small duplex he shared with his girlfriend, Evelyn. He collected food stamps and unemployment, which amounted to less than $200 a week. He began smoking again.

Whenever he thought about Marjorie, Roger was bitter. She'd never contacted him after his release from prison. During his incarceration, she'd visited him just once, a few weeks after her acquittal. Marjorie had shown up with one of her attorneys and, throughout the visit, she acted distant and standoffish. Despite Marjorie's coldness, Roger had believed they would get back together some day and share the good life again.

Then Roger learned of her bigamous marriage to Wally Hagen. Because—as he had told others—Marjorie had physical needs Roger could not meet, he had trouble imagining Marjorie with a much older man. He kept waiting for Marjorie to contact him. Roger remained genuinely amazed when she didn't.

As far as he knew, he and Marjorie never divorced. Certainly, Roger hadn't signed any papers. When first imprisoned, Roger had told attorney Arnold that he wouldn't divorce Marjorie because he loved her and he didn't want to destroy the marital privilege.

But he hadn't seen or spoken to Marjorie for seven years. His love for her had been replaced by disillusionment and the realization she had abandoned him. He didn't hesitate to tell others he'd "lost everything" because of his marriage to Marjorie. Despite the generosity Marjorie displayed in the so-called "murder contract," Roger had yet to receive a penny.

Roger called David Arnold in the spring of 1986 with a request. He wanted to hold a press conference in Minnesota and reveal the truth about the murder before Marjorie's release from prison later that year. Some who knew Roger said he wanted to even the score; others said he wanted money, nothing more.

"In essence he wanted to set the world straight," Arnold recalled. "You have to understand that at this point one of the things…he wanted was to show Waller and DeSanto up for what he thought they were. For having framed him, for having been pawns of the family. But there was no question that his setting the record straight was motivated by wanting to get Marge."

Roger's list of conditions included holding the press conference in Duluth, including all Minnesota news organizations, and plane fare and lodging—at the county's expense. "St. Louis County, my God, they spent enough money trying to find me a place to hang my hat. They can find me a place, the best place in Duluth to stay while I'm there," Roger told Arnold.

DeSanto and Waller were down in the Twin Cities on business in May and agreed to meet with Arnold and talk over Caldwell's proposition. DeSanto and Waller wanted a preview of what Caldwell intended to make public. Arnold couldn't give specifics, but said Roger had hinted that his statement would implicate Marjorie. The problem, however, was that Roger would have to admit he'd lied during his sworn confession. He wanted St. Louis County to waive any perjury charges.

DeSanto had already guessed that, but he told Arnold that a grant of immunity was out of the question. "A blanket offer of immunity would only taint the information," DeSanto said. "It would look like Caldwell was profiting from his dishonesty."

St. Louis County and the Duluth Police Department were interested in what Roger might say. DeSanto and Waller again told Arnold they wanted an outline of the items he planned to cover. No, Arnold told them. Roger would not entrust anyone with even a sample of the new evidence unless they could guarantee something in return.

"I told Arnold we weren't interested," DeSanto recalled. "We were curious about what Roger had to say. But he had lied to us before. There was no reason to believe he might not lie to us again." The state was not going to resurrect a case based on a flimsy promise from a convicted killer and admitted liar.

Several months later, DeSanto got a call from Congdon family attorney Barney Johnson, their first conversation since Marjorie's acquittal. Johnson's reason for calling surprised DeSanto. Chuck and Jennifer Johnson, represented by Barney Johnson, had been privately trying to negotiate a deal with Roger. Johnson asked if the county attorney's office was interested in being a part of these negotiations. The Johnsons hoped Roger would name other people involved in the murders.

DeSanto recalled his conversation with the Johnsons. "I can understand you wanting to know the truth, we all do," he told them. "And if you want to pay for that information that's up to you. But you have to understand that St. Louis County is not in a position to negotiate with Roger Caldwell in any way."

The Johnsons and Arnold had noticed Roger's dramatic mood swings during months of negotiations. First, he was despondent, saying he was the only family member who'd suffered and sought revenge against Marjorie for ruining his life. Then his depression had lifted and he demanded payment for his information, alluding to a "third party" involved in the murders. Roger told the Johnsons that since Marjorie had promised him money, which he never received, he would settle for $50,000.

He wanted to work, but a middle-aged convicted felon couldn't even find a job pumping gas. If only he had enough money to open a little business, he told Arnold. Something he could even pass on to his family. Roger would not provide the Johnsons with any sample information aside from his teaser, the oft-repeated comment that "there is no third party involved except Marjorie."

In an August 28 letter to Barney Johnson, David Arnold reiterated Roger's condition: Roger must be compensated by the family in exchange for truthful disclosure. "It's time for [the family] to be creative in meeting my monetary demands, if they feel they can't pay me for my time," Roger demanded. "The price is going up." Arnold's letter explained:

Roger feels that he has essentially lost ten years of his working life as a result of two miscarriages of justice—the first, his conviction premised upon inadequate evidence; the second, Marge's acquittal. Since he spent five years in prison based on inadequate proof, he feels he should at least be entitled to recover an income that he might have generated during that period of time.

Roger suspects that the family intends to use his truthful disclosures against Marge, but he does not intend to give them that kind of information unless there is a benefit in it for him. "If I help them, they ought to help me. It's like they're buying a business from me and then selling it to me for one dollar. There's got to be a way of doing it that will satisfy both sides." While not disclosing anything to me regarding his likely responses, he did indicate that "if the family is looking for information regarding the illegal activity of Marge, I can certainly provide it."

Marjorie had been housed in one of the Shakopee Women's Prison's "living units" since January 1985. The modern, story-and-a-half structures were divided into wings designed to hold four to seven minimum to moderate security inmates. Marjorie had been assigned a small private room equipped with a sink and toilet. She had access to a television and telephone in the lounge of her wing. During her stay it was rumored that she tried to arrange the purchase of television sets for all the inmates.

The prison at Shakopee required Marjorie, like all inmates, to work at least twelve hours a week in maintenance, industry, or the prison's food service. Food preparation and cleanup became her specialties. Marjorie also kept busy with college correspondence courses and craftwork. Prison officials recalled that she made a number of quilts while incarcerated.

During Marjorie's imprisonment, Wally lived in the couple's Airstream in a trailer park near Shakopee. This allowed him to visit Marjorie regularly; he was one of the few family members to do so.

Marjorie's release was set for October 1986. But twenty months into her sentence, Marjorie had yet to pay a penny of her $10,000 fine. Judge Schiefelbein threatened to do what he could to keep her in prison until someone paid the fine. Four days before her scheduled release, Wally paid off her fine. Wally's children later learned that their father had sold ham radio equipment—loaned to him by his youngest son—to assure her release. Marjorie was paroled on October 19. She and Wally attended the baptism of one of her grandchildren that very day; it was probably the last time she would ever see Dick LeRoy. They never spoke. Shortly after that Marjorie and Wally packed their belongings, set off for Nevada with their Airstream trailer, and wound up months later in Arizona. Marjorie wanted a new life somewhere warm, away from the scrutiny of the media and law enforcement.

Discussions continued between the Johnsons and Roger. Arnold told them that Roger kept repeating that "Charlie [Johnson] has what Caldwell wants and Caldwell has what Charlie wants." Very interested in Roger's "truthful statements," the Johnsons offered to pay Roger's out-of-pocket costs and Arnold's expenses for acting as Roger's advisor. The family also agreed to the conditions that no representative from the St. Louis County Attorney's Office or Duluth Police Department would be involved and no family members would use the new information against him. But the Johnsons wouldn't pay Roger for the story itself.

Roger's sworn statement would not be taped, although a court reporter would record and transcribe it. The statement would only be used as information by the family and any rights to the statement would be Roger's.

By the spring of 1987, the Johnsons had grown tired of the protracted negotiations. In a letter to Arnold, they reluctantly agreed to pay Roger the sum of $50,000 with some strict conditions of their own:

> I feel strongly that Mr. Caldwell should, as a moral and ethical matter, tell what he knows freely and unconditionally so that society can understand and know all who should be implicated in these crimes, and so that any unconcluded justice may be done. You have made it clear, however, that the only basis on which Mr. Caldwell will provide the additional implicating information would be on the payment of money. While it is clear that such a payment is distasteful, we have no choice but to deal with Mr. Caldwell on those terms.... There will be no money paid until evidence is produced which would be sufficient evidence on which a criminal prosecution could be based.

The Johnsons recommended that a criminal attorney without any ties to the Congdon family or the murders obtain and analyze Roger's full and unconditional sworn statement. The letter continued, "If the lawyer found that the evidence was so sufficient, we would pay to Mr. Caldwell upon receipt of the lawyer's opinion, a transcript of Mr. Caldwell's statement, and all other evidence received by said lawyer, the sum of $50,000."

In late April 1987, Roger and David Arnold were fast approaching a standoff with the family over Roger's demands. The family, now represented by their civil attorney, Rick Solum, refused to negotiate without some indication of what Roger would say. And Roger had upped the asking price to $100,000.

In his letter to the Johnsons, Solum advised that after his most recent conversation with Arnold, further negotiations were questionable. Solum had quoted in his letter, as best he could, Roger's recent statements and conditions as outlined by Arnold. Roger remained adamant that the family make his life "a little better" because he wanted "to leave something to someone else" when he died. Solum told the Johnsons that Roger insisted that there was no third party involved yet also stated that he could "give absolute testimony to implicate a third party—specifically, my wife."

Later, Arnold would say that Roger's comments regarding a third party were probably misinterpreted. According to Arnold, Roger consistently maintained that there was "no third party except for Marjorie." Only Roger knew the precise meaning of those confusing statements, and he had been unwilling to provide any clarification.

Solum's letter concluded, "Apparently Roger is now disclaiming the existence of any evidence as to a third person, the receipt of which was the only real motivation to go forward with some arrangement. Secondly, he apparently does not want to have whatever evidence he has screened in any way, insisting on a $100,000 cash payment to be delivered in Latrobe as a condition."

A meeting between Chuck Johnson, Arnold, Roger, and a mutually agreed upon independent attorney failed to take place. Negotiations broke off in May 1987. The Johnsons would not pay Roger's increased fee of $100,000, nor would they back down on their demand for a preview of the information he planned to divulge.

Chuck Johnson recalled, "I'm surprised that he didn't come back. If the guy's sitting there with food stamps and is living a pretty poor life you'd think he'd come back and say well how about ten thousand, or five thousand or fifteen or twenty. Or throw some evidence out and say here's a sample. He didn't try to sell the thing at all."

This was the last time anyone discussed Roger's story, Arnold said. "The family was convinced there was a third party involved and their only interest in doing this whole thing, paying him for his time and his statement was to bring someone to justice that was presumably out there walking the streets."

Roger never once discussed the negotiations with his own family.

Back in Pennsylvania, life went on pretty much as it had when Roger was in prison. Estranged from his first wife, Roger communicated with only one of his children, daughter Christi—Caren would not speak to her father and Scott had died of AIDS. Marjorie refused to have anything to do with him. He still talked about writing a book to tell his story. Roger enjoyed being useful and often drove his parents around, ran errands in their station wagon, and performed simple maintenance on the car.

Living off welfare and food stamps was quite a fall for a man who enjoyed spending money and had once counted on sharing his wife's inheritance. Howard recalled his brother as someone who liked to act like a big spender. "He liked to spend money even if he couldn't afford to," Howard said. He recalled one incident when their parents needed a new stove. Roger insisted his parents pick out a new gas range that was then delivered to the house. But Roger had only made a small down payment on the stove, leaving the remainder for his parents to pay.

Once, during Roger's marriage to Marjorie, Roger told his parents to pick out a new house that he and Marjorie would buy for them. His parents went house-hunting only to discover that their son and daughter-in-law had no money available from Marjorie's trust funds.

As for his brother's marriage to Marjorie, Howard thought Roger "had his eyes on her money." Another likely reason for the union was that, despite their outward differences, Roger and Marjorie shared a similar outlook on life. "Roger liked to play the big shot," Howard said. "He always had an attitude about him that he was a little bit better or a little bit smarter than everyone else. That rules didn't necessarily apply to him. That rules were made to be broken, and to get away with what he could get away with."

Howard visited Roger at his brother's apartment, located next door to a bar, on Monday, May 16, 1988. Roger and Evelyn, Roger's on-again, off-again girlfriend of five years, were being evicted at the end of the month. Howard had recently helped them move into a new apartment, and Evelyn was already living there. But because the couple fought frequently, Roger was currently staying at the old place.

Roger sat on the rug, the only furnishing left behind except for the kitchen appliances. His thinning gray hair, puffy, lined face, and bleary, drooping eyes belonged to a much older man. While he was only fifty-four years old, heavy drinking and five years in prison had left their marks on him. A pattern of purple bruises dotted his head, chest, and legs—he often fell while on a bender and his overuse of aspirin made him bruise easily. He'd suffered depression for many months and repeated his threat about what Howard might find the next time he dropped by.

"Don't be surprised if I'm dead when you get here."

Howard was tired of the threats, and said so. Roger had a lot to say when he was drinking, and Roger was drinking heavily these days. He didn't care if the beer was warm, as long as he had alcohol to drink.

"Roger, you're talking crazy. You don't even have a gun."

"I'm going to cut my wrist with my knife, and I'm going to bleed all over this dago's new carpet," Roger replied, referring to his Italian landlord. Roger was angry at the landlord, who also owned the bar adjacent to the apartment, because he could no longer mooch drinks.

The brothers talked awhile and Howard promised to stop by the next day with the usual six-pack of Old Milwaukee beer.

Howard's union meeting at the steel mill ran late on Tuesday, May 17, but he had promised Roger he would stop by. He went to the liquor store and bought the six-pack of Old Milwaukee he'd promised and headed to Roger's old apartment. When he arrived an hour late, he walked up to the back door and tried to peek into the kitchen. The evening shadows made it impossible to see inside. Howard knocked but there was no response.

Howard got back in his car and drove home to call his brother David. The next morning, David asked another police officer to check on Roger. David called Howard back with the news. "You were right. Roger's dead," David told him.

Clad only in a blue-and-white striped shirt and blue socks, Roger had used a straight-edged steak knife to slash deeply across the insides of both wrists, severing the veins. The slit to the right wrist also cut his arteries. There were no hesitation cuts. The knife had fallen to the floor near his right foot.

Roger had left three notes written in a shaky hand, two on index cards and one on a sheet of paper. The first note was written to his brother Howard, known as "Bud" to family and friends:

Dear Bud, How such smart people like you and I (ho ho) could not remember the Greek word for water is hydro is beyond me. Look in the big book where the glass is and you'll find as always (ho ho) that I was correct. I've always loved you Jr. Tell Evelyn that I did love her and of course the whole family.

Recently, Roger and his brother had been trying to finish a crossword puzzle. The "big book" rwas *Webster's Dictionary*.

The second note referred to Roger's doctor:

I tried to tell Joe what was happening in my life, but the dumb Hunky he is knew better. He was wrong. He was my last hope—Sorry for us both.

On the sheet of paper, Roger wrote:

Please excuse the handwriting, but as usual my mind is clouded with booze. I would like to write each of you a note, but I am too drunk to do it, and you have all made it very clear that you don't care. I love you all and always have. Tell Evelyn I loved her too. What you need to know is that I didn't kill those girls or—to my knowled [sic] ever harm a soul in my life. I am truly sorry to go this way, however the pain is more than I can take. Try to find it in your hearts to forgive.

Despite his confession to St. Louis County authorities, he died maintaining his innocence nearly eleven years after the murders. Two days later, he was buried in his hometown in one of the Caldwell family plots, a few miles from a farm his grandfather once owned. Roger's family wanted to keep the service small and private, so they did not publish his death notice in local papers. Only eight family members and *Minneapolis Star-Tribune* reporter Joe Kimball, who had covered the Glensheen killings from the beginning, attended the funeral service.

Roger's family, friends, and attorneys had known that he suffered severe bouts of depression from time to time. His lapse back into alcoholism was apparent to all who saw him. Nonetheless, his suicide came as a shock, even to the family members who had listened to his repeated suicide threats.

Based on his observations of his client at trial and in prison, Doug Thomson had never thought of Roger as suicidal. Thomson later said, "He was in prison for about four years...and he never once complained. He seemed to enjoy it."

After the negotiations with the Johnsons had fallen through, David Arnold and Roger had kept in touch, speaking by phone periodically. Although Roger's homecoming had been far from smooth, Roger had talked about his supportive girlfriend and family.

"First of all I was extremely surprised," Arnold said, "because he had been—seemed to be—somewhat upbeat at least during the most recent conversations I had with him. I realized that he had vacillated in these depressive cycles. But he had been through fairly traumatic things that would have been...far more depressing."

Those who knew him couldn't help but wonder about whatever secrets he may have taken to the grave. "Roger always denied to me that he was involved," said Doug

Thomson of his former client. "I didn't think he had guts enough to do it. Of course I never saw him when he had been drinking. I'm certain that somebody had to gain entrance through the front door—and somebody that they knew."

As for Roger's suicide note proclaiming his innocence, Arnold believed that Roger, knowing he was going to die, told the truth. Arnold had trouble imagining Roger being connected in any way with murder. But if Roger was somehow involved, Arnold said, "Roger would more likely have been a passive party going along on the ride or would have set about to burgle the place and it got out of hand. I still cannot permit myself to think that Roger could sit down and plan…this scheme of murder."

The afternoon of Roger's death, a thousand miles away in Minneapolis, Arnold returned from an out-of-town business trip. But it wasn't until the next morning, while scanning his phone message slips, that he found one dated Tuesday, May 17. The message said simply, "Roger Caldwell called."

The Mirror, the Stillwater prison newspaper, reported after his suicide that according to the inmates he had known, "the ordeal he suffered was tantamount to a delayed death sentence." Roger had maintained his innocence throughout his time at Stillwater but, after the Minnesota Supreme Court's overturned his conviction, he had told other inmates that he would consider accepting a plea agreement to avoid returning to prison.

Roger left behind one other document that, surprisingly, received little publicity. In his last will and testament, drafted while he was in prison, Roger singled out those he associated with his murder conviction and incarceration for special recognition:

> It is my intent and desire…that my named beneficiaries shall secure as much monetary damage as may be recoverable from any or all of the following sovereignties, entities or individuals: State of Minnesota; St. Louis County, State of Minnesota; St. Louis County Attorney's Office; City of Duluth, State of Minnesota; City of Duluth, Police Department; John DeSanto, Sergeant Gary Waller; any and all newspapers, radio and television broadcasting stations, their owners, station managers, news editors and publishers.

Roger also included a special provision for Marjorie:

> I devise and bequeath to my wife Marjorie LeRoy Caldwell, also known as Marjorie Congdon Caldwell, whom I love, the sum of one dollar in recognition of her abandonment of me during my time of dire need.

Whatever Roger had to say about Marjorie's involvement—or that of a third party—in the murder of Elisabeth Congdon and Velma Pietila, he took his secrets to the grave.

CHAPTER 25

Ashes to Ashes

MARJORIE HEARD ABOUT ROGER'S SUICIDE THROUGH RICK "quite some time after he had died." Later she claimed she had called Roger's family because, she said, "it was the decent thing to do, and [I] told them I was sorry he had committed suicide." Then Marjorie, who hadn't attended Roger's trial, had visited him only once in prison, had remarried without divorcing him, and had never contacted him after his release, said she told the Caldwells, "I was sorry that they hadn't seen fit to at least notify me."

Since her own release from prison, Marjorie, the daughter of an heiress, made her home in RV parks, living off Wally's pension and the annual $34,000 she received from the settlement with her children. The couple had moved around out west, staying in RV parks from Reno, Nevada, to Coolidge, Arizona.

They had returned to Minnesota once, for a June 1987 Hagen family reunion. Wally's children had been disappointed by their father's refusal to come without Marjorie. Then Wally failed to recognize his grandchildren, a crushing disappointment for Tom Hagen's teenage daughter, Heather. She had pushed for the reunion, hoping to reconnect with a grandfather who had been a stranger for nearly a decade. But Marjorie insisted on speaking for her husband and would not leave his side. The couple left only hours after they arrived. After the brief Friday night visit, Wally and Marjorie went back on Sunday to say goodbye. Following the reunion, Nancy tried several times to call her father but Marjorie would not allow her to speak with Wally. For his birthday, Nancy had to send cards to Ron Meshbesher to be forwarded to her father. The reunion was the last time the Hagen children saw their father alive.

None of Marjorie's Arizona neighbors suspected she was anything but a middle-aged housewife and grandmother. She was chatty, plump, and unimposing, given to gesturing and fussing over people. She and Wally had moved again, settling in Queen Valley, Arizona, just east of Phoenix, only two hours away from the spacious house in Tucson where Marjorie had spent winters as a child. Relocating from Minnesota could have been a fresh start, but Marjorie's financial problems began to recur in spring 1989, when she was investigated for check fraud.

The Hagens had taken their 1978 GMC motorhome to Isley's RV Service Center in Mesa, Arizona, several times in 1988. The routine maintenance and interior remodeling—including a $1,400 refrigerator, engine repair, body work, and walnut paneling, cabinetry, and steering wheel—had come to nearly $99,000. For an additional fee the Hagens also had their 1978 Volkswagen Thing painted yellow to match their motor home. Although they had possession of the vehicles, they had only paid approximately $15,000 of the total bill. When Isley's requested additional payments, Marjorie wrote a check for $55,000. It bounced. The service shop sued Marjorie and Wally for the amount still owed: $90,817. The Hagens fought back, hiring their own attorney who claimed the Hagens had stopped payment on the check because the repair shop had not finished the remodeling and repair of the motor home. The vehicle was eventually repossessed.

During this same period, the sheriff's department in Pinal County, where the Hagens lived, was investigating a number of suspicious fires. Detective Larry Placencio advised John DeSanto that the rash of fires overlapped with the time that the Hagens had moved to the county.

In one fire, a home that the Hagens had purchased was vandalized two days before they were scheduled to move in. Someone had put a water hose in the house and damaged the carpeting, and the walls had been spray painted with triple sixes, the satanic "mark of the beast." The vandals were never caught and the damage was written off as the work of youthful pranksters. The Hagens' insurance company paid for new carpeting and decorating. After the couple took possession of their house, a neighbor's windows were broken and an accelerant was thrown on a bed, setting her house ablaze. According to police reports, another incident involved a neighbor who owned an RV. The neighbor asked Marjorie to watch the RV while the neighbor was away, then later called and told Marjorie it was no longer necessary for her to continue caring for the vehicle. The RV burned the next day. Several months later, another resident reported that her RV was broken into and the sofa inside was set on fire. But police collected insufficient evidence to tie the Hagens to the fires, and no charges were ever filed.

In December 1989, Marjorie and Wally Hagen moved further south, driving their 1973 Revcon motor home into Ajo, Arizona. The quiet desert community would soon be plagued by a rash of arson fires.

Ajo lies 120 miles west of Tucson, at the foot of the Sauceda Mountains, less than an hour north of the Mexican border. Like the Iron Range in northern Minnesota, where Marjorie's grandfather Chester Congdon made his fortune, Ajo prospered with the advent of mining.

In Ajo, however, it was copper ore—not iron—which was extracted from an open-pit mine that yawned a mile-and-a-half wide. At the turn of the century, several copper companies worked the mine with limited success until the arrival of John Greenway, one of Congdon's business partners. In the early 1900s, Congdon invested in mining operations across the Southwest, including another copper mine in Bisbee, Arizona, southeast of Tucson. Greenway managed the Calumet and Arizona Mining Company, which was ultimately bought out by Phelps Dodge Corporation in 1931. The town of Ajo sprang up at the edge of "The Mine," as locals call the pit. At the height of production in the 1940s and '50s, The Mine produced twenty- to thirty-thousand tons of copper ore per day.

Marjorie claimed to have been in Ajo as a young girl. She told Norma Walker, owner of the Guest House Bed and Breakfast, that she had accompanied her mother on a visit to the Ajo mine. According to Marjorie, she and Elisabeth stayed at the inn, originally built by Phelps Dodge Corporation for visiting company officials. Foreign competition, however, undercut the U.S. copper mining industry, and by the 1980s, layoffs and closings were commonplace. Phelps Dodge closed down the mine in 1985, citing low copper prices and labor problems. The town, which had once claimed 5,500 residents, lost more than half its population.

But the community didn't lie down and die. Hundreds of adobe houses—once miners' homes—were put on the market, with two- and three-bedroom fixer-uppers available for under $30,000. "Retirement living at 1950s prices," boasted the sign welcoming visitors to Ajo, and retirees responded, boosting the population to nearly 5,000. Another sign of retirees—and snowbirds—are the motor homes. The local Chamber of Commerce estimates that at least one-third of Ajo's residents own RVs.

The Hagens paid $15,000 for one of the miners' homes, a four-room, one-bedroom white adobe house on Palo Verde Avenue. Marjorie took great pains to decorate the house with Southwestern and Mexican-style furnishings. Signs of her handiwork included a coyote painted on the mailbox and rosemaling around the ceiling of the tiny library.

"Marjorie and Wally went to Mexico often. She loved to shop down there," said Emma Skinner, owner of the Territorial House restaurant in Ajo and a friend of the Hagens'. "She liked the wood carvings and folk art, and she liked the bold Mexican colors in her home."

The Hagens enjoyed a quiet life of leisure, marked by frequent trips to the library and senior citizens' center. Wally and Marjorie enjoyed eating out, and residents usually saw them at Territorial House or Pizza Hut, often with books in hand. The couple became active at Immaculate Conception Catholic church, where they attended Mass daily. Marjorie regularly assisted with preparations for communion and participated in a women's prayer group. Her Volkswagen Thing became a common fixture in the church parking lot.

"She was always parked in her little yellow Thing in front of the church every morning at 8 A.M. when I opened the restaurant," said Skinner. Marjorie and other women from the church frequently ate lunch at Skinner's restaurant with the priest. The group often participated in lively theological discussions, which Marjorie particularly enjoyed. She packed the floor-to-ceiling bookshelves in her tiny library at home with serious books on religion. The Ajo rumor mill buzzed with a story that Marjorie had complained to the Vatican after a priest at Immaculate Conception objected to Wally's wheelchair blocking the church aisles and hadn't visited their house soon enough when Wally had been sick.

Marjorie organized a quilting circle and joined a group of women that met each week at Irma's Knit Knack shop, behind the local Dairy Queen. "Marjorie had started coming here every week to knit, crochet, and talk," said Knit Knack owner Irma Park. "She was very likable. You name it and she could talk about it to no end." Park praised Marjorie's beautiful quilts, recalling one elaborate quilt with appliqués that was displayed as part of a rural arts traveling exhibition. Mae Hall, a member of of Marjorie's quilting group, said Marjorie even planned to open a little shop to sell her quilts and other handicrafts.

Bud Klinefelter and his wife, Carol, owned an RV park and the Del Sur repair shop where the Hagens had work done on their Revcon motor home after they got into town. Marjorie paid the $850 repair bill with a bad check. The Klinefelters' daughter tracked the Hagens down in Mexico, and when Marjorie returned to Ajo, she gave the Klinefelters a check for the original amount plus $100 for the trouble she had caused. The second check bounced. Again, the Klinefelters pursued the Hagens in Mexico. Marge eventually paid the debt with a cashier's check.

Klinefelter decided he didn't want to do any more business with Marjorie. "I have a philosophy. When my stomach goes into a knot and the hair on the back of my head goes up, I don't talk to you. The first day I met her that happened to me. And my feelings about her never changed. Ever."

At the same time, Emma Skinner and her husband, George, were seeing a completely different side of Marjorie. George, a real estate agent, was introduced to Marjorie when she was looking for a house. "Marjorie and Wally came to the Territorial House to eat," he said. "You're not in the same area where Marjorie is without knowing she's there." Marjorie's outspokenness and animated discussions attracted notice in a small town. "She has a tremendous presence," he said, complimenting her.

The Skinners, like the Klinefelters, received bad checks from Marjorie. But George and Emma said that when Marjorie found out she made good on them. The couple said Marjorie tried to help other people, in particular poor people just across the border in Mexico. "She was always putting together goodies, always doing things for people down in Mexico," said George. "She was very alert to people in need."

Marjorie said that she and Wally had moved to Ajo because it was near Mexico, where they could get medicine for Wally's terminal cancer. "At that time everyone believed her," said Gabrielle David, editor of Ajo's weekly paper, the *Ajo Copper News*. Marjorie and Wally made frequent trips to Mexico, where drugs requiring a prescription in the United States were sold over the counter. The couple vacationed at Rocky Point, a resort town on the Sea of Cortez, in part because Marjorie believed it was good for Wally's health. When it came to her husband, "Marjorie was a protectionist," said

George Skinner. "She watched Wally's diet a lot and she would tell him what to eat," said Emma.

"She told me she had to take very good care of her husband because he had cancer and because she was afraid if anything happened to him she wouldn't be able to take care of herself financially," said Irma Park.

Marjorie told organizers of Ajo's fund-raising drive for an ambulance service that she wanted to be involved. She even offered to donate a used washing machine to a raffle to raise money for an ambulance. "Marjorie said she was interested in the drive because of Wally's health," said David. "She claimed to be a registered nurse." She told friends and acquaintances that she was giving Wally injections of a combination of vitamins she purchased in Mexico.

No matter what the status of Wally's health, Emma Skinner described the Hagens as an affectionate couple who enjoyed a loving relationship. One story in particular stuck in her mind. "I went to her house to return a quilt. I could hear the radio and the doors were open," she said. "I'm knocking on the door and no one answers. I'm saying 'Marge, Marge.' The bedroom door opens a little. She finally comes out. And she has on this cute little red negligee. It's four P.M. in the afternoon, and she has a glass of white wine in her hand."

Although some residents say Marjorie boasted that she and Wally had money, others say they never suspected Marjorie came from a wealthy family. The Hagens had no telephone and had to use their neighbors' phone across the street. Mae Hall said Marjorie never talked about her family with the women at the Knit Knack Shop and she definitely "wasn't a flashy dresser," preferring mumu-like dresses and sneakers. Her hair was usually in a tight bun and she still wore oversized glasses. Pima County Sheriff Lieutenant Tom Taylor, a former Ajo resident, said that to him she looked like the frumpy character who lived next door to the main character in a sitcom. "I don't think I've ever seen her dressed up," he said.

Taylor was investigating the arson fires plaguing Ajo. Some people thought kids were responsible. Some wondered whether a volunteer firefighter was setting fires only to put them out—until the day firefighters were battling one arson fire while another was set across town. Taylor said that the sheriff's department had first suspected juvenile gang members. But the fires had been set in abandoned houses and garages, similar to Marjorie's pattern in Minnesota.

In June 1990, Marjorie took her motor home to the Del Sur RV repair shop for more work. This time she gave the Klinefelters a $300 cash advance. Several weeks later the work was complete and Marjorie owed an additional $1,800. But when Bud Klinefelter called her to say the RV was ready, Marjorie suddenly wanted a remote start switch for the generator. Against his better judgment, he agreed to keep the motor home in the Del Sur yard until Monday.

Early Sunday morning, July 9, someone cut the eight-foot chain link fence guarding the property, stepped in, and set two motor homes on fire, including the Hagens'.

The fire narrowly missed the repair shop, damaged a customer's car and destroyed the Klinefelters' dump truck, along with the two RVs. The fence had been cut like a V and rolled back—the perpetrator had done a professional job, Bud Klinefelter said. He told sheriff's deputies that the fence had to have been cut by someone who had been in the military or in prison.

The Del Sur fire was a turning point in the investigation, said Lieutenant Taylor. He was sure he was investigating an arson for profit, and when he learned that Marjorie's motor home was one of the two that burned, he immediately focused on her as his prime suspect. At the point of entry, where the fence was cut, deputies found a tiny shoe print. "You looked at that shoe print and you knew it was made by a child or someone who was very small," Taylor said. "It turn[ed] out to match exactly the length of her shoe."

The Pima County Sheriff's Department stepped up its investigation and solicited the public's help. The *Ajo Copper News* ran a front-page ad two days after the fire, asking residents to "Arrest Arson" and included the National Arson Hotline number. But the arsonist eluded authorities and the fires continued, with nine more in just the month of December.

Shortly before Christmas Marjorie wrote to Wally's oldest son, Tom, to ask for money.

> After a few more tests the doctors determined there is no more to cut and no need to put him through more hospital stress. They feel that other than keeping him comfortable the only chance might be the clinic in Mexico we went to last year.
>
> [Although Wally's doctors gave him only four or five months to live] we have had almost 15 due they feel to his drive and what the Tijuana clinic was able to do. They are free to use some drugs that are not yet okayed in the U.S. They have agreed to take the Bear [Marjorie's nickname for Wally] starting on 30 Dec., if he is able to travel, for 3–4 weeks. In conversation they feel they may be able to give him another 6–8 months of good time. However they don't take Medicare or IBEW [Wally's union, the International Brotherhood of Electrical Workers] or delayed payment as do the U.S. hospitals and doctors. By upping the motor home mortgage and selling what we can we have raised $7,200 of the needed $10,000. The Masonic Lodge and the church in Ajo are trying to come up with some more but against your dads [sic] knowledge.
>
> I am asking you and Dick and Nancy if you can or will contribute anything at all. I've written to all mine also as I have no pride when it comes to something for 'The Bear.' If you can't for financial or personal reasons, I understand but felt I had to ask you.
>
> He is up in his wheelchair, wrapped in quilts and out in the sun for between 1–3 hours per day now depending how strong he is. The bowels are fine most of the time but the bladder is still out of control about 65 percent of the time.
>
> I'm so glad we have 73 degree weather and no god awful snow to fight, but would you believe we are chilly. Shows what dedicated Arizonians we have turned into! Merry Christmas to all of you and we will keep in touch about his progress or lack of.

None of the Hagen children would consider sending money to their father, and certainly not to Marjorie. They were convinced Marjorie was lying, as she had for years, about Wally's illnesses. If Marjorie were to be believed, their father had suffered from stomach cancer, Parkinson's disease, leukemia, deafness, and glaucoma, and had undergone several open heart surgeries.

Two weeks after Marjorie's letter, the *Ajo Copper News* printed another plea from the Pima County Sheriff's Department for citizens to come forward with any information. The sheriff's department, with the help of citizen volunteers, had begun videotaping the fire scenes to see if any of their suspects were among the onlookers. Deputies noticed that Marjorie was frequently present.

"We had this thing, it was kind of a joke in the town. One of these houses would burn, it was urban renewal Ajo-style, thanks to Marge Hagen," said Bud Klinefelter. Taylor said that after the arson fires some residents began calling the Ajo volunteer fire department "Hagen's Heroes."

An Ajo sheriff's deputy was making his rounds on March 24, 1991, when he spotted a blaze in an abandoned house on Palo Verde. The fire, which damaged a window and the attic before he extinguished it, was just two houses from the Hagens.

Later that night, around 10 P.M., the sheriff's department received a call from the Hagens' next-door neighbor. Mark Indvik, a U.S. Border Patrol officer, had been in bed when he heard a noise at the bedroom window: "Someone grabbing and yanking at it," he said. He looked out and saw Marjorie and the Hagens' dog Wulf walking from his house toward the alley. Indvik thought Wulf had gotten loose and come into his yard because the back gate was always left open. Back in bed five minutes later, he heard another noise at the window. This time it was Marjorie without her dog, walking back home through the alley. "I looked down at the window and she'd stuck a rag [in it] and I could smell the kerosene. The kerosene-soaked rag was wedged between the windowsill and frame."

Lieutenant Taylor decided to lay a trap. He believed Marjorie would return to finish what she had started. Five deputies were dispatched to set up surveillance of the Hagens' house and Indvik's. One deputy was assigned to the inside of Indvik's house, equipped with a camera, radio, and fire extinguisher. Two deputies staked out the alley in an unmarked vehicle and wore night-vision goggles. Another two deputies were on standby.

Shortly before 1 A.M., the deputies in the unmarked squad saw the Hagens' patio light go on and off. Seconds later, the deputies saw Marjorie and her dog leave the back yard and go into the alley. As she approached Indvik's driveway, the officers saw her stop and look around before entering the back yard. Detective Frank Alvillar, stationed in a back yard just west of the Indvik and Hagen residences, "saw a small flash consistent with a small type fire up against the rear of the residence. Approximately four or five seconds later I observed a bright white flash coming from the rear of 731 Palo Verde."

Billy Ned, the deputy stationed inside Indvik's house, saw Marjorie ignite the rag with a match. He took a picture, although the image was obscured by the window glass, and then another as Marjorie took off running out of the backyard. Indvik grabbed the fire extinguisher and put out the fire before it could damage the window. Outside, deputy Alvillar spotted "Marjorie Hagen exiting the rear entry/exit way to the backyard of 731 Palo Verde and start running east in the alleyway."

The deputies chased Marjorie down the alley before grabbing hold of her. She was wearing a jean jacket, long nightgown, and white tennis shoes.

"What are you doing?" Marjorie demanded. "I was only walking my dog." She said Wulf had gone into Indvik's backyard and she had gone in to get him.

Marjorie was arrested for arson for the fire at Indvik's house. In addition, "based on her M.O. and her proximity to the fire [at 701 Palo Verde,] we arrested her for that one as well," said Lieutenant Taylor. She was taken to the Ajo jail while investigators talked with her husband.

Wally said he had no idea what was going on and that his wife left the house to walk the dog. He blamed the incident on a misunderstanding. According to Wally, Wulf had snatched the rag from Indvik's windowsill and Marjorie was returning it.

"Wally was involved—if nothing more than as a passive participant," said Taylor. "We caught him coming outside of his house which was on the opposite side of the Indvik house, his robe on. Not like he'd just woken up."

The next day when deputies searched the Hagens' house they recovered a paper bag beneath the sink filled with cloth similar to the rag found on the windowsill. They also seized matches and several lanterns and lamps filled with kerosene. The kerosene-soaked rag consisted of cut strips of cloth—a pair of scissors discovered in a kitchen drawer appeared to have cloth fibers on the blades.

A Tucson grand jury indicted Marjorie on two counts of arson of an occupied structure on April 3, one for Indvik's house, one for the earlier fire on Palo Verde. The woman who had spent millions of dollars throughout her lifetime couldn't raise $50,000 dollars to free herself from jail. Her bond remained unpaid and pleas for money to her and Wally's children went unheeded.

While being held in the women's unit of the Pima County Jail in Tucson jail, she quickly earned a dubious nickname. Each inmate was given a nickname so that jail staff could talk freely about them. Marjorie's nickname was "Toad," one of the female jailers said, because she was "short, squat, and dumpy." Eleanor Baum, the corrections officer who coined the nickname, said it was also because Marjorie's oversized round glasses made her eyes look toadlike. Marjorie sat in jail for eight months.

Dean Hadfield, the Hagens' neighbor across the street, recalled that Marjorie had initially told him and his wife that Wally was dying of cancer and had three months to live. But when Marjorie was jailed, Wally was up and around, out of his wheelchair, and driving their car. He became known as something of a ladies' man. Wally frequently dined at local restaurants, including Kentucky Fried Chicken, where Marjorie had refused to let him eat. He flirted with the waitresses and pinched their behinds.

"He was most friendly and outgoing to women. He didn't pine away," Gabrielle David said. "It was not that unusual to see a woman toward his age bracket having a meal with him. I don't know whether they were merely sympathetic neighbors, people who walked by the table that he grabbed, or whether he had a girlfriend." More amazing than Wally's extroverted excesses was his sudden vigor. "When [Marjorie] was around he was frequently down in a wheelchair. When she wasn't around, within a week he was up, he was driving his vehicle, and he was walking erect unaided. It was a big change. Everyone noticed."

"[Before Marjorie's arrest] he was all hunched down in the wheelchair and she was tucking in blankets around him," said Ajo native Nydia Gonzales. "After she was arrested, suddenly he was walking in Pizza Hut with a beautiful woman."

"When Marjorie was in jail Wally is like a real person, he's real people. He's trucking all over town," said Bud Klinefelter. "He's cognizant of his surroundings. When you talk to him he's very alert."

Marjorie posted bail that winter. Mark Indvik wasn't pleased to have his neighbor back. "One day…I was walking up the sidewalk, and her dog came running up and he was barking at me. I told him to shut up. And she's standing back peeking around the corner looking at me."

That afternoon the sheriff's office called Indvik in response to a complaint by Marjorie. She claimed that Indvik had been walking up and down the sidewalk with a can, shaking the fence and agitating Wulf.

"I found out she made all these other complaints," Indvik said. "That I had wild parties, threw my trash in her yard. That's crazy."

Lieutenant Taylor recalled, "I know of three times when we had them say that someone was throwing a rock at their house or through their window." The Hagens eventually cemented over the windows of their house on the side facing Indvik. "There was another incident, an alleged traffic accident scraping their bumper. And none of it was verified."

Indvik wasn't the only one who suffered after Marjorie's release, but the other person wasn't complaining. "When she got out of jail, it wasn't a couple of weeks later and [Wally] was fumbling around. And it wasn't too long he was in a wheelchair," said Carol Klinefelter.

Dean Hadfield also said that Wally was soon back to being an invalid after Marjorie got home and gave him more pills. According to Hadfield, Marjorie was popping pills into Wally that made him sleep most of the time.

Whatever the reasons for Wally's relapse, his health problems resulted in numerous postponements of the arson trial. Marjorie's attorney, Edward Bolding, told the court that Marjorie had to care for her seriously ill husband.

On October 22, 1992, eighteen months after her arrest, Marjorie stood trial for arson. The trial was held in the Pima County Courthouse in Tucson, in a modern, darkly paneled, windowless courtroom distinguished by its unusual U-shaped layout. Deputy County Attorney Bill Dickinson, forty-nine, had been with the county attorney's office since 1978. An experienced prosecutor, Dickinson was one of two attorneys for the office who handled arson cases. He also supervised narcotics cases.

In his opening statement, prosecutor Dickinson noted that Marjorie had set fire to Mark Indvik's house while the residence was occupied by Indvik and another man. He also emphasized to jurors that "It's not required that the house burn to the ground in order to support the charge of arson." During testimony Dickinson would make sure the jurors learned of her previous arson conviction.

Bolding's opening statement alleged Marjorie had been mistreated by police at the time of her arrest and described her as community- and church-loving as well as "law-abiding."

"So, was Marjorie Hagen out walking her dog on the night of March 25th?" Bolding said. "Yes, she was. Guilty. Did Marjorie Hagen's dog get out and head over to Mark Indvik's house? Yes. Marjorie had just finished watching *The Ten Commandments* with her husband, and the dog needed to go outside. Guilty."

On October 23, 1992, twenty-eight-year-old border patrol agent Indvik was called as the prosecution's first witness. He testified that after he moved into the rented house next door to the Hagens, he frequently saw the couple out in their yard. He said that except for saying "hi" he never really talked to Marjorie or Wally. Indvik testified that he was unaware of any problems between himself and his neighbors.

"Nobody throwing garbage over the fence or anything of that sort?" Dickinson asked.

"No, sir."

Indvik testified about Marjorie first just pulling on his window, then returning later with the kerosene-soaked rag. He explained how, after he called police, a trap was planned.

"What were you supposed to do? What was the plan?" asked Dickinson.

He told jurors about Officer Billy Ned's having the camera and extinguisher ready, and how he was awakened about 2 A.M. "Be quiet, she's right here by the window," Ned whispered to Indvik.

Indvik continued, "[W]e could hear what sounded like a match being struck, and you could see a faint glow through the curtain, and then the next thing I know there was a huge ball of flame coming up from that rag. The flames went up at least a couple of feet."

"What did you do then?" Dickinson asked.

"Officer Ned threw the curtain back. I gave him time to take a couple pictures and then I hit the rag with the fire extinguisher."

The most melodramatic moment of the trial occurred when Wally testified. An ambulance crew brought Wally into the courtroom lying on a gurney, where he remained for his testimony. In a break with usual courtroom decorum, Wulf—claimed by the Hagens to be a hearing ear dog—was allowed to remain alongside Wally. Under questioning by Bolding, Wally explained that he needed the gurney because he had a couple bad discs surrounded by an inoperable tumor. Despite these claims, several jurors said afterward they spotted Wally get something from the car unaided during a break, then return to the stretcher.

Bolding wasn't finished with improbable medical testimony. "[C]an you talk about your health…back in March of 1991?"

Wally testified that he had "had cancer operations—colon, intestine, and two-thirds of my stomach—and eye operations."

"Who was the person who cared for your medical needs at that time?"

"Marjorie. She is a registered nurse." This story went back before Dick and Marjorie married, when she had claimed to be a nursing student at St. Louis University. Perhaps Wally believed her.

Bolding finally moved on from Wally's alleged ailments to Marjorie's. "Tell me about her arthritis in her hands."

"Well, she has had to give up what little sewing and stuff she'd done. If she happens to pick up a dish just right and it slips, why, she cannot close her fingers enough to stop it and it falls on the floor and breaks."

After eliciting further anecdotes about Marjorie's arthritis, Bolding came to his point. "[W]as Marjorie capable at that time of holding and striking a match out of one of these paper book matches?"

"Well, the match would just slide over. It wouldn't keep on the igniting part of the match. She couldn't hold it between her fingers."

Eventually Bolding asked Wally to describe the time period leading up to his wife's arrest.

"Well, when she got up [to walk the dog], I went into the kitchen and I said, 'I'll make hot water for tea and we'll have tea when you come back,' and so she started for the door, and I said, 'It's kind of chilly out there. Why don't you put my jacket on,' and I grabbed my jacket and threw it on her. It was hanging on the hook right alongside the kitchen door there. Then she snapped the leash on Wulf and took him out."

"And that's the last time you saw her before she was arrested?"

"Well, yes.... [A]nd then they threw this big light in my face. One of the fellows gave me a push. He said 'Put your hands behind your back,' and I said, 'I can't do that because I have got Parkinson's. I have to keep my hands out where they are free and I can keep my balance. Otherwise I have to lay out there on the floor.'"

On cross-examination, Dickinson revisited Wally's physical condition. He got Wally to admit that he and Marjorie had driven by car from Ajo for the trial, and that he had not come to Tucson by ambulance.

Wally spoke with reporters after he finished testifying, using what had become a time-honored refrain in Marjorie's life—she'd been framed. In a new twist, however, Wally made Wulf part of the setup. "I think someone put meat juice on the rag, and

Wulf took it off the windowsill. She was just returning it." He added, "Her mother was murdered you know, but Marge proved her innocence. And she will again. I'm standing by my wife."

When Marjorie took the stand after Wally she claimed to be "terrified" about testifying, but then immediately launched into one of her stories. She claimed to have a master's degree in theology from the University of the South.

Marjorie also claimed—as Wally had earlier—that she and Wally had been married for thirteen years. They had actually been married only eleven years, since August 1981.

Regarding Helen Hagen, Marjorie said, "She died of Alzheimer's." This wasn't true. Helen's doctor had expected her to live another twelve to fifteen years with Alzheimer's, and the coroner had listed her cause of death as pneumonia brought on by dehydration.

Marjorie testified about her grandchildren and other personal information, claiming only "some medical training," selling short her oft-repeated claims of being a registered nurse. After some additional background testimony, Bolding turned the subject back to Wally's health.

Marjorie testified that Wally had had an aneurysm which "started to leak, and… they had to replace the entire aorta from the heart all the way down to the legs." He had also "had four major cancer surgeries…four or five strokes… Parkinson's disease… [and] peripheral vascular disease."

Next Bolding asked Marjorie to describe her and Wally's life in Ajo.

"I belong to two church groups," she began. "We have Bible study on Tuesday night. When my hands are good enough, I do needlepoint. I do quilting, sewing, and I make a lot of my clothes. I do things for the grandchildren and the new babies. I paint, decorative painting, not a scene, but flowers and stuff. Wally cut me some borders for the kitchen and I painted designs on those…." This seemed at odds with Wally's testimony that she had had to give up her handicrafts because of her inability to hold things.

Bolding moved on, asking Marjorie about her health at the time of her arrest.

"I had angina. The doctor terms it severe unstable angina. I had arthritis…[and] three major cancer surgeries…[for] lymphatic cancer and I had scarring on both arms up to the armpits. I have it on my hips, down the leg, and from the point of the hip around under the buttocks. They couldn't do it all in one surgery. They did it three weeks in a row, and I ended up with fifteen hundred stitches for that." She may have had some scars in these regions, but they were from the nips and tucks she'd gotten during Roger's trial. But her troubles weren't over. "I am trying to avoid open-heart surgery…. I have one kidney that doesn't function at all and one that has a tumor in it."

Bolding then gave Marjorie an opportunity to explain how in March 1991 her arthritis made it difficult to perform normal tasks. She said her hands were achy and swollen in the morning so that until they limbered up, she could not turn on a faucet or brush her hair. Under prodding by Bolding, Marjorie said that the design of the windows in Indvik's house, similar to the Hagens', made them impossible to open without tools.

Next Bolding asked about Wulf. Marjorie testified that Wulf had been purchased to help Wally because of her husband's hearing problems. "[H]earing aids don't do much good for the type of deafness that he is progressively getting worse with."

Finally, Bolding got to the question that the jurors and Judge Dawley had been waiting to hear: "Okay, Marjorie, I need you to tell this jury what you did on the evening of March 24."

Marjorie said she and Wally ate dinner on trays in bed and watched *Sixty Minutes* and *The Ten Commandments*. When Wulf wanted to go out during the movie, Marjorie took him for a walk. "I didn't have him on a leash like I should have, and when we went out the back gate, he took off, and I heard him next door," she said. "I walked into Mark's yard...and he was up by the back of Mark's house." Marjorie said Wulf was scratching around and "grabbing at stuff." Although concerned about whether Wulf had caused damage to the house, Marjorie said she decided to wait until morning to speak with Indvik.

Marjorie took Wulf home and went to bed. Later the dog woke her up, and she took the dog out after discussing it with Wally. The dog ran off again.

"I went up to [Indvik's] house because that's where Wulf had gone earlier.... I put my hand out like this on the side of the house to feel my way and...all of a sudden there were blue lights and sparks.... It scared me to death...."

She complained about the way she was searched and handcuffed, calling it "a nightmare" and then said they threw her into a police car. Bolding next turned her testimony toward match books.

"My hands are too awkward on those little tiny matches. It's like at church. I have to use the long wooden stick." Her handicrafts apparently forgotten, she was back to being unable to use her fingers.

Bolding asked her about seeing something on Indvik's windowsill. Marjorie said that she hadn't been able to see anything. "I just felt something that wasn't like a window or a wall. It was soft." She said she thought it might have been a sweatshirt that Wulf had damaged.

Finally it was the prosecutor's turn to question Marjorie. Dickinson believed that Bolding had done a good job of coaching his client on courtroom demeanor. He said "she sat still and kept quiet" throughout the trial, uncharacteristic behavior for Marjorie. Of course, by then she had more courtroom experience than most people. Her only problem was that she volunteered information she wasn't asked for and sometimes had trouble answering questions directly.

Dickinson had to question her repeatedly about her criminal history in Minnesota during his cross-examination. "Is it not true, Mrs. Hagen, that you had been previously convicted of a felony?" Dickinson began.

"Well, everybody knows that. It's common knowledge," Marjorie said.

"Is it not true, Mrs. Hagen, that you have previously been convicted of a felony?"

Dickinson had to press Marjorie for a simple yes to his question, and the judge had to order her to answer the question. Then Dickinson had to press her to acknowledge the date of her conviction in Minnesota—February 9, 1984. Asked about when she and Wally had obtained Wulf, Marjorie said in about March 1991. They had brought him home from the pound, Marjorie testified. He had originally been named "Ugly" and he was a mutt—a malamute, German shepherd, and coyote mix. Marjorie didn't seem to be aware that Wulf's pedigree went against their pretense that he was a hearing ear dog.

Dickinson was, of course, most interested in the details of Marjorie's activities the night of the fire. "On March 24, how many times were you in Mr. Indvik's yard?"

"Before midnight, I can remember two. I may very well have been over either in the yard or in the alley outside earlier in the day. I don't remember."

"The first one was at what time?"

"I remember going during Sixty Minutes…."

"Was it daylight?"

"Yeah, it was. It was twilightish."

"The second time was when?"

"That would be during the Ten Commandments when there was a commercial break."

"Was it daylight?"

"No." Marjorie testified that the second time she went up by Indvik's house was because her dog was scrambling around.

"Did you touch the house?"

"I don't know."

"Did you touch the window?"

"I did later. I don't think I did then."

Marjorie did not consider Indvik a good neighbor, she said, because he threw garbage over the Hagens' fence and his yard was filthy. She said she and Wally had cleaned up Indvik's yard because "he never cut the weeds and there were a lot of Dairy Queen junk and beer cans in the yard and you don't like to live next door to it."

On Thursday, October 29, 1992, the jury found Marjorie guilty of attempted arson of an occupied structure. But in an unusual move, Marjorie wasn't immediately taken into custody. Instead, Pima County Superior Court Judge Frank Dawley granted Marjorie's request for twenty-four hours to drive Wally home to Ajo and arrange for nursing care. She would turn herself in at 5 P.M., Friday, October 30. Lieutenant Taylor had the Hagens' house under surveillance that night, concerned that the couple might flee to Mexico. The Hagens returned home about 9:30 P.M., and on Friday morning the only sign that something might be out of the ordinary was the lack of activity inside the house.

"The house was all closed up…which by everybody's recollection is pretty unusual," Taylor recalled. "But not enough for anybody to act."

At 1 P.M. that afternoon, Taylor got a call from Bolding. Marjorie would turn herself in at the local jail. Bolding then accused sheriff's deputies of stopping Marjorie six or seven times without reason during the drive back from Tucson. Lieutenant Taylor said he was concerned the couple would escape to Mexico, and Judge Dawley had agreed that deputies could detain the Hagens if they were headed south. Taylor told Bolding that Marjorie drove up next to a deputy sheriff who happened to be at a trading post west of Tucson. The deputy recognized the Hagens' Jeep and spoke to Marjorie. He called Ajo authorities who instructed him to send the Hagens on their way since they were driving in the right direction.

Sergeant John Gilmartin, one of Taylor's deputies, rode his bike past the Hagens' house shortly before 2 P.M. Friday and caught the scent of natural gas. He immediately contacted Lieutenant Taylor, who quickly went to Wally and Marjorie's home.

As Taylor walked up to the door he could also smell gas. He knocked, but no one answered. Then he heard Marjorie's voice from inside.

"What do you want?" she asked from the kitchen window. "What's the problem?"

"We've had a report of a gas leak," Taylor said. "Is everything all right?"

"Yes, everything's fine," Marjorie insisted. "The pilot light blew out. It's okay now."

"Is everyone all right?"

"Yes."

"Well, I'll see you later this afternoon," Taylor said before leaving.

Just before 4:30 P.M., Marjorie called Wally's son Tom in Minnesota and told him his father was dead. Tom's first reaction upon hearing the news was to tell Marjorie to "call the police." When she didn't respond, he said, "Well, if you can't call the police, call a doctor." It struck him as odd that Marjorie hadn't called anyone when his father was dying. After Marjorie finally agreed to call a doctor, Tom hung up and contacted the county sheriff's office in Ajo.

Marjorie had also notified Bolding and the Reverend Sid Sandusky, the minister at the Presbyterian church the couple had recently been attending. Sandusky immediately went to the Hagen house, where he discovered Wally lying on the waterbed in the couple's bedroom. "Wally had been dead for quite a while," said Sandusky. "She had bathed him."

Bolding presented Marjorie's postmortem care of Wally as an excuse for Marjorie not notifying police, stating that she had wanted to spend time with Wally. "She tried to get him presentable looking."

Since Marjorie had not followed through on her promise to Tom Hagen to call a doctor, Sandusky "called the clinic because I figured a doctor should come over and verify Wally was dead…. Marjorie seemed confused. She was not making sense."

Detective David Allen was the first law enforcement officer to arrive on the scene. Allen said Marjorie initially acted hyper and kept trying to tell Allen and other officers things she thought they should know. Marjorie made sure to tell the officers that she loved Wally. What would she do without him, she asked. But to Allen, it felt like Marjorie was putting on a performance. As the day progressed—and with Wally's body unmoved from the house—Allen noted Marjorie's voice sounded progressively more resigned.

When Taylor arrived, he noticed that all the windows and doors were now open. As he walked in the front door, he saw Marjorie talking with Reverend Sandusky.

"Where is Wally?" Taylor asked. Marjorie pointed to the bedroom. Taylor found Wally lying in the waterbed, covers up to his chin, obviously dead. Rigor mortis had already set in Wally's jaw, and it was Taylor's guess that he had been dead since that morning.

"Whenever I've seen [Marjorie] she's always been in control. And when I saw her this time it was like she was out of control," Taylor said. "My sense is she was on the edge because she wasn't sure how this thing was going to shake out."

Marjorie started talking with Taylor about a gas leak and how the pipe had been pinched off and was leaking. Taylor suspected Wally had been asphyxiated by the leaking gas. Natural gas utility workers inspected the Hagens' home, but found nothing wrong with the gas meter or gas lines—if gas was involved, it had been no accident. Neighbor Dean Hadfield told investigators that he had seen Marjorie cut a length of hose that day. Hadfield said that apparently the hose wasn't long enough, because Marjorie cut another piece of hose and taped the two pieces together. Taylor assigned a detective, who had a hidden tape recorder running, to stay with Marjorie.

Sheriff's deputies obtained a search warrant and gathered evidence including a vacuum hose, bottles of prescription medications, wrenches, pruning shears, garden hoses, and an antique kitchen stove made in 1924. A latent print was recovered from the gas line that fed the stove. Deputies also recovered a note detailing a suicide pact Wally had allegedly made with Marjorie.

The note, addressed to Bolding, began in Marjorie's handwriting. She proclaimed her innocence in the arson case, and stated that she and Wally were committing suicide because "with Wally's health and the type of political miscarriage of justice done to both of us we have no choice." The note continued, "When a reward creates a situation where an [sic] sworn law officer and his friend can create a set up to destroy the lives of two innocent people, and a prosecutor and a judge deliberately withhold information and facts in order to predjudice [sic] a jury, we are left with no choice."

Marjorie also noted that the couple wanted to be buried in a single coffin along with Wulf: "As we have only the three of us in life, we wish to have the three of us together in death."

A smaller part of the note, in Wally's handwriting, stated that "all material things that I have are to go to Richard LeRoy," and a postscript included Wally's declaration that "these decisions in this Letter made equaly [sic] between Marge and myself. To think that a reward can go to such extrems [sic] to make people do these things to neighbors. Marge and I care very much for each other and would like to be buried together."

At about 11 P.M. Hadfield intercepted Marjorie as she headed to the home of Tia Concha, another neighbor. Hadfield brought her to his house. He had first met Wally and Marjorie soon after the couple moved to Ajo. He and Wally had developed a close relationship, especially around religion, Hadfield later said. Wally would come and ask Hadfield to pray with him. However, if Wally stayed too long Marjorie would come and get him. Hadfield described Marjorie as the type of person who could not recognize when she had made a mistake. He also recalled Marjorie as an expert manipulator and a smooth talker who could deftly control the flow of conversation.

At the Hadfields', Marjorie had at first made a fuss about how she had been trying to keep Wally warm. She then used Hadfield's phone to call her attorney. After using the phone, she said she was hungry. Hadfield offered her food and something to drink.

"No, I'll just eat this apple," she said, holding up a large green apple she had brought with her. While Hadfield's wife tried to make her comfortable, Marjorie said, "I must have knocked the flex hose off the natural gas stove." After she ate the apple, Marjorie fell asleep. The Hadfields were unable to sleep and, at about 4 A.M., Pima County sheriff's deputies came to arrest Marjorie for the murder of Wally Hagen.

Edward Bolding publicly blamed police in part for Wally's death. He said that a combination of cancer, heart disease, and other illnesses—in addition to grief over Marjorie's arson conviction and police harassment—had killed Wally. Bolding again claimed that the Hagens had been stopped several times for no reason during their drive from court in Tucson back to their home in Ajo, adding several hours to the normal two-and-a-half-hour drive. "The trip killed him," said Bolding.

Within three weeks of Wally's death, prosecutors dropped the murder charges. Wally's autopsy results were not yet available and the prosecution was not ready to present its case to a grand jury. With the deadline for convening the grand jury approaching, prosecutors dropped the charges to avoid having them dismissed with prejudice, which would have closed the case permanently.

Eventually Wally's autopsy results disproved Bolding's claims and confirmed what the Hagen children had been certain of all along—Marjorie had invented her husband's cancer. The official cause of death was listed as "ingested toxic quantity of propoxyphene," a barbiturate that had been prescribed to Wally.

"He overdosed on drugs," said Lieutenant Taylor, "but they could have been self-administered. The note that was written, both sets of handwriting were on there, his and hers. And the fingerprint on the gas line was inconclusive." Since Marjorie had waited so long before notifying authorities, any gas in Wally's system would have dissipated before tests were conducted. None of the evidence—the overdose, the tantalizing hints about gas asphyxiation—was sufficient to build a murder case. The manner of death, which the coroner had the option to indicate as "homicide," "suicide," or "accidental," was marked as "undetermined."

The trial hadn't been the end of Marjorie's arson trouble. Additional charges were brought after the guilty verdict, and in May 1993 she pleaded no contest to a charge of criminal damage in excess of $10,000 in connection with the July 9, 1990, arson fires at the Del Sur RV shop.

At her sentencing on June 11, 1993, Bolding characterized his client as a woman in her sixties suffering from an assortment of serious health problems. "She's had lymphatic cancer where she had 1,500 stitches to take care of the operations that she had there," he told the court. "She has severe angina. She has hypertension. She suffers from…nonfunctioning kidneys, with dialysis being the next step there. She has a thyroid problem of a severe nature. She has severe arthritis, bursitis," which Bolding said Marjorie had suffered from for many years. "Mrs. Hagen, frankly, does not believe that she will survive a prison sentence." Bolding asked the court for a shorter sentence based on mitigating circumstances.

Dickinson argued that while Marjorie was attempting to portray herself as the victim, she was a woman convicted three times of setting fires. She had also committed insurance fraud in Minnesota, Dickinson continued, and, more recently, in Ajo. Both cases involved fires.

Marjorie should be portrayed, Dickinson said, as a manipulative firesetter and a danger to the community. "She sets fires to homes. She sets fires to homes in which people are sleeping. She is a danger. She is a menace," Dickinson told the court, requesting Marjorie be given a fifteen-year prison sentence. "All of us need to be protected from Marjorie Hagen, for as long as we can be protected from Marjorie Hagen."

Wally Hagen's three children sent a letter to Judge Dawley asking that he give Marjorie the maximum sentence. It read, in part:

> [It] is clear she has no remorse or any comprehension at all that arson, theft, fraud, and murder are things that are wrong! Marge obviously feels she is being picked on by society. That everybody else, including you, are responsible for Marge's problems…. She is indeed a career criminal and must be put away for the protection of society in general and us specifically."

Judge Dawley sentenced Marjorie to fifteen years, the maximum sentence for the attempted arson conviction, noting he found no mitigating circumstances in Marjorie's age and health concerns. "I do find that Mrs. Hagen is a threat and, despite her age and health problems, would remain a threat if not incarcerated." She was also ordered to pay approximately $39,000 in restitution to the Del Sur repair shop and the owners of the motorhome and car damaged in those fires. The prosecution decided not to charge her for Wally's death. That case was shelved by Pima County homicide detectives.

Marjorie was sent to the maximum security prison at Goodyear, Arizona. The women's unit is housed in a gray concrete single-story building surrounded by barbed wire, with only a few scattered palm trees outside for landscaping.

"I think she is the personification of evil," says Lieutenant Taylor. "She is the most sinister woman I have ever dealt with. I think she is a sociopath. The scary thing about her for me is that I can understand her burning down her motorhome for money. I can understand her setting the other fires. I can't understand her setting fire to an occupied residence. I can't understand her setting fire to the house next to hers, unless her house was going to be next and Wally was going to be in it—I'm sure that there was in her mind that Wally was outliving his usefulness."

Some in Ajo have said Marjorie changed their lives and the small town, perhaps permanently. "She has made the community a little more suspicious about people moving here," Gabrielle David said. "We're still a friendly town. But people are beginning to take what other people say with an extra grain of salt."

"She left her mark on this little town. She left a lot of anxiety and a lot of fear, because she basically put the community on a fearful edge," said Bud Klinefelter, who had two sons on the volunteer fire department. "We as a family were extremely tense and concerned. The law of averages said some fireman is going to get hurt sometime on a fire. I just dreaded to hear the goddamn fire alarms going off." His wife added, "Sunday nights I couldn't sleep."

Despite the arson conviction and murder accusations, the Skinners remained staunch supporters of Marjorie. The couple said she left a permanent mark on their lives as well, but a positive one. "Marjorie helped me to grow up some. I realize that in life people genuinely have got things crossed up. She helped me understand that perception is what needs to be negotiable. And my perception of her was always a good one," said George Skinner. "If there's a bad side to a person like that there's a good side. I'm glad I met Marge Congdon. She was important to both of our lives."

"I don't have to judge her. That's not my business," said Emma Skinner. "We lent a hand and tried to help her, and through her difficulties she taught my husband about life. I saw her as a bright star. She had a lot of pep and enthusiasm. She was outgoing and gregarious. The other side I don't know anything about."

National arson expert and psychologist Dr. Jessica Gaynor of San Francisco has studied numerous fire setters and arsonists. She reviewed Marjorie's personal history, news stories, and what little is known of Marjorie's biological family background. She speculated that Marjorie was a "classic sociopath" suffering from an antisocial personality disorder, a disorder that may lessen or remit over time, but will never disappear.

Antisocial personality disorders appear before the age of fifteen. Marjorie's behavior in childhood and early adolescence, specifically her history of lying, stealing, and breaking rules, supports the diagnosis. "So does her adult behavior," Dr. Gaynor said, "the chronic lying, the repeated failure to meet financial obligations, her estrangement from her children, and the manipulation of the significant people in her life."

Marjorie's fire setting, another form of antisocial behavior, is intriguing, Dr. Gaynor said, because most serial arsonists are men. Marjorie's background, however, matches some of the factors most associated with fire starters. She was the oldest child, grew up in a fatherless home, and has had difficulty with interpersonal relationships. But her profile differs from that of the typical female fire setter because she not only set fire to her own property, but targeted the property of others.

"What makes this so unusual is the fact that as well as committing property crime, Marjorie also allegedly committed violent crime," Gaynor said. "It's very rare for an arsonist to also commit violent crime."

The FBI classifies fires arsonists set using several categories: revenge, pyromania, malicious mischief, concealment of crime, and insurance fraud.

"Marjorie uses the same criminal vehicle, arson, for more than one reason," said Dr. Gaynor. "That makes this case intrinsically more interesting."

Once the murder investigation into Wally's death had closed, his body was finally released from the morgue. During the seven months Wally's body was kept in the morgue, a legal battle began over where Wally would be buried. While Marjorie did not oppose the decision by Wally's three children to cremate him, she wanted him buried in Arizona. Wally's children wanted to bury their father's ashes next to their mother. The legal battle that followed dragged on for more than three years.

The Hagens hired Arizona attorney Robert Hooker and argued that Marjorie and Wally's marriage was not valid. Shortly after the marriage, Wally's son, Tom, had asked one of Marjorie's attorneys if she was divorced from Roger. The attorney told him, "Maybe in Marjorie's mind she is." Records from the North Dakota Bureau of Criminal Investigation indicated that investigators had been unable to find any proof that Marjorie had ever divorced Roger. According to Marjorie, she had obtained a divorce in Tijuana, Mexico.

"Do you have any records of that trip?" Hooker asked Marjorie during a deposition for the civil suit.

"I did have."

"Until when?"

"Until my legal papers were stolen."

"By whom?"

"The Isley's Corporation." Isley's RV Service Center had seized an RV from Marjorie for lack of payment. However, the employees who inventoried the RV at the time of the seizure refuted Marjorie's assertion.

In an April 28, 1993, deposition, Marjorie was asked by Hooker, "Do you know what the purpose of a deposition is?"

"For you to snoop," she responded.

Bolding, still representing her, chimed in, "That's exactly right, Marge."

In a later deposition given by Nancy Hagen Kaufmann, Bolding asked, "Do you know that Wally has signed a writing saying that he wants to be buried in Arizona?"

"Are you referring to the suicide note?"

Bolding repeated, "Are you aware of any writing where Wally has stated that he wanted to be buried in Arizona?"

"Yes."

"And you chose not to want to follow that wish, is that correct?"

"Can I interject? I'm aware of the suicide note.... The only thing that it states is that he wishes to be buried in a common grave with Marge."

"And you choose not to accede to that wish?"

"My father belongs in Minnesota with his family."

"So you say he has no decision-making power in that connection?"

"I believe my father was told to write [whatever Marjorie] wanted, whatever document you have. I believe that my father would wish to be buried in Minnesota next to his wife...."

"What makes you believe he was told to sign that writing?"

"Twelve years of having Marge control my father." Kaufmann went on to state, "Your client has a tremendous amount of control over people, and she can talk anybody into doing anything, whether it's their legal wish or not. I do not believe if my father was allowed to be by himself for a few months and dry out from Marjorie, that he would wish to be buried in Arizona." Kaufmann said that her father had told her in 1980 that he wanted to be buried in Mound, Minnesota, next to his wife, Helen.

By late 1995, the Hagen children wanted some finality to their father's death. The three children reluctantly accepted what the judge had suggested—half of their father's ashes. A settlement was reached on December 19, 1995, but Wally's children had to wait until January 1996, to receive their half of their father's remains. The mortician did not send the ashes to Minnesota until after the Christmas holidays, concerned that they might get lost in the holiday mail.

On a blustery January day, Nancy went out to her mailbox and found a small brown box wrapped with brown tape. Wally's ashes were spilling out of a ripped corner of the box. Nancy gathered up the ashes and box, which she placed in a large plastic bag, and called her brother Tom. "Guess who's finally here," she told him.

Later that day, plastic bag in hand, Nancy met with a mortician to pick out an urn. She chose a medium-sized green marble urn shaped like a flower vase. Nancy then walked out to her blue van, opened the passenger door, and buckled in her father's remains.

Nancy's first stop was her mother's grave, where she set Wally's urn on top of the headstone, climbed into the van, and played a cassette of Christmas songs, a favorite collection of Helen's. "I let my father and mother have a little chat," she recalled. She then took the urn and visited the house where Wally and Helen had raised their family, after which Nancy took her father's remains to her house and placed the urn on the living room mantel.

The urn stayed at Nancy's for several days, then went to Tom's house, where the urn was decorated in Christmas red and green. Since Wally had been an avid basketball fan, Tom placed the urn on top of the TV when he watched University of Minnesota Golden Gophers games.

On January 19, 1996, a bitterly cold afternoon with a cloudless sky, Tom Hagen, Dick Hagen, and Nancy Hagen Kauffman, along with their spouses, children, and grandchildren, gathered to say goodbye to Wally. In an intimate memorial service held at Westwood Lutheran Church in St. Louis Park, Wally was eulogized as the prodigal father, home at last. The green marble urn rested at the front of the church next to a photo of Wally from a happier time, when he was a loving husband and father of three.

As the minister emphasized in the eulogy, Wally was home to stay after years of separation from his children and their families. The minister mentioned Marjorie, not as a loving wife, but as an evil force in Wally's life. "Is there evil in this world? Knowing what I know about Marjorie Caldwell, I have to answer my own question with 'Yes, there is evil in this world.'" He concluded, "It's the end of some of the twists, a resolution, a long struggle to win back Wally's ashes. And with this comes release, closure."

Wally Hagen's children, grandchildren, and great-grandchildren buried his remains alongside those of Helen in a cemetery not far from where the couple had raised their family.

CHAPTER 26

Prison Life

ARJORIE ENTERED PERRYVILLE PRISON AS INMATE #098685 on July 19, 1993. She was transferred several times in her first year: first to Florence, then to Tucson, and then to the Arizona Center for Women in Phoenix in August 1994, where she remained until May of 2000.

Over those six years she racked up twelve disciplinary violations, including one for refusing to work and the rest divided between lying to officials and disobeying orders. Nevertheless, she adapted to the structure of prison life, much as her second husband, Roger, had. She fancied herself a mother figure, eager to chat with and offer unsolicited advice to the other inmates.

Before going to prison, Marjorie had been an active volunteer at Immaculate Conception Catholic Church in Ajo. Prison staff even received a letter from Marjorie's former priest, praising her readiness to defend a just cause or wrongly accused person, her ability to find quick solutions in difficult situations, and her volunteer activities. Not surprisingly, then, Marjorie became involved in prison ministries.

Her work assignments, which paid between ten and fifty cents an hour—and for which she received positive evaluations—included chaplain clerk, law library clerk, clothing clerk, and education aide.

In June 1996, Marjorie made a $1,000 down payment on a 5,100-square-foot lot in Copper Crest, a gated community on the outskirts of Tucson. Of course, she never met the Copper Crest sales staff; Bolding, as her attorney and financial advisor, informed the salespeople that she wanted to buy the $29,950 lot. He also appeared for her at the closing in September 1996 and paid an additional $5,500 toward the down payment.

From her prison cell, Marjorie began designing her manufactured home and surrounding gardens. She contacted companies for production information, which she compiled in several notebooks along with her own house drawings and landscape sketches. The living room, dining room, and bedroom were to have cathedral ceilings with exposed rafters. Marjorie wanted a hand-carved, built-in bed. She spared no expense and overlooked no detail: the notebooks included plans for an L.L. Bean deluxe hammock to hang from the rafters; a $169 antiqued frolicking pig weathervane; $2,000 cast-iron wood stoves for the living room and bath; 1914 Hoosier-reproduction oak cabinets and work table for the screen porch; and an electrical outlet for a heating pad in her dog's bed.

Marjorie's landscaping plans were equally ambitious, particularly given the lot size. She sought a "landscape genius" to create the look of a "gingerbread cottage" hidden among various trees, flowers, and vines. "The house must nestle in the plantings," she instructed. Her ideal landscaper was someone like herself, who "has never completely grown up and has fun creating a mythical, fantasy, mad Ludwig of Bavaria, sort of landscape."

Marjorie wanted large trees, fruit trees, bird feeders, lattices covered with roses and vines, wildflowers, pansies, poppies, geraniums, lilies, lilacs, herbs, and many other varieties of flowers. But, she emphasized in her landscaping notes, "I do not wish to have either trees or plants put in with the idea of 'spectacular growth' over the next few years. I haven't *got* the time to wait, or waste, on 'spectacular growth.' I want it NOW!! Instant gratification is *just right*!!! Think hammocks and swings, when you consider tree sizes!!! Also, there can never be too many trees for me, or too many large rocks grouped near their bases, with bulbs, bushes, and wild flowers tucked among them."

Marjorie also instructed potential landscapers that "The house must be fragrant all year long from open windows and doors having the scent waft in! …Above *all* things, fragrance, fragrance, fragrance, and more fragrance. I *must* be able to sleep or bathe with windows open to beauty and fragrant odors."

Along with Marjorie's long lists of must haves, she was also adamant about what she didn't want. "ABSOLUTELY no glads, zinnias, sunflowers, marigold, or other stiff, stuck-up funeral flowers!!!" Marjorie's idea of a mystical fairyland of trees, plants, and flowers included one item that attracted special attention from Copper Crest management. Marjorie planned to place a full-sized painted carousel horse on a brass pole under one of the large trees.

Marjorie's sense of humor apparently stayed intact in prison. While working as a clothing clerk in 1999, she wrote the warden a letter with the heading of "naked inmates":

> While Lady Godiva was able to ride through Coventry stark naked, somehow I don't think it would be policy here at A.C.W. But since we have been out of medium, large, x-large, and 2x large underwear, large 3x and 4x t-shirts, and using towels destined for the dog kennels, we are not far from having women in the same boat as the aforementioned lady. Order after order has been given but we can not seem to get any of them signed off.

Marjorie taught English to Spanish-speaking inmates and organized and taught a course entitled "Spanish for Gringos." She was a popular teacher whose students described her in glowing terms: "the definition of a sweet teacher," "kind and patient," "someone very special," and "the world's greatest teacher." One even said "we all love you."

Not all the women felt the same way. Prison records indicate that in 1999, an inmate reported that Marjorie had encouraged other inmates to accuse staff of having sexual relations with inmates in order to get the Criminal Investigations Unit to back off. The inmate told prison officials that Marjorie was trying to have other inmates do her dirty work for her by making the false accusations.

Yet Marjorie's prison files also contained thank you letters to staff written in flowery language reminiscent of the overly generous gifts she bestowed on friends. She wrote of a Captain Karl:

> Of late he has had to don the armor of a knight, pull his trusty steed out of the barn, and ride to save the young and not so young damsels in distress on 14 yard! We truly do appreciate the times he saves us from fire breathing dragons who would send us back into our caves for the day, as well as seeing to it that the kitchen officers obey your orders as to diets, and don't go off on their own! The signs that are posted saying "inmates are students of our behavior," could very well have been created with Capt Karl in mind! Does he never raise his voice or loose his temper? Remarkable! Sometimes I think I would kill me if I were he, but instead he is ever polite, kind and competant [sic]!

In a letter praising "exemplary officers," Marjorie wrote:

> While we all tend to be quick to employ pen and paper against what we perceive as wrongs done us, hopefully we are equally quick to give credit and recognition where they are due! In that view, may I compliment you on these outstanding A.C.W. officers.... We are fortunate to have those, who after knowing the consumate [sic] horrors of the prison system attempt to build not only a safer world, but a more decent one. They do not brag nor brood or complain of superiors or the system, but do what they can wherever they may be placed. A single candle sometimes in the throes of darkness & despair! ...They may receive no buttons, rewards, or financial benefits for their efforts, but will at all times be remembered as beacons of life in an ever more hostile feeling between inmates and their largely politically motivated "keepers." Thank you for these few!

In prison, Marjorie continued to do handiwork, particularly needlepoint; apparently her fingers, unable to strike a match according to her and Wally's testimony at her arson trial, had recovered. She embroidered an altar cloth and donated it to the chapel at the Arizona Center for Women. Marjorie was still an avid reader, particularly of murder mysteries, and a frequent visitor to the prison library. Every month friends sent her ten to fourteen books, which she donated to the prison library.

Marjorie didn't have many visitors. While prison records indicate Bolding, visited only twice, officials suggest that not all of his visits—some for special circumstances—were recorded. Other than Bolding, Anthony Nevara, a minister, visited once in 1996. Her son Ricky and a woman named Carolyn Saenz were the only other people on her list of approved visitors, but records indicate neither ever stopped by to see Marjorie.

Five years after Wally's children buried their father, they received notice from the Arizona Board of Executive Clemency that Marjorie was seeking an early release from prison. Her fifteen-year sentence would not expire until February 2007, but she had an opportunity to request parole. Her initial appearance before the parole board was scheduled for November 15, 2001, at the Perryville Women's Prison in Goodyear, on the western outskirts of Phoenix.

Marjorie had started serving her sentence at the Perryville prison in 1993, so she had come full circle on May 5, 2000, when she was transferred from the Arizona Center for Women back to Perryville, which had been converted to an all-women's prison earlier that year.

She was housed in Santa Cruz, a medium security unit. While most inmates were incarcerated on drug charges, largely possession and trafficking, Marjorie was one of the eight women in a prison population of roughly 2,000 who had been convicted of arson.

Arizona has a hard-labor law, which meant that Marjorie had to work 40 hours a week, or work 20 hours and participate in programming for 20 hours per week. "We try to occupy [inmates'] time with productive kinds of activities from the time they get up to the time they go to bed," said a top prison official who asked to remain anonymous.

Due to her custody level and the classification of the unit where she lived, Marjorie was no longer allowed to knit, crochet, or do needlepoint. But she found other ways to keep busy. A fairly vigorous walker, Marjorie usually walked the track each morning out in the main yard. She continued to be an avid reader. Prison policy permitted inmates only seven personal books in their cell, and Marjorie received seven books each week. She would read the seven books and then donate them to the prison library so that she could get seven new ones. According to prison officials, Marjorie was one of the largest benefactors, among inmates, of books to the prison library.

As she had in previous prisons, Marjorie got involved with her fellow prisoners. "I think she fashioned herself as the mother [or] grandmother of the unit and tried to help the other inmates, assist them with their problems," a prison official said. "Marjorie particularly involved herself in health issues, speaking out on other inmates' behalf."

By the time of her first parole hearing in 2001, she was no longer viewed as a problem inmate. Since leaving A.C.W., she had not once violated a disciplinary code. That didn't mean that her behavior was without its rough spots, however. Although Marjorie liked to see herself as as a teacher and helper, prison officials said that she also tended to put herself above the other inmates. "She saw herself as the smart one, the educated one, the 'I know a lot of stuff and I'm willing to share it with you.'"

If Marjorie had a complaint, the "kites" she wrote to prison officials were seven or eight pages long. Marjorie complained more than once to prison officials because in the summer she wanted to get up and walk at 5 A.M., and the yard didn't open until 7. She complained about food and wanting more freedom during recreation time. One official recalled that Marjorie became convinced there was a huge conspiracy to not allow Catholic priests in to serve the inmates. Nevertheless, Marjorie, who sometimes went by the name Margaret, was considered neither a public nor institutional risk, at least on paper.

In support of her parole request, Marjorie had submitted a written release plan to the five-member board. In her plan, Marjorie did her best to portray herself as an exemplary prisoner and harmless grandmother and great-grandmother, who had seen the error of her ways.

> I am a woman of very close to 70 years old, to whom the prison experience has been a horror! When I was first incarcerated my mind was so very full of anger, frustration and the sorrow and stress of the recent death of my very loved husband, that there was no room left for either personal accountability or remorse for my action.

Marjorie said that after participating in individual and group therapy with staff psychologists, "I have come to an understanding of what brought me here to this place. I have become aware that through my extremely bad choices to solve my problems, many others through no fault of their own, have been made to suffer."

Marjorie also submitted program descriptions and copies of certificates indicating courses she had completed in prison, including Anger and Stress Management, Thinking Straight, a substance abuse education program, Inmate Legal Research, Spanish, and a twelve-step program called "Women Who Love Too Much." She noted that she had been an active volunteer in prison.

As for her release plans, Marjorie said she planned to live in Copper Crest. Her transportation would be a Dodge conversion van she owned outright. She had sufficient money to "assure me of enough income to live comfortably, but not lavishly, without a need to re-offend for financial reasons." For income she would count on Wally's union pension and approximately $34,000 a year from the civil settlement with her children, which had also been accumulating throughout her incarceration. Marjorie said her support network would include her church, priest, and self-help groups. Marjorie listed a simple short-term goal: "To re-enter society with the least amount of notice possible." She explained, "I am a very private person."

Her long-term goals included being "a contributing member" to society, "rather than a parasite." She planned to continue her volunteer literary work, serve on the Altar Guild and participate in other church work, teach quilting and needlepoint, visit shut-ins at hospitals and nursing homes, and deliver food for Meals on Wheels. Marjorie wanted to get a service dog and join a pet therapy group so she could take the dog on visits to hospital wards.

Marjorie also claimed to have been "blessed with a circle of caring friends and supportive children, who will stand with me on the outside, as they have during my incarceration." She lamented that she was doing prison time "rather than [having] a time of enjoyment of children, grandchildren, and yes, two great-grandchildren." In truth, of her seven children only Rick maintained contact with her. Other family members, including her daughter Rebecca and niece Clara, instead wrote letters urging the Arizona parole Board to keep Marjorie in prison.

Other family members sent letters opposing her release. Marjorie "should not be released from prison, as she is a con artist and a pathological liar," wrote Jennifer and Charles Johnson. "We believe she is a desperate and unbalanced person who would go to any length to get what she wants." The Johnsons feared that if Marjorie were released she would "latch onto another unsuspecting family and ruin their lives."

Rebecca said that her mother "is unable to live within her means…. Her behavior can often be described as irrational at best. It is difficult to put on paper how she succeeds at being so destructive. One would have to live through it, like I have to truly understand what I mean."

The sole letter in support of release was from Marjorie's attorney Edward Bolding. Bolding said that he had read the letters opposing her release and described them as "vitriol-laced opinion letters." He also provided additional details regarding his client's release plans. Bolding confirmed Marjorie's intent to live in Tucson when she got out of prison. Marjorie owned property in a manufactured home subdivision, Bolding said, and would have a home ready for her to move into upon release. He also said that he had handled all of Marjorie's finances since her incarceration. "I confirm and guarantee that she has more than adequate income for the purchase of the home, transportation for her medical and other needs, and for all items necessary for her living arrangements and medical bills. In addition, Marjorie will be eligible for Social Security benefits and Medicare."

But Bolding's written guarantee did not fit the facts. Earlier that year, Marjorie had fallen into a familiar pattern of behavior; she was behind on her mortgage payments. When a payment was late, Copper Crest developer Gene Jones would contact Bolding, who would apologize and, according to Jones, be "full of excuses" as to why Marjorie's payments were late. Bolding would then assure Jones that Marjorie would soon be receiving money from her family trust. Eventually Bolding would send a check on Marjorie's behalf to catch up on the mortgage. "Bolding was having trouble getting the money from her," said Jones. "He'd get three or four months behind, and I'd chase him and he'd send a check and apologize."

Tom Hagen and Nancy Hagen Kaufmann didn't only write letters opposing Marjorie's possible parole, they flew from Minnesota to Phoenix to attend the parole board hearing. "As long as Marjorie is on the loose, there is a real possibility she will set more fires, cheat more people out of money, and destroy more families," said Nancy.

The hearing took place in a prison classroom building in Marjorie's unit. Marjorie, dressed in a prison-issue orange shirt and pants and sneakers, had her hair tightly pulled back in a bun, her piercing eyes surrounded by her signature large round glasses. She sat at a table facing the board members, with the Hagens slightly behind her, to her left. Marjorie was visibly surprised to see Wally's children, and angered that they were permitted to testify.

Board members wanted Marjorie to demonstrate accountability for her crime and indicate she was sorry, and even the warden was on hand to hear what Marjorie had to say. But Marjorie consistently denied her involvement in the attempted arson. She deflected attention from her own culpability by berating Wally's children for turning their backs on their father in his time of medical need. Nancy and Tom both testified how Marjorie had hurt their family and set fires, and described their love for their father.

The parole board voted 4–0 to deny Marjorie's bid for early release, noting that Marjorie needed to further address her criminal behavior and take responsibility for her offense. After the hearing, Nancy Kaufmann and Tom Hagen thanked the board members. As the two went to retrieve their belongings from a prison locker, Bolding saw them leaving. "He yelled over at us, 'I hope you guys are proud of yourselves,'" Tom recalled. "He said we were there because we had 'children's remorse' for abandoning our father."

Although the forty-five-minute meeting was over, the proceedings were not. Unfortunately, the board's tape recording equipment had malfunctioned, failing to record a number of parole hearings that day, including Marjorie's. As a result, the board held another hearing on March 12, 2002. Marjorie had another opportunity to accept responsibility for her crime.

"Are you guilty of the arson?" one board member asked.

"I'm torn because no, I'm not, but I've been told to tell the board, 'yes,'" she responded. "Because you won't even hear me if I don't admit to it."

Asked for details of her crime, Marjorie said, "I had taken some stuff over from our yard to our neighbor—we had a young border patrolman living there in a little house…. And when I was over there, he and a bunch of his friends jumped on me and said that they felt I was trying to burn the house. There were no matches, there was [sic] no cigarettes, there was nothing to light, there was no flame, there was nothing. But they had had a series of fires within [Ajo]."

It was perhaps her most wildly divergent version yet. Marjorie then blamed her conviction on her inability to attend most of the trial and the jury's knowledge of her prior Minnesota arson conviction. Marjorie told board members she was only at the trial long enough to testify because of her late husband Wally's poor health. She said that Wally had died the day after the jury found her guilty, noting that "Wally had numerous strokes, he had open heart surgery for an aortic aneurism, he had five major cancer surgeries." These claims had already been disproved by his autopsy.

The parole board, however, was not interested in Wally's health, and pressed Marjorie for more information about the attempted arson. Board members wanted to know what evidence helped convince jurors Marjorie was guilty.

"But there was some evidence left behind of some attempt?" asked one member.

"No, there was nothing."

"Nothing?"

"I had a jacket that I had picked up that I believed belonged to the border patrolman. I'd taken it over and the windows on those houses opened out, you know the old fashioned ones with metal windows with the little glass panes. And I crammed it in there. We were not on good terms with him," Marjorie explained, still inventing new details.

Following Marjorie, Edward Bolding testified that Wally's children had come "on a personal vendetta because of some guilt they might feel in saying 'oh well, our father died, and therefore we believe Marjorie had something to do with it and therefore she's an evil woman.'" He emphatically told the board that Marjorie had been a "model prisoner" who had done everything she was supposed to do.

Bolding said that Marjorie was probably one of the oldest women in prison in Arizona, and "has completed every course, every program, every opportunity she has to better herself, to do what this board and other people call rehabilitation. What has she done to deserve being released from having to serve her full length of time, to deserve a parole, to deserve being out? Everything."

Both Bolding and Marjorie disputed statements by sheriff's deputies about the attempted arson.

"Miss Hagen, who's been my client and friend for eleven-and-a-half, twelve years now, I'm sorry to say, is living evidence of my failure as a trial lawyer," said Bolding. "She was charged with arson. When she testified, she, under oath admitted of course, that she had been previously convicted of the crime of arson. The jury decided that there was no evidence of burning, there were no flames, there was no, as Miss Hagen said, no cigarette lighter, no matches, no nothing." Bolding and Marjorie each blamed Wulf, the Hagens' so-called service dog, like she had at trial. Bolding said that Wulf picked up something and put it at the neighbor's house, and Marjorie had said Wulf ran into her neighbor's yard while she was running with him.

Other witnesses included Tom Hagen and Nancy Hagen Kaufmann, who had again flown from Minnesota to personally address board members.

"Please know that Marge can be a very sweet, charming, and convincing woman," Kaufmann testified. "I also believe her to be dangerous. Marge has no regard for life, laws, or rules. The only rules Marge follows are the ones she makes."

Tom Hagen testified that if Marjorie were let out she would be "a hazard to the community" and the people around her. He pointed out that none of Marjorie's immediate family members were present to testify on her behalf. Like his sister, he encouraged the board to remember that despite the fact Marjorie was seventy years old, "she could be ninety years old and she still would be an evil person."

Following their testimony, Marjorie launched into a tirade against them. "Nancy and Tom are on a personal vendetta. They hate me. They've hated me since I married their father. He was twenty-two years older than I. And they've done everything they possibly could to injure me."

Marjorie also insisted that she had not asked her children to come largely because of the expense. She admitted she did not get along with three of her children who had sued her to prevent her from receiving her Congdon family inheritance. "They took me to court to try and get the money away," Marjorie said. "I don't hate them. I hate what they did." Marjorie's comments about her children did not satisfy board members, who wondered why she did not at least have letters of support. Marjorie explained, "I didn't think about asking them to write a letter."

Again, the board unanimously denied Marjorie parole, citing her denial of responsibility for her "serious and violent offense."

Although Marjorie had other opportunities to renew her request for parole in September 2002 and March 2003, she waived both hearings.

Marjorie was not released on her early release date in May 2003 because of the nature of her crime; arson of an inhabited structure is considered use of a deadly weapon. She was also denied her provisional release, originally scheduled for August 23, 2003, because of opposition. Six individuals wrote in protest of her release, and several more phoned in their objections. She had also failed to secure a place to live once she left prison. Although she had claimed to have saved over $1.2 million while incarcerated, she was still behind on her payments for the Copper Crest lot, and construction of the house she had started designing in 1996 had yet to begin. The denial of her provisional release date changed her earned release date from February 19, 2004, to January 5, 2004. Barring the commission of a felony or a series of serious offenses, she was guaranteed to walk out the gates of Perryville on that date.

CHAPTER 27

Trouble in Tucson

ON JANUARY 5, 2004, A COOL, SUNNY MORNING in Perryville, Arizona, seventy-one-year-old Marjorie Hagen left her home of more than ten years—cell #110, a seven-by-twelve-foot room with a concrete floor, furnished with a steel bunk bed, sink, and toilet. She emerged from prison shortly after 9 A.M., shedding her prison-issue orange jumpsuit for civilian attire in a changing room that looked like a portable toilet, just inside the razor-wire fence. Hagen had received the change of clothes from her friend, Edward Bolding. He was no longer representing her. On January 5, 2003, he had been suspended for one year from practicing law in Arizona "for violation of his duties and obligations as a lawyer." The Arizona Supreme Court found in December 2002 that Bolding had become involved with a mentally ill female client with a drug addiction and had not protected her trust funds or kept proper records. Bolding had appealed, but on July 24, 2003, the Board of Disciplinary Appeals, according to the Texas Bar Journal, "entered an agreed judgment of active suspension" against him. Although he would at first apply to be reinstated after the one year was up, he eventually withdrew the application and remained suspended from practicing law.

For her release, Marjorie wore a cabled salmon-colored sweater, white shirt, and khaki pants, and her signature oversize round eyeglasses. Her hair was swept back from her face and forehead.

A prison guard helped Marjorie carry several boxes of personal effects to the waiting white Crown Victoria. Bolding had told prison officials that he was unavailable because of possible back surgery that day, but had arranged for a hired driver, Gene Reller, to take Marjorie from the prison to a rented apartment in Tuscon. Apparently Marjorie planned to live in the apartment until her dream house was built on the Copper Crest lot.

Marjorie appeared healthy as she walked to the car. She helped Reller load the boxes, and got in the passenger seat unassisted. Marjorie seemed anxious to leave, yet unconcerned, perhaps because she was not expecting anyone outside of the prison staff to witness her departure. She was one of the prison's most notorious inmates, and interview requests had poured in as her release approached; as she always had, she refused every one. Marjorie told Reller she did not want any photographs taken as they departed. She "hated the press," and wanted to be left alone.

A two-person television news crew from the Twin Cities, another from Duluth, and author Gail Feichtinger and her publisher stood just outside the prison's south gate. As the hired car approached the exit gate, Marjorie spotted the reporters and their cameras and ducked down, hiding under a briefcase. She called out instructions to Reller, and the car suddenly veered toward the entrance gate at the other end of the parking lot. The car sped out the gate and onto a public road, with the Twin Cities news crew in close pursuit. Reller then took the freeway heading toward Tucson, traveling fast enough to pass cars on the entrance ramp. The news van chased after the car and tried to drive beside it. Reller switched lanes to avoid the van. The TV crew reported they called off the pursuit when the Crown Victoria reached 100 miles per hour. Reller, however, denies he was ever speeding.

Marjorie was "friendly and talkative," Reller recalled, as they drove her to her new home. She told Reller that she had nine children, for some reason inflating her family's size. She left out any mention of her mother or having spent winters in Tucson as a child.

She and Reller talked about prison life. Marjorie said she had been an English tutor for the Hispanic inmates. She also said she had given inmates lessons in needlepoint and crochet.

"She made it sound as if she was a model prisoner," Reller said, "and everyone was sorry to see her go and wished her well." Some of the things she talked about "didn't jive," but she was very convincing with other stories, including how she ended up in prison.

Marjorie had supposedly committed a white collar crime in the name of love. She told Reller that her third husband, Wally, had been diagnosed with cancer and was dying. The treatment that could save him was available only in Switzerland and was very expensive. The couple was desperate, unable to pay for the treatment because Marjorie's money was tied up in family trust funds that she couldn't access. She was forced to commit arson, setting fire to the couple's RV, to collected the insurance money to pay for Wally's treatment. The treatment, Marjorie said, was successful, and Wally survived. In this version, obviously, she had not been investigated in connection with his death, or at one time charged with his murder.

Marjorie told the story so convincingly that Reller believed her. Next, she asked Reller about going grocery shopping, and she suggested that he cash a couple of checks for her. Despite Marjorie's assurances that she had the money, Reller declined. But when the two stopped at a Jack in the Box restaurant, Reller did pick up the tab for Marjorie's breakfast sandwich and coffee, with Marjorie's promise to pay him back. Not surprisingly, it was a promise she didn't keep.

Within hours of her release, a number of Ajo citizens claimed to have seen Marjorie in the tiny Arizona town. Rumors of her presence in Ajo were fueled for days by several fires that broke out in the city, each set by candles.

Dan Eastwood, who was visiting in-laws in Ajo at the time, was standing in their backyard shortly before noon on the day of Marjorie's release. Eastwood said a blue van, possibly a Ford Aerostar, with an old red-and-white Arizona license plate, "came cruising down the road."

The driver was a man much younger than the passenger and reminded Eastwood of pictures he'd seen of Rick LeRoy. In the passenger seat, which was closest to Eastwood, he saw an older woman, late 60s to early 70s, "just tall enough for her chin to clear the windowsill, wearing large frame eyeglasses…. She was looking out and turning her head around like a tourist fascinated to see the neighborhood, unlike someone who'd been living there awhile…. [She] looked a lot like Marjorie Congdon."

Late in the afternoon on the day of Marjorie's release, a fire damaged the Catholic church in Ajo, the same church where Marjorie had had a run-in with the priest years earlier. The fire started when candles in plastic containers melted too low, setting the candle stand on fire. Ajo fire chief Jim Bush said that the fire damaged the ceiling and a wall. As firefighters were standing outside the church watching the smoke come out, Bush said that one person quipped, "It sure didn't take her long to get back, did it?"

Bush said that no one knows why a dozen or more candles burned. Since the church is open until 8 P.M., anyone could have lit the candles while praying. Over the next few days, there were two more fires caused by candles, but there was no evidence to prove that they were anything but accidents.

In the years since Marjorie left Ajo, the small town had stepped up efforts to market to travelers passing through on the way to Mexico. Signs advertising clean restrooms and travelers insurance are everywhere, particularly along Ajo's main thoroughfare. In the days before and after Marjorie's release, many Ajo residents hoped that she would never return, while others still considered her their friend. Most residents agreed, however, that Marjorie was unlikely to ever call Ajo home again, and they speculated about where she would settle.

Newspaper editor Gabrielle David said that there was a general feeling among residents "that they don't believe she'll come back, but they also don't want her to return." David explained how the town felt after Hagen was convicted. "There was a sigh of relief. Today, there is some concern, but not with everyone. In fact, there are some people who still believe in [Hagen's] innocence."

Carol Klinefelter, whose RV sales and repair shop was vicitimized in a fire set by Hagen, was not among those who think Hagen innocent. "I feel sorry for anyone around here," Klinefelter said. "She'll be dangerous until the day she's dead." She later added, "I hope someone is keeping a close eye on her, because she's not to be trusted."

Bea Meyer, a Canadian native who has lived in Ajo since 1990, remembers the fires—and Marjorie. "Since she's getting out of prison, I think it crosses our mind she might have the nerve to come back here. I hope she doesn't come back." Myer remembered Marjorie as a very smart woman who could "charm the birds out of the trees."

When asked if she was frightened by the prospect of Hagen returning to Ajo, Meyer replied, "Not if I had a revolver with me."

Sue and Roland Shaw, residents of Ajo for twenty years, are equally concerned. "The woman is sick—there's no question about that," Sue Roland said. "I'm sorry she's out and hope she never comes back." Underscoring his wife's concern of Hagen's propensity to start fires, Roland added dryly, "We live in a wooden house."

As Marjorie had planned her new home and gardens from prison, she repeatedly fell behind on her mortgage payments. In 2004, after more than a year of late payments, Copper Crest's Gene Jones had grown tired of chasing down the money, particularly when he learned that Marjorie was also delinquent on $50 monthly homeowners association dues and on property taxes. "It was just a bunch of nonsense," Jones said. "Finally, it happened so often that I turned it over to an attorney."

While his attorney, Charles Whitehill, was threatening to conduct a trustee sale for lot 168, Jones saw an article in a Tucson paper about a Marjorie Hagen being released from prison. He was distressed to learn that it was the same Marjorie Hagen who planned to become a Copper Crest resident. "We were between a rock and a hard place because technically Marjorie had a right to complete the purchase of the lot," Jones said. But he thought that Marjorie moving in "would just destroy this place."

So Jones decided to try to buy back the lot, and he asked Whitehill to negotiate with Bolding, who was still advising Marjorie informally although suspended from practicing law. Marjorie's initial request was for $17,000, but the two men finally settled on $5,000 as the amount Jones would pay for Marjorie to deed back the lot. "I hated the idea of giving Marjorie $5,000," Jones said. "But I could not even take a five percent chance that she might want to move in."

Three weeks after her release from prison, Marjorie signed a release for lot 168, agreeing to sell the property back to Copper Crest. Whitehill met with Marjorie and Bolding for several hours in his Tucson office when she signed the papers. He described Marjorie as quiet and soft-spoken, and inconspicuously dressed. "If you didn't know the background, I would think that she was a very sweet little old lady," Whitehill said.

Jones ensured peace of mind for Copper Crest residents by insisting that the release include a clause prohibiting Marjorie "for the rest of her life from buying any lot or visiting any individual at Copper Crest Property Inc., and if she does, she agrees to a penalty of $100,000 per incident." Additionally, any violation would result in an immediate restraining order.

In addition to paying Marjorie $5,000, Jones had to pay back taxes and homeowner dues. But he said it was worth it to get Marjorie out of Copper Crest. "Rumors get floating around at the coffee klatches or in the jacuzzi or swimming pool.... And our seniors are our strongest sales people. We have happy contented seniors here. The prospect of having a murderer and arsonist in your midst would be more than they could take," said Jones.

This may have been the beginnning of the end for Marjorie and Bolding's long and ineffective attorney/client friendship. In May 2004, Marjorie would accuse Bolding of stealing from her. She told Tucson police that Bolding placed her personal possessions into storage when she began her prison sentence. After her release, she alleged that he refused to tell her where her belongings were located. She also claimed he had threatened her. She said there was a knock on her door around three in the afternoon. No one was there when she answered it, but a yellow piece of paper on the ground made threatening statements in Bolding's handwriting. In a strange role reversal, Marjorie would cooperate with authorities' ongoing investigation of her former attorney.

Since Copper Crest no longer welcomed her, Marjorie took up residence at Broadway Proper, a luxury senior apartment complex. Most people who met her after her release from prison had no idea she had been in prison or had ever had any legal problems. She called herself "Maggie Wallis" and told a number of her new friends and acquaintances that she was the widow of a well-to-do doctor; that the couple had lived in Pennsylvania, had a motor home, and used to travel to Arizona; and that she was a retired nurse who had worked with cancer patients.

As she had done throughout her life, Marjorie wove truth and fiction together as she created her new image. Perhaps Wallis was derived from her third husband's name. Her second husband had grown up in Pennsylvania. As a child, Marjorie, her mother and sister had spent winters in Tucson. The fantasy of being a nurse had roots going back over fifty years, when she had claimed to be taking nursing classes while dating Dick LeRoy, and she had continued that fiction into the early years of their marriage.

"Maggie" spoke little about her family, except to say she was estranged from them, and that she had seven children. A woman who volunteered with her recalled that Marjorie didn't like to talk about her children because there had been a falling out over money. Although Marjorie had bragged to some people that she had trust funds, other friends and acquaintances had no idea she had grown up surrounded by wealth. Certainly her appearance and attire did little to suggest money. Marjorie was typically dressed in colorful muumuus, often with decorative embroidery, or in pants with a large blouse worn outside. She wore little jewelry, minimal or no makeup, and comfortable shoes.

Surprisingly, Marjorie actually followed through on one part of her prison release plan. Shortly after her release, she contacted one of Tucson's greyhound organizations about adopting a greyhound that she could train as a service dog. Given the presence of the Tucson dog track, the city had a large active group of volunteers dedicated to finding homes for the retired racers.

In January 2004, Marjorie adopted a male greyhound, a dog who had suffered a broken leg while racing. The dog, Aloha Legacy, was a rare-hued greyhound, a handsome gray-blue color. Marjorie renamed him "Blueberry Hound" because, she told people, one day she turned her back on him when she opened the refrigerator, and he took a bag of blueberries. He ate the whole bag and made a big mess in the apartment.

Blueberry Hound became Marjorie's constant companion. She pampered her pet with homemade meals, keeping her refrigerator full of individual bags of chicken and hamburger. Reminiscent of her spending sprees on her children's clothes, she bought her dog numerous leash and collar sets, blankets, dog beds and pillows, jackets and vests, and even a raincoat and boots.

Carolyn Olson, vice president of the Greyhound Adoption League, had introduced Marjorie to Blueberry at one of the league's meet-and-greets at Petsmart. Olson stayed in touch with Marjorie after the adoption and checked up on the dog. Marjorie had no car at the time, and Olson was concerned about how Maggie would get around and about Blueberry walking in the Tucson heat. Marjorie told Olson not to worry because she had met a neighbor, Roger Sammis, who had a car and could transport her as needed. Sammis was also in his seventies and, despite a heart condition, was still active. The two had bonded, in part, through their mutual love of dogs, sometimes walking their dogs together.

In the summer of 2004, Marjorie told Olson that her ophthalmologist had given her permission to drive again. One acquaintance described her driving as "terrible," because she "wasn't paying attention," and weaved in and out of traffic. Marjorie purchased a green Volkswagen Beetle that had been restored even down to the headlight covers. She had the passenger seat removed so that Blueberry could get in and out easily, and she also had special padding installed in the back seat for him. Blueberry accompanied Marjorie nearly everywhere she went around Tucson, including to church, the doctor, library, and on trips to Mexico. The dog even accompanied her to the symphony, wearing a special tuxedo-style collar she had purchased for him.

Marjorie enrolled Blueberry in Handi-Dogs classes, intent on having her dog certified. In November 2004, Blueberry successfully completed classes in "record time," according to Olson, and became the first greyhound service dog in the country. "Marjorie and Blue became the ambassadors for greyhound rescue and Handi-Dogs, and we were all so proud of them," Olson said. Marjorie donated a quilt with an animal pattern, which she said she'd handcrafted, for a Greyhound Adoption Rescue fundraiser.

Marjorie and Blueberry Hound made regular public appearances. "Maggie was very impassioned about the greyhound cause and how she felt that greyhounds had been wronged," said a greyhound adoption volunteer. Marjorie could be gregarious and charming, an adept public speaker with a good sense of humor, according to attendees. She also solicited news coverage of Blueberry's accomplishments as a service dog. Local television stations and newspapers reported on their life together. Marjorie even detailed Blueberry's alleged heroics in an article she wrote (under the name Maggie Wallis) for *Greyhound Magazine*.

"Of all the accomplishments of the marvelous Blueberry Hound—winner at the racetrack…first Greyhound ever certified as a service dog by Handi-dogs, Inc., and beloved friend— perhaps the most impressive is that of rescuer of his human companion." Marjorie claimed that Blueberry saved her after she suffered a small stroke and fell in her living room. After she told him to get help, the dog went into the bathroom and pulled an assistance cord. Blueberry then went to the door of Marjorie's apartment, unlocked the door with his nose and mouth, turned the handle to open the door, and waited for help to arrive. An ambulance was called, and Blueberry rode with Marjorie to the hospital, wearing his service dog cape, and stayed with her in the emergency room. When she required laser surgery on her right eye to stop retinal bleeding, Marjorie wrote that "outfitted with a surgical gown, booties, and bouffant-style cap, Blueberry Hound accompanied me into the treatment room for my surgery." The magazine identified her as a retired nurse.

Marjorie also wrote a glowing tribute to Blueberry in the Handi-Dogs newsletter. "He has given his life to me so that I may have one." She called Blueberry her confidant, companion, and beloved friend, and claimed that he came to her at the start of her "long and difficult journey into growing darkness and disability from cancer, stroke, and increasing blindness." Marjorie also stated that he was like "glowing candles that light my growing darkness."

On November 20, 2005, Marjorie drew up a document that she filed with Broadway Proper, Carolyn Olson, one of Blueberry's vets, Arizona Greyhound Rescue, and an attorney. "In the event of either my sudden death or permanent incapacitation, I request that Caroline [sic] Olson be called to take my service dog, 'The Blueberry Hound', and that she take him…to be euthanized and cremated. In the case of my death I ask that I be cremated and his ashes mixed with mine." Marjorie stated that she had purchased a plot for herself and the dog at a Tucson pet cemetery, where she claimed her husband's ashes were. The handwritten document was reminiscent of her plans for herself, husband Wally, and their dog Wulf as given in the 1992 "suicide note."

In fall 2006, Marjorie moved from Broadway Proper into another upscale senior apartment complex on Tucson's East Side, Atria Bell Court Gardens. Located in a restored historic mansion, the apartment complex featured many amenities for its senior residents, including a heated pool, spa, sunroom and guest room suites, 24-hour onsite security, housekeeping services, and, through its affiliation with a home-care company, assisted living services. The marketing materials for Atria state that it "offers resort-style retirement living for the most discerning senior."

Marjorie made several changes to her 850-square-foot ground floor apartment before moving in, including removing the carpeting and replacing it with a scored concrete floor and taking down the window coverings. The apartment was sparsely furnished, with a big bed and corner set aside for Blueberry. An Atria resident who visited the apartment noted the lack of family photos on display other than a small photo album that Marjorie kept on top of her bedroom dresser containing photos of Wally. Marjorie's apartment also had a small backyard with a wrought iron fence, which provided a space for Blueberry. After moving in, Marjorie covered the surface of her patio with a half foot of sand, telling other Atria residents that sand was easier on Blueberrys' feet. "It was like the beach," one resident recalled.

She continued telling the story of her alleged stroke to employees and residents at her new home, claiming it had caused her to lose sight in one eye and that she was legally blind. On other occasions, she told people she had an inoperable tumor in her eye that had caused permanent blindness. Another Atria Belle Court Gardens resident reported sometimes seeing Marjorie and Blueberry out walking. "She certainly didn't rely on Blue as a seeing-eye dog," the resident said. "He was out on his own exploring."

When Marjorie moved into Atria, she had the money for the $1,750 deposit. However, when the $2,900 monthly rent came due, Marjorie couldn't pay it. She told management that she was having problems with her bank, and was going to change banks by year's end. Marjorie assured Atria management that she had 10 to 12 million dollars in a trust fund, and produced a copy of a letter from a trust associate with the private client group at US Bank. The letter stated that Marjorie C. Hagen (she had resumed using "Hagen" as her last name) "is the primary beneficiary of the Marjorie C. Hagen Income Trust Under Agreement. As the primary beneficiary, Ms. Hagen is entitled to the net income produced by the trust." Despite her assurances, Marjorie remained delinquent on her rent.

Throughout the time she lived at Atria in 2006 and 2007, management remained unaware of her troubled past, including her history of fire setting. Ironically, during her residence at Atria, there was a small fire in Marjorie's own apartment. At lunchtime one day, employees heard the smoke alarm in Marjorie's apartment. When no one answered the phone, housekeeping went inside, finding the apartment full of smoke and one of the electric burners on the stove left on. Atria staff located Marjorie in the complex's dining room with Blueberry. She told them, "I was cooking something for Blueberry. I could have sworn I turned the burner off."

Marjorie continued her friendship with Roger Sammis, volunteering to help him as he had helped her, with transportation to doctor appointments and errands. Following her usual pattern—Marjorie began to dominate Sammis and began making all his significant decisions. She persuaded him to open a joint checking account with her, allegedly after badmouthing his family members and telling him they were trying to steal from him. In early 2007, she went as far as to obtain power of attorney for him. She told friends that Sammis was estranged from his family, although Audrey stayed in touch and had spoken with Marjorie on a number of occasions.

Not a wealthy man, Sammis was expecting a small inheritance from a male friend's estate in New York. But Sammis' health deteriorated, and he died in a Tucson hospital on March 1, 2007, the day before the inheritance check was drafted. No autopsy was conducted since Sammis had died in a hospital. Marjorie arranged for Sammis' body to be released to Brings Funeral Home in Tucson, telling the funeral home that Sammis had no family, that she had power of attorney, and that she wanted him cremated immediately. Roger Sammis was allegedly cremated without his family even knowing that he had died, or that he had an inheritance. Sammis' ashes were given to Marjorie. Audrey would not find out about her brother's death until weeks later.

On March 19, 2007, Marjorie deposited the $11,181.04 inheritance check into the Bank of America account she had opened with Sammis. Detective Doug Musick of the

Tucson Police Department's fraud unit said Marjorie tried to exercise her power of attorney for Sammis and forged his signature on the inheritance. She then attempted to wire the money from the joint account to her personal account at Alliance Bank in Tucson. Officials at Alliance, suspicious about the transaction, put an extended hold on the transfer and alerted Tucson police. Tucson police discovered that on March 5, 2007, four days after Sammis' death, Marjorie Hagen had written a check from her Alliance account to the Brings Funeral Home in Tucson for $1,304, payment for Sammis' cremation. Not only had Sammis died the day before the date on the check that Marjorie presented the bank, but her power of attorney had expired when Sammis died. On March 21, 2007, Marjorie went to Alliance Bank, expecting that the wire transfer had been completed. When told that there was an extended hold on the money, Marjorie became irate, telling an employee she was so angry with the Bank of America manager that she was going to kill him and burn the bank down. Marjorie then went to the Bank of America and demanded to know why the money had not been transferred to her personal account. Bank officials informed Marjorie that they were uncomfortable with the check's endorsement. Marjorie was told to complete a limited power of attorney form—which needed to be signed by Marjorie and Sammis. With Sammis dead, Marjorie signed a new affidavit claiming that Sammis was alive and that she represented his financial interests.

On Thursday, March 22, 2007, Marjorie was arrested at her home, charged with forgery, theft, tampering with a computer, and fraudulent scheme and artifice. She was booked into the Pima County jail, her bond set at $250,000. Tucson police said Marjorie needed Sammis' inheritance money for unpaid rent and overdue bills. At that time of her arrest, Marjorie owed approximately $15,000 for past due rent and services at Atria Bell Court Gardens. She was also behind on payments for her new car, a 2006 Toyota Scion. Shortly after she was arrested and jailed, the car was repossessed.

After Marjorie's arrest, Blueberry Hound was retrieved from her apartment. The Greyhound Adoption League and Arizona Greyhound Rescue arranged for the dog to be placed with a foster family. When released from jail on April 25, 2007, on a $75,000 bond, Marjorie was determined to get Blueberry back, insisting she was Blueberry's legal owner and he had to be returned.

During Marjorie's time in jail, however, information had surfaced that Marjorie had not always been as caring about her dog as she wanted people to believe. Blueberry had gained an unhealthy amount of weight during the time he lived with Marjorie, according to greyhound rescue/adoption insiders and Atria residents. His weight had gone from eighty-five pounds to more than one hundred pounds; his daily diet included a pound of hamburger. These sources also reported that there were a number of occasions when Blueberry did not want to get up for Marjorie. Some people said they had seen Marjorie yanking on Blueberry's leash, even giving him a kick when he was too slow to get up. One of Marjorie's former neighbors recalled that when they were out walking their dogs, Marjorie sometimes let Blueberry off his leash to run loose. "We have a lot of coyotes around here. That didn't seem to matter to Maggie," the neighbor remembered. After being placed with a foster family, Blueberry slimmed down and was doing well, according to representatives for Arizona Greyhound Rescue and Greyhound Adoption League. Blueberry remained with his foster family.

Marjorie, outraged that Blueberry had not been returned to her, hired an attorney and, in June 2007, she filed a lawsuit against the Greyhound Adoption League and Arizona Greyhound Rescue to get Blueberry back. Marjorie claimed that although she arranged for the dog to be cared for by Mary Freeman of Arizona Greyhound Rescue following her arrest, the greyhound organizations would not return the dog. She claimed that without Blueberry, she "is at risk of injury and/or aggravation" of her serious medical conditions. Later that year Marjorie bought a $154,000 condominium in Tucson and adopted a greyhound service dog to replace Blueberry. According to her court-appointed attorney, Brick Storts, Marjorie was training the greyhound as a seeing eye dog.

Marjorie's own case was scheduled to go to trial on January 7, 2008. While Detective Musick acknowledged Marjorie's behavior was "consistent [with] but not identical to things that happened in the past," he pointed out that Sammis' cremation was a dead end for investigators. "We're just focusing on the fraud investigation right now. There's nothing to pursue on a murder angle."

After repeated delays due to Marjorie's health issues, including a right knee replacement in May 2008, her trial was rescheduled for November 18, 2008. The day before jury selection began, she pled guilty to attempted forgery as part of a plea bargain. She admitted that she endorsed and deposited an $11,181.04 check sent to Roger Sammis after he died. Marjorie told the judge she deposited the money into the bank account she and Sammis shared and then tried to transfer the money into her personal account. But Marjorie did not know that her power of attorney privileges for Sammis expired when he died, Storts said. He refuted allegations that Marjorie was cash poor at that time, stating that Marjorie had over $7,000 in her personal account and was receiving monthly trust fund payments.

Marjorie's health problems also delayed her sentencing, which was continued until March 4, 2009. Storts claimed his client had battled nonterminal cancer and provided evidence that she had degenerative athritis in both knees and was legally blind in one eye. He said Marjorie's sentencing was postponed so she could participate in a program at the Southern Arizona Association for the Visually Impaired. Shortly before Marjorie's sentencing, Storts was unaware of any pending surgery, but said that "Marjorie continues to think she has a lot of health problems," uses a walker, and no longer drives.

Although she could have received two-and-a-half years in prison, Marjorie was sentenced to three years of intensive probation. And while he let her off lightly, Pima County Superior Court Judge Clark Munger had rather harsh words for Marjorie at her sentencing. "You still haven't come to grips with the fact that you committed a crime," he told her. "It's that type of self-delusion that has landed you where you are."

Loose Ends

IN NOVEMBER 1982, VELMA PIETILA'S WIDOWER, LOREN PIETILA—along with the couple's three children, James, Lauren, and Karla—filed a $475,490 wrongful death lawsuit against the Congdon family. At the heart of the case was Glensheen's security, or lack thereof, at the time of the murders.

Security at the mansion had been minimal when the women were slain. A private security firm was on call, but there was no routine drive-by and no alarms or security systems had been installed. The household staff testified that they had few day-to-day security worries. They kept Glensheen's double front doors locked and checked the windows each night. Household servants and nursing staff occupied the main house while chauffeur Dick Kartes and gardener Bob Wyness and their families lived on the grounds, within sight of the mansion. But given what Congdon trustees believed was a previous attempt on Elisabeth Congdon's life (the infamous "marmalade incident"), the suit alleged that Glensheen should have had better security. Judge Jack Litman, who had presided over Roger Caldwell's trial, heard the case.

Defense attorney Gerald Brown, aided by the testimony of trustee Bill Van Evera, argued that adequate security measures were in place at the time of the murders. Glensheen had never been burglarized in its history, Brown told jurors. Glensheen was in a low crime neighborhood, situated off of a well-traveled main thoroughfare. The last reported crime in the area had occurred at least six years prior to the murders. Congdon family members would later say they didn't worry about Elisabeth's safety—at least when Marjorie wasn't around.

The Pietila family's attorney, David Sullivan, argued that the Congdon estate had been inadequately secured against a break-in like the one during which Velma Pietila was murdered. Nursing and household staff testified, and Sullivan contended, that police could respond faster than the security service hired by the trustees, that the staff was made up of older women, and that the chauffeur's and gardener's families wouldn't know what went on in the mansion without first being summoned by phone.

Deliberations began Monday afternoon, November 15, just one week after the trial opened. Jurors took less than four hours to reach a verdict that shocked the

Congdon family and trustees, finding the trustees and conservators liable for Velma Pietila's death and awarding her survivors $225,000.

On February 15, 1985, the Minnesota Supreme Court overturned the appellate court's decision that negligence by the Congdon trustees was a direct cause of the deaths of Velma Pietila and Elisabeth Congdon. The court held that "neither the trustees, the conservators, nor Elisabeth Congdon had a duty to take measures to guard against the murders perpetrated on June 26 or 27, 1977." No damages would be awarded to the Pietila family.

Loren Pietila had died on February 2, 1985, so he never knew about the appellate court's reversal. After Velma's death, he had moved to Tucson and studied painting at the University of Arizona. He gained recognition as a landscape artist of the Arizona desert and northern Minnesota. A showing of his paintings hung at the University of Minnesota Duluth's Tweed Museum of Art in 1984.

The Glensheen estate's last residents, gardener Robert Wyness and his wife Elsie, moved out of the gardener's cottage into an assisted living facility in February 2004. Wyness had been head gardener from 1945 until he retired in 1985. In an interview conducted by WDIO-TV in Duluth shortly after the move, Wyness discussed the day of the murders. "It was a shock I tell you, when that happened," he said. "Especially to Miss Congdon, she was such a wonderful [person]—she was like a sister to me, almost, you know…. [Marjorie] definitely was the one. Sure, they knew that right away…. To adopt the kids and then have that happen? It was crazy, you know." Mr. Wyness died of heart failure Friday, October 29, 2004. He was 89 years old.

Before Roger Caldwell left Minnesota to return to Latrobe, Pennsylvania, he gave his friend, attorney David Arnold, three boxes and a black satchel, all containing documents gathered during his time in prison. He then asked Arnold not to open the satchel until ten years after Caldwell's death. Arnold stored the satchel and boxes in his attic and gradually forgot about them until the authors asked about the satchel. In 2003, Mr. Arnold generously allowed the authors of this book access to all the contained documents. The boxes and satchel held copies of legal documents, many letters from family (particularly his parents, brother, and Christi O'Neil, whom Roger called his "darling daughter"), and Roger's awkward attempts at fiction and poetry—some of it clever, some rather bawdy. Much of the information in this book's chapter about Roger's time in prison comes from those documents. The authors found only two letters from Marjorie: one in which she complained about her current state while Roger awaited trial in a St. Louis County Jail, and another, more formal, letter that indicated that her attorney, Ron Meshbesher, had advised her not to contact Caldwell any further. The authors found no document indicating that Marjorie played any role in the killings at Glensheen—no "smoking gun."

After Roger Caldwell's suicide, one more tragedy awaited the Caldwell family. In August 1999, Roger's daughter, Christi O'Neil, age forty-five, murdered her sixty-five-year-old mother Martha Burns, Roger's first wife and high school sweetheart. Just as Roger confessed to have done to Elisabeth Congdon, O'Neil used a pillow to suffocate her mother. She then placed the body in a makeshift cardboard coffin, packed in seven-hundred pounds of salt, and surrounded it with stuffed animals and burning candles. A few days later, in a telephone call to her sister, O'Neil said that she had had a dream in which she smothered her mother with a pillow after her mother had tried to do the same to her. A week after her mother's death, as she left the house to go on a date, O'Neil allegedly looked over her shoulder to the house and called out, "See you later, Mom." A week after that, O'Neil used her car, a hose, and some duct tape to kill herself by carbon monoxide poisoning. She had lived with her mother in the same house they had once shared with Roger.

Doug Thomson, Roger Caldwell's criminal attorney, died in 2007 at the age of seventy-seven from complications due to Alzheimer's. Friends eulogized Thomson as a tenacious cross-examiner with a flair for fine clothes—at least once he bought a new pair of British shoes just for closing arguments. With his oratory skills, flashy clothes, and notorious sense of humor (readers will remember his "misdemeanor suit" quip at prosecutor John DeSanto's expense), Thompson was a force in the courtroom and is remembered by one judge as a lawyer who could "win cases that appeared to be absolute losers." His oratories were called "legendary," and he once said, "I'll defend anybody accused of anything, providing I control the case. I'm not going to be anyone's mouthpiece."

After her acquittal, Marjorie did receive part of her inheritance, including her mother's beloved diamond-and-sapphire ring. Jennifer Johnson learned that while Marjorie lived in Arizona, Marjorie pawned several pieces of jewelry, including the ring: the ring Marjorie often played with as a child; the ring that was stolen from Elisabeth's finger the night she was murdered; the ring that was found in Marjorie and Roger's Bloomington hotel room. Jennifer and Chuck tracked the ring to an Arizona pawn shop and bought it back.

Ironically, while under investigation for fraud in 2007, Marjorie herself (along with another former client) filed fraud charges against her former defense attorney Edward Bolding. Bolding was charged with stealing more than $350,000 from Marjorie's trust fund while she was in prison for arson, and taking over $400,000 in settlement money from the other victim and depositing it in his personal account. Appearing before Judge Hector Campoy, he requested to be released pending trial and to be supervised by Pima County's Pretrial Services agency. Marjorie testified that she was afraid of Bolding and begged Campoy to keep Bolding in jail. Bolding's attorney, Bob Hirsh stated in court documents that "the case against Mr. Bolding hangs on the claims of one victim who has distinguished herself as a serial killer and arsonist." Bolding was released with orders to keep his distance from his alleged victims.

Bolding was tried by the Arizona Attorney General's Office in December 2008 and represented himself at trial. He told the jury that Marjorie verbally agreed to pay him $500,000 to defend her in her arson case. He argued that the charges were a "total fabrication," and that Marjorie had "lived a life of crime with a reputation for not telling the truth." But jurors took less than a day to find Bolding guilty of two counts of fraudulent schemes and artifices and one count of obstruction of a criminal investigation. Bolding, facing a possible prison sentence of up to over twenty-seven years, failed to show for the reading of the verdicts, despite an arrest warrant. Sentencing is on hold indefinitely, as Bolding allegedly fled Arizona shortly after the trial concluded.

At the time of the Glensheen murder investigation, forensic investigation was not as advanced as it is today. Techniques for finding fingerprints now include a lumalight, which is used to enhance fingerprints left on surfaces as well as stains left by blood, semen, and other body fluids. Investigators also use a technique called *cyanoacrylate* or *super-glue* fuming to find fingerprints. Essentially, a piece of evidence, such as a weapon, is placed in an airtight chamber in which any strong adhesive containing cyanoacrylate is heated; the vapors cause a light colored dust to form on latent fingerprints, making them more observable and recoverable. In some cases, an entire room can be sealed off and fumed. Had these techniques been available in 1977, investigators and prosecutors certainly would have had more physical evidence to work with. And, of course, DNA testing is now available.

DNA is essentially a biological fingerprint and testing it eliminates 99.9999 percent of the population who doesn't have the same DNA signature. In the days before DNA testing, blood samples could be matched by type and enzyme group only, eliminating up to eighty percent of the population—and leaving twenty percent as possible suspects. Matching hairs was even more difficult. Without DNA testing, hairs were identified only by a visual test—easy for a defense attorney to refute in court.

When St. Louis County closed the books on the Congdon/Pietila murders, authorities returned all evidence that belonged to a specific person to that person, including Marjorie, Roger, and Ricky. Evidence belonging to the Congdon family was returned to the Congdon Office. All evidence remaining with the Duluth Police Department was scheduled to be destroyed—the county's normal procedure. Instead, when the property bureau officers called DeSanto for authorization to proceed with the destruction, DeSanto told them to put everything into boxes and send it to him. Then he simply put the boxes in his office file cabinet and his basement at home, where they sat for over fifteen years.

In January 2003, DeSanto and Gail Feichtinger discovered that the boxes of evidence contained items that could be tested for DNA. Among the evidence were known hair samples from the victims and the confessed killer as well as hairs from unknown persons found on and near the victims at the crime scene. Unfortunately, none of the unknown hair samples included the root, which is vital for DNA testing, so there were no DNA signatures to extract from them.

But DeSanto and Feichtinger also found the infamous Duluth Radisson envelope used to mail the coin stolen from Glensheen the night of the murders to Caldwell in Colorado, on the day the bodies were discovered. It was possible that the envelope's seal and stamps had preserved saliva from which DNA could be recovered. Luckily, the boxes also contained a known sample of Caldwell's saliva; without a comparison sample, the unknown sample would be nearly useless. In the absence of the blood evidence, which had been destroyed following the trials and appeals, this was the only chance left to bring modern DNA testing to the decades-old murder.

The publisher then sent the samples to Genetic Technologies, Inc., of Pacific, Missouri, to compare Roger's DNA from the known saliva sample with the DNA, if any, recovered from the saliva on the envelope or stamps. Although the envelope was treated with ninhydrin in 1977 in order to raise fingerprints—a method that contaminated the saliva and rendered investigators unable to perform secretor blood analysis—modern techniques allowed Genetic Technologies technicians to extract DNA from the saliva that remained on the envelope's seal. The stamps yielded no testable DNA.

According to Genetic Technologies' report, the DNA found on the seal belonged to a man (it showed both X and Y chromosomes; women only have X chromosomes). Due to degradation caused by the ninhydrin, technicians were only able to determine conclusive values under two of the nine genetic markers tested, but the values of both of those markers matched Caldwell's DNA. In their official summary of the lab analysis, Genetic Technologies states that "Based on the genetic information obtained by the samples submitted, Roger S. Caldwell cannot be excluded as a possible contributor of the genetic material recovered from [the envelope's seal]. The partial genetic profile obtained from [the envelope] is expected to occur in 1 in 106 in the Caucasian population and in approximately 1 in 614 in the African American population among unrelated individuals."

"Cannot be excluded" is hardly the statement a prosecutor would like to bring to court, but consider the following:

At Roger's original trial the prosecution could only present blood evidence. Blood had been recovered from the scene that did not belong to the victims. This blood belonged to the killer, who had been cut during his fight with Velma Pietila. It was type O, expected in 45 percent of the Caucasian population. It was enzyme group B, expected in 36 percent of the population. To find out the percentage of the population expected to have both of these traits, the individual percentages are simply multiplied; this is known as the product rule. Multiplying 45 percent by 36 percent yields 16 percent. There was a 16 percent chance that Roger would match the blood sample. He did.

The DNA tests provided more data to use with the product rule. The two markers found in the saliva DNA are expected in 1 in 106 of the Caucasian population, which is equivalent to .94 percent—less than 1 percent. The DNA was also male; while the force used in the murders implied a man, anyone could have licked the envelope. Defense theories about framing Roger included a woman sealing the envelope, but now it has been proven scientifically that a man sealed it. In 1977, 49 percent of the U.S. population was male: .94 percent times 49 percent is .46 percent. There was only a .46 percent chance that Roger would match the sample from the envelope. He did.

But the product rule can be taken even further. What are the chances that a single suspect would match both the original blood evidence and the new DNA evidence? Multiplying 16 percent by .46 percent yields .07 percent. Only .07 percent of the Caucasian population would be expected to match both the DNA from the envelope and the blood from Elisabeth Congdon's pillow case and bedspread. Roger Caldwell matches both the blood and DNA. This scientific evidence is a statistical smoking gun pointing at Roger as the one who both bled on the sheets in Elisabeth's bedroom and later sealed the envelope containing a coin stolen from that same bedroom.

If DNA evidence had been available in 1977, John DeSanto wouldn't have had to rely on a questionable fingerprint and disputed fingerprint analysis to link the envelope and coin directly with Roger Caldwell, placing him in Duluth at the time of the murders. Ron Meshbesher couldn't have used the shaky fingerprint evidence to help win Marjorie's acquittal. That same fingerprint evidence could not have been used to win an appeal for Caldwell, which ultimately gave him the leverage to bargain for his release by giving a confession that authorities have never been satisfied told the whole story. He would have remained in prison in Stillwater, perhaps for the rest of his life—and not gone back to Latrobe, Pennsylvania, to eventually kill himself. More time in prison might have convinced him that Marjorie had indeed betrayed him and would never come back. Perhaps then he could have been convinced to tell everything he knew about Marjorie and the murders at Glensheen.

Timeline of Key Events

September 29, 1881
Chester Adgate Congdon and Clara Bannister marry in Syracuse, New York.

April 22, 1894
Elisabeth Mannering Congdon is born.

1905 – 1909
The Congdons build Glensheen along the Duluth shore of Lake Superior.

July 14, 1932
Jacqueline Barnes is born in Tarboro, North Carolina.

October 1932
Elisabeth adopts Jacqueline Barnes and renames her Marjorie Mannering Congdon.

1947 – 1950
Marjorie attends Dana Hall prep school. Her letters home indicate she has trouble handling money.

Summer 1949
Marjorie is sent to the Menninger Clinic in Topeka, Kansas, because of her compulsive lying and irresponsibility with money. She is diagnosed as sociopathic.

1951 – 1970
Marjorie's marriage to Dick LeRoy. The couple has seven children, and Marjorie's money problems escalate. Her husband attempts to curb her appetites, going as far as contacting department stores and banks concerning her spending. Unable to do so effectively, Dick LeRoy ends the marriage.

May 23, 1974
Marjorie coerces Elisabeth into co-signing a $345,000 loan from Marquette National Bank of Minneapolis by duress, undue nfluence, and false pretenses (admitted by Marjorie during a civil lawsuit, August 6, 1975).

November 3, 1974
Elisabeth Congdon becomes mysteriously ill after a visit from Marjorie during which Marjorie fed her homemade marmalade. Elisabeth is found to have an elevated level of the drug meprobamate in her system. The Congdon family decides not to investigate the incident.

May 12, 1975
Marjorie is suspected of setting fire to her home in Marine On St. Croix along the Minnesota/Wisconsin border.

Summer 1975
Angry with bank officer Tom Welch, who handled her trust, Marjorie states in front of witnesses that she is, "going to take care of that bastard" and then allegedly calls someone in Chicago ("Hi, this is Marge LeRoy; I need someone taken care of"). Shortly after moving to Colorado, Marjorie is arrested on charges that she stole two cars from Minnesota by purchasing them with bad checks.

March 20, 1976
Marjorie marries Roger Sipe Caldwell.

April 1976
Roger Caldwell tells friends that within their first month of marriage, Marjorie had written over $7,000 worth of bad checks.

July 1976
Marjorie applies for a Carte Blanche credit card in the name of E.M. Congdon, forging her mother's signature and using her mother's credit rating to get the card. This credit card is then used by Marjorie, Roger, and her youngest son, Ricky.

September 29 & 30, 1976
On both days, fires are set inside the First National Bank of Englewood in Englewood, Colorado, shortly after Marjorie is seen in the bank. Marjorie had experienced problems with the bank earlier in 1976, and the bank had threatened legal action against her.

November 23, 1976
Marjorie makes false report of burglary and theft to Park County, Colorado, Sheriff's Department, claiming someone had broken into her ranch home and stolen over $80,000 in property. Aetna Insurance Company later pays Marjorie and Roger $74,529.60.

December 8, 1976

Marjorie and Roger attempt to open an account at Colorado National Bank by depositing a $35,000 check from Aetna made out to the Caldwells and the First Bank of Evergreen. Roger forges the Evergreen endorsement. Colorado National returns the check to Aetna because of the improper endorsement, and the Caldwells bounce all the counter checks they received for the new account.

December 1976

Marjorie writes New Mexico rancher Tim Singer a $4,600 bad check as a down payment for a $9,000 purchase of horses.

January 1977

Marjorie passes another bad check as payment for horses at the National Western Stock Show in Denver.

January 24, 1977

Marjorie passes a bad check in the amount of $656.87 for horse tack at the Hunt and Harness Shop in Denver.

February 11 – February 20, 1977

After he and Marjorie enjoy a ten-day fling at the plush Broadmoor Hotel in Colorado Springs, Colorado, Roger pays with a $6,000 bad check.

May 1977

Marjorie passes another bad check to Louise McConnell of Hillcroft Acres in Golden, Colorado, as payment for past due stable and board bill for the Caldwells' horses.

May 1977

Marjorie drafts a false "To Whom it may Concern" letter dated May 23, 1977, on stolen National Asthma Center stationery over the forged signature of Dr. Hyman Chai. It states that certain ranch properties are needed by her and Roger to take proper care of Marjorie's son, Ricky, who suffers from asthma. Roger takes the letter to Duluth on May 24 to meet with Congdon trustees to request $750,000. Roger later admits to the forgery.

June 1977

Marjorie and Roger pass over $100,000 worth of bad checks in Colorado. Roger meets with Congdon trustee Tom Congdon and asks for $250,000 to hire attorney F. Lee Bailey. During this meeting, Roger admits to defrauding Aetna Insurance Company, writing a bad check to the Broadmoor Hotel, and forging the letter from the Asthma Center, and also claims he and Marjorie had been passing bad checks, using expired gasoline credit cards, and putting slugs in soda machines "simply to stay alive."

June 7, 1977

Caldwell purchases $27.45 worth of flowers for his mother in Pennsylvania at Alpha Floral Company in Denver with a Carte Blanche credit card over the forged signature of Elisabeth Congdon.

June 18, 1977

Marjorie passes two bad checks, one for $6,000 (for the purchase of a horse) and another for $881.44 (for equipment, boarding, and training) to Melissa and Rick Lapin of Wildwood Farms in Englewood, Colorado.

June 23, 1977

Roger and Marjorie Caldwell receive $3,000 for pawning jewelry.

June 24, 1977

Marjorie has her hand-written "will" notarized. The document promises Roger Caldwell approximately $2.5 million of the enheritance "accruing to [Marjorie]" upon the death of Elisabeth Congdon.

June 27, 1977

Duluth, Minnesota: Elisabeth Congdon and her nurse, Velma Pietila, are found dead at Glensheen. Jewelry and a wicker suitcase have also been stolen from the mansion, as well as Pietila's car. By 8 a.m., Duluth Police have already begun their investigation and processing of the crime scene. By the end of the day, both bodies have been removed and autopsies begun. After brief interviews with Glensheen staff and Congdon family members, investigators already suspect Marjorie and Roger Caldwell.

Bloomington, Minnesota: At 8:30 a.m., maintenance personnel at the Minneapolis-St. Paul International Airport find Velma Pietila's car keys in a trash can outside the terminal. Later, another maintenance worker finds a parking stub, in the same trash can, stamped "0635 hours."

Golden, Colorado: When asked Roger's whereabouts, Marjorie first explains that he "just went out for some pop or Coke." Later, when asked the same question, she says that Roger is with her son Ricky, "in the mountains." She eventually provides six different alibis for Roger's whereabouts that weekend.

June 29, 1977

Morning: At 11:30 Duluth detectives interview Marjorie and Roger Caldwell. The top of Caldwell's right hand is extremely swollen and he has a cut on the right side of his upper lip. Later, Marjorie, Roger, and Ricky visit grounds at Glensheen but are not permitted inside the mansion.

Afternoon: Funeral for Velma Pietila.

June 30, 1977

Morning: Duluth Detective Gary Waller officially assigned to the case as lead investigator. Work continues on evidence for submittal to FBI and BCA labs.

Afternoon: Funeral for Elisabeth Congdon.

Evening: Duluth police search the Duluth Radisson hotel rooms of Marjorie and Roger Caldwell. During the search, police find a receipt dated June 27, 1977, from Host of Minneapolis (a gift shop at the Minneapolis International Airport) for a purchase totaling $56.16. The Caldwells decline a polygraph examination; other family members take the tests. Of those family members examined with polygraph, none show deception.

July 1, 1977

An interview of Host shop clerks at the Minneapolis-St. Paul International Airport verifies the receipt for $56.16 for the purchase of a garment bag. The clerks say a man fitting Roger Caldwell's description and carrying a wicker case made the purchase.

Gary Waller travels to Golden to extend the scope of the investigation.

July 2, 1977

Golden: A clerk at the Holland House Hotel alerts police to a Radisson Hotel envelope addressed to Roger Caldwell and postmarked "27 JUN, 1977, P.M., DULUTH, MN 558." After obtaining a warrant, police discover a 1,700-year-old Byzantine coin determined to be missing from a memorabilia case in Elisabeth Congdon's bedroom.

July 3 and 4, 1977

The investigation continues in Golden and Duluth. Duluth police interview Rick Leroy, who claims he did not see Roger Caldwell from Saturday, June 25, until the evening of Monday, June 27. When he finds out that the police have interviewed Rick, Roger becomes extremely angry with stepson Stephen LeRoy. Meanwhile, authorities in Duluth determine where the Caldwells are staying in the Twin Cities metro area.

July 5, 1977

Golden: Police execute search warrants for the Caldwells' rooms at the Holland House Hotel; a message slip with the Indianapolis Hyatt Regency's telephone number is found, but investigators are unable to determine its significance.

Bloomington: Host gift shop clerks are shown a photo lineup, and Roger Caldwell is identified. Caldwell is taken by ambulance from the Holiday Inn in Bloomington to Methodist Hospital after he loses consciousness shortly after having breakfast with Marjorie.

At 7 p.m., Duluth police detectives, along with detectives from the Bloomington Police Department and the Hennepin County Sheriff's Department, obtain a search warrant for Room 307, the Caldwell's room, at the Holiday Inn in Bloomington. During the execution of the search warrant, items including a garment bag (identical to the one purchased at the Minneapolis Host gift shop) and a wicker case (identical to one stolen from Glensheen) are found in the hotel room. Police also find a blue plastic pantyhose container filled with jewelry, including items later identified as taken from Elisabeth Congdon's body and bedroom.

At 10:15 p.m., Marjorie arrives outside of Room 307. Roger Caldwell is still being treated at Methodist Hospital. Marjorie is taken to another room, the search warrant is read to her, and she is questioned. After calling her attorney, David Arnold, she states that the jewelry items were given to her by her mother or were duplicates of jewelry belonging to her mother. Arnold and an associate arrive and prevent further questioning. After finding specific items in the Caldwells' hotel room, Duluth police and DeSanto decide to arrest Roger Caldwell.

July 6, 1977

Shortly after midnight at Methodist Hospital in St. Louis Park, Minnesota, Caldwell is questioned regarding his whereabouts during the time the crimes were committed at Glensheen. After refusing to answer, he is arrested for two counts of murder in the deaths of Elisabeth Congdon and Velma Pietila. His only comment after being told of his arrest is, "Oh."

July 9, 1977
Roger Caldwell makes his first appearance in St. Louis County District Court.

July 14, 1977
Detective Waller searches a safety deposit box opened by Roger Caldwell on June 28, 1977. Two documents are found: Power of attorney to Roger Caldwell from Marjorie Caldwell dated May 2, 1977, and Marjorie's handwritten will dated June 24, 1977.

August 5, 1977
Roger Caldwell is indicted in Duluth by a St. Louis County grand jury on two counts of murder in the first degree.

August 7, 1977
Marjorie reports to the Fridley, Minnesota, Police Department that she was attacked by a man "dressed like a cop" at her son Stephen's apartment. Marjorie claims that her assailant cut her with a razor after entering the apartment to serve her with some papers, and told her to stay away from Duluth and not help her husband. Marjorie has slash wounds and lacerations on the left side of her face and head and on her left breast and chest and left shoulder area. She is taken to Mercy Hospital in Coon Rapids where she is examined by Dr. James Sipe. In Dr. Sipe's opinion, the wounds have been self-inflicted.

February 27, 1978
Roger Caldwell enters a plea of not guilty.

March 30, 1978
Judge Litman orders the trial of Roger Caldwell moved to Crow Wing County, Brainerd, Minnesota.

April 10 – May 4, 1978
Jury selection for Caldwell's trial.

May 9 – June 30, 1978
Testimony presented during the trial of Roger Caldwell. The prosecution calls 103 witnesses; the defense calls 6.

July 5, 1978
Attorneys DeSanto and Thomson present their final arguments to the jury.

July, 8 1978
The jury returns verdicts finding Roger Caldwell guilty of two counts of murder in the first degree.

July 10, 1978
Roger Caldwell is sentenced to two consecutive life terms at Stillwater State Prison in Stillwater, Minnesota.

July 11, 1978
Marjorie Caldwell is arrested on charges of two counts of murder in the first degree and two counts conspiracy to commit murder.

August 18, 1978
Marjorie Caldwell is indicted by a St. Louis County grand jury on two counts of aiding and abetting murder in the first degree and two counts of conspiracy to commit murder.

September 20, 1978
Attorney Doug Thomson files notice of appeal of Roger Caldwell's conviction in Minnesota Supreme Court.

January 11, 1979
Minnesota Supreme Court orders Marjorie Caldwell's trial moved from St. Louis County to Dakota County.

April 3 – 24, 1979
Jury selection for Marjorie Caldwell's trial.

April 26 – July 13, 1979
Testimony is presented during the Marjorie Caldwell trial. The prosecution calls 112 witnesses; the defense calls 55 witnesses.

July 18, 1979
Prosecutor DeSanto presents closing argument to the Marjorie Caldwell jury.

July 19, 1979
Defense attorney Meshbesher presents closing argument to the Marjorie Caldwell jury.

July 21, 1979
The jury returns four verdicts of not guilty, acquitting Marjorie Caldwell of two charges of aiding and abetting murder in the first degree and two charges of conspiracy to commit murder.

July 24, 1979
Attorney Thomson files a motion in the Minnesota Supreme Court to stay further proceedings

on appeal of Roger Caldwell's conviction in order to remand the case to St. Louis County District Court for consideration of a new trial based on newly discovered evidence (presented at the Marjorie Caldwell trial).

August 16, 1979
Five of Marjorie Caldwell's seven children commence a civil lawsuit seeking to disinherit Marjorie from her inheritance on grounds that they can prove by a preponderance of the evidence that Marjorie was involved in the murders of Velma Pietila and Elisabeth Congdon.

September 20, 1979 & February 8, 1980
Post-conviction relief hearings on the issue of whether Roger Caldwell is entitled to a new trial because of new evidence are held before Judge Litman in Duluth, Minnesota.

March 26, 1980
Marjorie visits friend Helen Hagen at her room at Twin Birch Nursing Home. Marjorie hand feeds her friend, who is found in a coma the next day. Helen Hagen dies a few days later, on March 30, 1980.

April 21, 1980
Judge Litman rules that Roger Caldwell is not entitled to a new trial because of newly discovered evidence.

May 30, 1980
Roger Caldwell's defense attorney, Doug Thomson, files notice of appeal of Judge Litman's April 21 order in Minnesota Supreme Court.

August 7, 1981
Marjorie commits bigamy by marrying Wally Hagen, Helen Hagen's widower, in North Dakota without divorcing Roger Caldwell.

January 21, 1982
Candace Byers gives FBI Special Agent Bob Harvey a written statement that she was not truthful when she testified that she had seen Roger Caldwell at Golden, Colorado, on Sunday, June 26, 1977, at 10 P.M.

August 6, 1982
The Minnesota Supreme Court overturns Roger Caldwell's convictions on two counts of murder in the first degree because of the "fingerprint evidence."

September 1, 1982
After serving a total of five years and two months incarceration, Roger Caldwell is released from prison pending a new trial.

September 15, 1982
Fire destroys Marjorie and Wally Hagen's home in Mound, Minnesota (the "Cranberry House").

January, 16, 1983
Marjorie is arrested for arson of the Cranberry House.

March 20, 1983
Marjorie Caldwell charged with bigamy in North Dakota. State officials refuse to extradite her (she can only be arrested if she returns to the state).

July 1, 1983
Children of Marjorie Caldwell reach pretrial settlement in lawsuit to disinherit Marjorie so that no civil trial will proceed.

July 5, 1983
In accordance with a plea negotiation arrangement, Roger Caldwell pleads guilty to two counts of second-degree murder, makes a full confession, and is released from prison. His confession provides officials with no new information.

January 13, 1984
Marjorie is found guilty of the September 15, 1982, arson of the "Cranberry House" in Mound, Minnesota.

February 9, 1984
Marjorie is sentenced to twenty-one months at the State Women's Prison in Shakopee, Minnesota. She remains free pending appeal.

January 21, 1985
The Minnesota Court of Appeals upholds Marjorie's arson conviction and sentence.

January 25, 1985
Marjorie begins her prison term.

October 19, 1986
Marjorie is released from prison. She and her husband, Wally Hagen, eventually move to Ajo, Arizona.

May 18, 1988
Roger Caldwell commits suicide in his apartment in Latrobe, Pennsylvania.

March 24, 1991
Marjorie is arrested on arson charges in Ajo, Arizona.

October 12, 1992
Marjorie's Ajo, Arizona, arson trial begins.

October 29, 1992
Marjorie is convicted of attempted arson and sentenced to fifteen years in prison. The judge allows her a day to put her husband's affairs in order.

October 30, 1992
Wally Hagen is found dead in his Ajo, Arizona, home. Marjorie is arrested and charged with murder the next day, but charges are dropped when it is determined Wally died of a drug overdose and that his death could have been a suicide.

October 31, 1992
Marjorie begins her fifteen-year sentence at the state prison in Tucson, Arizona.

January 5, 2004
Marjorie's revised earned release date from Arizona State Women's Prison at Perryville in Goodyear, Arizona. She left prison at about 9 A.M. that morning in a hired car; the driver sped out of the parking lot once he saw television camera crews waiting at the exits. Marjorie relocated in Tucson, Arizona. She claimed to have saved about $1.2 million while in prison.

January 2004
Marjorie tells people she is a retired nurse named "Maggie Wallis" (she later returns to using "Hagen" and uses "Wallis" as her middle name). She also acquires a greyhound she calls "Blueberry Hound" and has him trained to become the first greyhound service dog in the country.

May 2004
Marjorie accuses her former attorney, Edward Bolding, of stealing from her.

April 2006
Bolding is arrested on charges he stole $750,000 from Marjorie and another client; he was released to await his trial after making bail.

March 1, 2007
Roger Sammis, an elderly gentleman who Marjorie had befriended, dies in Tucson. She had obtained power of attorney over Sammis' accounts.

March 5, 2007
Marjorie Hagen writes a check to the Brings Funeral Home in Tucson for $1,304, payment for Sammis' cremation.

March 19, 2007
Marjorie deposits a check for $11,181.04 that Roger Sammis had received as an inheritance.

March 22, 2007
Marjorie is arrested at her home, charged with forgery, theft, tampering with a computer, and fraudulent scheme and artifice. She is booked into the Pima County jail, her bond set at $250,000. With no body or evidence, Pima County officials cannot charge her in the death of Roger Sammis.

January 8, 2008
Marjorie's original trial date. The trial is postponed several times due to Marjorie's claims of illness.

November 17, 2008
The day before her trial is scheduled to start, Marjorie pleads guilty to attempted forgery as part of a plea agreement. Sentencing is delayed due to Marjorie's health problems.

December 17, 2008
Marjorie's former defense attorney, Edward Bolding, is convicted by a Pima County Superior Court jury of two counts of fraudulent schemes and artifices and one count of obstruction of a criminal investigation.

December 18, 2008
Bolding fails to appear for the reading of the verdicts, delayed a day because of his absence. Bolding reportedly fled Arizona shortly after the jury reached its verdicts.

March 4, 2009
Marjorie is sentenced to three years of intensive probation in the Sammis fraud case; she could have been sentenced to up to 2.5 years in prison, but her attorney lobbied for probation because of her age and poor health. She had surgery on her left eye two days before her sentencing (she claims to be legally blind) and arrived for her sentencing accompanied by a service dog.

Congdon Family Tree *

Chester Adgate Congdon (6/12/1853 – 11/21/1916)

Clara Hesperia Bannister Congdon (4/29/1854 – 7/12/1950)

Walter Bannister Congdon (11/5/1882 – 10/20/1949)

Edward Chester Congdon (5/20/1885 – 11/27/1940)

Marjorie Congdon [Dudley] (1/12/1887 – 10/11/1971)

Helen Clara Congdon [d'Autremont] (2/16/1889 – 5/19/1966)

John Congdon (1891 – 1893; *actual dates unavailable*)

Elisabeth Mannering Congdon (4/22/1894 - 6/27/1977)

Marjorie Mannering Congdon [LeRoy] [Caldwell] [Hagen] (ADOPTED)

Richard Webster LeRoy (DIVORCED)**

Stephen Brainard LeRoy

Peter Treworgy LeRoy

Suzanne Congdon LeRoy

Andrew Webster LeRoy

Rebecca Warner LeRoy

Heather Mannering LeRoy

Richard Webster LeRoy

Jennifer Susan Congdon [Johnson] (ADOPTED)

Robert Congdon (9/4/1898 – 6/12/1967)

*Abbreviated. Except for Elisabeth, all of Chester and Clara's children married and raised families. While Elisabeth never married, she was said to have had a number of suitors, including one in particular who gave her a diamond-and-sapphire ring to commemorate their friendship—the same ring stolen from her finger the night she was murdered. It was later found in her adopted daughter Marjorie's hotel room. (As a child, Marjorie was often reprimanded for taking the ring without permission.) Elisabeth's other daughter, Jennifer, married Charles Johnson and together they raised six children.

**Following her divorce from LeRoy, Marjorie married Roger Sipe Caldwell in 1976. After being acquitted of conspiracy to kill her mother, Marjorie married Wally Hagen in 1981, following the mysterious death of his wife Helen. Marjorie never divorced Caldwell and was later charged with bigamy in North Dakota.

Glensheen Crime Scene

(A partial view of Glensheen's second floor.)

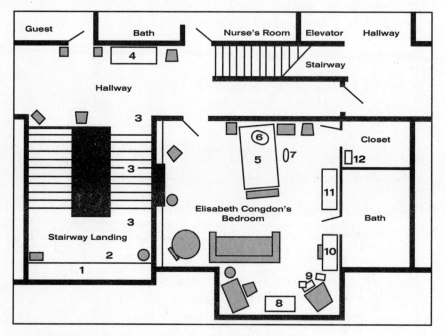

1. Window seat where nurse Velma Pietila's body was found.

2. Murder weapon #1: the candlestick, used to kill Velma Pietila.

3. Various items found on staircase and landings, including a key, broken eyeglass frames and lenses, earrings, the heel pad of a shoe, a woman's left shoe, hair pins, batteries and pieces of a broken flashlight, broken teeth, and pieces of hair.

4. The hallway bureau from which the candlestick was taken.

5. Bed where Elisabeth Congdon's body was found.

6. Murder weapon #2: a satin pillow found covering Elisabeth Congdon's face and stained with flecks of blood, one corner still crumpled, presumably from the killer's grip.

7. The pillow that supported Elisabeth's left arm as she slept.

8. Memorabilia case, from which a 1,700-year-old Byzantine coin was stolen; the coin was mailed from Duluth to Roger Caldwell in Golden, Colorado, in an envelope that appeared to have been addressed by Caldwell himself.

9. Empty jewelry boxes found on floor; most of their missing contents were found in Roger and Marjorie Caldwell's hotel room in Bloomington, Minnesota.

10. Vanity: rifled through by the intruder (or intruders) in search of jewelry.

11. Dresser: drawers opened as if searched, but contents found in perfect order.

12. Wicker suitcase: its smaller counterpart was found in Roger and Marjorie Caldwell's hotel room in Bloomington, Minnesota.

Glensheen's Floor Plan

(*Not shown: Glensheen's third floor and attic; nothing is believed to have occurred on those levels during the night of the murders.)

FIRST FLOOR

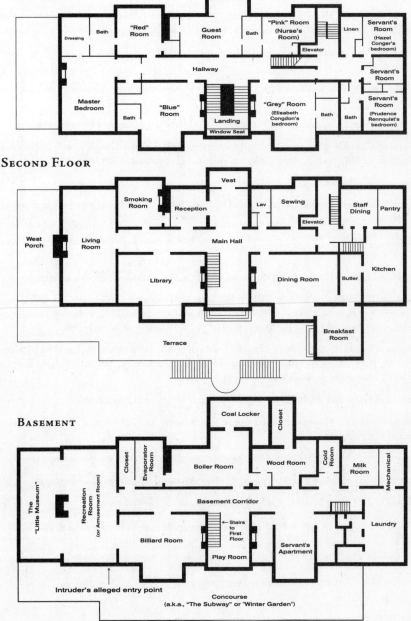

FIRST FLOOR

Dressing | Bath | "Red" Room | Guest Room | Bath | "Pink" Room (Nurse's Room) | Elevator | Linen | Servant's Room (Hazel Conger's bedroom)

Hallway

Master Bedroom | Bath | "Blue" Room | Landing · Window Seat | "Grey" Room (Elisabeth Congdon's bedroom) | Bath | Bath | Servant's Room · Servant's Room (Prudence Rennquist's bedroom)

SECOND FLOOR

Vest

Smoking Room | Reception | Lav | Sewing | Staff Dining | Pantry

Elevator

West Porch | Living Room | Main Hall | Kitchen

Library | Dining Room | Butler

Terrace | Breakfast Room

BASEMENT

Coal Locker | Closet

The "Little Museum" | Recreation Room (or Amusement Room) | Closet | Evaporator Room | Boiler Room | Wood Room | Cold Room | Milk Room | Mechanical

Basement Corridor

Billiard Room | ← Stairs to First Floor | Play Room | Servant's Apartment | Laundry

Intruder's alleged entry point

Concourse (a.k.a., "The Subway" or "Winter Garden")

Photo & Diagram Credits

All images are the copyrighted material of the sources mentioned below.

Crime scene and Glensheen diagrams (p. 418 – 419) by Tony Dierckins, based on drawings made by the Duluth Police Department and City of Duluth engineers provided by John DeSanto.

Cover photo and photo of Glensheen (p. 195), Swiftwater Farm (p. 198), prison photos (p. 215) and photo of Marjorie Hagen's car leaving prison (p. 216, bottom) by Tony Dierckins.

Photo of Glensheen's milk room (p. 197) and the Henri Harpignies painting (p. 202) by Scott Pearson.

Vintage postcard of Westhome (p. 198) courtesy of www.dupontcastle.com/castles/congdon.htm.

Photo of Chester Congdon (p. A2) courtesy of the Northeast Minnesota Historical Center.

Photo of Clara Congdon (p. 195), the Hesperia (p. 197), Chester Congdon with Robert and Elisabeth (p. 196), and Elisabeth Congdon (p. 196, right) courtesy Glensheen.

Photos of Elisabeth Congdon (p. 196, left) courtesy of Jennifer Congdon Johnson.

Photo of Marjorie Congdon, et. al, at Dana Hall (p. 199) from the 1948 Dana Hall high school yearbook.

Wedding photos (p. 199, 200) and photo of the LeRoy family (p. 200) courtesy of Richard "Dick" LeRoy.

Photo of Elisabeth Congdon and her nursing staff (p. 201) courtesy of Dennis Loberg.

Photo of Elisabeth Congdon (p. 201), crime scene and evidence photos (pp. 203–207), mug shot photo of Roger Caldwell (p. 209), photo of John DeSanto (p. 210), and images of Marjorie's handwritten will (p. 208) and forged letter (p. 202) courtesy of John DeSanto.

Photos of Velma Pietila (p. 201), Marjorie Caldwell (209), Marjorie Caldwell and Rick LeRoy (p. 209), Gary Waller, Ron Meshbesher, and Douglas Thomson (p. 210), and Roger Caldwell (p. 213), courtesy of the *Duluth News-Tribune*.

Photos of Helen and Wally Hagen (p. 212) courtesy of Tom and Julie Hagen.

Photo of Marjorie Hagen's antique stove in Ajo, Arizona (p. 212) courtesy the Pima County Sheriff's Department.

Booking photo of Marjorie Hagen (p. 213) courtesy of the Ajo, Arizona, Police Department.

Photo of Marjorie Hagen (p. 214) courtesy of the Arizona Department of Corrections.

Photos of the Hagen house in Ajo (p. 211) courtesy of Gail Feichtinger.

Photos of Marjorie Hagen walking out of prison on (p. 216, top) courtesy KARE-11 TV.

References

DOCUMENTS & INTERVIEWS:

The authors referenced literally hundreds of legal documents, court transcripts, and exhibits concerning both the criminal and civil actions surrounding the murders at Glensheen and the further legal problems and criminal activity of Marjorie Hagen. Other documents furnishing information for this book include diaries and letters provided by Congdon, LeRoy, Caldwell, and Hagen family members as well as other individuals and organizations. Further information was gathered by conducting interviews with Congdon, LeRoy, Caldwell, and Hagen family members, friends, acquaintances, bankers, investigators, civil attorneys, prosecutors, defense attorneys, judges, former jurors, and many others whose lives felt the impact of the events described within these pages. Marjorie Caldwell Hagen refused all offers to be interviewed.

BOOKS & PERIODICALS:

Berini, Nancy. "Glensheen in a New Light." *Lake Superior Port Cities*, Volume 4, Issue 1. 1982.

Boese, Donald L. *John C. Greenway and the Opening of the Western Mesabi*. Grand Rapids, Minnesota: Itasca Community College, 1975.

Boutan, Lisbeth. "Gardens of Glensheen." *Lake Superior Magazine*. April–May 1993.

Fourie, Ada. *Their Roots Run Deep*. Duluth, Minnesota: University of Minnesota Duluth, n.d.

Glensheen Staff. *Glensheen*. Duluth, Minnesota: Glensheen/University of Minnesota Duluth, 1980.

Hoover, Roy. *A Lake Superior Lawyer*. St. Paul, Minnesota: Superior Partners, 1997.

Icove, David J. and M. H. Estepp. "Motive-Based Offender Profiles of Arson and Fire-Related Crimes." *FBI Law Enforcement Bulletin*. April, 1987.

Icove, David J. and Philip R. Herbert. "Serial Arsonists: An Introduction." *The Police Chief*. December, 1980.

Kurian, George Thomas. *Datapedia of the United States: America Year by Year 1790-2000*. Lanham, Maryland: Burnam Press, 1994.

Lane, Michael. *Glensheen: The Construction Years*. Duluth, Minnesota: Glensheen/University of Minnesota Duluth., n.d.

Lykken, David Thoreson. *A Tremor in the Blood: Uses and Abuses of the Lie Detector*. New York: McGraw-Hill Book Company, 1981.

Marquis, Albert N., ed. *The Book of Minnesotans: A Biographic Dictionary of Leading Living Men of the State of Minnesota*. Chicago: Publisher Unknown, 1907.

Rider, Anthony Olen. "The Firesetter: A Psychological Profile." *FBI Law Enforcement Bulletin*. June–August 1980.

Scott, James. National Architects: Their Images upon Duluth, 1808-1916. Duluth, Minnesota: Published by the author, 1967.

Tenuta, James A. "Glensheen Opens Its Doors to the Past." *Lake Superior Port Cities*. Vol. I, Issue 3, Fall 1979.

Van Brunt, Walter, ed., *Duluth and St. Louis County: Their Story and People*. Chicago: American Historical Society, c1921.

Williams, J. Fletcher. *A History of the City of St. Paul to 1875*. St. Paul, Minnesota: Published in the collections of the Minnesota Historical Society, Volume 4, 1876.

NEWSPAPERS:

Ajo Copper News (Ajo, Arizona)

Arizona Daily Star (Tucson, Arizona)

Arizona Republic (Phoenix, Arizona)

Brainerd Daily Dispatch (Brainerd, Minnesota)

Chicago Sun-Times (Chicago, Illinois)

Duluth Herald (Duluth, Minnesota)

Duluth News-Tribune (Duluth, Minnesota)

Hastings Star Gazette (Hastings, Minnesota)

Milwaukee Journal (Milwaukee, Wisconsin)

Minneapolis Star-Tribune (Minneapolis, Minnesota)

Phoenix Gazette (Phoenix, Arizona)

St. Paul Pioneer Press (St. Paul, Minnesota)

Seattle Post-Intelligencer (Seattle, Washington)

Seattle Times (Seattle, Washington)

Tucson Citizen (Tucson, Arizona)

Yakima Herald Republic (Yakima, Washington)

The Associated Press

Glensheen Today

GLENSHEEN WAS GIVEN TO THE University of Minnesota Duluth by the heirs of Chester and Clara Congdon in 1968, but did not open to the public until after Elisabeth Congdon's death. (Chester's will allowed the home to remain available to his children as long as they were alive; Elisabeth was the last of the Congdon children and the only one to live in Glensheen her entire adult life). The University and the Congdon trustees share a common goal: to preserve Glensheen and use it for "public pursuits which might not otherwise be available because of growing pressure to budget demands upon public and educational institutions."

The mansion today closely resembles the way it looked November 24, 1908, when the Congdon family first moved in. It is listed on the National Register of Historic Places and has been featured on an episode of the A&E network's *American Castles* program. Glensheen was opened to the public as a museum on July 28, 1979. Over two million people have since visited the estate.

Glensheen offers a variety of tours, both guided and unguided, including the "Main House" tour of the first two floors, a "Bedroom Slippers" tour that allows visitors past the velvet ropes, and a "Third Floor and Attic Tour." Glensheen also hosts catered dinners, brunches, and other private events such as weddings. All private functions include full or partial tours for guests.

Glensheen also hosts many public events such as elegant New Year's Eve, Valentine's Day, and Mother's Day dinners, as well as free outdoor summer concerts, dinner theatre, and the annual Festival of Fine Art and Craft each August.

Glensheen is self-supporting. Revenues raised from tour and museum shop sales, memberships, donations, and grants pay for operational expenses and conservation/preservation efforts. For more information, contact:

Glensheen: The Historic Congdon Estate
3300 London Road
Duluth, MN 55804
1-888-454-GLEN ◆ www.d.umn.edu/glen/

About the Authors

Gail Feichtinger first researched the Glensheen murders as a crime reporter for the *Duluth News-Tribune* and *Duluth Herald* around the time Roger Caldwell bargained for his release. She obtained an exclusive interview following his release from prison by delivering Caldwell a pint of his favorite ice cream. Feichtinger was born in Stamford, Connecticut. She studied journalism at Southern Methodist University and received a B.A. from Carleton College. She has also reported for newspapers in Dallas, Texas, worked as a reporter and producer for Twin Cities Public Television, and was an assistant producer for the *MacNeil/Lehrer NewsHour*. Feichtinger obtained a law degree from William Mitchell College of Law in 1996. She now works as an assistant attorney general for the Minnesota Attorney General's office. She lives in Minneapolis with her husband, Bob Geiger, and their daughters, Alexandra and Elena. This is her first book.

Former Assistant St. Louis County Attorney **John DeSanto** prosecuted Roger Sipe Caldwell and Marjorie Caldwell for the crimes at Glensheen. DeSanto—along with his twin brother, Will—was born in Duluth, Minnesota. He graduated valedictorian from Duluth Cathedral High School in 1964, received a B.A. in psychology from the University of Minnesota Duluth in 1968, and—after serving two years in the U.S. Army—went on to study law at the University of Minnesota, graduating in 1973. In 2009 DeSanto was appointed trial court judge for Minnesota's Sixth Judicial District. His chambers are located in the St. Louis County Courthouse in Duluth, Minnesota, where he worked as a prosecutor for thirty-five years. During the three-and-a-half decades he prosecuted cases, DeSanto tried only one murder suspect who received an acquittal—Marjorie Caldwell. DeSanto and his wife, Lana, live in Duluth and are the parents of three adult children, Amy, Abby, and Adam.

As a Duluth Police Department detective, **Gary Waller** led the investigation of the crimes at Glensheen. Waller was born in Duluth, Minnesota, where he served in the police department for twenty-one years. Waller holds a B.A. in criminology from the University of Minnesota Duluth and an M.A. in management from the College of St. Scholastica. In 1986, he was elected St. Louis County Sheriff; he retired in 1999. He now operates a consulting service doing organizational and facility assessments. Like Waller, his father, Donald, served in the Duluth P.D. (for 25 years), as did his uncle Floyd Bowman and brother Roger, Duluth's former Chief of Police. Waller has two children, Bridget and Sean (a former Duluth police officer now serving in Oklahoma), and two stepchildren, Terry and Kathleen. He and his wife, Mary, live near Kettle River, Minnesota, enjoying time with their seven grandchildren.